advantage

Dear Valued Customer,

We realize you're a busy professional with deadlines to hit. Whether your goal is to learn a new technology or solve a critical problem, we want to be there to lend you a hand. Our primary objective is to provide you with the insight and knowledge you need to stay atop the highly competitive and ever-changing technology industry.

Wiley Publishing, Inc., offers books on a wide variety of technical categories, including security, data warehousing, software development tools, and networking — everything you need to reach your peak. Regardless of your level of expertise, the Wiley family of books has you covered.

- For Dummies® — The *fun* and *easy* way™ to learn
- The Weekend Crash Course® — The *fastest* way to learn a new tool or technology
- Visual — For those who prefer to learn a new topic *visually*
- The Bible — The *100% comprehensive* tutorial and reference
- The Wiley Professional list — *Practical* and *reliable* resources for IT professionals

The book you hold now, *The CISA® Prep Guide: Mastering the Certified Information Systems Auditor Exam,* is the first comprehensive and commercially available preparation guide to offer CISA study materials. The book provides definitions and background on all of the seven content areas of CISA, along with sample test questions and explanations of answers. Whether you are an information systems auditor, an IS audit manager, a CISSP® or SSCP® professional, or a professional who needs to get up to speed on IS systems, this book with its Boson-powered, interactive CD test-prep engines should provide all you need to know to prepare for the CISA exam.

Our commitment to you does not end at the last page of this book. We'd want to open a dialog with you to see what other solutions we can provide. Please be sure to visit us at www.wiley.com/compbooks to review our complete title list and explore the other resources we offer. If you have a comment, suggestion, or any other inquiry, please locate the "contact us" link at www.wiley.com.

Thank you for your support and we look forward to hearing from you and serving your needs again in the future.

Sincerely,

Richard K. Swadley
Vice President & Executive Group Publisher
Wiley Technology Publishing

15 HOUR WEEKEND CRASH COURSE

Visual

Bible

DUMMIES FOR

WILEY
Wiley Publishing, Inc.

The CISA® Prep Guide:
Mastering the Certified Information Systems Auditor Exam

John Kramer

Wiley Publishing, Inc.

Publisher: Bob Ipsen
Executive Editor: Carol A. Long
Editorial Manager: Kathryn A. Malm
Managing Editor: Angela Smith
New Media Editor: Brian Snapp
Text Design & Composition: Wiley Composition Services

This book is printed on acid-free paper. ∞

Published by Wiley Publishing, Inc., Indianapolis, Indiana
Published simultaneously in Canada

For general information on our other products and services please contact our Customer Care Department within the United States at (800) 762-2974, outside the United States at (317) 572-3993 or fax (317) 572-4002.

Wiley also publishes its books in a variety of electronic formats. Some content that appears in print may not be available in electronic books.

Library of Congress Cataloging-in-Publication Data:

ISBN 0-471-25032-5

Printed in the United States of America

10 9 8 7 6 5 4 3 2 1

Contents

Acknowledgments

I would like to thank my family — Nick, John, and my wife Linda — for putting up with me through the process of developing this book. Without their patience and understanding, this would not have been as easy or as enjoyable. I am also grateful to the many IS auditors whom I have met and worked with during my career in IS auditing. The association with other professionals who pursue excellence in their work is always a benefit to personal growth.

About the Author

John Kramer is the Information Security Manager and Security Architect for the UPMC Health System. He spent eight years working in information systems auditing for both large banking and investment and health care institutions. In both environments, he has been responsible for managing all phases of the IS audit programs, conducting risk assessments, and managing IS operations and audit functions. John has had the responsibility for the development and training of many IS auditors, several of whom have passed the CISA exam successfully. John has been a CISA since 1995. He is a former Vice President of the Pittsburgh ISACA chapter. He is also a CISSP. His formal education is in electrical engineering.

Introduction

Information systems auditing is a profession that is both rewarding and challenging. It allows the information systems auditor a unique view of the business processes and the supporting information technology that encompass a wide scope of understanding and perspective. This view is often one of the overall system and how it works; the big picture. IS auditing is frequently a stepping stone to management positions and careers within the business for which the auditor learns the systems and controls. Process knowledgeable system thinkers with inherent integrity and risk focus are often sought as reliable management material. The most sought after, globally accepted standard of certification for an IS auditor is that of CISA, Certified Information System Auditor. Since 1978, this designation means that the auditor is recognized as a certified professional. Earning the CISA designation shows that the auditor takes his profession seriously and is dedicated to establishing his reputation and career as a proficient professional.

CISAs are trained in all aspects of IS auditing and bound by a code of ethics to perform sensitive activities reliably and with integrity. The certification process was established to evaluate competency of IS auditors and provide a mechanism for encouraging IS auditors to maintain and enhance their knowledge of the IS auditing profession. CISA certification requires a broad knowledge of the information technology management processes and five years of experience in IS auditing, control, or security allowing for a few substitutions and waivers. It also depends on a basic understanding of generally accepted auditing practices as well as many of the basic processes used every day in information processing and business management.

The CISA certification is a pre-requisite for many audit and security job postings in the marketplace today. The majority (71 percent) of those holding a CISA certification surveyed in 2001 believe that obtaining this certification has helped to advance their careers. This opinion was borne out by a recent survey conducted by Foote Partners, which showed that CISAs received the highest salary bonuses among the 39 technical skills certification programs studied. Those possessing the CISA certification received a median 10 percent bonus (as a percent of base salary), the highest bonus amount attributed to a certification. Overall, the average bonus for all certifications tracked during the same time period was only 6.8 percent.

More than 10,000 individuals registered for the CISA exam in 2002, yet very little information is available about what IS auditors' work is all about. Becoming certified takes years of experience and exposure to information systems and risk and control techniques. There is no substitute for this work experience. My hope is that this book will give you insight into one person's perspective of how to perform this work, add value to the business organizations you are supporting as an IS auditor, and most importantly show you how to consolidate your understanding of the audit process into the successful passing of the CISA exam in June.

After you have received your certification, you will find that this book is a valuable reference and ongoing tool that you can use while practicing your trade as an IS audit professional. Technology is a fast-paced and ever-changing world where yesterday's bleeding edge is today's obsolete process. IS auditing techniques applied to the business processes' risks and controls do not change as much over time, however. They are more closely tied to human behavior and corporate governance, which mature and endure steadfastly over time. To know the IS audit profession is to understand how to go about getting the right results without necessarily having a full understanding of each and every technical solution that comes along. You don't need to know all of the technologies in the greatest detail to understand how the business processes require them for processing and how to control risks inherent in the technical solution to business problems. ISACA has created many excellent standards and control-assessment processes to provide the auditor with the tool needed to successfully apply risk and control examinations to the business processes, assisting them to improve and achieve the business objectives. The CISA certification is a proud moment for the audit professional, one which marks a milestone in a successful career path.

The ISACA Organization

The Information Systems Audit and Control Association (ISACA) was founded in 1969. With over 26,000 members in over 100 countries, it is the recognized world leader in IS governance, control, and assurance. The mission of ISACA is to support enterprise objectives through the development, provision, and promotion of research, standards, competencies, and practices for the effective governance, control, and assurance of information, systems, and technology. The Association helps IS audit, control, and security professionals focus not only on IS, IS risks, and security issues, but also on the relationship between IS and the business, business processes, and business risks. There are more than 160 local chapter organizations in cities across the globe that provide unique opportunities to leverage common experiences and further knowledge of the IS auditing profession.

The Examination

The CISA examination is administered once a year on a Saturday in early June. You must register at least a month in advance, and by registering early you can receive discounts on your registration fees. Discounts are also afforded to ISACA members for the test and study materials that are offered by ISACA. This is just one of the many benefits of membership to this international IS auditing professional organization. In 2002, the exam was given in over forty states in the United States and over seventy other countries worldwide, many in multiple locations in that country. You can pick a test center where you would like to take the test and the language that you would prefer the exam be given in. Two to three weeks before the exam date, you will be sent an admission ticket that must be presented for physical admission to the exam location. Local ISACA chapters often host the test and provide administration and logistics for the exam. Booklets are handed out and oral instructions are given at the start of the four-hour exam time frame during which you must answer 200 multiple-choice questions similar to the ones at the end of each chapter of this book.

Several supplemental resources are available to help in preparing for the exam. ISACA provides some study aids which can be purchased from their Web site. Technical books on the details of IS auditing and systems controls are relatively few, however. Your local ISACA chapter is an excellent source of information and can be a valuable resource for finding others to study with and share preparation for the exam with.

Obtaining and Maintaining Certification

Becoming a Certified Information Systems Auditor is a process of passing the exam described in this book, showing a commitment to the profession by agreeing to the professional ethics and continuing education requirements, and providing evidence of five years of IS audit, control, or security-related work experience. This is not a paper certification by any measure.

Criteria for Becoming a CISA

CISA certification is a process of assessing individuals for their skills and judgment related to IS audit, control, and security. In addition to passing the exam, the candidate must submit evidence of five (5) years of experience in the professional practice of IS audit, control, or security. Substitution and waivers of such experience may also be obtained that will apply to this five-year experience requirement as follows:

- A maximum of one year of experience may be substituted for
  - One year of other audit experience
  - One year of information systems experience and/or
  - An associate's degree (60 semester college credits or its equivalent)
- Two of the required five years of experience may be substituted for a bachelor's degree (120 semester college credits or its equivalent).
- One year of IS audit, control, or security experience may be substituted for each two years of experience as a full-time university instructor in a related field (e.g., computer science, accounting, IS auditing) with no maximum limitation to the two for one experience year substitution.

All related experience submitted as evidence for the certification as an IS auditor must have been gained within the ten years preceeding the application for certification or within five years from the date the candidate initially passed the exam. Individuals may choose to take and pass the CISA exam prior to meeting the experience requirements but will not be awarded the CISA designation until all the requirements are met. All experience will be independently verified with employers.

Maintaining Your CISA Certification

The CISA certification must be actively maintained by the individual who is awarded with this designation through a program of continuing educational pursuit and annual maintenance fees paid in full to ISACA. The continuing education policy requires that a certified individual earn and submit a minimum number of Continuing Professional Education (CPE) hours annually. CISAs must obtain and submit one hundred and twenty (120) CPEs over a three-year reporting period with a minimum of twenty (20) CPEs in any given year. Some CISAs are selected each year for an audit of their CPE credits and their applicability to the continuing education process. You must respond and submit any required supporting documentation if you are selected for this annual audit. For this reason, it is very important to keep separate and accurate records related to your continuing educational efforts related to maintaining your CISA certification.

The Certification Board may at its discretion revoke certification for a number of reasons. This action would be taken only after due and thorough consideration and for one of the following reasons:

- Falsifying or deliberately withholding relevant information.
- Intentionally misstating a material fact.
- Engaging in or assisting others in dishonest or inappropriate behavior in connection with the CISA exam or the certification process.
- Violating the Code of Ethics in any way.
- Failing to meet the Continuing Education requirements.
- Failing to pay annual CISA maintenance fees.

The Approach and Layout of This Book

The approach of this book is a blend of relating experiences and the transference of knowledge: Experiences in passing the CISA exam, years of performing IS audits, and audit management, as well as teaching entry-level IS auditors. My experiences are somewhat unique because they span both medical and financial business environments as both an auditor and audit manager. Recruiting junior auditors and training them to perform IS audits and eventually pass the CISA exam were both personally rewarding and instructive to the advancement my understanding of the IS audit profession. I have included information and relate my views about several of the standards and current direction of the ISACA organization and its evolving testing criteria. This firsthand knowledge of what works and what information is most relevant to the professional IS auditor uniquely positions you, the reader, to study for and pass the CISA exam and perform IS audits with confidence.

Organization of the Book

The text is organized according to the examination content areas that are currently defined for preparation and study for the CISA examination:

Chapter 1, "The IS Audit Process" (10 percent of test content).

Chapter 2, "Management, Planning, and Organization of Information Systems" (11 percent of test content).

Chapter 3, "Technical Infrastructure and Operational Practices" (13 percent of test content).

Chapter 4, "Protection of Information Assets" (25 percent of test content).

Chapter 5, "Disaster Recovery and Business Continuity" (10 percent of test content).

Chapter 6, "Business Application System Development, Acquisition, Implementation, and Maintenance" (16 percent of test content).

Chapter 7, "Business Process Evaluation and Risk Management" (15 percent of test content).

Appendix A, "Answers to Sample Exam Questions."

Appendix B, "What's on the CD-ROM."

Each chapter is accompanied by a series of sample questions that are in the same format as those found on the CISA examination. Answers are provided for each question along with an explanation of the answers in Appendix A.

Valuable reference material and glossaries of terms include information with which you will need to become familiar. Some of the author's favorite resources are listed at the end of each chapter to guide the candidate for further study and to use in performing IS audits.

The Companion CD-ROM

Included with this book is a CD-ROM containing all of the questions presented as samples, formatted in a similar fashion as those in the CISA exam. The Test Engine from Boson Software allows you to determine what categories or content areas you are strong and weak in, in order to narrow your study efforts as you prepare for the actual exam. You can review the correct answers after each question and time your test-taking abilities. Options for keeping track of your quiz-scoring include asking missed questions over again in subsequent quizzes and multiple quizzes using select content areas if desired. Scoring is tracked and graded as you progress. Instructions for loading and using the software are included in Appendix B of this book.

Who Should Read This Book

This book is not only a useful preparation guide for the CISA exam, but also will serve as a reference to best audit practices which can be subsequently adapted to the individual situation faced by an IS auditor in his or her work. It can be used to ensure that all aspects of risk and control have been considered when preparing for or performing an IS audit engagement. There are three main categories of readers for this comprehensive exam prep guide:

- Candidates who are planning on sitting for the CISA exam and who are looking for a comprehensive and practical guide to all of the knowledge required to achieve certification. This book is not designed to cover all of the details of every aspect of IS audit and control. Instead it provides a guide that will walk the candidate through all audit content areas at a high level, allowing the candidate to determine where they need to follow up with additional resources and fill in the gaps in their knowledge base.

- Students of IS management and auditing who need a comprehensive view of the process and control issues faced in the daily management of an IT process environment. Business operations rely on information systems and in many cases are totally dependent on the efficient and effective management of those systems for the success of the business. The study of IS management practices, in the pursuit of an information systems management career path, will necessarily cross the path of IS audit, and the correct application of controls over the business risks created when information systems are applied to business solutions.

- IS managers who want to educate themselves with a full understanding of the processes used to balance risks and controls in their complex and demanding IT environments. The management of these systems, the risks, and controls related to the implementation of them, in pursuit of the business objectives, can be better understood through the study of this guide as a business systems management leading practice guide. Successful IS managers are those that understand risks and manage them best. What better way to do this than through a full understanding of how the certified IS auditor would approach the evaluation of his or her business processes and controls?

Summary

Having passed the CISA exam and successfully trained others who have also passed the exam, the author believes the information provided in this book will serve as a vital foundation for studying Information Systems Auditing processes and techniques in preparation for the CISA exam. The candidate must be knowledgeable and experienced in information systems and their implementation as a pre-requisite to performing IS audits and becoming certified as an information systems auditor. Understanding basic business operations and management are also areas of knowledge the candidate must be familiar with. This preparation guide follows the exam content areas closely and calls out every subject matter that must be mastered by CISA exam candidates in order to pass the test. The information provided here, drawn from experience in applying this knowledge in actual practice and in various business settings, makes this book unique as a preparation to the exam and practice of Information Systems Auditing.

CHAPTER

1

The Information System Audit Process

Developing a risk-based IS audit process that can be implemented in accordance with generally accepted audit standards and guidelines will ensure that your organization's systems and information technology are adequately controlled and are meeting the needs of the business. This chapter will outline the steps necessary to implement such a process. Knowledge of this subject matter comprises 10 percent of the CISA exam content. Required knowledge for these processes are described in detail and some insight on managing the process to best meet the needs of the organization as well as to achieve reliable and defendable audit objectives and results will be explained. By the end of this chapter, you should have a working knowledge about the following tasks:

- Developing and implementing risk-based IS audit scopes and objectives in compliance with generally accepted audit standards that will ensure that information technology and business processes are adequately controlled to meet the organization's business objective

- Planning IS audits

- Obtaining sufficient, relevant, and reliable evidence to achieve the audit objectives

- Analyzing that evidence to identify the control weaknesses and to reach conclusions

- Reviewing the work performed to provide reasonable assurance that the audit objectives were achieved and the conclusions were appropriate

- Communicating the resultant audit findings and recommendations to key stakeholders

- Facilitating risk management and control practices within the organization

The IS audit process itself is similar to the System Development Life Cycle (SDLC) processes that you will audit. The successful deployment of an audit engagement consists of the following:

- Careful and methodical planning

- Determining the scope and objectives of the process

- Validating the plan, its scope, and objectives with the stakeholders

- Identifying the required resources

- Carrying out the planned tasks

- Documenting the steps and results along the way

- Validating or testing the results of the tasks

- Reporting the final results back to the process owner or stakeholders for their final agreement or approval

IS Auditing Standards

The Information Systems Audit and Control Association (ISACA) standards and guidelines for IS auditing and the code of professional ethics for certified IS auditors are the first references the CISA candidate must become familiar with. This information is the internationally recognized basis of all IS audit activity and provides the foundation of defendable and binding audit work. The standards define the mandatory requirements for IS auditing and reporting that the CISA certificate holders are required to follow. These standards are fairly straight forward and describe the basics of the IS auditing requirements:

- The responsibility, authority, and accountability of the IS audit function are appropriately documented in an audit charter or engagement letter.

- In all matters related to auditing, the IS auditor is independent of the auditee in attitude and appearance.

- The IS audit function is sufficiently independent of the area being audited to permit objective completion of the audit.

- The IS auditor must adhere to the Code of Professional Ethics of ISACA.

- Due professional care and observance of applicable professional auditing standards are exercised in all aspects of the IS auditor's work.

- The IS auditor is technically competent, having the skills and knowledge necessary to perform the auditor's work.

- The IS auditor must maintain technical competence through the appropriate continuing professional education.

- The IS auditor must plan the IS audit work in order to address the audit objectives and to comply with applicable professional auditing standards.

- IS audit staff are appropriately supervised to provide assurance that the audit objectives are accomplished and applicable professional auditing standards are met.

- During the course of the audit, the IS auditor obtains sufficient, reliable, relevant, and useful evidence to achieve the audit objectives effectively. In addition, the audit findings and conclusions are supported by the appropriate analysis and interpretation of this evidence.

- The IS auditor provides a report, in an appropriate form, to the intended recipients upon the completion of the audit work. The audit report must state the scope, objectives, period of coverage, and the nature and extent of the audit work performed. The report must identify the organization, the intended recipients, and any restrictions on its circulation. The report is to state the findings, conclusions, and recommendations, and any reservations or qualifications that the auditor has with respect to the audit.

- The IS auditor must request and evaluate appropriate information on previous relevant findings, conclusions, and recommendations to determine whether appropriate actions have been implemented in a timely manner.

Guidelines and procedures also are provided by ISACA that give examples and set requirements for work and reporting. These guidelines and procedures are considered the best practices and should be followed unless justification exists for deviating from them. The current version and details of these guidelines and procedures are available on the ISACA Web site at www.isaca.org and cover the following areas:

- Corporate governance of information systems
- Planning
- Use of the work of other auditors and experts
- Effect of involvement in the development, acquisition, implementation or maintenance process on the IS auditor's independence
- Audit evidence requirement
- Report content and form
- Use of computer-assisted audit techniques   *CAAT*
- Materiality concepts for auditing information systems
- Outsourcing of its activities to other organizations
- Audit documentation
- Audit sampling
- Due professional care
- Effect of pervasive controls
- Audit considerations for irregularities
- Audit charter
- Organizational relationship and independence
- Use of risk assessment in audit planning

In addition, several new guidelines and procedures are being developed and are in various stages of being moved into their final form. These subjects include

- The nonaudit role's effect on the IT auditor
- The third-party service provider's effect on IT controls
- The IT auditor's role in dealing with illegal acts and irregularities
- Auditing IT governance

The professional ethics code, which you agree to as a condition of your certification as an IS auditor, assures your employer and clients that you are above reproach and hold a high standard of integrity in your daily activities. These oaths should be seen as a guide to your behavior as you perform your task professionally.

CODE OF PROFESSIONAL ETHICS

INFORMATION SYSTEMS AUDITORS SHALL:

- ◆ Support the establishment of and compliance with appropriate standards, procedures, and controls for information systems.

- ◆ Comply with IS Auditing Standards as adopted by the Information Systems Audit and Control Association (ISACA).

- ◆ Serve in the interest of their employers, stockholders, clients, and the general public in a diligent, loyal, and honest manner, and shall not knowingly be a party to any illegal or improper activities.

- ◆ Maintain the confidentiality of information obtained in the course of their duties. This information shall not be used for personal benefit nor shall be released to inappropriate parties.

- ◆ Perform their duties in an independent and objective manner, and shall avoid activities that threaten, or may appear to threaten, their independence.

- ◆ Maintain their competency in the interrelated fields of auditing and information systems through their participation in professional development activities.

- ◆ Use due care to obtain and document sufficient client factual material on which to base conclusions and recommendations.

- ◆ Inform the appropriate parties of the results of the audit work performed.

- ◆ Support the education of management, clients, and the general public to enhance their understanding of auditing and information systems.

- ◆ Maintain high standards of conduct and character in both professional and personal activities.

You will need to get in the mind-set of basing your IS audit activities on these standards and performing your work within the code of ethics in order to pass the CISA exam. This code of ethics will be your guide and governing advice as you perform your work as an IS auditor. Failure to follow these standards is grounds for having your certification revoked. As you perform audit functions in a professional capacity, supporting the proper solutions based on your knowledge, integrity, and ethical standards will enable you to defend your actions as appropriate and to competently execute them. Many examples are provided throughout this book, but when you are unsure about a choice or decision from an ethical standpoint, it is always a signal that revisiting the professional code of ethics and using it to evaluate the choices available may be the right way to proceed.

residual risk

Risk-Based Approach

A recurring theme throughout the IS audit process is basing your audit approach on risk. It is important to fully understand the role that risk-based analysis has in the audit process because it is a primary differentiator in the exam question formats. A candidate must use a risk-based approach to pass the exam, because many of the exam questions rely on the candidate's ability to understand the best solution based on risk. It also should be used as the best practice for ensuring that the auditing you do is maximized in terms of value added to your employer and the organization being appraised by the audit process. This is the definition of "thinking like an auditor." The purpose of an audit is to identify risks and to ensure that the *residual risk* (risk remaining after controls are applied) is acceptable to management.

All activities in life have risk associated with them; some more than others. We are constantly doing a risk analysis hundreds of times a day in the normal course of our lives. If I push the speed limit will I get pulled over? Should I try this new product on the grocery shelf or buy the same brand as I always have? If I walk faster will I beat the traffic light at the corner? All actions have risk associated with them. It is the cost of doing any business at all. Consequences are evaluated, the probability of loss is computed, risks are weighed, then a choice is made.

Auditing is not about eliminating risks. It is intended to enable management to have a high level of confidence about what is going on. If risks were not being taken, there would be no decisions being made. Nothing would ever get done, which is not a good thing in a business process. Another way to look at it is with a financial savings analogy. The reason a high yield bond fund pays more interest in general is because the investor assumes a higher risk. More risk, more reward. No pain, no gain. However you want to look at it, there needs to be risks taken in business to make money. The businesses that manage their risks the best stand to be the most successful. Managing risk could mean monitoring the situation with no additional control actions taken, or it could mean reducing controls because the risks do not warrant the extent of the controls currently being applied. The old adage "don't spend $100 to solve a $10 problem" is what risk management is all about. Sometimes it is through sheer luck that business profits are obtained. Most well managed businesses do not depend upon luck for their profit margins. Auditing is designed to give management a view of the effectiveness of their processes and the associated controls and how well the risk is being managed. Auditing can be seen as a necessary fine-tuning process related to risk management.

Managing risk is what makes business successful. Unforeseen risks can be disastrous to a company. Understanding your pain threshold and having controls in place to ensure your risks match your tolerance for risk is what the audit process is all about. Accepting risk is a management decision. Insurance is a control that many choose to use and is a way of managing risk. Understanding the cost of the controls, both short term and in the long run, and determining the best solution in line with risk tolerance while weighing the potential gains are the skills an auditor will need to develop to be successful and to pass the CISA exam.

An auditor should consider three kinds of risk when planning an IT audit:

Inherent risk. The susceptibility of a business or process to make an error that is material in nature, assuming there were no internal controls. The inherent security risk of a default install of a UNIX system with no patches applied that is installed on a network is generally high. The inherent risk of a stand-alone PC is relatively low in comparison. Because the potential for material errors in IS areas with no controls in place is usually high, the inherent risk is usually high.

Control risk. The risk that the controls put in place will not prevent, correct, or detect errors on a timely basis. Log reviews may not result in timely detection or correction of errors, or they could result in errors easily missed—an example of control risk.

Detection risk. The risk that the IS auditor's substantive procedures will not detect an error that could be material. When the inherent and control risks are high, additional audit evidence should normally be obtained to offset the detection risk.

Know Your Business

The first step in getting a risk-based audit understanding is having a working knowledge of the business and its objectives. What are the business functions and objectives of the company? What is the current state of this type of business in general worldwide? Where does this company fit into the global marketplace for this line of business? What are the inherent risks in this business? Are there examples of risks that are in the news for this business type? What are the current and future trends for the products or services that this business provides? What does the financial market think about this company? Are their any surprises in their financial reports?

Identify risk and make sure residual risk is acceptable by management

Once you have a feel for the type of business, you need a level of understanding of the management culture of this particular business. What does the organization chart look like? Is it a flat or a very hierarchical organization structure? How does management react to bad news? How are the controls failures recognized and reported? What is the stated mission and vision of the company? What is the history of the executive team, their relative depth, and knowledge related to the business objectives? Is it a seasoned team with a track record of success or a newly formed team with no synergy? How much turnover is there in the company's management ranks? Does any of this background research identify the potential weaknesses or gaps that may result in "blind spots" for this organization?

For the IS/IT auditor, an additional aspect of the overall risk landscape is a base understanding of the processing model being utilized for performing the business processing. This will require experience or research into the best or common practices for this business type, models typically used for this kind of processing, and an understanding of the IS organization that is supporting the business. What is the auditee's overall IT architecture and technological direction? Are the systems being used for this business process appropriate based on the type of business, the business model, and the customers for this type of product or service? What is the maturity of the technical solutions being deployed and the company's apparent ability to use it successfully? Are there obvious deficiencies with the technical solutions being used? Is the technology appropriate for the type of business model being used? Are there complaints that are generally known about the way this company does business? What is the company's reputation for satisfying its customers? A quick walkthrough of the processing areas can usually speak volumes of the high level of risks that may need to be further investigated. The overall order, risk awareness, and control environment are easily identified with a little experience in IS audit risks and controls.

This preliminary investigation will position you to do several things:

- Understand the issues and current risks of the business.
- Speak to management intelligently about the business and gain their confidence in you as an auditor.
- Identify the hot spots that may require special attention in an audit through a cursory evaluation of controls.
- Understand the materiality of risks and potential control weaknesses.
- Know how to go about developing an audit scope that will add value to the business process by focusing on the risks most meaningful to management.

Controls

The CISA candidate must understand the various types of controls and their use. There are three basic kinds of controls.

Preventive Controls

Preventive controls are controls that are designed to prevent an error, omission, or negative act from occurring. Locking the door is a preventive control because it keeps the door from being opened. Any control that circumvents a risk from occurring is a preventive control. These are the best kinds of controls to put in place because the bad thing should never happen when a preventive control is applied to the risk. Taking positive actions and proactive steps based on previously identifying the risks are usually preventive controls. Putting procedures formally in place is another example of a preventive control. *Formally* implies that these procedures are in writing, monitored, and enforced.

Detective Controls

Detective controls are controls put in place to detect or indicate that an error or a bad thing has happened. An alarm on the door is a detective control because it tells you when the door has been opened but does not prevent someone from coming through the door. Reports and audit logs of activities are common examples or detective controls. Albeit after the fact, it is better to know some undesirable risk situation has occurred than to be unaware of the occurrence at all. Other examples of detective control activity include reconcilement of activities that have already occurred, such as bench reviews and periodic analysis of reports of transactions for discrepancies.

Corrective Controls

Corrective controls are those controls that enable a risk or deficiency to be corrected before a loss occurs. They are intended to fix an identified error after it has occurred and before the problem results in the consequence related to the risk. For example, if a computer process has a check subroutine that identifies an error and makes a correction before enabling the process to continue this would be considered a corrective control. A corrective control may be dependent upon a detective control to initially identify the error. Another example might be tied to a reasonableness check in an input program. Say, for example, that a medical billing process automatically checks for male users of a gynecological process at a medical facility. The program could stop and force an intervention either through a branching subroutine program that questions the input or through a human intervention subroutine that gives the input clerk an option to correct the error, should this situation occur. Implementation of this routine is a corrective control. An insurance policy is another perfect example of a corrective control. It steps in after the damage is done and fixes the problem.

Other types of control mentioned occasionally are deterrent control and risk transference as a control. Deterrent controls reduce the likelihood of a deliberate act to cause a loss or an error. Examples of deterrent controls would include barriers or warning signs (like login warning banners) to notify would be violators that causing a loss or an error is unacceptable. Another example, related to me by a friend, was when he changed an internal time card process at the workplace he managed, thus requiring the staff to fill out separate and lengthy reports for each time card error. This deterrent control quickly changed the behavior of the staff and reduced the risks and cost of inaccurate and incomplete time cards.

Risk transference is the process of paying someone else to assume the risk and to reimburse you should those risk situations actually result in loss. Many insurance companies aggregate the large loss portions of their business and cover this potential loss through reinsurance companies who specialize in assuming this risk. These are classified as corrective controls, because making the process whole by compensating for the losses incurred is a corrective action, which is assumed to be part of transferring the risk. If you wanted to split hairs, however, you could look at them separately.

In addition to understanding the risks of the organization and its business units, having a good grasp of the current, applicable, and cost effective controls that can mitigate risk is an important aspect of being able to successfully perform, audit, and make value-added recommendations. Recommendations that provide for the control of the risk without considering its impact and integration to the business process do not add much value to the business. Value-added recommendations will improve the process overall, while reducing the residual risk at the same time. It also is valuable to understand the limitations of controls and what they will and will not do to mitigate risks in various situations. Equally important is to understand how controls can work together in a way that one control can compensate for otherwise weak controls in isolation. Many times you will need to seek out *compensating controls* before you can determine if there is an actual exposure due to a single identified weak control. Compensating controls are controls that indirectly mitigate a risk and can therefore be seen as compensating for control weaknesses or the lack of controls directly acting upon a risk. Compensating controls are subjective and may require some circumstantial analysis before you are convinced that they are applicable.

Within IS auditing there are a few other ways to break down controls into subcategories that the CISA candidate must know.

General controls. Refers to controls that relate more to the general IS environment and to all IS applications as opposed to *application controls*, which affect the behavior of a particular application. Examples of general controls include:

- Environmental and physical security controls
- Production environment controls such as change control and library version control
- IS security policy
- IS development and deployment strategy
- Systems-wide planning for disaster recovery and business continuity

General controls can be manual or programmatic.

Pervasive IS controls. Refers to a subset of general controls that focus on the management and monitoring of information systems. Strong pervasive controls can contribute to assurance in an area where detailed controls by themselves would be weak. Weak pervasive controls can undermine otherwise strong detailed controls.

Detailed controls. Controls that apply to the acquisition, implementation, delivery, and support of specific applications and to general controls that are not pervasive in nature.

Types of Audit Engagements

Internal & External Auditing

There are basically two types of IS audits: those conducted by an internal audit function and those conducted by a third party or external auditors. Audits from external parties are usually performed to serve one of two purposes. Either they are initiated from within the company to obtain an independent and objective third-party opinion of the current state of risks or controls, or they are initiated because of external requirements (typically from a business partner or regulatory agency). The board of directors usually initiates the audits of internal governance or some other executive body as required by the committee's charter or oversight mission. In the case of public U.S. companies, the Securities and Exchange Commission (SEC) could federally mandate this oversight, or in the case of federally chartered financial institutions, the Office of the Comptroller of the Currency (OCC). A working knowledge of the requirements of the particular regulatory bodies that apply to the business that is the target of your audit assignment will be necessary in order for you to be sure that all of the requirements are met—a dry but necessary assignment.

SAS 70

If the service provided by a business is such that many buyers would likely seek "right to audit" clauses in their contracts, an alternative is for the provider company to get an independent third-party audit that will review their processes and provide assurance that they are adequate. This is referred to as a Statement on Auditing Standards (SAS) 70 audit and the scope of this service can be tailored to the specific needs of the contractual arrangements.

The SAS 70 for service organizations is an auditing standard developed by the American Institute of Certified Public Accountants (AICPA). SAS 70 is the authoritative guidance that enables service organizations, such as information systems processors, to disclose their processes and the related controls to their customers' auditors. It is important to understand that the service provider is the customer of the SAS 70 audit and the final report is their product. They may share it with their potential client, but the clients have no direct control of the scope of the SAS 70 audit. Careful review of the scope and objectives is important to those using a SAS 70 to gain reliance on provider services—caveat emptor! There are two types of SAS 70 reports and related audit efforts: types I and II. A type I SAS 70 depicts the organization's description of their controls at a specific point in time. The auditor performing the review will express an opinion on whether this description presents the controls fairly and whether these controls are suitably designed to achieve the specific control objectives defined in the scope of the report. No real substantive testing of the controls and processes takes place in a type I SAS 70 report.

A type II SAS 70 goes into the actual testing of these controls and is more exhaustive and therefore a more expensive option for the company's management. Typically the type II SAS 70 reports include the results of the testing of those controls and an opinion on the sufficient effectiveness to provide reasonable, but not absolute, assurance that the control objectives in the scope were achieved. These opinions only hold valid for the time period specified, which is typically over the past fiscal year, and they cannot be directly relied upon to predict the future performance of the company. Again, the scope and objectives of a SAS 70 is a variable negotiated by the party paying for the audit—the business owner—and may not represent all of the relevant risk areas or issues of the company.

The Audit Organization

In most corporate structures, an audit subcommittee of the board is charged with ensuring that the risks are being actively managed and audits are performed to keep them informed as to the current state of control and risk mitigation. This board committee is often the group that the internal audit department reports to formally, although they often report elsewhere administratively.

The auditor should have a clear mandate to perform the IS audit function. This mandate is documented in the audit charter. Wherever the charter exists for the entire audit function or internal department, for example, the IS audit mandate should be incorporated. The audit charter should clearly address the authority, accountability, and responsibility of the audit function.

External auditors may be engaged annually by the audit committee to review the company's finances and to give an opinion on the sufficiency of the bookkeeping and reporting processes. Today all the bookkeeping is done on computers, so in order to give an opinion on the financials, Certified Public Accountants (CPAs) and accounting firms first must get a comfort level on how well the IS processing environment performs and is being managed. If the information systems are not in order, how can the financials be relied on? Placing reliance on the systems that manage the company's financial information is the primary reason auditing and accounting firms need to perform an IS audit. Once assurance is gained that the systems processing the books have integrity and accuracy, an opinion can be provided on the numbers themselves.

The other reason to perform an external audit is because the company is providing a service for other companies and these other companies want some assurance that the service provider has good processes and is managing risks by appropriately by applying systems controls and good IS business practices. Various options are available to the organization providing services that a buyer wishes to audit. One option is to enable the buyer to come into their organization and perform an audit, perhaps on a periodic basis. Depending upon the rigor of the audit (a negotiated issue) and the level of risk being assumed through the purchase of this service, the buyer may require an audit that involves a lot of the provider company's time and resources to accommodate the audit (see Figure 1.1).

For independence purposes, staff members who are ideally positioned outside of the production-reporting structure should perform the internal audits. An example of a typical organization chart showing the placement of the audit function in relationship to the business process departments and the senior management is shown in Figure 1.1. This audit effort can be, in some cases, outsourced to external service providers, but the scope and objectives will remain the same. The internal audit function is intended to assist all members of the organization in discharging their responsibilities by analysis, appraisals, and recommendations for improvement concerning the activities reviewed. An internal audit ensures that the management and production teams are considering their risks and applying the controls as senior management intended.

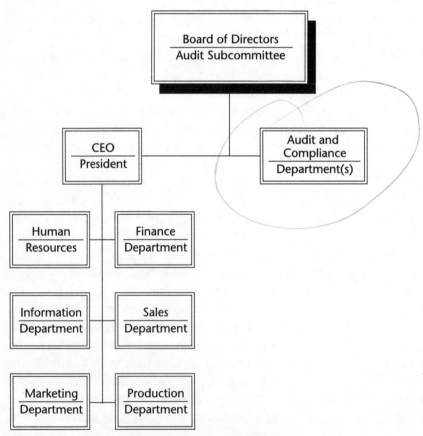

Figure 1.1 Audit organization reporting relationship.

Audit Planning

External audit planning is largely determined by the audit requirements of the paying party. Regulatory or contractual obligations also play a role in determining the scope of the external audits. In order to achieve the review objectives of the paying party, standard audit objectives are typically proposed for inclusion into the audit scope based on the experience of the external auditor. Due to cost factors, external audits tend to be of a higher level and broader in nature with less specific and detailed testing or narrow in scope when specific and detailed testing is required.

The scope of an internal audit is usually more tactically focused on high-risk areas or new and emerging risk areas. The annual revisiting of sensitive or critical operations also is a common focus of internal audits. This is especially true when an external audit or other regulatory recurring activities require that these processes are reviewed and relied upon for regular validation. The scope and objectives of the individual internal IS audit engagements generally support the overall audit plan for the organization in any given year. This plan should be based upon an annual risk assessment process.

This assessment process would follow classic quantitative risk assessment guidelines:

- Identify all of the relevant assets (information assets, processes the company is dependant upon, infrastructure that the company needs to perform daily operations, and so forth).

- Value the assets (cost to replace, reputation costs if unavailable, regulatory risk if not operating properly, and so forth).

- Identify the risks and threats associated with these assets (what can go wrong?)

- Identify the corporate tolerance for risk and the regulatory requirements for risk avoidance (discussed earlier).

- Identify the likelihood that these risks will actually happen (probability and expected frequency of occurrence).

- Identify the natural divisions and auditable entity groupings or reporting opportunities (based on political hierarchy, areas of responsibility, operating system groups, delineation of functional commonality, common processes, and so forth).

- Review the frequency and results of previous audits in given subject matter areas.

- Understand what amount of support the IS audit function will need to provide to non-IS audits for the audit department in the coming plan year.

- Assess the subset of the audit department's resources and budget available for performing IS audit reviews.

Materiality

Materiality is the concept of the relative significance or importance of a particular matter in the context of the whole organization. The assessment of what is material is a matter of professional judgment and includes the consideration of the effect of the error, omission, and so forth on the organization, which may arise from control weaknesses identified during the audit. The auditor needs to consider the overall or aggregate level of error acceptable to management (the pain threshold), and the potential result of the cumulative effect of a number of smaller errors, and so on. Understanding the quantity of transactions in a given time frame and the value of those transactions is a necessary input for determining the materiality of a control weakness on a transaction processing system. When the objective is to obtain a statement of assurance regarding IS controls, a control weakness is material if, as a result of the weakness, assurance cannot be given. Material control weaknesses should be considered a reason for issuing a qualified or adverse opinion depending on the audit objective. All material findings should be reported in the final audit report.

Irregularities

When planning an audit, the auditor is responsible for assessing the risk of fraud and incorporating the audit objectives and tests related to detecting irregularities. The category of *irregularities* such as fraud also includes the following:

- Acts that involve deception to obtain an illegal advantage

- Suppression or the omission of the effects of fraudulent transactions

- False recording of transactions without substance

- Manipulation, forgery, or falsification of records or documents

- Misappropriation or misuse of assets

- Acts that are noncompliant with existing agreements or contracts with third parties

- Errors arising from unauthorized access or use of IT systems

While there is no guarantee that the audit will identify existing irregularities, the audit plan should consider opportunities for employees to collude with other employees, management, or outsiders to create or hide fraudulent representations of material risks or the effectiveness of controls. The auditor must be familiar with the subject of fraud and the risk factors that contribute to the occurrence of fraud. The audit planning should take the following into consideration:

- Corporate ethics
- Adequacy of supervision
- Compensation and reward structures
- Vacation scheduling policies
- The history of the organization
- Management turnover and competency
- Previous audit reports and legal activity
- The competitive environment of the business environment and condition of the control structures
- The complexity, sophistication, and maturity of the technical solutions being applied to the business processes

The auditor will need to develop an ability to think like a fraud perpetrator in order to successfully seek out and identify risk factors that may need to be investigated for proper levels of control. A healthy suspicion is an attribute of a good auditor.

From all of this gathered information, an internal IS audit plan is devised and approved by the audit committee prior to any individual audit kick-off meeting. This plan is based on the current assessment of residual risk as outlined previously. During this planning process, preliminary scopes and objectives are identified for individual audits. High-level scope and coverage boundaries for a given audit are defined so that schedule times and resource allocation can be determined. It also is necessary for notification of the business units for audit timing and scheduling with the rest of their work schedules. These scopes should provide overall assurance to the audit committee that the material IS-related risks are assessed and reported on.

When planning an IS audit, it is important to focus on the goals and objectives of the audit. Always begin with the end in mind. Ask: "What needs to be evaluated in order to provide an opinion on the final goal or objective of the audit?" This is usually the point in the planning process where you have to realistically compromise. You must compromise between how much work you can actually perform according to your budget and time frame versus how much testing and sampling you will need to do in order to achieve a sufficient level of confidence on the opinion you intend to provide. Often, this exercise results in a narrowing of the scope in order for the audit to be successful.

A master planning document is often helpful to illustrate the process described previously. It can be used as a historical reference of the risk and controls decisions made and the overall risk assessment applicable at the time that the planning process was conducted for each year. In subsequent years, the rational for the decisions can be revisited and adjusted so you can more quickly and accurately get to the final draft of the plan and adapt to changes. Once the final IS audit plan has been reconciled with the other department efforts and approved for implementation, scheduling and notice to the client areas is the next step.

Scheduling

Schedules of individual audits, resources, the start and finish deadlines, and possible overlap of each audit all must be reconciled when developing a master IS audit schedule for the IS audit plan. Remember that time also must be allocated to vacations, training, departmental meetings, and other overhead-related time. Time allocation for an individual audit should include time for planning, fieldwork review, report writing, and post-audit follow-up. It is usually wise to set aside some time in reserve for unplanned issues that come up during the course of the year, either due to new risks or business issues that will require more work to satisfy the risk/control investigation that is warranted.

Clients should be given the opportunity to provide input into the final scope and goals of an audit plan and to the individual audits. There may be local concerns or newly emerging risk issues that the planning process was not aware of or did not account for that can be addressed by seeking out this input. Business unit management also should be given the courtesy of advance scheduling notice so that the disruption of the business processes is minimized.

Audit management may take the approach that audits should contain the element of surprise to ensure that the audit truly represents the actual control conditions by implementing their audits unannounced and capitalizing on the element of surprise. In some cases, gathering evidence before announcing an audit may be necessary to establish a known condition where IT management chronically disregards established controls. A poor control environment is not often correctable by advance notice of an audit, however. You may be able to fix up some issues cosmetically, but correcting the root problems requires basic process changes that advance notice will not enable an auditee to address. In fact, if the overall goal of the audit is to help the business and its management implement proper controls, improve performance, and assist with reaching the organization's common goals, then having the IS processes unit prepare for an audit by tightening the controls achieves much of this by itself. Actually it is more of a win-win scenario because the internal audit team then can report to management that controls are in place as desired, and the process and the business overall can benefit from the improved control position.

Self-Assessment Audits

When audit resources are limited or when the management culture is one that prefers to give guidance rather than evaluate compliance, a self-assessment audit is a good tool to use. These self-assessments can range from a white paper documenting the best practices or guidelines that a process area agrees to abide by to a formal checklist of tasks that the management completes and submits to the audit department declaring their level of compliance. Often, it is a blend of these assessments that usually involves little testing or validation on the part of audit as to the actual effectiveness of the controls. Depending on the regulatory requirements, this tool may not be acceptable for validating the controls. However, it may be similar to the collaborative efforts described previously in the win-win scenario. It does help foster cooperation and can result in a better understanding of the risks and willingness to apply the appropriate controls. When a process area seeks out audit help and consultation related to inherent risks and proper controls, this is a good way to establish a nonthreatening process to address the issues. Self-assessments can be a good head start for an area with a particularly difficult audit on the horizon and also gives the audit team a good beginning in creating a program for evaluating controls when a more formal review is requested.

Audit Staffing

Part of planning IS audits involves making auditor assignments. Schedules, individual audit timing, and skill requirements must all be juggled to satisfy the plan requirements. Aligning the audit and technical skill requirements with the skills of the available staff and the development goals of the team members requires thought and management skills. The Auditor in Charge (AIC), who will lead the individual audit, must be knowledgeable of the technology, risks, and audit techniques unique to the subject and be able to provide guidance and developmental assistance for staff auditors assisting in the fieldwork. The AIC will be responsible for the final product and will approve all of the work papers, testing, and results. The AIC will represent the audit department through the presentation of the final report and ensure that the opinions rendered represent both the risks and controls adequately. Their communication skills (both verbal and written) must be well developed enough to give management the sense that the audit effort is well managed and under control at all times.

There may be a requirement for skill sets that are not available from the existing staff. Opportunities for partnering with the IS department experts are ideal for building relationships and educating IS staff members on the control best practices while obtaining knowledge of technical subject matters, as long as independence can be maintained. In addition, opportunities for formal training and individual staff auditor development also exist. Care must be taken to ensure that the end result does not misrepresent the overall audit effort as inexperienced and unprofessional. Partnering with the external auditors to gain technical knowledge also is a viable option that pays off for the companies' external auditors because it enables them to more easily rely on the internal audit's assessment of controls. Additional planning time may need to be allocated to an audit where skills need to be developed before the audit can be conducted professionally.

Planning the Individual Audit

Once you have a particular audit assigned with a broad idea of the scope and the objectives defined, you will need to plan the audit. Planning an audit involves the following:

- Notifying the client and working out a schedule and pre-audit meetings
- Defining the scope and objectives
- Determining the corresponding business processes on which to focus
- Understanding the process and its technical components
- Understanding and validating the inherent risks and threats of the processes and components with the client
- Determining the desired controls or risk mitigants and validating expected controls and current residual risk with the client
- Identifying management tools that would validate or report on the proper functioning of the controls

- Performing a risk and control analysis to document the risk exposures and corresponding auditing priorities of the audit program components and their relevance to the scope and objectives

- Creating an audit program that incorporates the risk control analysis, gathers the evidence needed to determine the sufficiency of the existing controls and risk mitigants, and identifies the weaknesses

- Finalizing staff resource and skill requirements

- Determining the time allocation for the components of the audit based on the materiality of the risks, the various tasks associated with testing each component, and the skill level of the staff

- Establishing the framework of the work papers and fieldwork documentation

IS Audit Types

IS audits span the continuum from the general to the specific, which is discussed in detail in the rest of this prep guide. High-level audits of IS and production governance are useful to determine whether the management control organization exists to enable more specific IS processes to function efficiently. Evaluation of the business processes and the systems used to perform the business functions are covered in Chapter 7, "Business Process Evaluation and Risk Management." These types of reviews will analyze the efficiency and effectiveness of the business support systems and the implementation of risk management processes. High-level *general control* audits are intended to give overall comfort of processes, similar to SAS 70 type I audits.

At the next level, IS department audits will focus on the structure in place to match the business goals and objectives with the appropriate technologies and will use them with sufficient control to keep the risks and threats within acceptable limits. These audits are explained in Chapter 2, "Management, Planning, and Organization of Information Systems."

Audits of the overall technical infrastructure are important to assess the underlying transport layer of the information processing underpinnings. These audits review the operations procedures, hardware, and systems performance processes. Reviews of the various networks (voice, data Internet, and so on) and gaining assurance that the assets are managed properly through service level agreements, problem determination, and follow up are important aspects of the overall review of information system management. These audits are explained in detail in Chapter 3, "Technical Infrastructure and Operational Practices."

The security and protection of information assets can be reviewed at a security group level or scoped to specific platforms or data types. A review of the physical security and environmental controls is a popular audit to ensure that the more routine maintenance of data processing is occurring as expected. These subjects are covered in Chapter 4, "Protection of Information Assets." This is the largest part of the CISA exam and the most important aspect of all IS audit-related efforts.

Reviewing the companies' ability to continue operations after a disaster of business interruption has received renewed attention recently. Many aspects of acceptable risk have taken on new meaning after the tragedies of September 11, 2001. The entire process and audit programs for assessing the various processes are covered in Chapter 5, "Disaster Recovery and Business Continuity."

Reviewing the processes associated with application development and deployment can be targeted to the overall corporate process used, or more specifically, focused on the process used by a single group or business process. It may be targeted to a single application; or depending on the size and complexity of the technical solution, scope, and objectives, the audit might even focus on a subset of an application's development, implementation, acquisition, or maintenance process. An ideal engagement would be to review an implementation of an application as it is being deployed. This opportunity enables the business to ensure that the risks are identified up front and addressed when changes are comparatively easy to correct. These audits are defined in Chapter 6, "Business Application Systems Development, Acquisition, Implementation, and Maintenance," and are a major portion of the CISA exam.

Risk Assessment

All control techniques should be applied only commensurate with the risks and the associated costs in mind. Both the cost to implement and maintain the control and the costs related to a loss must be weighed in this assessment to determine the benefit of controls compared to losses that may be experienced. Risk is academically defined as

$$RISK = Threat \times Vulnerability \times Cost.$$

In a *quantitative* risk assessment, risks are identified by first looking into how much a single error would result in loss. Then, a determination is made as to what the cost would be in terms of recovery, loss of future business, reputation, fines, and so forth. Both direct and indirect losses need to be considered. After that, an estimation of how often this might realistically happen in a given year is computed. Multiplied together, this becomes the *Annual Loss Expectancy (ALE)* or *Estimated Annual Cost (EAC)* related to a particular risk. A quantitative risk assessment approach adds up these potential losses based on the measurement process described previously and places an overall value on the risk exposure using this as a benchmark to determine whether risk is acceptable, and if it has increased or decreased over a period of time.

A *qualitative* risk assessment, which is more widely used, does not require the determination of probabilities and an exhaustive cataloging of assets. In this process, threats are first identified. Threats are anything that can *go wrong* or *bad things* that may happen. It is the potential of an adverse effect to cause harm. Threats are a combination of intent, capability, and opportunity.

Vulnerabilities are weaknesses in systems or processes that provide potential points of exploitation, which would enable a threat to be carried out. Vulnerabilities can be measured in the likelihood or ease with which the vulnerability can be exploited (easier to do implies more vulnerable).

The risk is therefore the chance that the threat and the vulnerability result in an error combined with the impact or cost of that error, should it occur. Risks must be identified and then prioritized in order to apply your audit resources to the best and most efficient advantage. You will always want to demonstrate that you have risk ranked your audit testing steps and worked from highest risk to lowest risk until your resources run out. Several kinds of risks must be considered in IS audits.

There are many ways to gather process-, risk-, and control-related information when planning an audit. Often direct communication with the management is necessary at some point in this process to get their understanding of what the processes are and how they work. During this communication process, you can get their feel for what controls exist and what should be in place, thus getting a level set of inherent and residual risks before testing formally begins. Your planning objectives are to

- Define all of the relevant processes involved in managing the business in detail.

- Understand their inputs and outputs.

- Define the risks related to each of these processes.

- Seek an agreement on what control techniques a reasonable person would put in place to mitigate these risks, based on the risk tolerance of the business management.

- Identify tools that management uses to ensure that these controls are in place and working properly.

How much cost X how often X

Sometimes mapping out the processes using flowcharting tools or work flow block diagrams helps everyone get on the same page as to what the process is and enables the auditor to see where additional processes, which are not under the direct control of the management team responding to the audit, may impact the review. Scope and priority decisions are often necessary in this phase and decisions need to be made to expand the review into these tangential areas or to conclude that they are out of the scope of this audit.

CobiT

Understanding the concept of the control objectives is a necessary part of your audit planning and fieldwork efforts. Introduced in 1996, Control Objectives for Information and Technology (CobiT) is the single most revolutionary concept introduced by ISACA in recent years. Now in its third version, CobiT has implications that you will need to fully understand and become familiar with using in order to be successful as an IS auditor. Parts of CobiT are now considered to be an open standard for widespread use and adoption as an audit tool. CobiT is a catalog of control objectives that is divided into four domain areas. There are 34 high-level control objectives, which are broken down into 318 specific control objectives and defined to support this framework. A high-level view of the CobiT Framework is depicted in Figure 1.2.

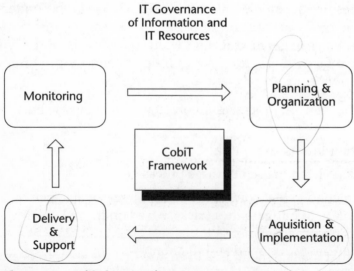

Figure 1.2   CobiT framework.

The control objectives are laid out into 34 naturally grouped sets of processes for which key and detailed level control objectives have been defined. A *control objective* can be defined as a goal that ensures that some set of risks does not occur. Control objectives almost can be thought of as the inverse of a risk. If a risk is the potential that something bad can happen, then a control objective ensures that the risk does not materialize. Looking at control objectives this way quickly enables you to get a catalog of potential risks to refer to when you are looking for items to consider in your risk assessment. This risk list can subsequently be used to define audit programs that are comprehensive and to ensure that the organization, through your audit and assessment of controls, meet their objectives. There are many interesting and unique risks to consider when you are planning an audit and assessing the risks of an IT process or system. Once identified, risks are considered to be applicable to the process or system that is the object of your audit scope. You must prioritize these risks in order to maximize your effort in reviewing how they are controlled. Risks to consider include the risk that

- Strategic IT plans are not properly defined and developed.
- Information architecture is not developed and deployed.
- Technological direction is not effectively planned and documented.
- The IT organization and its roles and responsibilities are not defined and documented.
- The company's IT investment is not managed properly.
- The IT control and management environment is not communicated and implemented effectively.
- IT personnel are not managed and trained.
- Contractual and regulatory requirements are not complied with.
- IT risks are not assessed and actively managed.
- IT projects are not managed correctly.
- Quality control processes are not sufficient or effective.
- Effective solutions do not result from requirements, analysis, and design processes.
- Application software is not acquired or maintained effectively.
- Technology architecture is not acquired or maintained effectively.
- IT procedures are not developed and maintained.
- Systems are not tested and implemented adequately.

- Changes to the IT environment are not appropriately managed.
- Service levels are not defined and managed.
- Third-party services are not managed effectively.
- Performance and capacity issues are identified and addressed.
- Continuity plans are not developed, tested, and maintained to meet the needs of the business in times of necessity.
- Systems security is not sufficient to meet the business needs.
- IT costs are not identified and attributed back to the users of the services.
- Users of the IT infrastructure do not get proper training.
- IT customers and users do not get adequate help and support for their problems and queries.
- The IT configuration is controlled and managed effectively.
- Problems and incidents are not identified, tracked, escalated, and resolved in an effective manner.
- Data is not managed and cared for properly.
- IT facilities are not maintained and secured effectively.
- Scheduling and other operations functions are not performed adequately.
- IT processes are not monitored to ensure that performance goals are met.
- Internal controls are not assessed and managed according to risks.
- Independent assurance of how well the previous risks are managed is not obtained.
- The audit function is independent and does not perform according to professional standards.

CobiT is very versatile and was created from an extensive source list that is both comprehensive and authoritative. It was designed with the business processes and objectives in mind so it would fit naturally into any existing IT environment. It is broken down in several layers of detail so the needs of the various levels of management and oversight requirements can all be best met. It can be used in several different ways in an organization:

Communications Tool.   "There is a method, here's how we look at the controls."

Organizational Tool. Identifies organizational structure best practices and ensures all necessary business process support elements have been considered.

Consensus Building Tool. Utilize the various levels of detail for the appropriate management structure.

Engagement "Scoping" Tool. "I want to review this process. What control objectives are involved?"

IT Self Assessment Tool. "How am I doing?"

EXAMPLE OF THE RISK CONTROL MATRIX TEMPLATE

Process. Define the grouping of activities that can be identified as a single logical process (that is, Managing Hardware Resources, Contingency Planning, Information Security, and so forth).

Control Objective (1). A control objective is one of the many goals that should be established to ensure process control. Each process will have at least one audit objective. Control objectives are defined here and are sequentially numbered throughout the Risk Control Matrix.

Risk Exposure. Document the result of not meeting the identified control objective; "What can go wrong." Potential exposures include financial loss, unauthorized or accidental destruction, disclosure, or the modification of data and other factors that would negatively impact your operation or the reputation of the organization. Ranking the risk on some kind of scale (1-10) is useful in prioritizing and subsequently determining the materiality of unsatisfactory conditions.

Control Technique(s). Measures implemented by management to ensure the fulfillment of the control objective, therefore mitigating the occurrence of the potential risk exposure. Control Techniques are detailed in this section and are sequentially numbered for each separate audit objective and related risk exposure.

Preventative. List those controls that are designed to prevent an error, omission, or negative act from occurring.

Detective. List those controls that indicate that an error, omission, or negative act has occurred.

Corrective. List those controls that correct identified errors, omissions, or negative acts.

Management Tools. Document any mechanisms that management utilizes to monitor the effectiveness of the various control techniques (reports, notifications, and so forth).

The latest enhancements to the CobiT toolset also include provisions for

- Maturity models for assessing your organizations control over processes in comparison with industry and international standards
- Critical success factors defining the most important implementation guidelines
- Key performance indicators that define measures that communicate to management whether the IT processes have met their business requirements

Although you do not need to go out and buy this tool in order to pass the CISA exam, you will find that its contents are very beneficial to your daily auditing tasks. You should encourage your clients to adopt this model because it is a *de facto* standard of the best control practices, and as an auditor, you can rely on it to keep you aware of all the things that need to be considered for your audits to be comprehensive and thorough.

It can be helpful to both the business and the auditor to create a risk control matrix with the auditee as part of the planning for the audit. If policy requires that all businesses understand and actively manage their risks, this type of documentation may already exist in the IT or business departments. This collection of process risks and controls can be a viable tool for prioritizing and defending risk-based decisions.

Audit Objectives and Scope

Defining the scope and objectives of an audit is the first formal step of an audit engagement. It sets the stage and identifies the key areas of results. The CISA candidate must understand how this scope definition places boundaries around the activities, reporting requirements, and obligations of the audit.

Ideally, the audit scope and objectives definition is a collaborative effort in which the management of the business and its processes is heavily involved. The more input you can get from the management related to their insight into the inherent risks of the processes, the controls in place, and the challenges they face on a daily basis, the more valuable and relevant your audit report will be. The necessary first step in planning of an audit is discussing the objectives of the auditee relevant to the audit area and the technology infrastructure. After some experience, you will quickly recognize that the audit has already begun and you are informally interviewing the auditee and forming an opinion of the control environment as you plan the audit and seek their input. Part of the planning process will encompass understanding the business requirements and environment as input to materiality decisions made when planning an audit.

Based on the assigned objectives, you will present the plan to the client, seek their concurrence, and entertain their suggestions for modification of the scope. Sometimes you will be asking for documentation or tours of the process to better understand the technology being used or the actual work-flow. Depending on whether this is a cyclical audit or not, you may be looking for how you might do things differently this time or how you will scale the scope down to something digestible in the time frame allotted to the audit. In all cases, it is important for management to understand how the risks can affect the business and how the controls might help make their jobs better or more profitable. If they do not agree with or at least understand the reasoning behind controlling risks to meet the business needs, you have a different kind of risk on your hands that may need to be addressed off-line with senior management. Risk assessment and prioritization of identified risks are all necessary steps in defining audit scope and objectives.

As you identify the risks and controls, both potential and existing, the IS auditor will need to consider the extent to which they will need to test existing controls in order to place reliance upon them. If the scope requires reliance on controls over a period of time, you will need to plan on gathering evidence and testing procedures across that period of time to test the effectiveness of the controls. Preliminary evaluation of these controls will be necessary to plan your testing and resource needs properly. For example, historic data may need to be reviewed through logs or other audit documentation and will therefore take additional time or testing processes compared to an audit with the scope's point that is time control evaluation.

The scope and objectives are typically presented to management in writing and formally presented in an audit engagement or kick-off meeting. Depending upon the preliminary agreements that may already have taken place, management may negotiate terms and conditions at this meeting. In this meeting, they should layout the concerns that need to be reviewed and the assurances they are seeking as a result of this engagement. This also is the time for deciding how ongoing communications will be managed during the course of the engagement in terms of frequency, length, detail of updates, and who should be the contacts.

Using the Work of Other Auditors

You may wish to include work performed by other auditors or subject matter experts as input to your audit work and to support your conclusions.

Use of this work may need to be specifically included into the audit charter and scope of the audit and should be considered when planning the audit. This is especially relevant when external auditors wish to rely on work performed by internal auditors. The independence and competence of other auditors will need to be taken into consideration as well as the scope and objectives of the audit being used, because input also will need to be taken into consideration. The usefulness and appropriateness of the information being reported as well as its relevance and the time frames of the work all are factors to be taken into consideration when choosing to utilize information provided by others for making your opinions and conclusions. Sufficient review of the other work in order to assess its relevance and applicability will need to be performed before committing to its use.

Impact of Outsourcing on IS Audits

When planning an IS audit where parts of the processes are managed by or delegated to third parties, special considerations must be made. The rights to audit may be unclear and an investigation into what contractual rights the company has to have audits preformed on the work done by the third party will need to be conducted. Available SAS 70 reports may need to suffice as the assessment of the controls and performance conclusions of the third party. The audit charter, its scope and objectives, will need to account for this situation and how it can be addressed in meeting the overall audit objectives. This must be agreed upon before the audit can begin. Audit steps and associated fieldwork may need to be performed with the cooperation and involvement of the third party in order to satisfy the scope and objectives of the audit. Additional risks may present themselves as inherent to the third-party relationship and limitations of control effectiveness due to the arrangement. Service level agreements, reliance on the audits performed by auditors, and the amount of access to the processes and relevant evidentiary information are considerations that may impact an audit of this nature.

Independence of an Auditor

It is important to clearly prove the independence of the auditor in relation to the subject matter being audited at all times. Processes under the direct control of the auditor cannot be audited without compromising independence. Any actual or perceived independence conflicts should be fully noted in the work papers and explained in the final report, should the auditor continue to be associated with the audit after these potential independence conflicts have arose. Factors to consider when assessing independence on a regular basis throughout the audit engagement include the following:

- Changes in personal relationships
- The financial interests of the auditor
- Opportunities for personal advantage or financial gain
- Prior work assignments and responsibilities

The perception of the auditor's attitude and the appearance of independence should be maintained at an adequate level throughout the engagement. Audit management should be consulted when it is perceived that the independence of the auditor may be impairing the audit. Audit management has the responsibility of reviewing and assessing the audit work for the potential independence compromise.

Audit Engagement

Once the goals and objectives are agreed to, they must be clearly stated in the *engagement letter*, which will be referred to throughout the audit engagement as a touchstone of direction and guidance over the work performed. This letter serves as the audit charter for this particular engagement and should confirm the following three key aspects in detail:

Responsibility. Demonstrated through the documentation of the scope, objectives, deliverables, and risk assessment related to the audit engagement. The independence of the auditor should be established in this document along with recognition of any specific auditee requirements related to the objectives or scope.

Authority. Establishes the right to access information necessary to form an opinion and limitations associated with that access. Evidence of the agreement between the auditor and the auditee to engage in the audit should be formally documented in this letter.

Accountability. Establishes the deliverables and target dates. The rights of the auditee should be delineated, and the communication and a process for the escalation of issues should be defined.

During the kick-off meeting, communication expectations are agreed upon between the audit team and the client management. Update meetings are scheduled and planned for, and the level of notification and interaction along with the requirements for successful audit completion are outlined.

Creating and Maintaining Work Papers

Your work papers are the internal set of documentation that houses all of the relevant information about the audit. It is the evidence and justification of your activities and conclusions. It should walk a reasonably competent IS auditor through your process in a sufficient amount of detail that would enable them to agree with your approach and directions and draw the same conclusions related to the findings and their relative materiality. If a legal case were ever to be brought against the auditee, you should be aware that the regulators can and have subpoenaed internal auditors' work papers into court. Work papers have the following basic sections:

- Cover sheet with history and signoff
- Key audit documents
- Background
- Planning and risk assessment
- Audit program
- Evidence
- Permanent files

Whether the work papers are hard copy or electronic, they will have this basic structure. With IS audits it is often more convenient or practical to gather evidence in a electronic fashion, but storing, retrieving, and proving the integrity of the gathered information needs to be considered when using electronic evidence. It is often difficult to produce a completely electronic set of work papers, but scanning and converting all of the paper-based documents is acceptable. Many regulators still find comfort is seeing information in writing in an ink-signed document when they are considering matters that are officially presented. It may take some time before this preference type changes.

There are opportunities through electronic work paper tools to cross reference findings to the evidence found on reports. A few currently available examples of work paper automation tools include

- Audit Leverage (www.auditleverage.com)
- AutoAudit (www.paisleyconsulting.com/)
- TeamMate (www.pwcglobal.com/)

Time management and scheduling also can be managed through many of these products. Often complex database management and infrastructures are required to maintain this type of tool for a large audit department, however.

Managing hard copy work papers involves a good filing and retrieval system as well as sign-out and document management processes. In addition, the life cycle of the audit work papers must be managed so that information is available historically when relevant or required for regulatory purposes and to be destroyed of properly when your destruction and purging policies and procedures call for it. You will need to understand and follow the legal and due care requirements for strongly securing work papers and work in progress. This information is a compilation of the control weaknesses of an audit area and should not be accessible without a legitimate *need to know.*

Due Care

Your work papers should always survive the *reasonably competent third party* test when you are unsure about the level of detail, quality, or sufficiency of the documentation. This concept is referred to as *Due Care* and is formally defined as ". . . the level of diligence that a prudent and competent person would exercise under a given set of circumstances," according to the ISACA IS Auditing Guideline on Due Professional Care.

Due Professional Care means exercising your professional judgment while conducting your audit work, something a person with a special skill set, such as a certified IS auditor, should be in practice of doing. Due Care is relevant to sample selection, evidence reliability decisions, computer-assisted audit techniques (CAATs) use, and conclusion relevance, and so forth.

This does not mean, however, that on occasion the wrong conclusions will not be drawn. Recipients of audit reports have an appropriate expectation that the work and conclusions were made with professional due care. IS auditors should not accept assignments where they cannot perform in the manner expected of a professional due to skill level, knowledge, or resource inadequacies, for example.

Cover Sheet

The cover sheet of the audit work papers is the table of contents for the audit. It provides an overview of the chronological and logical layout of the audit and the relevant memos related to the document through an indexing and cross-reference scheme. All relevant dates should be available on this cover sheet including the destruction date. The cover sheet or contents should enable a reviewer of the audit to quickly understand where they might find key documents and the time frame and resource information related to the audit. Tick mark legends or any other shorthand used throughout the work papers should be identified on the cover sheet, because it is a standard place to reference the navigation nuances of the work. If this is a hard copy work paper set, this might be where the review and final sign-off of the audit are evidenced. Depending upon the review process implemented by the AIC, you may initial the sampling of the audit work and date those reviews directly on the cover sheet. Budget allocations and final resource use also can be tracked here as a reminder to future audit engagements of any overruns or variances that were experienced during the audit.

Key Documents

Located directly behind the cover page should be the key documents relevant to the audit. These might include the following:

- Engagement, planning, and scheduling memos to the client
- Pre-audit documentation requests given to the client to expedite the testing and review process
- Internal control questionnaires, which are tools that are used to gather preliminary state information related to the existing controls, policy, and procedures
- Organizational charts and lists of key personnel and their roles
- Any major correspondence agreement of the scope, objectives, risks, or existing controls with the client management
- Contracts or legal agreements relevant to the audit
- Summary of the risk and control weaknesses identified. This is a working document that is used at the end of the audit to aggregate issues into common themes and pervasive control weaknesses for report writing and management communication purposes
- Closing meeting minutes; notification of control weaknesses to management; and documentation related to the final disposition of audit findings used to formulate the final report
- Final audit report (best position may be first in the document list)

Background

This work paper section has several uses depending on the audit department culture. It may be used to carry forward comments to alert the next audit team of outstanding issues that need to be considered for inclusion in future audits. It could include key documentation that will help the auditor understand the business, processes, or technical architecture that impacts this audit, which is relevant to understanding of the material risk issues for this audit. Sometimes abstracts of company documents, sales brochures, and presentation documentation related to the auditee's process are stored here to give the auditor a sense of the final product or service that this organization provides. Historical information related to mergers, acquisitions, or technological upgrades and process changes will often be documented here to set a baseline of why certain risks are higher in this situation.

At times it is important to use the background section for administrative content such as travel directions, good places to stay and eat, pitfalls experienced by the audit team in performing the audit, tips for making the audit easier for those repeating the audit in future cycles, and so on. In general, the background should inform the reviewer of all the information needed to adequately understand the business, process, technical, risk, and control situation.

Planning and Risk Assessment

This section of the work papers is for housing all of the efforts and information gathered to understand the processes and technology relevant to the agreed scope and objectives. Individual audit risk assessments should supply the overall audit risks assessment and planning tools mentioned earlier.

Audit Program

Once all of the relevant technical processes are identified and the extent of the involvement of these processes is understood for the purposes of planning the audit, they can be separated into logical subdivisions of the audit program. These divisions are based on the expertise required, geographical divisions, managerial responsibility divisions, or some method that worked well in the prior audit approaches. Evidence of approval by the audit management with their assessment of risks and planned scope and objectives should be well documented in this section.

The audit program is a high-level description of the audit work to be performed. It is a series of audit steps designed to meet the audit's objectives by identifying the process-related risks, determining the controls that are in place to mitigate that risk, and testing those controls for effectiveness and sufficiency to successfully mitigate the risk to an acceptable level. The collection of all audit steps that must be performed to reach the desired conclusions is called the audit program. This program should be prepared in advance of the fieldwork and include sections for testing, evaluation, and conclusions for all of the significant risk areas that were identified and approved for inclusion in the audit's scope and objectives. As dictated by the style and format used by your audit organization, assignments, and the work allocation of auditors of particular sections will be documented in the audit's program sections of the work papers.

Some programs are organized by process, thus exploring all of the risks and control objectives for a particular process. This is a useful way of developing an audit program when different managers are accountable for separate processes, because it enables the audit to focus on areas divided by a manager and provides a vehicle for prioritizing risks for a single process.

Another organizational style is by risk or control objective. In this manner, a particular risk can be fully explored across all relevant processes and functions, thus enabling an aggregate view of the impact of a particular control objective. This type of audit program approach typically is used by upper management in order to understand the impact of changes or the exposure that requires a broad corporate view of a particular issue.

Provisions for tracking risk/control weaknesses and for aggregating them in a summary format also should be planned for in work paper layout. In addition, standard locations for making notes on program steps, such as when noting the percentage of steps complete, filling out the auditor date of completion and management review, and making comments, should be part of the format adopted in an audit program. Each section should provide an approach that would enable a reasonably competent third-party auditor to follow through with your process and draw the same conclusions. Tying the testing and related findings directly back to the risks and drawing conclusions and making recommendations that support the business needs is the best way to ensure this is done.

Test Work and Evidence

All test work relevant to the evaluation of controls should be evidenced in the work papers including

- Information about the sources of the test information
- Who performed the work
- A description of the testing procedure
- The rational for the testing approach
- The conclusions drawn from the testing exercise

Sufficient levels of spot-checking by the AIC also should be noted in the work papers in order to strengthen the validity of the test work and associated conclusions. Evidence, as a result of the testing activities performed by the auditor, will be the main tool used to draw and support conclusions on the effectiveness of the existing controls and will be the basis for recommendations for improving the control environment.

Post-Audit Checklist

More of an administrative section of the work papers, the post audit checklist section will evidence that all of the I's were dotted and T's crossed. In this section, you may find several items: test work reviews, sign-offs related to risks, report acceptances, recommendation agreements, action items, target dates, follow-up information, clearing of review notes, logging and filing of audit results, or possibly audit committee reporting instruments. Total resource usage and budget reconciliation as well as destruction of prior work papers and clean up of information that does not support the objectives of the audit could be included in the post-audit checklist items.

Fieldwork

IS audit fieldwork is performed to ensure that the business needs are being met through the systems, processes, and IT infrastructure and their associated controls. This is accomplished by challenging the effectiveness of existing controls and by identifying the need for improved controls to meet the control objectives. Fieldwork is associated with every program step in the audit program. It represents testing that looks at the controls in a particular place at a point in time. If the audit scope covers a span of time, evidence will need to be gathered that represents that particular span of time. If the audit time frame is inclusive of the present, then what is observed and the evidence that is gathered is representative of what should be concluded on during the present, regardless of whether issues are corrected or changed during the audit. Professional judgment will be called to the test here once again.

Once a program has been further delineated into program steps in some structure, the auditor must decide how best to obtain the information and evidence necessary to opine on the condition of the controls.

Control Objectives and Audit Approach

A typical audit program section will identify the control objectives that must be met and will target a particular process that must be reviewed for that objective. Using the planning and risk assessment and control objective information gathered earlier, you should already have preliminary information available on the particular process, its functions, the technologies involved, the current controls in place, and any special circumstances that you want to be sure to review when performing the field work. The steps that are necessary to guide the auditor into forming an objective opinion are listed in terms of the tests that need to be performed, questions that need to be answered, and so forth. From this point, it is up to the auditor to conduct the fieldwork necessary to conclude the process. The auditor performing the work must determine how much more they need to understand about the audited area in order to draw a professional conclusion on the state of risk and control.

Referencing

Throughout your fieldwork, you will be referencing other documentation to support your work. You will need to determine a reference-indexing scheme that will easily relate to the steps in your audit program. For example, reports and forms are items that will be gathered as evidence that is reviewed and possibly notated, then indexed and referenced as supporting evidence when drawing conclusions. If using electronic work papers, the audit process will need to differentiate those items of evidence that are maintained electronically from those found on hard copy. A separate coding scheme may identify them easily so reviews can quickly be performed. Whether your evidence is in an electronic or hard copy form, you also may want to adopt a color-coding scheme through highlighting. This scheme can be used, perhaps, for further identifying sections of the referenced evidence relevant to a particular issue to easily enable a reviewer to identify what part of the evidence supports the referenced issue. Good tick mark legend practices will be very beneficial in keeping your work paper references easily understood and defendable.

Obtaining Evidence to Achieve the Audit Objectives

Evidence is gathered and used as a basis for forming an audit opinion. The more independent the evidence source is, the more reliable it is, and it can be depended on to make conclusions. For example, documentation provided from customers on the service they are receiving is more reliable than data presented by the management on the customer satisfaction level.

When planning an audit the auditor should take into account the kind of evidence that will be required, its use in achieving the audit objectives, and its reliability. The auditor should choose the best evidence available that is consistent with the importance of the audit objective. The evidence should be sufficient, reliable, relevant, and useful in forming opinions and drawing conclusions. When sufficient evidence cannot be obtained, this must be documented in the work papers. Evidence can be obtained through rough manual audit procedures, CAATs, or both.

There are several ways to gather evidence in the fieldwork process. All methods used to gather evidence should be recorded on the evidence or in the work papers so a reviewer can determine how to repeat the process if necessary, and so that a determination can be made as to the independence of the evidence's source. In all cases, it is important to document your understanding of the area being audited, its systems and technology, and the control environment because it is the basis for your conclusions.

Flowcharts

Flowcharts are a great way to get an understanding of the business processes. Pictures are worth a thousand words when it comes to understanding the interactions of various processes and how the transaction flow has dependencies and branches that run in various directions. Often seeing the "big picture" helps to identify possible risk points and other influencing factors that were not initially considered until a pictorial view was assessed. A flowchart may be documented in the work papers and subsequently used as a road map to be referenced repeatedly so a reviewer can identify why particular concerns warrant assessment, such as those concerns you have during the course of your fieldwork. Flowcharts also can be a useful tool when making a recommendation on improving a process by showing steps and their interaction both before and after the proposed changes. There are many popular software tools available for documenting process flows.

Documentation Reviews

Most audit work involves some level of documentation review. Many times this requires reading through policies, procedures, standards, training materials, customer and sales information, reports to regulatory bodies, legal agreements, contracts, and so on, to determine whether the information is fair, accurate, and sufficient to be used for the purpose represented by management. At times when the documentation is rather lengthy, it is advisable to include only excerpts or the table of contents when evidencing these items into the work papers to keep the work papers manageable. When regulatory issues are involved, it is sometimes necessary to include the entire copy of the document and to footnote it with comments as it is reviewed. In all cases, conclusions in the work paper referencing the documentation review must conclude with the testing performed relevant to the audit objective at hand.

Narratives

Narratives are the paragraphs of written word that explain observations, interviews, or tours conducted by the auditor in pursuit of the audit objective. Most fieldwork contains some level of narrative, because it is in the narrative where the conclusions are drawn and the assessments are made as to the sufficiency of the controls in place. Care must be taken to contain the amount of narrative included in the fieldwork. Too much verbiage can be hard to follow and may leave the reviewer uncertain as to whether they understand the root issues and would draw the same conclusions. If during a narrative you call out a control weakness, some kind of highlighting or tick mark format is typically used to enable a reviewer to quickly spot the section of the narrative where an opinion was made that a weakness exists.

Interview

Interviewing is a common technique used in auditing. Talking is the natural way people communicate, and it is the natural method used in preliminary planning and risk assessment. The documentation of interviews should follow a line of questioning that is relevant to the determination of the process and its related risks and controls. As the auditee explains the process, how it works, and what they do to ensure its risks are being managed, opportunities for testing and evidence gathering present themselves. "Can I get a copy of that report?" "Do you have a sample form that shows how that input is gathered?" "Can you show me the minutes from that meeting?" "Is it possible for me to look through those logs myself and review the actions taken based on the results?" These are all questions that will come from the auditor during an interview. Validating the processes, policies, and procedures by first listening to the auditee's explanation and by subsequently confirming through independent assessment is all part of the overall technique of interviewing auditees.

Observation

Observation also is a useful technique when reviewing a process with many people or steps are involved. It enables the auditor to compare in real time how well policies and procedures are followed and whether there are circumstances not seen as routine that impact the risk control equation. Observation can be simply inventorying tapes at an off-site storage facility, or physically verifying that an Uninterruptible Power Supply (UPS) system is powered up and in working condition. Care must be taken in applying the observation technique to avoid interference with production processing. You also must consider the impact that your presence might have on the actual steps being taken and whether those steps are actually the ones used when no one is watching. Opportunities to observe unnoticed can circumvent alterations in a process due to the auditor's presence.

Observation is often helpful when creating flow diagrams and when determining what the process flow should be. Comparing this to procedures and other documentation will often point out deficiencies in control techniques or the need for supplementing those techniques with other ones. Before engaging in an observation session, you will need to give some thought as to what you are looking for and what you will need to see in order to successfully conclude your observation work. Using a reminder checklist or key points documented in advance will enable you to stay focused during the distraction of an observation of a process in progress.

Inspection

Inspection is a form of observation that usually includes some advance criteria that is expected. Often a checklist of expectations is reviewed and reconciled during an inspection so that a gap analysis between what was observed and what is expected can be formulated. Reviewing the configuration files of an operating system against a list of best practices is a form of inspection.

Confirmation

Confirmation implies validating information already gathered from another source. For example, reports depicting that a controlled environment at an off-site storage facility has the required physical security, logging and monitoring of environmental controls, and storage procedures in place and is working well should be confirmed by a field visit to the site. The risks related to not meeting these objectives are of a material nature and would jeopardize the reliance on the facility to enable accurate and timely disaster recovery of the business processes. Cross-referencing the evidence obtained by multiple techniques enables you to perform a confirmation indirectly throughout your fieldwork.

Reperformance

Reperformance is when a process or transaction flow, for example, are reperformed by or under the direct supervision of the auditor to ensure that the results match those reported in the first instance of the transaction process. Reperformance often is coupled with a sampling technique. During the implementation of a new process, reperformance of the electronic transaction processing is a viable way to validate that the process works as designed. When auditing a transaction process, this technique serves to ensure that the controls are working as they are designed to do. A variation on reperformance is to introduce a known error into the process and to see if the controls actions and results are as expected. Other such testing techniques will be examined later when we discuss test work in more detail.

Monitoring

Monitoring is the ongoing input of evidence for a time period sufficient in length to meet the needs of the audit objective. Sometimes obtaining direct evidence is not possible and observing a particular time period of a process is not sufficient to ensure that the controls are working properly. Thus, an audit step must be designed to monitor a process or transaction flow over a period of time to ensure that controls are working properly. This is especially the case when many smaller processes or transactions are involved.

Test Work

Test work is shown the sections of the fieldwork that formally step through a test designed to determine whether the controls are working. Testing is a basic building block of fieldwork. It is a scientific process that involves understanding a process and the expected results—whether they are control related or actual computational results—and performing the work to see if the results support the hypothesis. Because reperformance and the testing of large amounts of transactions or data is usually prohibitive, some kind of population sampling is usually performed in a sufficient quality and quantity to extrapolate the results of the testing into a reliable conclusion for the entire population of items.

Substantive Testing

This type of testing is used to *substantiate* the integrity of the actual processing. It is used to ensure that processes, not controls, are working as designed and give reliable results.

Compliance Testing

A compliance test determines if controls are working as designed. As policies and procedures are created, documented compliance testing looks for compliance to these management directives.

CAATs

Computer Assisted Auditing Techniques (CAATs) are useful when large amounts of data are involved or complex relationships of related data need to be reviewed programmatically to glean appropriate evidence from the aggregated data. CAATs can really be any electronic audit tool such as a standard data examination tool like spreadsheet software or a custom tool built and tested for a single purpose. It may be necessary to use a computer-aided audit technique when no directly tangible evidence can be readily obtained. The use of computer-aided tools can enable the auditor to assess a large amount of data quickly and efficiently, however proper planning is still important. Unless it is a test that you will use often, the time and expense of developing a defendable and reliable CAAT may outweigh the benefit for a single audit effort. Some of the functionality you will be able to make use of with CAATs include:

- Avoidance of a sampling error by addressing 100 percent of population
- Stratification of data
- Aging of the transactions and data
- Recalculation (reperformance)
- Exceptions identification
- Fraud detections (via isolated variances)
- Extraction of the subsets of data
- Linkage of data for analysis
- Identification of duplicate transactions
- Audit trail analysis

CAATs may require a more invasive approach to auditing and will require close communication and agreement with the auditee. Data file copies may need to be exported off line in order not to interrupt the production use of the data. In addition, strict controls will need to be placed on the extracted data to establish and maintain its integrity. If technical staff is involved with developing and performing tests related to the use of CAATs, due care related to the integrity of the data and additional controls over the audit testing processes may need to be considered.

Additional steps to ensure that source code and object code match and that file and data definitions are available may be appropriate in planning and executing CAAT-based reviews. Changes caused by the interaction of the production system and the CAAT tools to both the production environment and the CAAT tools need to be fully understood before reliance on the technique can be made and before risks to the production environment are introduced. Full description of the CAATS processes and input/output should be documented in the work papers.

Management Control Reports

Reports used by management to ensure that the controls are working or to be used as detective controls for identifying when errors occurred are often gathered through a sampling and are evidenced in the fieldwork. Management reports are gathered to confirm statistical or performance data and to evidence communication between line management and other areas affected by their work. Often these are identified as control mechanisms during interviews, at which point representative copies are requested. If the control mechanism supported by the reports is material or significant to the audit objective and kept in archive as evidence, a sampling may be an appropriate review process.

Sampling

Sampling is an appropriate way to meet the requirements that audit evidence is *sufficient, reliable, relevant, useful, and supported by appropriate analysis.* Sampling is the process of applying the audit process to less than 100 percent of the audit items population in order to form an opinion on the control environment. The sampling process has several defined steps:

1. Determine the objectives of the test.
2. Define the population.
3. Determine the confidence level.
4. Determine the precision.
5. Determine the expected standard deviation.
6. Compute the sample size.
7. Document the sampling procedure.
8. Select the audit samples.
9. Evaluate the sample results.
10. Reach an overall conclusion based on the sampling.

There are several types of sampling applicable to IS audits and several related definitions that you must know:

Attribute.   An aspect of an element of the total population. For example, the attribute in the sample of those items without proper signatures is improper signatures. Attributes are binomial (for example, yes or no).

Population.   Also known as the universe or field, this is the aggregate total of items to choose from and about which information is desired.

Confidence Interval.   A range of values that defines the upper and lower limits between which the actual population is believed to lay compared to the sample statistic. For example, if the results of a 95 percent confidence level sample produces a confidence interval between 200 and 300, and the auditor were to repeatedly pull samples of the same size and calculate a confidence level of 95 percent, then 95 percent of the intervals would encompass the actual population value.

Confidence Level or Degree of Assurance.   The probability that the results of a sample are reasonable results related to the population as a whole. It is an estimate of the degree of certainty that a population average will be within the precision level selected. Confidence levels are usually expressed as a percentage. A 95 percent confidence level means that if a repeated sampling was conducted, the actual value would fall within the confidence interval about 95 percent of the time.

Standard Deviation.   The degree to which individual values in a list vary from the mean (average) of all values in the list. The lower the standard deviation, the less individual items vary from the mean and the more reliable the mean.

Precision.   The range or tolerance estimated that the population would be represented at the confidence level. For example, if there is a 95 percent confidence that the average value is X, then there is a 5 percent risk that the average number is greater than X and a 5 percent risk that the average number is less than X.

Probability.   The ratio of the frequency of certain events to the frequency of all possible events in a series, usually expressed as a percentage of all events in the series.

Random Statistical.   This is a selection process that utilizes a random selection of a sample population from which every item has an equal chance of being selected for applying the audit process. Use of a random number generator would be a way of performing such a selection. Your work papers should document the process used to generate the random number sequence.

Systematic Statistical.   This is a selection process that utilizes a fixed interval between selection items with the first selection being a random selection. For example, selecting every n^{th} item for applying the audit process. The mathematical method used and the rational should be documented in you work papers.

Haphazard Nonstatistical.   This sampling technique does not rely on any methodology or basis for selection. It should not be used to form a reliable conclusion on a population of items.

Judgmental Nonstatistical.   This also is referred to as exception sampling. You may pick items over a certain value or outside of some normal definition boundaries for examination. Often in a financial transaction, this also is a way to focus on higher risk items by picking those transactions that represent a high dollar value for closer inspection. The results from audits of samples chosen with this method cannot be extrapolated over the entire population of items to be sampled. Attribute sampling mentioned previously is a judgmental nonstatistical sampling method.

Sampling Risk.   Sampling risk is the risk that arises from the possibility that the sample size does not represent the population, resulting in a conclusion that would not have been made had the entire population been examined. This error can occur in two ways: 1) the conclusion results in an incorrect acceptance of the test because the population is misrepresented by the sample, and 2) the conclusion results in an incorrect rejection of the test of the sample when testing the entire population would have resulted in an acceptable outcome.

The auditor should use a sampling method that is representative of the population relative to the characteristic for which the population is being tested. *Stratification*, a process of subdividing the larger population into smaller ones with common attributes, may be considered as a way to narrow the population and to increase the confidence of the testing, depending on the audit objective for which the test is designed. The larger the sample sizes, the less error that can be expected; however, some amount of error must be expected when applying a sampling technique of any kind. The auditor should consider whether the expected error rate will exceed the tolerable error rate when determining what to sample and what size sample is sufficient. Sampling procedures and determinations used in defining the sample method must be properly documented in the work papers in order for the samples and overall conclusion to be defendable. In determining these methods and processes, care must be exercised to show that bias has been avoided and that sample size is sufficient.

Preparing Exhibits

Exhibits should be included in a section of the work paper and organized so that references can be easily made to the audit program. An indexing scheme calls out or indexes an exhibit based on the exhibit's location in the work papers where it was first referenced. This helps to logically order the exhibits in a sequential order. For example, if audit Step 3 is the first time an exhibit of a certain report is used in the audit work, it might be labeled "EX-3-1" for the first exhibit in audit Step 3. Subsequent references to the exhibit then will continue to use this number as an exhibit identifier. It is helpful in large or frequently performed audits to also note additional information in the labeling of the audit exhibit, such as the auditor who gathered the evidence, the technique used to obtain the evidence (from who, how, by what extraction method, and so on), and the date it was obtained. Provisions in the labeling also should accommodate places for initialing by the reviewer to evidence approval and sufficiency of the exhibit to meet the audit objectives.

Identifying Conditions and Defining Reportable Findings

As audit work is performed, evidence is reviewed, and work papers are documented, the auditor forms an opinion on whether the controls in place are sufficient to mitigate the risks to a level that meets the audit objective and business needs of the auditee. Deficiencies between the expected or required control effectiveness and the desired level of control are referred to as control weaknesses. Weaknesses can be systemic across the audit area or specific and unique to a single test or piece of audit work. During the course of the audit work, all deficiencies should be noted in and annotated with work paper shorthand for review and summarizing.

At times, weaknesses are pronounced and significant, requiring the auditor to consider bringing the issues immediately to management's attention for correction or disposition. Depending on the prior audit arrangements and the nature of the audit, this is a prudent course of action. If irregularities are identified that could involve an illegal act, the auditor should either consider seeking legal advice directly or recommend that management do so. Identifying the appropriate level of management or the appropriate responsible person to report issues of this nature to can be tricky and may take some special considerations and professional judgment. Again, outside legal counsel or audit committee reporting may need to be considered to appropriately handle situations like this. It is important to validate the concerns and double check the evidence and audit process without alarming those involved before confronting management in order to avoid embarrassment and risking the loss of confidence in the audit team. Reporting irregularities needs careful consideration because of the potential for further abuse from identified weaknesses, loss of customer confidence, company reputation damage, and the affect on employees not directly involved with the irregularity. External reporting of illegal acts may be a legal or regulatory obligation. Approval for this kind of reporting should be sought from audit management and the appropriate level of management prior to proceeding. The majority of the routine concerns can be raised in the ongoing and periodic status communications between the auditor and management. Even if satisfactorily corrected and addressed, these weaknesses and related findings should be reported as part of the audit. When audits are performed to place reliance over a period of time, a determination must be made as to when the weakness existed in comparison to the effective time period the audit is covering.

Conclusions

An important aspect of all testing and fieldwork is to draw a conclusion based on the evidence reviewed. This can be a difficult part of the audit for an inexperienced auditor. The conclusion is the actual value that comes out of the audit process, without which there is no reason to audit. It is the step most agonized over by auditors, because it is where their opinion and professional training is ultimately put to the test. The CISA candidate must be familiar with the process of determining, from the evidence presented and tests performed, what their professional opinion is about the sufficiency of the controls relevant to the risk culture of the management and the materiality of the particular finding. Even when there are no findings of weakness, or especially when there is no weakness found, the auditor must clearly state this finding when writing their concluding opinion about the test or fieldwork before they are done with the audit program step. When weaknesses are noted, some planning will help position the weaknesses to help you formulate findings and reportable items.

Identification of Control Weaknesses

The identification of the control weaknesses results in the recording of a single incident of a failure or deficiency in the controls. It is important to begin to transition your thinking from the technical to a management level of communication when identifying weaknesses and documenting them. You should be able to state as part of the weakness documentation what you expected to find or what the condition should have been to draw attention to the magnitude of the difference between that and the found condition. These findings form the basis of the audit report and the overall opinion rendered as the primary deliverable of the audit work.

Summarizing Identified Weaknesses into Findings

Once you have gone through the audit program and addressed the audit program steps sufficiently to have an end point for all of the items that needed to be reviewed, you can begin to analyze the weaknesses and look for findings that may be reportable. Using a notation methodology that preserves information about the audit step and the particular test where the weakness was identified, you can place all of the weaknesses onto a separate document to help you focus only on the weaknesses and to determine whether any common themes or weaknesses are shared. Prioritization based on materiality also can begin to take place during this analysis.

When multiple weaknesses are related to the same root control deficiency, you should note that these items are actually different examples of the same audit finding and should be addressed as a single issue because the solution will cover all of the weaknesses identified. During this step, there should be open communication among the auditee management to validate the issues identified and to ensure that there were no misrepresentations during the course of the audit work. As root issues are identified, audit findings are formulated from an overall understanding of the materiality, risk prioritization, audit objectives, scope and risk tolerance, and the weaknesses identified into reportable findings. Now you are prepared to draft the findings into a reportable format.

Reportable findings contain five specific parts in their presentation format:

What is the condition that was found?   State the situation in clear nonjargon language.

What should be the state of the condition?   What would you expect to see in a well-controlled situation?

Why is the auditee at risk?   Why is this important?

What is the significance of the condition?   What is the potential downside impact of the condition to the auditee if not addressed?

Recommendation.   What do you propose that might better mitigate the risk exposure identified by this finding?

Your finding should take this format in its final form, but before you make any recommendations you will need to do some root cause analysis to make your recommendations value added.

Root Cause Analysis

Root case analysis is a process performed on the weakness findings to answer the question: *Why?* Before you make a value added recommendation, you must understand what the root issues are and what the symptoms are. Correcting a symptom will not solve the weakness effectively and result in a long-term solution. Often, you must peel back through several layers of *cause and effect* scenarios to get to the real cause of the weakness or deficiency. Generally, control weaknesses are symptoms and a collection of them will help you identify the root cause.

Another popular method to get to a root cause is to start with a symptom and ask *why* three to five times to get to the real cause that needs to be addressed in order to change the identified symptomatic outcome. This exercise may lead to root causes that are outside either the control of the affected or audit area or beyond the scope of audit's influence. Alternate recommendations that are within the control of the management affected by the audit should be provided in order to provide actionable results that can be implemented to mitigate the risks.

Value-Added Recommendations

Your recommendations for addressing risk control weaknesses will need to be realistic and cost/benefit positive to the auditee in order for your work to be seen as adding value to the auditee management. The auditee management may dismiss your recommendations where the cost of the solution exceeds the potential loss, should the risk go unchecked. Many questions in the CISA exam will test your ability to determine the cost beneficial recommendation and will ask you to evaluate whether it is *worth it* or not. Sometimes this involves understanding the cost of the solution and the cost of the problem over a period of time to define the best long-term control recommendation.

Reasonable Assurance through a Review of Work

In applying due professional care to their work papers, the IS auditor will have their work checked by another auditor to ensure that their conclusions are sound and will stand up to review. Through this second review, the accuracy of the conclusions and identified weaknesses can be reasonably assured. The expectation of a second opinion of their work prior to the issuance of findings and reports keep the IS auditor focused on thorough and understandable documentation and testing work.

The AIC and the Next Level Review of the Work Performed

Wherever feasible, all work papers should be reviewed and approved by another auditor, preferably the next higher level of management in the audit organization. If an audit manager performs a section of the audit work, this section should be reviewed by at least one staff auditor or a peer manager to ensure that all of the work performed reasonably meets the *reasonably competent third party* test. Work paper comments and concerns related to unclear procedures or conclusions or related to the sufficiency of the evidence should be documented and discussed with the auditor performing the work. These review comments should be presented and cleared in a manner that will not remain part of the permanent work paper files. Notation of the presentation and subsequent clearing of the review comments should be recorded in the chronological log without recording the substance of the comments discussed. After having reviewed the work and satisfactorily addressed and cleared all of review comments, the reviewer's should initial the work to provide the assurance necessary to achieve a reliable audit result.

Peer Review

Peer review of audit work is an excellent way to benchmark your audit work with other auditors and audit teams. By using this technique consistently, improvements can be achieved as methods are challenged and procedures improved upon. A peer review of the audit work also is a good way of establishing common ground and relationships with external and internal auditor pairings. Joint audits between internal and external audit teams also serve this purpose well.

Communicating Audit Results and Facilitating Change

The audit report plays a unique and influential role in communicating with auditee management. These reports are what the client management pays for when funding an audit. The purpose of an audit report is to inform, persuade, and get results. Readers expect a direct, straightforward, and factual presentation of the results of the audit. Brief statements should be used to encapsulate key ideas and to summarize supporting data. The reports should be issued in a timely manner so they are relevant and useful to the recipients.

The report should flow from the audit test work, findings, and conclusions, and logically compile the work identified in the previous sections into a final result. The report phase is separate and distinct from the audit work phase, and the mind-set and approach are actually intended to be somewhat separate, possibly isolated from one another. You should not perform audit work with the report in mind. The report content should be determined from the results from the test work, which is synthesized and aggregated into a management-specific view of the material details after the test work is performed and the conclusions are made. The report is a summary and conclusion of the root concerns identified in the audit test work, which is reformatted into language that will be understandable and actionable to the management audience, for which it is intended. Audit reporting represents a shifting of gears and change of the mind-set into a management frame of reference. The report must use the appropriate tone and strategy commensurate with the materiality and significance of the information being presented. Language should be carefully selected to emphasize varying degrees of significance among the issues presented.

The content must be objective and relevant to the business in order to motivate the audience to act on the recommendations. The overall tone should be constructive, giving credit where possible and balancing the negative with the positive.

Effective reports provide realistic and actionable recommendations with descriptions that are brief and provide measurable results. The overall cost of the solution compared to the risk of loss potential must be clearly recognizable to the reader in order to motivate them to act on the recommendations.

Your aggregated weaknesses list should be prioritized and summarized into key findings and root issues. From this reduction, items of significance should be moved to the top of the list and opportunities for grouping the findings, either by their root causes or by those with a common solution, should be considered.

Overall conclusions should be drawn and the key supporting points should be identified and rephrased to cohesively present the overall conclusion.

Report Layout

Audit reports should contain the following:

1. Report title (organization and/or area audited)
2. Recipients of the report
3. Date the report was issued—effective period covered by the audit and preparing auditor(s)
4. Scope
5. Objectives of the engagement
6. Coverage period
7. Brief description of work performed
8. Background information
9. Overall audit conclusion
10. Findings, recommendations, and responses listed from the highest material risk to the lowest material risk

The report should initially describe the scope and objectives of the audit and provide information about whether the audit objectives were satisfactorily met. Legal or regulatory requirements related to this audit also should be defined in this report when laying out the scope and objectives of the audit. After describing the scope, objectives, and effective time frame of the audit engagement, a description of the work performed helps to represent to the reader what was done to reach the conclusions made in this report. This does not require a detailed explanation of the entire body of the test work, just an overview of what was tested, the systems and audit areas covered in the audit, and the kinds of testing techniques and methodologies used. Any circumstances that limited or expanded the scope should be described in this section of the report.

Any relevant background information related to the audit should be inserted next. This information may be used to set the tone of the audit or to provide information about why or what specific issues were involved, thus setting the stage for a better understanding of the business risk environment and what transpired leading up to this audit engagement.

An overall conclusion or opinion on the audit objectives as a whole then should be offered before describing the individual reportable findings in any detail. Depending on the nature of the audit, it may be appropriate to make this conclusion for the given time frame that is covered by the audit and to state that as a qualifier to the opinion and conclusion being made. In the same manner, any reservations or caveats to the opinion also can be included as necessary so that the reader has an understanding of where the opinion does or does not apply. Any overarching recommendations for corrective action should be made at this point as well. Any substantial changes that were made to the environment or processes during the audit or before the final issuance of the report that affect the overall response desired from senior management as a result of issuing the report should be mentioned. For example, it is not unusual for significant material items to have been resolved or corrected before the final report is issued, due to their potential impact on the business. They are, however, reportable in the audit report because at the time of the audit they were not properly addressed, and as mentioned earlier, an audit is a snapshot in time.

Findings

Because the overall audit conclusion and reportable findings are described in the final report, a few things must be kept in mind to achieve the goals of informing, persuading, and getting results. Most important is that you must write with the consideration of the audience in mind. This is a different audience than the one you have been dealing with during the audit up to this point. This audience does not necessarily understand a lot of technical jargon and detailed control analysis lingo. They want to see full subject/verb/object sentences that have been spell checked (no kidding). If you do not want to turn them off, you will need to reread your report several times, taking a hard look at eliminating negative language out of your report. Rephrasing problems as challenges is the kind of changes you need to make to produce a receptive nondefensive response to your report. A trick I was taught is to do a *find* on every instance of the characters *n* and *o* together in the report. Look for ways to turn the sentence around. Instead of talking about what was *not* being done, report what *needs* to be done to better control the process. It seems simple, but it really works.

All findings of a material nature should be included in the report. The auditor will have to exercise their professional judgment on what is material and should therefore be included as a reportable item.

Responses

Preliminary drafts of the report may be created for response and validation of findings prior to final issuance of the report. You may need to help guide the management in crafting their responses to meet the needs of this new audience as well. Senior management does not want to hear about excuses and rationalizations as to why things are the way they are. A weakness has been identified and they are uncomfortable. The responses from their departmental staff need to be clear, forthright, and actionable, and have deadlines associated with them that seem reasonable given the materiality of the situation and the complexity of the solution. Suggested changes to departmental responses can help move the process to a positive actionable conclusion when possible. I often send reminders when seeking the response to management stating:

Your responses should include

- Description of the action to be taken to resolve the issue
- The name of the person responsible for completing the action
- The target date for completion of the action

Follow-Up

Follow-up is the reperformance of the audit tests to ensure resolution and is handled differently in every organization, depending on the materiality of the issue, the resource availability, and proximity of the auditors to the process. Certainly board reportable findings probably need to be followed up on periodically through their satisfactory conclusion on a frequent basis to enable updates to be presented to the audit committee of the board of directors. Follow-up information, test work, evidence, and conclusions should be housed in the work papers of the original audit if possible, so an entire package is available for review and support of any legal requirements that may arise.

Resources

The following resources are useful in helping you to understand the information system audit process.

Publication

Report Writing for Internal Auditors, Angela J. Maniak (McGraw-Hill, 1990).

Web Sites

- www.aicpa.org/index.htm
- www.ncua.gov/ref/ffiec/ffiec_handbook.html
- www.isaca.org/cobit.htm
- www.isaca.org/stand1.htm
- www.isaca.org/standard/code2.htm
- www.sas70.com/
- www.theiia.org/itaudit/

Sample Questions

The following questions and answers are a sample of what the CISA exam content might look like on the subject matter covered in this chapter. The format, style, and layout of the question and answer choices should give you a better understanding of the exam question format. In addition, it should enable you to become comfortable with the multiple choice style, where the best answer must be chosen from a set of four answers, some of which also may be technically correct. Answers are provided with explanations on the right and wrong answers in Appendix A, which will help you understand the intent of the question and the correct response.

1. When planning an IS audit, which of the following factors is *least* likely to be relevant to the scope of the engagement?

   A. The concerns of management for ensuring that controls are sufficient and working properly

   B. The amount of controls currently in place

   C. The type of business, management culture, and risk tolerance

   D. The complexity of the technology used by the business in performing the business functions

2. Which of the following *best* describes how a CISA should treat guidance from the IS audit standards?

   A. IS audit standards are to be treated as guidelines for building binding audit work when applicable.

   B. A CISA should provide input to the audit process when defendable audit work is required.

   C. IS audit standards are mandatory requirements, unless justification exists for deviating from the standards.

   D. IS audit standards are necessary only when regulatory or legal requirements dictate that they must be applied.

3. Which of the following is *not* a guideline published for giving direction to IS auditors?

   A. The IT auditor's role in dealing with illegal acts and irregularities

   B. Third-party service provider's effect on IT controls

   C. Auditing IT governance

   D. Completion of the audits when your independence is compromised

4. Which of the following is *not* part of the IS auditor's code of ethics?

   A. Serve the interest of the employers in a diligent loyal and honest manner.

   B. Maintain the standards of conduct and the appearance of independence through the use of audit information for personal gain.

   C. Maintain competency in the interrelated fields of audit and information systems.

   D. Use due care to document factual client information on which to base conclusions and recommendations.

5. Due care can *best* be described as

   A. A level of diligence that a prudent and competent person would exercise under a given set of circumstances

   B. A level of best effort provided by applying professional judgment

   C. A guarantee that no wrong conclusions are made during the course of the audit work

   D. Someone with a lesser skill level that provides a similar level of detail or quality of work

6. In a risk-based audit approach, an IS auditor must consider the inherent risk and

   A. How to eliminate the risk through an application of controls

   B. Whether the risk is material, regardless of management's tolerance for risk

   C. The balance of the loss potential and the cost to implement controls

   D. Residual risk being higher than the insurance coverage purchased

7. Which of the following is *not* a definition of a risk type?

   A. The susceptibility of a business to make an error that is material where no controls are in place

   B. The risk that the controls will not prevent, detect, or correct a risk on a timely basis

   C. The risk that the auditors who are testing procedures will not detect an error that could be material

   D. The risk that the materiality of the finding will not affect the outcome of the audit report

8. What part of the audited businesses background is *least* likely to be relevant when assessing risk and planning an IS audit?

   A. A mature technology set in place to perform the business processing functions

   B. The management structure and culture and their relative depth and knowledge of the business processes

   C. The type of business and the appropriate model of transaction processing typically used in this type of business

   D. The company's reputation for customer satisfaction and the amount of booked business in the processing cue

9. Which statement *best* describes the difference between a detective control and a corrective control?

   A. Neither control stops errors from occurring. One control type is applied sooner than the other.

   B. One control is used to keep errors from resulting in loss, and the other is used to warn of danger.

   C. One is used as a reasonableness check, and the other is used to make management aware that an error has occurred.

   D. One control is used to identify that an error has occurred and the other fixes the problems before a loss occurs.

10. Which of the following controls is *not* an example of a pervasive general control?

    A. IS security policy

    B. Humidity controls in the data center

    C. System-wide change control procedures

    D. IS strategic direction, mission, and vision statements

11. One of the *most* important reasons for having the audit organization report to the audit committee of the board is because

    A. Their budgets are more easily managed separate from the other budgets of the organization

    B. The departments resources cannot easily be redirected and used for other projects

    C. The internal audit function is to assist all parts of the organization and no one reporting manager should get priority on this help and support

    D. The audit organization must be independent from influence from reporting structures that do not enable them to communicate directly with the audit committee

12. Which of the following is *not* a method to identify risks?

    A. Identify the risks, then determine the likelihood of occurrence and cost of a loss.

    B. Identify the threats, their associated vulnerabilities, and the cost of losses.

    C. Identify the vulnerabilities and effort to correct, based on the industry's best practices.

    D. Seek managements risk tolerance and determine what threats exist that exceed that tolerance.

13. What is the correct formula for annual loss expectancy?

    A. Total actual direct losses divided by the number of years it has been experienced

    B. Indirect and direct potential loss cost times the number of times it might possibly occur

    C. Direct and indirect loss cost estimates times the number of times the loss may occur in a year

    D. The overall value of the risk exposure times the probability for all assets divided by the number of years the asset is held

14. When an audit finding is considered material, it means that

    A. In terms of all possible risk and management risk tolerance, this finding is significant.

    B. It has actual substance in terms of hard assets.

C. It is important to the audit in terms of the audit objectives and findings related to them.

D. Management cares about this kind of finding so it needs to be reported regardless of the risk.

15. Which of the following is *not* considered an irregularity or illegal act?

A. Recording transactions that did not happen

B. Misusing assets

C. Omitting the effects of fraudulent transactions

D. None of the above

16. When identifying the potential for irregularities, the auditor should consider

A. If a vacation policy exists that requires fixed periods of vacation to be mandatory

B. How much money is devoted to the payroll

C. Whether the best practices are deployed in the IS environment

D. What kind of firewall is installed at the Internet

17. Some audit managements choose to use the element of surprise to

A. Scare the auditees and to see if there are procedures that can be used as a backup

B. Ensure that staffing is sufficient to manage an audit and daily processing simultaneously

C. Ensure that supervision is appropriate during surprise inspections

D. Ensure that policies and procedures coincide with the actual practices in place

18. Which of the following is *not* a reason to be concerned about auditor independence?

A. The auditor starts dating the change control librarian.

B. The auditor invests in the business spin-off of the company.

C. The auditor used to manage the same business process at a different company.

D. The auditor is working as consultant for the implementation portion of the project being audited.

19. Control objectives are defined in an audit program to

    A. Give the auditor a view of the big picture of what the key control issue are based on the risk and management input

    B. Enable the auditor to scope the audit to only those issues identified in the control objective

    C. Keep the management from changing the scope of the audit

    D. Define what testing steps need to be performed in the program

20. An audit charter serves the following primary purpose:

    A. To describe the audit process used by the auditors

    B. To document the mission and business plan of the audit department

    C. To explain the code of ethics used by the auditor

    D. To provide a clear mandate to perform the audit function in terms of authority and responsibilities

21. In order to meet the requirements of audit, evidence sampling must be

    A. Of a 95 percent or higher confidence level, based on repeated pulls of similar sample sizes

    B. Sufficient, reliable, relevant, and useful, and supported by the appropriate analysis

    C. Within two standard deviations of the mean for the entire population of the data

    D. A random selection of the population in which every item has an equal chance of being selected

22. Audit evidence can take many forms. When determining the types required for an audit, the auditor must consider

    A. CAATs, flowcharts, and narratives

    B. Interviews, observations, and reperformance testing

    C. The best evidence available that is consistent with the importance of the audit objectives

    D. Inspection, confirmation, and substantive testing

23. The primary thing to consider when planning for the use of CAATs in an audit program is

    A. Whether the sampling error will be at an unacceptable level

    B. Whether you can trust the programmer who developed the tools of the CAATs

    C. Whether the source and object codes of the programs of the CAATs match

    D. The extent of the invasive access necessary to the production environment

24. The *most* important aspect of drawing conclusions in an audit report is to

    A. Prove your initial assumptions were correct.

    B. Identify control weakness based on test work performed.

    C. Obtain the goals of the audit objectives and to form an opinion on the sufficiency of the control environment.

    D. Determine why the client is at risk at the end of each step.

25. Some things to consider when determining what reportable findings should be are

    A. How many findings there are and how long the report would be if all findings were included

    B. The materiality of the findings in relevance to the audit objectives and management's tolerance for risk

    C. How the recommendations will affect the process and future audit work

    D. Whether the test samples were sufficient to support the conclusions

26. The primary objective of performing a root cause analysis is to

    A. Ask why three times.

    B. Perform an analysis that justifies the recommendations.

    C. Determine the costs and benefits of the proposed recommendations.

    D. Ensure that you are not trying to address symptoms rather than the real problem that needs to be solved.

27. The primary reason for reviewing audit work is to

    A. Ensure that the conclusions, testing, and results were performed with due professional care.

    B. Ensure that the findings are sufficient to warrant the final report rating.

    C. Ensure that all of the work is completed and checked by a supervisor.

    D. Ensure that all of the audits are consistent in style and technique.

CHAPTER

2

Management, Planning, and Organization of Information Systems

Now that you have a solid foundation in the audit process itself, the approach to the subsequent chapters will differ slightly from the first. The rest of the material in this book is about *what* to audit not *how* to do it. It will be assumed that you understand how to identify risks and build an audit plan from the information provided. Testing tips will be provided, in some cases, but mostly there will be a description of what the key issues are and *what should be* in place. This can be used as a reference against what you find (*what is*) when evaluating these processes in a business setting. The intent here is to impart knowledge about the practices themselves with the understanding that what is determined to be material and which findings are significant will be the result of your risk assessment and management communication processes. Once you have an understanding of the expected processes and what *should be* found in practice, you then will be able to build an audit program that looks for the related control weaknesses in support of your particular audit objectives. The audit objectives may be pointed out as we go along but in most cases, the objective will be to ensure that these processes are in place, working efficiently, and designed to meet the tactical and strategic needs of the business. Keywords to look for are *needs to be, should be, is responsible*, and *are required* in some form.

This domain chapter covers auditing of the pervasive audit controls and control objective areas related to strategy, policy, procedures, standards, and those practices related to the management, planning, and organization of the information systems. Knowledge of this subject matter comprises *11 percent* of the CISA exam content. By the end of this chapter, you should understand the following as part of your working knowledge toolkit:

- Auditing IS organizations and their personnel structures
- Auditing IS management practices used to ensure compliance with policies, procedures, and standards
- Auditing the policies procedures and standards and the processes used to create and maintain them
- Auditing the IS strategy and evaluating its support of the business objectives

Evaluate the IS Strategy and Alignment with the Business Objectives

At the very root of this process is a business with needs, goals, and a mission. As described in the previous chapter, it is very important for you to have a good understanding of these items first. Any intelligence that you can gather about the company direction, culture, or long-range plans will be helpful for developing value-added audit strategies of the IS planning and management aspects of the business. Knowing the vision of the business owners and decision makers will help you determine whether the IS direction lines up with the corporate direction and enable you to make suggestions that will be readily embraced by upper management.

The senior management of the organization is responsible for providing direction and guidance to the rest of the organization. Their hopes and dreams should be translated in writing to the vision and mission documentation. You will need to determine what that guidance is when it exists in a documented form. You may investigate annual reports for such information or find it on Web pages or corporate literature. Validating these goals with the senior management is useful in establishing their applicability to the IS organization and the interpretations individual management members may have of the overall mission of the company. This could help you identify areas of focus for your audit.

Your goal will be to evaluate the IS strategy and direction and how well it is being managed. Seek documentation of the mission of the IS organization. Evaluate how it supports the business needs and mission. Look at how the tactical or short-term goals of the organization help the business' short-term direction succeed. Any divergence in the two paths is worth noting and following up on. If the plans are not well documented or well developed, there should be concerns. If they exist but are not well known to the IS organization staff due to poor communication techniques or an inconsistent application of the goal model, there may be concerns as well. Audit testing will involve observation, interviews, and reports reviewing the audit testing techniques.

The IS strategy should be communicated, perhaps annually, to the IS management and staff in the form of strategic and tactical plans. Look for confirmation that this has occurred. Evaluate any processes that exist to ensure that this process occurs on a periodic basis in a way that is documented and well communicated. Look for evidence that the business goals and strategies of the IS organization are input to and supported by this process. This approach would ideally be a structured one that has a life cycle of repeatable steps. These steps should include the assessment of what exists in terms of process automation, functionality, cost, and processes, and should provide for adjustment through a strategic planning process when the inevitable changes do occur. Also included should be the steps to align the IS plan with the business needs. The IS strategy and direction should be evaluated for their effectiveness as well as with a reasonableness test.

Part of the strategic IS planning must include information about the IS business model, its staffing and organizational structure, and the pervasive controls it visualizes for managing and monitoring the IS processes put into place to meet the business needs. Any assumptions or strategies related to any unique business model variations also should receive the audit's attention. These include outsourcing, in-sourcing, third-party relationships, unique manpower management techniques, or market-related activities of the business cycle that create special situations and therefore associated risks.

You also will need to assess the strategic planning process for how well it incorporates the future direction of technology and its impact on the planning process. Are there alternatives identified or optionally available should a strategic direction hit a dead end? Consider the recognition for eventual obsolescence of technologies in the IS strategy. How flexible, scalable, or technologically risky is the strategic direction? Does the plan provide for growth that will support the long-term plans of the business? Are infrastructure contingencies built into the design? Are there obvious single points of failure that may create a catastrophic outage if equipment failed, for example? Does the direction encourage standardization and take advantage of economies of scale, or does it encourage a high degree of entrepreneurial experimentation that may not integrate in the long run and become expensive to support in the long-term view? Is there a process that keeps abreast of the regulatory issues looking for how they may change the direction of the IS strategy and plan for compliance-related adjustments?

Most importantly you need to be looking for alignment of the IS strategy to the businesses model and its needs. Do not overlook the basic concern that the IS strategy will support the business well and has the proper overall control environment in place to accommodate the business strategy as you understand it. There should be evidence of established relationships between the IS functions and the business functions to ensure that the business needs are input to the IS strategic planning process and are actively being addressed as a result. This liaison and communication structure should be integral to the daily processes of managing the technology and address both the business unit functions and needs and the internal needs of the various subgroups of the IS organization as well. A high-level assessment of the business process functionality and workflow compared to the complexity, flexibility, maturity, and performance of the IS strategy will provide you with a big picture assessment and reasonableness check. Your evaluation should map out the strengths and weaknesses of the existing approach to strategic planning and compare it to ideal processes to identify possible reportable weaknesses.

Systems Architecture

Part of the strategic planning of the information systems must include a master plan of the IT architecture. The model should be kept current, be well documented, and be maintained for accuracy and completeness as changes occur and the direction evolves. Your evaluation will need to determine that the architecture supports the needs of the business. This systems map should include the data model as well as the infrastructure configuration. Knowing where data is, how it is created, what the data attributes are, and what dependencies exist for data interaction, help build an efficient process flow and identify opportunities for optimization and innovation. The term used to define a full explanation of data elements and all their attributes and syntax rules is a *data dictionary*. This is most often used in relation to complex database and process modeling applications. Having a well-documented data dictionary that incorporates the data classification process is a best practice that evidences a good control structure.

Data classification is the process of valuing the data in terms of importance to the company, sensitivity to legal or privacy requirements, and is usually the responsibility of the data owner. Having this information will be very important for the security of the data, because it is a key to identifying who has a need to know this data. This identification lays the groundwork for the access rules so that the proper security controls can be put into place. Understanding the data relationship and its value classifications also is helpful when trying to understand the relationship of the various data elements and the process flow. This will be covered in more depth when policies and security management is discussed, but the security levels of each type of data classification should be well understood and reflected in the architecture and the related decisions for handling the data.

Evaluate the IS Organizational Structure

The IS organizational structure should be the result of considered and measurable planning and forethought. There should be built-in, appropriate provisions for the natural segregation of duties so that opportunities for collusion and loss of control over important processing functions do not occur. The interaction of subgroups within the department should be efficient and conducive to smooth operations due to the organizational structure that has been put in place. The IS organizational structure should represent the best plan for meeting the business needs of the organization through technology and processes. Oversight of the IS organization and its functions is ideally done through a steering committee with senior management involvement or representation at a minimum to ensure this alignment occurs. Organization charts should show clear lines of authority and responsibility so that there are no opportunities for confusion regarding who is accountable for the key functions. This accountability and authority should be clearly defined in the corporate level policy and come directly from senior management so that there is no doubt as to the support and mandate of the IS function to perform their duties. The process for bringing technology issues to senior management's attention for resolution and ensuring that the IS function regularly reconciles with management's direction should be readily evident.

Roles and Responsibilities

Through a system that includes an organizational structure, written job descriptions, clear lines of reporting, and documented responsibilities and accountabilities, the IS organization should have described the job functions of all individuals. This process will have accounted all of the job functions that need to be performed to meet the mission of the IS organization as the responsibility of one or more job descriptions. These roles and responsibilities should be well documented and effectively communicated to the people to whom the assignment and accountabilities have been given. It should be evident that everyone knows his or her role and the expectations of his or her management. Some degree of responsibility for security and internal controls should be part of everyone's job description. Reminders to increase awareness of control and security responsibilities are ideally part of every performance review.

Segregation of duties is defined as giving different and separated job functions to separate people so that there is a reduced risk of inappropriate actions or errors because no one person has exclusive control over a process or transaction. Examples that are easiest to understand are financial in nature. Typically, the purchasing and receiving of material are separated so that a different person from the initiator of this financial transaction concludes it in the operation. Usually, it is appropriate to separate, initiate, and approve actions for high-risk or high-value transactions to ensure that there is reduced chance for error or irregularities. Access to certain IS functions also should be restricted based on job function to ensure that change control and data management is properly managed.

The roles of the various information processing functions are all very important and hold unique responsibilities. Application programmers have the role of developing applications to meet the business user's needs. They should be able to change the application based on direction from the application owner's representatives. However, this should not happen while the application is active in a production environment and being relied on for data integrity. Data and production control personnel should prevent this kind of access and ensure the integrity of the production data and environment. Computer operators should not have access to modify the application code, production data, or the operating systems code. They are the independent processors of the application and system processes, but they cannot change the intended functions or prevent operations from occurring as designed. Systems programmers should not be able to modify applications or their intended functions because they do not represent the business owner's needs or requirements for the application functions. For the same reasons, they should never be able to modify the production data either. A librarian function should independently manage all data and back ups to ensure these items are objectively handled and stored securely. This describes an ideal representation of what should happen in a large environment. It is not always followed in smaller shops, but the rational for the segregation of responsibilities is nonetheless important and compensating controls should be investigated and recommended wherever appropriate.

Compensating controls are those that are put into place to make up for an existing situation that introduces an unavoidable risk.

Database Administration

The Database Administrator (DBA) defines and maintains the data structures in database systems. Their role includes

- Specifying data definitions
- Preparing programs to create data
- Sizing tables and storage requirements for database systems
- Testing and evaluating queries and table joins
- Implementing access controls, update controls, and concurrence controls
- Performing database optimization and tuning
- Monitoring database and space usage
- Defining and initiating database back up and recovery procedures

Database administrators are able to access data and its structures by definition or their role. Because passwords are often stored in database tables, DBAs often have access to passwords as well. Segregation of duties and procedures to offset fraudulent and irregular activities will need to be considered. Review of the logs of DBA activities by supervisors should be considered in addition to tools, to identify data misuse.

Change control processes should isolate production code and data from an application and system programmer's direct access in order to ensure that they have integrity at all times. Anytime either the production code or data is exposed to undocumented or ad-hoc access or modification, their integrity must be suspect. Data entry functions should be segregated from programming functions for the same integrity assurance. Security functions should be separated from code or data modification functions to ensure independence. Change management functions should serve as the impartial gatekeeper, ensuring that the process is followed without fail. Computer users should not be able to modify code or have access to any of the programming functions. Programmers should not be able to perform user functions in production. This segregation must be maintained at all times and is especially important to watch when reviewing the testing of new development, as shown in Figure 2.1.

**Access Control Profile
Suggested for Medium to Large
Computing Environments**

Resources / Users	Application Data		Application Functions	Program Libraries		Job Libraries		System Utilities	System Libraries
	Production	Test		Production	Test	Production	Test		
Application Users	Yes	Restricted	Yes	No	No	No	No	No	No
Computer Operators	Yes*	No	No	No	No	No	Restricted	Restricted	No
Application Programmers	Restricted	Yes	Read	Read	Yes	Restricted	Yes	Restricted	No
System Programmers	Restricted	Restricted	No	Restricted	Restricted	Restricted	Restricted	Restricted	Restricted
Librarian Function	No	No	No	Yes	Yes	Yes	Yes	Restricted	No

Key: Yes _____ All Access Allowed (within Application Parameters)
No _____ No Access Allowed
Restricted _____ Restricted or Troubleshooting Access Allowed
Read _____ Read-Only Access Allowed
* Through Authorized Production Jobs Only

Figure 2.1   Access segregation for medium to large environments.

Other areas concerning the IS auditor are responsibilities that directly impact the control environment itself and those that need to be reviewed. This review not only ensures that responsibilities are defined and being performed, because they will most likely interview those performing these functions as part of the subsequent evaluation of the inherent control infrastructure. Ensuring that the quality assurance duties are assigned and well provided for will be a key aspect of evaluating development and implementation controls. Responsibilities for security, both physical and logical, will need to be described in detail and the persons fulfilling these roles must be interviewed when these functions and processes are evaluated for sufficient controls and segregation. You will need to ensure that there are assignments for the role of data owner or steward as part of the job descriptions. This role must be a clear responsibility to ensure that the required functions of classifying the data and approving the access security are being adequately performed. In a similar fashion, clear ownership of systems and daily processing must be documented so that the decision makers are identified and known.

Qualification and Training of the IS Staff

Staffing practices and succession planning should be reviewed to ensure they are documented and meeting the needs of the business. It important to keep track of open positions, required and approved positions, as well as the ongoing efforts to maintain a well-trained workforce to perform the IS functions. Understanding the cross training and back up responsibilities of all the key functions should be part of this analysis. Plans for succession should be identified for the key positions that must be kept filled at all times for the efficient functioning of the operation. An assessment of the adequacy of the staffing levels and the ability to attract and maintain these levels also will need to be performed.

To the extent that contract staff is used to fulfill assignments, the contract agreement will need to be reviewed to ensure that adequately qualified people are provided in a timely fashion and at a reasonable rate to meet the needs of the business. The contracts and performance of these personnel will need to be actively managed to ensure that the results are achieved and assets are protected.

The performance of the employees should be documented and managed through appropriate supervision, goals and work assignments, feedback, performance evaluations, and skills development. Professional development and training assessments should be part of this continual process. Standards of performance also should be established and measured against to ensure that fair and quantifiable assessments can be obtained. From a controls perspective, there are a few human resource practices that you should see in a well-controlled IS organization. You should determine whether a requirement for periodic job rotation is advisable, especially in jobs requiring a high degree of risk or exposure to potentially fraudulent opportunities. Job rotation helps keep a person from being put into a position where a fraud or malicious act can be perpetuated through human intervention. By changing job responsibilities periodically, the opportunity to identify collusion and irregularities, and to expose nonstandard activities is created. The other type of job rotation is a requirement for vacations that will at least annually replace a regular employee with someone else, affording additional opportunity to identify possible fraudulent or irregular activities.

Training practices and education of the key team members along with the provisions for continuing education must be assessed. A gap analysis starting with an understanding of the level of education, experience, and knowledge of subject matter that each job function requires must be performed. A subsequent mapping of the existing skill levels and background of each person currently holding these positions as well as provisions for periodic training and continued education also must be considered. Membership in professional organizations that support and promote development in a particular field of endeavor is often desirable to evidence commitment to quality and excellence. The assessment of training and qualifications also must include functional back up personnel who may perform the function at some point.

Background checks and other security issues related to the hiring practices of the IS organization are considerations for the assessment of the overall staff management processes. Requirements for staff clearances related to the sensitivity of the particular job functions should be documented and used in assessing candidates as part of the hiring process. Often those people with criminal records or large amounts of debt are not suitable for positions where a high level of trust is part of the daily functional job requirements. When internal transfers or promotions result in a potential placement of an internal candidate that was not previously subject to these background investigations, these clearances should be obtained before the job is offered to them. A minimum set of requirements should be satisfied for all hiring decisions made, and the satisfaction of these requirements should be documented as part of the hiring process.

Part of the human resources processes you will be assessing as an IS auditor will include what levels of security awareness training is performed both initially and periodically to ensure that all employees understand their obligations to protect the assets. Often is it prudent to have the employee sign a form signifying that they have read the related policies and understand the requirements. A best practice is to sign-off on acknowledgement of security policy requirements annually.

When a job change or termination occurs, timely actions should be performed according to documented procedures to ensure that access rights and possession of keys and privileges are adjusted to reflect the new *need to know*. Consideration should be given to changing group access codes and passwords for all systems where shared knowledge can be brought back only into line in this manner. This may require rekeying locks in the physical security environment. Exit interviews, recovery of company property, and arrangements for final pay should all be issues covered in every termination processed. A checklist used to ensure that all items were considered is often a great way to ensure that these items are addressed, especially when this process is not performed very often and is performed sometimes under stressful conditions. A completed *termination checklist* also can be used to evidence that all required steps were performed adequately.

Evaluating IS Policies, Standards, and Procedures

There are three levels of documentation that you will need to evaluate in order to determine how well the overall pervasive control of the documented guidance and direction is being managed in the IS organization. Each level is distinct and needs to be examined for different attributes. The top level of this documentation is policy. Policy is a mandate and directive from the top of the organization. Its purpose is to influence behavior. From it, management provides the overarching principles under which the business operates. It should not vary in its message or enforcement model. Policies should withstand the test of time and are often ideals requiring interpretation.

The next level of documentation is the standard used to guide the daily operations and management decisions. Standards are not mandates but common ground where uniform actions will lead to predictable results. Without standards, costs get out of control and management of information systems is rarely efficient and effective. In fact, getting control of what is going on, from a process and functions standpoint, is largely why standards are necessary and desirable. Standards tend to be more dynamic than policy and often are more technologically specific.

The third level of documentation you will assess as an IS auditor are procedures. Guidelines and direction of how to get things done are included in this category of documentation. Procedures are process specific and detail the steps taken to achieve an objective. Procedures include operations manuals, user manuals, and all manner of process documentation.

Policy

Policy should be the unchanging framework and basis for all other documentation and actions of all employees. Often policy is short in length and subject to interpretation. Policy should be applicable to the entire organization and not change significantly year after year. Subject matter worthy of inclusion as policy includes

- Ethics, values, integrity, and principles
- Mission and vision of the entire organization
- Management's philosophy and style
- Quality and service commitments
- The accountability and direction provided by the board of directors

- Responsibility and accountability for the protection of the shareholders' assets and business goals

- Operational style and business segment direction

- Legal and regulatory commitments

- Overarching directives related to control, security, financial, or human resource framework issues

The establishment of policies should be a carefully considered process and changes should be formally approved at the highest levels of the organization and through well-documented processes. A documented review of the policies should be performed periodically to ensure that they remain applicable and relevant. Communication of these policies should be pervasive and all employees should have access to the information. Implementation and consistent enforcement of policy should be provided for as part of the governance of the business. In order for a policy to be effective as a control, it must be written down and communicated. IS policies should align and support the overall business policy. It should ensure that the IS functions will be carried out in an efficient and effective manner and meet the businesses needs and goals. Commitment to quality, ethical behavior, protection of assets, and regulatory compliance should be evident in the documentation. Responsibilities for performance against the policies' requirements should be clearly defined in the policy. The basis for the control framework and security authority should be documented in the IS policies with strong ties to overall business directives. Many issue-specific policies will need to be evaluated and considered to ensure they are appropriately documented and supported. This will effectively enable these issues to be addressed in a proper manner.

When evaluating policies, you should consider whether they are sufficient in scope and coverage. IS policies should at minimum cover all topics related to the high-risk control objectives identified in your risk analysis. There should be a process in place that identifies all legal and regulatory issues that are applicable to the IS organization. An ongoing effort to stay informed of the requirements of these issues should be formally assigned. A review of the IS polices, to ensure that these issues are appropriately addressed through policy, also should be performed formally and periodically. The majority of topics covered in IS policy will be related to security. Items to consider for policy include the following:

- High-level security policy evidencing authority and responsibilities

- Disaster recovery and business continuity planning

- Ethical behavior and acceptable use

- Service commitment and management
- Data valuation and classification
- Data protection and disposal
- Information ownership and its related roles and responsibilities
- Access control and authorization
- Internet security, data protection, and virus protection as appropriate
- Email use, expectation of privacy, and data ownership position
- Intellectual property rights, copy protection, data transfer, and so forth
- Operations and systems responsibility
- Problem management
- Change management
- Data and network management
- Security awareness and user obligations issues
- Training and human resource policy
- Security incident reporting and response
- Legal and regulatory issues (for example, in healthcare—naming a security and privacy officer)

You also must evaluate how well the IS polices are communicated and maintained in order to form an opinion on their adequacy. The documentation format of a policy should include

- The bright line principle or policy statement
- Why this principle is needed and where it is applicable—possibly through a background section
- Definitions necessary to understand the context of the policy
- Responsibilities of various members of the organization related to the policy
- Enforcement authority and consequences for noncompliance
- Information on where to go for more information, such as related policies, standards, and procedures
- Who is responsible for maintaining the review of the policy
- The owner and last review date

There are many leading practice books and Web sites available against which you can measure the policies you are evaluating.

Standards

At the next level of documentation detail, IS standards will provide direction in a more detailed and specific manner. Evaluation of industry leading practices is a useful technique to use when reviewing standards and performing a gap analysis to determine their sufficiency. Care should be exercised to ensure that a working knowledge of the unique business needs is applied to this review. A lack of standards where there is not a business need for them or where the technologies are immature or limited in deployment may not be cost justifiable or pertinent in terms of material risk to the organization. Standards should reflect the majority view of the IS organization. If most of the organization is doing things in a way that is different than the documented standard, it is not really the standard, is it? Standards should be reviewed regularly, because you would expect them to change more often than policies.

Standards may be a catalog of the best or leading practices and, depending on the organization's direction related to enforcement versus giving only guidance, they may be no more than that. As part of the evaluation, the IS auditor should evaluate the enforcement and realistic application of standards. There may be a significant difference between what is actually happening in practice and the documented standard. This should be reconciled as part of the review process. Guidelines should be written in a way that clearly explains the boundaries between what must be done and what may be a good way to get things done. When standards are written as absolutes with enforcement statements contained in them, an effort should be undertaken as part of the evaluation to determine the extent to which this standard is deployed and how well that deployment is being enforced in practice. Individual and technological items of concern or confusion determined during the course of an audit review are often opportunities for new standards that have not been previously identified.

Procedures

Procedures are documents that spell out how to get a process completed. Most often they are specific to an individual subgroup within IS, unless it is an organization-wide issue where the procedure is applicable to the entire IS organization. Procedures are important for disaster recovery (DR) and business continuity planning (BCP). Consideration should be given to how these procedures will be performed by a less knowledgeable employee when they are being created. Often a little more detail that is common knowledge to those who perform the tasks everyday can be very useful when the tasks have to be performed under stressful conditions by persons unfamiliar with the tasks. As with all of the documentation listed previously, authorship, maintenance responsibilities, and additional information sections should be included in the documented procedures to be most useful to the reader. As with standards, procedures should reflect the way something is currently being done and should be reviewed for relevance and accuracy when compared to the current process. Keeping in mind the reuse of procedures for DR/BCP purposes, a procedure that does not reflect the current practice may result in undesirable results, especially if applied by a less knowledgeable individual. As processes change, the revision of procedures should be part of the completion of that change. Look for evidence that this happens as a matter of course in the change control process as a leading practice.

Evaluating Third-Party Services Selection and Management

The evaluation of governance over third-party relationships is an important part of forming an opinion on management oversight and monitoring effectiveness. When management makes a decision to use outside parties to perform functions, there are several common reasons for doing so. The big reason is money. It is increasingly popular to involve other parties in the business process for a variety of good reasons. If the rationale for using an outside party is one of cost, you should review the cost justification and draw conclusions on the merit of the cost and benefit analysis supporting the third-party arrangement. Another primary reason for using third-party services is a classic buy versus build decision. Maybe the skill levels required for a new task are not available in-house and would require a significant recruiting effort. Perhaps the investment in the equipment required to perform a service requires a large up-front capital commitment. Many times, it makes more sense to rent a service rather than buy it and pay the ongoing costs of supporting that service. Valid rationales include the simple fact that it is not a core competency of the primary business and the service is best left to individuals who can focus on the excellence of that service as their primary offering. Many times when new ventures are embarked upon, strategic alliances and partnerships are formed with third parties. There are potential benefits for all parties involved and the risk is distributed at the same time. Keep in mind, however, that in all cases the risks to the business are the responsibility of that business. While losses can be absorbed by other businesses because of how the deal is structured, loss of consumer confidence in the core business and its services also will result when problems occur.

There are trade-offs to consider when making any third-party decision. As an IS auditor, you will need to review these trade-offs, looking for risks and ensuring that they are understood by management, have been appropriately considered, and are being accepted or mitigated by additional controls. Risks to consider include processes that are now out of the IS organization's direct control. Confidentiality, integrity, and availability—the three basic principles of information security—come to mind first. Making sure that the performance levels meet your auditee's needs and that they have recourse should the arrangement not live up to the businesses needs and standards is another key issue to consider. You should expect to see a process in place for management to receive input on how the process is meeting their needs on a regular basis in a way that monitors the entire process and the third-party-managed services, both separately and collectively. If the focus is too narrow, on the service in a stand-alone fashion, for example, the overall business objectives may not be met in a satisfactory manner while still achieving the goals of the third-party relationship.

The process that a business should use to engage a third-party service follows common SDLC methodologies. During your review, you should investigate and gather evidence of the following steps:

1. Define the business objectives and requirements.

2. Identify the necessary technologies for the delivery of the requirements.

3. Perform a baseline risk assessment, analyze the rational, and document the business decision.

4. Specify delivery and control requirements based on the entire business process flow.

5. Perform due diligence in selecting potential vendors, validating control, and accessing delivery abilities.

6. Define contractual, service-level, and insurance agreements.

7. Document procedures, responsibilities, controls, and monitoring mechanisms.

8. Execute an agreement and plan transition implementation.

9. Perform an ongoing relationship management and monitoring.

As you assess a third-party relationship, an important item you will need to find is the identity of the person in the business that is responsible for the relationship and the ongoing management of the agreement. This is a key aspect of third-party relationships that is often overlooked as one of those "assumed to be taken care of" issues that result in the ball being dropped. This person should be able to prove through documentation that all third-party relationships and interfaces with the IS organization are identified. They should be knowledgeable of the service level agreements, the contract, and the insurance in place for this relationship. The qualifications of the third party should be assessed and defendable, preferably through a selection process that shows that there was a best-case analysis performed when the selection process occurred. Naturally, contractual agreements should be in place and well documented. You will want to review this documentation and compare it to your risk scenarios to ensure that all bases are well covered. The contract should hold the third party responsible for performing the functions required in the manner and quality required to meet the IS organization's business need. There should be appropriate and necessary clauses that ensure the business can retain ownership of intellectual property, which would remain an ongoing concern should the third-party relationship go sour. Exit arrangements should be clearly defined as part of the agreement, and requirements for both parties to initiate and satisfy dissolution of the agreement should be spelled out in detail. Requirements to perform due diligence related to security and regulatory concerns that affect the business should be required as part of the third-party contractual agreement. This is where you want to see a *right to audit* clause in the agreement. The control objectives of the business can be extended into the third-party extension of their process in this manner. Liabilities for nonperformance against these requirements, including penalties, should be agreed upon contractually.

Contract Management

Managing this contract and the relationship of the third-party arrangement should be an assigned task as previously mentioned. This is often poorly followed through, leaving many vulnerabilities and risk exposures to the business. Just because it was agreed to at a management level does not mean the skills and support were available at the functional performance end of the relationship. It should not be assumed that the contract would be acted against without any monitoring process in place. For example, one company received benefits well in excess of the salary paid for a full-time person to implement an effort put in place to ensure that contractual obligations were being met with insurance claims processes for employees healthcare. Had the process not been in place, the overcharging would have gone unchecked to the loss of the business. This monitoring should be evidenced through reports and actual physical checking, performed by the person responsible for contract management.

You will have to use professional due care to determine whether the oversight of the third party is adequate, based on the materiality of each individual issue. Contract management includes a periodic review of performance, risk mitigation, new risks and threats, changes in needs and support requirements, and the ability to manage the relationship in a mutually satisfactory fashion. Management should have procedures in place to ensure that all of this is done in a consistent acceptable manner that ensures a good working relationship while meeting the criteria and goals of the engagement.

Service Level Agreements

Service Level Agreements (SLAs) are a good tool to use for managing processes and defining expectations and recourse. They are applicable to external processing arrangements of all kinds, both internal to the business and with external third parties. Formal SLAs should contain several elements and complete books and training curriculum should exist to train a person to develop and manage SLAs. An SLA defines what the service is, at what level (quality, quantity, frequency, and so forth) it will be performed, and what recourse exists if this does not happen in the simplest terms. It is a negotiated document that recognizes the limitations and cost of the work to be performed and how to manage nonstandard items that come up during the course of the relationship. It defines the responsibilities of both parties. Items to consider when reviewing an SLA include

- Scope of work or service performed
- Expectations/definition of normal service
- Processes for handling exceptions and changes to normal service provisioning, restrictions, and so forth
- Costs and charges for the various service levels
- Measurement criteria and reporting commitments against those criteria (frequency, response time, and so forth)
- Definitions of acceptable service deliverables, response times, and processes for addressing customer service support (this might include escalation procedures, penalties, and so forth)
- Continuity and disaster recovery planning, security, legal requirements, and so forth as appropriate
- Process for renegotiating based on the changing situation of either party, such as capacity or growth requirements on changing needs
- Retention and storage of media, logs, and historical information
- Notification processes and commitments for "out of bounds" conditions

Evaluating Project Management

All projects managed by the IS organization should have a well-defined and documented framework as their basis that you will need to assess. A generally adopted project management methodology for managing the resources, budgeting time, and achieving milestones with the project management sponsor's approval ensures that sufficient governance is in place for the objectives to be met and deliverables produced in an efficient and effective manner. In order to understand what parts of a project management framework need assessment from a management oversight perspective, you will need to have a working knowledge of the various steps of managing a project.

Project management involves project scope and objective definitions, managing constraints and resources availability to achieve the objectives. In order to develop a project, participation from the affected departments is required to define the required deliverables. The user department or project sponsor provides the authority for implementation of the project and has an approval role that should be evident at various sign-off milestones during the project. The responsibility for the sponsorship, project management, and project team members should be clearly assigned. The project management methodology should provide a clearly written work statement that defines the scope and objectives of the project before it is undertaken. Approval of the project plan, its approach and implementation requirements, and time frames should be obtained from the sponsor. Approval from users or management also should be obtained at various milestones or checkpoints of phase completion, providing interim validation that the project is proceeding according the intentions of the project sponsor or authority. The project manager will develop a project plan that breaks down the project into a time line or list to map out the tasks that need to be completed to receive the end goal. This plan will be used to manage and monitor the project throughout its life and will serve as the primary control mechanism for tracking times, costs, resources, and deliverables. A full understanding of the individual tasks required to achieve the objective will be required to perform this successfully. The detail aspects of each task also will need to be defined:

- How much effort is required to perform each task?
- How many resources are necessary to perform this effort?
- Is there any opportunity for getting the work done faster by applying multiple resources to the task or to work multiple tasks concurrently?

- Are there other tasks that need to be done before this particular task?

- What are the costs associated with the materials and manpower to complete each task?

- What is the estimated time span needed to perform a unit of this task's type?

- What other steps of the overall objective are waiting for this task to complete before they can begin?

All of this information needs to be compiled for each subtask and possibly at an interim milestone or at roll-up points, where subtasks can be rolled up into a major component of the overall project plan so the entire project can be managed properly and in a well-controlled manner. In addition, planning steps for assuring the quality of the product, training of the users, testing of the implementations or modifications, and post implementation reviews and analysis should all be considered as necessary steps when the project scope warrants them. Again, professional judgment will be called upon to determine the sufficiency of the project plan at hand.

A system providing quality assurance throughout the project life should be evident when reviewing information technology projects. This will include testing and approval of the steps prior to all implementation phases. It will support the accreditation of systems against requirements defined early in the planning phase and related to internal controls and security prior to go-live.

A risk assessment process used to manage risks throughout the project life cycle would evidence a strong commitment to achieving the project goals and minimizing the risks to the sponsor and the management team. Risks will need to be assessed in an ongoing fashion, adjusting project parameters, such as resource levels, costs, task time completion estimates, and deliverable milestones, along the way to show that good control processes are in place.

Each project will need to be reviewed on a case-by-case basis during the audits of those particular projects. When assessing the overall management processes, however, you will be looking for an overall consistent management approach to handling projects in general. Sampling the documentation of projects completed or in progress will give you a body of evidence from which to draw a conclusion on the project management framework deployed by the IS organization.

Evaluating Change Management

The governance of change management and the IS organizations philosophy related to managing change provides a good big picture view of the overall control environment and practices actually embraced by an IS organization. A fully implemented change control methodology ensures that the segregation of duties and access to production is strictly controlled, maintained, and provable in an IS audit. This segregation will follow the guidelines defined previously in Figure 2.1. The change of control ensures that there is a clear separation between the production environment and any testing or pilot environments and ensures that the production data has integrity and is not accessed by users or programmers directly. A well-developed change control process puts a gatekeeper between systems development and the production of hardware, software code, and data. This gatekeeper has several roles:

- Ensures that changes have been approved by process owner
- Ensures that changes have been thoroughly tested for deployment in the live production environment
- Ensures that back-off procedures are available, should the change fail
- Checks that the impacts of the changes have been considered and communicated to the affected parties
- Ensures that corresponding disaster recovery processes have been updated prior to the implementation of the change
- Determines that the source and object code match when applicable
- Records the change and provides an audit trail of the code movement
- Promotes the change to production in an independent and impartial manner
- Determines the success or failure of the change and initiates the back-off procedure when required

This is only part of the overall change control process, however. A well-managed change control process starts well before a change is introduced to the change control operators. There should be evidence of a change request initiation and control processes. These processes capture and record requests while ensuring that the requests are well documented and supported by user or management authorization. These requests should be categorized and prioritized and should include a process for managing expedited or emergency changes. All changes should pass through these control processes and be documented and considered as they are evaluated for introduction into the production environment. This includes routine changes and environmental changes to systems supporting the processes such as power supplies and HVAC systems. Part of the review of changes should ensure that the impact to the environment and functionality has been assessed. Items to consider include

- Interaction with other applications or components
- Increased cycles to existing equipment such as CPUs
- Storage requirements
- Back up and tape requirements
- Power and heat dissipation loads
- Wiring and equipment placement
- Sufficient user notification of changes and related outage impacts for deploying the change
- User training and functionality related to process changes
- Disaster recovery procedure changes
- Documentation and process procedures changes
- Planning and scheduling of the changes reviewing opportunities for aggregating changes to minimize downtime, while being mindful of the need to compartmentalize the changes should a partial back-off be deemed necessary

Change control management processes should ensure that only authorized persons perform maintenance on systems and that the actions taken are documented as an audit trail for subsequent problem determination processes. Formal procedures for ensuring that regression testing and authorization for all changes should be followed and integrated with the overall configuration management process. Opportunities for disaster recovery documentation, updates to procedures, and operations manual documentation changes should not be missed. A follow-up process that ensures the changes made meet its objectives to the requestor's satisfaction to close the communication loop should be a final step in the process.

Evaluating Problem Management

When reviewing the problem management processes, you will be assessing the IS organization's ability to identify, examine, and resolve problems that occur in the IS environment. Well-managed governance over the processes and structure that makes up a problem resolution and escalation process can help the IS auditor get an overall comfort level with how unidentified problems may be handled when they occur in areas not previously known or experienced. A problem management system should capture and document all events that are not standard operational events. It should force these events through an evaluation process that determines their cause and the resolution of the issue, tracking the record of the problem through to its conclusion. Ideally, problem tickets are automatically opened when production application programs abnormally end (ABEND), populating the problem tracking system with the available documentation that can facilitate the issue's resolution. This process may be interrelated to the change control process because the changes may cause problems that can be resolved by changes made to the production systems.

It is important to capture and record events that are not obvious problems because they can be symptoms that can lead to a root problem. Only by gathering these seemingly unrelated events and correlating them over time will they lead to a root problem through an in-depth analysis. Problems should be assigned to the affected areas for review and resolution. This resolution process should be documented and tracked to ensure that all of the problems have a resolution and to enable learning from mistakes and the prevention of future problems based on similar circumstances.

When problems are identified and initially recorded, time stamping should be utilized to ensure that follow-up of the problems occurs in a timely manner. Severity or criticality will need to be assessed and associated with each ticketed event to facilitate the proper prioritization and escalation of the resolution efforts. A problem management system must track the resolution of problems and escalate them so they will get more attention when certain criteria are met. The criteria could include severity, number of occurrences, impact to the organization, and the amount of time lapsed since the problem occurred, assuming that the problem remains outstanding. The exact procedure and sequence of escalation to who and under what set of circumstances should be written down and communicated in a manner that ensures everyone involved knows the process and can respond according to the procedure. This procedure may include trigger mechanisms for more serious problem situations such as the declaration of disaster and building evacuation. The procedures should provide guidance for the prioritization of efforts, should multiple problems occur simultaneously. Your evaluation of IS management's ability to manage problems will take all of these issues into consideration as you evaluate them along side the relative business risks apparent to the organization.

How well problems are tracked and recorded historically also is part of this evaluation. You should be able to pull sample problems from a recorded log and follow them through to a satisfactory conclusion. Knowing how many problems occur over a typical period, how many are currently being work on, and what the average resolution time is are all good metrics to consider when evaluating problem management systems. Part of your review will be to determine that adequate feedback and follow-up processes are implemented to close the loop of problems leading to or resulting from changes in configurations, hardware, software, or processes. The management system should provide for the transferal or reassignment of problems to different responsible parties throughout the life cycle of the event/resolution cycle, without the loss of pertinent information needed to close the problem successfully. The ability to get adequate reports and metrics from the process also should be evaluated. The IS organization's practices for giving priority to outstanding problems, informing everyone who needs to know the status, and actively pursuing problem resolution are aspects of the process from which you will be able to draw your conclusions on the sufficiency of the process.

Evaluating Quality Management

Quality management is the process of assuring that the IS functions are performed in a quality manner with quality output as the goal. The management of the organization should oversee the development and implementation of an overall quality plan that has the quality aspects of the long-range IS plans and continuous improvements as its objectives. There should be a standard approach for both general and individual project quality assurance activities. This approach will specifically define metrics and processes used for determining quality and assessing it over time for improvements or slippage. Quality measurement activities include reviewing the process and product and sampling, measurements against standards, and monitoring the quality of outputs, and tracking it in documented records.

The management should implement this plan and use its output to improve processes and products over time. Responsibilities for quality management activities should be clearly assigned and an evaluation of the adherence to the quality plan should be part of a periodic review. To ensure that quality processes are developed by the IS organization, part of this plan should be the adoption of a Systems Development Life Cycle (SDLC) methodology. The SDLC methodology should be sufficient for driving the processes of development, purchase, deployment, and maintenance of systems in the organization. Understanding the SDLC methodology is fundamental to many aspects of information technology and will be a guiding process in your IS audit work, providing you with guidance for cause and effect analysis of the process life cycles. In fact, the applicability of SDLC methodologies as a way to look at processes is pervasive throughout many management processes and, as you have seen, is referred to in this book several times as a way to look at processes in general.

System Development Life Cycle (SDLC)

SDLC methodology is the life cycle of systems development activities and, in a cyclical fashion, describes all of the standard acceptable processes utilized to develop and manage technology systems from inception through retirement. There are many versions of the overall process in use, some are more detailed and robust than others. By describing a fully detailed process, you will see how the cycle flows and be able to recognize smaller scale versions of the cycle when they are presented to you. In reviewing the management and planning aspects of an IS organization, you will be most interested in finding documented standards and procedures that espouse a common organized approach, which provides the controls structure necessary to enable the successful development of projects. An SDLC flow follows these steps:

- A new idea is generated for a system or improvement.
- The idea is preliminarily accepted for potential funding by a sponsor, owner, or user group.
- Problem analysis:
  - The feasibility of the idea is investigated and data is gathered and analyzed related to the cost and benefits, along with other alternative courses of action.
  - Classic problem definition and current state analysis is performed and documented to understand the primary problem that is to be solved using root cause analysis techniques.
  - The constraints of existing and potentially future solutions are identified.
  - The resultant idea feasibility and options for moving forward are documented and presented to the sponsor for approval.

- Solution design:

  - If approved for further study, criteria are developed for a successful implementation and are documented along with the functional requirements for the system to meet the needs of the sponsor and the proposed idea.

  - Processes are defined by system flowcharts and data flow diagrams to better understand the possible solutions and project tasks involved with deploying the various solutions.

  - Various solutions are analyzed, buy versus build analysis is performed, software acquisition strategies are investigated, and in-house versus contract services are reviewed as options.

  - The technical feasibility of the various solutions is examined and reconciled with the organizations infrastructure, data model, current and planed system architectures, configurations, and so forth.

  - The economic feasibility also is examined of the top choices for solutions and compared to ROIs and the budgeted resources available.

  - Risk analysis of the various options, including security and control concerns, are documented and prepared for the final proposal along with recommendations for risk mitigation.

  - Solution proposals are made with recommendations of the systems development goals, costs, and deliverables expectations for approval by system owner/sponsor.

- System design:

  - Based on the approved and agreed upon scope and constraints, the system is designed and developed considering users needs, data requirements, functional and processing requirements, training, interfaces, inputs, outputs, internal and application controls, audit trails, availability, data integrity, security requirements, and reports.

  - Requests for Proposals (RFPs) are designed and submitted as appropriate and contracts are negotiated with various providers and vendors. For contract programmers, a specific contract language ensures that the adequate controls over deliverables, quality, performance to standards, and workmanship, as well as supportability issues exist.

- Project plans are built defining the required resources, time-frames, deliverable milestones, and so forth. This is the point where review criteria is developed and agreed upon to ensure that design goals are met.

- Mock-ups and a cost-benefit analysis are presented for approval and final sign-off of development by the departments of management and the affected users.

- System development:

  - Equipment is purchased and installed properly.

  - Systems are developed in the test environments.

  - Programming occurs either through internal or contract resources.

  - Several iterations of programming and testing are staged and integrated to achieve the final objectives.

  - The testing staged includes unit testing, integration testing, regression testing, hardware and component testing, load and stress testing, pilot testing, user acceptance testing, performance testing, and total system testing. This testing should have provisions for protecting sensitive data in the testing phases. The testing duties should be segregated from development tasks as much as possible to ensure the fair analysis and testing of the resultant system or programming components.

  - User screens are developed and tested.

  - Initial systems documentation is produced.

  - Test data is processed for the required objectives testing.

  - Facilities planning and implementation is developed with acceptance procedures defined for all of the environment and support needs.

- System implementation:

  - Based on approval and sign-off, implementation and production deployment is planned.

  - File conversion is performed to populate the final system.

  - Systems conversion is planned and executed using pilot, parallel, or full-system cutover methodologies.

  - User and operations manuals are documented and completed.

- Users and operators are trained.
- The final cutover is created, involving close interaction and communication with the system users.

■ Maintenance and modifications:

- The system undergoes routine maintenance and bug fixes with scheduled improvements prepared over time using mini-SDLCs.
- An ongoing, operational use and utilization of system occurs.
- The periodic assessment of design and performance based on the needs and changes in technologies also occurs.

■ Cycle repeats:

- A new idea is generated for the improved system to better meet the needs of the owner/sponsor of the user group.

Key aspects of every SDLC deployment are the involvement and input of the users and owners of the system and their approval at key milestones along the critical path of the project. As an IS auditor, you should be reviewing change initiation and systems development processes to ensure they are being primarily driven by the needs of the business organization. This ongoing communication and input is a key measure of the good controls because there is reduced chance for progress to get off track and for results to be out of alignment with expectations.

Rapid Application Development (RAD) also is a methodology often used that is worth some discussion. RAD employs an iterative process that quickly moves from design to prototype and testing with refinement along the way. While this approach is not without merit and can bring a system to productive use quickly, its use can be risky and deserves special attention from an audit perspective. This methodology can be problematic from an audit and control perspective due to the subjectiveness of the criteria, development, planning, and testing. Because perceptions and expectations change with the iterative process, scopes can creep and the overall objective can be elusive. A further concern is that it is difficult to successfully engage business process owners throughout a RAD process, leaving much of the iterative steps up to the design and deploy teams, compromising the independence of the testing and incremental improvements. Because RAD approaches are very dynamic by definition, the overall level of documentation is often very poor and good final versions of process documentation never seem to get completed.

The standards and procedures for SDLC implementations should provide for the basic functional and operational requirements that you would expect as good practice. Quality processes like testing and evaluation of results against functional requirements and standards should be evidenced throughout the SDLC process and indeed any quality management process. Requirements for safety, security, regulatory compliance, compatibility adherence to the overall vision and configuration, and the satisfaction of business requirements should be required in the documentation of the adopted SDLC methodology.

Quality Assurance Standards and Procedures

There also should be procedures and standards in place for the tasks and processes defined in the SDLC steps, which are implemented as part of the management oversight process you are evaluating. A partial list of potential standards and associated procedures of this nature includes the following:

- Hardware planning, obsolescence and capacity standards, and purchase procedures
- Proper hardware installation, configuration, and hardening practices
- Test environment establishment, usage, and documentation
- Testing standards, parallel/pilot testing, unit testing, aggregated program testing, stress testing, and the segregation of duties during testing, and so forth
- Code migration, test partitioning, storage, and back up
- Coding and program specifications and documentation techniques
- Naming of conventions and data dictionary standards
- Configuration design requirements and format standards
- Purchasing, bidding, and selecting a vendor
- Maintenance, upgrades, and patch application
- Key performance measurements, and other quality metrics
- Customer communication, report formatting, and so on
- User training and documentation
- Change control and production data migration

Depending on the maturity of the IS organization, the amount of this type of development work performed and the materiality of the work effort and projects to the organization, these procedures slide on a scale from "must have" to "would be nice." Once again, your professional judgment is the arbiter along with feedback and communication with the client. While all of these procedures and their content will be discussed in detail in the individual sections pertaining to the actual work, just having the procedures that you can point to and guide the operations are the controls with which the management and oversight review is primarily concerned.

Evaluating Performance Management

The IS organization's ability to identify Key Performance Indicators (KPIs), report on them, and adjust direction based on these results is part of the evaluation of the overall IS organization's management capabilities. There should be documented processes in place to assess the performance of information services on a routine basis. The needs of the business and the various service agreements will provide the input necessary to understand what should be measured and reported from the timeliness, quantity, and quality perspectives. The assessment completed through this performance reporting mechanism should compare the results of the IS deliverables to the needs of the business. It should measure the success or failure to meet the business objectives in a quantitative manner against previously identified benchmarks for a quick read of the organization's overall health and to provide insight to potential problem areas quickly.

When reviewing the management's effectiveness and control over the performance management aspects of the organization, you will want to determine how well the business needs are matched with the deliverables, what processes are in place to track and communicate the performance, and how effective the mechanisms are to correct or escalate situations that are out of the acceptable boundaries of performance. For instance, you should expect to find a proactive monitoring process in place that routinely measures output and compares it to acceptable benchmarks, identifies an unacceptable performance, and initiates corrective measures as part of an ideal control process for performance management.

Key Performance Indicators (KPIs)

The first part of this equation is the measurement of the performance. What is the metric used to identify the services or deliverables of the organization? There are usually many to track. Sometimes this can be reduced to what parameter, when it changes, and causes of concern in the management ranks. These items are typically measured in some way so that the management concerns can be headed off. Measures of output quantity, quality, efficiency, timeliness, mean time between failures (MTBF), and service level metrics are all performance indicators that should be recorded and tracked over time. Many times, a few key performance indicators tell much of the story of how the organization is running and represent the overall performance as a whole. Often, customer complaints are a key measurement tool and get immediate attention and reaction from management when these issues are presented to them directly. Using KPIs, management is able to assess the temperature and health of the organization quickly and drill down to other metrics and reports when alerted by these indicators that something is amiss. This good control practice is indicative of well-planned and proactive management structures.

KPIs can be set up in morning reports or summary screens that can be used as a dashboard to guide management into where the problem areas are and where their focus needs to be directed. Executive Information Systems (EIS) are designed to provide this single view functionality for senior management to use in monitoring the business and making decisions. The auditor should seek out the key indicators that management uses and examine how they are presented, communicated, and maintained to run the business. You also will need to evaluate how well the KPIs represent the underlying performance and whether there are material control-related issues that might go unnoticed with the continued use of the existing summary information to represent the organizations performance measurements overall.

Performance Measurement Techniques

There are many ways to measure the performance of an IS organization—some are subjective and some are discreet objective measurements. Some are not as obvious to a management team focused only on the bottom line and require a risk-based perspective to realize their need and usefulness. Modeling tools may be usefully employed as a way of understanding how multiple changes and the related dynamics might impact business needs and deliverables. This technique, as well as others, can be used for predictive analysis and proactive performance management.

There are many aspects of the IS organization that are worthy of some type of measurement, and as the IS auditor, you should expect to see a robust item list from which to determine the overall management governance in place. Some of the more popular measurement techniques include:

- Measurements of the workload, both historically over the past shift day, week, and month, and projected work in the queue to be used in anticipation of peaks and valleys in a demand curve. This is typically captured from shift summary reports or machine counters that are read and recorded on a routine cycle. Often, the data can be gathered automatically from log data or through consoles that are used to monitor throughput and the success or failure of completed procedures or operational tasks.

- Capacity monitoring and measurement of various flavors, including but not limited to, CPU usage and cycles, storage availability, and the use of various media types (DASD, disk, tape, off-site, bandwidth, number of concurrent users, and so on) is an important aspect of the business to keep an eye on. Again, automated monitoring technologies or log messaging can be used to gather this information. Manufacturers do not usually recommend running IT equipment at 100 percent load. They recognize that throughput varies during a production cycle and bursts or peaks in load and throughput occur throughout the process. There also is a recognition that growth occurs over time and special situations can result in additional capacity needs. It is important to monitor capacity for these reasons and to ensure that the equipment is running with an ample reserve capacity to accommodate unanticipated spikes in resource requirements. Knowing how the workloads translate into resource requirements and therefore affect the reserve capacity variances also is an issue that the IS auditor should question to see how well management has a grip on the proactive management of the capacity issues.

■ Customer satisfaction is a good measurement of performance but often a difficult one to get objective data on. There are many ways to gather anecdotal information of customer satisfaction and certainly, perceptions are very important, but quantifiable data cannot usually be gathered with a high degree of confidence in its reliability. For example, satisfaction can be ascertained by monitoring help desk calls or complaints to a complaint line. Keeping track of problems reported, length of time problem remains outstanding, number of outstanding problems, impacts to users from problems in duration, and severity all fit into this category. Response time for users and system availability to users also can be indirect measures of user satisfaction. Routine surveys of user comments and feedback over time can give a measurement relative to the previous input as to whether perceptions are getting better or worse.

■ The most common measurement is against known deliverables and service levels agreed to in a performance commitment of some kind, such as an SLA. In fact, a primary reason for developing an SLA is to reach agreement on what is measurable, what the benchmarks and standards are for those measurements, and what the action plans are to be should variances occur that are unacceptable to one party or the other. These measurements often take the form of delivery times and deadlines of a clock-based nature, such as reports delivered by 3 P.M., checks processed by end of business day on Friday, or month-end financial books closed by the third business day of the following month. Measuring quantities of a deliverable is usually geared toward satisfaction of an inputted request for a deliverable, such as a report or copies of a brochure, 25 Gb of storage made available, some fixed amount of CPU cycles consumed, paper used, tapes sent off-site and stored, and so forth.

Evaluating Capacity Management

Capacity management is more than just keeping track of when you are about to run out of disk space, tapes in the library, or exceed a fixed percent utilization of a processor. Good management practices are proactive and seek out changes so they are planned for and anticipated. Here you should be finding procedures and processes in place that tie into the annual budgeting processes and strategic planning against the mission of the various business units being supported by the IS organization. Knowing where the capacities are going, the rate at which they are changing, and being able to capitalize on opportunities to adjust capacity in ways that optimize expenditures and economies of scale are indicative of well run IS organizations.

During the budget cycle, there should be a process to identify the coming years' anticipated expansion or contraction of resource requirements from the businesses being supported. This information should be gathered and analyzed, and you should be looking for opportunities to make strategic decisions to add value while limiting impact to the organization's overall direction as a whole. Knowing that the capacity planned for will enable you to save money by buying at a time when the market rates are favorable or when a larger unit will give a better price break for the whole years needs, are often significant cost issues in the IT business. Commitments and contract pricing are often linked to the length of commitment and penalties for severing relationships that can be optimized by proactive planning efforts. Of course, follow-through on these kinds of efforts is equally important and requires rigor and discipline from IS management as well as the contract management issues mentioned previously. You will want to evaluate how well this information is used and tracked in order to draw conclusions on the effectiveness of the capacity management processes.

Economic Performance Practices

You must evaluate the annual budgeting processes of the IS organization to ensure it is properly funded to perform the tasks it is assigned. This can be a very subjective task, as most IS organizations tend to be under funded compared to the technological desires and demands of the business organizations. The process used for determining needs and establishing the fiscal budget should be reviewed. Projects and support needs should be prioritized and appropriately analyzed for costs. Capacity requirements and associated costs should be budgeted for in the months that the needs are required so that the IS organizations can successfully meet their service agreements. The manner in which revenues flow in and out of the IS organization will need to be evaluated for consistency, equity, accuracy, and reasonableness. Well-managed IS organizations will have documented charge back or allocation processes published that capture enough of the processing details related to each supported business to equitably redistribute all costs plus charges for administrative overhead as applicable to the business units consuming the resources. New projects should have budgeting processes built into them to capture both expense and capital costs as well as ongoing maintenance, growth, and support costs for future budget cycles.

When analyzing the IS budgeting process, you must be aware of the capital projects and ongoing operating expenses. There are accounting rules governing what can be and should be capitalized and what can be treated as operating expenses. This use of capital funding versus expense and operating monies depends on the fiscal strategies of the finance organization and senior management. The best way to think expenditures that can be capitalized is to relate them to brick and mortar examples of capital investments. When a company invests in a large capital item like a building, for example, the standard practice is to amortize the capital costs over a long period of time, allocating a portion of the total up front cost to the subsequent productive years that the asset has a useful life. While the initial capital investment can be large, the impact to the financial reporting in that fiscal year is limited to the portion of the total cost that is depreciated against that year's budget. Items that are categorized as operating expenses, however, go directly to the bottom line of that year's expenses. There is no depreciation or ongoing amortization of the expenditure to account for in future years, but the cost must be fully explained in that year's budget.

SOP 98-1

SOP 98-1 is an accounting statement of position that defines how information technology software development or acquisition costs are to be expensed or capitalized. If you are building a process or software for internal use only, like other capital items that can reasonably be depreciated over time, accounting guidance offered by the AICPA allows for the capitalization of many of the line items expended in the building of this software. This advice is provided as Statement of Position (SOP) 98-1. Any software or process that adds substantive new functionality to the IT process falls into this guidance. This statement breaks down the cycle of software development into three stages, or a short form of an SDLC: preliminary project, development, and post implementation.

There are certain items that can be capitalized in each phase and those that cannot. At the time of go-live or post implementation, the aggregate capital costs of creating this item then are depreciated over the useful life of the tool, software product, or process. Keeping good track of what is expense and what is capital will be part of what you will expect to see in your evaluation of management's governance. Ideally, there will be a project database system that holds the activities for all IS projects. This system would have direct links to the financial system and be used to track the capital and expense allocations accurately. Clearly, standards and procedures related to this process will need to be documented and followed by everyone to be a defendable process.

Work hours and other costs that cannot be capitalized are generally those that do not directly contribute as material input to the asset being developed. They include such items as

- Current state assessments and evaluations of feasibility
- Alternatives evaluation and development
- Gathering of requirements
- Any training costs related to the project
- Costs for data conversion unless those costs are for the development of a tool that will be used more than once for conversion, hence, software development that can be capitalized
- Maintenance costs associated with existing systems where no substantive additional functionality results (such as bug fixes)
- Administrative and overhead costs

Project work that must be capitalized includes design, coding, installation, testing, data conversion software, and maintenance that results in new functionality. Costs that can be capitalized also include direct material and services costs as well as payroll and payroll-related expenses for employees who actually are spending time on this project. Capitalization should begin when management authorizes and commits to funding the project, indicating it is likely to be completed and should end when the software or process is ready for productive use. Amortization of the capitalized costs should begin when the phases dealing with capitalization move to productive use.

Expense Monitoring

The monitoring of expenditures against the planned budget is an important control function that should be apparent in your review of the management processes. Routinely generated reports and records that are scrutinized and followed up on regularly would indicate the proper oversight of the money management processes. Ideally, there are processes that tie all of the costs back to the associated services, deliverables, and planned projects, so that a benefit can be determined, a return on investment identified, and realistic costs of doing business can be determined. Management controls should be in place for addressing situations where the benefits do not justify the cost being expended for a particular deliverable or project. These processes also should produce forecasting information to manage budget issues proactively, such as meeting budget expectations and documenting explanations for major variances and KPIs in the financial aspects of the business that will be followed closely by most organizations. A risk-based approach to evaluating this information would be to identify large outstanding costs and variances and to see what process is being followed to review and adjust financial expectations based on that procedure.

Evaluating Information Security Management

Management oversight of information security processes will need to be evaluated when you are trying to form an opinion of how well the overall management function is being performed. There is currently much debate in the information security industry over how much security is enough and how to justify the cost of security. Finding ways to quantify the investment in security and return on this investment is an appropriate management focus. Information security appropriateness in terms of effort and expenditures is not easy to quantify, however. Referring to a Forrester Research study citing average expenditures on IT security at 0.0025 percent, Richard Clark, the Cybersecurity Czar reporting to the President of the United States, recently said, "If you spend [only] 0.0025 percent of revenue on IT security, you will be hacked and you deserve to be hacked."

Security of information assets has only recently begun to get adequate focus and attention because of the federal legislation in the United States and world events. It has always been more of a focus legislatively in the European Union. Many Pacific Rim countries still have little in the way of laws that govern security violations and penalties. There are many laws in the United States related to privacy and security of information. The primary laws that concern the privacy of personal information and the security related to it are the Gramm-Leach-Bliley Act of 1999 (GLB) and the Health Information Portability and Accountability Act of 1996 (HIPAA). The former is applicable to financial institutions and the latter to health care providers, payers, and related organizations. Both were established to address the concerns of citizens over the privacy of their personal information.

The root concerns of information security are identification, authentication, and authorization. *Identification* is the process of validating that a person is who they say they are. This may see trivial but its importance cannot be understated. Establishing the identity of a person in an enrollment process, recording it with an audit trail, and ensuring that the person has an understanding of the expectations of acceptable use is the basis for all other security tasks. *Authentication* is the process of proving that identification when accessing the system. This is done through some type of a mechanism that substitutes for the initial identification process. The most common method is to provide a password. Other authentication devices could be physical tokens, keys of some kind, or the biometric aspects of the person, which are registered and established as representing that person in the enrollment process. *Authorization* is the granting of permissions to that identity with access to particular data and functions after they have been authenticated.

Like auditing, information security management cannot be responsible for the elimination of all security risks. The systems, applications, and business processes are not theirs to manage, and as we discussed earlier, risks are inherent in all business transactions. The information security function is one of expert consultant and advisor to business management. Knowledge of the best practices, risks, threats, and countermeasures are brought to bear by the information security manager to help business management make informed risk-based decisions. It is the business and senior IS organization management that makes the decisions based on this input and others to run the business.

Information security management is a matter of risk assessment, follow through, and application of due diligence. When evaluating the management of information security, your first task is to become aware of any regulatory requirements that are applicable to the IS organization you are assessing or the businesses it is supporting. As with any strategic planning process, there should be a risk identification exercise completed by management that identifies the acceptable risks of this particular set of business processes, that is subsequently prioritized and risk ranked, based on the culture of the business and its management, the existing control state, and other factors mentioned in Chapter 1. Understanding the applicable threats, the vulnerabilities unique to the organization and business at hand, and the relative costs of reducing the risks to acceptable levels sets the stage for adequate information security planning and management of the function.

The overall information security plan will be the blueprint for the information security-related activities. This will necessarily be a dynamic plan that is periodically revisited and adjusted as changes occur in the threat-vulnerability landscape. The information technology security plan should have several of the following common elements:

- Periodic risk assessments and evaluations of current security status
- Incident identification and response, and follow-up processes
- Policy, standards, and leading practices of identification creation and communication
- Security awareness and training processes
- Communication-related security activities (phone or dial-up, Internet, trading partner connectivity, and so forth)
- Data access control activities, such as information ownership, data classification, firewall management, content control tool administration, and so forth
- User account administration activities including adding users, modifying access needs, terminating accounts, periodically revalidating access needs, resetting password, and managing accounts and data access pairings
- Systems security activities, such as security plan and configuration documentation, implementation of minimum-security baselines, hardening of systems, maintenance of proper patch levels on systems, and investigation of new technologies
- Monitoring activities, such as network- and host-based intrusion detection implementation and management, and gathering log activity and reviewing it for violations in security policy
- Business partner access and risk management through vehicles like trust agreements, third party security assessments, and so on
- New project security design, participation, and implementation including risk assessment and the recommendations of appropriate security technology commensurate with the risk
- Security architecture design and implementation for the network, data systems, and interfaces

As with all other aspects of management, there are a few key items to focus on. You should evaluate any available documentation in terms of policies, procedures, and standards. Determine whether they are sufficient for the environment and appropriate commensurate with the risks and management's risk tolerance position. Analyze the strategy and mission that is being followed by information security, including plans and projects. Ensure that the priorities of management are understood and being addressed. Make sure that new and emerging threats are being considered in a timely manner and that the plans of the information security organization are being adjusted accordingly. Determine whether the stated deadlines and project milestones are realistic and appropriately funded, given the available resources and obstacles for the project plans. Identify any KPIs or process metrics used to encapsulate the performance of the information security processes and evaluate them. Draw conclusions on how well they represent the activities of the information security staff, whether they are communicated and understood by management, and if they are meeting the needs of the decision makers running the business.

Evaluating Business Continuity Management

As with most technical functions, you will be evaluating from a management perspective; the review of the business continuity management begins with a review of the applicable policies in place and corporate culture and risk tolerance related to this subject. Based on current studies, this is an area of risk mitigation that often gets a lot more lip service that action. This is especially true where systems and processes are large and complex, which is rightly so because fail-over processing can be an expensive proposition. Business continuity planning can be thought of as an insurance policy against service disruption. Management's philosophy and strategies towards disaster recovery and service continuity must be understood before you will be able to assess the sufficiency of the continuity planning efforts that you will be analyzing adequately. This philosophy should be reconciled for consistency with the quality and service commitments stated in the overall business mission and goals documentation. Management can be understandably hesitant to fund business continuity preparedness because it can be argued that it may never be needed. It only takes one situation like a natural disaster or terrorist act, both of which are unanticipated and out of the management's control by nature, to understand the need and value of investing in continuity preparedness and the need to plan for alternative courses of action.

To ensure that risks and potential disruptions, which a business needs protection against, have been properly considered in the business continuity decision-making process, you will need to review the business impact analysis that has been completed and the related documentation. Business impact analysis is a process where each business function, IS operation, information system, and application is analyzed for the impact of its unavailability or disruption of processing capability. This analysis must involve the business owners and the management that is responsible for meeting the business objectives resulting from these provided services. In this impact analysis process, the business needs and tolerable margins for error are identified and documented. The resultant risks to the business caused by disruption from minor failures in service level up through major regional disasters are examined to determine the impact to the business at the various failure levels and scenarios. The results of this impact analysis will yield potential costs and losses for the various scenarios and provide a basis for evaluating the tolerance of unavailability for the given time spans and severity of disruption.

Proper management of the business continuity process will ensure that a business impact analysis has been performed to a specific level of detail and depth with the involvement of business leaders and management. The management process will require documentation for these decisions and will accumulate all of the input into an overall strategy, prioritizing the various components into a comprehensive Business Continuity Plan (BCP) document. The IS organization will be required to prepare alternative courses of action that will meet the business objectives and the stated tolerance for unavailability defined by the business management that they support. There will be decision hierarchies described within this plan that define who can declare a disaster at the various disruption levels, and this plan will adhere to the published BCP and disaster recovery policies issued by the organization.

It also is important to ensure that manual business continuity processes exist, are documented, practiced, and prepared for by the business units. Disruptions will inevitably happen. Depending on the tolerance of the business process for disruption, there needs to be alternative processing procedures available for use while the IS organization is busy recovering the information technology. This is not an IS organization issue but is a critical element of any recovery process and management would not be performing proper due diligence if it did to look to the business managers to support the business-in-progress while IT recovery was in progress.

Once the tolerable limits of unavailability by the business organizations is known and documented, IS management will be expected to oversee the creation of achievable recovery plans that include all necessary aspects of the IS process and related elements (such as interfaces to return to an acceptable service level in the time frames identified by the business owners). This planning should be documented, exercised, modified based on the results of the testing conducted and reported on to senior management and the business organizations so that the current state of recoverability is known to the affected parties at all times. The current limits of the recovery process should be used to adjust the expectations of the business organizations and cyclical iterations of needs, and the recovery capabilities will need to be assessed and evaluated until satisfactory processes are established.

The management of IS continuity processes will need to manage many issues related to the dynamic nature of both the businesses and the IS configuration. As an auditor, you will need to evaluate the processes in place for modifying processes and expectations as change management processes introduce variations to business needs, IT infrastructure, and systems. Ensuring that these changes are captured and translated into the plans in place will be a mark of good business continuity management. This will trickle down to the hardware, software, supplies, documentation, testing, and training prepared for the various disruption scenarios.

Obviously, standard elements of disaster recovery and business continuity planning should not be overlooked in your evaluation of the management of these processes. These include

- Processes for inventorying all relevant information technology and systems; determining how they interact, their relative needs for recovery capabilities, and the dependencies of these systems on each other and external factors; and for reconciling of all of these interactions along with their business requirements into a prioritized list of what steps a recovery process should follow

- Processes for identifying hot sites, cold sites, or warm sites from which to recover when warranted, and ensuring that a relationship exists with an alternative processing arrangement

- Training for both the users, to employ alternative procedures during recovery situations, and IT personnel, to perform the recovery of technologies

- Maintaining the viability of the recovery plan through testing, review, and modification processes on a periodic and documented basis

- Communicating the realistic expectations and alternatives for business continuity along with responsibilities and tasks required during recovery scenarios to all affected parties

- Sufficiently and properly storing back up media and related processes including current recovery documentation, procedures, and stop gap processes for services that may be temporarily set aside in the throws of a recovery-in-progress, such as a security audit and management oversight processes

- Ensuring that all applicable legislative and regulatory issues are considered and appropriately addressed in the planning and execution of recovery processes

- Ensuring that processes have been considered, documented, and tested to recover the business processes, transactions, and operations to the point of the failure

- Appropriately protecting processing and information assets during recovery processing

Evaluating IS Management Practices and Policy Compliance

In this chapter, we have reviewed the many aspects of the management of IS organizations and their subprocesses. This chapter has covered the following:

- IS organization's relationship to the rest of the organization

- How this overall need best results in proper system architecture planning

- Staff roles and segregation

- Policies, standards, and leading practices

- Third-party services management

- Contracts and service level agreements

- Project management practices

- Change management practices

- Problem management practices

- Quality assurance management
- The System Development Life Cycle
- Performance measurement and management techniques
- Security and business continuity management

The details of these individual processes will be described in the subsequent chapters. These details will provide you with a view of the audit-related activities you will need to perform to obtain a comfort level with each of these areas detailed processes and their related controls. Oversight and governance of these processes, and ensuring that these processes exist and are being managed and monitored appropriately are the primary focus of this section of the exam and book content. Making sure that the big picture is being managed as well as the detailed processes are all part of the evaluation of the overall IS organization.

Resources

- *Information Security Policies Made Easy Version 9,* Charles Cresson Wood (PentaSafe, 2002).
- Bits Framework: Managing Technology Risk for Information Technology (IT) Service Provider Relationships, October 2001. (www.bai.org/pdf/BITS-update-120901.pdf, for example.)
- FFIEC guidance, "Risk Management of Outsourced Technology Services," issued November 28, 2000.
- AICPA Issues SOP 98-1 for "Internal-Use" Computer Software Accounting, March 5, 1998 (www.aicpa.org/news/p030598a.htm).
- Information regarding the Gramm-Leach-Bliley Act of 1999 (www.senate.gov/~banking/conf/).
- U.S. Department of Health and Human Services—Administrative Simplification (http://aspe.hhs.gov/admnsimp/).
- RSA: Cybersecurity Czar Urges Cooperation, Spending—*InfoWorld Daily News,* February 19, 2002, article 1197.
- *Information Systems Security Officer Guide,* Dr. Gerald L. Kovacich, Butterworth-Heinemann, 1998.

Sample Questions

Here is a sampling of questions in the format of the CISA exam. These questions are related to the management, planning, and the organization of information systems, and will help test your understanding of this subject. Answers with explanations are provided in Appendix A.

1. Which criteria would an IS auditor consider to be the *most* important aspect of an organization's IS strategy?

    A. It includes a mission statement.

    B. It identifies a mechanism for charging for its services.

    C. It includes a Web-based e-commerce strategy.

    D. It supports the business objectives.

2. From a segregation of duties standpoint, which of the following job functions should be performed by change control personnel?

    I.   Verifying that the source and object code match before moving code into production

    II. Scheduling jobs to run in the production environment

    III. Making changes to production code and data when programs fail

    IV. Applying operating system patches

    A. I only

    B. I, II, and III

    C. II and IV only

    D. I and IV only

3. In a database management environment, which of the following functions should *not* be performed by the database administrator?

    A. Sizing table space and memory allocations

    B. Testing queries and consulting on table join limitations

    C. Reviewing logs for fraudulent activity or access errors

    D. Performing back ups and recovery procedures

4. Many organizations require employees to take a mandatory one to two full weeks of contiguous vacation each year because

A. The organization wants to ensure that their employee's quality of life provides for happy employees in the workplace.

B. The organizations wants to ensure that potential errors in process or irregularities in processing are identified by forcing a person into the job function as a replacement periodically.

C. The organization wants to ensure that the benefits provided by the company are fully used to enable full employment of replacement staff as much as possible.

D. The organization wants to ensure that their employees are fully cross-trained and able to take over other functions in case of a major disruption or disaster.

5. Which of the following would be *most* important in evaluating an IS organization's structure?

I. Human Resource policies that adequately describe job functions and duties sufficiently

II. Organization charts that identify clear reporting and authority lines

III. System configurations that are well documented in the system architecture

IV. Training requirements and provisions for cross training that are documented along with roles and responsibilities

A. I and II only

B. I, II, III, and IV

C. I, II, and IV only

D. II and III only

6. In a review of Human Resource policies in an IS organization, an IS auditor would be most concerned with the absence of

   A. Requirements for job rotation on a periodic basis

   B. A process for exit interviews to understand the employees' perception of management

   C. The requirement for employees to sign a form signifying that they have read policies

   D. The existence of a termination checklist requiring that keys and company property are obtained and all access permissions are to be revoked upon termination

7. A System Development Life Cycle can be *best* described as

   A. A process used by programmers to document SOP 98-1 compliance

   B. A methodology used to guide the process of software creation project management

   C. A system design methodology that includes all the steps in problem definition, solution identification, testing, implementation, and maintenance of the solution

   D. A process used to manage change control and approval cycles in a development environment

8. What is the *primary* difference between policies and standards?

   A. Policies provide a high-level framework and standards are more dynamic and specific.

   B. Policies take longer to write and are harder to implement than standards.

   C. Standards require interpretation and must have associated procedures.

   D. Policies describe how to do things and standards provide best practices guidance.

9. Which of the following is *not* a standard?

    A. Approved access control methodologies

    B. How to request a new account

    C. Minimum security baseline for hardening a UNIX server

    D. Description of acceptable back up and recovery methods for production data

10. Which of the following are *not* key considerations when reviewing third-party services agreements?

    A. Provisions exist to retain ownership of intellectual property and assets.

    B. The lowest price possible is obtained for the service rendered.

    C. Business continuity planning and processes are part of the signed agreement.

    D. Security and regulatory concerns are identified as risks during negotiations.

11. When evaluating project management, which of the following would you be *least* concerned in seeing evidenced?

    A. Well-defined project scope and objectives

    B. Costs identified with the resources allocated to the project

    C. Timelines with achievable milestones

    D. Sponsorship and approval by business process management

12. When evaluating a change control process, the IS auditor would be *most* concerned if he or she observed the following:

    A. Change control personnel permitting systems programmers to patch operating systems

    B. Computer operators running jobs that edit production data

    C. Application programmers correcting data errors in production

    D. Change control personnel copying code from the production for testing purposes

13. During the review of a problem management system, it is determined that several problems have been outstanding and unresolved for an excessively long period. Which of the following reasons is *most* questionable to the IS auditor reviewing the management controls of this process?

    A. The problem has been sent to the vendor who will send a fix with the next software release.

    B. The problem has been determined to be a user error and has been referred to the business unit for correction and additional training.

    C. The problem is intermittent and after researching, remains outstanding until reoccurrence.

    D. The problem is seen as a low risk issue and is therefore low on the priority list to be addressed.

14. During the problem analysis and solution design phases of an SDLC methodology, which of the following steps would you be most concerned with finding?

    A. Current state analysis and documentation processes

    B. Entity relationship diagramming and process flow definitions

    C. Pilot testing of planned solutions

    D. Gathering of functional requirements from business sponsors

15. What is the *primary* concern that an IS auditor should consider when reviewing Executive Information Systems (EIS)?

    A. Ensure that senior management actually uses the system to monitor the IS organization.

    B. Ensure that the information being provided is accurate and timely.

    C. Ensure that the information provided fairly summarizes the actual performance of the IS organization so that indicators will be representative of the detailed tracking and monitoring systems.

    D. Ensure that MTBFs are kept to a minimum and within acceptable boundaries.

16. SOP 98-1 is an accounting position that needs to be considered by the IS auditor *primarily* because

    A. The AICPA requires all auditors to be aware and comment on this statement of position.

    B. Management may be capitalizing software development tasks that should be expensed.

    C. Keeping track of development efforts from a capital and expense perspective is indicative of good management of IS organizations.

    D. SOP 98-1 tracking systems are required to be interfaced directly to accounting systems and may introduce opportunities for fraudulent accounting.

17. When reviewing the management processes for overseeing budgeting and spending, the IS auditor should be *least* concerned with which of the following items?

    A. Ensuring that all spending is reconciled to a budgeted line item and the variances to budget are explained

    B. Ensuring that all of the budgeted money is spent in a budget year

    C. Ensuring that expenditures are recorded and reported on budgets to IS organizational management

    D. Ensuring that SOP 98-1 provisions are adequately documented and appropriately allocated

18. When evaluating information security management, which of the following are *not* items the IS auditor would consider commenting on as a potential control weakness?

    A. A security program had not been developed using a risk-based approach.

    B. The information security officer does not accept responsibility for security decisions in the organization.

    C. The use of intrusion detection technologies has not been considered for use in the security program.

    D. Account administration processes do not require agreement to acceptable behavior guidelines from all persons requesting accounts.

19. In evaluating business continuity management, what three factors are considered important aspects of the overall management of the program by the IS auditor?

   I. Impact to the businesses has been studied and agreed to from the business management as a basis from which to understand the continuity needs.

   II. Interactions of all affected processes have been identified so that priorities for recovery can be determined.

   III. Recovery tests have been successful and determined to fully meet the needs of the business.

    IV. Contracts have been negotiated with hot site vendors, enabling for the immediate declarations of disaster to result in quicker recovery times.

    V. The procedures required to manage the business processes without the information systems have been well documented and moved off-site to provide for interim recovery processing.

   A. I, II, and III

   B. I, III, and IV

   C. II, IV, and V

   D. I, II, and V

20. Which of the following sets of documentation would an IS auditor expect to find at the off-site facility for business continuity and recovery processes?

   I. User manuals and training documentation

   II. Current systems configurations

   III. Current systems and application code

   IV. Operational procedures and required forms and supplies for processing

   A. II, III, and IV only

   B. I, II, and III only

   C. I, III, and IV only

   D. All of the above

CHAPTER 3

Technical Infrastructure and Operational Practices

This chapter covers the technical and operational infrastructure of the IS organization. It will explore the risks, controls, systems, and processes involved in building and maintaining IS processing and infrastructure systems to support the objectives of a business. Knowledge of best practices related to hardware, software, and the ongoing IS operational processes will help you understand how to evaluate the effectiveness and efficiency of the organization that you are reviewing and enable you to understand how to answer the CISA exam questions from an auditors perspective. This subject matter comprises 13 percent of the exam's content and this next level of detail presented here will build on the management oversight of these areas described in Chapter 2. In order to master these subject areas for the CISA exam and to perform the IS audits in these areas, you will need to gain a working knowledge in the following subject areas:

- Development/acquisition, installation, and maintenance of systems software and utilities

- Acquisition, installation, and maintenance of hardware

- Acquisition, installation, and maintenance of network infrastructure

- IS operational practices and support functions used in daily operations and management of information systems
- Systems performance and monitoring

Evaluating Systems Software

IS software and utilities are defined as operating systems that translate user and application needs into hardware actions and the utilities that assist and support the operating system in performing these tasks. The primary difference between software applications and operating system software is that the applications are the user interface and the point of access to the data being manipulated by the process. Applications use operating systems to operate or control the hardware and network resources of the computer, but the operating systems are not accessed directly by the user.

When evaluating the development or acquisition of these systems, it is most important to understand the requirements of the user applications and the mission of meeting the business objectives so support by the systems software can be appropriately examined. In many cases, there are dependencies inherent in the applications software design that require certain operating system platforms and database systems to be used in order for the applications processing functionality to operate effectively. Applications are so interdependent on their support systems that they often will not function without the correct types and versions of database and operating system software supporting them. In many cases, the audit review of the operating and support systems is a matter of determining what the application was designed to operate on and ensuring that this is indeed what is being used or understanding the rationale for deviating from the recommended configuration.

Operating Systems

Application server operating systems (O/S) have matured into a few common brands over the last several years. Microsoft NT, Windows 2000 and XP, variants of the UNIX operating system, Mainframe O/S (typically IBM), VMS, and a handful of others are the most common. Because of the requirements for interoperability of various application systems and the need for every system to communicate on a common framework, processes that do not enable interoperability have fallen out of favor for most large companies. Audit programs and security checklists are readily available on the Internet for the specific review of a wide variety of these operating systems and their possible applications. This chapter will not go into that level of detail because the version levels change quickly, thus invalidating books with detailed audit steps for a particular operating system revision level.

Some unique needs and specialized proprietary systems require off-brand or isolated operating and database systems. This may be required due to peripheral equipment restrictions, such as medical device interfaces or financial institutions check readers, for example. Ongoing maintenance of these systems tends to be expensive and support is hard to find as a cost competitive commodity, which is unlike the more common systems. When specialized systems are required to support a similar application, the audit issues tend to be more of an application interface and interoperability one than an issue with the O/S itself. Indeed, the IS auditor probably does not have the skills to review the unique O/S scenarios without specialized training, which may be required, depending on the assessed risks.

At a high level, a review of the operating systems is one of ensuring that the system code is kept current, has integrity, and changes are tested for compatibility with the applications using it. Old code levels may have known vulnerabilities for which exploits are trivial to execute, because they are widely know and well documented. Current code is not an absolute requirement, however. Testing of the newer levels with the application and other interface software must be performed or validated with the applications and vendors equipment; otherwise, additional risks are introduced into the process. Many times a risk-based decision to upgrade or stay at current levels must be made. "If it's not broke, don't fix it" applies here. The same situation applies to patching for a bug or security fixes and where upgrades will provide for increased functionality of these systems. When seeking to determine whether current patches have been applied, also check to see if the cure may be worse that the disease. Testing cycles, regression testing, load testing, and migration of code through the phase of a mature change control process had better be warranted by the risk exposure of not applying the fix, or it should be questioned as being prudent by the auditor. This especially requires scrutiny when operating system functionality increases do not directly improve the application functionality or business processes being supported by the system. This is a good reason for the user and owner delegates to be required to approve all the changes, even those at this level of system complexity.

One compelling reason to upgrade the operating systems is to maintain supportability from the vendor. However, even this reason needs to be weighed against the risk of staying at the current level. Many systems continue to operate well in today's environment without any vendor support.

When decisions are made to forgo vendor support in lieu of making changes, you should insist on documented decisions and criteria that explain the risks and resultant decisions. Alternatives and contingencies should be planned for ahead of time in cases like this as well.

When evaluating O/S code and changes, you will want to gain assurance that the code applied and in use has integrity and its source can be verified. You cannot assume that compromised systems have O/S code that has any integrity or can be relied upon. Shrink-wrapped code from the vendor should be copied and stored off-site for when back up corruption occurs and for cases where IS operations is unsure how far back in the back up rotation the contamination might have occurred when trying to restore system code. Good back up schemes, where valid code is saved before changes are applied, along with good baseline back ups kept in reserve, would indicate a well thought out operating system control process.

At times, applications will need to get the operating system to perform functions in a more direct manner than is easily permitted by the provided O/S application interface. Application programming exits and Application Programming Interface (API) points will be used to issue commands directly to the O/S on behalf of the user processes. Care should be taken to evaluate these exit points and fully understand their function and any risks created by introducing these modification points to the otherwise isolated operating systems layer. This includes any custom coding done that could be accessed by users directly and not through an application interface. One common auditing requirement when evaluating applications is to ensure that the users cannot break out of the application interface and get an operating systems command line prompt for this exact reason.

Determining who and what systems have logical access to the O/S code and enabling changes or modifications to it will be required along with an understanding of what level of expertise and back up needs are required for the management of support and maintenance of the processes. Review of the change logs, where changes have occurred, and the reasoning behind these changes will be on your list of items to check out. A log of changes to operating systems becomes a controversial issue in reviews like this. Yes, those with access to O/S code also have access to logs to cover their tracks in fraudulent application of these privileges. Yes, you could insist that logs are made inaccessible to systems programmers or only available to their supervisors, but this is extra work, requires modifications to standard operating system functions, and may add more risk than it mitigates. There are ways around all of these scenarios created by a persistent system programmer with nefarious intent. Standard practices and manual procedures for code migration along with supervision oversight are sometimes all that can be expected as control measures. Job rotation, training of back up personnel, and enforced vacation policies may help mitigate these risks better than trying to force hard controls that promote distrust and tension among the system support staff.

Other system operations access requirements to O/S need to be evaluated and privileges assessed as part of this review. Tape back up processes typically need a fairly extensive amount of privilege, and depending on the control schemes afforded by the operating system or a corresponding security overlay program, those initiating this process may be able to escalate their privileges to a rather extensive level. Operator, help desk, media librarian, account administration, and scheduling are all systems-related job functions for which logical access will need to be reviewed and assessed for excessive privilege. If a subset of root or administrator privileges must be made available to these functions for some job aspect, access should be limited and managed from a *least privilege* perspective.

You also must be very aware of the default accounts that come with the O/S from the vendor with passwords that are compiled into lists all over the Internet. This chapter does not go into a strong password discussion here, but the account passwords with access to root O/S privileges should be closely guarded, changed more frequently than others are changed, and known to an absolute minimum number of personnel necessary to perform the function adequately and safely. In some cases, you cannot rename or otherwise disable the administrator or root access account by design, and the number of password tries cannot be limited to lockout attempts to gain access either. These IDs are sitting ducks for brute force access attempts. Logging access attempts and monitoring the logs, creating overly complex passwords and storing them under physical security measures, and subsequently using equivalent accounts, which are not as obvious to potential hackers, are all techniques worth considering. Services provided by the operating system that are not absolutely necessary to perform the business processes needed on this server should be turned off and future patches and upgrades should revisit this issue to ensure they stay that way.

Other aspects of the O/S ongoing operations worthy of considerations for risk mitigation are routine clean-up activities and monitoring. What kind of utility programs are deployed to ensure that the baseline code has not been altered, for example, and how are log files purged or saved in case they are needed for review later on? How long are logs kept and who maintains custody over them? If a scheduled job runs periodically to clean up temporary files or do log clean-up, what permissions do these programs run with and are there opportunities to exploit this process to escalate access from a hacker ID that gets on to the system? On UNIX systems, there are often issues with file permission changes that occur to files after a root user or process owned by some account touches the file. What process is in place to ensure that this file ownership change is reset to maintain the security and integrity of the system?

Database Management Systems

Databases are complex application data support structures that sit logically between the operating system and the application. They provide the framework for data storage and retrieval through data tables that are linked together by sharing common data elements or keys. Databases are interfaced from application front ends that provide application users the information they need to do their job. Unique views that meet the needs specific to a user profile are made available while maintaining the larger body of data to suit other needs simultaneously. As with other operating systems, support software, and system utilities, there must be compatibility between the database and the application design making the process of selection a relatively minor decision. Usually major database dependant applications are developed to provide you some amount of choice between the several popular and standard databases on the market. IS organizations will usually choose a common database subsystem to economize on the training and expertise required to support them. Similar to one-off operating systems, support and maintenance as well as interoperability can paint an application developer into a corner quickly if they are not developing them for a widely available database system. Your review will start with an understanding of the applications needs and requirements for database support similar to the operating system discussion previously.

When evaluating a database system, you will want to get a complete understanding of the data, the relationship of the various data elements, and any other design-related considerations, such as use cases and interactions with other systems. Understanding the design approach will help you assess potential risks and control weaknesses when comparing the plan and design to the actual use of the system. Data dictionary definitions and sizing considerations will be part of a knowledge base you will need to gather. Knowing the relative security classifications given to the elements by the data owner also will be required for this type of review. Databases are best created with an architectural plan for the tables, views, and user's transaction needs because the complexity can get difficult to maintain quickly if proper planning is not an integral part of the design/build cycle. The concept of normalization implies that consideration has been given to keeping the tables and the need to join them to get the necessary data views from the system as simple as possible. Depending on the level of detail required by the audit review, you might go as far as mapping out the functional requirements and processing flows of the business processes to the database tables and views, determining whether they are designed efficiently and effectively. This would be a rather tedious and subjective effort and hindsight is always 20-20. At a minimum, you will want to examine the initialization parameters for the database and evaluate the security baselines and their related control aspects.

When transactions occur in a database system that is used simultaneously by more than one person, it is important that safeguards are put in place to lock the data elements that are being changed from the other users so that these transactions can be completed without the other users corrupting the data during the actual change process. This can be complicated by multi-tier client/server configurations. It is even more complex when multiple databases are involved and need to be updated simultaneously. Often other users are presented with the last known value for an element involved in such a transaction and then are refreshed with the new data when available. How this process of data locking occurs should be assessed for risks, based upon the business use and requirements for the data. A transaction log that enables the unwinding of processes gone amuck is one thing you will want to see turned on when you examine the control parameters.

Sizing and tuning of a database system are normal functions of the DBA. Ideally, planning enables for the size of field level elements to be determined and the growth of data to be managed in a methodical fashion, but this may not be the case in the real world. Changes in the needs of the business users and expansion at rates unpredictable to the original design occur routinely. Therefore, a process for handling these issues without corrupting the data and its structures or unnecessarily impacting the users needs to exist. You should review how well this process is managed when determining whether effective and efficient processes are present that do not negatively impact the business users. A process also should be in place to monitor table space routinely so that limits are not reached during business transaction processing. Exceeding table size limits often results in the stoppage of processing until the situation is remedied or becomes worse.

A review of the database installation process will determine whether proper security has been considered and implemented as part of the development cycle. Default passwords need to be changed on all out-of-the-box accounts. Any services that are not specifically needed should be turned off. Care should be taken to ensure that DBA back doors (you know they have some built in) are protected and modified to limit access appropriately after code is moved from testing into production. In cases where processes or applications access the database as an interface during normal processing, access rights and the controls of these interfaces need to be examined closely for appropriate configuration. More often than not, these connections are done with DBA root-level privileges and countermeasures need to be put into place to ensure that this access path is not exploited or stolen by lesser deserving accounts or processes. Any remote access parameters or interface points will need to be examined to ensure that authentic and legitimate connections are established and maintained. Any opportunities for encrypted transmission sessions should be reviewed for applicability, risk, and overhead considerations.

Databases can keep track of the data relationships that routinely get established amongst the various tables using a reference table that lists pointers or placeholders to manage the process. Over time, this reference table can get corrupted or confused. Routinely, these tables need to be cleaned up and accounted for to get the system back to a normalized state. You must determine how this process is performed and assess the security and integrity checks inherent in the process to see if they are sufficient and commensurate with the risk.

Often the access and modification rules change for database access as the development process moves along the sandbox, test, quality control, approval, and production domain continuum. Assess how the permissions have been adjusted to ensure that the same access levels by developers do not end up in the production system instance of the database that they enjoyed in the development sandbox. Databases use system-level communication protocols to do business with operating systems, users, mid-tier servers, and other processes. They listen at certain published ports for messages and cues from other applications interfaces. Investigate what ports are used to establish these communications and how readily these ports can be spoofed, commandeered, and inappropriately exploited. Ensure that all appropriate auditing logs have been initialized and are being monitored for irregular activity.

Another aspect of database assessment is a review of who has access to the ability to write queries against the data. Queries are command-line instructions that present results based on the rules defined in the statement. A query may involve joining several tables with their related data to get a result that meets the writer's criteria. Care must be taken to ensure that the results of these queries are secured from other system and application users. There also is a possibility that, through the query creation process, users who would normally not have access to certain information can aggregate data and get at results from queries but not through application views or screens they have the permission to see. All of these issues must be considered when evaluating the security of databases:

- Panel- or screen-level user access
- Table and elements security based on data classification
- Access to queries stored for frequent use
- Access to results of queries created and run by others

Sorting all this out, on many levels, can be very complex and confusing. This is in addition to all of the system-level access issues related to installation and routine maintenance of the database management system.

Multi-Tier Client/Server Configuration Implications

When process applications operate across multiple systems, there are many considerations to evaluate to ensure that the operations are secure and efficient. Placing a server between the user and the end process involves having a process act as a proxy for the user in performing their intended action on the host or back-end system. Most of this hand off of the processing and surrogate access is transparent to the end user. Reasons for operating in this manner include the off-loading of processing cycles needed for manipulating the transaction from the back-end server to the middle tier. Multi-tier architecture also can increase maintainability and flexibility, and is conducive to object-oriented programming techniques enabling scalable expansion to occur more readily. By channeling many users to a few mid-tier servers and then to smaller in number but larger data stores, data can be transacted efficiently and effectively for all users involved.

Security isolation is another excellent reason for proxying a user's access to a back-end process. Anytime a secure portion of a network is accessed from a lesser secure portion of the network, the security of the more secure space is lowered to that of the lesser because it cannot be anymore secure than the weakest security directly allowed to affect the data it holds. Proxies are used to maintain the level of security in a particular network segment by not enabling less secure access into that zone. The proxy is a trusted agent and ensures that security violations do not occur by performing only the tasks it is permitted to do.

Other reasons for mid-tiered specialization also may include specialized processing servers where unique tasks are aggregated and performed in a higher throughput, concentrated fashion. SSL accelerators and Citrix servers are examples of this type of use of intermediate servers providing a concentration of services that enable the back-end processing to focus on other needs. A mid-tier server also can house business logic and rules that are executed and maintained separately from the database server. Quite often, a set of frequently applied processes or computationally intense processes of an unpredictable nature, due to the process being driven by ad hoc user requests, makes mid-tier processing more expedient to use and less taxing on the back-end servers. The placement of business logic in the middle tier also can simplify change control of these business rules and help to ensure that everyone is using the same processing logic as well as to provide for the asynchronous queuing of requests to the database level of the process. It also enables different tiers to be developed in different programming languages.

When multi-tiered systems are employed to perform a business transaction, additional audit review steps will be needed to ensure that the transactions occur as expected. Isolation of the processes will be an issue that needs to be examined carefully. How does the middle tier processor maintain the ownership of transactions it is handing off and keep track of who asked for what? How does it maintain the state so that a process, which is being handed off, does not think it has been abandoned or dropped? What happens to a transaction if the connection does in fact get dropped? For database transactions using a middle tier server, there is a process known as a *commit* that locks the fields and commits to the change, keeping every related field suspended during the cycles where the change is actually occurring. Complex checks and balances ensure that all of this happened correctly. If the transaction set cannot be completed successfully, because of a dropped session, for example, a *roll back* process puts everything back to where it was. These processes are required because many things are changing at once and the whole set of changes must all conclude successfully for the transaction to be successful. For multiple databases, a process known as a two phase commit, where a prepare phase initiates the locking process requesting that all involved processes agree to commit or roll back operations for a given transaction. Subsequently, the commit phase actually performs the distributed change, checking all participants for notification of a successful commit before concluding or requesting a roll back from all participants.

Other issues to be concerned with, when reviewing tiered client/server systems, are the ways that compatibility is maintained between the various components as maintenance is applied and system upgrades change one system that impacts another. Many times, these complex environments are difficult to simulate in a test environment, especially to the volume levels of actual usage and with simulation databases being the size of the actual system in use. Representative testing and extrapolation of those tests obviously introduce some risk and need to be weighed against the alternative costs of extensive test environments. The best way to get a full understanding of the process and possible risk points is often to fall back on the data flow diagram method of tracing the process, looking for opportunities for things to go wrong and asking "what if?" questions.

Maintaining coordination and synchronization of all of the distributed processing pieces is another challenge that should be assessed. Single points of failure can cause breaks in processing that need to be reviewed for roll back and orphaned process resolution. Disaster recovery implications of partial failures and the need to recover partial segments of the process must be planned for when determining alternative processing methods. What if the user tier is still intact, but the middle tier cannot perform its function? You also must consider the ramifications of process request interception, man-in-the-middle attacks, and replay attacks when processes traverse untrustworthy network segments in performing their designed functions.

Security Packages

Two types of security packages need to be considered when evaluating a technical infrastructure. The details of the various security tools and their use are covered in the chapter on information asset protection. One type of security package is security that is added to applications and operating systems for an additional level of protection. It is an unfortunate fact that prior to September 11, 2001, most application and operating systems software was not built with security as a high priority business requirement. Rather, it was an obstacle to selling software, resulting in the relatively few security features being shipped in disabled default security configurations. This less than robust security resulted in the need to purchase and apply security overlay systems that would sit on top of operating systems and applications to supplement the security and get it to an acceptable auditing and security level.

Another type of security package is a solution set designed to address a particular type of problem in the environment. Virus protection, VPN solutions, firewalls, email security, Web content control, encryption schemes for various storage needs, and security suites are examples of these point solution tools. A review of any of these types of packaged solutions always starts with an understanding of what problem they are being put in place to solve. These packages rarely just drop in to the existing environment without causing some compromises and changes to business processes.

Understanding the materiality of the issues that need to be addressed helps the IS auditor to understand the risk reduction afforded by the counter-measure being applied.

If you are assessing the acquisition and implementation process, you will need to compare the business need for the added control against the options available to meet that need and the subsequent choice made along with the rationale for that choice. Often, there are few real choices available to meet a particular need from a security perspective. That is not to say that there are not many choices. However, once the constraints of the local environment (scale, compatibility with other tools, complimentary functionality, and so on) and administrative requirements (cost/benefit, ongoing maintenance costs, user impact, and so on) are assessed against the available options, the short list develops rather quickly. With overlay packages, the choices are usually very few. An IBM mainframe security overlay choice set includes RACF, ACF-2, and Top Secret, for example. For some applications and applications suites, the choices are even fewer. This can make the evaluation of the selection process easy, but implementation may not meet all of the requirement criteria because of the limited options available.

A major support component of the selection criteria you should expect to see documented for these choices is the IS organization's security architecture and how well the considered components compliment the overall strategy for security and control across the enterprise. The support and enforcement philosophy of the IS organization, stemming from the business policy, provides the input needed to make decisions on what tools to deploy, with a realistic assessment of the willingness to support the ongoing requirements for sufficiently monitoring administrative tasks to keep these systems relevant and useful. Security is all about compromise. Trade-off decisions must be made between ease of use and relative security. There is no absolute security. The most secure system does not enable users to access it. What kind of compromises must be made to put this additional control in place and use it effectively? How much labor is required to perform this additional function correctly? What kind of policies and standards support the deployment of and enforcement coming from this toolset? Is reporting in place, and to the right people, to ensure that the tool is being used objectively and fairly? What controls are in place to ensure that patches, updates, and signature files are updated regularly? How about when bug and virus identification warrant out-of-cycle updates?

Most of these overlay tools require administration that will need to be managed from a segregated function to be most effective in adding a level of control. How is this process being managed? Is it sufficient to mitigate the risk to acceptable levels? Adding security packages to existing processes add a layer of maintenance upkeep as well. Changes to either system will need to be tested to ensure that the implications of those changes are understood on both the system and the security package. It has been said that it is seven times cheaper to build security at the beginning of a system's design, and this is part of the reason. All of these items need to be considered as a selection and acquisition process being assessed.

Implementation process evaluation takes the same path as the previous implementation processes that we have discussed. You should expect to see complete project plans with realistic milestones, resource allocations, and sponsorship. Security baseline hardening, a process of configuring the security of the system to align with leading practices for optimum security, should be applied to ensure that the default passwords have been addressed, known vulnerabilities are patched, and unnecessary services have been turned off. Testing and piloting are the good best practices that you should see used as part of the detailed planning and implementation documents you review. Processes may need to be developed for interacting with these tools. Work flows for forms to be used to request access, modify rules, and to get enrolled as a user should all be thought through and developed into useable processes ending in a piloting and sponsor approval phase. There also are both the user's and the operator's perspective on training and manuals that need to be considered. Post-implementation reviews should identify problem areas and address any shortfalls in meeting the original goals and security needs that were originally identified as reasons for pursuing these solutions in the first place.

An operational review will assess the toolset's effectiveness to meet the control criteria for which it was designed. Key performance indicators should be identified to enable management to monitor the tool efficiently and in a meaningful manner. Problem reporting should be assessed to ensure that performance meets the service levels acceptable to the organization and typical for product implementations of its type. Audit testing procedures to ensure that processes and controls are effective may be utilized to get firsthand knowledge of the control in action. Reports will need to be assessed for their accuracy and usefulness in providing the information necessary to properly assess the tool. Reviews of maintenance and upgrade records should bear out a rigorously executed change control process that is timely and addresses the business needs. Upstream and downstream impact to the business processes should be assessed to ensure that the security/access compromise decision is worthwhile in terms of risk mitigated versus burden to the user. In addition, you also should ensure that the contingency plans have considered the failure of these tools or the disruption of service options that may need to be put in place for various scenarios of unavailability and security compromise. In addition, because technology and especially security solutions are very dynamic environmental variables, you should expect to see a vigilant watch over the effectiveness of this solution as the business processes evolve and mature. As situations change, yesterday's solution may not always be tomorrow's panacea. An ongoing validation process should be present that ensures the current process has not been outdated by newer solutions, which are more economical, effective, or reliable than processes that have met the needs in the past.

Operations Management Consoles

Operations management consoles and related software suites are used to organize and manage complex processing environments efficiently and affectively, at least that is what the sales brochures say. These tools typically use agents placed on individual processing systems to keep tabs on the health and maintenance of these systems, reporting to the main console via Simple Network Management Protocol (SNMP). A single console then can track adherence to the predefined business rules and monitor job functions by querying the agent for a status and heartbeat signal. Messaging provides for the notification of problems to those remote from the system via email or pager (for example, to get someone's attention to situations that are outside of a defined allowable range). The deployment criteria for a successful installation of operations consoles are that all of these rules need to be defined by persons intimately knowledgeable with the business processes, the system's configuration, and the IS organization's management philosophies. The other issue is this is a slow developmental process, not a big bang implementation. It usually involves a gradual deployment of agents and the tuning out of false positives. It also includes developing new IS business processes and changes in job functions and responsibilities. All of this occurs with a backdrop of pressure to show success and provide value for a complex and expensive project.

When performing the assessment of a processing system that utilizes one of these operational centralization tools, there are many items to add to your review task list. Let's first cover the acquisition and implementation process review. Assuming that the processing needs are large enough to justify the need for this kind of tool, this will be a big project to assess. These tools make sense only for IS organizations that begin as large and complex organizations. These solutions usually make them more so. System solutions of this type include products from IBM—Tivoli, CA—Unicenter, and some other hybrid solutions from major software/

hardware vendors. They require a large commitment of resources and money to make them work well.

The acquisition process review starts with an evaluation of the requirements and criteria. Focus on what the problem to be solved is and how it has been defined. These problem statements should be clear and precise. Scope creep begins early in this type of project. The selection process will necessarily include vendor demonstrations and evaluations of not only functional capability, but also deployment planning, logistics, and support teams provided by or through the vendors. You should evaluate the promises of performance and support carefully to ensure that all parties understand the risks, perceived benefits, and necessary commitments to implement successfully. Ongoing support should be identified up front and agreed to by the IS organization's management in order for a project like this to stand any chance of success. Classic project review steps also apply here. Good documentation should occur, where all of the phases are described in detail, according to their milestones, resource allocations, and so forth. One particular twist to pay attention to is training and knowledge transfer for the staff who will be managing and further developing the tool functionality as it matures after the start up team leaves. The realistic first phase functionality should be simple and able to demonstrate clear success, or these projects can get mired down quickly. How will the existing staff transition from old processes to new ones? Will retraining and going back to fill existing positions enable a new support staff to hit the ground running?

Installation review should evidence a good installation team, time allocated for addressing scope creep, and a realistic adjustment to the deployment plan as issues crop up when reality does not line up with the assumptions made during the project planning. Progress should be tracked formally with reporting to program sponsors performed at regular intervals that ideally include meetings to explain the process and answer questions as the project progresses. These large system overlay deployments are multimonth engagements. With consulting or contracted services, people change and the project's direction can tend to drift. Look out for the substitution of expert contract staff with the entry-level persons leaving less support and progress than originally planned.

The performance of the console management and control processes against the previously defined project objectives should be assessed. Reports and messaging outputs should be evaluated for timeliness, accuracy, and usefulness. Compatibility will be an issue with some aspect of the integration, unless all hardware and software are of a standards predictable nature, which is not usually the case. You will want to investigate the implications of bridges and interfaces as well as translations and work-arounds developed to address incompatibilities determining the gaps in requirements and delivery capabilities. Plans for functionality expansion should be assessed against the progress made to date to assess the feasibility of the goals based on resources and outstanding issues. Problems should be analyzed for root issues that are hidden from the people who are looking at the project too closely to appreciate them. These problems are quite often political in nature, in the final analysis.

Of course, you will want to evaluate the tool's performance and its ability to help solve problems, along with how well the processes are documented and proceduralized. Review the maintenance needs and how well they are being addressed, along with the problem logs related to performance and support. Review any security controls put in place to ensure that the tool is used only by qualified persons and well-developed processes. Tools like this are very powerful and can shut down the entire process effectively and completely. This should be a consideration when determining the need for the network segregation of these devices and the access control permissions issued and how they are administered. Alternative processing and contingency planning should be thoroughly considered because dependency on this tool type can leave old manual processes forgotten along the way. Opportunities for single points of failure also should be analyzed in the deployment process and BRP considerations.

A console that accumulates information and manages processes centrally is an ideal opportunity for providing key performance indicators of the process overall and other statistical- and metric-related feeds. You should assess this as a possible control tool for better providing management of the service levels and for meeting the business objectives. This may be the silver lining to this tool implementation and provide you with the ability to manage the process at a new level over time.

Most add-on tools create issues of their own. One would hope that they would solve more problems than they create, or at least more materially risky problems than they create. You will want to assess the overall problem and risk situation with an eye toward new high-risk weaknesses that crop up due to the new systems and processes. This is not to say that you should not also be looking for opportunities to applaud good controls and risk mitigation when you find it. One of the talents of good IS auditing is to look at all items from a skeptical viewpoint but also seek to identify the things that are working well and give credit wherever possible and in equal measure at a minimum. One downfall of most IS auditing is that the skeptical view usually gets the better of the auditor, and negativity then carries through to the reporting and the relationship in general. This seldom results in a win-win situation.

Evaluating Hardware Acquisition, Installation, and Maintenance

Hardware can mean many things, so let's start with some clarifying definitions. In this section, we will limit the discussion to processing hardware such as servers, storage devices, and large systems used in data center operations. Network hardware, such as routers, switches, and hubs, are covered in the network infrastructure section, but the processes will be similar. Desktop-related hardware and office equipment, such as personal printers, faxes, and scanners, for example, are not covered in this topic directly. However, when evaluating the hardware acquisition strategy and approach, considering opportunities for large volume, economies of scale, and decision processes is usually a good sign that collective bargaining is being used to reduce costs and standardize models. This usually has the effect of reducing maintenance and support costs for large numbers of smaller devices such as printers and fax machines. Typically, when settling bulk deals for commodity items (such as desktop workstations), there are several model types or option classes provided to the user community to address the variability of the user's needs. Standard, deluxe, and power user models provide some selection and the ability to tailor the needs to the devices offered, while still taking advantage of common platforms, maintenance and support structures, and pricing.

Computer data center hardware falls into a few main categories: processors, storage (both disk and removable media devices), and other I/O devices such as large printers of various types, check sorters, consoles, and similar I/O devices. Use of this equipment will be driven by user- and application-specific factors that will need to be reviewed to ensure that the right equipment is acquired and installed to meet those needs. How the users will interface with the application also may drive the need for the hardware solutions. Users who require a wireless terminal or device for accessing applications will have different hardware needs than those who only need a keypunch operator to enter batches of information from a day's business receipts of registration slips, for example.

For large systems, your evaluation will begin by understanding or applying your already developed understanding of the overall business objectives and requirements being used to make the necessary hardware decisions. Knowing the existing constraints and application boundaries will be required to assess the acquisition process and determine whether risks are being overlooked. The hardware selection process is easy to follow once you have ensured that all of the application and use case needs are known and have been translated into terms of the hardware requirements needed to make them function properly. Risks also can be introduced into the process when the selection process is being executed. Items to consider as input to this assessment process include

- Current and future labor and support expertise availability

- All of the relevant application-based requirements of the hardware performance, such as response time, turnaround time, throughput, capacity, peak volumes, and compatibility limitations

- Application requirements for memory, storage space, processing speed, interface cards, capability to handle specialized protocols or peripheral interface cabling, and physical distance limitations to other communicating devices

- User interface requirements such as the proximity of output to users, numbers of concurrent users, sophistication of the user's interface needs, and tolerance for unavailability

- Existing environmental support facilities availability and space capacity for housing hardware and support infrastructure

- Time and cost constraints based on the process, production deadlines, the project, or the company's business culture

This information will describe the requirements' boundaries within which you should expect to see the acquisition process functioning. Anything that you see that is outside of this initial set of constraints will be a concern that will need to be investigated and analyzed for its potential to introduce material risks to the process and the organization.

Depending on how often the same requirements come up throughout the acquisition process in general, you may expect to see procedures documented with these criteria defined as given constraints to be considered in all of the purchases made. Some level of purchasing guidance and procedures should exist to provide a general direction of the approved processes to ensure that the financial and budgeting requirements are met consistently. Capitalization of hardware and other SOP 98-1-related issues should be captured routinely by following such documented procedures, for example. These procedures also should tie the process of project planning and identification of hardware needs back to the budgeting and acquisition processes in a manner that ensures efficient and effective hardware sourcing. Specifications and preparation for the bidding process and criteria for evaluating proposals also should be documented into procedures for the fair and efficient execution of those processes.

The planning and budgeting process should anticipate a potential impact caused by obsolescence, upgrades, expansion, and growth, and it should provide evidence that these things have been considered through the documented acknowledgement of them as part of the process. This is required to provide for the control of the process adequately. Valid review questions will help to determine that the hardware planning is part of the acquisition process: How long will this last? When is the next upgrade anticipated? Have you anticipated the impact of new business? Is there room for growth? How much maintenance or support is required or available for this growth?

With the needs well defined and the constraints understood and documented, the selection of hardware that meets these needs must follow a bidding, selection, and acceptance process. The hardware selection requirements will need to be documented into a Request for Proposal (RFP) document that will be sent to the vendors who are identified as capable and willing to respond to the bidding process. This may require meeting with the vendors initially to determine their viability as potential vendors, but care should be exercised to ensure that an unfair advantage of one vendor over the next is not gained by this interaction and its subsequent influence on the requirements' definitions.

Bid packages are sent out with a deadline for final bid submission and strict guidelines to follow for response format and content. Ideally, there will be no opportunity during this period for vendors to get an inside track on providing favorable responses through contact to the evaluating parties or by asking questions that may give them an advantage over others in formulating a bid response. All questions should be circulated to the other bidders to keep everyone at the same level of understanding. Sometimes it is best to invite all vendors on the bidders list to meet with the bid solicitors initially so that everyone hears the same pitch, benefits from the questions asked by others, and is able to hear the answers at the same time. Procedures requiring an evenhanded management of this process will ensure that a well-controlled process occurs, and if this process occurs, you should ask for evidence that it is being followed consistently.

An analysis of the bids should occur after the close of the bidding deadline and should be based on the responses received and the ability of the vendors to effectively comply with the bidding process requirements. Noncompliant responses will need to be evaluated closely to determine whether they are acceptable to honor and what implication this may have to the other bidders. Typically, this is the starting point of some negotiation as an apples-to-apples comparison is sought and pricing is dickered over. A final deal then is struck and the contracts are finalized. You will want to review the contract for material purchases to ensure that they fairly address the particular risk areas you are now aware of according to the situation at hand. Attention to details such as the delivery dates, the commitments and payouts based on these dates, testing and acceptance, and any liability-related language or considerations that need to be addressed also will be required.

As an IS auditor, you also will need to step back from the entire process and ensure that the overall hardware selection process makes sense from a business perspective and meets the originally specified needs in a satisfactory manner. A good price on a product that does not fit into the environment is a bad decision. Duplicative maintenance training and spare parts inventories can diminish the value of an otherwise sweet deal. The old adage, "If it looks to good to be true, it probably is" fits here. You will quickly develop a sense of risk, poor process, or deployment, and be able to give it the smell test to determine how deep you need to dig into a review quickly as you gain experience in this area. Skepticism is the auditor's friend. Trust but verify your findings.

Installation

The evaluation of hardware installation is a relatively easy assessment for the IS auditor. Clearly, a plan must exist to which this hardware installation is being applied. Adding hardware without any plan or justification and documented analysis is a red flag. A review of the plans should reveal a configuration that this hardware fits into well. Where a "field fit" is required, allowances for variations in completion times and the potential outcomes variability should be evident in the plan. Placement and location decisions should consider all of the classic needs, such as power, cooling, physical security, and maintenance access to the extent required by the situation. Humidity control, physical security, power filtering, or the continuous availability of power requirements should all be understood and provided for to the level necessary to meet the manufacturer's needs and the businesses requirements. Any unaddressed requirements or missing controls should draw your attention for follow-up.

How the introduction of this hardware into existing processes affects the workflow also will need to be considered. Returning back again to the big picture, how does processing need to be adjusted due to this equipment? Does the process change? Is this still the most efficient way to flow the work? Does this hardware mean that other changes are required because the overall layout no longer makes sense?

Hardware installation also involves logistical planning for which you should seek evidence. The timing of its installation can impact other processes, deliverables, and service levels of existing processes. Outages may be required to cut over utilities or to place equipment physically. Cables running under raised floors tend to get messy over time, even in the most well controlled environment. Running new power and data lines can inadvertently cause repeat interruptions in service to equipment not even connected to the existing process. Change control planning should be found in use here to ensure that all contingencies and operations have been notified and considered.

Depending on the local codes and practices, multiple craft trades may need to be involved and coordinated. Floor tiles will need cutouts made in them, cooling will need to be readjusted in the data center, and power will need to be redistributed. The potential impact on the user will also need to be planned. Integration of the hardware changes with software changes, application conversions, and user-related system availability needs will all need to be input into a master matrix for decision management by the data center manager to ensure the best fit for all needs. Your evaluation will assess how well prepared these hardware installations are and will review past instances of hardware implementations for variances from documented procedures and prudent best practices.

Maintenance

The evaluation of the hardware maintenance is a matter of evidencing proper planning and execution against those plans. Planning maintenance can be seen as the first step in the life cycle of this process. When reviewing this process, you will begin by gathering an inventory of what items need maintenance. A quick risk assessment of those items may provide an opportunity for narrowing your efforts to a smaller inventory. However, be aware of seemingly insignificant items, without which the whole process comes to its knees. Intimate knowledge of these processes may be required for this analysis, and a knowledgeable operator can be invaluable in helping point out risk areas that might be otherwise overlooked or problem areas with the existing layouts or configurations that result in otherwise unexpected problems. Most staff level personnel inherently evaluate risk because these items cause problems for them in their daily work and they want as a smooth process as you do. Thus, assurance of a win-win situation can bring benefits all around.

Now that you have identified the items to consider for maintenance, you will need to gather the requirements for the maintenance of these items in terms of frequency and quality. Find out whether there are rec-ommended maintenance routines provided and recommended by the vendor. In classic "what is, what should be" gap analysis fashion, this information will be used to build a matrix of the expected maintenance behaviors that you will want to see in practice. Performance against these requirements may involve contracts with periodic servicing ven-dors, contingency contracts to provide for required downtime limitation parameters dictated by service level agreements, or manufacturers-recommended maintenance practices. Following the manufacturers-recommended maintenance schedules may be required to ensure valid warranties or to guarantee performance levels promised by the product specifications.

Ensuring that qualified personnel are available for performing the maintenance required will be an objective of the review as you assess the overall hardware maintenance process. In addition, cross training the available maintenance personnel, determining the single source depen-dencies of either the parts or service personnel, finding hard-to-find parts, and comparing the documented failure rates being experienced with sim-ilar experiences in other organization's or manufacturer's benchmarks information also will help you assess the overall efficiency and effective-ness of the process you are evaluating. You also may want to identify the physical security and personnel security clearance aspects of using con-tract employees for servicing the equipment. Equipment that leaves the premises for servicing that contains classified data should have the confi-dentiality and integrity of the data, which could be potentially lost. Ensur-ing that data is wiped from devices that are retired, obsolete, or swapped out will need to be monitored. Service organizations that are not bonded to protect the company from security breaches may expose the client to risks worth considering as material.

You will want to gather evidence on the levels of service being per-formed, the contracts that are in place to ensure service availability, and the up-time statistics on maintenance, response time records, documen-tation on problems outstanding, MTBF calculations, and customer sat-isfaction measurements should be tied to hardware maintenance as applicable. For example, you may find that not much of this kind of information is being routinely gathered and recorded on servers. Every situation will require that different levels of diligence be applied to them to mitigate the perceived risks. These decisions will be based on risk tolerance and actual experience of historical events that require proper maintenance attention.

Evaluating Network Infrastructure

We will assume that you will not be auditing the acquisition and installation of a base network infrastructure being installed from scratch. More likely, you may be involved with auditing an expansion to or a major change in an existing infrastructure. With any networking configuration that you evaluate, there are a few key principles that you will replay in the review process. Not surprisingly, they follow the basic SDLC methodology lines of reasoning. If the systems are supported by effective management, problems will arise and be resolved as a matter of due course. The primary objectives of any network-related review are to ensure that

- Proper and sufficient levels of engineering and architecture disciplines were employed in the planning and design of the network.
- The resources in use are well supported and maintained.
- The system is monitored and issues are properly being addressed.
- Adequate controls are in place to ensure the security, availability, and survivability of the network based on risk.

Voice Networks

Voice networks interface with the public telephone system and are very important to the ongoing operations of any business. Phone systems existed long before computer networks were invented and their needs and requirements are better understood due to the system's relative maturity. Public telephone infrastructures deal with disaster recovery all the time, have support and troubleshooting processes, and are so well entrenched in our daily lives, we seldom question the availability of a dial tone. As phone systems grow and the functionality demands increase in a business, increased complexity and the required internal infrastructure force the IS organization to manage the process and to insure the effective and efficient use of the resources and the availability of the systems.

By now, the routine should be evident for the IS audit reviews preliminary tasks. What are the business needs? What is the organizational structure in place for this subset of the organization? Organizational charts, job descriptions, financial tracking, billing processes, problem tracking, and resolution processes documentation are all basic preliminary documentation sets that you will want to gather to set up the review. Request configuration and layout drawings and examine them for engineering practices that would be indicative of a meticulously maintained environment. This would include good change control evidenced right on the drawings, such as evidence that the engineering drawings and actual field installations are not the same and a reconcilement process to ensure that the drawings will be reflective of the actual environment when needed. Disaster recovery documentation is usually an excellent indicator of the depth of the management team, the amount of discipline actually practiced, and amount of attention given to the viability of the processes in the real world.

Ask about plans for future growth and the current growth rates. What is on the drawing board in terms of change in the next 12 months? Does the existing network need major changes to accommodate this growth? Will there be staffing and support issues due to the plans that are being developed? How will the management and the maintenance processes change as a result, if applicable? Ask about monitoring processes and the results of problem reports and subsequent follow-up. Is there evidence of a timely follow-up? Are customers getting a good turnaround for their reported problems and relocation requests? Is there a process in place to quantify these issues and adjust the workforce as user need waxes and wanes? Throughout this process, you should be building a risk matrix, identifying the potential problem areas to focus on as you dig into the details of the systems and their management.

From a management and personnel perspective, you will need to ensure that job functions are all identified, clearly understood, and assigned, and that those who have been assigned these jobs understand their accountabilities. This process applies across the entire range of functions—it does not just apply to the staff and workers. If management authority and direction were presented as a mixed message to the staff, poor performance would not be an unexpected result. Part of the management assessment that you will perform includes ensuring that performance reviews occur for both staff and third-party support and personnel issues are being addressed in a timely manner along with the proper segregation of duties considerations. You also will want to assure that contract personnel are escorted when accessing equipment or that some similar control is in place to insure accountability for physical and logical access. You should expect to see thoroughly documented termination procedures that include changing passwords, keys, and access to system support consoles and PBX equipment. In fact, access codes should be changed periodically as a matter of due diligence for all devices that offer remote exploitation opportunities, which could easily go unnoticed. Management should have processes in place to regulate these issues and address them in a timely manner. How is this done and what evidence can be found that this is being managed properly? What are the key regulations and what risks to the organization do these regulations represent? Are the regulations sufficiently mitigated with control processes in place and operating?

You should assess the configuration and system layout. Is it structured to meet the needs of the business and corporate objectives? Does it provide for scaling and growth? Are opportunities available for simplifying the cost and system layout that have not been addressed? How might outages that currently impact the users be better addressed by changes in layout and minimize downtime? Are reconfigurations feasible without disrupting the business' needs? Look for system redundancy and fail-over strategies. Ask about user requirements for special services such as flexible bandwidth, mobile access, variable user populations, and out of the norm uptime requirements, and assess the configurations designed to accommodate these needs. Does the configuration make logical sense or is it a patchwork of different designs and strategies? What are the biggest risks to the voice system? How are they being addressed? Are the disaster recovery plans formally documented and tested periodically? Do the drawings used to make troubleshooting decisions reflect the major changes and maintenance that has been presented in the change management and problem-related service orders you reviewed?

Look at the financial reporting and cost management structures. Are the costs captured representative of the total costs being experienced? How well do these costs get reported and allocated to the users of the service? How are billing errors managed? Does the process meet the needs of the business in the way it is performed? Are all of the assets accounted for and fairly represented by the financial picture? Do buy versus lease decisions apply, and if so, how does the reporting and amortization of the system change as a result? Review any service provider contractual arrangements that may move costs or recovery on investments out to future fiscal years for possible risks and control weaknesses. Ensure that the maintenance agreements are current and that the costs are reasonable and appropriate based on the current equipment in use and service levels required. Make sure that this information accurately translates to the fiscal reporting reviewed in the previous steps. Assess the details of the billing information and its support systems. Is it sufficient to support the billing to the users? Does it make problem resolution and customer questions difficult to address? How are these issues resolved to the satisfaction of all the involved parties? If package service deals are provided, do they match the service actually being provided? How are the costs reconciled over the entire usage for the system? How are special business requirements and needs accommodated and charged?

Assess the quality control aspects of the voice network management process. What metrics are used to indicate problems in quality and the user experience? Are they sufficient to indicate the overall health of the system or are there problems that may go unnoticed based on the information currently being monitored? What process is in place to ensure that economies of scale are reassessed periodically, based on user statistics, so that the line sizing and device utilization are rebalanced periodically to provide the maximum value to the user population based on service need?

Assess the daily operations and management of the systems. How is the workload managed and distributed among the staff to ensure that tasks are accomplished in a timely manner and to the end users' satisfaction? Is the training of the staff sufficient to support the needs of the organization and its service levels? What are the service level agreements in place and how are they managed, monitored, and reported on? You should review the reports provided on service performance and determine that they fairly and accurately represent the performance of the systems. How are spares managed and controlled? What evidence exists to support that maintenance work orders are being managed and tracked, thus ensuring not only that the equipment and inventories are being well maintained but also that the work is done in an efficient and cost effective manner? Look at the daily operational issues and assess the effectiveness of the performance of the tasks. How well is traffic flow and work assignment managed? What key performance indicators are used to ensure that these processes are controlled sufficiently?

Review the security controls in place for both the system and the use of the system. Are there policies in place that define the acceptable use of the system? Are they enforced? How well does this process actually work? Tour the equipment rooms and assess physical security aspect of the control process. Are the doors locked? What type of access controls monitor who gets into the rooms where the equipment is housed? Who else beside the voice personnel have access to these places? Do obvious single points of failure situations based on equipment placement or the routing of lines present themselves during the tour? What is the maintenance condition of these equipment rooms? Look for dirty, cluttered, and poorly maintained environments. How well are wires and termination boxes labeled? Do the *as built* drawings match what is out in the field? Fire hazards and poor ventilation should be addressed by the appropriate environmental controls. You should assess the power conditioning needs and controls in place for devices such as surge protection and UPS.

The logical access security of telecommunication systems is no different from other computer systems and will need to be evaluated to determine whether proper controls are in place. Have the default passwords of the accounts that access routing and interface devices been changed? Is access limited to those who have a need to know? How often are the passwords changed? Have strong authentication mechanisms been considered? Where are the vulnerable points of the systems logical access? Turning off unnecessary services or controlling those that can be taken advantage of should also be a point of review for these systems. Are unnecessary services disabled on the voice systems? Can a redirected dial tone be gained from an outside phone such that the billing for the call hits the system instead of the originator? What controls are in place to deter services theft? Can the voice mail system be spoofed into providing unauthorized access to either stored messages or outbound phone lines? Has a logical mapping of inputs and output been performed to account for all lines in use and on the bill? Are fax lines and modem lines identified well enough to provide sufficient control over misuse of these tools for unauthorized data network access? Policies and user-related expectations and the associated education are also valid evaluation points for this type of review. What are the policies related to voice systems and their use and how well do the processes in place enforce these policies? What review processes are employed on a regular basis to identify irregularities and the misuse of the system? What reporting and follow-up is a result of this process? Is misuse reported appropriately and addressed appropriately? What interfaces into the controlling devices exist and how is this access limited effectively?

PBX devices and phone switches are the primary interfaces between the outside lines and the internal wiring of a voice communication system. There is some amount of intelligence in these devices and they are typically managed by a computer interface. Depending on the style and model of the device, the actual audit program will differ. How this control system is protected from unauthorized access and disruptions will be of interest in your review. Hardware and software changes control also will require assessment. The list goes on and on. You will need to budget your time and decide where the risks are to best provide a review that adds value and appropriately meets the review objectives, investigating the nuances of the particular situations you are faced with as you go.

Data Networks

Data networks also are unique to the business requirement and the legacy of the early attempts to deploy and grow interconnected systems into a useable infrastructure. Seldom are networks installed entirely of new components and reflecting a single cohesive strategy. There are many network design topologies that you should be familiar with from a CISA testing perspective; star, Ethernet, token ring, and bus, for example. Understanding their differences may be important for testing but not as important as understanding what you are looking at in your audit and why it needs to be configured like it is from a business and strategy perspective. You must seek to understand the network architecture and design in order to evaluate all of the pieces in relative detail. What are the goals of the organization that drive the need for networking? If you are unfamiliar with network design and configuration strategies, you will need to educate yourself on this first. In the mean time, you can be gathering the available documentation and reviewing it. System configurations, device lists with models and microcode levels, quantities and the placement of devices, and network line diagrams depicting the separation of the various subnets are all a good start for this review process. Knowing which protocols are in use and what security controls are in place also will be helpful information. If firewalls, *Access Control Lists (ACL)* on routers and switches, network intrusion detection, or proxies are deployed, take note of their locations and the segments that are protected by them as well as the rules governing them. Pinpointing the locations of sensitive and confidential data on the network and the mission critical processes will begin to point out where redundancy, disaster recovery, spare capacity, and single points of failure may introduce risk to the business processes. An overview of the data flow for critical business processes will help you understand how the network configuration and security countermeasures are supposed to work to help in the business process. A best practice is to have a security plan for each business process that defines this data flow and its expected behavior. This plan also would baseline the network components the process expects to interact with along its journey and how the controls work.

You also should assess the definition of the outermost boundary or perimeter of the network. Where is the logical line drawn exactly and what is the difference from a security and control perspective for devices existing on either side of this fence? Are there other boundaries that need to be understood to evaluate the network fairly? Drawing a line around the perimeter, based on where the rules and policies are applicable, will help you understand the difference between an intranet or internal network to the organization and an extranet used by business partners and value-added resellers of services, for example. Any segregation within the perimeter also should be noted for further evaluation during this process. Determine where the other boundaries and segments are delineated. Are *De-Militarized Zones (DMZ)* used to secure transition from more secure and lesser secure network segments? DMZs are small staging segments of network space that enable the limited movement of data and isolate trusted traffic from untrustworthy traffic. In the DMZ on an Internet to company boundary, one might find, for example:

- Proxy servers to disintermediate the public from trusted zone access
- Authentication servers for validating identity and determining levels of authorization for users seeking access
- Mail servers to hand off and receive email delivery without enabling access into the network
- VPN and extranet edge devices
- Intrusion detection monitoring devices
- Other intermediary hand-off servers such as FTP servers or remote access servers
- Zone-specific DNS servers

DMZs separate network segments by logically making the access rules different. This separation is usually managed by a rule enforcement device, such as a firewall or routing device, with an ACL used to filter packets and restrict traffic. DMZs are the halfway point between two such control devices and the designated areas of quasi trust and access. If you think of them as neutral drop-off points, such as a mailroom or a guard station, you will soon understand how they could prevent the direct passing of traffic and where risks and vulnerabilities may occur as you are reviewing data flow diagrams. A DMZ is usually a network segment that sandwiches itself between two firewalls and creates a middle space between other network segments for traffic hand-offs. If access is allowed directly from one zone to the next, logically the security of the two segments is the same by definition. In fact, unless the packets or processing request is terminated and resourced from a trusted agent within the DMZ, you could argue that the security has been compromised. This is because you can never be sure a payload is without a hidden nefarious content, unless it was intercepted and recreated from scratch by a trusted source. You will need to map all of this out and determine whether the security architecture meets the security and separation needs of the business processes with these issues in mind.

As you build an evidence list and plan the testing steps for your review of the data network, you also will need to gather some basic documentation. Which policies are applicable to the networks and related matters and are they sufficient to meet the business needs, if enforced properly? Do *Acceptable Use* policies exist, ones that cover intellectual property, downloading from lesser secure networks, virus protection, and the like? Are security breaches defined, how to react to them, and the roles and authority of an incident response team established by these policies? What business needs and strategies are supported by the network and its configuration? Have any risk assessments been performed and documented that would substantiate the need for extra measures of redundancy of the contingencies? Your work papers should include a gap analysis of the policy and standard documentation against best practices for similar IS organizations. In addition, you also should interview both technicians and users of the environment to get their input on the effectiveness and relative enforcement of the policies actually being employed.

Are there sufficient job descriptions and an assignment of tasks and accountabilities to ensure that every job has an owner and every one knows who is responsible for what tasks? For the people managing the network, are all of the proper human resource-related issues being addressed properly? These issues would include performance reviews, mandatory vacations, duty segregation, cross training, training in general, background clearance checks, termination procedures, and procedures and documentation in general. If contract personnel are used, review the contracts for the appropriate items to mitigate risk and insure a satisfactory performance.

Look at the equipment that is being used to push packets around on the network. If there is a mix of different kinds and vintages of equipment, investigate the reasons behind this. Is it part of a strategy or the result of a low cost bidding and vendor *du jour* patchwork systems management? Complexity of this nature is hard to support because expertise is required on many products and interfacing will lead to some level of incompatibility to be sure. Investigate the various technologies in use to understand the rationale for deploying them. Sometimes you will find older technologies mixed with newer ones in use on the same network, for good reasons. The network plan may call for older, less functional, and slower products to be used where demand can tolerate them, and the newer devices may be placed in areas of high demand or where low fault-tolerance exists. A phase-out strategy may be in use that replaces components over time, as resources permit. Make note of any limitations these situations may introduce into the network and determine whether they could add risk or impact business processes negatively. Compare the configurations of the network to the best practice strategies for supporting businesses of similar size, security needs, and operational requirements, which you previously determined. Question any identified gaps found for possible mismatch and business supportability concerns.

In addition, you should look at the problem identification, tracking, and resolution processes and supporting documentation. Ask the network support staff their opinion about what are the major issues and problems. Draw conclusions on the sufficiency to address the needs of the business and its users. Review the change control processes and determine whether the testing and back-off processes will sufficiently protect the business from disruption while meeting the requirements of the necessary change management tasks. Assess the maintenance requirements, processes, and service records to ensure that the corrective actions are taken in a timely and effective manner. Review the monitoring and management tools in place to control the network and to keep it running at peak performance. Are the tools monitoring the right indicators and providing information that can effectively be used to address performance and irregularities? How well are these processes supported with staff compared to the requirements for meeting the service levels? Review the performance service levels and any documentation that shows changes over time for signs of degradation or poor performance history.

Look closely at the security tools in place to control data traffic flowing across the various network segments. Are they planned and strategically tied together to meet the data flow needs and business model? Walk through some of the more material data flows and ensure that the data is appropriately protected by the configuration and security controls in place. Do the rule sets used on the control devices provide for the necessary security control, based on your understanding of the need and functionality of the countermeasure being used? Look at these rule sets and ensure that they are built to deny by default traffic that is not required for a business purpose. Are the security and other network devices deployed such that only the minimum amount of necessary services is turned on? Make sure that these tools are being kept current in terms of patch levels and required updates to signature files. Have baseline snapshots been taken of the configurations or have tools such as Tripwire been implemented to ensure that changes do not occur without notice? Are copies of these configurations stored off site for disaster recovery purposes along with other pertinent documentation? Have the default accounts been changed and is the access to network devices controlled sufficiently to ensure that it is limited to those with a need to know? You should complete your review on the adequacy of the security based on the planning, design, and implementation of the network devices and security tools.

If possible, run a security tool that will scan the network to identify potential vulnerabilities and determine the applicability of these findings to the risk profile of the business process. This is an ideal opportunity for a CAAT tool, by the way. If network vulnerability scanners are being used already by the network or security staff, ask to see the results of the scanning efforts and identify the actions taken, based on these results. You should expect to find a risk-based scheme for prioritizing the results of network vulnerability reviews and proactive extrapolation of these items into the identification and resolution of root problems through the analysis of these findings. Watch for the reactionary fixing of symptoms that do not address core problems. Mature network intrusion and vulnerability analysis processes will gather symptomatic data from several sources, firewall logs, network- and host-based intrusion detection equipment, and traffic monitoring tools, to determine a more accurate picture of what is actually going on at the transport layer.

In addition, you should assess the bandwidth provided on the various network segments against the business needs on those segments. Identify the reports used to communicate and manage network performance and assess their adequacy. Look for KPIs and review the history of these indicators to see if major changes or issues have occurred that warrant an investigation or explanation. Verify that the reports include information on capacity, latency, traffic patterns, and trouble areas and ensure that variances are escalated as appropriate to management. Ensure that the security tools are being actively monitored and the results from this monitoring are being proactively investigated to prevent problems. Review the networking devices for proper configuration and ensure that routing decisions are being made to minimize cost and maximize throughput. Ensure that the devices are sized to meet the business needs and burst throughput that is required.

In addition, you should determine what back up and contingency planning processes are used to prepare for disruptions from failures or outages. Review the existing process and procedures documentation, planning and business impact information, and back up compilations. Ensure that network recovery is considered as an integral part of the various business process recovery plans as well. Where single points of failure have been mitigated with fail-over and high availability schemes, you must determine the frequency with which these schemes have been tested and exercised. Identify how power is supplied to the key networking components and ensure that uninterruptible power is used as required to provide network support during power glitches. Assess the need for supplemental battery power to these UPS schemes, battery life, testing of battery back up, and so forth. Identify any gaps in the alternative networking arrangements that exist in the network and draw conclusions on the potential residual risks that may need to be brought to the attention of management in an audit report.

Evaluating IS Operational Practices

Operational practices are the tasks performed in daily operation of the processing components of the IS organization. It is the business end of data processing, and as such, it can be thought of from a business perspective instead of from a technical or hardware/software view. As a service provider, the IS organization has made commitments to the businesses it is providing for and supporting. These commitments need to be thoroughly documented in order for the IS organization to understand the related deliverables and time frames, and in order for the business to understand what is and is not within the scope of the performance expectations. Usually, the professionalism of computer operations can be tied directly to the quality of this documentation and the understanding and expectations management between the provider and the user for these services. This professionalism is a strong indicator of the control and risk management environment. When reviewing computer operations and evaluating the processes and performance, you should get a sense for the depth to which the rules are established for performing routine tasks. Observe how rigorously they are followed, as part of the operations culture, in general. This will be an early warning system for your audit of how well the overall review will turn out.

Operational practices are a people management issue. You cannot expect operators to know intuitively what the right thing is to do next. Operators of computer systems work hours that cover the entire 24 × 7 spectrum, often with little supervision or management interaction. Just keeping up on what is happening during daylight is a big deal for these dedicated staffers. Management decisions and strategic direction are seen as interference to getting the job done for the most part. Checklists, duty rosters, and turnover documentation are the operator's guiding tools. Long periods of boredom punctuated by short stretches of high stress and panic are the daily routine. Human resource processes called out repetitively in this prep guide should be closely assessed in particular for these individuals. Job rotation and training are important to keep them challenged and engaged in the support processes, which are so necessary to the success of the IS organization's mission. Ensuring that responsibilities, authority, and procedures are well documented and clearly understood will be important keys to mitigating the potential risk to the operations that this staff can introduce.

Computer Operations

Computer operations are the impartial and objective execution of tasks defined by business and support process owners. Typical tasks include answering routine systems messages, monitoring processes and system functions to ensure they complete correctly, and notifying support personnel when they do not. Starting back ups, initiating clean-up jobs, rebooting systems, and acknowledging messages from peripheral and support devises (such as printers, tape drives, power supplies, cooling equipment, disk drives, interfaces, and communication links) all require the operator to have a procedure available depicting the expected responses to various situations that inevitably will occur on their shift. Your review will begin by determining what the tasks are that the operators are expected to perform and what kind of support documentation exists related to these tasks. Assessing gaps between SLAs and the operator's expected tasks may give you some insight into overlooked items and the critical path of various tasks performed by the operations staff. As with all IS organizational tasks, understanding the key performance metrics for the functions being reviewed and assessing the integrity, accuracy, and usefulness of those measurements will help you understand how well the process is being performed and managed. Look at these statistics to ensure that the right things are being monitored from a risk-based point of view. You also must ensure that these statistics are being reported and followed up on properly to provide a good control of the environment.

The segregation of duties will be a major assessment point for operational reviews. Operators have many responsibilities and may indeed be in charge at times when they are on duty. Understanding their escalation procedures and their realistic ability to perform against these documented processes will help you understand how realistically the segregation of duties is actually maintained on off shifts. Depending on the size of the shop and the resources available, computer operators can be asked to wear many hats. These hats may at different times include:

- Loading operating systems to computers by booting or Initial Program Load (IPL) processes
- Initiating programs to run on computer systems
- Monitoring jobs and making notes of their completion status
- Loading printers and handling print-output distribution tasks
- Loading scratch tapes into tape drives and managing tape librarian functions

- Checking engineering and supporting staff into and out of the data processing area, and escorting them during their work

- Testing environmental control systems and logging the status of systems' health

- Performing escalation and notification tasks when processing ends abnormally (ABEND)

- Performing some change control functions and acting as a gatekeeper to various levels of system access

- Answering calls and helping users

- Performing some troubleshooting and problem analysis

- Managing operations schedules and reordering workloads to meet service schedules and deadlines

- Responding to routine interventions on the systems to keep processes moving

- Assuring physical access integrity to the data center space by acting as a monitor, guard, and key control

- Documenting irregularities for examination and follow-up through problem reporting processes

- Tracking statistical measurements of processing and reporting those metrics to management

- Making a fail over and swap out of equipment decisions and performing these changes to keep production commitments

- Performing asset control functions by inventory and checking out all the equipment entering and leaving the computer room

Clearly, if an operator had all of these responsibilities in an operation of any size, not only would they be very busy, but there would be serious concerns from an auditing, segregation of duties, and conflict of interest perspective that too much unchecked authority had been given to a single set of job functions. Several compensating controls would have to be put in place to get any comfort that this situation could go on without introducing significant risk to the IS organization. Let's examine some of the natural divisions of labor, what these jobs entail, and how they should be best controlled and managed.

Some of the more traditional tasks of a computer operator include initializing jobs and monitoring their progress and completion. From a schedule provided to them, the operators would run down the list and kick-off processes. When prompted by the system that these tasks had ended, they would follow the procedure, perform any related functions such as notification or verification, and go to the next item on their list. When things went wrong, they would consult their back-out, restart procedures, and attempt to right the process, based on the instruction provided to them and developed by others. They would perform only against these instructions, making notes along the way of the success or failure to provide the process owners insight into what worked, what did not, and why. Problems would be duly recorded in problem tracking systems and reported and turned over to the next shift. Either the operators relieving the list of the last shift would continue the resolution efforts, or they would pass on the information to the persons who manage the process to resolve the problem and provide fixes through the change control processes. The operator's tasks are separated in this example from any access to program code (other than *execute* access), application functionality, or job script content. A job function for operator tasks only, fully segregated from other tasks, would perform only actions defined and pre-built by others and have no ability of its own to manipulate code or data except through programs built by others. However, unless the organization is very large, there is usually more to performing the operator's job than this and some compromise must be struck between resource utilization and security.

Printer Operators

For example, it is common for computer operators to also serve as the printer and tape drive attendants in some fashion. These devices are all central to an IS operation and on off-shifts the staff might likely support all of these areas. Printers need routine maintenance, cleared of paper jams occasionally, and the output needs burst into individual reports from a continuous printer feed and sorted, perhaps into pick-up bins or shelves, maybe handed to users who come to a distribution point to pick it up. The print queues, where the print jobs are electronically spooled while awaiting printing, need to be actively managed. Print jobs are sorted by the output paper requirements, job priorities, and routed to available printing devices. Printer availability and uptime should be monitored and reported on. Along with possibly managing the check stock, and other specialized stock based on the process (stock certificates or other negotiable stock), the operator also would have access to the output from programs run on the computer systems. Being able to also run these programs as well puts a single person in charge of processes where they could inject nefarious code and gather up the evidence of this happening to keep it from possibly becoming known to the actual owners or users of the application.

Consideration of the possible compensating controls needed to bring the risks of this excess access rights and privileges situation back to acceptable levels will be needed. These controls might include computer system logs that are sent to and reviewed by management or other IS operations oversight functions, who either track the programs submitted by the operators or the output coming off the printers or both, and then reconciling these logs against reported work to identify any variances that may need an explanation. Good control of the access to programs and code that does not enable operators access beyond execution privileges also is a possible mitigating control, but it would need to be thoroughly investigated to ensure that backdoor access could not be gained. Back up processing usually involves a significant amount of access privilege for computer operators, and if interrupted cleverly, it could leave wide-open access to systems and access to program code.

Media Library Management

In a similar situation, tape operations holds out even more risk when its duties are combined with the duties of a computer operator. A review of tape or media library operations can be an audit in and of itself for large IS organizations. The tape librarian is charged with maintaining the security and integrity of the removable media library, which includes keeping copies of all the code and data that is moved to removable storage locations for archive purposes. There should be routine back up copies of all the important information created, stored, and used by computer operations. Sometimes, these copies are produced to create back ups that are moved off site for recovery needs as necessary. Sometimes, the purpose is to create copies of data or code for removal from the operations center, based on the business needs or technical support requirements of the process. It is prudent to make copies of any information that, if the original was lost or corrupted, would disrupt the processing operations or impact the users.

When reviewing the media management operations, your objectives will be to ensure that the library function provides the necessary access to removable media while insuring the restrictions of access to those who should not be able to remove the data from the premises. You also will determine whether there is a sufficient back up process in place to enable the timely recovery of production code and data, should this be necessary due to processing errors or data corruption. You also will be assessing the overall organization and management practices of the library to ensure that good inventory management practices are employed and that the locations and contents of media are indeed those expected by the system users. Off-site storage facilities also should be assessed to ensure that those locations are managed properly for environmental controls, security, and library management processes.

Tapes are a source of incoming code and data to the systems processes. Data can be input when new clients are added in bulk to existing applications or when systems conversions are performed, by adding new systems code along with the accompanying production data. Patches and system updates can come into the system via tapes and other removable media. New versions of code and test code created by programmers on test systems, perhaps not part of the data center operations domain, also are introduced into the process through the tape library. Your review of incoming media should ensure that it is logged, recorded, and used for the intended processing. Care should be exercised to ensure that external input data is not erroneously introduced into the production environment without being reviewed and checked through the internal change control processes. The movement of media out of the library also must be carefully controlled. Logs should exist detailing who, what, when, and why for all media leaving the premises. There should be a check in place to ensure that the person handling the media is authorized and otherwise has a need to know.

Back ups of the production processes can be managed in several ways. The two most popular methods are full back ups and incremental back ups. Full back ups capture the entire set of application code and related data and store them together. In this way, an entire instance of a process can be recovered if necessary. Remember when reviewing contingency planning aspects of the back ups that any scheme will provide only recovery to the point in time when the back up was produced, and any processing that occurs after this copy is made will need to be recovered by some other means. The other method is to use incremental back ups to supplement less frequent full back ups. This process copies those things that have changed since the last back up and copies those items to storage. Restoration then is accomplished by laying down the last full back up and adding the incremental changes to the desired recovery point. This method is used for large systems where full back ups take a long time and possibly require that the system is unavailable during the back up process.

Part of the tape librarian function is to retire the older tapes and make them available for reuse by staging them to be overwritten when called for by the programs. Scratching a tape, as this is referred to, does not actually erase the data but only rewrites some header information and flags it as available. A robust media management program will be required to keep track of tape aging, cataloging information that spans multiple pieces of media without getting the sequencing mixed up, and managing check-in and sign-out tasks while keeping the library in order, all the while. Being able to control the jobs that are running on the system and the data coming into and out of the library can provide opportunities for unchecked access to data and processes to which the operator has no legitimate business need without compensating controls being put in place. Knowing that a particular step in the payroll job has just completed running and getting access to a copy of that file on tape may be an issue for senior management and the human resources department. Additional controls could include close monitoring and logging of all operator processing activities and very tight tape inventory processes. Supervision over operator activities is an additional control that is assumed in most of these cases. As with the printer example cited previously, a clear risk analysis should be performed if not by the IS organization, then at least by your audit process to point out these risks fairly and to seek a management decision on better controlling or accepting the risks.

The overall inventory and library aspects of the storage should be reviewed by spot-checking from the catalog to the racks of stored media and by pulling selected media from storage and cross checking it to the catalog listings. Working with the librarian, allowances should be given for work in progress and movement off site. Work backlogs can cause unexpected delays in processing because the necessary data is not correctly placed in the storage rack system. You should review the outstanding work and the ability to stay caught up with the needs of the processing.

You also will want to assess any offsite storage locations and processes and inspect how they are managed. Look at the vendor relationships and contracts to ensure that they are sufficient to meet the demands of storage size, unscheduled media availability, right to audit, security and environmental controls, and support provisions. Assess the manner in which the media is boxed up and moved to ensure that the data is protected from physical and environmental abuse as well as being protected from theft and misplacement. Visit the off-site storage location if possible to see firsthand what kind of security and environment exist for the storage. Pay attention to excessive dampness or vermin. Look into the cataloging and storage methodologies to ensure that the media could be picked out of the mix and returned quickly, should individual application recovery become necessary. Ensure that media being returned to the processing center is checked in and returned to its proper location, based on whether the media is expired or being returned for use.

Physical Access to Operations Areas

The physical access enforcement duties also can fall onto the operators at times. This applies to asset inventory and management functions as well. These tasks can be distracting from the computer operations monitoring, causing the neglect of the process or worse yet, the physical access tasks may be neglected in favor of the operations monitoring, enabling inappropriate physical access and egress to occur. Familiarity with the engineering and support staff eventually relaxes the guard of operators over time, who see the security tasks as not really adding value and interfering with their primary function. Lax security and poor audit trails end up being the result. Spot checks of security conditions and alarms on doors that sound when blocked open can help mitigate the risk of overlooking that proper security is in place at all times. Checking sign-in logs and matching maintenance and change records to access entries can help show that the security tasks are taken seriously. Strict control of temporary badges for vendors and visitors should be maintained, reconciled, and inventoried on a regular basis and be accompanied with reporting to validate the review. Insisting that badges are displayed and visible and making a practice of challenging anyone who is unknown and not escorted should be encouraged as a compensating control as well. Routine walkthroughs by management and staff, possibly checking environmental controls or power to systems, also will deter unchecked activity from proliferating.

The concerns with operators also acting in a trouble determination capacity or fielding help desk calls relate to the fox watching the chicken coup. If they are the cause of the problem, you will never know it. Problem reporting needs to be segregated from the activities that could be causing the problems to ensure that an objective and balanced performance of the function occurs. As tasks are combined to achieve operating economies and efficiencies, risks and tradeoffs must be recognized and carefully considered. As you review the operations of IS organizations and understand the current combination of roles and responsibilities, you will need to identify opportunities to circumvent access restrictions and otherwise defeat good behavior expectations and to question whether these risks have been considered and accepted or to recommend additional controls. Looking at situations from the perspective of what could go wrong is part of thinking like an auditor. You will need to consider carefully the materiality of the potential risk situations as you weigh its ability to be reported and overall risk. Resist the temptation to identify improbable sets of circumstances and insist on remediation. Remember that businesses must inherently have some amount of risk or there would not be a business opportunity. Reducing risk to an acceptable level for management is the objective, not the elimination of all risk. You can chase "who is watching the watchers?" backwards almost indefinitely, but you will quickly find that you have to trust someone eventually and that the risk was reduced to an acceptable level much earlier in the exercise than where you ended up.

Help Desk and User Support

Help desk functions are very important to business users because these functions are their portal to the IS organization and to getting their needs to satisfactorily perform the business functions. Your review of this set of processes should be approached with this in mind. The objective of this review will be to determine how well the user's needs are being met. Aside from the routine assessment of the HR management issues of clearly defining tasks and roles and responsibilities, along with the staff scheduling and coverage needs, training and procedures will be an important aspect of the people end of the user support business that you will want to assess. When user support personnel are not knowledgeable, a bad user experience will likely result. This training and education must cover many aspects of the user interface requirements. One aspect is that the knowledge sent to the various platforms and the business applications ideally must be accompanied by prompting scripts to ensure that the right questions are asked in the right order. Highly sophisticated user support solutions include artificial intelligence engines that adjust the questioning as answers are input from the support person, thus narrowing the search to the most likely resolution as the questioning continues. These processes "learn" from the feedback and input to improve this likelihood of getting the correct response over time. Other training includes basic phone manners, dealing with irate customers in a courteous manner, and the use of problem reporting and tracking systems. Sufficient and sustained training also will be a key metric to consider.

The various metrics gathered and monitored will be another key area that you will want to review to understand the performance of the support and help desk processes. Review these metrics for trends in service and their ability to meet the user's needs effectively. Understanding what level of service has been committed to and how the performance against this SLA is measured, will be important to drawing a conclusion on the effectiveness of these IS organization services. Measurements of performance for the help desk staff can include:

- Elapsed time to pick up the calls
- Rate at which calls are abandoned (by users for poor response, presumably)

- Amount of time spent on the calls
- Number of calls handled per hour
- Number of calls per person
- Number of calls per shift
- Problem management statistics related to that subsystem

The primary concern of most users seeking help is the length of time they have to wait and the kind of response they get when they do get through. Many techniques can be used to improve on this experience. Web page-based Frequently Asked Questions (FAQs) could help answer questions without a phone call or wait. These questions also can be augmented with capabilities to send messages and get responses through email for less urgent queries. Note that the response to these queries also should be evaluated for timeliness, accuracy, and conversational tone. Some programs will allow for an automated service, such as a password reset, to be completely managed from Web-based forms or processes. Clearly, security and integrity concerns will be added to your list if this service is found to be in use. Phone prompting to segregate calls by type can be helpful when a subset of the client population needs to be directed to a particular support person or desk. Care should be taken to ensure that the user's experience is not impacted negatively by long prompting instructional messages and the need to sit through lengthy choice lists before an action can be taken. Informational messages via the Web or front ending the phone answering system can reduce the need to interface with a support person for notifications that need to be spread widely, such as outages or impacts, which might prompt a high volume of calls otherwise. Message relevancy and recency used in these techniques will need to be monitored to guarantee maximum effectiveness. Forms submittal and automation of requests is a popular solution overtaking requests by phone as well. Some users will always prefer to talk to a live body, however.

Job Scheduling

Job scheduling is the process of managing the traffic on systems that are shared by multiple application processes. If the programs are all running on separate dedicated machines or logical partitions (LPARs) of the same machine, scheduling may be nothing more than planning for downtime or back up processes to run. On large systems with many programs running on a single system, prioritization and planning are required in order to process against the various and diverse business requirements and to meet deadlines. Reruns and restarts must be taken into consideration as well as rush requests and unique events sequencing. Often the scheduling task can become very complex when multiple systems require multiple processing tasks to be completed and timed so that all of the interactive needs of the diverse business lines can be met. When reviewing the scheduling process, you can best begin by gaining a full understanding of the commitments and business requirements of the function. You also will need a quick course in the tools and steps the scheduler uses to perform the function. Make sure that you seek to understand the limitation of the tools so that unrealistic recommendations for improvement do not result in embarrassment.

The processes for initiating scheduling requests should be examined to ensure that the requests acted on are valid and originate from people and processes with valid business authority to request such scheduling. Audit trails and documentation should accompany the requests to prove their legitimate authority and accountability. Any abilities to circumvent this control by requesting that the jobs be scheduled in time frames not acceptable to the business owners or by enabling people without the authority to request jobs to run should be identified. In addition, conclusions should be made on the sufficiency of the controls in place at the time of the review. Fixed schedules should be established and result in a routine that is relatively static. This enables the scheduler to focus on the exceptions in the processing routine and increases the operation's efficiencies. Actual processing completion times and output results should be compared to the scheduled expectations on a regular basis to identify areas of concern, such as missed deadlines and opportunities for improvement. Opportunities to optimize processing, through job scheduling and the reconfiguration of processing routines, should be evaluated periodically as demands drift over time and situations require revisiting.

Remember that audits are a snapshot in time and look at the present conditions and historical evidence. While change in processes to correct identified deficiencies may occur during the review process, if material weaknesses were observed during the review, they reflect the state of control at the time of the audit. You are obligated by your ethical commitments to report the current state so that management can fairly assess the performance of the processes and the related controls at review time. You should encourage improvements in processes as you review them and work with management to give credit for improvements and proactive problem resolutions wherever you can. Inclusion of weaknesses in the final reports can be handled in many ways; some have more impact than others. One technique is to mention improvements along the way in commentary sections, thus avoiding specifically calling out a weakness and requiring a response and action plan. This solution may be appropriate if the issue was already addressed. However, you will need to use your professional judgment in these matters and consider your personal reputation, as well as the audit relationship with the client, as you determine the best way to handle these matters.

Configuration Management

When reviewing the management of an IS operations center, you may find material risk in the way the configurations are established and maintained for the various components and their layout. Management of this subject requires knowledge of the facilities, its capabilities, and the operating specifications of the components, as well as the business process flow. There are several interactive components to consider when evaluating the layout of an operation center's configuration. The primary consideration is the logical placement of equipment based on the workflow or natural groupings of equipment. Floor loading capacities, the proximity to cooling equipment, power supplies, fire detection, and humidification devices may need to be considered as well. Cabling requirements, including run length, diverse paths, cabling tray fill rates, and electrical noise interference considerations are all necessary input to the configuration solutions you will be examining. Your assessment should determine that all of these issues are routinely considered as decisions are made. Overloading the circuits and running environmental support equipment without adequate reserve capacity are indicative of improper planning and configuration. Evidence of planning that enables growth and flexibility should be obtained. As systems planners identify new needs and logical configuration requirements, a process that is in place should ensure that proper configuration management practices are called upon in advance of the production deadlines necessary to put the equipment online. Change control processes should validate that the proper planning of facilities and configurations were part of the systems development life cycle. Maintenance considerations, including access to equipment and additional tasks added to the maintenance schedule, should be part of the planning process. Finally, a sanity check—stepping back and assessing the overall configuration against the root business needs—will enable you to summarize the effectiveness of these processes and any risk that may be residual from the configuration.

Asset Management

The evaluation of asset management is one of inventory control. It starts with identifying the computing assets of the IS organization. This identification may require some agreements on assumptions to determine the proper scope of the review. A decision will need to be made as to whether user equipment will be included in the review and where the line will be drawn. Will desktop computers be included or is this a departmental issue? How about the phones, faxes, printers, and other peripheral devices managed locally (scanners and palm devices, for example)? This decision sometimes depends on the capitalization practices employed in the business and the IS organization. Assets where the purchasing and asset depreciation occurs centrally also may be part of the review. Setting aside the acquisition process, which was covered previously, you will want to understand how the assets are managed financially to get a picture in your mind of what constitutes materiality for this evaluation. Costs can add up quickly for small desktop items in use everywhere, and poor control of these assets can be material in nature when looked at in total. Depreciation schedules should be considered and a determination must be made as to the realistic useful life of the equipment in use. Examine the disposal process and any related write-off procedures to ensure that the assets are not carried on the books beyond their actual use. Periodic reconciliation of actual assets and those on depreciation schedules will provide you with a comfort level that this process is well under control.

Furthermore, you also should inquire as to the tagging and tracking methods used to identify computing assets and mark them as property of the organization. Ideally, this should be a pervasive process ensuring that all relevant assets are tagged and recorded. Tags should not be easily removable and certainly should not be merely supplied with devices along with a requirement that the end user will affix them to the device. All material assets need to be accounted for and managed. You should review the inventory listings and the actual equipment in use for categories of equipment that may be left out of the process for some reason. Spot-checking several items to ensure that the purchase dates and residual costs seem reasonable may pay dividends in your analysis.

You will want to understand how upgrades to equipment are handled, what happens to the displaced equipment, and how it may be redeployed. In addition, there also are information securities concerns related to residual information, which may be confidential or sensitive, to address as part of this review. Simple things such as preprogrammed numbers on a fax machine from another area that handles confidential information can cause serious concern if not corrected when equipment is exchanged. Of course, a process will need to be documented for the equipment disposal and the scrubbing of sensitive data that this equipment may contain. A testing process that insures a complete purging to the level that mitigates the risk sufficiently should be in place. There are many data recovery techniques for extracting data from a hard drive on which the files have previously been deleted. You may need to become familiar with these techniques to assess whether the risk has been sufficiently mitigated or not. Overwriting the data several times may still not provide sufficient obliteration of data, depending on the perception of risk by management. This applies to all types of storage devices, disk drives, magnetic tapes, CDs, and so forth. Physical destruction may be necessary to ensure that security breeches do not occur in some cases. Often, charitable donations are considered as an outlet for PCs and desktop equipment that has outlived their usefulness in the business setting. You should examine the actual processes involved and the contractual obligations of all parties to ensure that security is not compromised. Part of your physical inspection tour of the facilities may turn up storage rooms of old equipment that either has not been written off of the books yet or has not been redeployed to productive use. You will need to question the status of these items and validate their tracking on the asset management systems that may be available.

You will probably encounter situations where equipment has been leased rather than purchased outright. If fact, you should expect to see a lease versus buy analysis as part of the rationale for obtaining depreciable assets in the first place. The decisions to go in either direction will be both financial and strategic and should have a basis in the overall business objectives and mission. Documentation should exist that bears out a process and the associated decisions sufficiently to ensure that a methodical approach is taken. As you conclude on the effectiveness of the asset management processes, your primary objectives will be to ensure that the assets are stated fairly, that the assets are managed appropriately, and that data remains secure because of these processes.

Change Management

Change management is the key control process in an IS organization upon which many security- and quality-related audit opinions depend. In order to be considered as a reliable control technique, a change control process must include several strictly adhered to attributes:

- All requested changes to systems and software must be documented and considered. *All* means all, not most.
- Changes must be tied back to the business needs.

- Changes must be approved by the business owner or his or her empowered representatives.

- Success or failure of the application of the change must be recorded.

- Failed changes must be backed off in a way that returns the configuration to its prior state.

- Part of the change process must be to amend all documentation and software copies that existed in a current state before the change was applied.

- Some kind of testing should occur before implementing changes to a production system.

- Changes should be applied by neutral and objective people and processes to ensure that only the approved changes are applied in the manner approved. This implies that restricted access to production data and programs and a segregation of duties occurs.

- Live production data should not be used to test changes because it risks the data's integrity.

- Testing should ensure that the production systems and data will not be negatively impacted by the change.

You should expect to find a change control process that gates changes into the production environment for any IS operational review that you perform. As mentioned previously, this may be an ideal place to start any evaluation of an IS organization, because all of the roads lead through change control eventually. Without a solid change control program in place, many other controls are rendered inconsequential in having any beneficial affect on the insuring the quality performance and data integrity. Your test work should review historical changes and trace the process back to its origination point, ensuring that the appropriate steps and approvals were completed along the way.

Change control processes are typically managed through automated tools to ensure that source and object code are matched and that all movement and code versions are accounted for and recorded. Manual processes do not provide the same level of assurance that changes have not occurred outside of the control mechanism as an automated one will. Access permissions of the files, which would need to be protected to ensure that changes are limited to working within the process, would have to be painstakingly reviewed and examined to gain the same level of confidence that an automated control process would otherwise provide. This kind of access review would not be possible to perform without accessing the systems in some fashion, thereby jeopardizing the production systems integrity in order to perform the review—a sticky problem to be sure.

Whether manual or automatic processes are used, there should be documented procedures for emergency changes. Emergency changes occur even in the most well planned development initiatives. If a change control process does not enable immediate corrective action to occur and this process does not provide for authorization and approvals to catch up to the change later, the business will not be successful in meeting its obligations. For this reason, it is important to segregate the duties of the change control librarian from other tasks because this role then can be charged with insuring that the backward notification and post change approvals occur. It is preferred that these emergency changes be automatically trapped and identified. A possible control technique is to notify the owners automatically to ensure that all changes, even those that happen in very busy and stressful situations, will get recorded and reviewed. The discipline of recording and reviewing all of these changes must be evidenced by process procedures and logs that indicate this process is used continuously.

Part of the change process should be the review of change preparedness prior to scheduling or proceeding with the change. The person accountable for operations will ideally assess all of the changes to be scheduled and the compatibility or interference of these changes with other scheduled tasks and changes. Changes that have not been adequately tested, documented, or reviewed with the user's representatives for possible impact to the business should be deferred until these processes have been completed. A checklist of acceptance criteria and a regularly schedule change control meeting is a good way to ensure that all of the items have been considered and everyone involved knows what the plans are. Possible checkpoints to consider include:

- Testing and sponsor acceptance of change
- Back out procedures and programs that are available and tested
- Resource usage changes and plans to accommodate them, including disk and tape storage, CPU usage, job scheduling, production control process changes, and so on
- Operator training and procedural manual documentation updates
- User training and user manual documentation updates
- Business continuity planning impact and recovery procedures and documentation updates, along with updates to off-site data planned for use in recovery
- Security changes and modification to security baselines and plans
- Interface changes and notification to other processes that depend on or feed this changing system

- User impact of the changes and possible business process workarounds to accommodate downtimes

- Notification and coordination of all necessary resources and support teams to implement the change

The process of preparing for changing the production code also should be examined. There are several ways to manage the assurance of integrity to the code in production at all times while providing for changes or modifications to that code at the same time. The preferred method would be to copy the production code into a test domain for modification and to subsequently move the modified version back into production. Version control and keeping track of movement in and out of the production domains can be complicated by having more than one copy of the production code signed out at a time due to the multiple changes being developed simultaneously. Integrated testing will need to be performed to ensure that these changes do not impact each other or the underlying code when both are applied. Even when emergency changes are required, care must be taken to provide for production code integrity and back out capabilities. Copies of production before and after changes are applied should be maintained until assurance is received that the change will be left as part of the new production code set. Knowing what version the change was built for may be a required validation step. If the changes occur frequently enough, there may be a question as to whether the fix is applicable to the code presently in production and not built for an earlier version.

Another way change control is maintained, and this is especially prevalent for Web page code, is to maintain a Quality Control (QC) copy of the production code that is always a mirror of what is in production. In this manner, copies and evaluation of the production code set can take place without directly impacting the actual code in use. Additional care must be taken to ensure the synchronization of the production and QC code sets at all times. This additional step provides for an ability to reload the production code quickly into production, should some type of integrity breech or corruption occur. This is the reason for this technique's popularity for Internet facing programs, which are vulnerable, based on their placement into a hostile and untrustworthy environment.

Finally, you should be interested in reviewing the back up processes for the various versions of code in test, staging, and production, which collectively make up the change control system. Changes and back ups should be coordinated so that it is possible to recover systems through a combination of restoring the back up and reapplying the changes that have occurred since the back up occurred. Changes will need to be maintained separately from other code in order to accomplish this type of recovery scheme, and a process to ensure that only those changes between back ups are staged in this manner will need to be developed.

Evaluating System Performance

A system's performance evaluation is a review of how well the processes perform against industry benchmarks or in comparison to similar processes and against the management's expectations. Performance can mean different things to different people, so your first step will be to understand what particular aspects of performance are included in your scope and objectives. Usually, this comes down to understanding the Service Level Agreement (SLA) and whether the deadlines and commitments are being met. You also may need to understand the process in a broader sense to ensure that the metrics used for managing the business adequately represent the processing's performance and that the risks are managed appropriately. If this is the objective, you will need to inventory all of the potential control and measurement points available to the IS process management and assess the best combination of performance indicators to gather data from in order to form your opinion. These control points will break down into several broad categories such as people, hardware, software, processes, and deliverables. In all cases, when performance fails, an investigation and follow-up to determine an appropriate corrective action should be evidenced and reviewed as part of your evaluation.

Monitoring Techniques, Processes, and Tools

For people performance management, you will be assessing staffing, training, and performance in terms of units of output per time unit of effort expended. This will be measured against historical trends and comparable industry benchmarks where available. Several companies make a business of providing IT benchmarking services and consulting practices. In addition, many IT specialty focus groups and newsletters provide benchmark information to newsgroup subscribers. Finding relatively comparable examples may take some effort and extrapolation, however. Processes and tools for monitoring and measuring performance will vary, depending on the tasks and the processes with which the staff members are interacting. Labor-related tasks in computer processing environments break down into support of the processes (tape jockeys, print handlers, operators, schedulers, user support, and so forth) and technical support of the systems themselves (programmers, service engineers, field engineers, change control, and so forth). Tapes per shift, pages per hour, and calls per person are some of the metrics that may be key in developing a monitoring program for the support staff performance management and control. You will need to identify the appropriate units of measurement from your knowledge of what meeting the business needs means in each case you encounter. Project management techniques are probably the best tool to use for managing and tracking performance of the technical support staff. Development and technical support does not break down into units per hour types of measurement in most cases.

Hardware performance metrics include system utilization, percent busy, response times, uptime statistics, and mean time between failure, to name a few. When reviewing hardware performance, you will need to keep in mind what, of the available metrics, are not only meaningful from a performance perspective, but also from the perspective of what is material to the business processing. Statistics can be interpreted in many ways to support conclusions that widely vary. When in doubt, always apply the auditor's best friend for a sanity check, otherwise known as the question, "So what?" By seeking the root concerns of the issues identified and by questioning the gravity of the results you are reviewing in this way, you will support a balanced approach that seeks only to identify the material risk exposures and to address them, rather than chasing statistics and performance measurements that do not significantly affect the processes.

Software performance can be measured against the functional requirement expectations for which the software was originally designed. Knowing the design's limitations and the actual usage in practice will enable you to perform a gap analysis of the actual versus expected performance measurements. Because relatively few actual software implementations are textbook simple, identifying the reasons for implementation variations from the recommended installation will be necessary to get a meaningful comparison. Once again, you will need to see information on the performance over time and understand any changes that might have an effect on this performance in order to be able to opine on software performance metrics. The challenge will be to ensure that the software is running with a hardware configuration that is supported for its use so that there is no question as to whether the performance issues are software bound or hardware bound. Software/hardware performance tools will be covered in more detail in the systems development chapter. If the software performance metrics are tabulated and monitored routinely to gauge the operation's performance, your evaluation should identify the integrity and value of these metrics to ensure that they are control parameters that can effectively be used to manage the operations.

Processes are monitored to gauge operational performance most often because they represent the business needs most directly. Completion of tasks and measurements such as response time and availability are black and white issues that are either meeting the need or not meeting the need. They are usually tied directly to SLAs and reported as KPIs because they are not complex enough to understand and to represent the success or failure to the IS organization most directly. The throughput of transactions is a common measurement. Performance management tools usually are imbedded in either the hardware or software and the report generation of process monitoring is a standard feature required in these and most turnkey processes as well. Your evaluation will most likely depend on the designer's view of process monitoring variables, and the outcomes of these monitoring tools should be reviewed to ensure the consistent performance of the processes based on the predefined definitions. Where variations from expected outcomes exist in the historical reporting of this information, you should look for corrective action that was timely and effective in bringing the processes back in line with the organization's expectations.

Performance based on the output of the IT processes is the simplest and most effective method for monitoring and managing an IS organization's performance. Once the outputs are identified and the quality and quantity of those outputs is agreed upon through the SLA's, the agreed upon metrics are either met or not, which is an easy to understand performance indicator. Understanding exactly what the output needs to be to satisfy the business needs is a much more difficult problem than it first appears to be, however.

Capacity Planning

Capacity planning is required to manage an IS organization effectively because it reduces the impact of the growth-related changes on the business and its users. Your objectives in a review of capacity planning are to ensure that a planning process exists, which enables the workload and service obligations to be met by providing sufficient capacity in a cost effective manner while limiting the impact to the users. Good control over this process will involve a proactive solicitation of future demands for services and it will translate that into a strategic plan for managing the capacity of the processing facilities. Periodic renegotiation of the SLAs provides an excellent vehicle for validating service requirements and identifying the organization's changing needs. Budget cycles also will drive the need to understand the next fiscal years requirements and may be a good trigger event for assessing the overall capacity and direction for the operation's requirements.

When evaluating the process of planning for capacity, you will expect to see the identification of the business needs as part of a process that is performed periodically. These needs can be identified through the direct solicitation of the business owners or users. Obtaining this information also may be accomplished through the evaluation of the delivered services over time to show growth and the need for the expansion or adjustment of the capacities based on historical trending and the extrapolation of these trends into the future. Contracts and agreements also can be used to identify the future needs and capabilities for performance, which will have to be met in order for the IS organization to be successful. The evaluation of performance may be additional input to the decision-making process used to identify future size and capacities of systems.

Risk is introduced into the capacity planning processes when change occurs either without notice or too quickly to avoid an undesirable impact to the end users. You will expect to see controls in place that not only measure the existing capacities and track them over time but that also measure control techniques providing for the anticipation of change. Anticipation of changes can be an inexact science and therefore should be revisited regularly, adjusting plans as conditions shift. Good control processes will regularly challenge those assumptions used to make the capacity planning decisions and will give the best chance for accuracy in the process.

A thorough knowledge of the standard sizing options available for equipment and licensing will be required to anticipate when the changes will be needed to keep the operations running smoothly and effectively. Keeping capacity in reserve for unanticipated bursts in demand will be part of the cushion that you will assess when determining the risks being assumed in the capacity planning process. Tight schedules and the little chance for error will require more flexibility in capacity in order to reduce risks and ensure the successful completion of the business requirements. An understanding of the limitations that existing configurations present should be documented and used as a basis for comparison to current usage monitoring so that performance does not suffer and the changes can be appropriately anticipated. Performance should not be affected negatively because of the capacity planning deficiencies. Problem logs and deliverable cycles may need to be assessed to ensure this is not the case.

Finally, the cost effectiveness aspects of the capacity planning evaluation will determine what decisions for expansions and changes are being made in a way that adds the most value to the process with the least cost amount. Spending for capacity, where preplanning may have avoided such costs can be assessed by looking at how far out the planning cycle is occurring and assessing how effective the planning has been in the past by avoiding unnecessary and costly upgrades to the capacities of the various IT components. The planning process should anticipate the changes in needs effectively and enable for economic decision making that provides low cost solutions with maximum capacity. Reviewing the alternative scenarios may be counter productive, so care must be taken to ensure that the best information available is used to make these judgment calls.

Problem Management

The objective of a problem management system review is to ensure that all problems are identified, logged, and resolved. Another objective is to ensure that through this problem management process, corrections are made that prevent problems from reoccurring (that is, that the IS organization learns from its mistakes). Problem identification can be accomplished in several ways, all of which should be evaluated as potential input to the process. Where a process has a known procedural flow and measurable outcomes, problems can be defined as any deviation from the expected flow and outcome. Ideally, this deviation will be trapped through automated problem management processes that ensure all exceptions are identified as problems without human intervention. Seemingly inconsequential exceptions do not get logged as problems when people are required to decide whether these exceptions are worthy of being defined as a problem. The effort necessary to log and track these problems outweighs the value of reporting too many busy operators. Users also report problems typically through the help desk or user support facilities. Understanding the real problem can be a challenge when dealing with users who do not have a technical background. Other business processes up and down the process flow continuum may identify problems that do not directly affect the originating process. The result will be a flawed outcome to the overall process and the need being identified as a problem as well.

In order to manage problems well, a tracking and logging system will need to be put in place. This system will need to maintain a history of all problems in a database to be useful for analyzing problems. Some of the required attributes about the problems that will need to be captured include times, system, a description of problem, and an audit trail of the escalation and referral will need to be tracked from detection through resolution. This information should be captured in a standard format and separated into fixed field positions in the database so that reporting and queries can be performed against the aggregated data. Your review should assess the data fields that are recorded in the problem tracking process and evaluate the sufficiency of the information for analytical and investigative purposes. Any canned or customizable reporting capabilities should be assessed for functionality and relevance.

The ability to refer problems to areas where they can be appropriately addressed without loosing the pertinent information will be an important attribute of a good problem management system. Various departments should have access to the problem system, such as operational areas, the help desk, scheduling, and programming so that as the problems are assigned and investigated, each additional piece of information can be added to the problem. The problems then can be effectively reassigned without the loss of information, should root cause analysis point the resolution to a different group other than the one originally assigned to the problem. All potential problem solving groups in the IS organization should be required to access the system routinely and resolve the issues assigned to them in a timely manner. System oversight should ensure that the problems not being addressed are escalated to management for follow-up and notification of the business process owners. A good method to ensure that problems are being proactively managed is to pull all of the responsible parties together for a weekly meeting that reviews all outstanding or difficult problems or those particularly impacting the organization as a whole. Often this meeting can coincide with the change control planning meetings held by the operations group, because problem resolution usually results in changes to correct the problem. The tracking and resolution of the problems will need to be evidenced clearly for the auditor to believe that issues are being addressed effectively. All problem resolution should be recorded in the problem system in a way that allows for understanding problem-related information by application or by an information processing subsystem. The analysis of the overall problem levels related to individual systems and processes then can be used to identify and justify necessary changes to the production systems though systems development efforts.

The overall and elapsed time spent on a problem, as well as the time spent in individual areas, should all be tracked and reported on so that the cost of problems can be identified. By understanding the overall cost of problems, the IS organization positions itself to better manage problem prevention and to understand the costs and benefits of doing it right the first time. You should assess the processes in place to use the problem tracking system as a KPI and determine what kinds of analysis are routinely preformed from the problem data. A proactive IS organization will closely review this information for opportunities to improve the processes it manages.

Service Level Agreements (SLAs)

Service Level Agreements (SLAs) are the glue that holds the business relationship together with the IT processing. Managing the services provided to the customer is a critical piece of the IS organization business, because it is the point from which the relationship is managed. Your evaluation of this process will be two fold. First, you will need to look at the process from the customer's perspective to ensure their requirements are understood by IS operations and are being met. Second, you will need to look at the relationship from the IS organization's perspective to ensure that the business' expectations are not exceeding the agreement and that demand changes are being appropriately managed and accounted for through the identification of all provided services and the associated costs of those services.

In large and complex IS organizations, managing customer relationships is a full-time job for many individuals who act as client service managers and customer liaisons to the IS organization subgroups. This is a necessary analyst position that translates the business issues into technical ones. Personnel who hold this position can explain the technical issues to businesses in such a way that they can understand them as well. This person acts as a negotiator and arbiter when disputes or conflict arises. They are ideally positioned to contribute to the development and maintenance of an SLA between these two parties as they straddle the fence between the business and computer operations worlds. Whether the organization is large or small, you should seek a business relationship representative that fills this role when performing an evaluation of the service level management processes.

This role will identify all of the business requirements, including deliverables, time frames and target dates, support coverage requirements, response and escalation for questions and problems, and any other parameters that are important to the particular business process and work flow. This list of requirements then will be reconciled with the IS organizations view of the cost of support, reasonableness of the request, and scheduling and labor force requirements to meet the needs and satisfy the customer. Once both parties reach a general agreement, there will be a document, which is signed and subsequently used to measure performance and expectations going forward. Common elements of a service level agreement include

- Purpose, definitions, and limitations of scope
- Services to be provided
- Availability, throughput, response, or other deliverables commitments and methods of reporting and monitoring
- Communication and reporting relationships and methods
- Requirements of the client receiving services
- Problem identification and escalation processes

- Methods for costing out additional or new services and requesting changes

- Basis for charges and methods for assessing penalties and charging for services not covered in the agreement

- Renewal, annual review, and methods for changing or renegotiating service level commitments

There are many others aspect of an agreement to provide services that could be documented as part of an SLA. In previous chapters, contingency planning, security, and regulatory obligations also were mentioned. The variations are limited only by the uniqueness of each individual arrangement and by the needs of the business and the support organizations. When evaluating SLAs, the control objective is to determine that all expectations are documented and that a means exists for measuring the delivery against these expectations, including reporting mechanisms, so that both parties are aware of the relative success or failure of meeting the objectives. You will not only be reviewing the content of the SLA to assess how it introduces or mitigates risk in the business process, but you also will be reviewing how to use it as a tool for understanding the commitments and expectations. Poorly documented services will result in dissatisfaction, confusion, and an all around ineffective business performance, because the expectations are not written down and therefore cannot be met well.

Resources

- www.google.com
- www.auditnet.org/asapind.htm
- www.theiia.org/itaudit/
- www.itsecurity.com/papers/fulllist.htm

Sample Questions

Here is a sampling of questions in the format of the CISA exam. These questions are related to the technical infrastructure and operational practices, and will help test your understanding of this subject. Answers with explanations are provided in Appendix A.

1. The *best* way to understand the security configuration of an operating system is to

   A. Consult the vendor's installation manuals

   B. Review the security plan for the system

   C. Interview the systems programmer who installed the software

   D. Review the system-generated configuration parameters

2. What three things are the most important security controls that should be present when reviewing an operating systems security?

   I. The code comes from a trusted source.

   II. Audit logging is turned on.

   III. Unnecessary services are turned off.

   IV. The default passwords are changed.

   V. Systems administrators do not have any more access than they need to in order to perform their job.

   A. I, II, and III

   B. III, IV, and V

   C. I, III, and IV

   D. I, II, and IV

3. Databases are complex to evaluate from a risk perspective because

   A. Access controls for application views, query permissions, field level table access, as well as access to reports and query results must be reviewed to assess the security of data.

   B. They can have complex data structures that may be joined through several keys.

   C. Data definitions must be maintained in order to understand the data classifications.

   D. Data flows and data normalization processes make both table sizing and transaction mapping difficult.

4. In a two-phase commit database transaction, the roll back process is initiated

   A. When the client and server cannot agree on a communication protocol

   B. In multi-tier architectures that need to reject a proxy request

   C. When a committed transaction cannot be completed by all participating servers and clients involved

   D. When ownership of the session cannot be assured and committed to

5. Which of the following is *not* a design consideration to investigate when reviewing security packages?

   A. What kind of changes and compromises must occur to existing processes

   B. How well the security updates and patches are maintained on the security package

   C. What weaknesses and deficiencies cause a security package to be considered

   D. What kind of support effort will be required to maintain the product adequately

6. Which of the following is *not* normally a concern when reviewing the implementation of an operation console system?

   A. Whether the expertise to implement the system is being provided by the vendor to backfill existing functions, enabling the existing staff to learn the new systems

   B. Whether the scope and goals of the implementation plan are being met in a cost effective and timely manner

   C. Whether the KPIs used to manage the business will be improved by the implementation process

   D. Understanding how well the console will interface with other operations components and what compatibility issues exist

7. Which of the following will *not* be information that you would expect to find documented when evaluating a computer hardware installation project?

    A. Procedures for defining the requirements and submitting the requests for proposals and bids

    D. How the hardware installation has improved the process throughputs

    C. Functional requirements for the hardware based on the business plans and needs

    D. Placement and location decisions for equipment installations

8. Which of the following is the *most* effective method of assessing the controls over the hardware maintenance process?

    A. Look at the hardware and assess whether the maintenance is current and that the equipment is well kept.

    B. Following the recommended maintenance tasks and maintenance schedules, determine that the procedures are carried out and evidenced as completed by logging and dating the actual maintenance efforts.

    C. Identify the required maintenance procedures from the vendor's information and ensure that these processes are addressed by the IS organization's procedures.

    D. Look at the problem logs and validate whether maintenance processes are determining the mean time between failures when compared to the industry averages.

9. When reviewing voice systems maintenance processes, which of the following is the *least* critical to the audit objective of ensuring customer satisfaction?

    A. Ensuring that as-built drawing modifications are made to the copy of the drawings kept in the office

    B. Ensuring that the support staff is knowledgeable and available to perform the necessary maintenance tasks

    C. Ensuring that the physical security of the PBX devices is managed properly

    D. Ensuring that planning and configurations provide for flexibility with minimal impact to the user base

10. Which of the following should an IS auditor review when performing an assessment of a PBX?

    I. Ensure that the dial-in numbers enabling toll-free outbound access are turned off.

    II. Ensure that voicemail systems do not enable access to phone lines through hijacking.

    III. Ensure that the access codes for the maintenance ports have been changed from the default.

    IV. Ensure that outbound toll numbers, such as 900 numbers, are restricted.

    V. Ensure that excessive phone usage is flagged and investigated for fraud.

    A. I, II, III, and IV only

    B. II, III, and IV only

    C. II, III, IV, and V only

    D. I, II, III, IV, and V

11. Which of the following would you not expect to find in an Internet DMZ?

    A. DNS servers that advertise addresses to the Internet

    B. Mail relay servers that receive incoming mail and push outgoing mail

    C. Web servers containing content and business logic

    D. Proxy servers that authenticate access requests to internal content

12. When reviewing data network architecture, which of the following is not a *primary* review criteria for the IS auditor?

    A. All router access is controlled by secure authentication methods.

    B. Network routing enables the efficient flow of the businesses critical traffic.

    C. Protocols that are not needed for the business and administration of the network are disabled.

    D. VLANs using layer 2 switching techniques are employed to secure the traffic of critical data.

13. In a well-segregated operational environment, which of the following scenarios would you expect to see?

   A. Computer operators responding to systems messages and initiating problem tickets for failed jobs

   B. Change control librarians making modifications to code only when notified of errors by the application programmers

   C. Tape librarians managing print queues and reloading paper for printers as well as loading off-site storage containers with back up tapes

   D. Operators assisting system programmers with troubleshooting the operating system by adjusting parameters while the programmers observed the results

14. What are the *most* important criteria to assess when reviewing job descriptions?

   A. The job functions are all defined for the work that needs done, and training is required

   B. Clear authority is established and everyone knows who holds what roles in the organization

   C. Vacations are mandated and job rotation is provided for

   D. Performance is monitored and raises are based on goals that are defined jointly

15. The primary purpose of key performance indicators are to

   A. Give management the ability to make sure that the staff is doing their work

   B. Monitor the capacity of the systems equipment and process performance metrics

   C. Provide management with a tool to gauge the overall health of the process and to point to potential trouble spots

   D. Enable operators to know when things are going wrong and whether the SLA is being met

16. In a media management system review, the IS auditor does *not* need to concern themselves with

    A. Whether the systems catalog accurately reflects the physical library's location of the media

    B. Whether the media is accessed by only those individuals with a "need to know"

    C. Whether the media is accurately identified for movement off site for back up purposes

    D. Whether the system adequately retires media and provides for its recycling in a secure manner

17. What is the *most* important aspect of a change control system?

    A. All changes are documented and approved.

    B. Changes are managed through automated tools, preventing access from people.

    C. Copies of production are maintained in case the change fails.

    D. Quality is ensured through testing and approval.

18. When emergency changes are identified during a change control review, what should the IS auditor also expect to find?

    A. A control weakness, because these actions should not be allowed to occur and it should be reported

    B. That the changes were applied as necessary and the related problems tickets were logged

    C. Disciplinary actions related to enabling the changes to occur without approval by the system owner

    D. A process for notifying the system owner of the changes and all associated actions taken with explanation

19. Which characteristics of a problem management system are important to the IS auditors review?

    I.   All problems are tracked through to conclusion.

    II. All problems are initiated automatically, thus ensuring that the correct data is captured.

    III. Escalation processes ensure that problems do not sit unresolved.

    IV. All relative IS operation areas have access to the system to review and address the problems.

    V.   Statistics can be gathered from the system to facilitate the analysis of the IS problems.

    A. I, II, III, IV, and V

    B. I, III, IV, and V only

    C. II, III, IV, and V only

    D. I, III, and V only

20. Critical aspects of an SLA review include all of these items except

    A. An annual review and revalidation of the business needs

    B. Ensuring that the expected services are clearly defined

    C. Ensuring that monitoring and escalation procedures are in place

    D. Ensuring that the service provider is supplying service to all customers equitably

CHAPTER
4

Protection of
Information Assets

Reviewing and assessing the information asset protection systems of an IS organization follows a hierarchical flow from policies down through the specific actions taken to enforce them. There are many concepts to understand and the technological solutions can be complex. Dynamic industry driven solutions continue to tout a "silver bullet" but none ever really exists. Keeping up with security threats and countermeasures requires a continuous education and understanding. This chapter covers the basic concepts so your "knowledge toolbox" can be outfitted and applied to the situations that you will face as a certified IS auditor, however diverse they may be. Again for this chapter, the focus will not be on the technical details of how all of this security technology works under the hood. Rather, it assumes that you have some base knowledge of these issues and will be geared more toward identifying the risk and control points and the overall audit approach you should take for evaluating these processes and systems. The systems' inner workings and the exact technology used to secure them will change over time, probably in the time it takes you to read this chapter.

Knowledge of the entire body of the security audit subject matter comprises 25 percent of the CISA exam content. Some of the exam questions will likely be basic technical background information that will not be covered here, because this chapter assumes that you are at least conversant in those technologies and can hold you own in a discussion about them with management. By the end of this chapter, you also should have understand the following basics:

- What the review objectives are for in the information asset protection evaluations

- How an information security program should be developed and designed

- The role of information security management in the IS organization

- How polices and standards relate to security

- The concepts of identity, authentication, and authorization

- Various access control methods and best practices related to managing them effectively

- Various authentication methods, their pros and cons, and how to evaluate their use

- Evaluation of security architecture and its components

- Various network- and host-based security countermeasures and their evaluation

- Security awareness and the role it plays in information security overall

- Protecting information assets through environmental controls

- Protecting information assets through physical security measures

- The interdependency of all of these functions and the natural order of their usefulness

You can reference many good books about security concept theory and how the solutions to threats exploiting them are designed. These books layout the theoretical processes behind the various cryptographic tools and detection schemes used when building a comprehensive security architecture. I have referenced some of the more popular and common ones (as of this writing) in the resources section at the end of this chapter. Please review them if you feel your knowledge about these subjects is not sufficient to grasp the overview of their use, which will be assumed here. These resources also are helpful if your interest is peaked by this topic and you want to understand the technology in more depth. Knowing this information in detail is most important to the technician and designer of these systems, but familiarity with them will be required for you as an auditor to interact successfully with these people.

An IS auditor does not have to be intimately familiar with every nuance of every style of problem solving to know whether the problem is being solved well and whether there is a sufficient management process in place to ensure that problems are being addressed in a risk-based manner. In order to provide overall comfort that the control structure is in place, policies, procedures, and people are more important factors than the details of a technical solution. Good problem recognition, tracking, and correction processes will go a long way toward ensuring that the risks are adequately identified and addressed, commensurate with the potential loss or threat created by these risk scenarios. As mentioned previously, security is not absolute and will never be a complete solution. Security is about compromise and is mostly a people problem in the final analysis. All of the basic audit techniques and methods of looking at process apply here. This is just a new set of processes to apply those formulas to and a different set of risks to consider for controls.

Security Risks and Review Objectives

Access to IS resources should be controlled in order to protect them against unauthorized use, modifications, loss, or damage. Proper controls over the information asset access will assist in the prevention, detection, or correction of deliberate or accidental errors or exposure caused by inappropriate access or data manipulation. These are the basic objectives and rationale for assessing security. At an even more basic level, the CIA model of information security (Confidentiality, Integrity, and Availability) is always instructive.

Remember that most audit activity has its roots in gaining assurance that the company's financial reports are accurate and reflect the actual fiduciary picture of the business to outside concerns. Auditing is a way for a third party, regulator, investor, business partner, shareholder, or whomever to send in a reasonably knowledgeable professional (you) to assess for them that what they are being told is good information. The data that this group is using to make business decisions must have integrity for this to be the case. Integrity means that the data is accurate, unchanged, and represents what is really happening inside the business processes and, by extension, for the customers and suppliers of those processes. Integrity also implies that the data has not been altered or modified outside of normal processing, and when it has, it is because the process meant it to be done and only for the reason that it was meant to be was it altered. An objective of a security review, therefore, is to assure data integrity.

In order for a business to be profitable, there need to be risks assumed by the businesses, which this book covered in Chapter 1. Business decisions are made to take risks and make money, based on this decision-making process. The spread between the residual risk everyone else in the same business takes and your business risk exposure is typically analogous to the business' profit margin. If you manage risk better, you are most likely to be more profitable and successful. If other businesses knew how your business could make a better product or one of the same quality but for lower cost, they would do so as well, cutting into your available market share, driving the price of the product down, and causing your profit margin would suffer. It is imperative that data used to run your business is classified so that everyone involved understands which data has been determined to be worthy of maintaining as confidential and which information can be exposed that will not impact the success of the business. The rank and file workers do not know what is important to management, unless they are explicitly told through security levels assigned to the data. Trade secrets are only one representative aspect of the need for confidentiality. Customers also expect that their data is kept private. Without that trust, they will take their business elsewhere, which also will affect your profit margin. In fact, unfavorable press exposure, public relations faux pas, and corporate embarrassment can easily cause a run on the bank, so to speak, resulting in plummeting stock valuations and a loss of confidence in the business by the consumer. All of these are significant risk factors to consider when determining security classifications. The way to protect yourself from the often over reactive situations related to public opinion is to ensure that the data remains confidential when it has been classified as such. Therefore, the evaluation objective of ensuring that data is classified and access to this data is limited to those who have been identified with a need to know are often the target of an information asset protection review.

Information systems are now the lifeblood of most businesses. Turn off the computer and the phone and try to conduct business for even a half hour. It can no longer be done in most organizations of any size. Business revolves around data in many forms and it simply must be available in order to do work. Information availability means it is recoverable when disruption or disaster strikes. However, it also means that this data is available to the clerk when necessary to perform their function, instead of being inaccessible due to onerous security restrictions being set in place. Also of concern are the poorly applied controls where classifications have incorrectly labeled the clerk as not needing to know the data, therefore leaving the clerk unable to do their job because of the access profile assigned to them. *Available* also means that the systems have not been prevented from performing their job because someone inadvertently pulled the wrong plug, or launched a denial or service attack against their old boyfriend, bringing down the business process at the same time. Therefore, one of the objectives of an information asset protection assessment is to ensure that the data is available to those with a *need to know*, when they need it to perform their functions. Availability can be thought of as the inverse of access restriction, because making information unavailable to those who have no business accessing the data also helps make it available to those who do need access to it.

Other corollaries to the basic CIA premises of information security include identification, authentication, non-repudiation, privacy, authorization, and accountability. These terms will be explained as their applicability presents itself throughout this chapter. Their use is more of a special case subset of the three basic principles and control objectives. As you will see, basic management, business decisions, and enforcement of those decisions through people processes are the primary way to establish and maintain the controls necessary to ensure that these objectives are met.

The Security Officer's Role

Evaluation of the information security processes of an IS organization will begin by finding out who is in charge. As part of your background investigation and information gathering process, you will seek out policies, procedures, and standards that may exist and are related to the subject of information security and security in general. More importantly, you will want to find out the following from the security officer: What gives them the authority to perform their job function? Where does this authority come from? What limitations or restrictions are attached to it, based on the political environment, business model, and the overall mission and vision of the senior management? One common misconception is the assumption that it is the security officer's responsibility to ensure that all security is in place and functioning properly, regardless of the business decisions made. This simply cannot be the case. Businesses make risk-based decisions related to their business processes every day and some of those decisions involve taking chances with security to get the job done. Security cannot be perfect and will always involve trade-off and compromise. The security officer's role should be to consider the effects of the business decisions being considered and to bring their security expertise to the table, by offering alternatives or advice on potential ramifications and possible results of these decisions. In this way, the business owners can make informed, risk-based decisions, being fully aware of the potential downside consequences of the decisions they own and for which are ultimately responsible. The security management's role is one of being a subject matter expert and consultant to the business for their decision-making processes. They also serve as the implementer of those business decisions, as it relates to security functions in an independent and objective manner to ensure an unbiased adherence to the decisions made by the management.

The security officer's role can, however, be defined in a variety of permutations from the textbook model, and they can all work well for an organization, depending on the authority and mission of the security function. The keys to understanding the particular situation you are assessing lies in the documentation of the security officer's role and job description and the mandate in the policy; these items should be clear and appropriately defined. You will want to evaluate what authority this position has been given by assessing these items, the security policies, any organization charts that are applicable, and by possibly interviewing senior management to gain an understanding of their vision for this role. Make sure to ask about limits of authority, if you get the opportunity to question management about the role. Management support for unpopular decisions that must be made by this position will be a key to their success. Knowing who reports to whom, all of the related job descriptions, and ensuring that all jobs have been assigned will be part of this review, like all of the other reviews you will perform.

Your evaluation will include a gap analysis between the responsibilities and accountabilities assigned to the security management (and hence their staff), and those of a best practice situation or otherwise comprehensive list of items to consider. In this way, you can find out who has been assigned to each of the security functions that needs to be performed and can follow up with the right person to ensure that each function is being managed effectively. It is best to do this up front before any other assessments have been made to avoid a finger pointing session when vulnerabilities and weaknesses are uncovered later on in the review process. Make sure that you can track these assignments back to documented proof or you will have to conclude that the assignment is arbitrary and ambiguous, leading to possible noncompliance because of unclear task assignments. A list of possible functions to consider for ownership determination includes:

- Assuring that all security-related audit concerns are followed up on and addressed in a timely manner
- Championing new security-related policies and nurturing them through the policy creation process

- Developing security standards to give direction to the organization for technically specific issues and emerging technologies

- Ensuring that contingency planning programs are developed, maintained, and tested to the satisfaction of the business owners

- Developing the overall security architecture for the IS organization and ensuring that the systems and components existing and planned will fit the architecture, support the security direction of the organization as a whole, and determine what compromises or accommodations will be necessary as a result of noncompliant business decisions

- Developing the overall security program, which includes periodic risk assessments, the planning of countermeasures, and controls deployment to reduce identified risks to acceptable levels based on input from the business owners

- Implementing the various components of the security program, managing the budgets and staff scheduling for those implementation projects, and managing the resultant processes

- Ensuring that security-related problems are identified, tracked, and resolved in a timely manner and in a way that prevents the problem and those similar to it from reoccurring

- Managing the security staff, ensuring that they are properly trained and have the tools, authority, and clearly assigned tasks necessary to be successful

- Ensuring that the security tasks are performed for the IS organization in a manner that preserves independence, ethical behavior, and a segregation of duties to properly control security where full-time security assignments are not employed

- Ensuring that all employees are routinely made aware of security policy, their respective obligations, and accountabilities for the protection of information assets through awareness programs and training related to information security

- Developing processes to ensure that application and systems administrators are compliant with the information security policies and standards in the discharge of their job functions; developing procedures as required to facilitate this process

- Ensuring that all users of the information assets are uniquely identified and assigned access levels commensurate with the direction of the business process owners, and that those users' accounts are managed in a timely and customer responsive fashion

- Developing processes to ensure that security is considered to be an integral part of all changes and before the introduction of new systems and components into the IS organization and its configurations

- Implementing processes to assess the security measures against risk guidelines for new and existing systems and their relative threats and vulnerabilities

Once you have identified the responsible person for these tasks to be evidenced in writing, your subsequent review tasks will involve ensuring that these tasks are being performed in a risk-based fashion and documented appropriately to show adequate compliance and effectiveness of performance against leading practice expectations.

Privacy Risk

Privacy is an increasingly visible topic and important to users and clients alike. In assuring privacy as business processes gather sensitive data and provide opportunities to leverage aggregated data to the detriment of users and clients, it becomes important to review this risk, its assessment, and control. Keeping data private implies sharing only what is necessary and avoiding unnecessary data exposure to those without a need to know, however, it is more than that. It also implies doing the right thing when it comes to accessing and providing data based on the wishes of the data owner, which sometimes can get into decisions of moral and ethical use of data. Consent is the buzzword used by the HIPAA regulations to draw a line between data access that should be permitted and that which should not be allowed based on what is considered appropriate, presumably to the person doing the consenting. Consent of all the users and clients on an individual basis can be a monumental task, especially when data is fragmented and spread across the enterprise for various business purposes, some of which the owner may not fully understand. Gramm-Leach-Bliley, another U.S.-based privacy regulation recently enacted to ensure financial privacy, was implemented to ensure that a customer's nonpublic financial information is not bought, sold, or otherwise disclosed to businesses looking for opportunities to provide services and to increase their potential customer list without the expressed consent of the client.

The risk to the business is the inability to adequately identify and classify customer-related data that is nonpublic or personal in nature—a data classification risk. Other risks include the subsequent ability to treat data classified as applicable to the privacy regulations (the U.S.-based laws mentioned here are merely representative examples of laws in many countries), with sufficient security and access controls to prevent disclosure unless the consent is obtained. There are many tangential risks such as the ability to track and manage consents and to provide proof or reporting that the appropriate consents where agreed to or that special exemptions, written into these laws and others, are applicable to the situations being investigated for compliance. These risks are pointed out here because they are currently hot button topics for businesses as citizen privacy rights movements continue to gain momentum. Awareness of the appropriate behavior in the nonelectronic aspect of data handling and management also must be considered for potential compliance-related exposures. Security officers and their teams cannot be held responsible to solve these problems in isolation of the business decisions and processes, however. There are many administrative business processes, which must be considered and assessed for the appropriate handling and identification of this data. Consent forms, disclosures, disposal, and marketing and advertising practices are all on the long list of processes and procedures to consider that have little to do with information security traditionally.

The Security Program

The plan or outline of information asset protection tasks, duties, and projects can be collectively referred to as the *security program*. This program is the roadmap of the security processes. The security officer has the responsibility to create and maintain this program in a way that addresses all of the relative business risks. This makes business awareness one of the security officer's accountabilities.

Your evaluation will assess the security program for the following attributes:

- Is based on a documented risk assessment that identifies all relevant information asset security threats

- Documents management's risk tolerance and position on dealing with these threats in general

- Identifies all of the necessary elements of the security program, including an inventory of information assets, the classification of those assets, and a pairing of which threats apply to which assets

- Is a baseline assessment of the existing vulnerabilities relevant to each information asset, based on the product, its configuration, and the way it is currently being managed

- Documents the existing controls in place to mitigate the risks that are identified by analyzing the previous threats, vulnerabilities, and management tolerance for risk

- Identifies the gaps between what *is* and what *should be* in terms of security controls and countermeasures

- Develops project plans for projects and processes necessary to improve the existing situation and move toward a more optimum security posture

- Develops metrics and key performance measurement instruments for assessing security activities and the maintenance of the existing service levels and controls

- Provides the basis for funding and labor requirement justifications

- Is revised and reviewed periodically, ideally by an independent third party with security professionals on staff to validate the program and its progress

Without some version of this ideal security program, there will always be questions about whether the time and effort for security is being spent wisely and whether there is justification for the funding and compromise necessary to implement a security program. The risk assessment and establishment of the functional requirements is really no more that a SDLC methodology applied to the problem of what do we need to do about security? Once the risks are identified and an agreement is reached with management about how secure they want to be, the rest is a matter of priorities, time allocation, and resources. All of the project requirements usually boil down to the good-cheap-fast triangle. You cannot satisfy all three elements simultaneously. If the desire is for a good and cheap solution, it will most likely take a long time to implement. If time is short and it has to be a high quality product, it will most likely be rather expensive. If the available funding is limited and time is constrained, then the product's quality will have to be the variable that is adjusted downward. By establishing the security quality requirements of the business and documenting that decision, the other two sides of the good-cheap-fast triangle then can be better assessed and defended, and the project can move forward when time and money become more of a concern.

Along with the project plans, baseline assessments, and risk analysis, the overall security program will consist of the definition of the security team and their roles and responsibilities. Even if this is only a one person team, the mission and services provided should be documented and available as a reminder to everyone of what the expectations and roles that these functions serve are in the IS organization. Job descriptions, organizational charts, and all of the other human resources-related processes mentioned in previous chapters apply here, too. It is very important to have these responsibilities well documented—more for what they are not than what they are. Information security tends to be a job that nobody wants to take responsibility for and everyone would like to think of it as someone else's worry. In fact, it is everyone's concern and should be written into the job description of every employee in the organization with very few exceptions, if any. Being able to point to the services provided, maybe even a Service Level Agreement (SLA) of sorts with the IS organization, helps all parties concerned keep their respective expectations clear and focused. The segregation of duties will need to be closely considered along with independence and the reporting relationships. Security teams that report to people whose primary accountability is production may have difficulty getting support for tough calls on security controls that could impact production deadlines, for example. Clearly, training and knowledge of the security technologies and their implementation in practice will be the evaluation criteria that will need to be assessed for you to conclude on the security efforts adequately.

Finally, you will want to assess the overall communication strategy of this security program, its commitments to providing services, and the commitment of management to support the program. Security needs visibility in order to be successful. It is constantly a battle to keep security awareness on everyone's minds.

Policy and Standards

Security policy is a subdivision of the corporate policy and governance strategy. It should take its authority from the corporate mission and the company's ownership or board of directors. The overarching security directive policy can be rather simple and succinct. In fact, the shorter the policies are in general, the greater the chance that they are going to be concise, easy to understand, and clear. The umbrella policy, as it is often referred to, should state that all information assets belong to the company, are important, and will be secured based on data classification and risk. It also should name a person to carry out these directives by formally giving the information security officer the ability to do what is necessary to ensure that this policy is enforced throughout the company. Other information security policies located at the corporate level should establish the corporate direction on various second tier issues. These policies will declare the company's intention to protect information assets by statements that will

- Establish virus protection processes for the organization.

- Establish data classification and information ownership responsibilities and processes.

- Establish acceptable use parameters for employees and the processes for enforcing them, along with penalty definitions so that all employees clearly understand the consequences for noncompliance.

- Establish security training and confidentiality expectations and programs.

- Establish security control processes that will be used by the company to protect information assets by identifying the ownership for the assets within the organization.

- Establish what expectations the privacy information systems users should have when using company systems, such as email, and will define the ownership of data on this system.

- Define expectations for intellectual property rights and ownership of data, which may touch not only on using the data or programs of others without license or agreement but also determining who owns the programs and data created by the employees for the company's use.

- Establish the expectations and programs related to contingency planning and process recoverability.

- Establish the authority and accountability of employees and agents of management for the protection of the information assets.

When evaluating security polices for sufficiency and completeness, you will need to keep in mind the business goals and management style as well as the type of products or services the company you are assessing provides. You will likely see that regulated businesses such as financial institutions will have different expectations for policy content than you would see for a computer game software developer, for example. These expectations may revolve around the kinds of risks that management sees or about which they wish to make a statement. If you are going to recommend that a policy needs to be created, you will need to be prepared to describe the risk associated with not having the policy in place. Security policies reflect the management's direction and to create a policy that is going to be seen as unnecessary by management will likely result in an ineffective policy that will not be followed. Ideally, security policies are relatively few and short and provide a high-level direction. They should stand the test of time, thus requiring infrequent updating, and should state the general corporate direction, leaving the interpretation of the details up to the departments or standards adopted to address particular theme variations. As long as the authority for protecting the information assets is established and the processes and means to achieve this protection are clearly established, the security policies will have done their job.

There are, however, many things that will need to be documented as IS security standards, and the list will depend on the business, its processing model, its customers and users, and the environment in which it operates both technically and politically. Standards should be created for every IS security decision made and process that is established, which needs to be communicated throughout the IS organization or the entire user base, depending on the subject matter. Standards provide a basis for the efficient operations of the IS organization. When standards are established, communicated effectively, and followed, they provide a guide for the organization to use rather than reinventing the wheel every time similar situations requiring decisions related to this subject surface. As you assess the IS organization and get a feel for the kind of security processes that are involved with controlling access and protecting the information assets, many opportunities for standardizing decisions will make themselves apparent.

One of the primary reasons standardization is so important for security-related decision making can be described with an explanation of the security architecture models and the theory of how security works. Security of information varies on a sliding scale from public information that everyone knows to highly confidential data that is so important that only the originator of the final decision should have access to all of the data necessary to make the same decision. Highly secure data is compartmentalized in this fashion to keep the aggregation of data from exposing the decision or the processes involved. This is usually more of a national defense approach to information security than one used in commercial businesses. All data has an intrinsic value to its owner and it should be labeled or classified as to its value so that it can be properly protected as it moves around the information systems of a business. If the data is so important that it will not be moving around the system; it probably will not be classified at all and will be locked away physically on a stand-alone system that is air gapped from the network or any outside communication connectivity. Access to data must be based on an individual user's or processes' need to know that data and have clearance to access that data, which is based on the permission of the owner who is granting access. Unless the data owners are willing to grant permission to each user individually, access is grouped and granted to everyone who has that particular job function or role within the organization. This example is one aspect of why standards are necessary to provide a common ground for operating securely.

The theory describes users with a particular level of clearance or permission to access data and the data of the same level of security, which exists in a zone or security level where common amounts of protection are given to all data at this level. If data at this level was made available to users or processes with a lower level of security clearance, the data could no longer be considered as secure at the higher level, because data can only be as secure as the lowest level of clearance that has access to it. This is an around about way of explaining the time worn security adage that "information security is only as strong as its weakest link." The point of this digression is that if every security decision about a particular technology or set of circumstances were different within an IS organization, then the worst or least secure decision would be the best security that the organization would have, as related to the matter under discussion. Standards are, therefore, desirable to set a lower limit related to the security decisions and to establish a baseline set of expectations for security control on a particular technology scenario or subject matter. Whenever technologies present themselves that have the potential to be used in various ways, all of which have different security consequences, you should expect to see a statement of position or standard documented to establish the minimum acceptable security outcome of the possible decisions that may result.

Security standards also will include the official position on many of the building blocks of systems as well. There should be standards related to how access is granted and who should have control and authority based on the policy's directions. These directions would be interpretations of the policy applicable to all users and systems within the authority of the standards making body. In this way, other subsets of the organization can interpret the policy differently, as long as jurisdictions do not overlap and each interpretation can coexist while still meeting the spirit of the policy. Other subjects that could call for a standard may include:

- Standards for the acceptable identification criteria of users to the system
- Definitions of the system's development parameters including
  - Naming conventions
  - Password requirements
  - Testing requirements

- New systems requirements
- Access and domain restrictions
- Approved methods for making interfaces and connections
- Approved coding and documentation methods
- Criteria for change control and system acceptance

- Standard positions on authentication solutions such as
  - PKI
  - Biometrics
  - Smart cards
  - Digital certificates
  - Security hardware tokens
  - Passwords

- Standard positions on encryption solutions such as
  - Virtual private networking, client to server, and LAN to LAN
  - Database encryption
  - Laptop encryption
  - Email encryption
  - Data storage encryption

- Minimum security-baseline standards for the various operating systems and network-attached devices
- Standards for the acceptable physical security and environmental controls related to processing systems
- Standards related to contingency planning and recovery processes
- Standards related to the various processes and procedures, which support any particular system or process in the organization, that would benefit from a common approach or published methodology

Your evaluation of the security-related standards will require that you have a comprehensive understanding of the systems and technologies in use and that you can discern where the risks exist due to the lack of standards in order to provide a security baseline from which you can evaluate. You will want to assess the existing standards for the ability to provide an unambiguous statement of direction and the ability to describe the problem for which the standard should be applied. Knowing where to go for more information and who is responsible for maintaining the standard should new and unique scenarios come to the forefront, causing the standard to be reviewed for possible revision, also needs to be evidenced somewhere in the body of each standard.

Finally, and most importantly, you will want to understand how these standards are enforced and what the consequences are for noncompliance. While these standards are not mandates, there must be some consequences for not using them or they will be meaningless. For example, if the standards are not followed, additional proof will be required for acceptance into the production environment or the support or service levels cannot be guaranteed. However, if disregard for the standards does not result in some consequences, then the whole purpose of creating the standards and interpreting policy to provide common ground is a waste of time. Penalties will, of course, depend on the culture of the organization and should be commensurate with the intended results to be gained by the standard being reviewed.

In addition, while you will want to see that good enforcement mechanisms are in place for standards designed to provide controls and protection over the information assets, you will need to seek evidence of their effective enforcement when it is described as part of a policy or standard. Without actual examples of when this enforcement mechanism was used in practice, you must be suspicious of the effectiveness that the enforcement process actually has in its daily operations. You also will want to see a fair and equitable application of this enforcement across the spectrum of users and employees. If management is treated differently for violating policy or standards than clerical employees, for example, you will be unable to conclude that the standard has been fully implemented or that the risks are in fact mitigated through this control mechanism. There also may be legal liability concerns to address as well.

Some documentation is referred to as being a set of standards or even a policy, but it is actually a guidance or procedural. While best practices give direction, unless they are described as a standard practice and are adopted by the organization as the acceptable practice, they are little more than a convenient guide of doing something that may be recommended but does not necessarily need to be done. This information can be identified by the language found in the documentation that describes a way of accomplishing an objective but leaves the door open to using other methods and describes all methods as equally acceptable. No enforcement statement or consequences also are a clue. When the documentation lists the steps for accomplishing an end, this is usually a procedure. Procedures typically will walk a user through how to achieve an objective. Sometimes procedures are included in a standard to show the reader how to be compliant

with the standard in the most forthright manner. You may see other opportunities to go back and review the existing policies for weaknesses and
deficiencies as you proceed through the security review, but at this level
you really just want to establish authority, accountability, and ownership.

Periodic Security Assessments and Planning

After you have assessed the policy and directives that establish the security
function in the IS organization you are evaluating, you will want to gain an
understanding that this security function is doing the right things using a
risk-prioritized approach. A best practice for assessing this is to have an
independent and objective assessment of the state of the security conducted by a third party and to have this evaluation become the basis for
determining where the gaps are and what priorities should be to close
them. This exercise should be repeated periodically and used as a report
card to evidence, in an independent fashion, the improvements or progress
achieved over time or to point out the inability to do so to management for
corrective action. Many companies will feel that they do not want to fund
an effort like this, that their data is too sensitive to risk this kind of exposure, that they can perform this assessment sufficiently in house, or that
they are afraid the testers will use the information to later compromise the
organization's systems. These fears are unfounded for the most part,
assuming that qualified and reputable firms are retained for the testing.
Certainly in today's market, there are many vendors to choose from that
will provide the IS organization with a good service at a reasonable price,
as long as the organization is selective and specific about what it is asked
for and an agreement is configured in a way that it meets the organization's security and confidentiality requirements.

A large accounting and consulting firm does not need to be used for a
professional result. However, an effort must be made to ensure that the
final report is well written, presented in a positive manner, and accepted
by management as actionable and not seen as a ruse or pretense for getting
funding for concerns that are not justifiable. A lot of education may be necessary up front so the "ignore it and maybe it will go away" management
mentality can be adequately addressed. You will want to evaluate what
kind of assessment is being performed to ensure that you are not contracting for a penetration study, which is a different engagement. Penetration
studies, which these efforts are collectively called in error, are attacks on
your system with the aim of gaining access to a trophy of some sort, a file,
or password, for example. These studies typically ask little about your system up front and are designed to test your defenses. Once breached, the
game is over and the report is written about how the system was breached

and what needs to be improved to close the hole. You will probably get some suggestions for improvement that were noticed along the way, but you will not get much more than that in terms of identifying improvement needs or other items worth correcting to develop a robust security defense posture.

A vulnerability assessment is an open book test where you will need to show the contracted team all of the organization's inner workings so they can recommend design and approach changes that will help you meet the business needs that the IS organization is supporting. Of course, this assumes that the contracted service is bonded, trusted, and ideally looking for a long-term relationship with the organization. Contracts and nondisclosure documentation will need a lawyer's review to make everyone comfortable with letting their guard down for you to look around. With the proper levels of trust established, this kind of arrangement will enable an objective third party to ask the stupid questions and to point out issues that may be obvious to them but overlooked to those too close to the problem to see it from the proper perspective. The result can be an actionable punch list that can be prioritized with easily checked off items and strategic initiatives that will need to be funded and planned over the course of several years. These service providers also will be in a position to help sell the needs and benefits to management and to explain the consequences of not accepting the recommendations with firsthand evidence of results of ignoring the weaknesses and vulnerabilities. Whether the IS organization fully embraces this approach or some other version as mentioned previously, as an IS auditor, you will want to see some sort of risk assessment process performed to benchmark the current state and the risk-control status periodically thereafter. IS auditors should expect to see the risk criteria well documented and in line with the risk tolerance and acceptance levels that were previously identified with management.

Risk assessment, in whatever form you find it, will be a necessary basis for moving forward in the evaluation of an asset protection program. The security officer will have to know what they are protecting these assets from in order to expect to be successful in doing so. Using risk assessment formulas as the basis for building a security plan is defendable and will most adequately address the issues identified from highest to lowest risk. Without this approach, you will find lower risk issues being addressed with all available resources, with the higher risk issues, which are not the focus of the day, being ignored. This is not to say that a risk-based approach will not be able to accommodate fire fighting, which inevitably crops up during the normal course of business. Those items will become high risk for the duration of the management's attention span or the time it takes to get the fire under control. In a risk-based approach, the security plan then will migrate from the tactical back to the strategic as the threat or vulnerability is adequately addressed. The plan's attention then will turns back to the building blocks, which will eventually result in a robust and pervasive solution set that can be relied upon to mitigate new risk threat combinations as they occur. Your assessment of the risk-based approaches and the measurement of risks and threats are fundamental audit activities that should be the initial part of any assessment you undertake.

Designing Security from the Start

One of the better approaches that you can hope to come across during your assessment of information protection processes or any systems development effort, for that matter, is the recognition that security needs to be part of the initial solution identification process for the business solutions and an integral part of the system's design and development life cycle. Studies have shown sevenfold cost differences between installing proper security controls after a process is brought to production compared to designing these same solutions into the process from the beginning. You should expect to find a requirement for this security integration and forethought in the standards and polices related to systems development. Systems development should be a process that gets buy in at the top of the organization. Thoughtful consideration should be given to all aspects of embarking on a significant investment. This process should include an evaluation of the market's potential, user need, and criteria; the possible profitability and the life cycle predictions for the product line; as well as regulatory and security considerations that will need to be addressed in order for the solution to be acceptable to the organization from a business risk point of view.

A best practice is for a senior level product review committee to meet periodically and review proposals for new products and systems, assessing their potential return on investments (ROI) and potential for improving the company's business prospects overall. The security officer should attend this meeting and an assessment of whether the proposal has considered and addressed the inherent security risks and potential impact to the systems overall security architecture should be part of the decision process during the review of the proposed systems. Contingency planning, proper regulatory control considerations, and a security sensitive design should all be required for a product with equal footing to evaluate criteria such as the ROI and potential profits and client opportunities that are considered as rationale for giving the go ahead to new investment initiatives. Security involvement should continue to be evident throughout the development and testing cycles to ensure that the product implemented in production is as well controlled as the design had envisioned. This inclusion will assure that the product's functionality is not compromised or sacrificed because of the late entry of security into the process.

In a similar fashion of checking that the estimated ROI is actually achieved in production, security should be validated or accredited in a live production configuration. All of the relevant administrative processes should be explored during this project assessment to ensure that the security controls' cure is not worse that the disease. Often, lofty promises made by eager development and marketing people will leave out the intense manual effort and ongoing administration some of the proposed security solutions will require to be maintained in proper working order. When done correctly, meaning deploying an application or proposed solution with all of the appropriate controls and proper security measures in place, the ROI of a proposed system can change significantly and will not look quite as attractive as it was first presented without the inclusion of necessary security considerations. On top of that, retrofitting security controls into the process at a point in the process when design is well underway, or worse yet, completed, or during the first production control review, will be much more expensive, shooting large holes in the return and profitability assumptions. Therefore, you always should conclude on the inclusion of security considerations whenever you review a systems implementation or design project.

Identification, Authentication, and Authorization

Whether you are reviewing systems, applications, or networks, one of your top priorities will be the interface points with the user. The majority of risk will always lie with the people who will be using the IS systems that you are evaluating. People do not always follow rational processes and cannot be depended upon to follow policies and rules at all times. Our fallible human nature makes us naturally curious beings that often want to explore our environment, sometimes beyond where we have permission to go. Systems are predictable, on the other hand, and will follow the rules given to them. When an error occurs, it can be reproduced because the same thing will happen over again, absent from human intervention.

As you go about evaluating the human interface to systems, you will need to be aware of the security-related characteristics of the individuals and their usage patterns. This starts with ". . . just exactly who is this person anyway?" The user's identity is the key aspect of access that must be focused on first and foremost in the security evaluations. Unauthorized access usually begins with identity theft or masquerading as someone you are not. The escalation of privileges, social engineering, and physical theft, for that matter, are all identity issues at their root. Privileges are associated with individuals. There is an implicit assumption that the individual is who they say they are at the point in the process where these permissions are handed out. Because none of this happens in the physical world where human recognition processes would be used, surrogate processes are used to approximate the human ones in the logical environment. Identification and how it is established is your first step in investigating the access and control of the computing resources assignments.

You will want to assess the processes that are used to identify people and note how this identity is validated and recorded. You will have to ask yourself what constitutes the sufficient identification of a person and to whom is it being validated. Signing up on a Web page as Daffy Duck is a favorite example used to illustrate how identity can be misrepresented when few controls are in place. Is a picture ID sufficient proof of identity? Does identification need to be established in person? Does a background check need to be performed? Should a government entity be used to validate identity before credentials are issued? All of these questions require risk-based decisions by the management of the organization. You should determine the reasoning behind accepting a level of risk associated with the identification methods that are used. This will help you to understand how important being accountable for the actions taken by any given user actually is to the business and management decision makers.

There are factors related to time and money that must be considered as well as convenience issues to examine when evaluating the adequacy of the processes established for identity management. Face-to-face identification is a strong process but requires a lot of time and administration overhead to be managed properly. Systems that are used to establish the identity of users can be deployed in fixed locations but without an attendant, ensuring that the procedures are properly performed by those identifying themselves, spoofing and masquerading can result. Using the hiring process through a supervisor or human resource department can be a reasonable control as long as the actual issuance of the ID to the preidentified person can be validated through some kind of control process that provides a reasonable assurance that the ID is not misapplied.

Another good way to manage the control of identity that is currently popular is to trap a key personal secret phrase. This phrase can subsequently be used to match the response given later to validate the person's identity when account servicing is required. Many ways to apply this can be circumvented with a little social engineering, so risks and due diligence must be considered. Having the enrollee pick from a series of questions and applying a personal answer to the selected question may seem like a lot of work to reach identity verification. However, it works a lot more securely than using a mother's maiden name or date of birth, both of which are easily obtained in today's wired world. A weak authentication process can invalidate many downstream security controls that wrongly assume the user's identity has been established in a thorough manner.

Once identity is established, accounts must be assigned and maintained in a manner that links these surrogate tokens of identity, usually referred to as an ID or User Account, to the individual for the duration of their use of the system. IDs are typically issued to the user or to their supervisor for issuing to the user. Making sure the ID is issued to the person whose identity it was established for may be an additional identification exercise. When the surrogate identity is presented to the system for use, it will need to be authenticated by some act that proves the ID belongs to the person it represents. This process is referred to as authentication and can take place only after an initial identification process has occurred and IDs have been established. The most common mechanism used for this purpose is a password. Known only to the person it was issued to, it revalidates the identity and authenticates the user as the person to which the identity was validated originally.

When an account or ID for a user is established, certain rights or permissions then can be associated with that account, which entitles the holder to perform tasks and access information on the information systems. These entitlements represent what that account, and hence, the user is authorized to do or see. Authorization is, therefore, the process of matching access rights or functional permissions to an account.

Need to Know

A basic premise of security controls is that users should be given only access to those things that they have a *need to know* about. This is referred to by many catch phrases such as *least privilege* and the *default deny* access model. All of these terms imply that access is available only to users after it has been specifically granted to them, presumably by the data owner or their representative, and that no more access than is necessary to perform the job function has been granted to them. When you are reviewing security controls, this will be a natural benchmark against which to measure the access you are evaluating. If access is allowed more widely than would be granted using this principle, you will have a more in-depth investigation task and additional risks to consider. The idea that if you do not need to know it, you should not have access to it is more of a military compartmentalization of a security view of access. However, if data is fairly and uniformly classified along with a pairing of that access to roles and user profiles by the data owners and stewards, then not needing to know becomes a conscious decision of the data owner and not a subjective value judgment about an individual. Having a need to know or right to access data does not necessarily mean that the user will always use their data rights appropriately either. This is an inherent limitation of granting access rights to data and assuring appropriate use through information systems. Unless some kind of inference engine or business rules-based activity analysis can be performed on logs of actions to identify inappropriate but authorized use, access permission rights are as close to the absolute security controls as you can hope for from a technical perspective. The rest of the control is a people-based problem.

Security Controls Economics

This might be a good place to digress quickly and help you understand the law of diminishing returns when it comes to security and controls in general. This law is commonly referred to as the 80-20 rule and can be used as rough guidance of how much control is actually cost effective. Naturally, this all comes down to a management decision and business risk models. Information asset security and control issues will generally range from the simple to the complex and their solutions run along the same continuum. Some vulnerabilities are easily corrected by turning off unnecessary services, for example, and it costs relatively little to implement these controls. Solutions costs are usually proportional to their complexity and not necessarily to the risk exposure, thus, the more complex the issue, the more expensive a solution is to both implement and maintain.

As a general rule of thumb, you will find that 80 percent of the solutions related to a security problem you encounter can be solved with the first 20 percent of the cost that it would take to solve the issue in its entirety, if that were even possible. The last 20 percent of the solution— the users or whatever variable you are trying to gain control over by applying a solution— will consume the other 80 percent of the costs. The reason for this is that within the last 20 percent of the problem's range, you will find all the oddball issues that require special case analysis and custom solution design. This is where the costs explode and the actual return is diminished, which also gives you insight into why security is never an absolute 100 percent solution. Somewhere along this curve, the cost to fix exceeds the cost of loss, should the threat you are trying to prevent actually happen to occur. Ideal security exists at the point where the cost to correct is less that the cost of loss and where the majority of the risks, say 80 percent, can be addressed by the control that is being implemented.

This brings up another important security concept referred to as *defense in depth*. If you run the numbers, you will see that adding layers of 80 percent solutions on top of one another can quickly address a large number of the potential vulnerability points, while still keeping the costs below the 100 percent solution of any one fully implemented countermeasure. If you can solve 80 percent of the problem with the first solution at 20 percent of the cost, and 80 percent of the residual problem with another 20 percent of the cost, you will have solved 96 percent of the problem at 40 percent of the cost to solve it with only one defense layer. This is bit of an over simplification, of course, but the general idea is still applicable. You will see that the achievement of a complete security solution will approach infinitely expensive implementation costs if pursued in full measure. *Layered security* provides the additional benefit of creating multiple and uniquely different barriers to overcome in order to compromise the target information assets you seek to protect. When relying on a single defense mechanism, all of your eggs are in one basket. If the basket becomes compromised, you will loose all of the eggs. With different solutions being applied to the same problem, no one exploit will likely give an intruder a full compromise position. The downside is, however, the total cost and overhead of deploying multiple solutions. Costs like maintenance, training, and support must be considered when determining the cost-benefit equation on these layered strategies. When performing an audit on information security, look at solutions and countermeasures as potentially single points of failure in the security armor. Also seek to understand what is happening to control the 20 percent that got away and what mitigating controls are in place to address these issues.

Role-Based Access

Role-based access controls are a type of security compromise that provides administrative benefits at the cost of granular and specific access control. When evaluating role-based access controls, you will first want to get an understanding of the basis and rationale for categorizing the access permissions and functionality that are allowed in certain roles or groups and will want to identify who made the decision for such groupings. The decisions for grouping the permissions into such roles should always be tied back to the data owner or their stewards. These sets of permissions or roles should make business process sense in terms of functional cohesiveness as well. The reason this is important has to do with the nature of the compromise that is implicitly agreed to when roles are implemented.

You can think about the access permissions granted to an individual as a set of privileges that provides them with the ability to perform their job function, no more, and no less. This is the most granular and specific set of permissions that can be given to the individual and still enable them to adequately perform their functions within the organization. Making a set like this for each individual and tailoring it to their unique job functions could be very time consuming and difficult to administer. Furthermore, there also are lots of opportunities for error and drift over time as people adjust their job performance and duties and subsequent access requirements in daily operations. Remember that an important aspect of any access control review will be to ensure that these permissions are tuned up periodically so that they accurately reflect the access needed by the individual(s) to perform their functions.

By creating a group of these sets, a less granular role is created, the administration of access can be simplified, and the total number of access profiles can be reduced. The trade off, however, is that not all of the permissions of the role will be an exact fit for any one individual assigned to that role. Assuming that this book is not talking about completely overlapping and redundant job performance characteristics, there will always be more functionality available to the individual on average than they will need to perform their function, however, the administration will be simplified to these aggregate roles. There must be an understanding that individual users can never have less access permission granted to them than they need to perform their tasks, otherwise they would be ineffective workers and unable to perform their duties. Because of this, the band of compromise that is defined by the roles access aggregation must always err on the upside of enabling more access than necessary rather then less. Sometimes this is deemed unacceptable to management, and the decision is made to manage the roles for sensitive access permission sets with a one-to-one relationship to the users for which they are assigned. This also can be considered as role-based access, enabling anyone with that function the same set of permissions. By creating and maintaining access roles instead of individual access profiles, the application or process now is positioned to enable an individual to assume several roles, moving into one and then the other while still maintaining a segregation of duties among the various roles. This will require the individual to change roles and subsequently their permissions to play a different role within the access control scheme.

Care must be taken when reviewing the decision to allow individuals the ability to have the access permissions of multiple roles concurrently. The risk of aggregated access, when the total access permission set that multiple roles provides enables access that should not be granted to one function, will possibly require an assessment of what mitigating controls might be applied to reduce the risks back to an acceptable level.

Evaluating Account Administration

The processes and procedures of administrating the users' accounts will be found in every system and application where access is permitted. The main functions performed in providing this service should be independent of the application modification and data access functions to ensure that only the users identified and approved by the data owner and stewards actually receive the accounts. These accounts should contain only the permissions defined to the individuals' preapproved role in the organization. The account administration function often serves as the first point of contact for the users who are interfacing with the applications, therefore making customer service a big part of the administrator's process.

Documentation of the procedures followed by the account administration staff should describe the processes used to perform the tasks of adding, modifying, and deleting the accounts. Routine maintenance functions, such as the termination of accounts and cleanup of dormant accounts, should be evidenced in these procedures as well. The procedures should be updated and reviewed periodically for accuracy and applicability to current processes. Job descriptions will need to be gathered and assessed for the proper segregation of responsibilities and completeness of administrative duty assignments as part of your evaluation. Proper training and management support also will be expectations that the IS auditor will have to ensure that the service levels are met and the commitments of throughput and availability of accounts are in line with the needs of the business processes.

Some standard attributes of account building and maintenance can be described here and reviewed as relevant when the risks warrant for not only account administration processes but also for application and operating system access controls. Most systems and applications provide several restrictions that the IS auditor will want to assess for their use and applicability in controlling access. The time of day and day of week restrictions limit access to systems and may be desirable to restrict access outside the working hours. Care must be exercised when using this control because of the emergency or contingency access requirements. Password strength and aging will be covered later but also are parameters that are configured within each system or application. Consideration may be warranted for more stringent controls to accounts with sensitive or extensive access, such as systems administrator accounts, for example. You may even see the workstation restrictions in use, and then you will need to evaluate the process used to manage the access limitation for a given ID to certain specific terminals. Naming conventions for the IDs will need to be reviewed to ensure they are well controlled and managed. Consideration should be given to ensure that the account names cannot be used to understand who the user is, what their function might be, or the permissions associated with a particular ID. Account names, such as "Administrator," are obvious magnets for those trying to compromise a system.

User Account Management

Account management begins with the identity management processes that were discussed earlier. Evaluate the procedures used to identify and validate new users and ensure they are sufficient for the risk tolerance and business model used in the particular IS organization you are reviewing. Once the identity is established, a record keeping process that manages this ID will track the user's account information and access permissions over the course of the useful life of the account. Any special secrets or codes established during this identification process, along with any demographic and contact information, will be registered in the record keeping system for use in revalidation, should that become necessary at some point in the life of the account. An effort should be made to ensure that the accounts are given to first-time users, along with any other information they will need to know about how to use the application or process to which the account gives them access. This also should include security awareness information about acceptable use and warnings about the consequences of security violations. A best practice would be to include the provision of proactive security education on issues like how to recognize security violations or breaches, how to report incidents, and the guidelines on creating secure passwords.

Requests for access will come into the account administration process in some formally documented form. These requests should be approved before they are processed. This approval can either be obtained as part of the workflow of the request form, as it is routed from the originator to the account administrator, or as a subsequent step that is managed through the account administrator's process. Approval of this request needs to be tied back to the application's management or ownership in some way. The ability to approve access requests may be (and often is) delegated to the supervisor of the users for the subset of the application functionality used in the work area supervised by the manager. When roles are used as an access control methodology, each role will have an owner or steward, which will validate that the person requesting the account does indeed fit into the role being requested as an access profile for that person. Approvals will need to be evidenced and tracked in the record of the account so that there is an audit trail of management decisions for granting access.

Passwords are established for accounts so that they can be accessed initially. These passwords should be used only one time and then expire immediately at the first log on. This will require the user to establish a password of their design and choosing, thereby ensuring that their account cannot be used anyone else. The process of establishing first-use passwords will be a security vulnerability that will need to be evaluated. Passwords used for this first-time use should not follow a known pattern, which can be easily used to pirate accounts that have been built but not distributed or logged into yet. The distribution of these passwords and the associated accounts also will be the subject of investigation by the IS auditor. Secure physical measures will ensure that the accounts go to the person who has a previously established identity and association with that account. You should investigate what happens when these accounts cannot be delivered and need to be returned and situations where accounts are created in advance and are held for new hires. Processes that validate the user's identity by asking them their secret code at first log in will mitigate the risks substantially.

Requests for the modification of existing accounts' permissions will follow the same workflow processes that new accounts will take. The only difference will be the password establishment process, which is not usually required for modified accounts. However, the permission and approval process will need to be evaluated. You also will need to review the modifications from a job functionality perspective. When a person changes jobs, that person may require a change in their access permissions to perform the new set of tasks that describe their new job. Their old or previous job permissions should be removed from the access profile they had previously as soon as possible. If this does not occur, the access permissions of this user will add up, possibly exposing the process to an inappropriate access capability because of the aggregation of permissions. A person moving from purchasing to receiving and then to the billing department, for example, could write their own ticket with all of those permissions aggregated into one person's access profile. This is another reason why the access profile for applications needs to be reviewed periodically by the business management to ensure that only those with a need to know are actually getting access to the roles and profile necessary for them to perform their functions.

In situations where roles-based access is used to manage account access, you must determine what deviations are required in the administration process when the modification requests fall outside of the established roles and access groupings. When the job function of a person changes but it is not moving cleanly into another previously established role, there may be a need for a new role to be created or an existing role may need to be modified as necessary. Data owners should provide oversight and approval for any modification to existing roles or the creation of new access roles for their application or system. Opportunities for the verification and notification of role changes should be explored through independent means as a best practice to ensure that these job function changes are indeed valid. Human resource and the payroll processes and systems provide opportunities for ensuring that such changes are valid and these systems also can be used to ensure that all of the job function changes are recognized and result in a realignment of the system access permissions. You should look at the processes used to notify the account administrators of changes and assess the controls used to ensure that they are complete, accurate, valid, and timely. You also should ensure that these changes are adequately recorded in this person's record so that a permanent audit trail exists of each individual's access permission history over the life of the account.

Termination processes are another part of the routine account management process that is performed on a regular basis. Processes and procedures must be set in place that support the immediate and sustained termination of access for situations where it is required to preserve the system's security. You will want to evaluate what is considered to be adequate authority to initiate this process and ensure that access is terminated only in the appropriate cases. Typically, account administrators will develop relationships with administration personnel in other departments who routinely interact with them in their daily processes. These people will be the ones who request new accounts and otherwise manage the departmental aspect of a user's needs. They also will be seen as an authority and validation checkpoint for any requests coming from that department. These relationships should be documented and formalized in order to provide back up documentation of the established authority role. The Human Resources department can be used as an adequate checkpoint for the termination requests when these requests are coming from unknown or untrustworthy sources.

In addition, there also should be routine termination processes that occur based on the reports from valid sources. Human resource and supervisory labor rosters used by the management processes are the best sources to leverage for this information. These reports should be used as a trigger to initiate the termination and cleanup procedures. Evidence should be available to the IS auditor that provides assurance that adequate and timely termination processes are being performed regularly and recorded. The disposition of the information that resides in the user's personal allocation of file space, as well as those files flagged as being created or owned by this user ID, will need to be reviewed to guarantee that the confidentiality and privacy policies are honored. Depending on the organization's policy, email storage may need addressed in this manner as well.

There also should be policies that require accounts, which have not been used for some extended period, to expire. This best practice keeps the accounts that have been missed from the termination process for some reason from lying around like a loaded gun. Subsequent clean up processes will move any disabled accounts into a terminated status and will subsequently close the accounts and purge any related files. You will need to evaluate this process to ensure it is being performed consistently and to assess whether the time frames between last use, disabling, and final termination are sufficient to address the risk tolerance of management and support the documented policies on this subject. Additionally, a best practice is to have all temporary, vendors, and other nonemployee accounts created with a limited lifetime, thus enforcing a revalidation of the needs periodically. There should be evidence that an authorized representative of the organization approves any revalidation of this access type. Audit trails should exist that clearly establish the accountability and security expectations of these accounts so that legal liability is established or transferred in a manner that satisfies the inherent risks of such transient access.

From an efficiency and performance perspective, you may want to assess any available KPIs or recommend some that enable management to understand how well the account administration services are being provided and the level of customer satisfaction that is related to the account administration process. Labor productivity and turn around of requests are typical measurement points for assessing the performance of the administrators.

Single Sign-On Solutions

Several kinds of solutions in the marketplace today are loosely described as single sign-on solutions, each with its own limitations. Some get between your request for access and the end application and sign on for you; others create an environment where all of the accounts and passwords are the same for a given individual. Anytime access is made easier the security risks go up, which is to be expected as part of the balance between security and access. When evaluating single sign-on solutions, the IS auditor will seek to identify single points of failure resulting from the implementation and opportunities for intruders to leverage the ease of use features enabling the compromise of access. When scripting is used to imitate the user sign-on process, access to the scripts and the ability to compromise and subvert them will need to be evaluated. When tokens are used to validate authority and sign on, as in a Kerberos implementation, you will want to evaluate the application process flows and various parameters used to issue and pass the tokens, assessing their adequacy for the purpose at hand. Expiration of tokens, and interception and replay risks should be addressed in the design of the process you are evaluating, for example.

You also will want to review the repository of the sign-on information, user record entries, and rules engines used to manage the central process. Security of this server and its contents, along with the business rules and their build processes and related documentation will all be on your list of items to review for proper design, documentation, and controls. Assessing the implementation of a project to deploy single sign on would follow the similar project and SDLC audit steps described in previous chapters. Clear expectations of functionality will be important because these solutions are often over promised and under delivered based on the current market hype and search for a silver bullet to solve the user interface problem across the enterprise. Enrollment and identity establishment processes are very important to the single sign-on solution. This is because once these accounts have been established, the control that validated the user for each separate access need, which is used in a decentralized log on methodology, can no longer ensure that the person using the ID is the same exact person.

Application Design Security

As we have discussed, building security into the application design is the right way to implement security. When you are reviewing the application design processes for security, there are several key attributes that will reinforce that the security processes are being considered adequately in the SDLC methodology being utilized. Systems should be designed to include as many of the following items as possible, depending on the control objectives of the particular application:

- Users should not be able to break out of the user session of the application and get to a system command line interface. They also should not be able to get out of the application user interface and roam around the internal application file structure at will.

- Access to business functions that need to be segregated in the physical world also should be segregated in the logical world as well. Testing should be performed by people knowledgeable about the business to ensure this issue has been appropriately addressed.

- Sign-on processes should not show passwords as they are being typed and the ability to display the last user will need to be assessed for its pluses and minuses in the particular environment where the application is typically deployed. On one hand, knowing that the last log on at a personal workstation was someone other than the person the workstation is assigned to may be interesting information. For kiosks or public workstations, however, knowing the last person's ID is one of the pieces of information that an intruder would need to put together enough information to compromise someone's access.

- Other password-related parameters to include in design considerations are

  - Aging of passwords

  - Password reuse history files and checking routines

  - Strength requirements (use of numbers, mixed case, special characters, and so on)

  - Password length requirements

  - Password strength checking routines

- The granularity of access control built into the application based on the data classification and user functionality should be commensurate with the risk and need to control that access

- Limitation of access to utilities and support functions that permit access at a systems administration level

- Log on warning banners should be displayed that deter the inappropriate use of systems and warn of the consequences for doing so

Let's discuss some of these in more detail so that you can get a sense of the leading practices that then can be used as benchmarks for your review and gap analysis of the application design processes.

Application and Data Access

Both during an application's design and its use, access to the data and the application code needs to be controlled based on a need to know. Focusing first on the data, the owner should determine what level of sensitivity the data elements have and then provide support and approval for building control processes that apply the level of security required to maintain the integrity, confidentiality, and availability of that data based on its classification. Processes should be documented assuring that decision-making processes determined the appropriate data classification and that the access controls were built to protect the data at that level. This data, once classified, needs to be secured in every format it exists in, whether on paper or electronically, in the test domains and in production. Logging and review of the access may be a necessary control, depending on the sensitivity of the data in question. Rules for accessing this data will need to be developed as part of the design and implementation of the application. These rules will be the control that ensures the owner's wishes for access limitation are carried out, and therefore need the owner's approval to be considered appropriately designed. Once the functionality of the application is built in a test or pilot scenario, the access criteria approved by the sponsor or owner should be formally validated and reported on. There may be a need to show that the higher levels of data classification are treated in increasingly more secure and demonstrably different ways to prove that the security controls increase as the data classification moves from public to confidential. The data access capabilities of the systems and database administrators will need to be scrutinized. Although the controls over DBAs and Sysadmins are somewhat limited in usefulness, these roles should only be accessing the data when appropriate to do so, through the enforcement of manual procedures to that effect, if necessary. Consideration of controls for the data must include file, and data element level permission controls and the management of them, as well as security over the back up processes and possibly the use of encryption as a security control.

Looking at the application code and the underlying operating and database systems, the application design process should make every effort to ensure that this data cannot be manipulated or altered by the application's business users unless designed as part of the functionality. The favorite way to do this is through buffer overflows, which exploit bad software design and sometimes give the users access to functionality and the administrator level, that they are not authorized to have. This evaluation also means looking at each file, directory, utility, and function, and determining what the appropriate access is and who should be able to have that access or permission. These decisions then must be documented and used as guidance for building security into the system and subsequently used as testing criteria to ensure that it is indeed what the final product behaves like. Some data about the users such as IDs, passwords, and security permissions may need to be encrypted at rest and in transit to ensure their integrity and confidentiality. Tables where this information is housed should have access logs associated with them that go above and beyond the normal access control logging provided for the rest of the application code. Attempts to access through the use of non-administrator IDs should be seen as attempted security breaches and treated as incidents for follow-up.

All forms of confidentially classified information also should be treated the same whether they exist as paper design documentation, test code, pilot code, training program code, or production quality versions of the application code set. Mechanisms should be set in place that track the access to all of these forms commensurate with the risk-based security decisions referenced earlier to validate that the security exists in practice and is what was determined in the planning design stages. Controls over sensitive functionality, such as DBA functions and powerful systems utilities, should be documented and managed to limit the access to as few personnel as reasonably possible, without risking the ability to perform under contingency situations. Functionality that puts the data at risk will need special consideration as described in the database locking and roll back processes discussed in an earlier chapter.

Information Ownership and Custodianship

The responsibilities of information ownership include processes that identify, label, and protect the data. At the point where the data that is important to the business process is created, it should be tagged with the correct classification that will enable the users and processes to afford the appropriate protection and controls over it, thus keeping it confidential and accurate. Knowing who should access this data is necessary in order to provide access in a controlled manner. This will be important when you need to define access permissions that are restricted to only those who have a need to know. Users must be categorized into access roles or permissions sets and matched with the data they will need to access. Pairing these access permission rights to the data classifications is the responsibility of the data owners or custodians.

Review of Access

Reviewing the access control processes periodically will be necessary to keep them in synchronization with the changes to the data quality and users' needs. Whether the user roles are defined or access is granted on an individual basis, the IS auditor should expect to see a process in place for periodically validating the access to ensure that it remains appropriate to the needs of the business. These ownership reviews should be documented and driven by policies and procedures that describe the required processes in sufficient detail to ensure that the activity is done thoroughly and in consideration of all the applicable review criteria. These criteria should include the validation of the information classification, the validation of the job functions being performed by the individuals holding the access rights, and the appropriateness of those access rights for access based on the job functions with which they are paired. Knowledge of the business processes and the needs for data access by these functions requires that a businessperson be involved in this evaluation. You will want to get some explanation if you see this process being performed without business people being involved. Review of the personnel with access may turn up accounts for terminated employees who still have access or access may still be available to individuals whose roles have changed since the last review. This periodic review provides an excellent opportunity to tune up the account and access permissions changes that may have fallen through the cracks of the normal process for managing people and data.

Data Classification

In order to economically apply security controls to data, the value of that data must be known. Just as you would not spend $100 to solve a $10 problem, you cannot adequately secure data unless you know its value. Value is assigned by the data owner or delegated to others from their authority. Data classifications schemas should be simple and easy to understand, but they also must exist formally and be documented as a policy in order to ensure that everyone in the business and IS organizations has the same understanding about the data's value as the person assigning that data's value. If you cannot find documented evidence of a valuation process, you will need to question how the IS organization can fairly secure data and be able to differentiate the security requirements that need to be applied. The alternative is a high level of security controls for all data, which does not treat confidential data any differently than public data in the eyes of the lawyers. Knowing the data's value makes determining the security countermeasure a simple matter of balancing risks. The cost to control access versus the potential loss are business decisions that can be adequately defended and justified with known values of protection and loss mapped to the data's classifications.

The primary consideration when reviewing data classification is therefore that there is a documented requirement for classifying information assets and that this classification differentiates data levels so that security and controls can be applied at varying levels of rigor or intensity. It will be important to draw a distinction between data that is publicly available, which the IS auditor will be able to validate readily, and other more sensitive data that should be more closely controlled and protected. The rationale for placing information into the various levels or categories is a business decision that may be part of your review, if your objectives call for it. There may be regulatory requirements or the customers may have some right or ability to self-declare the classification that you may need to take into consideration. Keep in mind that you may need to follow this data through several applications in the process flow to ensure that the security and protection decisions made by the data owner are honored along the way. As data flow crosses network and system boundaries, especially to different legal entities, this monitoring becomes extremely important and difficult. Most important is the establishment of a formal classification process and a way to label the data or notify others of the classification decisions that have been made. Trust agreements may be necessary in order to protect the data across legal boundaries.

Data labeling sounds like a great idea and a necessary step to protect the data until you try to practically perform it in a real-world business application. Removable media is about the only data storage or transport mechanism that can be labeled with the classification of the data contained on it. This labeling should be done to ensure that all data leaving the premises can be adequately protected by properly labeling it at the highest level of classification that the collection of data on the media represents. It is very difficult to label data passing through electronic transmissions and stored in temporary caches, however. As impractical as individual data labeling seems, it is important that a mechanism is used for enabling the data users and processor to understand the quality of the data that is being manipulated so that the proper control behaviors can be observed. Sometimes this is done by assuming that all of the data from a given application is classified as the highest level of classification for the data managed by that process or application. As an auditor, you will need to see how this is managed for each case that you evaluate. In addition, you will have to determine whether the classification decisions are made consistently across the organization, hopefully based on common criteria, and documented so that these decisions can be communicated to people making security and control decisions about the data transport, storage, and manipulation. Your conclusions should be based upon the reasonable competent man rule that guides auditors into making rational common sense assessments about the sufficiency of controls. Keep in mind that all data sensitive classifications should have a time limit or life span. There should be an assessment of the need to maintain high levels of security classification for data that has existed for an extended period. You may find that an automatically expiring statute of limitations is a sufficient process for managing this issue. Disposal policies and procedures will be a useful sanity check and should align with the overall decision for maintaining the security classifications.

Evaluating Logical Access Controls

Control of the access to data and systems is a major part of information security and the primary objective of any audit reviewing data for integrity and confidentiality. There are many ways to control access and many devices and programs on which to control it. Different configurations lend themselves to different solutions that will work best or be sufficient to mitigate the risk to an acceptable level. Let's begin by reviewing several techniques used to control access logically.

Good Passwords

Passwords are the most common and widely used means of controlling logical access and are used as a control mechanism for physical access as well. A combination lock is really a password-controlled access device, if you think about it. Anyone knowing the password gets in. The assumption must be made that knowing the password is equivalent to the identity validation originally performed when the user enrolled and was given the account. Of course, this is a flawed argument, because many things can happen to a password to expose it as the secret managed by the actual holder of the identity. The following discussion assumes that for access control use, the first thing you will check is to ensure that passwords are required when a password control scheme is used. Blank spaces, or hitting enter, should not be considered a valid password. Policies should require the usage of passwords as a minimum access control requirement and may spell out some of the password use criteria described here for all of the users and system developers to be aware of and perform against.

One argument used against good password necessity is that you also would need the user's ID as well to gain access to a system. Some may even go so far as to claim that ID plus a password is two-factor authentication. Do not buy it. If there is sufficient evidence that the IDs cannot be easily guessed, you might consider this argument, but this is not usually the case. Many systems, including Microsoft and others, preload the last used account name on a terminal access screen, leaving only the password in question. Additionally, it is common for naming conventions for user IDs to be a simple algorithm that is easily discerned by looking at only a few IDs and knowing a little about the person's name and job function, for instance. Procedures and standards, which are available to internal staff, may describe the algorithm in enough detail in invalidate any argument about the ID's confidentiality. You will need to perform several simple tests for yourself and understand the algorithm used to conclude on the sufficiency of the ID uniqueness as a control.

So for the sake of argument, let's assume that the ID can be gleaned from email names or some other ID's naming convention clue. Passwords then become the only thing standing between an intruder and the data. "Hard to guess" becomes a good control, so does "not too many chances at guessing are available." This is why password strength and the number of attempts or tries are important password parameters to review in your control assessment. Standard practice for number of tries is three, as in "three strikes and you're out." While some systems reset automatically, the disablement of an account should ideally be set to stay locked out until a call is placed to a person for intervention. This task is often handled by the help desk, which should be keeping records of this security event for historical and tracking purposes. The help desk then can validate the user's identity and determine that intruder access is not being attempted. If the system resets itself or does not lock out at all, an intruder can methodically try many password combinations until the correct one is found. Some systems make subsequent tries wait a longer period, and keep extending this interval to deter automated hacking attempts. The quality of the responses received from the system when attempting to gain access also are important to review because of the information that may be inadvertently given away about the access attempt. Knowing that the password is too long or that the ID was incorrect may seem helpful to keep legitimate users from getting frustrated, but it also helps the intruder to narrow their search for the right password combination in order to gain access.

How strong the password is will determine the security of this control and it should be examined against the best practices. The strength of a password means how long it is, how complex it is, or in other words, how hard it is to guess. A system's password criteria can include

- Mixed case alpha characters (capital and lowercase together)
- One or many numeric characters
- Special characters up to and including the ones you get when you first hold down the <Alt> key on the keyboard
- Testing against the use of common words by checking passwords being proposed by users against a dictionary systematically
- Syntax restrictions against repeated letters or numbers
- Requirements for a password's lifetime that possibly vary, depending on the sensitivity of the account profile (a more sensitive user profile changes more frequently)

- Requirements for preserving the history of old passwords and not enabling reuse immediately, for a length of time, or ever

- Requirements for minimum length (six to eight characters is common, some systems have design restraints that must be accommodated)

First time or initial passwords also are a consideration as mentioned previously. Account administration and the person handing the account and password to the user for the first time may be able to know what the account and password are. The first use of the system or application should force the user to pick their own password based on guidance given in policy or through automated password strength checking processes that manage the quality of the password. By the same measure, initial passwords should be unique in some way to keep unused accounts from being stolen and used by unauthorized persons when not activated right away.

Passwords are meant to be kept secret and doing this is harder with complex and long passwords. Users should be given guidance to make acronyms from phrases or sentences in order to clue them into remembering their passwords. You should ensure that the documentation of passwords in anyway is not allowed. Self-adhesive notes found under the keyboard or on a computer monitor can usually be found during an inspection of the work areas and is a cause for concern about the security awareness education levels. Often, user IDs are used for systems interfacing and process accessing that requires an ID and password be presented for a system-to-system communication session. This results in a hard-coded access pair that can easily be stolen and used elsewhere. Users also will attempt to script their log on process at their workstation to facilitate ease of access to the system for themselves. This problem needs close review for the appropriate compensating controls, such as physical ones and password aging, or it should be disallowed altogether (which is even better).

There is no right answer as to how much is enough for password controls. It will depend on the business needs and risk appetite of the business. The better question is, "Are passwords enough of a control for protecting this data?" The problem with passwords is that they are an inherently poor and risky control measure in the first place and many arguments can be made on either side of the password control parameters. Changing passwords frequently is a controversial issue with users and security professionals alike, but it is a control practice that has been widely adopted. In theory, no password can be trusted more than once, because it can be captured and replayed, even if encrypted. Password aging can limit the exposure of a user's password by limiting its life span. Keeping track of recently used passwords and not enabling the user to switch back and forth between two passwords is another way to ensure that the passwords are not traded around and commonly known. Histories of the old passwords need to be maintained and checked against the new passwords in order to control this aspect of password resetting. Some have argued that a good strong password is sufficient control and should not be changed unless the user suspects it has been compromised. Passwords will be around for a long time and the debate will no doubt continue. Your professional opinion will depend on your assessment of the needs versus the controls and your own good judgment.

Strong Authentication

When passwords are not enough of a control to mitigate the identified risks, something stronger is called into action. Strong authentication augments a password with other authentication mechanisms, which are designed to more strongly tie the user's identity in the physical world to their surrogate identification in the logical world. Two or more identity factors can be brought to bear at the time of authentication to increase the assurance that the ID of a user is being used appropriately by that authorized user. These additional factors can include the biometric attributes of the physical person, or something that they possess physically. The buzz phrase is "something you know, something you have, or something you are." Multiple instances of the same factors often is misconstrued as strong authentication and called on to validate a person's identity. Does two separate passwords imply a strong authentication? These passwords are two factors, but they are both knowledge based and weak at best. You will have to decide the answer in your particular situation based on the risks inherent in the processes that are being controlled. Physical tokens that are in the possession of an authorized user include items that plug into the system such as smart cards, dongles, and keys (a physically locked room and a password is two-factor authentication if you can prove good key control). Physical tokens also can include calculator-like processing devices, which compute a return code that is either a response to a challenge or based on a seed or key. This seed or key proves that the token device is unique, that it belongs to the system's control process, and is based on the secret entered by the user, which is held by the identity to whom it was issued.

Evaluation of these systems that manage the multifactor control access to other systems will always include similar tasks, regardless of their style. First, you will want to ensure that all of the authentication factors were issued or registered to the same identity or person through records created at the time of issuance. You will want to answer, "How is this validated and evidenced?" You also should be concerned with the storage and control over the validation system and record archives, because the physical access and controls will need to be sufficient to avoid compromise. Any tokens, cards, and other physical devices used will require inventory control processes that include physically secure distribution and return processes. If the device maintains a configurable secret, then you will want to ensure that these devices are well controlled and managed in a way that no two devices are alike and that spoofing or masquerading is not possible. Biometric authentication factors will cause privacy concerns among users and control over the information gathered about them during the registration process will need to be examined carefully. How the authentication system interfaces with the business process systems that it is making the control decision for also will have to be evaluated for the secure identification of these devices and their relative communications channels and processes. The decision-making process of the authentication system, how it was designed to work, and how it works in practice will need to be understood so that conclusions about the sufficiency of this process to control access can be determined. Naturally, the roles, responsibilities, procedures, maintenance and support, performance and capacity planning, and all of the other standard systems relevant to the control objectives also will need to be considered when ensuring that a controlled and efficient process is being used.

PKI and Digital Signatures

Public Key Infrastructure (PKI) is a framework for managing digital certificates that are issued to users and systems for identification and access control. Digital certificates are small pieces of encrypted code that are created and registered to validate the identity of a user or system to another party through an independent validation by a third party that is presumably independent and acts as an authority in this validation process. The digital certificate is registered to a Certificate Authority (CA) who can vouch for the identity it represents and corroborate your story that you are who you say you are. There are several problems with this scheme and it should not be taken at face value and proof positive of an identity. An IS audit of a PKI system will involve reviewing the CA and the controls and policies they maintain as well as those used internally to the IS organization for managing the keys and their use. There are many examples of the process for a PKI, and these explanations will not be replayed here. Any of the primary vendors, such as VeriSign, will teach you more than you want to know about the subject and the various process flows.

Evaluating a PKI will include all of the standard security and control audit objectives of any access control and transaction processing system. It also will involve the testing of the distribution and management systems for certificates to ensure that they are sound and well-managed processes. Definitions of the policies and of the scope and authority for the certificate management and enforcement processes also must be understood and compared to the actual practices and business needs of the particular application it is serving. The procedures for managing all of these functions and evidence of the controls will be required as well. These are relatively simple processes to review but are relatively involved in terms of the labor and processes required to implement them thoroughly and in a manner that covers all possible user options and issues. Companies that sell PKI solutions will tell you how easy it is to implement this solution, and technically it is relatively easy to put in place. The changes to the business processes are the human behavioral aspects of integrating a certificate into the transaction flow that involves interaction with people processes, which are not trivial issues.

The most important thing, which the vendors will not tell you readily, is that relatively few of these systems are in full productive use in the business world. Reasons for their poor acceptance include the complexity, cost, and administrative overhead involved with successfully deploying and maintaining a PKI. Like the previous review of the physical token discussion, inventory and the control of the certificates will be an important part of this review. One weakness of digital certificates is that if the identification process is poorly performed and managed, then the relative validity of the rest of the process is unstable. Another weakness is that the certificates are accessed by a PIN or password, therefore the strength of the entire process is ultimately tied back to the password (a weak control). Another is that unless an even more complex solution is considered up front, the certificate is installed on a computer workstation or other device. For example, roaming certificates can be installed on a smart card, which can actually be a rather strong solution. However, a certificate resident on a computer only actually identifies the computer, not the user. In addition, like a credit card, the digital certificates must be managed actively. Expired certificates must be revoked and all systems that are expected to accept them must be notified when changes to a certificate's validity occur. Users will find out sooner or later that their certificates have been compromised, lost, or stolen, and they will need to replace them for these reasons as well as for routine expiration. All of this things must be managed in a timely manner in order to protect the processes depending on a certificate's validation. The final point is the need to provide historical proof for the actions validated through the certificates. These certificates require that expired certificates and all of the other categories of the old certificates mentioned previously need to be maintained somewhere and be reproducible, along with certifiable time frames during with they were valid. This is due to the fact that the whole purpose of the certificate is to prove not only before but after the fact that the transaction happened as expected and is recorded so that the owner cannot deny that it occurred. This concept is referred to as non-repudiation.

Non-Repudiation

Non-repudiation seems to be a concept that is unique to the digital world because no physical world, legal agreement equivalency really exists. This concept refers to proving the double negative that you cannot say that you did not do it. In theory, if your transaction has a digital signature that provides non-repudiation associated with it, you could never claim that the transaction did not occur, because it can be proved that it did occur because it was witnessed by the certificate's validation through an independent third-party CA. In the physical world, this concept has never been fully adopted because the requirement for signatures and their use as proof have never been a hard and fast rule in most societies. If a signed transaction is denied, thus violating a contract in the physical world, the legal implications are penalties and recompensation, however, the argument is never about proving whether it actually happened or not. Proving that a digital signature can be tied to the actual physical equivalent of signing a contract has not been established. Furthermore, proving a transaction happened using a PKI model has not been validated by any case law at this time. Proving this transaction occurred would require educating a jury on a very technical subject matter, and it would result in a translation of the issue into the physical world that they could understand and can make decisions about. The many layers of technology and the logical assumptions required in order to follow a proof argument results in this being a tenuous argument at best. Without the promise of proof and non-repudiation, you have to ask why bother going to all of the trouble to begin with? If the objective of the review you are conducting is to ensure that this can be substantiated, you will need to closely follow the transaction flow and look for opportunities for things to go wrong. At the end of the review process, you might be able to conclude that that particular transaction would, in all likelihood be provable in court, but that will not mean that other transactions would or that a jury would accept the argument. It will be very important as a result of this and other concerns with PKI to ask many hard questions up front as to what the purpose and intentions are for the PKI installation and what the business problems are that are to be solved by its implementation. If they are authentication based, your process for review will differ from a review intended to prove protected transmissions through encryption methodologies.

Biometric Access Controls

Biometrics authentication continues to mature, but it is still not readily accepted in commercial production for an audit review. The human parts used to validate identity include face recognition, iris scanning, eye retina geometry scanning, hand geometry scanning, fingerprint mapping and matching, keystroke cadence matching, voice recognition, and probably some sort of body fluid matching, if you look hard enough. The concern over the usefulness of such metrics is related to the matching process of the registered sample pattern to the live person. The system approximates the real specimen, thus error is introduced into the process. Because humans are dynamic in nature, the source biometric changes somewhat over time. A moving target and an approximation of a sample captured at some time in the past force the matching process to accept a certain amount of error in order to be useful at all. False positive acceptance and false negative rejection will need to be measured as part of your evaluation to determine how well the process works and whether the error acceptance ranges introduce unacceptable risk. The initial expectation is that these biometric solutions are used when extraordinary controls are required, so high error rates are less acceptable than they would be under less demanding conditions. On top of that, there will always be some people that the process will just not work for, such as the handicapped, for example. Therefore, alternative processes will need to be present and working as viable alternatives that add to the evaluation and review process as well as to the management and overhead for biometric solutions of the organization. Privacy of the registered information related to the user's biometrics will be a priority for the users and may be an object of your review. Strong physical and logical security measures, along with strict disposal and data sharing criteria, also will need to be examined. Reviewing the controls on the data repository also is required.

You will want to view this authentication device as a potential single point of failure and explore what the contingency plans are for unavailability or the disruption of its process. Look for disaster recovery alternatives if access dependency is placed on this authentication method. The registration process will be interesting to you because it is the point at which the identity is established and linked to the biometric that will be the match for the presented identity going forward. The records of identity registration and any problems encountered during this process also should be reviewed. Attention should be given to the registration process so that the gathered samples have integrity. Evaluation of a biometric authentication process will likely include a review of the practical success of the process in performing the intended function and the acceptance of this method of authentication by the user population at large. Opportunities to circumvent the control and complaints about acceptance or rejection rates of the system should be investigated and reviewed for remediation and follow-up processes along with the related documentation. Change control procedures that protect the established benchmark measurements will lead to a better control process overall and more user satisfaction. All of the other standard IS process review routines related to SDLC, Human Resources, KPIs, and planning, maintenance, and problem management apply here as always.

Network User Access

Evaluation of the controls over network access could mean either control over being able to get on the network as a network user or being able to modify the network as a network administrator. Network device access will be addressed in the discussion of network infrastructure security. The network user access, however, is a base privilege of the application users for some configurations and must be successfully negotiated before the user can gain access to the application servers and other services on the network such as remote access devices, Web services, or printers and file servers. Network user access is controlled by the controls of the network operating system, typically Microsoft NT domain controllers, Microsoft active directory services, or a Novell network operating system, of a similar domain control scheme. Account administration for these accounts will require a basic identity management system that you will usually find tied to the production application account management process. Quite often, email services also will be an attribute of the base access to an IS organization's network infrastructure and the related services it provides. Your assessment of this scenario will follow the review for account administration processes outlined previously. There also may be additional items to review that are unique to the services and privileges available to a network user that are not covered in an application account administration review, which will need to be identified and included in your testing and analysis steps.

Identifying the services that are available to a user is a basic step for assessing the access control of any process, application, or system. Once you have determined what the possible ranges of the permissions are, you will want to identify any natural groupings of these services that are offered to users as a profile. Categorization of these services by their profiles, if possible, will enable you to better understand the next review phase. This next phase is where you match users up to the profiles and determine how the rights to be granted these profiles are decided upon, what job functions deserve which access profiles, and where the special cases and exceptions are. Any access that requires the additional downstream access granularity to be determined before the access can be properly managed on the downstream device or service will warrant an investigation. How this information and the request for it gets passed along in a timely manner to meet the needs of the business making the request for access will need to be investigated. Feedback mechanisms, turnaround time, approval process flows, and record keeping will all be on your short list of control objectives in this assessment.

Information Security Architecture

Information security architecture is a concept that covers all of the security-related items discussed in this chapter tied into a strategy that is cohesive and considerate of all of the risks and controls. Security architecture has to be a consideration that is integrated with the functionality of an infrastructure during all design phases in order for it to best serve the needs of the business and system users. An evaluation of security architecture will include a review of the risk assessment methodology used to baseline the current state and will analyze the best practices for the business against this current state of the assessment to determine any gaps that need addressing. A security architecture that recognizes the business risks and implements countermeasures, processes, and procedures that provides appropriate controls for those risks is what you will be looking for in this assessment. Documentation of the data classifications, sensitive data locations, and inherent risks should be available to show that the architect understands what it is they are trying to protect. Integration of the various solutions for securing the environment that encompass host-based as well as network-based and application-based controls should be found.

A design process should exist that ensures the chosen tools work well together, compliment each others strengths, and compensate for each other's weaknesses, to provide a security in-depth solution that stands up well to the task of providing the level of security and protection required to meet the businesses needs. Enterprise security architecture will separate information into logical network zones to protect the data and to isolate users based on the need to know and the security classification of the data. Because security tends to seek the least common denominator, grouping the servers into zones enables a designer to limit this compromise of security to discreet levels, which can still meet the needs of the business while not watering down the security to unacceptable levels for more sensitive applications. The design will, therefore, focus on the perimeter lines that delineate the break between these zones and ensure that integrity is maintained and the rules for crossing that border in or out are well understood and preserved. Security architecture will provide for standard security services of authentication, authorization, auditing, and intrusion detection as part of this border patrol and will be designed with the best practices, worst case analysis, and the business risks in mind.

Security Plans and Compliance

An excellent benchmark of a good security process is to have security plans defined and documented for each and every system that makes up the total IS organization processing infrastructure. This includes not only infrastructure-like systems and networks but also applications and their interfaces. The security plan for a system or infrastructure provides an overview of the security controls as well as documents the business processes and expected performance and behavior characteristics of the process and its users. It should be the basis for the review and approval of a system's security prior to implementing it into the processing environment. Evaluation of a security plan design and approval process will assess the processes of gathering, documenting, reviewing, and maintaining of all the security plans. It also will include an evaluation of how well these plans cover the actual equipment in place, the extent to which these plans reflect the current configurations, and an inventory match of the systems in the environment to those on record with the security plans. Exceptions will need to be examined for risk exposure and commented on as appropriate.

Security plans should explain the business process and the data quality. These plans should identify all of the people involved in the target system: the systems support organization, the owners, the data stewards, and the user population. Enough information about each person or group should be provided so that they can be identified, their responsibilities and accountabilities clearly documented, and so that they can be contacted and communicated with should the need arise when availability or compromise issues related to this system occurs. Understanding the business purposes of the process that this system supports, who the typical users are, and what other processes may be dependant upon this one will give the operations and security staff a sense of how important the system is when referring to the security plan. It also will tell them what to do when there is a problem related to the proper functioning of this system.

An evaluation will first need to look at the policy requirements for producing and maintaining security plans. This management process should be a required step in the formal implementation of any SDLC methodology. Because systems and processes change over time, part of the change control process also should have a requirement to update and seek renewed approval of the security plan when changes are significant enough to warrant such an action. Substantial security changes, functionality modifications, or changes in support or authorization personnel are some examples where the security plan should be revised and resubmitted. Subsequent procedures will be required on the types of documentation to include in a security plan, possibly through some templates that will guide the plan's author through the process of building and gaining approval for it. In this way, examples can be provided and a standard format can be used, facilitating an easier review and consistent reference of the documentation.

Risk assessments are an important part of understanding the system security needs and the residual risks related to the countermeasures that may be deployed to mitigate unacceptable risks. Evidence of this risk identification process and the subsequent identification of acceptable levels of controls should be a required part of the documentation. Differences between the acceptable level of control and any compromise position taken during the actual implementation of the system covered by the plan also should be noted and approved by the data and systems owners as well as by the security management.

The procedure should require the review and approval of both the security manager and the businesses owner so all are in agreement that the risks and controls are fairly represented both in need and delivery against that need. Templates and procedures for the security plans should require that all controls are documented and explained. This includes management controls, technical controls, and operational controls. Diagrams and explanations should be required that clearly draw the system's boundaries and walk the reader through the transactions and process flow that are performed by the system. Maintenance requirements, such as update histories and processes for a periodic review of the existing security plans, should be provided for as part of the routine maintenance processes of the security plans.

Data used by or passing through this system should be identified and the identification of its security classification should be a requirement for inclusion in the security plan documentation. The owners of that data should be noted and their approval of the security controls in place on this system needs to be evidenced through their concurrence with the plan as part of the documentation. The security plan documentation should be part of the evidence trail that tracks the data flow and ensures that the control of highly classified data is managed as intended by the data owner. Any regulatory restrictions or legal compliance requirements that need to be observed and maintained by this system should be documented, along with proof that the control requirements have been satisfied.

The support for the system and its functional components should be documented, along with the security baseline hardening procedures performed on each of the components and subsets of the systems that make up a single security plan. Guidance on what constitutes a single plan and what needs to be viewed as requiring separate plans should be determined in advance and provided as part of the procedural and authoring guidance documentation. Any external connection points and interfaces should be identified, along with any processing dependencies and expectations for systems upstream and downstream in the overall process. The data type, format, and quality should be noted at each entrance and exit point of the defined system's boundary. This is especially important for dial up and other external connection dependencies.

Systems should be labeled and depicted in the documentation in such a way that the operations staff can walk up to them and place their hands on them according to the documentation provided in the security plan. Naming conventions, equipment layouts, and overall configuration diagrams will help these readers understand what is supposed to be happening and will identify any differences between that and what they are currently observing. This may become necessary should a security breach in progress need the most direct of control measures to be applied, such as pulling the plug.

Security plans are living documents by necessity. As patches get applied and operating parameters change the expected controls, the security plan will need to be updated. Knowing what controls were in place historically at a point in time for a forensic examination, for example, makes a chronological change control record of the plan a required part of the documentation. You should be able to tie all major system upgrades and security changes from your review of the change control process back to the security plan, which ensures that timely updates are occurring to enable the proper reaction and support for the system by the security and operations staff. The processes used for the development, testing, and review of the users' needs may be helpful in understanding the limitations and problems with the system, should they arise in daily operations. Consideration also should be given to including this information in the security plan.

You will want to assess the security plan requirements in the environment you are evaluating against these best practices and use your best judgment to determine whether the gaps found are material in nature or significant enough to warrant comment resulting from your review. However, having good requirements for security and system documentation is only part of the evaluation process. The hardest part of the procedures and documentation for any IS organization is to actually produce the written documents that are required and to maintain them. This takes a diligence and discipline that often is lost in today's short business cycles, rapid design methodologies, and time to market deadline shrinkage. You will want to sample the actual security plans on file and review them for the proper content, authorization, and approvals. Evaluate the content against the standards requirements to determine if they are being built and maintained properly. As mentioned previously, you may want to compare the plan's currency with the change control documentation for the same system to see how well these changes are being updated. Finally, actual security testing of the system and a comparison of the results to the plan documentation may be warranted in high-risk systems or in situations where your objectives require a high level of confidence that this information is being maintained.

The final part of this evaluation will be to reconcile the population of security plans to the population of systems that require them. You may want to identify the process for managing these inventories and reconcile them periodically as a way to ensure that this is an ongoing process to be actively managed.

Review and Accreditation of Systems

In order for an information system to adequately meet the needs of a business, the business' management and data ownership must approve of the system and agree that its implementation is capable of satisfying the needs of the business. This approval is the basis for all action taken on the business' behalf. The business leaders understand their risks, their tolerance to accept risk, and their accountabilities to the clients and stakeholders better than anyone else. They must, therefore, ultimately approve the systems that will be performing functions in support of their business. Before computers, these businesses hired a labor force to produce those same outputs and computations who were responsible to ensure that the output was adequate. Using an information system to perform the same process is no different; the business leaders are still responsible for the quality and quantity of the output. If you hire a poorly qualified subcontractor to produce for you and they do not perform to your customer's expectations, it is your responsibility to address the problem, not your customers. If the computer system you commission to perform a service for your business does not meet the data control expectations of confidentiality, integrity, or availability, the business is accountable for these errors in the eyes of the customer. Any business that relies on a system or third party without doing their homework and approving the process in advance gets what they deserve. These are the root reasons to test and approve system implementations and even changes to existing systems, for that matter. Relying on systems design and operations staff to test and approve a system without any business oversight is akin to letting the fox watch the chicken coop. Testing and accreditation must be performed by a knowledgeable party that represents the business and data owner's interests.

When evaluating this process for the business client, the hardest part may be getting this point about responsibility for testing and approval across to them. They do not understand systems and see the development and systems support staff as the only knowledgeable party in this matter that they know. Certainly, several vendors will insist that others are not qualified to judge their work and test it sufficiently. You should expect to see a validation process in place that will ensure that the design criteria and functional requirements are met for major system deployments and upgrades that are being turned over to production for use. Your evaluation should assess the processes used for this systems testing to ensure that the methodology is sound and that the results are documented fairly to meet the needs, which were set up as qualifying criteria before the testing was conducted.

Security testing is part of that assessment. It should cover basic best practice security controls, along with ensuring that policies and standards are adequately met, regulatory issues are addressed in the design and accounted for in the testing results, and that the testing bears out the quality of controls necessary to meet the needs of the business. Security testing can be very complex and encompass any or all of the security- and control-related issues that are only touched upon in this chapter. All of this will naturally depend on the risk that needs to be protected against, which is another reason why the scope of the testing must be a business management decision.

If the SDLC process used for development identifies the range of security and control risks and the possible mitigants from in the analysis phase, as it should have, your assessment is merely a matter of checking to see that those items were satisfactorily addressed during testing and performing some spot reviews of some of the results in order to validate the process. Security testing may be as involved as performing penetration testing and rigorous attack processes, testing code and configurations to see if they can be compromised. But in a business environment, this is not usually the case. Regardless of the level of testing, which will hopefully be a risk-based decision, there is an absolute need for evidencing the sponsor's approval for the final product so that the risk can appropriately be transferred back to the business accountable for the process.

Host-Based Security

At the server or information system component level, there are lots of security-related efforts required to keep a tight control on the information assets. This area frequently receives support attention from systems administrators who tend to react to operating system choices and their relative usefulness and popularity with religions fervor. However, except for the functional performance nuances such as scalability, interoperability, and applicability to special situations, these hosts can be seen as relatively similar from a risk and control perspective. When evaluating host-based security, you will need to understand the business process that is to be accomplished by the device just as you would for all other review processes you undertake. If you do not know where you are going, you will not know when you have reached your goal. Each host will have primary tasks that was put in place to accomplish, although there may be many functions that a host device is tasked to support and perform. Your evaluation of the operations and maintenance of this host device will be greatly simplified if fewer purposes or services are supported on it.

For every function or task that a host is expected to accommodate, there are certain controls that will govern that transaction or task. Services will be required from this host and the permissions for access, the execution of the process, and the manipulation of the code and data are a natural part of each isolatable process or function. The more functional requirements a server has, the better the chance that one of the processes required services or permission settings will be in direct conflict with the successful mission completion of an adjacent process or task requirement on the same server. Some of this is unavoidable, of course. Some of it also can be isolated through logical partitioning and virtual machine instances. At the operating system and hardware layer, the compromise required to have these processes coexist in harmony may or may not create other sets of issues.

Your evaluation of host-based security controls and processes will involve the identification of each service or process task required of each device or host in the inventory encompassing your review objective's scope. You should understand what services, configuration settings, and access permissions are required by each service and look for a potential conflict of the various processes or services offered on a particular device or conflicting control requirements that result from coexistent services. You then will need to review the configuration settings and services open and permitted on the device and perform a gap analysis compared to a leading practice configuration. You should question any open ports or services running on the devices that are not explicitly needed to perform the business functions being supported. Explore the impact of turning off each unnecessary service and understand what possible needs it may serve or the conflicts that may arise.

Minimum Security Baselines (MSBs)

Setting the services and security settings to the minimum necessary needed to perform the required functionality, along with configuring the device for optimum security control, while still enabling the business functions to operate unimpeded, defines the *minimum security baseline (MSB)* for that device. This baseline setting process will include

- Ensuring that all code is up-to-date and any available security patches for the operating system have been tested and applied with the required business system configuration, providing for the ongoing maintenance of proper security levels

- Ensuring that all unnecessary services are turned off and otherwise disabled, thus minimizing the functionality of the operating system to only the processes required for the applications and functions it is directly supporting

- Resetting any default passwords where possible to avoid opportunities for compromise; restricting guest and anonymous access; and renaming default accounts were possible, to deter use

- Using nonstandard ports to hide easily compromised services and communications where possible

- Using encryption to protect sensitive data at rest and in transit wherever practical

- Turning on the required level of logging and audit trail capturing to evidence any unauthorized activity

- Providing for the routine monitoring and analysis of log and audit information

- Implementing access control restrictions on users and processes that enable only access to data and services necessary to perform the authorized functions by

  - Carefully planning trust relationships and group access

  - Separating user access directories from the operating system and production code libraries where possible

  - Avoiding the use of privileged accounts for most tasks and paying special attention to the protection of administrator or root access accounts and passwords

  - Putting tight control on all critical files and directories

  - Ensuring that the permissions set for ownership and access of all files and directories relates closely to their designed use and the business owner's intended permissions

- Setting password parameters as strongly as possible without impacting users, which include

  - Unsuccessful attempt lockouts

  - Strength requirements for passwords

  - History and reuse of password allowances

  - Parameters for the expiration of passwords

- Setting the default access to everything that is not explicitly necessary to a deny status

- Implementing settings and configuration parameters to meet best practice security recommendations from vendors and security organizations wherever possible, with justification and explanation for situations where they cannot be accommodated

- Establishing sufficient back up and recover procedures and processes to appropriately mitigate the risks, including the creation and maintenance of restore disks to reestablish the hardened operating system instances in a timely manner

- Limiting access to utility functions and operating system services to the minimum administrative and necessary support staff

- Providing for the appropriate physical security control to servers and command consoles access as applicable

- Limiting the ability to boot servers remotely or from a local floppy drive in order to prevent gaining unauthorized control over systems

- Limiting log on banner information and password enumeration during log on.
- Providing warning banners prior to log in to deter unauthorized use
- Providing for adequate and sustained virus protection

You should expect to see this level of documentation provided as a guideline for all administrators to use as a checklist for hardening and installing operating systems with the variations identified for the unique settings and services available to whatever particular operating system that may be installed. Look for evidence that these baseline guidance documents are reviewed periodically and kept up-to-date as this dynamic process changes and as new bugs are identified and new versions of the operating systems become available. Naturally, you also will see proof that these documented practices were actually implemented and validated prior to the introduction of the server into the production environment.

You also will want to investigate the resources and processes used to establish these MSBs and any techniques that are used to validate them as currently installed baselines, by comparing the existing configurations against historic ones and the documented guidelines, to ensure that the deviations are minimal. The administrators should have a process in place to check the baseline security, and when exceptions are found they should be identified and addressed in a timely manner. If no process is in use, you may want to recommend one in your report.

The tools available to perform the identification of the variance from the best practices are used extensively in the IS audit business as well as in the security management space. Many of the popular tools available include Bindview, Kane security analyzer, Symantec Enterprise Security Manager, and PentaSafe's security manager tool, to name only a few. This is a growth industry and like all software competition, the providing vendors leap frog each other in functionality and quality of product all the time. Most large IS audit organizations use one or more of these tools to increase the thoroughness and efficiency of their audit teams in performing a platform security analysis. Without using these tools, looking through all of the files for permission settings on a UNIX instance can be a long and tedious effort. These tools also enable someone without an in-depth knowledge of each and every variation of the operating system to provide a high-level analysis of whether the proper security practices are in place and being followed without a full understanding of each parameter's configuration setting. This is possible because the tools are designed by experts in these fields who built the items to make the job of the IS auditor simplified. However, this is not a substitute for learning these differences or the proper security settings and reasons for their use. These differences merely aide you in identifying the relevant and important ones from a security and control perspective. Before a recommendation for changes can be legitimately made and defended, the IS auditor will have to understand the ramifications of making any change. The IS auditor also should be able to articulate the risk-based benefits of adjusting the permissions or settings, compared to the amount of work it will take to change them and maintain them in the new configuration.

Whether tools for assessment and maintenance of MSBs are available or not, you will need to ascertain whether the proper security controls, based on leading practice security baselines, are being deployed on the server's operating system and processing environment or not. Then, you can conclude on the effectiveness of the system's management and security practices. As with any other gap analysis review effort, you first will need to gain agreement on what *should be* found in terms of the proper settings and practices. Only then will you be in a position to explore *what is* in place in order to determine whether the previously agreed upon benchmark situation is indeed in practice. To perform a gap analysis against your own ideas of what the MSB is would imply that you know more about the business and its risks than those charged with performing these functions. This is not a recommended way to facilitate change in an organization. You should spend as much time as necessary gaining agreement with the administration and operations management on what the risks and business needs are and how they translate into adequate protection and operations practices before the actual server support and maintenance review is performed. If you do not, the resultant adversarial tension will not result in a better-controlled environment. Any review also should determine the processes for keeping the MSBs in place going forward. Change control processes are an ideal place to look for opportunities for ensuring that as changes are made, checks are performed to ensure that any established MSBs are kept at acceptable levels. Keeping the MSBs in place should be part of the testing and turnover process. As with any process with a life cycle, a review of the existing baselines also should be periodically performed to tune up the expectations and validate that they continue to reflect the security and leading practice needs of the business processes risk tolerance.

Host-Based Intrusion Detection

Intrusion detection can be managed on the host or network level. Unlike network intrusion detection, which analyzes traffic patterns in transmission, host-based intrusion identification and notification looks only at transactions and events that occur on a particular device on the network. This is typically accomplished by an agent piece of software, resident on the device, reviewing the logs on the device and comparing the information to either attack signatures in a pattern-matching detective mode, or against allowable access control lists and expected behavior permissions in a more proactive approach. Results of these comparisons can be communicated back to a command console where logging and notification to the administrator takes place, or the information may be fed to log accumulation server and the comparisons may take place at this central location. Typically, the source of the signatures or rules is centrally managed so that the changes and updates can be pushed from a central location out to the various agents. Logs must be actively managed to ensure they are a viable and reliable source of information to compare and draw conclusions from. This log integrity process also includes the archiving and purging of log files, so they do not become too large and impact the system. They are, however, preserved for evidence should further analysis be necessary.

Your review of host-based intrusion detection (HID) will determine the efficiency and effectiveness of the intrusion and response processes by following these steps. First, you must gain an understanding of the rationale for using host-based detection methods instead of the more broadly applicable network intrusion detection methods. You would expect to see a risk-based analysis, which resulted in a determination that the host-based methods were necessary to ensure this particular server or device, were protected sufficiently as opposed to a network-wide perspective of attack. Host-based intrusion can be deployed on each server on the network, but unless all of the servers use and purposes are very similar, the traffic patterns and risks will be different for each device to which HID is applied. Either the effectiveness of the host-based intrusion solution will be designed to identify common activities on all devices, thereby limiting its usefulness to the least common denominator, or there will be a customization effort required for each and every host agent, and the analysis and maintenance will be complicated and involved. Reaction to attacks will need to be tailored to the individual signature matches to fully realize the benefit of this approach.

Once you understand the purpose and goals to be achieved by the deployment of HID processes, you can focus on understanding what devices this applies to on the network. In addition, you will want to ensure that all of the devices that meet the criteria for protection and control, identified in the first step, are being protected in this manner. Methods for identifying new devices that require the HID protection and assessing gradual changes to existing devices to ensure that as the needs change, the HID deployment is periodically revalidated, also will be part of your review.

In addition, you also will need to gain an understanding of the mechanics behind this protection scheme. What the detection signatures or rules look like and how well will they serve the purpose of identifying the violations or events that are significant, when they occur, will need to be determined. Any potential control weaknesses that might exist, which prevent the identification of target events or sequences of events from happening or that might diminish the effectiveness of the identification process, if not addressed, will need to be identified. How the rules and signatures are made available to the agents for the comparison process will need to be understood and reviewed for any control weaknesses. How the individual rules are differentiated so that different servers are watching for unique events will need to be determined. You must assess whether this scheme is designed to give the expected results, based on your understanding of the goals and efforts made to meet those goals. Review any evidence available that substantiates that this detection process control is in place and working properly.

When reviewing the rules used for flagging events and actions, you first need to determine what events are required to be identified and why they will warrant notification if they do occur. There are many routine events that may be worthy of being monitored in this manner. Unsuccessful log in attempts, access to critical files, modification to operating systems files, and access to data through nonstandard methods are all examples of rules that could be set up for a match with the event logs. You then should determine why these events cannot be prevented by a more direct control method if the events are after the fact transgressions of the rules. The rules base also should be reviewed for overly complex scenarios and those for which the risks do not warrant this level of control. Part of the IS audit function is to comment on over control as well under control. It does not happen very often, but an opportunity to recommend reducing controls to match the business risk tolerance may help save the company money and provide a value-added service that is seen as a positive event from an IS audit report, which is always a welcome change. Host-based intrusion detection systems need to look at each log entry as they occur, and as a result these systems consume a large amount of CPU cycles in the process. Any unnecessary review activity will impact the processing capabilities without much benefit and should therefore be limited for efficiencies sake.

Part of the review of the signatures or rules will be to determine what the resultant action will be when there is a match to the rule. What happens when there is a trigger event? Who is notified or are there automatic procedures that are triggered to take place? What are the security implications of the scripted process taking off? How the notification process is carried out and what fallback or escalation processes should be initiated if this initial notification fails are all issues that will need to be evaluated. Reviewing the evidence from past situations where this has occurred and determining how well the process served the needs will be part of your evaluation. Identify how this reporting process integrates with other detection and response processes, especially the security incident response process.

Finally, you will need to determine how the maintenance and upkeep of these systems ensures that they remain effective tools for identifying intrusion on an ongoing basis. Intrusion detection systems take a lot of tuning and the weeding out of false positives and negatives to finally narrow the output into a useable set of information to take on action. This action then must be a reliable and integral part of the overall monitoring and response process to get the full effect of these trigger mechanisms' usefulness in controlling security in the IS organization. Without monitoring and response that is acted upon in a timely basis, there is not a lot of real control that an HID system actually provides.

Desktop Controls

When evaluating the desktop controls, you will look to see just what the user is allowed to do and compare it to their needs and the associated business risks whose permissions may present. Several of these issues were discussed previously. Access to removable disk drives can damage an organization in two ways. On one hand, data that is confidential or sensitive to the business or IS organization can be copied and removed from the premises using the ability to access removable disks or to burn CDs. On the other hand, viruses and nonlicensed software as well as games, screen savers, and applications, which will disrupt not only personal productivity but cause problems for systems and desktop performance issues, can come from the users by way of removable media drives on the workstation. Another review point for user access is the connection to the Internet. Downloading from the Internet has dangers like those described with removable drives, except they can happen a lot more quickly and do a lot more damage because they can be masked easily by the user. Innocent acknowledgement of a screen update by clicking an OK button can enable a Distributed Denial of Service (DDOS) bot program to be installed on the desktop, making it an unwilling accomplice to coordinated attacks against unsuspecting devices half-way around the world. Just getting access to certain services and processes from the desktop may be risky if the user does not have a need to know or if access from the location of this particular desktop could lead to exposure of very sensitive information.

All of these items, along with making sure that those desktop configurations are built for the needs of the end user's business function, will be evaluated when you are reviewing the desktop controls that are in place. Too many things going on at the desktop presentation layer can slow down the user's experience to the point where work cannot be performed at all. If there is not enough access on a worker's desktop to the programs and icon they need to perform the job, they cannot fulfill their mission. Decisions about letting users install software on their own desktops will need to be weighed against the risks of doing so and the potential impact to the system and those around them. There will always be power users and important people who will insist on extended capability. The monitoring and management of these permissions needs to be tracked and documented to be most effective. Assurance that virus protection and other standard minimum controls are not circumvented will need to be evaluated in order to conclude that the risks are properly managed when it comes to controlling desktop views and content on the PC.

Evaluating Network Infrastructure Security

As mentioned previously in the section covering the audit and review of network infrastructure in the previous chapter, you will need to understand the network configurations and their intended purposes in order to effectively review a network from a security control perspective. If the assessment has the objective of network device access, the process will be quite different. Your review, in this case, will start with an assessment of the network devices and the control capabilities of these devices. Routers, switches, hubs, and access points such as VPN concentrators, radius dial up servers, firewalls, and proxy devices may all be on the list of components you will want to inventory and analyze for control capability. Physical access security will be very important for this review as well and is discussed in detail a little later on in this chapter. Human resource processes for administrators will be a focus for this evaluation, because administrators have a very powerful set of access permissions and can cause catastrophic, system-wide problems if controls are not in place to manage this access and handle personnel issues such as unfriendly terminations with sensitivity. Many of these devices are not seen as needing account administration processes associated with them, so you will need to understand how access is being managed and controlled. Naturally, you also will want to get a status of the security patching processes employed with each of these devices so you can be assured that the known security vulnerabilities are being addressed in a timely manner. Access cannot be controlled if bypassing the access control is an available means of gaining access.

All access points for each of these devices will need to be identified to assess the overall control environment for the network device access. Modems connected directly to maintenance ports are notorious security control bypass points for which you should look. Understanding the communication protocols and ports used for access into these devices when they are on the network also will give you some insight to how access might be gained and the needs to be controlled. HTTP access for reporting on a network device also may provide opportunities for denial-of-service scenarios because they can be impacted by Web-based attacks inadvertently. The more services permitted on the device, the more avenues of access that are provided, and the more investigation you will need to perform to identify potential weaknesses in the controls. You should determine what kind of account and password schemes are used, who manages them, and what procedures are in place to ensure that the accounts are kept up-to-date and that passwords management is being addressed appropriately. Assess the process for changing passwords when team members leave and other procedures to ensure that only those with a current need for access can do so.

An ideal solution would be an external access control like a token or smart card device that independently validates the credentials for access to the network device. You also should explore the need and use of time of day and day of week control parameters, keeping in mind the need for emergency servicing capabilities. Secure Shell (SSH) or IPSec also may be solutions that provide an encrypted and authenticated access session. Methods to establish encryption tunnels like these should be established prior to the presentation of the credentials to ensure that they remain secret. Once you have determined the existing methods for accessing the devices, a gap analysis can be performed against the criteria of a strong authentication and encrypted transmission of the credentials and service traffic the administrator is providing to the device being reviewed. The relative placement of each of these devices may be a contributing factor in this analysis. Network Address Translation (NAT) may provide some protection by obscuring the device from other access points. An Access Control List (ACL) is a table of permissions maintained by the routers and other similar devices that is used to check permissions when determining whether to permit data transmissions or access to configuration tables, for example. A review of the control parameters defined for controlling the behavior of traffic passing through the network device also may point out certain local services, such as Telnet and TFTP, that could be prohibited to provide additional security to downstream devices.

Each device will have its own unique challenges and limitations. It will be important to make sure that the recommendations you make provide practical approaches to the problems and make sense when viewed in total as a holistic solution for network administration to embrace. Often, compromise must be made for some of the more challenging situations in order to keep the overall solution simple enough that it will be used and is workable in daily operations and does not disrupt the required flow of the information traffic. If not, the network administrators will disable the controls so they can get their work done and serve their customers, leaving this situation in worse shape than when the control review started.

Firewalls

The evaluation of a firewall is meaningless outside of the context of a review of the entire network environment and the overall security architecture. Perimeter definitions and boundary lines as well as the scope and purpose of the firewall will need preliminary information to adequately determine the effectiveness of a firewall as a control mechanism. A firewall can be deployed in several ways and many things can loosely be seen as serving the firewall function. A firewall is a network perimeter gate that has some intelligence associated with it (commonly referred to as a rule set) to enable some network traffic to pass through while denying other traffic access. If you think of a firewall as a gate in a fence, you will see that knowing what the definition of the perimeter is or where the fence line is will be very important to understanding the effectiveness of the firewall or gate in keeping the traffic controlled. This is where the term *backdoor* comes from, referring to alternative access (around the fence and gate) points. The strongest gate in the world is ineffective in keeping control when someone can walk around the fence altogether. You must be able to articulate what needs protection and what all of the access points are in order to assess the security controls properly. This included modems and physical access points as well.

Once you know what you are trying to protect and the line you are trying to defend, you then can move toward understanding what kinds of traffic should be allowed, from who, and under what circumstances (location of origin or source, for example) this kind of access should be permitted. You also may be interested in knowing what you do not want to allow, but it is much better from a security standpoint to just assume that what you do not want to allow, you will just deny by default. This is one of the primary rules of good security practice, "That which is not allowed is denied."

Firewalls can be hardware devices with minimal operating systems pre-built into them called appliances. They also can be servers with a regular operating system installed (and hardened) with firewall software running as the only application on the system. Firewalls can be an application running on a server with a lot of other processes and applications such as the popular personal firewalls might operate on a workstation. Firewalls might be a proxy device, a Virtual Private Network (VPN) concentrator, or a router of various configurations. Firewalls may be configured with high availability in mind and may share the workload with clustered devices to keep the traffic moving. Business continuity requirements may demand that the firewall configuration includes a heartbeat monitor output that is tied to a second fail-over firewall device to ensure that the process remains available in a failure scenario. You will need to understand the business needs very well to determine whether a material control weakness may result from a design that does not include these elements.

The style and configuration of the firewalls also varies a great deal. Packet-filtering firewalls perform a comparison of incoming traffic to a list of allowed protocols, origination points, and destination points, much like a bouncer at an exclusive club. If you are not on the list, then you do not get in. This can be problematic with redirection and protocol changes that can occur throughout the process flow of a connected session. Stateful inspection firewalls remember session information and track their activity maintaining the state as the session changes during its lifetime. Proxies filter and separate requests inbound to them and forward requests going outbound from them, thereby segregating the connection from going all the way through the network to the next network layer. Some firewalls are configured with two network cards in a dual-homed configuration, presenting themselves as a crossover point between two sets of network addresses. Some systems utilize Network Address Translation (or NATing) to create unpublished IP addresses that are hidden from the Internet and secured through obscurity.

All of these techniques and configuration schemes may play a role in your evaluation of the firewall and its configuration on the network, but you will need to understand the control objectives to determine whether the existing scheme works or whether there may be a better approach. Design planning and related documentation may be your biggest concern when it comes to firewall reviews. What decisions were made and why will be important questions that should be supported with good risk analysis and business owner input to ensure that it adequately meets the needs and represents the control requirements from a business perspective. For example, it may be better to respond to an attempted access with a disconnect rather that just simply dropping the packet, if the goal is to deter access attempts rather than hide the firewall through a no response reaction to attempts to ping it. The decision to log information that was dropped or rejected may need to include its usefulness for intrusion detection analysis, if that is part of the objective of the firewall deployment. Other devices may be doing that job or otherwise covering that risk already. It all depends on what set of tasks the firewall is put in place to accomplish.

Walking access and connection scenarios through the firewall and related DMZ or network security layers will help you understand any pitfalls or vulnerabilities in the existing configurations. Understanding the limitations and security MSBs of the device being used as the firewall also will be valid testing steps to perform. An appliance will not have the vulnerabilities and security patching needs of a firewall dependant on a regular operating system and associated hardware. A software firewall will have the potential of being violated or circumvented by other software that also resides on the same server that it is meant to protect. Anytime software other than the minimum necessary to perform the firewall services resides on a firewall device, compromise is a potential danger. Baselining tools, such as Tripwire, can be effective for monitoring the integrity of the system, but it will add a layer of complexity and need for management as well.

You will want to run through several "what if" scenarios with the firewall design and administration team to understand how the failure and recovery processes work. Check to see if the planned sequence of events has been tested or if they are theoretical only. An important risk-based business decision will be deciding what state the process will fail in. Failing in an open state effectively leaves the door open with no protection, which is good for getting traffic through, and bad for security control. Failing in a safe or closed position effectively closes the gate and does not allow any traffic to pass, which is good for security but no business passes. Different types of traffic and business scenarios will need to be evaluated to ensure that both the business and security needs are being met by the firewall configuration and rule set. It is important to note that a firewall steps through the rule set it uses to control traffic from top to bottom looking for a matching condition to make a determination, and then it moves on to the next packet. For this reason, the relative order of the rules in the rule set can affect the firewall's behavior. Just because a rule exists does not necessarily mean it is ever acted upon. You should always make sure that the firewall has a clean up rule at the bottom of the list to ensure that every-thing that has not been approved is denied.

Blocking traffic on both directions with the firewall is a necessary pro-tection measure for ensuring the integrity of the boundary. It is just as important that access to a less secure zone on the network is appropriately restricted from the more secure zone as that access to more secure areas is protected from the lesser one. If an Internet firewall is the target of your review, you will want to ensure that attacks cannot be launched from inside the network because of liability and that nefarious server-sharing is not set up for the rest of the world to enjoy from the organization's site internally as well. In addition, you also may want to investigate the proac-tive identification of expected protocols and services at destination addresses and ports as an additional measure to ensure that access is con-trolled adequately. Opening up port 80 to a Web server may seem like the expected thing to do, but if someone uses it to access the network by using FTP protocols, this opening will result in unnecessary exposure. You must keep in mind that the decisions about how much checking and how spe-cific the rule set should be need to be risk-based because all security deci-sions involve a trade-off with convenience. In this case, more specific traffic checking will be more of a burden on the firewall and may degrade its per-formance. You also will need to check the placement and subsequent per-formance of the rule set to insure the expected outcomes.

Testing and checking the performance are the best practice elements of firewall change control procedures as well, along with well-documented back off plans should those changes not work out. Fixing one problem but creating impact in two other areas as a result is a common occurrence with firewall changes. The more complex the rule set gets, the more difficult it will be to manage this issue. Firewall purists like to see the minimum num-ber of rules possible for this reason. Again, a compromise may be involved to achieve this goal. Rules can be combined to simplify the processing of the rule set and improve performance. But now, source, destination, protocol, and service in Scenario "A" share the permissions of the source, destination, protocol, and service for Scenario "B." Expect to see more opportunities to find risk-based analysis and business-considered decision-making processes that are carefully considered and fully documented as part of your review.

You also will want to assess how the clean up and revalidation of the rule sets is managed on a firewall because they tend to expand and creep over time. Periodic reviews to determine an active need for the existing rules is an ongoing effort that you should find in progress. This process should include the identification of contacts and data owners or stewards who can speak of the continued need for holes in the firewall defense. You also may find testing and probing of the firewall from both directions by the security group to be a process that is in place. This process determines the weaknesses that may be overlooked or identifies the general state of the servers that can now be "seen" from the less secure network zone. Classic problem tracking and reporting processes should accompany this process, along with the active participation of the business and application support staff sponsoring these access holes.

As you can see, a firewall is a piece of the network security puzzle that does not tell any kind of security story by itself. Your conclusions and reporting about the firewall sufficiency must be put in context with the overall security architecture, the goals and objective of the protection, and the organization's risk-based needs. Some compromises knowingly made that relate to the firewall security and its configuration may well be mitigated at another layer of the security plan, using defense in depth. Do not get trapped into expecting perfect security and assuming that unless all opportunities for security are acted upon, weakness will result. Day-to-day operations and the relative difficulty of affecting a control point at one layer of the defense rather than another may have a perfectly logical and actually better rationale than you would find by looking at a firewall or any other security device or subsystem in isolation. Always step back and look at the big picture when you are formulating your report and ask yourself, "So what?" Make sure the weaknesses that you have identified are truly material and that the recommendations you are considering will really add value before approaching management with them.

Demilitarized Zones (DMZs)

The audit evaluation of a Demilitarized Zone (DMZ) will be another part of the overall assessment of the network security infrastructure. DMZs are intended to be neutral zones between two network layers (Network Segment A and Network Segment B) to facilitate the transition of information from one level to the other in a safe, controlled manner. Generally, devices that reside in this middle zone are considered to be vulnerable and untrustworthy from the more secure security layer's perspective. A DMZ is logically separated from Segments A and B by one or more firewalls. In a single firewall configuration, the network segment designated as the DMZ is connected to the firewall and isolated from A and B by addressing and the rule set on the firewall. This firewall is potentially a single point of failure and compromise and can affect performance in this configuration, which can provide an economical solution, however. In a two-firewall configuration, each separate firewall has a different rule set and recognizes the devices sitting in the DMZ between them. Ideally, no data passes directly from the firewall-separating Segment A from the DMZ through the firewall separating the DMZ from Segment B.

The devices in the DMZ are designed to be endpoints of a communication flow such that transactions cannot cross completely through the firewall-DMZ-firewall configuration. Firewall B trusts the devices in the DMZ but not Segment A. The devices in the DMZ are dual homed, equipped with two sets of Network Interface Cards (NICs). The one side does not even know about the other side, thus making it impossible to "see" through to the other side unless the device in the DMZ is compromised. Dropping off files or requests for information in a DMZ for pick up or handling from the other side is primarily how the process is designed to function.

Your evaluation of the DMZ and related devices will include an assessment of the firewall(s) to fully understand the rule sets and trust relationships that exist between the various network segments and devices. Any scenarios that provide a complete pass through will be a concern that needs more explanation. You will want to investigate each device that resides in the DMZ to understand its purpose and configuration. Hardening will be critical for these devices, and the baselining software, which notifies the operations support staff when unauthorized changes occur, will be a best practice you should expect to see deployed. Any services not explicitly needed should be turned off.

Reporting and support processes often require a compromise that leads to difficulty in DMZ device design and security. Physically plugging a workstation into these devices to maintain them is the most secure method of support and ensures that remote changes cannot be made. This requires some additional considerations for troubleshooting and off-hours support, however. NAT will probably be used to hide address ranges from the other zones. You will want to investigate how DNS servers are configured to manage name resolution, what extent this information can be queried from the different zones, and what kind of security intelligence might be available to compromise the security controls.

You should assume that any device in the DMZ will be compromised at some point. Look at the application and information recovery plans with this perspective in mind. How will defaced Web pages and compromised DNS servers be recognized and reloaded? What kind of alternative processes will the business rely on while these servers are being rebuilt and unavailable due to a virus contamination, for example? What checks are in place to periodically validate the integrity of the code that resides on servers in the DMZ? How do change control practices ensure that the access to and integrity of server software is addressed in a controlled and secure manner?

Application and business logic exposure to these devices should be kept to a minimum because of the opportunity for compromise. Look at the transaction flow and determine whether the business logic is at risk by exposure to processes coming from the DMZ devices. If encryption and decryption are part of the process schema, where does this occur along the transaction path and is there exposed, unencrypted information on some segments of the network that are not protected by the firewall separation from the untrusted zones? If encryption accelerators are used to speed up the encryption/decryption process, make sure that they are configured properly, maintained securely, and do not introduce additional risk points to the secure network. If the encrypted data is passed through to the next network layer, are there potential opportunities for compromise from the pass through of the multiple layers of protection? Or, does the information get handed off to a secondary process that isolates requests from being made directly to the network zone where the protected data is stored? If the DMZ is a point of authentication and access control, you will need to understand how the ACLs and identity information is protected and what processes are used for updating this information without exposing it to compromise. Most requests for information from users, even after they are authenticated, are separated from the process directly accessing the data stores using a reverse proxy in the secure processes.

Proxies

Proxies are among the devices that typically reside in a DMZ and are used to separate user access needs from that actual data retrieval process. A proxy is a type of firewall that only enables certain traffic to be recognized. Forward proxying is a process where the user, sitting inside the secure network, accesses the services on the untrusted Internet by using the proxy server as their surrogate and making the request for them. They are protected from the untrustworthy network segment through this isolation—their address is not part of the actual request for service made to the provider. From the service provider on the Internet, for example, all they know about the requestor is the proxy device and its address. Control logic within the proxy can be alert to the type of traffic and the expected response to further protect it and the users it is proxy from any unwanted packets and payloads.

Reverse proxies separate inbound requests and users from directly reaching the protected zone of the IS organization's network. A hand off occurs and the proxy makes the request to the business logic layer and retrieves the response on the requestor's behalf. Control logic can again be used to ensure that the user is identified and meets the predetermined business criteria for getting the results for which they are authorized.

Evaluation of the controls and objectives of a proxy implementation will be straightforward. Once you know the process of the business, you will be able to understand the data controls that are to be implemented with the proxy and be able to review the proxy configuration to get a firsthand look at how the design is intended to secure the transactions and to separate the users from the requested services. You must assess whether the process works as designed and how well the design mitigates the risks that it has been put in place to control. Look around the DMZ for potential ways to get through to the secured inside service or to bypass the outgoing controls. The difficult part of the proxy's deployment is managing the effect that changes in general will have on the success of the transaction flow in maintaining the separation and transaction flow controls that worked well when the proxy was first deployed. As the processes mature and functionality changes, the control requirements will need to be constantly reviewed to ensure they remain in place and are tested each time changes are made to any part of the process that might affect the security of the end-to-end transaction. Software updates and patches also will affect the security and operability of the proxy schemes, which can easily become complex and difficult to troubleshoot when many hops and processes not completely in the designers control are involved.

Evaluating Encryption Techniques

Encryption is the process of scrambling information with a seed code segment and unscrambling the mess at the other end by using the same seed in reverse, in the simplest terms. It is used to protect information from being viewed, even when access is permitted or in cases where access controls cannot be properly applied, such as when data traverses the Internet, for example. This technique can be used to protect information while still enabling it to be transported and stored by others without compromising its confidentiality. The decision to encrypt information should be made based on a need, which is identified through a risk analysis and threat and vulnerability assessment. Once a determination is made to protect information through encryption during its life cycle, the solution must be persistent wherever the information's path presents the environmental circumstances where encryption is warranted. Two primary encryption scenarios exist: protecting the data in transit and protecting it at rest. Let's talk about information at rest first.

Information at rest is most often in need of protection through encryption while it is being stored on a portable storage media. If the media cannot be moved and is physically secure, other controls should be sufficient to protect its confidentiality, namely the physical and logical access controls within the IS organization's environment. The only exception to this may be if a decision is made not to trust the administration or operations staff who have access to information, as is the case in password files, personnel and payroll data, or in national security matters, perhaps. Removable media may be transported by a courier or shipping service, however, and this media needs to be protected while in transit, much like the electronic transmission over an untrusted path would be. Other examples for portable media storage devices, which are by far the highest risk and most often exploited, are personal devices such as laptop computers, PDAs, and digital assistant types of devices. These devices are often used by executives, house very sensitive information, are prone to being left behind or stolen, and are protected by people who, let's face it, are not at the top of the security awareness food chain. Getting these leaders to change their habits is often difficult and encryption is complex and foreign to most of them. These areas are where information at rest needs to be encrypted to appropriately protect it, nonetheless. Protection at this level, if it is used appropriately, will ensure that the information is unusable if it falls into the wrong hands. You will want to check policies and standards related to encryption and its applicability to certain use cases in the organization and then sample some of those cases to see if the policies are effective.

As with transmission encryption, there is an ongoing debate about what level of encryption is strong enough. This was highlighted by the U.S. government's decisions, which were recently lifted, to treat 128-bit encryption as munitions and ban its export from the country. Some experts with massively parallel equipment have cracked 128-bit encryption and have set the bar even higher. The reality is that most petty thieves and opportunists would not know 40-bit from 128-bit encryption and would reformat the hard drive and sell it for pocket money. Those who would try to attack the system for the data in this manner would not have to try as hard and would attack the IS organization's infrastructure using social engineering techniques instead. It is much easier to get the data that way and a lot less work. The bottom line is that there needs to be a realistic risk assessment associated with a decision to add the burden of encryption to any process and the end has to justify the means. Password protection on Microsoft Word or Excel can be easily broken by anyone who knows how, but it effectively deters casual snooping and may be a sufficient control, depending on the risk exposure. The risk assessment process includes reviewing the threat, the opportunity, and motive, and the amount of time exposed, as well as the probability that the event will occur. Encryption is not being downplayed, however, this chapter is only suggesting that the need should be realistically assessed. If encryption is so difficult that the executive holding the laptop writes the key on a yellow sticky inside the device, what has effectively been protected?

Encryption during the transmission of data is further complicated by the fact that the sending and receiving ends of the "encrypted pipe" need to know the same secret in order to encrypt and decrypt the data flowing between them. The fact that the line between these ends is untrustworthy (or encryption would not be necessary) means that exchanging this secret must be handled either through some other trusted path or be encrypted itself. The larger the key or secret, the stronger the protection can be but the more computationally intensive the process is to process the data. The better the chance that the key is only known by the sender and receiver and the shorter its life cycle is, the less need there is for strong encryption solutions.

Encryption that is present machine to machine is used extensively on the Internet to maintain trust and confidentiality between two locations. There is not much to evaluating an SSL process because of the standard nature of the process. Unless the systems have been compromised and tampered with, a session is negotiated and the port for the traffic is moved to the secure channel and the two servers go about their business using the negotiated key. Digital certificates and certificate authorities are used to pass keys around in a public key-private key exchange scenario, which is a relatively standard process. For example, you may be interested in the validation and storage processes, but only if they are unique or different than normal for a Web server.

Virtual Private Networks (VPNs)

A Virtual Private Network (VPN) is an encryption technology that is receiving a lot of attention as a network security solution. It is a good way of establishing an encryption tunnel between a client and a gateway or a concentrator server, thus enabling traffic to pass over an untrustworthy network such as the Internet. Unlike SSL, which is session specific, these encryption tunnels are established by point to point and all traffic across the communication link is encrypted. Ideal for remote connections to a trusted network segment, VPNs give the end user the freedom to perform many functions securely through the established tunnel. This tunnel is established by authenticating and key negotiation like most encryption processes, and it can be set up to operate in a single tunnel or split tunnel modes. The client's software must be distributed and installed before the tunnel can be established. This requirement can present some logistics problems and user training issues, but it also acts as a control to keep the access limited to those knowledgeable about the process.

The split tunnel mode enables the end user to maintain a second access path or tunnel to the Internet while securing select traffic to the host gateway via a second albeit encrypted link across the Internet as well. The danger here is that the workstation can now act as a relay between the host and the Internet, which provides an opportunity for violating their trust, and it also can act as a source of attack should the workstation become compromised. This configuration should be discouraged during connections to a secure network from a workstation whose security controls cannot be guaranteed. For the same reasons, it is very important to have a strong policy and requirements for the quality of the controls over any connecting workstation on the client end of a VPN. Connecting to a network through a VPN makes the client device virtually an extension of the host network. Because the security of any network is only as strong as its weakest link, due diligence must be shown to ensure that this client does not become a source of compromise or weakened security. Personal firewalls and virus protection that scan all incoming files and is maintained in an up-to-date status are a minimum set of controls that should be required and validated as operational when establishing the connection.

Authentication schemes also will be part of the review of VPNs from an IS controls perspective. The simplest solution is to provide the client software and to include a shared key for authenticating back to the gateway device. Not only is this a poor security control solution, but when users leave or terminate their relationship a new shared key must be issued to reestablish access that is limited to those with a need to know. Strong authentication through a token or smart card reader is ideal for establishing a trusted outpost of the secure network, but an administrative effort is required to maintain the additional account aspects. Ensuring that the client device is well controlled may be problematic due to the remoteness of the device and potential ownership or legal aspects of the controlling external devices. Trust and confidentiality agreements signed by the end user are a good control to use for placing the responsibility of client end controls on them and for assuring that the accountability is defined up front and known to all parties involved. As long as the VPN product set is a commercially viable tool and it is deployed with the proper testing and security accreditation processes in place, there should be little concern as to how the encryption process actually works and maintains the transmission's security.

There is a lot of academic information to review about how encryption works and about "Bob" and "Alice" trading keys and information back and forth, but you will be more interested in the administration of the process and the procedures used to ensure its integrity in an IS audit. Technical purists will disagree with this book here, but the human side of the process is always the weakest link and encryption schemes quickly become exposed by the human element of the processes involved. Human nature and forgetfulness are usually the highest risk factors and processes need to be built to compensate for human behavior. Knowing how the keys are exchanged, what process keeps them safe, how the keys are synchronized, and what process expires these keys when they are lost or stolen is far more important than how long it would take to break a 112-bit key in a brute force hardware attack if you threw 10 million dollars at the problem (10^{12} years, est.). You will obviously be looking to ensure that the encryption algorithm is a commercially viable and reputable one and not home grown and untested. However, whether it is triple DES or Twofish will not make a whole lot of difference, unless there are compatibility issues to consider. More important will be the basic blocking and tackling of IS organizational processes and controls to deploy and protect the process through good change control and access controls accompanied by well-documented procedures, standards, and policies to back them up. That, in one sentence, is the essence of the successful IS audit evaluations you will perform.

To summarize your evaluation of encryption efforts, compile a list of needs that drive the encryption process. You should determine what scheme is used and understand the way it works and its relative administration processes. Look for policies, standards, and procedures that support the process. Do not forget about the education and training for users and support staff. Review the existing processes to ensure they follow the procedures, assuming the procedures are sound and reflect the proper controls and support requirements. Also ensure that processes are in place to cover for the human failures that are bound to happen along the way.

Web Access Controls

Access to Web-based data and files is a complex evaluation that will require a fairly in-depth knowledge of Web servers and networking configurations, along with an understanding of the limitations and workings of the particular Web server software and operating systems being used to provide the services. In the most simplistic terms, you will need to identify the services and data available and the control requirements for each of them, and then ensure that this is indeed the level of control being provided in the live configuration. Because the software often is not designed with security as default criteria, there can be many hidden scenarios for exploiting access that even the designers were not aware of when the software was made available for commercial use. Placement of the Web server and the use of proxies and firewalls to protect them will be part of the overall security review and may impact the access control assessment as well. A Web server with all unnecessary services turned off and administrative privileges limited to only those persons with physical access to the device is still vulnerable to compromise in today's environment. This does not mean that access cannot be evaluated and controlled, but it only reinforces that there is no absolute security.

As with all other reviews, your best place to start is with understanding of the purpose and goals of the business needs for Web access. This should be closely followed by the more traditional review of the hardware and operating system hardening efforts to ensure that defaults are not being used for passwords, all patches are applied or at least being evaluated regularly, and unnecessary services are turned off. This includes coding that may invoke services that introduce vulnerabilities not seen without a close examination of the code. A review of the SDLC methodology employed in the design and implementation of the Web pages and the Web services software package's integration with the operating system will help you understand the overall control perspective carried throughout the implementation effort. Flow diagrams that provide data interaction with the client server transaction flows as information is presented and users get redirected will be important to understanding where the security weaknesses may exist and where the logical controls points for the flow should be. Data classification and the segregation need for more sensitive data access from pubic data access must be determined and documented so that the controls are effectively implemented while providing for maximum accessibility and convenience.

Content Management and Web Access Control

In addition, you also may get involved with evaluating the process that manages access to Web content and the Internet. These are two completely different content management areas: One faces inward and the other faces outward. Content management is the process of ensuring that the users are accessing only the subset of the content that is meant for them if approved for their access. Whether managing content on a Web server to ensure that only those with permission get access or managing intranet access through a surf control tool of some sort, you first will need to determine how the authentication and authorization processes are managed. This most likely involves an account or some identification schema and some way to prove that identity, possibly through the use of a password. Next, you should evaluate this system according to the account administration guidelines outlined previously. You then will need to understand what the options or divisions are for parsing out various accesses to users. No matter what the scenario is to be controlled, there has to be rules by which access control decisions are made. Look at the documentation and determine its adequacy and how easily it can be translated into access rules. If the roles are unclear, access will be unsatisfactory to either the provider or the receiver, and it may all be a matter of misunderstanding.

For Web access control, there will need to be a control mechanism that prevents uncontrolled roaming on the Web server from taking place. Clearly there should be a separation of the operating system and utility code from the business and programming logic and a separation of the user accessible information and content from the rest mentioned here. This is typically managed through file permissions and can be covered by MSBs for Web server installations. The partitioning of the user information and the business logic may be further separated through proxying and firewall isolation onto other servers to further ensure that users or other unauthorized individuals cannot gain access to the business processes. Once again, you will want to see that clearly defined rules are in place, which delineate what needs to be protected and to what level that it should be occurring. This delineation should be based on business risk and be the result of the involvement of the data steward or owner if possible. Review the access decisions and compare them to similar access to data that is not Web based, if possible, to ensure that access rules have been applied and the data is valued consistently. People tend to loose their brains when if comes to Web access for some reason, and they assume the rules are altogether different. Perhaps because of the new form factor and complex and expensive controls required to do it right, there is often a gap in data valuation and control requirements that needs brought to management's attention to throttle back the zeal for instantaneous Web-based access to all data, even when this data is confidential or financial in nature.

Unless a commercial package that manages access control is being used, you will need to determine how the control mechanism is designed to work and evaluate whether it is meeting the need and its design criteria. Good documentation is always a plus when trying to figure out design specifications against actual field use of software and this case is no different. You may want to test a few scenarios to see how well the control actually works and whether any control weaknesses are obvious. Problem logs and user feedback records may help point you in the right direction. If a commercial package is used for control, you will need to research that package to understand its functionality and potential limitations in order to adequately assess whether it is able to meet the needs of the business control demands, and if it is being deployed properly to facilitate that end well.

Surf control is not really a security issue but tends to fall in this category, depending on the management philosophy and how the controls are managed. Outbound access to the Internet, while nice to have, is not critical for many of today's network-connected jobs. Certainly those job functions that depend on the ability to get to the World Wide Web are few. The security issues are, however, productivity and bandwidth utilization issues for the IS organization. While Internet access often is seen as a perk or benefit, it can be costly to the business. The potential for sexually harassing, racially insensitive, or religiously fanatic activity makes Web access a problem for most businesses to manage, while still allowing some leeway to surf the Internet. Thus enters surf controls or 'net nanny products. These tools are filters on outbound activity that can monitor, restrict, log, and even parse out access limited only by the labor the organization is willing to expend on managing the process. Understanding the control criteria may be more of a political exercise for this Web content management than the controlling of an inbound scenario.

Time of day controls, controls over the amount of time spent surfing, and the blocking of sites related to over 70 different categories of subject matter are just a few of the controls that can be used to limit Internet access. Some companies work full time reviewing Web sites and keeping the blocking lists accurate and up-to-date. Some studies indicate that the vast majority of porn site hits and e-shopping occurs during business hours. If you are evaluating an organization's process for controlling these activities, you will want to look into the rules for control as mentioned previously and then how this control is administered. You should look at the sanction policy to ensure that it is being applied fairly and evenly to all employees. Any action to penalize a violator may be legally challenged and if the application of penalties is not administered in a manner that closely follows predefined and well-publicized rules for employees; it may not be defendable. Look into the logging processes and assess the level of evidence that is maintained, how long it is kept, and the physical security controls used to preserve its integrity. Identify how the content restrictions are matched to the user classes or roles. You also may be asked to assess any metrics of productivity or bandwidth consumption both before and after deployment to give management some indication of their return on investment. Besides the liability exposure of unchecked Internet activity, productivity improvements are the main promise of these control providers. Being able to show improvement is a key to getting acceptance for many projects.

Email Security

The use of email security is limited by the need to keep this kind of communication private. It also is constrained by the complexity of the solutions that are available. Being able to turn security on and off, depending on the intended recipient or content of the email, make security an overhead to normal communications that often is just ignored. There can really be no expectation of privacy and confidentiality for standard email because the packets are like postcards that can be read at any point along the path from sender to receiver. In addition, mail servers and transfer agents store and forward mail along the way, thus providing many opportunities for copies to get left behind. Digital certificates can provide some assurance that the email you receive actually originated from the person listed as the originator, but otherwise you really have no assurance that this is the case either.

Your evaluation of email security will entail a detailed definition of scope in order to limit the review to those things that are classified as needing security. Has all email been secured to protect those items that need confidential treatment or is the intention to provide a feature that can be invoked when necessary? If it is incumbent on the sender to determine the quality of the data and to invoke the proper set of controls as necessary, your review also should include an assessment of the training and policy requirements documented about these choices and the related procedures available to the user community. It may be difficult to provide definitive assurance that these data identification and control processes are carried out in all cases without some kind of filter and gate process being applied to outbound email content at a perimeter control point. Unless the need is great enough to warrant the overhead and inconvenience of reviewing all outbound email through a keyword filter that identifies potential misapplication of the security requirements, email will continue to be a medium of information exchange that is difficult to police. Attachments can be restricted and certain types of attachments can be quarantined based on their size or file extension, for example, but outbound text can only be indirectly controlled through user education and awareness.

The use of security labeling and notices is a control often debated in security circles because of its relative weak control properties. Legal precedent has not been firmly established to provide assurance that this method mitigates any risk at all. With the transparency of email and its widespread use in the business environment, it is hard to imagine this changing any time in the near future.

Encryption schemes and methods for accessing mail through Web portals are some of the more common methods of providing security to email today. These encryption schemes build into the popular Web application front ends seamlessly and will protect the payload through the delivery channel path. This does nothing to prevent access at the source and destination ends, however. The portal method provides the capability to use SSL encryption and strong authentication if necessary as controls to viewing email content. Other processes beside the email application then are used to provide the controls. The email content is just a service provided by the Web portal and the review of this method is really a Web access review.

Virus Protection

The evaluation of a virus protection program will consist of two phases: One program focuses on the systems and the other on the users. Damage to computer systems from viral infections is the single largest computer hazard-related cost experienced by businesses today. Cost estimates from the more extensive virus infections such as Sircam and Nimda reached into the billions of dollars worldwide. Viruses, worms, and blended threat contamination techniques move throughout the network based on the exploitation of known holes and vulnerabilities, depending largely upon users who unwittingly help the process along. Human nature is the primary vulnerability that is preyed upon to get the malware to spread and can be expected to continue as an avenue to circumvent otherwise well-designed and implemented system controls for the foreseeable future. Your evaluation will begin with a review of the applicable polices and procedures available to systems management and users as well. There should be policy requiring virus protection on all systems that are capable of hosting this kind of protection. The policy should require that virus protection is kept up to date, and that it remains active at all times and scans all incoming files at a minimum. Workstations should not be able to connect to the network, even (or especially) from remote locations without first enabling virus protection.

A well managed IS organization will standardize on a virus protection package and centrally manage the deployment of the latest code and signature updates. A best practice would be to ensure the protection is installed and active at the time of log in through a checking routine or software push at initial log on. SMS is a tool frequently used for this purpose in a Microsoft shop, but scripting to check, set defaults, and update files can be installed and maintained easily enough. You will want to ensure that the policy is written in a way to sufficiently cover all means of introducing viruses into the network and that it ensures the protection of each opportunity to do so. Common ways that should be addressed by the policy are the downloading of software and files from the Internet, the introduction of viruses from external media and floppy disks, and, of course, through email systems.

Internet access brings with it certain behavioral responsibilities in order to keep a production environment clean of nefarious code. Several ways exist to gain unauthorized access and to destroy or corrupt data and programs as the result of user actions taken on the Internet with unanticipated results associated with them. Connections to chat rooms, clicking on Web pages, and innocently clicking on an "OK" button to make a screen go away that is blocking your view are all potentially actions that can invite viruses and Trojans into your system. Without a screening device that checks all incoming data for known virus signatures (there are over 60,000 as of this writing), exploits that are known and were long ago corrected on other systems can find their way onto your hard disk and spread damage far and wide. The policy you evaluate should notify users of these potential dangers and require them to avoid behavior that puts the systems at risk and to scan all incoming files for known virus signatures. In addition, acceptable use policies also may be a place to look for coverage of this issue.

Any time data can be introduced into a computer system, there is a chance that files other than those intended can come along for the ride. In addition, Trojans, which are code that is imbedded into existing files or camouflaged from users, may be attached to files that are seemingly legitimate and serving the needs of the business or users. New software sent directly from manufacturers has been known to have virus problems associated with it. IS auditors, who by the nature of their job are constantly looking at documentation and files obtained from various outside sources, are particularly susceptible to virus infection and spreading. This is a very precarious position to be in from a reputation standpoint, when you are recommending these controls and are causing the problem at the same time. Some policies may require that all files are scanned, or that they must be cleared centrally. Downloading from diskettes may be prohibited and external drives may be routinely disabled or removed from user workstations. You will need to review the policies and make a judgment call on their sufficiency based upon the environment, culture, and business model in each case. Certainly nothing should be introduced into the production environment without first scanning it for a potential virus signature presence. Part of the security awareness training presented to users should describe the potential for virus problems from diskettes and teach habits of scanning before opening files. Trading programs and games around in the office is frequently the cause of viruses being introduced in this manner.

Email is the primary vehicle for virus migration in the business and operational environments today. There are many technical avenues, but the people problem cannot be overstated. Most companies standardize and centralize email traffic within their network to manage the content as belonging to company business and to control viruses. New email coming into a workstation should always be checked for viruses. However, that is not enough. Email servers and relays can become unwitting accomplices to the spread of infection across the Internet. Even without being compromised directly, they can dutifully take a bad situation and make it worse by doing the job they were designed for without reviewing or questioning activity or content. There should be alerts and checks built into a system to stop the pervasive and rapid spread of a virus by recognizing attempts to send large volumes of email out through a mail server. Additionally, virus protection software should be on all of these servers to scan all mail traversing its cues for virus characteristics. Procedures should be set in place to ensure that the virus alerts are reacted to quickly, signature updates are applied in a timely manner, and the proactive review and blocking of suspicious activity is manned and monitored regularly. Logs should be reviewed for evidence that this is occurring within a reasonable time after the alerts are sent from watchdog organizations. Consideration should be given to blocking known virus-bearing attachments such as VBS scripts and executables.

However, even all of this is not enough to stem the tide of spreading viruses in the email systems. Human behavior is unpredictable and will keep challenging any process put in place to protect it from itself no matter how hard you try. People are naturally curious and want to be helpful when possible. It is therefore very important to educate users on the dangers of opening mail from unknown sources and permitting installs and access to their system by launching programs for which that they cannot validate the quality of the code. Users will need to be constantly reminded not to do things that they would otherwise see as harmless fun. The creators of malicious code depend on that kind of behavior to propagate their wares. Caution and suspicion must be taught and the consequences of letting your guard down must be presented in a manner that drives home the need for thinking twice about opening mail attachments, for example.

You should inspect problem reports and help desk logs for virus-related activity to get a feel for how well the policies and procedures are working in the user community. Finding out how consistently protection is applied and what tools are used to ensure it is a pervasive control that will help you conclude on the protection at hand. Do not introduce viruses to test the controls. Ask about dial in and other external connection points to determine whether any vulnerabilities or situations that are not as well controlled as the primary process flows exist. These back channels are typically where viruses eventually get through because they are not the routine control focus and represent the other 20 percent of the problem that gets less attention. Laptops and other portable devices, which are not always connected to the network, also are primary suspects for introducing a weak link in the virus protection armor. Again, there should be policy and enforcement mechanisms in place to ensure that there is an expectation of virus protection for all applicable devices connected to the network from all of the many possible scenarios or a weakest link will surely result.

Logging and Monitoring

Your evaluation of the IS controls over the infrastructure and its security will necessarily include the logging and monitoring of certain activities for violations of security policy. This assessment begins with an understanding of the policies, which are to be enforced at a level of detail that will enable you to translate the log entries of operating systems and applications into positive or negative compliance event occurrences. All system devices that have the capability to log events should be evaluated for the benefit and need to have their logging features enabled and producing useable log information. The bad news is that logs that are not reviewed and analyzed by humans or automated processes for events are a complete waste of time and effort. Therefore, part of the preliminary understanding you will need in your review of the logging situation is what the expectations are in relation to logging from a practical operations management perspective. It is not uncommon to see the impractical mandate for pervasive logging and monitoring accompanied with the requirement for the daily review of all this information, but little follow-up support to actually make this happen from a labor and time allocation perspective. Realistic expectations and practical applications must be the guiding directives. Before finding fault with the IS organization for not adhering to the requirement, look for opportunities to recommend automated exception-based log analysis tools, where possible, as a value-added recommendation.

Access to the logs needs to be secured by the administrators of the systems, wherever this may be practical or possible. Other control processes, such as exporting the logs to log servers or write-only media formats, are some of the ways this can be done without falling into the circular logic trap of administrative access and root trust issues. Manual procedures and management oversight are other ways to address the risk of logs that are not completely secured from anyone but the objective reviewer function. How the logs are time stamped and evidenced as the original also will be part of your review. Being able to synchronize several logs from different sources may be a necessary part of the logging implementation standards you will expect to see documented so that a correlation of events can occur during forensic examinations across multiple systems. How much information is kept and how long it is maintained are risk-based decisions that should be formally determined and proceduralized for operations to manage their processes against. You should review the actual log retention processes to ensure they meet the requirements that are documented.

Evaluating which systems need to have their activity logged and what portion of the log requires a review may be a reasonable compromise to logging everything and reviewing it in detail. Using risk assessment techniques to determine how much and to what quality the logging should occur in the first place are practical measures that would indicate an honest effort for providing some level of useful log monitoring capability. You will want to review the decision and risk identification process to ensure that the assessment was performed to a satisfactory level of due care. In some cases as mentioned previously, there are macro control points that will alert the operations monitoring function of violations in a sufficient time frame to enable a proper response without extensive monitoring at the micro level for all devices. This involves a rigorous analysis and the design of a comprehensive logging and monitoring solution that will require review and assessment on your part to ensure that the controls are effective in meeting the need.

Your evaluation will involve an assessment of what monitoring is actually taking place and what happens due to the monitoring processes. Responding to out-of-bounds conditions will be a vital part of the logging process, but this does not necessarily mean you have your eyes glued around the clock to a computer monitor. If that requirement does exist, it is best managed by a Security Service Provider (SSP), which manages many customers' needs simultaneously. Not only do the economics of this service make sense, but the expertise and day-to-day exposure to incidents and their responses provide a better all around value to the IS organization. The expertise to recognize log entries as evidence of undesirable behavior on the part of a user or unauthorized person takes a fair amount of skill and is not exciting work. If controls are in place to prevent a situation from occurring, the time spent making sure the control remains viable is probably more productive that that used looking to see if the control stopped working and when.

Each subunit of the IS organization may have unique and special ways of managing their logs and different ideas of what is important to look for when monitoring their systems. Best practice monitoring and logging processes will ensure that a common objective can be supported by these efforts and determine that gaps in coverage are not created by a piecemeal approach to the overall vigilance activity. All monitoring that is not continuous or automatic should be performed with a randomized timing pattern to prevent routines that can be learned and avoided by those trying to circumvent the controls. Metrics showing the results from log monitoring and review activity are a good indicator to show that the process is being performed and to enable management to recognize escalated issues that may appear to be routine to those who overlook them due to repeated exposure to the activities. The roles and responsibilities for logging, reviewing, and archiving logs should be explicit and the related procedures should be as specific as possible to provide predictable outcomes. Job rotation and substitution will not be needed only to maintain the sanity of the reviewers but ensures that collusion opportunities are minimized. Continued education on state of the art threats and countermeasures also will help keep the task interesting and the staff members engaged.

Network Intrusion Detection

Network Intrusion Detection Systems (NIDS) are another way to monitor for unauthorized and disruptive activity on information systems. In NIDS, the network traffic gets scanned and filtered, looking for behaviors that are suspicious or add up to an attack signature, much like virus protection does. More advanced NIDS systems use sophisticated aggregation and analysis processes to show seemingly unrelated activity in different areas as the pattern of a coordinated attack in progress. An evaluation of this monitoring process will involve many familiar steps. Understanding the functional requirements of what you are assessing is the first step of every review you will perform as an IS auditor. In this case, that means knowing what you are monitoring for and what is supposed to happen when it is found.

A classic problem of NIDS deployments is that there are several false positive and false negative alerts that need to be sorted through to make useable sense of the information streaming out to the management console. In-depth knowledge of the expected normal behavior is vital in determining whether the output from the sensors should be ignored or investigated. There will be a need to investigate all activity at least once to determine whether it is a normal occurrence in the business process or evidence of illicit activity. When you review the NIDS implementation, you will want to keep this in mind and see how these issues are investigated and addressed, because new issues will come up a long time after installation is complete and before normal activity baselines can be effectively established. You also should understand the expectations for the system, examine the support and rule sets of the system, and determine whether those expectations are realistic based on the other factors. Many times these systems are oversold as a panacea and under delivered, giving management a justifiable cause for concern about their investments and the ability of network and security groups to protect the data. By its nature this is a detective system, not a preventative one, and it can look only for matches to known attacks and problem scenarios. New situations will not find their way into the signature file until after they have been recognized as undesirable and coded into the database as something to look out for. How quickly new situations are recognized and addressed also will be the subject of your analysis.

In addition, the architecture and configuration also will be of interest because of the way that a NIDS system works. Unlike host-based detection systems, NIDS sits on a wire and looks at passing data in both directions. If the traffic does not pass by, it does not know anything about the packets and therefore sees nothing wrong. For this reason, it is often better to set up several "engines" that feed a central monitoring and response console so that more territory can be covered. Like the old joke where the repair man charges exorbitant rates to adjust one screw and claims the money is justified because he knew which screw to turn, knowing what segments to put the detection engines on is a major success factor for a NIDS implementation. As you review the network and security architecture for the location and relative protection needs of the critical data and systems, you will see natural choke point locations for the placement of these monitoring system engines. One analogy that is easy to identify with is looking at the placement of the monitoring points in the same way you would look at the placement of monitoring cameras in a physical security system. You would probably locate a camera at the front door to see who was knocking. Most likely, you also would put a monitoring camera in the hallway leading to the critical data storage too. While it is a little more complicated than that, you need to understand the predominant traffic patterns to know where is most advantageous for the protection of your systems. This may change as the processes change too, so revisiting this issue periodically would be good practice that you would want to see evidenced.

In addition to all of the classic operational management, problem logging, change control, and process documentation you will review, you should look closely at the way rules are developed and how the triggers are set up to alarm you of problems in progress. As with most evaluations of IS organizations, procedures and responsibilities should be clearly documented and well known to all parties involved. Monitoring may not be addressed around the clock, but the system will need to alert someone when it sees a match on its suspect list, and the network and security people had better be prepared to respond and take action. You should review the process for notification and escalation to determine whether the possible risks exposed by the detection tool are supported with response capabilities commensurate with the potential losses if a response is not timely.

There will be a periodic update file from the vendor that keeps the new hacker attacks as part of the signatures database that the system uses to look for matches. In addition, there also should be customized rules built into the system as well that are unique to the business or situational risks of the particular organization you are evaluating. Reviewing these condition statements and what set of circumstances set off the alerts will help you understand the nature of the risks and other controls that may help mitigate the risks. This is important when considering the placement of the detection devices and other controls that also may be warranted. Rules can be designed to alert when a combination or sequence of events occurs. If it is not understood that the Internet router filters one of these elements out and will never be seen on the interior of the network, for example, the detection system will never flag the condition even if the rest of the evidence is there to act upon. This depends on how the rule is designed, but you can see that these solutions are all highly interrelated with other controls and need to be deployed and maintained as a cohesive system of layered security.

Incident Response

Unfortunately, there is no such thing as perfect security if you want to open the doors for business. Preventative controls will never completely solve the security problems and incidents that are bound to occur. Much like contingency planning, it is a matter of when not if, statistically. The security incident response process is the cornerstone of any complete security program that will be used and refined as the business processes it supports changes, as the tools for gathering evidence and controlling security matures, and as the threat morphs to get around those controls as they exist today. It is a never ending cycle.

When tasked with evaluating an incident response process, you would be well served to look up the latest best practices seen as expert advice in the information security space at the time of the review. This process is maturing rapidly and new threats have expanded the need for forensics and ongoing monitoring a great deal since online access in all its permutations have developed over the last few years. New technologies such as wireless networks bring drive-by network attacks into the realm of reality, which was an unthinkable situation only a few years back.

Some of the expected procedures do not really change, however, and the basic infrastructure will adapt to the current need if it is well established and supported. This process starts at the top of the organization. Senior management must support the activity and provide for the education and training necessary to react quickly in times of need. To adequately determine if the processes in place will meet those needs, you must understand the management requirements from an incident response process by asking some probing questions related to management's expectations. Being prepared to perform a forensic post mortem analysis is a lot different from a support and readiness requirements perspective than pulling the plug on an attack in progress or enabling the businesses to continue operations while minimizing the an attack's effect in real time. Remember the response to incidents is after or during the fact—it is not preventative. The house is already on fire or burned badly by the time this process kicks in. Management will be angry and frustrated so the response needs to be rehearsed and scripted well before it is needed. All of the right people must be identified up front and asked about the extent to which they see their authority, will lend their authority to the process, and will involve themselves directly in some span of the potential scenarios. Role-playing, drills, and mock incidents may seem silly but will help all parties understand their role during a real incident.

The legal department, human resource department, public relation department, business leaders, process owners, data stewards, and operational staff all have vital roles in responding effectively to security incidents. The roles and limits of response will need to be documented and communicated so that everyone is on the same page. Who can say what to the media and how the information will be managed to put the organization in the best light should not be left up to chance or circumstance. Communication with the business clients and other legs of the business will be important to getting the process back on its feet and minimizing disruption. Consideration should be given to tie these processes together with the contingency planning and disaster recovery processes for synergistic opportunities.

The process of incident documentation should look to other problem reporting in the IS organization for ideas on coordination, the reuse of similar services, and providing for common needs. The security of the information related to these problems may be quite different from a hardware failure report and needs to be kept with tighter controls for access to it. Recognizing security events and escalating them to security incidents with the appropriate investigation will be based on knowledge that can only be developed over time and involves a lot of user awareness training, because some security incidents look like harmless process burps by the perpetrator's design. An investigation and follow-up of the unexplained phenomena will be a discipline that will be difficult to measure but should be tracked as part of the follow-up investigation from auditing problem reporting processes. Your evaluation of the documentation and reporting of events should include an assessment of reports and follow-up of the events to ensure that the information was captured and preserved, showing the recovery steps and actions taken for analysis. It also will include a review of what kind of prospective analysis is actually done from the historic information gathered during the security incidents so the IS organization can learn from the mistakes of the past. You should determine what changes are made to the process and procedures because of incident analysis in order to prevent them from happening again in the future and to improve the overall incident response process. Your overall opinion on the incident response will conclude on the design and implementation of the process, how effectively and efficiently it is used, and how well the results of its use is in adding value to the IS organizational process overall.

Security Testing Tools

Information security programs do provide opportunities to be proactive and need to be evaluated as well. Testing security controls and assessing their effectiveness is one way to do this. New vulnerabilities are uncovered all of the time and as they are identified, the staff tasked with responsibility for information security must determine if the new vulnerability applies to their systems. One way to do this is to test the network and systems for the vulnerability with a security-scanning tool. It is better to find out by your own hand than at the hands of an attacker. Scanning the systems and networks for security vulnerabilities also is a good way to catch exposures that have drifted into existence over time, through insufficiently tested changes being applied or through unanticipated downstream results of a change to an indirectly connected system or process.

There are many scanning and vulnerability tools on the market and the quality leapfrogs on the various vendor and shareware tools release by release. You may want to familiarize yourself with these tools and their functionality. They are an excellent way to test security as part of an information security audit and can be used with few concerns of impacting production with the proper planning and approval. Many of these tools are priced based on the IP address range being scanned and you may need to negotiate a special roaming license for audit purposes to enable you to move around with it and not pay a per address fee for using it. Most security tool vendors have deals like this for audit use. Some of the functionality of these tools includes scanning for known and documented security best practices, recommended configurations, password strengths, and vulnerabilities unique to various common operating systems often automatically identified by the tool as it analyses the target IP address.

Many user friendly reporting features will explain the risk of the vulnerability or setting position, show the resource links for further study, and practically write your audit report for you. This would be a big mistake, of course, because the tool does not understand the business rationale for the current situation and may need to be taught what is acceptable from a risk standpoint before the output can make legitimate recommendations for improving on the current situation. Some of these tools even go so far as to provide a button to click that says something innocent and inviting like "fix this now?" A big mistake can be created by choosing this option. If the tool has permissions to do this because it was installed as a root or system administrator process, the results can be catastrophic to the business process that was running fine up to that point in time. Also you should remember that as an IS auditor, your job is to recommend and advise (usually with lots of "I'd do my homework first, if I were you, but. . . " caveats included) and not to directly affect anything that is in place in a system you are evaluating, which is a career limiting move for sure.

Security scanning tools do not identify all of the problems and are not without flaws themselves; they are only tools not definitive proof. You may have to find special tools for each operating system type if they are not standard systems or if the tools for the broader range of operating system scans are unavailable. The use of these scanners as a proactive security tool by the IS organization should be investigated and how the results are measured and reported should be assessed. Ensuring that there is no risk introduced to the operations from this process will be part of your evaluation. Ensuring that the results are further investigated before acting on them also will be a risk mitigation effort you will want to see in place. Policy should be in place to support this effort for the people accountable for security. Scanning the system with a vulnerability scanner should be prohibited in the IS organization otherwise and treated as a security breach. Care should be taken, and permissions formally sought, before using such a tool as part of an audit testing procedure. Your assessment should determine that the tools are in good order and up-to-date, and are being deployed in the right places (see the discussion on NIDS placement) and used by competent and trained personnel. You should evaluate the results of that scanning for accuracy and thoroughness and review the actions taken because of the scanning to ensure that the process is a value-added one to the organization and justifies the effort being expended on it.

This section also has touched on the use of these tools as audit tools. You should be expected to prove the same levels of competency, planning, thoroughness, and careful analysis of results as you would expect to find being deployed by the clients you evaluate if using these tools are part of applying your craft as an IS auditor. Several times, the author has recommended organizations invest in a similar tool and apply it proactively and he has used the opportunity to teach the tool, its use, and its reporting functionality, and the benefits of this proactive approach during the audit process. This approach can lead to a win-win relationship going forward.

Third-Party Connections

An evaluation of the third-party connections to an IS organization's systems and networks involves a review of any external entry point for accessing systems and data, which could mean modems on workstations or access directly into servers. It also may cover a review of networked business partners and the myriad of connection schemes used to exchange files and conduct business electronically. This section will review several of the more popular methods and some of the controls and risks associated with each connection method.

Modem connections are usually the largest risk because they are easy to deploy and can be connected by users and vendors alike. You must determine what policies exist to direct the behavior related to modem connections. Some of this assessment will involve reviewing what the remote connectivity solutions, which are available to employees, are for accessing work from outside the office. Many workers, such as executives, sales staff, information systems support, and company support who work from home arrangements, legitimately need to connect from remote locations on a regular basis. If no centrally managed solution is provided for these employees to securely access the work systems, the network's safety is at the mercy of these users' security awareness behaviors and diligence. Unless tools and training are provided to them and controls are firmly set in place to monitor and enforce the configuration and use of the access tools, security exposures will become a problem.

Without any policy and management direction on modem connections, there will be no effective way to manage the security of these access methods or to review the controls related to them. Policy decisions about how to access from outside the work environment and the network properly will be high on your list of items to gather before your audit evaluation can begin in earnest. Whether the policy direction is to prohibit remote connectivity that occurs outside of a centralized access system or not, you will need to understand the mechanisms that are in place to enforce the decisions and keep unauthorized access from occurring. Modems come as standard equipment built into laptop PCs, for example, and you cannot really ban them altogether. Monitoring and enforcement activities coordinated through phone system processes may be one example of controls that could identify unauthorized access of this kind. Other phone line-related controls should be considered as well, because without a phone line this kind of access cannot occur. Requests for lines to be used for data system connectivity should be approved by the IS security department. Perhaps, phone systems can recognize data transfer, when compared to voice traffic, and can log and report on it for follow-up, control it through access lists, or filter it out like a firewall and deny this type of traffic across those lines.

Strong physical and facility level controls need to be set in place at the same time because a thwarted user might take matters in their own hands and have a phone company install a line and bill it to themselves directly, if nothing prevents them from doing so. You will want to examine the various administrative controls over the phone line requests and installation to ensure these risks are appropriately mitigated. Another scenario to watch for along the same lines is to identify and control the repurposing of fax lines as a network traffic channel for moving data instead of fax traffic. Obviously, there should be rigorous controls over the unattended wall jacks that enable network access from common areas and conference rooms. These jacks should be in a disabled state normally and only activated when necessary and for the duration of need. IP addresses used by these ports should be given special monitoring and tracking attention when in use due to the connection's transient nature.

If modems are permitted to access the network, some guidelines and controls are necessary in order to ensure the connections are securely managed. Incoming target numbers should be changed periodically and communicated to the senders to ensure that other unauthorized parties are not using the connection. Incoming numbers also may be configured to use a dial back mechanism, which draws from a known list of source numbers to ensure that the originators are legitimate connection source locations by reestablishing connection attempts outbound to the expected phone number associated with a trusted location. Other controls to consider are related to authentication. Using domain level verification of identity ensures that users are known to the system. Local authentication with a strong password is a minimum requirement, but it cannot provide assurance of the controls when alterable by the end user. You should expect to see some kind of written agreement on file between the IS organization and the end user, agreeing to manage the security parameters and access controls appropriately, in order to mitigate these risks related to user-managed access. These controls should include strong security measures for the remote device connecting from the other end of the line. Current virus protections, using firewalls for undesirable access based on a predetermined rule set, and limitations of pass through network connections to other networks are a few of the possible parameters that should be documented in this trust agreement. It also should reinforce the need to behave according to the acceptable use policy of the network that they are connecting to as well.

The kind of business and the traffic related to it should be understood by the IS organization for any remote access request so assurances can be made that the access method is appropriate for the data type exchange being requested. Support requirements and data inputs to production systems will be viewed quite differently than an office worker's need to check email and work with office software remotely. This also will be important for business contingency planning purposes, should the connectivity be lost for some reason and the production schedules are impacted as a result. Legitimate business needs and appropriate security controls sum up the requirements for modem access. Many organizations have taken the position to not allow them, in which case the review becomes one of an enforcement of policy and fair and evenhanded sanctioning evidence.

Other kinds of external connections need to be evaluated besides those coming in on the phone lines. Network connections to the IS network from the business partners have the same risk exposures of being used by unauthorized persons, and providing an access path to other networks reduces the security level of the IS organizations network by exposing it to less secure environments. These connections should be known, registered, and controlled similar to the previous discussion. Access control schemes and firewall controls on traffic to ensure that the transfer of data is predictable and authorized will be of primary concern when reviewing these connections. Legal trust agreements of liability, responsibility, and service levels should be set in place and available for the auditor's inspection. Recourse for unavailability, back up requirements, and alternative provisions for doing business are good practice controls that should be evaluated along with the access and security controls of these connections.

Evaluating Security Awareness

Evaluating security awareness involves understanding what the educational requirements are according to a policy and other sources, assessing the delivery mechanisms designed to carry messages to the users, reviewing the tracking and monitoring of the message delivery to ensure that it is being performed, and measuring the effectiveness and feedback processes used to reinvent the process throughout a continual life cycle.

Knowing what the message is that needs to get across to the users will be a two-phase effort. First, you will want to assess what existing policies and regulatory requirements exist that require user participation in order to achieve compliance. This will include basic computer workstation behavior expectations, the identification of different security classes related to data (in all forms), and how the user is expected to treat each data class when they come across it in their daily business routines. This portion of the review should supply you with a comprehensive list of do's and don'ts for users to be educated about. Next, you will want to see a process that divides this data up for the appropriate classes of users so that the message is relevant and particular to each type of user's needs. Here again, you must make a judgment call, but some of the extremely technical detail will not be useful or interesting to average users. In addition, the executive user base may need a different message than the janitorial support staff. Some security awareness material will clearly be applicable to all users no matter what their role is in the organization. Having the right message aimed at the user is a key success factor in achieving security awareness.

The delivery mechanism is another area where the user's needs should be matched to the tools available to best make a successful learning style match. Pamphlets and fliers will help users carry the message to the user's workplace. Lectures and slide presentations may cover several users at once and could provide a live person to which questions and discussion can be directed. Online delivery solutions can provide access at all times and on an individual basis, thus overcoming the scheduling difficulties of lectures and presentations. Contests with prizes and testing can keep interest going long after the initial information is taught. Trinkets and handout gimmicks could provide prominent reminders at the workstation about the importance of good security behavior. All of these mechanisms have pluses and minuses and each have their own place in a well-rounded awareness program. Your review will determine that all options have been considered and are being deployed as appropriate to the situations that best meet the user's needs.

Knowing what has been done to the delivery a security awareness message and who has received that message may be an important part of evidencing the compliance to a requirement or policy to provide security awareness training to the user community. HIPAA, for example, makes security awareness training a requirement in both the privacy and security regulations. Even if tracking the delivery is not required for compliance, it is still a good practice to use for ensuring the effectiveness and response to various program delivery and content combinations provided by the security training group. How the users are tied to the program's delivery may be subjectively estimated or rigorously tracked for each user through formal attendance and competency testing processes. Being able to measure the effectiveness of a particular delivery approach will require that an attendance and subsequent testing process show how well the key concepts are being retained. Reporting and follow-up to ensure complete user population coverage may be a review item, if compliance drives the awareness program. You will want to review who has responsibilities for the various elements of this process and determine how their job performance is measured to conclude on the overall effectiveness of the process.

Measuring the awareness program's effectiveness may be more elusive that you think at first, due to the difficulty in measuring successful knowledge transfer. Having users notify the help desk of suspected security events may indicate that they got the message and might be seen as a useful metric. Running password checking tools and tracking password strength over time may be another. Having testing processes built into the training will give some level of comfort as well, but it will not assess if the issue's terms have been retained longer. Questionnaires and surveys after the fact also are an effective way of gauging success or failure in getting the message across. No matter what metric is used to show the program's success, your task will be to assess the rationale for using this particular set of measurements and to evaluate the measurement's results to ensure that it fairly and accurately represents what it is reporting to management about the program.

Social Engineering

A significant part of security awareness training will be to instill a healthy suspicion about requests to access data and processes where authorization has not obviously been given. Alerting people to the flaw in human nature of trying to be helpful, even if it means bending the rules a little bit, is an important part of assuring that access is limited to only those with a demonstrated need to know. This is often the attack method used to gain sufficient information for exploiting other access points in the systems when hacking attempts are made. Evaluating the prevention, detection, and avoidance of social engineering techniques will involve a review of the educational material related to identifying and recognizing these techniques in progress. Deployment of systems to facilitate the reporting and follow-up of the security events and the users' education on these processes and their use also will be part of your investigation. Each of these efforts will have different components targeted at various user types and support areas where higher access privileges are available and attacks are more often targeted.

Social engineering is the art of using false identity assumptions to gain privileges related to the assumed identity. Playing on the social nature of others, the perpetrator will assume a role or identity and make access requests or attempts based on that assumed role. Policies will need to be reviewed to ensure that guidance and direction are given on these activities and that recourse for attempting them is part of the enforcement process. Some of these policies will relate to physical security, some to IS organization operations procedures, some to human resources processes, and some to help desk procedures. These policies should require that the actions taken by users and support personnel, in situations where information or access requests are made, are responded to in a prescribed manner. Doing so will remove the temptation of the user or personnel to interpret the request in ways that might harm the organization by falling for the hacker's social engineering ploy. A wide range of activities exist that can be considered social engineering:

- Assuming the possession of a device or piece of information physically and walking out with it like it belongs to you
- Phone calls from people claiming to be VIPs, vendors, or support personnel, asking for information that is not publicly available
- Following other people through security doors (called piggy backing) and not providing credentials to a guard or checkpoint system like others do to pass
- Attempts at excuses for the lack of access codes, badges, keys, tokens, and so forth ("I forgot my key, can I borrow yours?")
- Mingling with a crowd and moving past a security checkpoint as part of the crowd, acting as a now part of the group ("Can I bum a smoke?")

- Attempts to gain access to information by dropping names and providing incomplete information, asking open-ended questions with the opportunity for some one to fill in the blank ("I was just asked by the Vice President . . . umm . . . What's his name again? Tall guy, . . . ?")

- Looking over someone's shoulder or on their desk to pick up information that exceeds their privilege levels. Includes shoulder surfing, reading documents off the printer and fax, dumpster diving and trash perusal, mailroom snooping, and so forth

- Trojans and software that tricks users into thinking they are using legitimate tools while the software steals their information. Includes fake front end GUIs, keystroke loggers, surveys and registration gambits, and so forth ("Ever enter a contest on the Internet hoping to win a prize?")

- Identity theft from a number of sources subsequently used to establish credentials and privileges by assuming the identity of another individual. This is the number one crime on the Internet today

While it is difficult to teach people to react differently than they usually would due to human nature—behaving without thinking—it is important to impress upon people the risks of being helpful instead of being mindful of the policy and requirements to protect assets first and being helpful to others for these issues second. Education on the common gambits and resultant losses may stick in their minds, especially when they can see themselves in similar situations. As mentioned previously, a strong policy with strict enforcement may help to serve as a deterrent. Making sure it is easy to report suspected situations without making it threatening for users to do so (possibly through anonymity) will help to promote proactive incident responses to situations about which you have educated them. The awareness training related to social engineering should be reviewed as part of the overall awareness training review. Ensuring that the support staff—especially the phone support personnel—are trained to recognize attempts to gain access in this way and are taught to strictly require all users follow the process that protects them as well as the organizations assets, will be the primary objective of an evaluation related to social engineering controls. Your evaluation of this program will probably not be able to tie results to the effort to put a process in place in a measurable and direct way. However, the concepts of this program needs to be well understood by you, the seasoned IS auditor, because they may be techniques that one may use to test procedures for compliance and manual control processes, and because a great risk exists for information loss through this access method. Left unchecked, the vulnerabilities can become material.

Evaluating Environmental Controls

The environment that an IS organization exists in physically is the support system for the processes and keeps them functioning to meet the business needs. Without controls on this environment, the entire operation is put at risk. Eating, drinking, or smoking in a data center may seem harmless, but it exposes the operations to potentially disastrous consequences with a relatively simple turn of events. When things are working well, there seems to be very little need for focusing on the support areas. However, when procedures and attention to detail are lacking, downtime and impact on customers can easily be the result. A review of the support systems for computer operations centers, such as power and cooling equipment, Uninterruptible Power Supplies (UPS), and battery systems as well as environmental control systems, should be performed when assessing an information systems process.

As an IS auditor, you will need to put your knowledge of social engineering skills to the test to disarm the tendency of maintenance personnel to distrust an auditor and hide information from them. Helping these employees solve their problems is always a conversation starter and it will not be a false promise in most cases. You will need to build your understanding of what should be occurring and expected for support and maintenance of these systems in order to position you to compare this to what you find in practice when you review these systems individually. Maintenance costs actually experienced compared to the expected or budgeted costs also can tell a story to the IS auditor. Where problem situations are identified, you will need to follow-up to see how the process of addressing issues like these are dealt with procedurally, and you will need to evaluate the effectiveness of this process firsthand.

Speaking of firsthand, at this point a little walk around tour may be in order. You should compare what you are seeing and hearing from interviews and documentation to what is actually on the floor or in the closet. Neatness counts. Maintenance schedules that are posted on equipment is a good sign that this stuff is being taken seriously. It also facilitates knowledge transfer among different service personnel and provides for quick troubleshooting assistance. If equipment looks to be in disrepair and appears not to have been serviced according to the documentation you have been presented with, there may be issues to discuss further. Be careful that you are not lead down the path here. Unless you know what you are doing, there are many pitfalls to reviewing industrial support systems and maintenance people love to lead you right into them. Physically dangerous and dirty situations are a favorite. Dirty does not mean poorly maintained. Yes, neatness counts, but sometimes not fixing it because it is not broken can be a wise philosophy as long as it is done with planning and forethought. People skills may serve you better here if you are not maintenance savvy. Actual failure rates and uptime are the key performance indicators and unless you have a risk-related reason to dig into this deeply, you should depend primarily on how well the problem reporting and planning, and scheduling and reported execution is performed in order to make your assessment.

Electrical Power

When reviewing the electrical power that supplies an IS organization and the network, you will be concerned with the quality and availability of that power. In large manufacturing installations in the early days of power generation, where the dependency on electrical power meant the difference between turning out a product and shutting down the operations, designs included power feeds from completely separate generating facilities to prevent disruption from an upstream failure at the generating station. Today, electrical distribution grids are tied together to ensure there is little dependency and impact from the loss of a single generation plant. In a similar way, an IS organization is very dependant on the availability of clean and continuous electricity to perform its functions and deliver against expectations. As you evaluate the IS organization, you will need to become familiar with what the local power companies track record is for providing good, clean power.

The electricity is expected to be at a certain voltage and computer power supplies step that voltage down to the voltage needed by the chips to make the systems work. The output of the system is predictable, largely because the voltage applied is predictable. If the voltage supplied to the processing systems is outside a range of tolerance, unexpected results may occur or the process could simply fail to operate. Typically, electrical devices are used to make the power smooth and predictable, thus keeping changes in the incoming line from resulting in unacceptable power to the systems. Some systems will tolerate variance better than other systems. Problem and maintenance logs will give you some insight as to whether there are ongoing problems in this area. Depending on the risk, you may want to ask about the monitoring and measurement charts for the quality of the incoming power. The facilities operations staff should be monitoring such metrics.

Electrical noise is a higher frequency signal that also is coming into the computer equipment from power lines and any wire for that matter. All wires will inherently behave as antennas. Unless these wires are shielded by grounded, electrically conductive barriers to drain off the high-frequency signals that being introduced through the air, the wires will receive and react to these transmissions. Depending upon the signal that is supposed to be on the wire, these spurious signals may add or subtract from the intended signal. Too much variance will change the results of the intended transmission and compromise its integrity. Sources of noise are usually found in electrical motors and rotating machinery. Copy machines, elevators, compressors, fans, printers, and any electrical equipment that starts and stops can create electrical noise that may impact the data or power signal. Cable trays may be used as the grounding shield and certainly shielded wire is used extensively in the IS industry for this reason. Optical fiber is a transmission of light and not an electrical signal and is therefore not affected by electrical noise. Some sensitive equipment can be affected by radio transmissions and even cell phone signals. Use of wireless devices often is discouraged in hospitals and data centers for this reason.

The most common concern you will find in the evaluation of electrical power will be its continued availability. Power failures will cause a break in the process and if not handled gracefully, these failures can leave data and transaction in quite a mess. Continuous and uninterruptible power is a critical need for processes that simply cannot have the rug pulled out from underneath them, without impacting the quality of the output. Back up generators are one way of providing power to a process, should the main source of power fail. If your evaluation includes a review of back up generators, you will want to ensure you understand what they are put in place to provide power for and what is actually being powered from them. You may identify a mismatch and deviation from the initial purpose that can jeopardize the ongoing production needs if demand outstrips supply. Generator equipment is expensive, requires maintenance, and should be tested regularly to ensure it will function when called upon to perform. Switching procedures should be documented and practiced that support the capability of running operations with the generator without impacting the public or street power feeds. These procedures need to be reviewed carefully because crossing power feeds with utilities can cause a catastrophic failure.

Uninterruptible Power Supplies (UPS) come in all sizes from under the desk units the size of a shoe box to large systems that fill several rooms. If you are reviewing a data center of any size and the processing is critical to the business, you should expect to review UPS system installation. UPS equipment can work in several ways and may or may not have a battery back up associated with it. The primary function of UPS is to smooth out the incoming power so that its predictability can be relied upon for the operation's processing needs. Filtering the power can be done through transformers or by using capacitors and coils to choke the variations out of the incoming signal and to clamp the voltage within a controlled range. An even better way to get predictable power is to generate your own by driving a motor with the incoming power and turning a generator with it for a clean source of local power, which is referred to as a motor-generator (M-G) set. Another way to ensure clean power is available is to recreate a clean sine wane signal by electronically reproducing it inside a UPS device powered by the incoming power. Whichever way it is done, the resultant output should be a predictable and controlled power signal that is not impacted by variations caused by external environmental factors. These systems by themselves will not help, should the incoming power fail completely, however. You will get some ride through from the momentum on an M-G set that will keep power flowing through minor disruptions, but outages of a longer duration will result in a power loss without battery back up. A comprehensive solution will utilize all three components of power conditioning: A UPS to clean the power, a battery back up to provide ride through for temporary outages, and a generator that will come on line and take over during long or persistent outages.

Battery systems are designed based on the load and expected duration of the need to supply that load. When assessing battery back up systems, you will need to understand how much power is needed and for how long in order to determine whether the battery system is of the proper size. Power needs change over time and large battery complexes require substantial investment and facilities infrastructure, therefore you may find a mismatch between the current need and the existing battery support capability. Batteries that are discharged too quickly or too extensively can be damaged and become a safety hazard as well. Batteries must be recharged and maintained at a proper voltage in order for them to perform properly when needed. Some batteries are sealed and do not present many maintenance issues. Some wet cell lead-acid battery installations are very large and require the routine interaction with acid and explosive gases. Wet cell batteries are common in large installations and the battery rooms should be explosion-proof installations that support the UPS and generator configuration at that site. The charging process results in the production of hydrogen gas, which is given off of the battery as it charges. The water levels and the correct acid concentrations must be maintained and monitored to keep these systems at the ready. Any battery will have a memory and tends to settle in at a lower than designed voltage level after using it. The voltages must be elevated periodically to keep the output voltage at an optimum level. Your review should ensure that this is occurring and that the output availability is measured and tested periodically. A best practice is to use the entire battery generator back up configuration on a regular schedule to ensure it will function as a unit and provide the necessary power alternative, should the need arise. These systems tend to be forgotten and determining IS operations diligence should be part of your evaluation and control objective assessment.

Temperature

Temperature controls within the processing environment should be recorded and controlled. Too much heat causes the premature failure of systems and may be indicative of a malfunction that needs immediate attention. It also is an early warning system for fire detection as well. Knowing the history and trends of temperatures can give an indicator on the overall health of the systems and processing performance, depending on how focused the sensors are and what is contributing to the heat. Under-temperature situations are typically not as problematic but may indicate an environmental systems failure that needs to be addressed. Sudden swings in temperature also will cause malfunctions of the systems and storage media. Media storage temperatures must be taken into consideration before putting the media to use. If you do not acclimatize a tape cartridge to operating temperatures first, for example, breaking or stretching the tape may result because of the mechanical nature of the reading device interaction, thus causing loss of data. In closed areas with little ventilation, power supplies can generate a lot of heat that will build up. The insulation on wires can become brittle from prolonged heat exposure and the resultant deterioration can lead to breakage and mechanical failure of the wire as well as exposure to electrical shock hazards. The storage of potentially flammable materials and those that give off flammable vapors in and around heat generating equipment also be taken into consideration. Depending on the kind of equipment and the manufacturer's tolerance range for the operating temperature, processing results may become erratic or unacceptable when operating temperatures stray too far from the suggested range. Furthermore, warranties and repair contracts on equipment may be impacted by operating the equipment in environments that are too hot or cold. Records of the effective implementation of appropriate controls on environmental temperatures should be evidenced, along with an assessment of the constraints and limitations that need to be managed to in order for you to gain a comfort level on the protection of equipment from temperature-related environmental issues.

Fire Suppression

Fires can be devastating and leave an operation in ruins and planning is required to prevent this from happening. Your evaluation of the information processing systems and support areas should ensure that proper safeguards and planning are in place to provide the best protection from fire damage to equipment and personnel. Just like in school, drills should be performed and practiced periodically. Building exits should be clearly marked and evacuation routes posted and taught to all employees. Fire extinguishers of the correct type should be available for extinguishing manageable fires. Spraying water (Type A extinguisher) on an electrical fire will do a lot of damage to the electrical equipment. Different types of extinguishers are required to put different types of fires out. Employees should be taught the procedures for evacuation and damage control as well as how to use the fire protection equipment. Shutdown procedures should be documented and emergency power off switches should be provided in case of a fire. Any special equipment for fire protection or suppression, or personnel safety in case of fire should be inspected and be of an approved quality. Evidence of the inspection, testing, and practice drills also should be available for your review.

Fire suppression equipment will range from handheld extinguishers to large built-in systems. These large systems may be the focus of some of the CISA exam test questions. There are three basic types of suppression systems: wet pipe, dry pipe, and Halon. Halon is a gas that displaces the oxygen in a room to extinguish a fire. Large canisters of Halon gas are set up in a sealed space such as a data center and are triggered by a fire-sensing device. The gas fills the room, puts out the fire, and an evacuation cycle then is performed by air handling equipment to purge the room of the Halon gas. Humans can survive exposure to Halon 1301. Halon 1301 has been determined to be destructive of the Earth's ozone layer, however, and is not being made any more. It is legal to have it, use it, and even recharge an existing system with it. New systems cannot be installed, however. The cost of replacement gas has gone up tenfold in the last 15 years. The testing of such an expensive product takes some planning and possibly substitution. Rooms must be well-sealed in order for a gaseous extinguishing solution to be effective. Another alternative gas that can be used in a similar manner is CO_2, but the effect on humans is deadly.

The more standard method of fire suppression is the water sprinkler system. Excessive heat opens an overhead valve that melts when too much heat is applied to it. Water then is sprayed out over the fire, extinguishing it (assuming the fire is controllable by water and not a petroleum fire, for example). This is the most reliable and safest fire extinguishing method available. The clean up and restoration following a discharge are a negative factor in use of this solution, however, but it may be preferable to fire damage. For this reason, you may find covers for equipment in some installations for protecting gear that you do not want to get wet. The question is though how do you get the covers on in time? This is accomplished by using a dry pipe system instead using of a wet one.

In a wet pipe system, the water is sitting in the pipe right at the spray head, under pressure, and ready to go. The dry pipe system is essentially the same, except compressed air is contained in the section of pipe over the protection area initially. These systems can be set up to trigger in a two-stage manner, thus giving the occupants time to assess whether there is a false alarm or situation that is controllable. It also provides a lag time for covering equipment that might be ruined by water. There are times when age and exposure to elements will cause premature failure of trigger mechanisms. This failure can cause an unexpected disaster if no opportunities to check the initial alarm situation are provided ahead of the sprinkler system being fully engaged in dispensing water. Timing is everything, as they say, and there are advantages and disadvantages to each of these systems in their reaction time and ability to react to stop from unnecessarily triggering as well as their cost to implement.

New systems for fire management are being invented and investigated all the time. Exotic gases and fine mist water systems are some of the systems in development. As you review the operations center and draw conclusions on the sufficiency of the fire suppression system, look around for fire hazards and business processes that provide the potential for high-risk fire situations. Sometimes, a little clean up can be recommended as a way to reduce the risk and to change the conclusions that might otherwise be drawn. Prompt trash removal and routine storage practices are worth evaluating for opportunities to reduce risk. Look at the risk and the practical application of the fire detection and reaction systems and procedures and how well they are tested. Keep in mind the human factor and the probable panic and reactive response in which a real fire will likely result. Determine whether the systems and processes for fire detection suppression and response will save lives first and protect investments second. Exits should not be locked or blocked and the exits paths should be accessible from any point in the building unimpeded. People are the most important asset of any organization.

Humidity

An aspect of the physical environment that must be evaluated in a server room, equipment closet, or data center is the amount of moisture or humidity present. Either too much or too little can cause operational problems for the equipment. Monitoring the humidity levels should be done, especially in areas where human traffic can create static electricity hazards for computer equipment. Air conditioning systems work primarily by drying out the air. It is easier to cool dry air than it is to cool air that is heavy with moisture. Dry air makes static electricity a problem and static electricity will build up on isolated surfaces, causing discharges of a high voltage that can destroy sensitive electronics and circuits that are small enough to be destroyed by relatively small currents. Raised-floor data centers should have their floor grid electrically grounded to dissipate the buildup of static electricity. Grounding straps, which are wristbands with leads that that can attach the service technician to an electrical ground, should be required when technicians are working on equipment. Humidifiers may be required to put moisture back into the air in some cases where humidity is often measured to be below acceptable levels.

Humidity can create problems in the other extreme, too. Water leakage also can destroy electrical equipment. Calcification from water evaporation can build up on humidification systems, causing them to fail and to leak water into the room and the floors below. Other sources of water that computer equipment must be protected from include drainage systems, restroom facilities, chilled-water cooling systems, and even fire suppression sprinkler systems. Sensors placed directly on the floor, which will alert the operations staff of water presence, should be used where these systems coexist with computer equipment. Covers to protect unaffected equipment in case the fire suppression system activates could be a good investment and save a more costly recovery process as indicated previously. Often, electrical closets are located near elevator shafts and other raceways that run facilities systems from floor to floor in a building. These runs often move supply and return water lines to facilities and systems as well.

Part of your inspection tour should include a look into these areas as well as the basement cabling entrance areas for excessive humidity or the presence of water. Flooding and standing water are not only electrical hazards but can be the beginning of serious human health and safety issues as well. Standing water can breed disease and insects and can be particularly problematic in areas that are not frequently visited by staff. Depending on the facilities proximity to flood plains, rising water and flooding situations may be an occurrence for which the evacuation of power down procedures will need to be invoked to protect the staff and equipment. Water sensors should be tied to an alarm system that is monitored centrally for the notification and dispatch of corrective measures. Records of the testing and validation of the working systems should be part of the maintenance records you would expect to see during your assessment.

Maintenance

Maintenance of the environmental systems supporting the information processes should be evaluated during the evaluation of that system to ensure that the support is designed and built adequately to preserve its intended environmental support functions and is based on the IS operations needs at the facility. These systems cannot be put in place and then forgotten because they will degrade from disuse and not work properly when called on to support emergency needs. You should expect to see routine testing and recording of the results of those test procedures so that the relative health of these systems is known at all times and periodically validated. Maintenance records, including recording the replacement of parts, system upgrades, and other processes you would expect to see mapped out through similar change control processes on an information system, also should be tracked and recorded relative to these systems as well. Due care to ensure that maintenance is performed by properly trained and qualified personnel will be important to accrediting the processes and in keeping the insurance carriers happy about relying on them as mitigants to limit losses they will ultimately cover should disasters occur. You should determine that similar quality of service controls are in place for your assurances as well.

Evaluating Physical Access Controls and Procedures

Physical access to systems and processes is an important aspect of evaluating the overall control of the information assets. A portion of every security-related review should look at the physical security of the devices along with the logical aspects of control. Without good physical controls, a device can simply be unplugged and carried off. A denial of service and complete loss of current data will result. Physical security is hard to enforce with technical people because they see their functions as more intellectual and scientific than, well, physical. No one likes confrontation and physical security requires confrontation and deterrence to effectively turn back the attempts of unauthorized access, either directly through brute force or using social engineering techniques. Aggressive behavior often begets more aggressive behavior, which can escalate into violence and physical harm, causing someone to get hurt. The best way to prevent this from happening is to ensure that the proper controls are in place and policies and procedures are thoroughly documented, communicated, and followed by everyone in the IS organization.

Your evaluation can add value by assisting the management in seeing these control requirements as a way of minimizing risk to their employees as well as their information assets and as good business practice at the same time. Testing to ensure that the procedures are followed will be important, because the road to loss is paved with good procedures that are not followed. Always begin with an assessment of the requirements for physical security through tours and site visits. Compile a short list of concerns and needs that must be addressed in order to satisfy your review of the residual risk exposures from your initial inspection. Ask about the location and the history of events in the local community that may indicate the presence of risk that you may not have considered. Look at the situation from an attacker's point of view and ask yourself how you would gain access if you were tasked with doing so without permission. Unauthorized access can be gained in very ingenuous ways and determined perpetrators will try them all in order to find the weakest entry point to gain access. You should review your list with the physical security management to determine whether these risks have been considered or addressed by some control that you may have overlooked. Attempt to qualify the risk for any gaps that may exist between your list of exposures and the controls that exist to mitigate the physical security risks.

There are several risk-control scenarios and each one will differ, depending on the situation and the organization's appetite for risk. Some of the items that could be deployed to reduce risk include doors, locks, fences gates, monitoring access points with closed circuit televisions and recording devices, guards, access logs, badges, keys, walls that span the entire floor to ceiling space (raised-floor access cavities), man traps, anti-pass back mechanisms, data center anonymity, and discreet signage. Each and every one of these controls will not be effective without supporting policy and procedures that require personnel to keep them functional and effective in performing the task for which they were designed. For example, propped open security doors cannot prevent access. As with all IS audit risks, the human factor cannot be overstated. Formally documenting the list of allowed access and thinking through procedures when situations are presented that are outside of these boundaries are human processes without which the physical controls will have limited effectiveness.

In order to form an opinion on the effectiveness of any control you evaluate, you will want to see examples of the control being successfully used to mitigate the risk its implementation was intended to control. This is more difficult to do with physical controls than logical ones, because audit trails are more difficult to obtain. Some of the physical controls have electronic components, which may provide opportunities to automatically record access attempts, but control effectiveness of a fence is difficult to prove directly. Other systems must, therefore, be used to indirectly validate their effectiveness. Guard stations and the maintenance of security reports and sign in logs are very important measurement tools for this reason, and their consistent use and accuracy should be part of your test procedures. Sometimes, these records will be depended upon to reconstruct a sequence of events for a security investigation that, at the time of recording the access, seemed extremely routine and unnecessary.

To summarize, you must identify the risks and threats, perform a gap analysis of the existing controls to those risks, identify opportunities to measure performance of those controls, and evaluate this performance against expectations for the effectiveness of the control. Be creative and flexible in looking for risks and opportunities to compromise the systems and challenge the performance against the documented procedures to gain assurance that they are being performed against consistently.

Visitor and Vendor Access

The physical security control process is complicated by the fact that physical access is routinely necessary by many individuals who do not have an ongoing need to know or right to access the IS organization on a regular basis. Visitors and vendors fall into this category. The reasons for needing access are many, all of them legitimate to a point, and usually are valid for only a subset of the complete physical access range being controlled at the perimeter only. Identification badges and permission for restricted areas should be supported with physical controls. Unless there are ways to partition access and limit it through controls that subdivide the physical space into discrete units of physical access, other mitigating controls will be necessary to limit access while providing for the business needs of servicing equipment or showing clients around.

The registration and recording the access needs are an important step in identifying the access requirements and authenticating the requestor.

Prearranged expectations with entrance control guard stations is a good way of ensuring that social engineering attempts are not used to gain physical access. No one should be allowed into a controlled area unless previously authorized. Badges clearly identifying visitors and temporary access limitations should be used at all times. Employees should be required by policy to challenge anyone out of the bounds of their permitted access in a nonthreatening manner. Check in and check out times should be reviewed against the predetermined expectations by check point personnel who should alert the authorities of any suspected variances.

Any equipment or material coming in or going out should be assessed for possible risks. This can be a difficult issue to manage with visitors and clients, but a vendor's equipment should be reviewed to ensure that integrity of the change control process is maintained and the equipment leaving the premises does not contain sensitive data. If consistent inspection is not seen as a control that is commensurate with the risk exposure, a random inspection of contents may be an option that provides some control while permitting most access with lesser constraints. For example, this method of limited review has been adopted by the airline industry for passenger belongings since the terrorist attacks of September 11, 2001. The inspection results should be recorded and maintained as evidence of the effectiveness of the control for analysis and audit purposes.

The Physical Location, Security Measures, and Visibility Profile

The physical location is one place in information security practice where security by obscurity is an acceptable practice. High profile computer operations provide an obvious target for terrorists, political activists, or anyone who is looking for a place to start when launching an attack. No different than the grade school sign taped to the back stating "Kick me," drawing attention to computer processing is asking for trouble. Your evaluation should identify signs, phonebook listings, lobby marquees, and registration desk areas that clearly point the way to a data center as risks that need to be addressed. Only those with a need to know should be provided direction to the processing facilities.

In addition, you also will want to evaluate the location itself for putting the process in harms way. Locating a processing facility in a flood plain, next to a hazardous or flammable material storage site, on an earthquake fault line, or where airline or rail traffic provides potential dangers are examples of poor planning that create risk for the IS organization. If any physical risk situations are identified during your review, determine whether these risks have been recognized and what compensating controls have been considered and deployed. Also, you should review the insurance coverage to ensure that these risks are covered by the policy. Alternative processing and contingency planning considerations also will play a big role when locations are less than ideal. Accessibility to and availability of the supplies needed to continue operations may be part of this consideration as well, especially for critical operations that could impact the physical safety of people if they were to be cut off.

Of course, you also will want to evaluate the physical protection provided from the environment where the processing is located as well. Fencing and gates should be adequate based on the location's risk. Guards or attendants that check credentials and log activity are a best practice for controlling access and deterring theft. Lighting and surveillance cameras will enable the guards to observe trouble from a safe location. Recording and monitoring will provide an audit trail of people coming and going and equipment movement, which should be reviewed for completeness and accuracy along with the associated procedures that describe the authorizations and any escalation practices. Man trap entrance controls and other key card processes should be used to ensure that physical security of the processing personnel and information also is provided.

Personnel Safety

The safety of personnel will be an aspect of the physical security evaluation that is almost assumed to be an integral part of any security process. As you tour the facility and look for areas of risk or poor controls, you will naturally have an eye open to physical dangers to personnel—you do it without thinking or your own personal safety. There may not even be policy that describes personnel safety as a priority, because it is assumed to be the case without being documented. Some areas to be aware of may be worth mentioning here, however.

Emergency evacuation plans and procedures should exist that prioritize personnel safety above physical and intellectual assets and include floor plans and evacuation routes. These plans and procedures should be tied closely to the contingency planning procedures and ensuring everyone's safety should be a primary concern. Handicap evacuation and access, first aid kit locations and instructions, and call trees and authority notification procedures for adverting a shut down in case of a false alarm should all be included in this plan. Emergency procedure awareness and training should be part of the training that everyone receives periodically. Escape and emergency exit doors should be available and include fail safe and override controls to meet the local building and safety codes on doors. You will want to be familiar with these local requirements and check them for compliance. Exits should not be locked or chained, even when that makes sense from a physical security of assets perspective. Alarms can be put in place to alert door opening while still providing for safe passage in case of fire or other disaster. Testing of the procedures and safety mechanisms should be routinely performed and documented.

Working conditions should be reasonable and provide break times and locations where employees can rest and eat. Schedules should be reasonable as well. Some of this will be a judgment call and you will need to be familiar with comparable situations in order to substantiate any recommendations in this area. Policies should exist that ensure that people do not feel threatened or harassed in the workplace, and policies related to workplace violence, abuse, drug and alcohol use, and sexual harassment should all be part of the human resource process. This concern may extend beyond the immediate work place, for example, where employees come and go at all hours supporting the operations process in remote areas or ones where crime rates are high. If employees are not treated well, the quality of the work will suffer and should be easily supportable, should you recognize weaknesses in this subject area. Make sure that you fully explore all of the circumstances and available options before announcing your review findings and recommendations, which may be based only on partial investigations.

Hard Copy Information Protection

The security controls of information in hard copy form should mirror that of electronic copies because the data valuation is the same. This is often overlooked in an IS evaluation and is seen as being more related to the management of the business process than the IS security's area of responsibility. Once a hard copy is generated and carried away from the printing device, electronic controls have no effect on the protection of the data's confidentiality. A few things that the information systems can do should be reviewed, however. Departmental and business process procedures should document the proper handling of the printed material and base the expected behavior on the value or classification of the data. Devices that routinely receive sensitive or classified information for printing, such as a fax or printer, should be in a physically secure location and be marked in some way to differentiate them from output devices that do not receive sensitive information so they are not mistaken. Suppressing the ability to print or forward information may be a control worth considering in some sensitive locations.

All output should be labeled either through special stock paper based on the data's classification or through watermarks, headers, or footers within the documents to clearly identify the data's value and who is authorized to handle or read it. Users should be instructed on how to dispose of printed material properly and be provided with ways of reporting violations anonymously, should they observe them occurring. Shredding stations or separate disposal provisions should be created for areas where large volumes of confidential material are routinely processed and disposed of. For example, light tables may be worth considering in order to ensure that the inadvertent disposal of important documentation does not occur by inspecting discarded envelopes for overlooked documents. When evaluating the security controls for output, you will need to interview the business users to understand their routines and for what their output is used. You also should ask about storage, retention, and physical controls to understand where the physical exposure of the information might create weakness. Also, you should review the disposal and retention policies to ensure that they require proper handling and compare those requirements to the field observations you have made.

Resources

Handbook of Information Security Management, Micki Krause and Harold F. Tipton, eds. (CRC Press / Auerbach Publications, 1999).

The CISSP Prep Guide—Mastering the Ten Domains of Computer Security, Ronald Krutz and Russell Vines (John Wiley & Sons, 2001).

Secrets and Lies: Digital Security in a Networked World, Bruce Schneier (John Wiley & Sons, 2000).

Information Security Policies Made Easy Version 9, Charles C. Wood (PentaSafe, 2002).

Hacking Exposed, Stuart McClure, Joel Scambray, and George Kurtz (Osborne/McGraw Hill, 1999).

Surviving Security—How to Integrate People, Process, and Technology, Mandy Andress (Sams Publishing, 2002).

Information Security Architecture—An Integrated Approach to Security in the Organization, Jan Killmeyer Tudor (CRC Press / Auerbach Publications, 2001).

Information Security Architecture—Design, Deployment & Operations Christopher M. King, Curtis E. Dalton, and T. Ertem Osmanoglu (Osborne/McGraw Hill, 2001).

NIST Special Publication 800-18—Guide for Developing Security Plans for Information Technology Systems, Marianne Swanson, December 1998.

Sample Questions

Here is a sampling of questions in the format of the CISA exam. These questions are related to the protection of information assets, and will help test your understanding of this subject. Answers with explanations are provided in Appendix A.

1. What is the *most* important aspect of performing an evaluation of information security controls on a process or system?

   A. Ensuring that the best practice control techniques are being utilized properly

   B. Understanding the businesses functional requirements of the process to ensure that they can be accomplished

   C. Ensuring that the deployed controls work as part of the overall security architecture program

   D. Making sure that access is strictly controlled based on a need to know

2. The concept of data integrity implies that

   A. Access has not been given to those who do not have a need to know

   B. Data can be accessed by processes when necesssary to support the business function

   C. Data has not been altered or modified outside of the expected and approved processing steps

   D. Data has not been made available to processes for which the data classification has not been accredited

3. When reviewing security and business risks, it is *most* important to keep in mind that

   A. Business risks are not as important as the security exposures to potential hackers.

   B. The customer's expectation of privacy should take precedent over the businesses risk tolerance when considering security controls.

   C. Data classification should determine the security controls requirements.

   D. Some compromise of the security controls to accommodate the businesses risk tolerance is a necessary part of doing business.

4. When evaluating the role of the information security officer, you should be *most* concerned to find that

    A. The security officer's role was not well documented as part of the job description.

    B. The security officer's role is defined as a key decision maker on a new product review committee.

    C. Part of the defined role was the accountability for ensuring that the security controls kept any security breaches from occurring.

    D. The authority for carrying out the role of a security officer was not explicitly tied to the organization's policy.

5. When reviewing an information system to assess its privacy risks, an IS auditor would consider all of the following *except*

    A. Ensuring that the appropriate consent has been obtained from the customer before the release of sensitive data

    B. The business needs for the client data within the processes

    C. Proper disclosures to the customer of what the data is used for and how it will be protected

    D. The laws and regulations relevant to the industry for privacy controls on customer data

6. While reviewing an information security program, the IS auditor determines that the best practices have not been followed as guidelines for developing the program. Which of the following would be the *least* important factor to consider when determining the recommendation related to changes for the program?

    A. Whether a risk assessment was part of the determination of what the program elements should be

    B. Whether the security officer had documented polices and procedures to direct the program

    C. Whether the architectural design of the security deployed an in-depth state-of-the-art defense

    D. Whether any inventory of the existing controls for managing security threats has been done

7. Policy for information security is a primary requirement for establishing control in an IS organization. Which of the following is *not* a reason why this is the case?

   A. A policy establishes the steps required to put security in place.

   B. A policy establishes the authority and accountability to get the security job done.

   C. A policy sets the expectations for the employee's behavior as it relates to security.

   D. The policy provides the mandate for putting the security program elements in place.

8. During an IS audit, the IS auditor determines that there is a control weakness due to the lack of available standards. When developing the findings and recommendation for the audit report, which of the following items should *not* be considered for inclusion as reasons for improving standards in the organization?

   A. Standards provide common ground that will increase the efficiency of the operations

   B. Standards creation is an industry best practice

   C. Standards ensure that individual policy interpretation will not result in the establishment of weaker security overall by lowering the minimum security level

   D. Standards provide simplified solutions to problems, enabling leverage of fewer solutions and economies of scale

9. During your review of an information security risk assessment, which of the following elements would you be *least* concerned with if no evidence was available to substantiate it?

   A. The exercise of risk assessment is reperformed periodically.

   B. The threats and vulnerabilities have been determined.

   C. The existing controls have been inventoried and assessed for their effectiveness.

   D. The risk assessment included a tactical as well as a strategic initiatives assessment.

10. When making a recommendation to establish a product review process that includes the security officer as part of the approval team, what should your *strongest* argument in the recommendation be?

    A. Security that is built into a process as part of the initial design can be seven times cheaper than the cost of implementing it after the product is in production.

    B. Plans should be documented and defended to upper management before they are used to implement a new program.

    C. The return on investment for products should be assessed prior to starting development so that these returns can be compared to actual gains after the product has been implemented.

    D. Plans should be evaluated to ensure that they follow the SDLC methodology standard in the organization and that the methodology has input from information security.

11. When reviewing the identification process used to establish user accounts, what is the *most* important aspect of the process?

    A. All of the relevant information is gathered about the person establishing the identity.

    B. Proof is provided to strongly tie the individual presenting themselves as the person for whom the ID is being established.

    C. Authorization is obtained for all accounts provided for the individual who is requesting access.

    D. The individual is given the opportunity to change their password immediately upon first log in.

12. The security concept of *need to know* implies all of the following *except*

    A. All access allowed within a permission set or role that is approved on a need to know basis can be viewed, copied, or modified because of the permissions granted.

    B. Access is required to perform the assigned functions supporting the business process.

    C. Data owners and their stewards have explicitly determined that the access by this role or person is acceptable.

    D. The least amount of privilege necessary to perform the function has been granted to the role or person receiving this permission.

13. An IS auditor would expect to see a defense in-depth approach to security or would recommend that one be adopted for all of the following reasons *except*

   A. It provides several different security mechanisms that increase the difficulty for hackers and intruders due to the increased knowledge required for compromise.

   B. More complex security solutions can lead to higher requirements for training and related support costs including audit requirements.

   C. Security solutions never completely solve a problem and a defense in-depth approach provides opportunities to address residual risk from one solution with another solution.

   D. Costs can be reduced by multiple iterations of solving most of a problem at a minimal cost and then applying another economic solution to address most of the remaining exposure rather than the extensive and expensive application of one solution set.

14. When reviewing role-based access, which of the following parameters should the IS auditor be *least* concerned with?

   A. Business functions and job descriptions provide the input to determine that the accesses defined are sufficient to performing the required tasks.

   B. The defined role is applicable to a job function or set of job functions that provides a categorization of need that defines a role.

   C. The access permissions of a particular role are reconciled to the actual functions performed on a periodic basis.

   D. The establishment of new roles is reviewed and approved by the data owner or steward.

15. During an evaluation of an account administration process, what should an IS auditor be most concerned about finding?

   A. Employee terminations that did not result in the closing of computer accounts in a timely fashion

   B. Time-of-day restrictions that were not used to limit access to systems

   C. Password aging that was not forced on accounts providing access to the network

   D. Accounts, which were supposed to have been suspended from disuse, were not followed up on and deleted

16. When evaluating a single sign on implementation, what single factor adds the *most* risk and provides concern for the IS auditor in their review?

    A. The fact that password resets must be effectively propagated across all systems in some way for single sign on to work properly

    B. The issue of systems administrators making changes to a system managed by the single sign on solution, thus putting the accounts out of synchronization

    C. The concern that single sign on cannot be effectively achieved unless roles and access needs are defined for all systems on which the user may need to perform their functions

    D. The concern that, if compromised, the single sign on access provides a wide range of access where access had been more limited previously

17. When reviewing application design processes for information security controls, which of the following is *least* likely to be of concern to an IS auditor?

    A. The SDLC methodology does not require that security is considered as part of the design criteria.

    B. The testing of the application coding does not consider the security requirements identified in the design phase of the system's development process.

    C. The sample data used for testing and design is not adequately segregated from the production version of the data.

    D. Access permissions of testing and design personnel permits data modification in the test environment.

18. Which of the following are data classification controls?

    I. Labeling the removable media containing classified data with the highest level of data sensitivity contained on the media

    II. Publishing a policy that defines what data classifications are and how these classifications are to be applied

    III. Encrypting data when it is being transmitted across the Internet

    IV. Treating all forms of a given data classification as equal in terms of protection requirements

    V. Regulatory requirements to protect customer data from disclosure without prior consent

A. I, II, and IV only

B. I, II, III, and IV only

C. I, II, III, IV, and V

D. I, II, IV, and V only

19. Which of the following is not a password control?

A. Requiring that a password have a minimum length and complexity

B. Encrypting passwords when in transit and at rest

C. Limiting the reuse of passwords through the use of a history file

D. Limiting the number of unique sessions an account can initiate

20. When evaluating strong authentication usage, what should an IS auditor be *most* concerned with?

A. Ensuring that the two factors are maintained in separate databases to ensure segregation

B. Determining the identification process for each factor and ensuring they are synchronized

C. Reviewing the biometric aspects of strong authentication or acceptable type I and type II error rates

D. Reviewing the physical controls related to the storage of the physical tokens or card stock supplies

21. During a review of a PKI, the IS auditor determines that non-repudiation cannot be assured for a set of transactions. This most likely means that

A. The certificate authority will not stand behind the validation of the certificate used at the time when the transaction occurred.

B. The user's certificate was compromised or was expired when the time the transaction occurred.

C. In reviewing the transaction flow and the security related to the use of the certification, it cannot be conclusively proven that no other person could have possibly been responsible for the transaction that had occurred.

D. The transaction did not go through as anticipated, causing a roll back of the request and negating the signed transaction.

22. Which of the following would an IS auditor expect to see as part of an information security architecture?

I. Evidence of the application of a defense in-depth strategy

II. A risk-based approach to the application and location of the security controls

III. A plan that takes into consideration the business needs and processes

IV. The inclusion of the management and operational controls as well as technical controls

A. I, II, and IV only

B. I, II, III, and IV

C. II and IV only

D. I, II, and III only

23. When performing a review of the host-based security controls, the risk factors that need to be considered are

I. The value of the data contained on the server being secured

II. The functions and tasks required of the server

III. The services that are not needed in the configuration of the server

IV. The operating system type and its vulnerabilities

V. Requirements for encryption related to the services provided by the server

A. I, II, III, IV, and V

B. I, II, and IV only

C. II, III, and V only

D. III, IV, and V only

24. Minimum security baselines (MSBs) and host-based intrusion detection relate to each other in what important aspect?

A. They both are security controls that apply to a device (server) as opposed to network-based controls.

B. Host-based intrusion detection cannot be successfully implemented unless MSBs are adequately maintained on the same device.

C. Host-based intrusion detection controls can be used in place of applying MSBs on the same device.

D. They should both be implemented on all servers as part of a robust security architecture.

25. During a network security review, the IS auditor determines that the firewall rule set is incorrectly built to protect the organization from the risks that are unacceptable to the business. The IS auditor should

A. Immediately notify the IS organization management so corrections can be made to prevent further vulnerability.

B. Discuss the issue with audit management and prepare the findings and a recommendation for their report.

C. Point out the deficiency to the firewall support staff, but note the state the controls were found in at the time of the review.

D. Look at the rest of the controls to ensure that the risk has not been mitigated by some other method before doing anything.

26. What is the *primary* purpose of a DMZ in network architecture?

A. To provide a place where authentication can occur before enabling access to sensitive data

B. To separate business logic from classified data

C. To provide a neutral zone where transaction requests can be made and honored without affecting the security of either adjacent zone

D. To provide a location for proxy servers and drop off servers to reside without reducing the security of the more secure adjacent network zone

27. When evaluating the encryption used to protect a data transmission over the Internet, which of the following is *not* a relevant security control?

A. Virtual private network

B. Message digest

C. Digital certificate technologies

D. Secure sockets layer technologies

28. Network intrusion detection and incident response are important parts of any security program. What aspects of an audit review *must* be included when evaluating these programs?

    I. Proper staff levels and training of the staff to react and respond to issues as they present themselves

    II. Establishment of a need for using either of these techniques based on the possibility of them actually being required

    III. The response time requirements and the ability of the program in place to meet those needs

    IV. Management's commitment to the programs and their support for enabling them to function when necessary

    A. I, II, III, and IV

    B. I, II, and IV only

    C. II, III, and IV only

    D. I, III, and IV only

29. While evaluating third-party connections in an organization, an IS auditor discovers PCAnywhere software resident on a financial worker's desktop workstation. Which of the following controls would be seen as the *strongest* risk mitigate to unauthorized network access in this situation?

    A. The software is used only for the remote control of the workstation and access must be authenticated by dial up server controls first.

    B. The software may be correctly configured to use network authentication prior to enabling connection through a modem to it.

    C. The modem is unplugged and only connected when needed.

    D. The software is configured to use dial back and only enables outgoing connections made to known numbers.

30. In an evaluation of virus protection processes, which three controls cover the *most* risk out of those listed here?

    A. Virus protection deployed on every workstation, the blocking of dangerous attachments in all email at the mail servers, and a strong user education program about email viruses

    B. Virus protection active on all mail servers, the blocking of dangerous attachments in all email at the mail servers, and a strong user education program about email viruses

C. A strong user education program about email viruses and virus
   protection that is actively enforced on all workstations, and the
   blocking of dangerous attachments in all emails at the mail
   servers

D. Virus protection on all mail servers, the blocking of dangerous
   attachments in all emails at the mail servers, and virus protection
   that is actively enforced on all workstations

31. Which of the following is *not* a control to address the risks associ-
    ated with social engineering attempts?

    A. Asking for a name of person to call back, documenting all of the
       requests, and validating the person by some means before grant-
       ing access

    B. Adding the physical security responsibilities to the system's sup-
       port people because they know who needs access to the opera-
       tions center best

    C. Following the rules for access and permissions at all times to
       avoid opportunities for allowing your guard to be down

    D. Developing a healthy suspicion and learn to "think like an
       attacker"

32. What is the *most* important control concern associated with the log-
    ging and monitoring of system or network activity?

    A. Ensuring that the information is time synchronized so forensic
       analysis can be accurately performed

    B. The placement of the sensors and protection of the logs from the
       systems administrator's access

    C. Developing exception-based reporting and log correlation
       processes to reduce the amount of log review required

    D. Having the staff support available to read through the logs and
       take action on the results found

33. When evaluating personnel safety controls in an IS operation, what
    is the *best* method to use for evaluating its sufficiency?

    A. Obtaining copies of the safety and emergency evacuation manual
       to evidence compliance with the requirement for procedures and
       documentation

    B. Reviewing the records of testing of personal safety devices and
       their maintenance histories

C. Spot interviewing a few passing IS staff personnel and asking them about their knowledge of the safety measures and procedures

D. Looking for posted evacuation signs and personal safety equipment stored in easily accessible locations to the users

34. What is the *most* challenging aspect of evaluating physical security controls in an IS organization?

   A. Assessing all of the numerous controls and ensuring that each one is managed properly

   B. Determining how to assess flexible situations such as security movement and the belongings of VIPs and visitors

   C. Being able to obtain proof of the physical security controls effectiveness in preventing or deterring unauthorized acts

   D. Touring the physical site and inspecting the controls to ensure that they are functioning properly

35. In a review of the environmental controls, all of the following are factors that need to be considered *except*

   A. The need for power continuity and the deployment of UPS, batteries, and generators as applicable

   B. The maintenance and testing schedule recorded for the fire suppression systems that protect the information systems

   C. Personnel evacuation plans and emergency exit routes posted in the operations center

   D. Moisture and temperature monitoring and tracking over time

10%

CHAPTER 5

Disaster Recovery and Business Continuity

Ten percent of the CISA exam's content is concerned with your knowledge of this subject matter, but for the businesses you evaluate, this will be one of the most important subjects they can address in order to protect their business from complete ruin. The importance of Disaster Recovery Planning (DRP) and Business Continuity Planning (BCP) can mean the difference between a viable business and a footnote on a ledger, should disaster strike a company. Make no mistake about it, this is a hard sell for management. The terrorist attack on the U.S. Pentagon and the World Trade Center on September 11, 2001, is a stark reminder of the devastating impact that unexpected calamity can have on a business. Some businesses continued with little disruption, others will never reopen.

The process of building, deploying, testing, and maintaining adequate recovery and continuity plans start at the top of the organization but also will involve extensive analysis and participation from many aspects of the organization. You should expect to see an ongoing process and commitment for building, maintaining, and testing plans to ensure business continuity and to see continuous involvement at many levels of the organization in order for you to conclude that the process is adequate. Do not expect to see completely successful tests, reported on in detail and tied up with a bow.

[handwritten: Continuous plan, no milestone]

Half of those companies with a well-developed plan do not have tests that meet most of their objectives on a regular basis. DRP and BCP are continuous processes, not achieved milestones or goals that can be set on a shelf until needed.

In order to effectively review the BCP process, you will need to know something about how to build one, what kind of support it takes to manage such a process, and what kind of outcomes should be expected to show you put a good faith effort toward being prepared to use a process that no one hopes they will ever need. By the end of this chapter, you should be able to

- Describe why these processes are needed to senior management in a way they will understand.

- Be able to assess the business impact analysis and requirements definition processes for completeness and adequacy.

- Review the project plan for building a BCP process and conclude on its sufficiency.

- Evaluate the process of risk assessment for determining BCP and DRP needs.

- Review the planning documentation and procedures to conclude on their completeness and effectiveness.

- Review the testing processes and determine if they are planned, carried out, documented, and followed up on in an appropriate manner for the business under review.

- Evaluate the human resource planning aspects of the recovery process to ensure that communication and human assets are planned for as part of the processes.

- Understand the various types of recovery and contingency options available to an IS organization to use in your review of different situations that you may come across.

- Understand the relative importance of various data classifications, application needs, and recovery priorities to aid in your evaluation of continuity and recovery processes.

- Understand the various infrastructure implications of recovery and loss that will be input to the planning and testing of the recovery scenarios.

Let's start by reviewing the management's end of the process and its requirements and decisions.

The Business Case for Continuity Planning

There are several three letter acronyms (TLAs) related to these processes collectively that you will need some level of familiarity with to be conversant with management about contingency planning. These acronyms all amount to roughly the same thing with some twists, depending on the focus of the presenter. Disaster Recovery Planning (DRP) is more of a technological recovery of information systems and infrastructure from a catastrophic failure. This failure could be a natural disaster, massive power outage, or anything really that keeps the operations from being able to continue their mission in their present location. Business Continuity Planning (BCP) and Business Recovery Planning (BRP) are used interchangeably to refer to the recovery of business processes to keep the organization operational in the face of lost technical systems, while the DRP process kicks in, for example. Crises Management Planning (CMP) is the whole process of manning the recovery process, doing the damage control, and marshaling resources to affect a successful recovery, thus dealing with the crisis in a planned manner. No matter how you slice it, it is a big project and cannot be effective unless senior management buy in occurs first.

If management is committed to having an ongoing and viable business, they need to manage risk to be successful as this book has now reviewed many times. Day in and day out, disruptions may occur that impact the ability of the business to perform "business as usual" and processes must be adjusted to compensate for these disruptions to get back to an optimum business state. Part of every business' strategic planning process should be a risk assessment that identifies the possibilities for catastrophic occurrences and the potential loss to the business and need for mitigating those losses in order for the business to keep its doors open. The senior management or business stakeholders should be asked directly about their tolerance for these losses and the need for planning for addressing recovery loss that may occur. Many levels of loss (the building, information system, business process, entire complex, key personnel, or communications system, for example) may shape this discussion, requiring some up front planning of potential recovery scenarios, costs, and recovery times to get management's attention on this issue.

Time is money, as they say, so the key issue that will get their attention is, "How long can you be without?" How long can a business can be down and what the downtime costs are should be numbers that can be estimated and presented to management for an executive decision. The indirect issue relates to the revenue impact when the customer's view of the business changes and the loss of future business occurs when customers see the company as one that cannot be relied upon to service their ongoing business requirements. At some point, the outage loss costs will exhaust the available resources of the company and it folds. The nine largest airlines estimated they lost between $100 million and $250 million a day after the September 11, 2001 tragedies. In fact, some airlines are now facing bankruptcy. It does not take long for losses to add up when incoming revenues come to a screeching halt at the same time that the operational costs are rising. In order for you to adequately assess the planning processes, you will need to know the acceptable recovery time frame based on the tolerance for loss. As a rough estimate, you can take the annual revenues of the business, divide it by 260 (business days in a year), and use that number as the first day's loss. Things will get worse in some kind of geometric progression from there until the loss consumes the company's reserves and borrowing capacity. Loss estimates and downtime costs must be compared to recovery estimate time frames and costs to determine what constitutes an acceptable risk to management. The loss of future business due to the public media coverage and customers turning to other suppliers to meet their needs also must figure into the equation. For a management that does not tolerate any downtime and assumes it will not happen to them, this becomes a trap because the cost of that level of redundancy and preparedness is very high. Compromise is the order of the day and reasonable acceptance of some loss and delay is inevitable, relating back to the application of the familiar 80-20 rule. You cannot adequately assess DRP and BCP without management's direction on loss acceptance and downtime tolerance.

These decisions need to be evidenced for the CMP group to use as marching orders. The failure to find that these decisions have been made and documented constitutes a material weakness in the BCP and DRP processes. A thorough risk assessment may be required to make these decisions properly and the risks and risk factors need a periodic reassessment as the processes and risks change over time. If management is committed and has directed the business and IS organization to accommodate their direction through policy statements and a level of expectation that is quantifiable, achievable, and funded, you can begin your review of the components of the recovery plans against that direction. Adequate budgets for planning, testing, and ongoing support of contingency preparedness processes are another way to demonstrate that there is necessary support of the disaster recovery commitments required to be prepared when the inevitable occurs. Some percentage of the IS organization's budget should be clearly marked for the ongoing care and feeding of the DRP process.

Regulators have been concerned with management's commitment to addressing contingency planning enough to have created requirements that auditors and compliance organizations can use to insist on the proper level of management oversight in these matters. The Office of the Comptroller of the Currency (OCC) issued banking circular 177 in 1983 to require that financial institutions provide proper planning for service interruptions. Since then, Gramm-Leach-Bliley and any external auditor preparing a SAS 70 has required contingency plans as well as the Federal Deposit Insurance Corporation's (FDIC) comptroller handbook and the Federal Financial Institutions Examinations Council (FFIEC) examination manuals requiring recovery planning as evidence of applied due diligence to protecting a depositor's funds. Recent HIPAA regulations require that the medical community drafts and tests contingency plans for their businesses as well. Many regulated utilities are required to have recovery plans due to directives from the Federal Communication Commission (FCC), the Environmental Protection Agency (EPA), State Departments of Environmental Services and Public Utility Commissions, Continuity of Operations Planning (COOP) directives produced by the Office on Management and Budget (OMB) for federal departments and agencies. Part of your pre-audit work will be to identify what relevant laws and regulator requirements are related to the particular business segment that you will be involved with as preparation for your engagement.

The Process of Planning for Adequate Recovery and Continuity

The planning for recovery and continuity is very important and a time consuming step of the process. Just as you cannot control what you cannot measure, you cannot recover what you have not planned for. Several commercial packages are available in the marketplace that provide a plan development methodology and even templates to use in building the required risk analysis and inventory tables you will need to adequately plan for recovery of IS business processes. In addition, many consultants also are available to assist an organization in the preparation of disaster recovery planning and associated documentation. Most of their help is provided through the facilitation of meetings and guiding the various business and systems managers through the process, asking the right questions, and challenging assumptions to ensure that the identified needs will accurately reflect what ends up being a blueprint to recover against.

An eight-step process is suggested for the recovery plan preparation process that moves from the strategic direction to the tactical follow through of the detailed plan testing and training. The concept that makes this process most successful is to have the plan built with the end user's perspective in mind. Regardless of what is going on with "the man behind the curtain," if the end user or customers see the process as equivalent to their expectations, then the recovery process has been successful and bought for the organization the necessary breathing room to fully implement reparations. The following are the eight steps:

Project vision.   Begin with the end in mind. Know what your requirements are for recovery time, loss tolerance, and management's vision of what needs to be recovered. At a high level, an understanding of what the possible loss scenarios are that the plan is being built for and what limitations or assumptions are inherent in the design before moving forward is needed. Knowing the business' core competencies and the senior management's expectations on recovery capabilities and budget constraint are necessary elements that need input into the project's vision.

Risk assessment.   What would happen if . . . ? Define the risk scenarios and likely outcome situations that would require a recovery plan be implemented. Although it was unlikely that you would have thought to consider someone flying an airplane into your building as part of a risk assessment prior to September 11, 2001, you must realize that there are many other reasons why a suite in an office building might become uninhabitable or suffer from the loss of all services or access. It is important to be thinking forward so that the plan is not built for this year's process and IS organizational structure. Your planning may need to look out several years to hit the mark. An honest assessment or recovery competencies might be timely at this point to help identify areas where the recovery efforts can be handled internally and where outside help will definitely be needed. An interdependency matrix will facilitate a better understanding of what the order of recovery is so that downstream dependant processes can lend their priority and risk ranking to the predecessor processes it needs to get back on line. Data classification and processing priorities may drive this matrix and identify the dependencies that challenge assumptions about what will need to be brought back on-line first.

Recovery strategy development.   Each set of resources or processes have several possible recovery strategies that will need to be defined to some level of detail in order to compare these strategies for their relative merits, costs, and time requirements. Level of difficulty; and time necessary for planning, advance notice, and preparation; along with the availability or reliability of solutions will be part of this analysis. Cost-benefit analysis is called for here. This strategy development will need to begin the process of reintegrating the various business unit recovery views into a cohesive and workable recovery plan for the organization as a whole. Tolerances for downtimes will need to be matched to the integrated recovery strategies as well. If the processing has several options for recovery time frames of 24 hours, 48 hours, and a week, all with associated costs, but the business does not need to be back on line for two weeks without undue losses, the slower and most likely less expensive option may be best. The strategies for a given resource across different business units also can now be reviewed for common solutions and synergy.

Plan development.   From the vision, risk assessment, and strategy, a plan can be developed to lay out the decisions and processes necessary to make those decisions into a testable and viable recovery plan. Documentation of the plan will be important and compromises along the way will need to be reconciled to the vision and risk decisions. The plan documentation will

- Lay out the vision, requirements, and assumptions
- Define the teams who will develop the components of the process
- Describe the action plans with levels of detail to be added as work and testing progresses
- Provide an inventory of all the vital records and locations of the back ups
- Provide an inventory of all the critical applications operating processes
- Document all of the system's software configurations
- Provide an inventory of all of the computers, systems, and other related resources
- Document telecommunication requirements
- Document plan maintenance and testing procedures
- Provide information from the last few tests and their results

Maintain the plan.   Maintenance of the plan will be triggered by the testing and evaluation of the plan as well as by the change procedures within the IS organization that will necessitate corresponding changes to the recovery planning of the system experiencing the change. Additionally, a six-month review cycle is suggested for reviewing the plan for other changes and maintenance that may be required. This could include call trees, personnel changes, or vendor relationships, as well as the overall resynchronization of business unit changes for their possible impact to the recovery plan overall.

Training. All levels of the organization will need to know about the plan, what is in it for them, what their roles are, and what is expected of them when a disaster is declared. Copies will need to be distributed to a select group of management and subsequent version control processes will need to be established and maintained. Staff awareness at the business unit level will involve communication strategies, call in processes, and off-site gathering plans from which to assess, triage, and begin the recovery processes.

Testing. The plan will need to be tested at many levels, with the eventual goal being an integrated test that measures the organization's ability to recover all of the pieces in the order and time frames necessary for a successful recovery. Business unit and partial testing processes will be a natural start. Expectations, problem identification, and plan revisions should be formally documented and commented on to management so everyone is aware of the current state or recovery capability for the proper strategic decision making and continued support. It is a never-ending cycle.

Plan approval from senior management. An important element from an audit's perspective, senior management must approve of the plan and its representation of their direction defined in step one. The final plan that meets their expectations is the version whose copy needs to be propagated and stored off-site and from which the recovery process needs to be directed.

In order to assess the planning process, you will need to review the asset and process inventories that are available, in order to size the recovery effort. Everyone in the entire organization may need to be involved in reviewing the processes and workflows to see how an upstream and downstream resource unavailability may impact their part of the overall process. Six major categories of resources define what will need to be inventoried and assessed, with various levels of additional detail included as necessary to fully determine the impact and recovery needs. Comprehensive inventories will be required for the following:

- Information and data
- Technology and systems
- Telecommunications systems— voice and data networking needs
- Processes and the related procedures
- People
- Facilities

As mentioned previously, the planning process must look forward a year or more because that is the realistic target time frame for having a fully developed and workable recovery plan from the initial planning phase. Each business unit will need a representative risk assessment that includes all of the previous inventory elements. For each of these elements, interviews and surveys will be required, along with hard asset inventories to determine what the emergency requirements for each resource are and what the time critical nature of their availability might be to the overall process. Impact analysis then can be performed on these subprocesses. Process flow diagramming will be an excellent technique for logically looking at the information needs and following them through the business transactions. Drawing logical perimeters around the subunits of the business or work process will enable both the auditor and recovery planner to subdivide the process into digestible chunks for analysis, testing, and follow-up. Natural lines of division may follow other audit divisible boundaries, which were discussed in Chapter 1, using reporting lines or other business or product boundaries.

When reviewing the contingency planning efforts of an organization, you should expect to see evidence of a process similar to the one previously described having been used to develop the recovery plan of record. The tasks related to identifying a comprehensive set of the components necessary to recover not only the IS portion of the business, but the business itself, either by a subprocess or in its entirety, will enable the review to span both the business and IS reporting lines of the organization. Scope management will require that the audit evaluation objectives are defined in advance so that the resultant review and opinion do not misrepresent or mislead. Time will need to be allocated to understanding the business needs thoroughly, even if the scope of review encompasses only the IS aspects, because your opinion on IS preparedness must be relevant to the business processes and cannot be concluded on in a vacuum. Additionally, being able to recover the IS processes without a business recovery and alternative workflow strategy determined in advance will not keep the business in operation or meet the business' service and client needs.

Evaluating Business Impact Analysis and the Requirements-Definition Processes

How do you determine if the recovery and continuity planning are sufficient to meet the needs of the business? One way is to review the process used to get to the plan for that recovery and assess if the proper steps were taken in making the decisions and determining if all of the relevant components have been considered in drafting the plans. The plans should be built around one or more of the loss scenarios used and determine what will be recovered, showing how extensive a loss was contemplated when the plan's development was contemplated. This will be very important for showing the extent of the anticipated recovery and management's commitment toward supporting the ongoing needs of the business in forming a due diligence perspective.

Business Impact Analysis (BIA) is a matter of looking at each subprocess and determining the impact to the rest of the operations if loss or impairment of that subprocess were to occur. The BIA also should be performed by determining what the impact to the business would be as the result of the potential disaster or disruption scenarios that are being contemplated. What would be affected if there was sudden and sustained loss of power to the facilities, for example? What would fail first and how far would the generators take you in continuing to provide service? This analysis goes hand in hand with a single point of failure assessment, a process used to identify the weakest link in a system so that preventive adjustments can be made to reduce possible downtime situations.

Many assumptions will need to be made to get to a fully developed loss scenario and each one of these assumptions needs to be documented and challenged for their reasonableness along the way. The matrix of process and service interdependencies will be developed because of this analysis and you should expect to see such a matrix documented and used to further develop the various recovery scenarios in the subsequent phases of the planning process. This resultant matrix then will describe what must be recovered and in what order this recovery has to take place in order for the entire system to get back on its feet and so that the recovery time of the most cortical processes is minimized.

For the IS organization, a determination will need to be made of each application and process as to how much downtime is tolerable to meet the various service level commitments. The SLAs will need to be reviewed for language that deals with disruptions and disasters to ensure there are acknowledgements for these disruptive possibilities. Penalties will need to be assessed and subsequently used as input to the cost and benefit analysis of the various recovery options with which the business and IS organizations will be faced. The downtime tolerance for each system and application also will need to be determined through interviews with the business management and the review of the applicable SLAs. A labeling system, which tags every process and application as to its recovery tolerance value, is the recommended shorthand method to be used for the subsequent recovery scheduling and prioritization exercises. Ranges of tolerance may be the best way to simplify this process. Downtime tolerance, which ranges in minutes, hours, days, and weeks, may seem oversimplified but is often sufficient to make the first cut at the recovery priorities. The prerequisites for the lower tolerance recovery items then will need to be reviewed to ensure they share a similar rating to the systems that they support or that support them. A process that must be brought back up in two hours will not do so if the process that feeds it can only be recovered after a six-hour recovery process of its own.

An evaluation of the interdependencies of each major process and the examination of the downtime assessments and recovery times frame estimates will provide you with an overall picture of what needs to be recovered, when, and how long it will take to achieve this overall recovery. Assumptions that may seem unrealistic should be closely examined for possible material impact to the overall expectations of the likelihood of the recovery success. The dependencies also will need to be examined for their impact to the overall recovery requirements of the business processes. Alternative methods of regaining productivity for a critical application may need to be developed as interim substitution of a predecessor process with an unacceptably long recovery time frame.

Each logical subsystem should have the following components associated with its BIA and related requirements definition:

- Determination of an acceptable outage or unavailability time frame

- Understanding of the business impact from the unavailability of this part of the process

- Documentation on the dependencies of this subprocess on the viability of other subprocesses

- Documentation of what other subprocesses are dependent on the one under analysis for operation

- Understanding of what level of substitution or work-around processes may be acceptable as an interim solution to the given subprocesses unavailability, the associated costs, and a determination of how long this replacement solution might be acceptable for use

- Description of the various recovery solutions, complete with time and cost estimates and the resource requirements necessary to affect each solution

- Categorization of a recovery priority for this particular subprocess in relation to the other parts of the recovery puzzle and in relation to the recovery process as a whole

- The identification of any assumptions or constraints that were used to get to these possible solutions and the justification for making them

- An optimum recovery path decision based on the input from the previous factors, including a cost and benefit analysis of the various options on the table

The plan that you review will no doubt be some variation of this list of expected development and analysis processes. Therefore, you will need to use your professional judgment to determine whether the identification of the need is sufficient in adequately representing the potential impact of a disruption on the business processes and whether the proposed recovery plans are realistic and adequately represented by the estimated costs, time frames, and resource requirements.

The final part of the recovery needs assessment is the aggregation of the subprocess needs and requirements into a master list. This master list will depict the recovery action plan that needs to be developed and tested to prepare the organization for recovery under circumstances similar to those used as assumptions for this exercise. This big picture view may have forced some reassessment of the requirements or a reanalysis of the definition of the acceptable downtime at this stage of the planning process. A frank assessment of the aggregate costs and overall recovery time frames needed to affect a workable recovery will often force you to rethink what is acceptable to the business while still being able to survive an outage. Be careful to look for adjusted assumptions of loss or for the severity of disaster scenario as a way to make the planning process more achievable. This short cut can lead to major disappointment, especially if the original recovery scenarios were widely communicated and agreed on by management. The result could be an expectation for the ability to recover in the broader scenario, while the development of the final plan is targeted toward a narrower definition of disaster. This gap should be identified and reviewed with management, if found, to ensure that there is no material misrepresentation of the recovery capabilities.

Evaluating Media and Documentation Back Up Procedures

Processes that create back up copies of the computer programs and data will be an obvious part of the contingency planning that will need to be evaluated in order to form an opinion on the sufficiency of the DRP. The processes you observe should be in place in such a way as to make these back ups easily available for recovery when needed with a minimal amount of extra steps necessary to make them available and useful to the recovery process. There are two main uses for back up copies of programs and data: One is the recovery from loss, disruption, or disaster, which is either partial or extensive; and the second is for archival and historical record-keeping purposes, such as an audit trail perhaps. The change control procedures must be closely coordinated with the back up process and the DRP so that the available recovery data and program code will most closely represent the processing that was occurring at the time of disruption. Some thought must be given to the recovery limitations—how the gap between what occurred since the last back ups occurred and the time of disruption, and what process will be used to return to where the process was left at the time of disruption—enabling the process to move forward from that point.

Schedules for moving back up data off-site will need to be planned so that the copies do not remain in the same general area as the current production version of the data for long time periods. Until a copy that can be used for recovery is produced at the off-site facility and ready for use as a recovery aide, those back ups should not be considered as available for planning purposes. Some businesses keep cycles of stored data on-site for incidental recovery from failed changes, for example, and subsequently moves them to storage off-site for archival and safekeeping after some time period. This scheme limits the usefulness of the data that is off-site for recovery purposes. This off-site data becomes less current each time a back up copy is made that is not moved to a location where it would be available to recover from a disruption. The possibility also exists that the data stored locally at the processing facility may become unavailable if the facility becomes unusable. The testing plans must consider the complete recall time frame, which includes staging, loading, and acclimatizing the media before it can be used in the recovery process. All of these considerations will influence the size of the gap between what is actually available to recover from and the state of the information at the time of the disruption or loss.

Back up copies of computer information typically are created as full back ups or incremental back ups of changes that have occurred since the last full back up. These incremental back ups are used to speed up the process of making back ups to reduce the delay to processing time and the unavailability of systems during the back up process. If recovery is needed using incremental back ups, the last full back up is recovered first. Then, the incremental changes are applied one at a time until the current data version is obtained, or at least as close as one can get, given the changes that have occurred since any back up was made at all. The physical location and sequencing of all of these various data versions will need to be part of the potential recovery scenarios considered, as the options are sorted out and interim reworking processes are devised. Methods for quickly identifying the media required for the timely recovery of processes in an emergency in a population of other archives and back ups should be considered and addressed as part of the planning process, possibly through some kind of segregation or labeling scheme. Evidence of these considerations should be found when reviewing the emergency operations procedures in the recovery manual.

The business processes you will review need to show the realization that the data being entered into the systems will not be recoverable until a copy is made and moved off-site to a recovery facility or back up storage site. This also applies to hard copies of the transactions prior to an electronic back up of the data being made. This perspective will enable a recovery to the point of failure. Extremely time-critical systems will mirror the data and replicate it off-site automatically, using disk copy routines that are part of the production process. This approach will ensure the maximum availability of the transaction information for recovery, if a disruption should occur. You will want to determine what kind of back up scheme is being used and compare it with the criticality of the data and the requirements for its availability in the recovery plans, in order to assess whether the back up process meets the business' requirements for data availability. Proper recovery planning will show that the examination of all possible scenarios for the time of the disaster to the time of the recovery planning has been considered. All possible combinations of circumstances and worst case scenarios will have been walked through at least on paper to determine the optimum storage cycles. This is another case where changes may be required, either to the expectations for recovery or in the back up processes, in order to get them to better meet the needs of the business should they be called on to put the systems back into production following a disruption.

The storage locations used for recovery data will be one of your points of interest when reviewing a recovery plan. This is often the same location used for archival storage, but it may be different if recovery times are critical and archival storage is remote to the planned recovery site. Moving data to and from the storage location can impact the critical path of the recovery timing. Like all storage facilities, requirements for fire proof, climate-controlled, and secure areas exist. Accessibility at all hours also must be a contractual obligation so that this media can be moved to the recovery process at any time after a disruption occurs. Electronic vaulting is an attractive albeit more expensive option to look for as well. The downtime is greatly reduced, and depending on the recovery site agreement and configuration, the recovery can be well underway before operators arrive on-site to man the consoles. In fact, with remote console control, recovery can be a simplified matter of setting up an Emergency Operations Center (EOC) and finalizing the operations transition to the alternate site.

As all processes evolve, improvements are made and changes occur. Each one of these instances of change creates a need to update the recovery plans and associated procedures. The concern that little may be known of the processes or changes recently occurring in the IS organization must be addressed within the DRP's development and maintenance, and it should be reviewed by the IS auditor in their evaluation of the process. As an IS auditor, you should evaluate how the determination is made to include the system and process changes into the DRP revisions. Revising the DRP documentation also should be a periodic process, absent from any routine updates, to ensure that the plan remains a viable road map from which to direct the recovery of the business. Opportunities to automatically include updates to the recovery manuals from the change control request forms and service or maintenance request forms is a best practice. The recovery manuals found at the point of storage and recovery will be of most interest to the IS auditor performing this evaluation. Copies available on-site will be of little relevance in times of disaster. Evidence of a maintenance trail should be documented so that the updates are logged and a history of the updates is evident. Any information related to testing and results of that testing will be invaluable to those trying to get the process to work during an emergency recovery.

Records of what data is necessary to recover the various processes will be vital for those trying to round up the media necessary to create a successful recovery. The prioritization of the process recovery steps should tie back to the media staging processes, so time is not lost sorting through media to organize it in a similar priority sequence. The results of the recovery testing will bear out the needs for data and the sequence of its need. Identification of individual files and directories stored on media may be necessary for expediting a partial systems recovery and to avoid the need for scanning large volumes to look for individual files. Changes to the back up process may be necessary to optimize the recovery from those copies. Marking copy dates onto the media will be critical to quickly finding the most relevant versions of the recovery files to use for data restoration. Media will continuously stream into and out of the off-site recovery storage area. As this data moves into and out of the available recovery window, an emergency will eventually freeze the window and those items in that space will need to represent a viable set of information from which a recovery can be achieved. This information set should be quickly identifiable and the associated documentation relative to that set of data should be right along side of it. This documentation should include file and program listings and the changes that it represents, which have not been incorporated into the recovery manual at that particular point in time.

Methods for moving documentation describing the media and process changes ranging from an interim staging availability to the full recovery manual documentation set should be evaluated for the completeness of the documentation and the timeliness of the updates. Media with no corresponding documentation related to it at the recovery location will slow down the recovery process and possibly introduce data integrity errors or worse. Documentation related to the processes and procedures will require a similar discipline for ensuring that current and viable processing is adequately represented by that documentation at the recovery staging facility. This includes operator's manuals for all of the equipment and vendor manuals on packaged software as well. Telecommunications and interface equipment may require set up and configuration as the interfaces get swung over to the back up processes, so information on getting these protocols established and the lines working properly also will be required. Versions of the recovery manual that exist off-site should be used for testing the recovery process. This is an ideal way to ensure that the documentation staged for recovery purposes can effectively meet the needs of describing the processes and recovery steps. You should assess the gap between what is documented off-site and the current information available on location to determine the adequacy of the off-site information.

It also should be noted that hard copy information, checklists, and forms will be in very short supply immediately following a disaster and a recovery plan on a disk will not do you much good without a computer to plug it in to. Items used everyday on people's desktops also will be missing from the recovery process. This included notes and shortcut process procedures tacked up by operators stations, in top drawers of desks, and posted by the phones and fax machines. Phone listings and items that change frequently will be difficult to trap in hard copy form and made available to the recovery team. Placing the recovery location on the routine distribution lists of information that gets sent to IT and the corporate managers within the organization will go a long way toward giving the recovery center a start at returning to normal and knowing where things left off. Some of this information, such as executive emergency phone numbers will be sensitive, and the need to restrict their distribution may require some creativity. Frequently changed information, time sensitive information, and privileged sensitive information may have to be stored and distributed separately from the bulk of the business recovery information. Procedure and policy manuals also should be routinely copied to this storage location for use during the recovery process. Testing teams should periodically clear the distributed material as part of the readiness process and to keep hard copy documentation current.

Evaluating Recovery Plans, Documentation, and Maintenance

human life is most important

In order to evaluate a recovery plan, you will need to obtain a copy that is intended to be used as the recovery plan for the business. It must be as complete a copy as available, and if the manual is divided up and distributed across several groups a consolidated manual may be required for you to conclude on the overall process. Ideally, this manual will be obtained from the designated EOC or location from where a recovery would be managed from, possibly a storage locker with the recovery media. The layout of a typical recovery manual was described earlier; let's dig into each section, describe the content, and what your expectations should be of them.

The introduction to the manual should state clearly what assumptions were made in the development of the manual so that the reader can quickly ascertain any gaps or discrepancies between the disaster they are trying to recover from and the one the manual was developed to address. Change logs and dates depicting the currentness of the documentation in hand also will be helpful in determining the usefulness of the documentation when comparing it to the existing emergency.

The initial steps of alerting management, ensuring the safety of the immediate personnel, and the declaring a disaster should be covered in the manual's introductory section. Activation criteria and procedures for mobilizing the recovery teams as well as formally declaring a disaster to people outside of the organization who are prepared to step up and assist in the process will need to be included in the introductory section of the recovery manual. In addition to assumptions and scope limitations, the recovery documentation should include several sections that will walk the reader through the necessary steps to affect a recovery; not all of these steps will be technical in nature. The inclusion of personnel rosters with phone numbers will be helpful for search and rescue operations. Emergency teams should be designated in advance and the team's roles and the initial steps they should take should be assigned to groups and documented in the front of the recovery manual. Call trees and emergency-gathering locations should be documented so the communication process and an orderly assembly of the personnel can be established to organize the staff and manage the recovery process.

Administration of the recovery process will need to be proceduralized so that the process can be established without a lot of advanced planning or discussion. The locations for command and control posts or EOC(s) and the necessary supplies and critical communications arrangements will need to be documented along with the inventories and services availability for these control locations. Processes for alerting management and possibly media, along with other pertinent external entities also should be included in the manual. Procedures for assessing damage, performing triage and damage control, and reestablishing communication with suppliers and clients also should be documented. Coordinating the recovery operations and logistical scheduling of help and resources will be a major task that requires specific assignment and dedicated personnel to manage it in the first hours of a crisis.

The next section should describe the various recovery teams that need to be established and what their roles will be. The designated staff and initial procedures will be outlined along with communication information and locations for supplies, equipment, and facilities for carrying out their designated tasks. These recovery teams may include

- A command and control center team

- Damage assessment and recovery coordination teams

- Alternative processing facilities and vendor notification teams

- A technical recovery team

- Departmental recovery teams

- Administrative recovery teams

- A management team

- A regulatory and media communication team

The assembly of these teams should be described in this section to get the recovery process quickly underway. The command and control team will staff the EOC and manage the recovery operations. They will act as the nerve center and provide consolidated status information to management for decision-making processes. They also will communicate with the various teams and feed information back and forth to facilitate problem identification and resolution. This includes providing recovery documentation to those who need it to perform the various recovery steps and procedures as well as directing resource needs and conflict resolution. The EOC should be identified in advance and preparations should be planned out to meet the need of the crisis management team who may be dug in for the long haul during a crisis. Several white boards and flip charts will be required to map out strategies and track hot-listed items. Communication devices of all imaginable types also will need to be available. Television, radios, cell phones, faxes, and multi-channel radios all with access to generator power will be among the requirements. Separate and dedicated phone lines for outbound calls that do not go through an IS organizational switch may be necessary for the survivability of the EOC. Geographical location maps with medical services and alternative routes marked on them also may be appropriate. Food, water, and rest room facilities along with showers and cots may be necessary preparations as well. Meeting rooms and hotline areas will be necessary stations in the EOC. The ability to trap and track problems and progress should be developed as part of the testing process and expanded upon in the EOC as needed.

Damage assessment and control will be one of the first orders of business and the documentation should direct that this activity occurs as a parallel exercise to getting the business and communication processes reestablished. Knowledgeable staff members will need to be deployed to determine how much damage has occurred, what the extent of the repairs that are required will be, and the estimated time frames and costs for getting operations and business back to normal. Determining what is salvageable as well as determining what can be put back into service immediately will take close coordination with the business recovery teams and the EOC so that cohesive business resumption strategies can be mapped out. Additionally, assessments will need to be made of any efforts that will be required to stabilize the existing situation to reduce or eliminate further damage or loss. Some equipment may need to be moved and reactivated as soon as possible. Other equipment may need to be secured and protected until prerequisite processes first can be restored. These assessments will be communicated back to the EOC, where the management and technical support teams can plot the best direction based on available resources, time, and cost factors. Security arrangements also will be determined based on these assessments and preliminary insurance contact and coverage determinations will be made based on this input coming from this review of the current situation.

The technical recovery teams will work with the alternative processing groups to reestablish the technical infrastructure necessary to get the operations back up and running. These teams will have several responsibilities related to management of the back up center operations and recovery to the primary site at the same time. These responsibilities include:

- Operation of the back up center
- Logistics and the transportation of supplies
- Support of the operations
- Specialized resources operations
- Creation of the architecture and network for the back up center
- Restoration and recovery of the original operations center

These teams will consist of communication professionals and data center operations management who can use the available media and equipment manuals to establish information systems at the recovery processing site. Or they can alternatively oversee repairs to the existing facilities and equipment depending on the assessed damage and estimated repair time frames and costs. Contingency planning is the creation of a set of documentation that enables the business processes to be put back into a state of usability and repair from some yet to be experienced disruption. Planning for an unknown future loss of the ability to produce a product or service must provide for the ability to recreate the production environment in a different location, with possibly different people than those who currently perform the tasks. Step-by-step procedures for not only the recovery but for the operation of equipment and processes will be necessary in order to accomplish this. It must be assumed that those who are most familiar with the day-to-day operations and processing steps may not be available and their routines will need to be documented so that a reasonable and knowledgeable person could adequately perform the same process and get similar results.

The unavailability of staff may seem to be a morbid thought, but there are many less dramatic reasons for requiring this approach. Natural disasters often take a heavy toll on people's daily lives, their homes, and their families, which will likely take precedence over the recovery of a business process with which they also may be associated. It should not be assumed that staff will devote themselves to the recovery of the business first and families second. This is an example of an unreasonable assumption in the contingency planning process. There may be reasons that more knowledgeable people will be required to dedicate their efforts with the rebuilding process at the main site, while others will be required to continue the processing and the back up facility. Good procedural documentation will be necessary to assist those less familiar with the processes and allow the ability to adequately recover while still producing.

The procedures for performing routine processes therefore should be found as part of the documentation set available to the recovery process. The location and state of maintenance for this set of documentation will be critical to its ability to assist in affecting such a recovery, however. This documentation set has to be current and relevant to the recovery process, which is not necessarily the process used in the primary processing situation. Any assumptions and substitutions agreed to as described in the previous section will need to be worked into the documentation to avoid confusion and interpretation at the time of need. It must be kept in mind that those using the documentation will be less familiar with it and inherent knowledge of those who perform these tasks routinely should not be assumed. As a relative outsider, the IS auditor will be ideally positioned to review the documentation and determine its usefulness to those who may be expected to be performing the processing from the back up site. Over documentation is impossible in these cases. Keep in mind that these procedures will be used by people who are preoccupied with many distractions and under stressful conditions, so the format should be clear and easy to follow.

The departmental recovery teams will be busy trying to implement the manual procedures available to them from their portion of the recovery process to keep the business wheels turning while recovery efforts are underway. Deployment of these procedures will be based on the initial damage assessments and needs determinations for what each business needs to get back into production and to get back into their particular place of business for normal operations to resume. They also will be reassigning staff to assess damage in their particular department; and identifying what the priorities are to their business, their customers, and their staff to keep things held together; repair to a state of normalcy; and move forward with the business if possible. All of these procedures and task lists should be documented in the recovery plan and available for your review. Manual procedures should be inherently risk based and developed to first assess the situation and resources available and then to initiate actions based on the needs of the process and availability of the various resources required to continue doing business. The plan documentation should describe these assessment and prioritization processes, referring to hard copy process procedures for missing electronic ones as they are identified. Access to forms, checklists, and stationary as well as work-around processes should be documented along with inventories of the available supplies and their locations. The business recovery team should be gathering the transaction documentation on what had occurred up until the time of disruption for reentry and reconcilement for input records to be used to reestablish the business after the point of failure.

A person on the department's recovery team also should be identified during the process to disseminate information to the departmental team members and to act as the designated departmental spokesperson to the EOC. If deadlines will be missed and service levels not met, this person will be working with suppliers and vendors as well as the customers to let them know and to communicate and inform. Communications should initially be managed centrally to entities outside of the organization. Both the public relations and the legal departments should have input to an honest and forthright message that does not evade the issues. Once sanctioned by the management team, this same message should be the basis for other departmental communications so a consistent message is delivered to everyone.

The administrative recovery team has several issues that will need to be addressed as part of the recovery effort. Documentation will be both critical and sensitive at the same time. Losses will need to be measured for insurance coverage and contacts will need to be made with the insurance representatives. Protection from further damage will need to be implemented as soon as possible. This may require guards and patrols, but it may also require cutting checks to local repair trades to keep things from getting worse or covering exposed but salvageable equipment. Keeping a recovery operation going involves the outlay of funds and the authority to do so. Ensuring that good money is not being thrown after bad will involve the trust and involvement of the crisis management team. However, controls over these expenses and access to the funds will be the tasks of the administrative recovery teams. The need to meet payrolls will continue and scheduled payments and bill paying will have to get back on track as soon as possible. The assessment of repair and communication of this status to management will fall on the shoulders of the administrative staff as they assess recovery operations, funding requirements, and mounting losses in the face of the disruption. Their participation will be critical in helping to determine the right course of action when cost and benefit decisions are required at various points in the recovery process. Continuing to maintain the books on any business that does get processed during the recovery may need to be logged and recorded using manual fall back processes that will require reconcilement at a later point in the recovery. Contractual obligations will need to be continuously assessed, keeping an eye on penalty clauses and possible recourse options.

Part of the administrative recovery team will be the human resource support team, and they have many tasks and processes to manage as well. They will assist in getting personnel to the right tasks and monitoring available resources to perform these tasks. This will include an ongoing assessment of the state of well being of workers who may have several personal priorities conflicting with the business needs in addition to stress, exhaustion, morale, trauma, and need for counseling, depending on the circumstances. They also will be looked to for fielding concerns about continued pay and benefits, some of whom may need special provisions provided for depending on the nature of the disruption. Monitoring worker productivity will be a helpful indicator of concerns mentioned previously, but it may be difficult due to workers performing tasks not part of their normal routines. On-the-spot training may be part of their role in the recovery process as well.

The management team will need to focus on ensuring that the right things get done while exposing the company to the minimum amount of risk. Interim policies may need to be implemented to get the job done. Ensuring that all necessary tasks are appropriately delegated, given the resource situation, while not burning out key people that are critical to the recovery success will be important. The role of "coach" and "cheerleader" will be necessary to keep from being hands on while encouraging everyone to do their best. Business plans and the original recovery plans may need to be modified and new assignments and strategic decisions made as the progress evolves. All of this will be the responsibility of the management team during the recovery process. Focusing on the bottom line and communicating this status as mouthpiece for the organization also may be tasks that need to be prioritized with the others. This team will need to be located in close proximity to the EOC, either physically or from a communication line so continuous updates and status can be conveyed. Tables and charts depicting key decision points and critical milestones should be prepared in advance to give the management team a head start on the predetermined factors that will be important to organizational recovery and success. This kind of information will serve as valuable checklists to help management ensure that all bases are being covered and that items seemingly insignificant in the heat of the situation do not get forgotten. Checklists such as these are a best practice that should be found in the departmental and IS organization's procedures as well. Simple and straightforward lists and tables will be the most effective instruments for quickly working through all of the planned items.

Regulatory and media communication issues will be an ongoing concern and involve the organization's designated spokesperson. This may be a high-ranking official depending on the situation, or it might involve regular updates from an EOC staff member. Communications related to employees, and their family members as well as vendors, customers, and media with incoming queries, will need to be managed as well as official statements. Help desk functionality, in some capacity, will need to be provided for to keep these attempts to get access to information from interfering with the recovery efforts. If regulatory notification is required based on the processes or type of business you are reviewing, the proper forms and notices should be prepared in advance along with the possible communication language, contact names, and decision tables. This should be done in order to prevent the wrong message from being sent out for the wrong reasons, to prevent confusion and miscommunication. Decisions for this regulatory notification should involve the management team.

Evaluating Alternative Business Processing Plans and Associated Training

There are many acceptable and alternative arrangements that can be used to provide for the businesses processing needs. First, let's discuss various data center processing site alternatives. There are four basic types of recovery facilities, all with their own costs and downtime constraints to consider:

Cold site.   This approach involves outfitting an environmentally conditioned and prewired computer room with co-located office space that is suitable for the necessary processing, with equipment that is either salvaged or shipped from the vendors and used to recreate the processing environment. The advantages are clearly cost related because minimal subscription costs for the space are required and the agreements maintained with the vendors to promise the provision of equipment and set up or configuration services when needed and then on a best case basis are minimal. Configurations would not need to be maintained and updated and continuous synchronization with the existing facilities is not an issue because the business provides and installs the equipment. The disadvantages are the time to prepare for use, which could be weeks. Equipment availability and set up also are potential sticking points. Costs will add up quickly for on-demand services in potentially short supplies at the time of a widespread disaster. Having configuration diagrams and set up maps in hard copy forms will be critical to the success, debugging, and ringing out all of the communication and the start up issues could be extensive.

Hot site.   This vendor-supported solution performs recovery and testing services routinely from an established recovery location. Equipment supplies have been previously contracted for to meet the needs of the business recovery. These facilities are well equipped with all of the meeting rooms and storage space necessary to manage a recovery. Testing is routinely performed here and workable solutions are programmed into the set up checklists managed by the facilities staff in preparation of your arrival. Communications are quickly reconfigured to fit your last known needs. The advantages are the minimal downtime and assurance of a workable solution due to the testing processes that are inherent with a contractual arrangement such as this. Opportunities and commitments to test and evolve the recovery processes through these contractual arrangements also are a plus. The disadvantages include the cost and effort needed to manage system and communication changes, both here and at the home site, and the renegotiation of contracts to enable the expansion of the IS organization's business in order to be prepared for recovery at any point along the growth path.

Mobile or portable site.   Used extensively in the September 11, 2001, disasters in the United States, mobile processing sites are similar to cold sites in their cost but add the flexibility of putting the processing in the parking lot adjacent to the recovery process. Mobile sites thereby minimize the costs of staffing and facilitating the recovery. Typically, these facilities are trailers trucked to the site and built to meet the needs on-site. There are limitations to how much can practically be recovered to these mobile sites, however. They also are an excellent option for augmenting office space or the command centers.

Dual site.   For large operations, the best way to operate and reduce risk is to split the operations center into dual sites that can back each other up and reduce the risk of loss at any one location. The risk of impact to daily processing from complex changes and upgrades to systems may be reduced because the operational needs can be shifted to the alternative site without affecting normal operations. High availability fail over schemes also can be deployed and provide redundancy for minor hardware failures and local outages, without impacting large portions of the operations. Often, operations can shift report servers and test configurations into the production environment without extensively impacting the users during outages or failures at one of the sites. The advantages are little or no downtime. In fact, critical operations may need this kind of hot fail over configuration even if located at a single site for some applications. The configurations remain current at all times because they are maintained as part of the daily operations. Back up planning is minimized for the business operations, thus reducing cost and effort on that side of the equation as well. The downside is that catastrophic errors made by support teams or vendors can impact both sites simultaneously, bringing down the entire operations if strict change implementation is not practiced diligently using a staged migration strategy. In addition, the ongoing costs may be higher due to the costs of additional facilities and support personnel. Some redundancy in equipment may require increased costs over cold site options but not over the hot site ones. Redundant network connection points also may create maintenance, network routing, and fail over issues that would not otherwise have to be addressed. Overall, this option has higher ongoing costs at a greatly reduced risk.

Reciprocal agreement. An agreement with a company of similar processing size, need, or rough geographical location can often commit to sharing each others space in times of need as a low cost variation of a hot site arrangement. Facilities may be ready to go or easily modified to meet the organization's need. Physical distance will be a factor in arranging with another company; too close and the businesses may be impacted by the same disaster, too far away and the recovery planning and customer support may not be economically feasible. Shared planning and training also can reduce costs and facilitate preparedness.

No plan. This is an alternative that may be adopted intentionally by an organization, using the rationale that insurance coverage and cost of recovery more than compensate for the cost of developing and maintaining a recovery plan and its associated support. You will want to review the assumptions and calculations supporting this decision. Advantages include no recurring costs or investment for back up or recovery processes. Insurance costs may dramatically increase, however, for the equivalent protection to an organization with a well-developed and tested recovery plan. Other downside risks include protracted outage lengths, if recovery is possible at all. There may be a reduced discipline to document processes and configurations, thus making rebuilding more difficult and returning the process to the point of failure impossible. Customers will definitely be impacted and you should expect to be able to review an impact analysis of the business case scenarios for client retention and public relations repair based on this decision and its long-term cost to the viability of the business.

Along with the processing site alternatives described previously, several other alternative decisions will need to be determined and documented in advance of a real disaster. This must be done in order to minimize the decisions necessary and the paralysis to the business, which can result from being forced to make decisions in a crisis when success hangs in the balance. Logistics decisions, communication decisions, labor reallocation, priority alternatives, and numerous other issues will have multiple alternative paths and some amount of thought must be given to these issues in advance in order to facilitate a recovery that will not be chaotic. Each decision for an alternative will carry certain risks and impacts that need to be evaluated and compared for their contribution to the overall risk and the need to accept a compromise as a necessary part of getting the recovery accomplished. Be sure to ask about desktop alternatives during your review as well. Work space and user access methods may create a long delay if preplanning has not been applied to determine the best alternative for providing a large number of potentially complex devices and their associated connectivity.

Shared processing has already been mentioned as an alternative that may be viable. Arrangements with a vendor or contractor to produce or process business may be acceptable as an interim alternative. Contracts related to these agreements will need to be reviewed with an eye towards the potential response times, which may become necessary to accommodate sudden needs and the associated influx of demand related to getting the disrupted business back into a mode of satisfying its customers. Drawing from the organization's inventories may help cushion downtime impact to customers, but manual processes will need to be developed and tested for keeping track of the work performed during a time when the accounting systems may be unavailable.

Business Processing Alternatives

Alternative business processing plans for the continuity of processing also will need to be evaluated along with alternatives to the IS organization's recovery. Personnel not directly involved with data center operations also will need a place from which to conduct business and perform their duties. Recovery centers with workstations, which are configured and ready to go, is an expensive investment that may not be justifiable as a stand-alone expense. Each business will need to determine and document how it will process its workload in case they lose the primary facilities used normally to conduct business. Understanding what functions are critical and those that are optional will be an exercise that could limit the need for workspace and connectivity. These needs will change depending on the length of the outage and business factors such as the monthly or scheduled delivery cycles, which may require changes in the minimum labor force requirements. Training facilities can often be pressed into service for an alternative workspace, but network connectivity may need to be reconfigured to point to the recovery center in a recovery scenario. Disperse operations will increase errors due to communication breakdowns and may introduce some logistical workflow situations that would not be ordinarily encountered. Testing and practice for these scenarios will help drive out these issues to the awareness of the recovery planning teams. Determining what is a critical function that must be manned and what can be deferred until the situation improves will be required to enable the business to scale its labor force requirements based on the severity and duration of the disruption. No one wants to consider their function as optional or marginally necessary, so management involvement will be needed to make final resource requirement determinations.

Once the workforce levels have been determined, they should be documented into the recovery plan and show what level of disruption will be required for each level of recovery support, which is roughly defined in the planning documentation. Locations then will need to be identified that will support this level of the workforce requirement, along with the necessary office accessories for the basic operational functions deemed vital to each business subunit. As mentioned continuously, emphasis on the manual processes should be assumed as the inventories and checklists are prepared for putting these alternative business-processing spaces into operations. Communication and network connectivity are major considerations and solutions will need to be thought through and planned. Forms and procedures along with desktop needs will have to be adequately provided for in order to perform most modern office tasks. Standard desktop configurations for a business process can vary widely, and without familiar icons and client software loaded on a workstation and available to the users, delays will occur.

Clearly, manual processing may be the first alternative considered during a service disruption. Any plans for processing in this manner need to consider the potential volumes and the ability for manual processes to manage even a subset of normal levels. There may be situations that obligate some amount of manual processing to occur in order to meet a commitment or delivery, or perhaps to create a natural breaking point in the process from which to begin the recovery process. When planning for these situations, businesses must take into account the effect that any processing outside of the automated controls the process may depend on could have on the integrity of the system and data. The integrity issue becomes very important with all recovery activities because normal controls are often unavailable and open access is more the norm. A post review of the access and processing should be planned for as part of the recovery process in order to reestablish the integrity necessary for financial auditors to place reliance on the accounting and record keeping processes. All of the alternative processing solutions must integrate an understanding of the fragility of the data's integrity along with the need to get back to controlled processing as quickly as possible. Controls over access and data integrity can severely impact the ability to quickly recover, however, and additional risk will need to be accepted to affect a quick recovery in all probability. These risks should be documented and instances of less than desirable control recorded as the recovery proceeds so that a proper reconcilement and review can be performed after the alternative processing is no longer necessary. Opportunities for reducing risk and better alternative processes, enabling quick recovery times while managing risk effectively, should be evaluated as part of the testing and audit review process and not as part of the recovery effort.

Insurance plays a large role in recovery preparedness as it does in all risk management for that matter. Insurance policies that recognize the potential loss and impact of risk situations and adequately compensate the company, should these situations occur, are important to the overall risk management process because they effectively transfer that risk to the insurance carrier. Many aspects of loss are related to service disruption; however, some may not be apparent or quantifiable before a disruption occurs. Every analysis of contingency planning and business continuity will involve reviewing the insurance coverage as a necessary component for ensuring that the more catastrophic levels of loss are not realized without recourse. Often, these tranches of risk coverage are more affordable than the more comprehensive coverage of an insurance policy that begins to cover at lower loss levels. A review of the insurance coverage should include an assessment of any obligations the organization may need to honor in order to fully qualify for compensation should the loss occur. It will be important to evaluate the compliance to these prerequisites in order to rely on the insurance coverage as part of the recovery risk mitigation.

Training Evaluation

Training for recovery is a part of everyone's job in the organization. People are the single most important factor to a successful recovery. For some, it is a matter of understanding their evacuation route and the use of safety equipment in their work areas. Individual staff members who are unaware of what to do in a disaster can complicate a safe shutdown and evacuation and make the situation worse. Contingency preparedness training will include basic awareness training on the facility's safety and emergency procedures in addition to teaching the steps to take for recovery. Prevention of and being able to stop a disaster before it gets out of hand are your best controls for minimizing the disruption risk.

Your assessment of recovery training should approach the issue from two directions. First, as previously mentioned, you will want to evaluate what the organization's staff knows about their roles related to recovery and whether they will on average, do what is necessary to support the plan that you have already reviewed and understand to be the road map for the organization's recovery. Any gaps between your understanding of the plan and the average worker's perception of what they should be doing if a disruption occurs will need to be evaluated for material difference and possibly reported on. Workers should clearly understand what their evacuation route is, what they should be gathering on the way out (if possible), what shutdown procedures they should be performing, and any corrective measures they should attempt before initiating shutdown procedures. These procedures and related decision guidance should be documented in procedure manuals that everyone is familiar with and readily available to workers and supervisors at a moment's notice. Reminder cards and laminated handout procedures are an excellent technique to ensure that these procedures, which will not be referred to very often, are available for reference in times of crisis. Processes that routinely remind people of the recovery and evacuation procedures and enable for questions and a discussion will be a best practice that you may encounter. These training and review sessions are an ideal opportunity to identify differences between the historical recovery procedures and current needs driving an update notification and follow-up procedure that can tune the recovery process to the current organizational practices.

The other aspect of a training review will start from the recovery plan perspective and look to see that all of the plan's elements have been covered in the training given to the staff who will need to respond to the individual plan requirements. The plan should detail how disasters will be declared, for example, and who is authorized to do so. Follow-up analysis should validate that those individuals understand their responsibilities related to the activation of the recovery process and know what to do and the sequence of events that will occur. Each step that is targeted for a responsible group or function should be known to that group or function, as well as how all of the related tasks fit together, what to do if dependant processes or prerequisite tasks are not carried out by others, and how to recognize this. The ability to execute at least the initial portions of the plan without having the full recovery plan in hand may be important for reducing reaction time and expediting the recovery process. Each business unit should know their portions of the recovery plan. They should have tested the interaction of their carrying out their plan steps with other portions of the recovery and have all materials and procedures staged and ready to take their individual business units from the point of failure to a recovered and reconciled processing status. The most evident aspect of the recovery plan training will be the results of any testing that occurs. Testing and practice are the only real ways to know if the alternative processing measures will work effectively enough to keep the business going and to limit its losses during a full recovery.

Cross-functional training as part of the operational routines as well as current documentation of the recovery process (due to testing) and the daily operational practices will be necessary should key people be unavailable to assist in the recovery efforts. Substitution personnel will require familiarization to the unique way an operation performs its processes to minimize the learning curve associated with taking over for missing or unavailable personnel. Training materials should assume this is the case to be most effective in meeting the needs of the recovery process.

Evaluating Testing Methods, Results Reporting, and Follow-Up Processes

Testing the recovery plans is an ongoing and evolutionary process that involves many stages and matures only after several trials and modifications based on the results. Tests should be initially unit specific with the goal of moving quickly toward integrated recovery testing that includes participation from the business unit teams to simulate the actual processing required to keep the business going. Reporting to management and those who depend upon the test's success is a very important part of the testing process. Because of its evolutionary nature, the need to continually communicate the current state of preparedness and the rate of progress toward fully integrated recovery testing will be required for daily risk management and decision making. This also will be a critical control point that helps the IS auditor conclude on the overall program and its effectiveness. Some of the more recent reports should be included in the recovery documentation that is stored off-site so those performing recovery will have an idea about the relative state of recoverability, should the need to use the plan arise before it is successful on a repetitive basis. The follow-up efforts, which address issues and discrepancies discovered during the testing exercises, is the only way to get from an initial test to a functional recovery process.

Your evaluation criteria will include ensuring that the testing shows continuous improvement, is a realistic preparation for a disruption that may actually occur, and is reported on objectively to management so that the current state is clearly understood. Often, an ideal way to form an opinion on testing and recoverability progress is to observe a test directly and possibly even participate in some way as a scribe or by keeping track of problem reports, for example. In this way, an internal auditor can get a firsthand look at how the plans translate into actionable tasks and can add valuable experience to their audit tool kit for subsequent reference at the same time. This observation technique also will be invaluable when reviewing the objectiveness of the report's content and the accuracy of the reported success and time frames achieved.

Testing of a recovery plan should be an integral part of the responsibilities that the crisis management and planning team have. Each subunit with recovery responsibilities and a plan documentation that can be tested in relative isolation should be chartered with testing their documented plan and evaluating that test's results against predetermined success milestones. They then should report back to the overall recovery coordination and testing oversight team with the results and issues identified for each progressively comprehensive testing scenario. Inputs from outside of the testing subunit can be simulated so that testing does not have to be conducted concurrently or depend on the success of other testing in order to reach a conclusion or to make progress.

The team responsible for the overall recovery effort should coordinate all testing and results to effectively manage the process. They should determine what rate of progress will be necessary to successfully achieve the desired recovery capabilities, in what time frame, and assess test results against the criteria. Progress may depend on the availability of resources to perform sufficient testing, where testing conflicts with the production schedules. The testing may require manning a mock recovery center and a balance must be struck to not leave the live production processing with less than adequate support and at risk, while continuing to perform the testing sequences, making sufficient progress on the contingency planning goals. Each test should be formally scheduled so that resource commitments, goals, and potential milestones can be set in advance that will map to the progression expectations for the overall plan. Senior management should be advised of the plans for testing, the projected rate of progress towards a recoverable business and IS operation, along with the costs, resource commitments, and risks associated with the exposures and projected recovery success time frames.

Planning a test involves preparing the EOC for the simulation test and using a command post like it to monitor the progress of the various subteams towards the goals of the particular testing phase. Flow diagrams, mapped out on white boards or posted where all teams can see them, will help the communication and coordination of the testing process. As interim milestones are achieved, progress can be noted on these charts, giving those who need to be involved in subsequent steps notification of relative progress and a sense of when their part is coming up in the sequence of events. Separate stations representing the various operational work teams may be the best way to recreate a mini-operational environment, where each team can perform their part of the overall sequence of recovery steps while enabling communication and the overall processes by being gathered in a common room. Communications and workstation preparations may initially be done for the command center prior to testing but will eventually need to be built from scratch just as they would be during an actual disruption, for example. Your evaluation should assess the preparations for testing and note any deviations from what might be realistically expected during a disruption. Timing of the preparation and any unrecoverable issues also should be noted as well.

Testing the plans for recovery will involve integrating the business transaction processing into the recovery process at some point in the maturation of the testing. Entering business transactions and getting business results will be a milestone showing that actual work can be conducted with the recovered systems. It will be very important to ensure that the test system's instances and test data are segregated from live production to maintain the integrity of the production systems and data. Data that is moved from the off-site media storage should not be reintroduced into the production environment under any circumstances, especially once alterations have been made. If data is obtained from the live production environment to force a successful test conclusion, it should remain outside of the production environment as well. At the same time, the data and system code used in the recovery testing will need protection from confidentiality breaches, where access controls and roles segregation may be less stringent than in the actual production environment. Ensuring that all copies of the information and any changes to the system code or data are destroyed and wiped from systems should be part of the conclusion of any testing procedures. Direct supervision over the access and segregation variations should be applied to testing processes so that control concerns are not introduced. If the systems are loaded by hot-site vendors, additional controls may need to be explored so that access and residual data are managed appropriately. With smaller than normal groups of people attempting to recreate a complete production environment, there are bound to be segregation and control situations that would not normally be of concern. Due care must be applied to ensure that operators do not take advantage and inappropriately abuse these situations.

Your evaluation should assess the preparation and planning involved with the testing. Any recommendations you may have to facilitate the smoother performance of the exercise or to ensure a more realistic approach that improves the chance for success during an actual event will be value added. Overemphasis on the controls and exposed risks should not be the primary objective of an auditor evaluating the recovery testing processes. Instead, your role as an auditor will be one of ensuring that outstanding items are identified, ensuring these items are recorded for follow-up, and ensuring the test fairly represents the true state of recovery capability and preparedness of the recovery teams. Disaster recovery is not measured by risk control and exposure—the risk is not recovering quickly and effectively enough. Control expectations will naturally be reduced in these emergencies and your evaluation of the process and vulnerabilities should be adjusted accordingly. If you are involved with the direct observation of the testing, review the issues and problem logs periodically along with the workflow and progress expectations to ensure that progress is made. If progress has not occurred, you should ensure that accurate issues and concerns are documented that will enable the corrective actions necessary to remove any roadblocks in the subsequent testing.

One of the most overlooked and yet critical aspects of testing that needs to be evaluated during an assessment of BCP testing is the process flow and the impact to the business from a disruption. How well a business can assess the related impacts, understand the implications to the clients and users, and use that information to correctly focus on priorities that address the business impact, will ultimately determine how successful the business will be after a disruption occurs. Viewing the needs and requirements of the recovery from the client's perspective and integrating those considerations into the IT recovery perspective will help to ensure the process focuses on the business needs appropriately. Business impact analysis should define these needs and requirements and should therefore be used as a measurement of testing success and testing goals and criteria. A successful IS organization recovery with disenfranchised customers will not be a win for the business in the long view.

Reporting Evaluation

At the conclusion of a test, a report documenting the test should be prepared and presented to senior management and those affected by the recovery plan. Opportunities to respond to outstanding issues may be required prior to the report's issuance to management, which is not unlike an audit report. In fact, an internal audit may be the ideal vehicle for producing an objective synopsis of the tests conducted and forming an opinion on the rate of progress and overall state of preparedness for inclusion in a management report. Goals for the test should be determined prior to conducting the test and the results and reporting should measure progress toward those goals. The goal of recovery without intervention or "back-door" assistance for existing operations should be a primary objective. Timely recovery and the ability to process production will initially be secondary objectives. Many of the daily IS operational routines, including problem identification and tracking, change control, scheduling, and operations, will have to be recreated to effectively manage the testing process and to provide an audit trail of the recovery exercise. Personnel may need to be sequestered in order to provide a realistic simulation of the conditions, and each test may span multiple shifts requiring logistical support, not only for the recovery operations but also for the reporting and tracking processes required to adequately document the recovery process and its progress.

Documentation of the testing efforts should include recording all recovery steps taken, the elapsed time for each step, the problems that were encountered, the work-around fixes or resolutions deployed, and an analysis of the progress against the predetermined goals. The order of recovery steps and the intended goals should be submitted to the recovery planning team to ensure that progress is tracked and interrelated issues with other testing teams can be coordinated. A review of the progress toward the overall goal should be included as part of the report given to senior management after each testing exercise is completed. Notations of progress on previous sticking points and additional stumbling blocks should be noted along with the planned follow-up items and next steps.

The points in the execution of the recovery test where recovery can not be effectively completed due to impassible issues should be noted and alternative testing scenarios should be explored with the remaining scheduled testing time so that progress can be maximized and scheduling disruptions kept to a minimum.

Follow-Up

After the test process, a review of the results and an honest assessment of what went wrong are vital parts of the ongoing life cycle of contingency planning. Meetings should be documented where problem logs and milestone charts are analyzed and modifications to the approach are suggested for subsequent testing. The lessons learned should be shared with similar functional groups within the organization to minimize "reinventing the wheel." An assessment of the progress against the goals, how realistic the goals are in the time frames estimated, and the rates of expected progress against historic progress will all be instrumental in adjusting expectations and providing insight for the next set of milestones that need to be set. The required modifications to the documentation and processes should be assigned and addressed in a timely fashion in order to get the useable documentation in as close to a state of readiness as possible, as soon as it is practical. Moving this documentation set to the recovery site and other distribution points will evidence another step toward an achievable recovery plan.

Resetting all of the processes so they are ready to be reinitialized in a real situation or another drill will be time critical if the window of exposure leaves the recovery process vulnerable and unable to be used until replenished. All problems and issues identified need to be cleared and resolved, along with any related process changes and task scripting for use in the next recovery process. The revised approaches need to be communicated extensively to recovery team members. This is a process that team members do not perform regularly and they will barely be able to remember what they did the last time, let alone internalize the changes that have been determined at meetings after the fact, which they may not remember or did not participate in directly.

An overall assessment of the downtime and recovery time frames experienced should be evaluated against the risk assessment and acceptable losses used to initially set the boundaries and justification of the contingency planning effort. This reconcilement exercise must result in either an adjustment to the time frame expectations, increased funding for quicker turnaround, or decreased expectations in what can be accomplished given the time frames and resources. This is the classic good-cheap-fast triangle once again. Your evaluation of the follow-up process should assess all of these issues and determine that they are managed effectively and in a manner that will result in a more successful test the next time, and are targeted at the eventual goal of sustainable recovery. There will always be room for improvement and even if sustainable recovery is the norm, cross training and integration with the operational changes will keep the need to periodic testing on the IS organizational priority list continuously.

Resources

- www.infosyssec.org/infosyssec/buscon1.htm
- www.ncua.gov/ref/ffiec/ffiec_handbook.html
- www.itpapers.com/cgi/SearchIT.pl?search=disaster+recovery

Sample Questions

Here is a sampling of questions in the format of the CISA exam. These questions are related to disaster recovery and business continuity, and will help test your understanding of this subject. Answers with explanations are provided in Appendix A.

1. An IS auditor is reviewing an organization's contingency planning and recoverability. What is the *most* important factor to consider for the success of the recovery plan?

   A. The plan has identified all of the critical applications required to be covered for the business to survive.

   B. The plan is stored off-site.

   C. The process is supported by senior management and funded adequately.

   D. Back ups are made and moved off-site regularly.

2. When reviewing business impacts of possible disruption scenarios, which of the following criteria should be considered?

   I. The likelihood customers will take their business somewhere else and return

   II. The potential losses in terms of buildings and equipment

   III. The costs associated with redeploying a process to replace the one that is lost

   IV. The time it would take to fully recover and return to processing

   V. The losses of current business from not meeting existing commitments

   A. I, II, and III only

   B. I, II, III, IV, and V

   C. I, II, III, and V only

   D. II, III, IV, and V only

3. An IS auditor determines that external consulting was used to create a recovery plan. Which of the following actions would be *most* appropriate for the IS auditor to take?

   A. Review the costs and contract deliverables for the consulting engagement and assess the adequacy of the contract.

   B. Review the methodology used by the firm and assess its appropriateness for the engaged organization.

   C. Ensure that the decisions made by the consultant seemed reasonable for the given business and organizational structure.

   D. Review the resultant plan and ensure that the business and IS staff were involved in inputting to the final product.

4. When reviewing a business and systems recovery plan, which of the following will be *most* important to find within the contents of the plan?

   A. Simple checklists depicting the steps that need to be taken to affect a recovery

   B. Change control information related to what has changed since the last plan update

   C. Call trees depicting the recovery teams and their contact information

   D. Inventories of hardware and equipment used on-site

5. When reviewing the rationale for recovery options and decisions, which of the following *best* describes the correct approach for determining the appropriate direction for recovery planning?

   A. Planning for a recovery scenario that will not be costly to implement a solution for while still meeting the requirement for a recovery plan

   B. Looking at all options for the worst case disaster scenario and picking the solution that is cheapest while still meeting the needs of the business

   C. Determining the downtime associated with each recovery option and deciding on the one that will recover the business most quickly

   D. Determining the most likely disaster situation and picking the solution that most closely represents the existing processing configuration

6. A business continuity plan should address the recovery of

    A. All mission critical computer applications

    B. Only those applications related to generating revenue for the business

    C. All applications needing recovery within the first 24 hours after a disruption

    D. Applications and processes determined by management to be high priority to management

7. Which of the following application attributes are *not* relevant when determining the priority order for recovery?

    A. The dependency of the critical applications on the output of this particular application

    B. The need for the critical applications to be recovered in order to supply input to this application

    C. The importance of this application to the business processing needs

    D. How much downtime is acceptable to the users of this the application

8. To be effective for disaster recovery, back up copies of computer information should be

    A. Stored on-site in the production environment in a fireproof and watertight container

    B. A series of incremental back ups labeled and stored properly in the media library

    C. Moved off-site as quickly as possible

    D. Labeled and cataloged, corresponding to the recovery plans, and sent to the location specified in the plan

9. When evaluating recovery plan documentation, an IS auditor determines that the plan's execution will result in the exposure of sensitive data to team members that do not have a need to know for this data. The auditor should

    A. Notify management of a material weakness in their final audit report.

    B. Recommend that stronger controls be applied to the data management during the recovery process.

C. Focus their efforts on the recoverability of the business processes and note the control weakness for follow-up after the recovery is complete.

D. Review the procedures for compensating controls or manual processes to control access during recovery.

10. Incorporating systems and process changes into a recovery plan is an important part of keeping it relevant and viable for the recovery of the business process. Which of the following approaches would *best* meet the needs of the business for ensuring that the changes are appropriately incorporated into the recovery plan documentation?

A. Testing the plan and making changes only as necessary to support the recovery plan process requirements

B. Sending all IS operational changes to the recovery site for inclusion into the recovery documentation

C. Updating the documentation during the periodic review of the plan and incorporating only the relevant changes

D. Making the business unit recovery teams accountable for their respective portions of the recovery plans and related updates

11. When reviewing a systems disaster recovery plan, an IS auditor should look for operations procedures that

A. Have been approved by senior management

B. Follow the procedures used by the IS organization in normal production

C. Describe how to perform the successful operation of the recovered subset of operations

D. Describe all aspects of the current process in detail

12. The declaration of a disaster that invokes a recovery plan process should be

A. Made by the IS organizational manager as soon as the need is identified

B. Documented as a process requiring formal approval and an audit trail to provide evidence of the decision

C. Only done after a repair and restore has been tried and has failed

D. A decision of the business senior management after considering all alternatives, risks, and costs

13. When reviewing the information recovery procedures, an IS auditor would be *least* concerned with finding procedures that

    A. Lay down the last complete back up and then all of the subsequent incremental back ups that are available

    B. Recover all available information from the available back up tapes and move forward with the available information

    C. Use hard copy transaction records to return the transactions processing history to the time of disaster from the last available back up

    D. Use the best information available and reconcile the inventories to understand the transactions that may have been lost during the disaster or disruption

14. The most important aspect of a recovery plan in the initial hours of a recovery process will be that

    A. Call lists and rosters are included for contacting the recovery teams.

    B. People have been trained what to do and where to meet to gather and begin recovery without the documented plan.

    C. A disaster is declared by management and the EOC is activated as a control center.

    D. Testing results have been included to show current recoverability.

15. When reviewing a recovery plan, an IS auditor will be *least* concerned with plans for managing the press and media by

    A. Providing a location away from the immediate action where the media and press can be briefed periodically by the designated spokesperson, and allowed the opportunity to ask questions

    B. Providing space for the press and media inside the Emergency Operations Center (EOC) with immediate access to recovery teams

    C. Using a policy to tell the media and press as little as possible and denying all rumors with a "no comment" reply

    D. Using a policy that encourages the media to talk to the workers and ask questions as they come in and out of the recovery area as a way to communicate without interfering with management and the recovery process

16. What is the primary advantage of a hot site over a cold site for recovery planning?

    A. There is less work to do at the time of disaster because the site management will prepare it for you.

    B. Communications have already been tested, thus providing for a higher probability of success.

    C. Testing has occurred at this location in the past, so recovery teams are more familiar with the facilities and how to go about affecting a recovery.

    D. Downtime is minimized because equipment does not have to be configured and installed.

17. When reviewing the plans for business operation recovery, an IS auditor would be *most* concerned to find which of the following unaddressed by the plan?

    A. That there is adequate space for accommodating the business staff in an alternate site

    B. That computer workstations are available with the latest technology on them with which to perform the business processes

    C. That a desktop appropriate for the processing of the recovered business can be made available

    D. That connectivity to the EOC is provided for the business desktops for communication

18. When observing the testing of recovery in a dual-site, operational, recovery plan configurations, what should an IS auditor expect to see?

    A. Business continues as it normally would with no downtime or disruption

    B. Additional equipment being quickly turned on and added to the configuration at the surviving site to accommodate full processing with minimal disruption

    C. Two identical sets of processing equipment set up for hot fail over from one site to the other with no impact on the users

    D. A procedure that sheds some testing, reporting, and lesser essential functions, allowing for the concentration of the surviving site on the critical business processing to be performed

19. When reviewing the recovery testing reports to management, an IS auditor will be *most* concerned if the following is not part of the report:

    A. An assessment of the time it takes to recover compared to the management expectations for recovery and a gap analysis of the potential impact that any shortfall may have on management's risk or loss expectations

    B. A comprehensive list of all of the problems and the resultant assigned action items

    C. A description of the process used to test the recovery, depicting the assumptions made about the recovery situation that was being tested

    D. A list of planned goals or milestones with an analysis of the ones that were achieved and those that were not successfully tested

CHAPTER
6

Business Application Systems Development, Acquisition, Implementation, and Maintenance

This chapter and the associated CISA exam content area cover the evaluation and assessment of building and maintaining those applications that businesses use to perform their work. Knowledge of this subject matter creates 16 percent of the exam content. We have covered many of these items previously in a slightly different context, but the concepts are worth revisiting here—not only because they are equally applicable but because they are universal concepts that need to be mastered by the *information systems* (IS) auditor, and the review and repetition will begin to solidify your required understanding of these principles for continuous use as part of your auditing toolkit. Under the hood, the more seasoned and experienced IS auditors normally perform detailed business application auditing. This situation occurs because you must first understand the general concepts that we covered in previous content areas in order to apply those same principles to the development disciplines required in application development. The new concepts that are unique to these user interface systems will have these principles applied to them, as well. Developers' methodologies must also be well known to the IS auditor in order for them to adequately and effectively compare the work they are reviewing to those models.

The processes by which application systems are developed or acquired will follow many familiar workflows and testing techniques that the IS auditor uses. They will ensure that proper diligence was applied to each of these steps so that the resulting application will meet the needs and objectives of the business organization while protecting the data and integrity of the business throughout the design and implementation phases. By the end of this chapter, you should be able to:

- Understand the applicability of the various development methodologies and tools, such as prototyping, *rapid application development* (RAD), *systems development life cycle* (SDLC), *object-oriented design* (OOD) techniques, and so on

- Review an application development and implementation process for appropriate use of:

  - Application design and architecture based on the associated risks and controls inherent with each approach

  - Application change control both during development and in the post-implementation phases

  - Segregation of duties principles during the development and designed into the systems under development

  - Input and output controls

  - Quality assurance and testing techniques and methodologies

  - Protection of code and data during development and testing

  - Flowcharting, entity relationship diagramming, and modeling

  - Built-in controls using file structures, interface design, and reporting

- Apply your knowledge of project management principles, techniques, and practices to the evaluation of their use in the application's build or buy, implementation, and maintenance processes

- Assess proper build versus buy decision-making and the related vendor evaluation and contract negotiations

- Assess the adequacy of data conversion, the integration of new systems, and ongoing system maintenance processes

- Review programming and testing processes at a high level for adequate approach and applied controls

I have found that being a programmer is not a requirement for reviewing this kind of work. A project management understanding is a requirement, however. It also helps to have the ability to think through the logical application of the process steps like a programmer might. In order to understand why deviations to what seems like a better-controlled way of doing things are being employed, the IS auditor must keep an open mind to understanding why the logic behind the chosen and better approach might not be the more controlled one for any one particular development effort.

Evaluation Approach

When tasked with the evaluation of a development effort, it will be very important to fully understand the scope and objectives for which your assigned review is intended. Is it to understand the efficiency and effectiveness of the software development that has already been concluded? Is it to opine on the overall process used by an organization for all development methods (therefore focusing on the methodologies involved with perhaps some samples cases used to validate the methods as examples)? As with all evaluation engagements, knowing the scope of the review will help set the boundaries and enable you to direct your resources appropriately on those tasks that are most likely to result in reaching the right areas of focus and meeting the needs of the business that is engaging you for the review. Generally, the type of review can be classified as either proactive—where you review the processes used before or at the initial stages of the process—or detective, where a review assesses performance after a project is completed. After-the-fact auditing, also referred to as bayoneting the wounded, is often less useful to those who need guidance most but is often used because management is not alerted to project problems until they are significant enough to appear on the radar. An internal audit organization might review the overall development methodology used as one of its regularly scheduled audits to avoid being put in the situation of a Monday morning quarterback and offering solutions that were not apparent at the time of the development process compromise.

If the target is one particular applications development effort, the scope should be clearly understood—and limits of any review assessment activities should be documented and agreed to before beginning the fieldwork, if possible. If a standard and approved methodology has been documented for an organization and the review is one of execution against that methodology, then the objectives are a little less ambiguous and more straightforward. Knowing the rules used as the development and quality standards is a first step toward this kind of audit, and a little legwork to determine the de facto standards and how they might differ from the documented standards will serve you well in avoiding pitfalls along the way. As you review these efforts, you will want to understand the authorities and decision makers as well as the project management team's scope of influence across the entire project so that boundaries can be best applied and your recommendations can serve successfully for those involved. Be wary of attempts to use the audit effort to pit one point of view or political faction against another by not committing to judgmental calls or premature conclusions before hearing all sides of the story and the rationale for approach and methodology.

One way to evaluate development processes is to be involved with the development process as a team member, keeping an eye on proper process execution along the way and ensuring that proper controls are built into the systems as they are developed. This approach also provides the IS auditor with a firsthand view of the compromises and risks assumed along the way and gives them an opportunity to bring their risk management expertise directly into the decision-making process. IS auditors attend development meetings, take note of progress against milestones, observe the change management and problem-solving processes for proper documentation and control, and assess the documentation quality while it is in progress. There are some concerns and pitfalls with this approach, however. Independence is the primary issue. Where the IS audit function is involved with the decisions and is complicit to compromises made during the development, it is in a difficult position when it comes to criticizing these situations down the road. The function will not be able to audit this system in the future when it represents its own work. This approach can also consume a lot of IS audit resource time with few direct deliverables to show for the time invested. Not everything that occurs in a development process is audit relative or interesting to IS audit, but even when using good judgment and triage, using time efficiently is difficult at best. It does provide excellent opportunities to develop relationships with software developers and can lead to a better controls environment all around within an IS organization. Testing and corrective actions occur in more real time as well, and value-added opportunities might outweigh the independence concerns if resources are available and IS auditing ethics are strictly observed and monitored to some extent.

Often, an internal application review related to application development will involve the normal maintenance and ongoing enhancement efforts of an existing production application currently used in the business with the objective of ensuring that its integrity and support are sufficient to keep the application viable and effective in supporting the business needs. Many smaller development and maintenance cycles will be part of this type of review, and change control and prioritization of fixes will become the primary scope items for inclusion in fieldwork procedures. Objectives will focus more closely on the translation of problems and evolving business needs into product enhancements that keep the business competitive and profitable. Ensuring that data integrity is protected while development and testing are conducted will be a primary control concern.

I have divided this chapter into a classic SDLC methodology in order to show how each section relates to audit techniques and fieldwork tasks necessary for the review of each associated SDLC step. Each section has several items that require good practice to be followed and testing that will reveal how well this goal has been accomplished for the development assignment at hand. First, let's review some of the various ways in which development can occur successfully and how their management affects the reviews that you will need to conduct. Subsequently, you will then be able to apply the relevant subsections to the various development methods as applicable.

Systems Development Approaches and Management

There was a time when most development efforts followed a life cycle that had documented and predefined reasons for all tasks and efforts that loosely followed the scientific methods taught in grade schools in the 1960s and early 1970s. Requirements were defined and identified; hypotheses were formed and tested; evaluation of experimental results was documented; and decisions were made in order to obtain a desired result. Systems were broken down into structured subcomponents that were further analyzed for their root processes, which were then reassembled into overall solutions. This method is still the most predictable for achieving results but is often short cycled due to time and money constraints in modern business environments. The scientific approach failed to appropriately involve the end user's point of view as well, resulting in solutions that were not user friendly. While they were technically effective, they resulted in over-engineered or needlessly complex solutions.

The e-commerce era swung development approach styles to the other extreme, promoting rapid design with little documentation and often buggy code that could not scale. The tendency of users and abusers to try things with the code that it was not designed for resulted in unexpected and often erroneous results. The ubiquitous buffer overflow security vulnerabilities that are prevalent throughout modern PC coding efforts is the obvious example. Getting it to the market, finding out what the problems are, and selling upgrades that fix these problems for even more money is an approach popularized by many well-known operating system vendors today. This prototyping and incremental development style can work well if user expectations are managed and evolution is understood and accepted by the sponsoring business along with the associated risks.

The *system development life cycle* (SDLC) approach in the classic sense represents the scientific method—a structured technique that will be the basis of this chapter's evaluation methodology. This method takes the problem and breaks down the requirements and needs into well-defined and documented criteria that are then used to identify possible solutions. The possible solutions are compared to the standard for achieving a solution to the problem and then to the integration of other problem-solving subsets. The result is an overall solution that meets all of the criteria in a structured and measured fashion. All attributes, activities, and outcomes are predetermined and solved as part of the problem analysis. This process tends to be more of a process-oriented development methodology.

Rapid application development (RAD), where modeling and prototyping is used to quickly get a version into the hands of the users for feedback and modification, is popular today because a working model of the final solution is more quickly available for evaluation. Problems are solved iteratively, and the final design evolves as representative user groups evaluate and assess the functionality and performance of interim prototypes and modeled solutions. Scope creep can be problematic as new ideas are sparked by partial and workaround solutions, leading to Rube Goldberg complexity if sanity checks are not a frequent part of the design process. This process tends to be more of a data oriented development methodology.

Object-oriented programming designs methodologies strive to develop modular, reusable subsets of code and functionality that can subsequently be reassembled and used as building blocks for other purposes as utility programs with stand-alone functionality and requirements. Another method worth mentioning is CASE, or computer-aided systems engineering. With this method, a set of programs aid in the design based on inputted parameters and requirements definitions. This method is useful when working within a well-defined programming environment where interfaces and database interaction must be consistently managed and enforced.

Project Management

Project management practices were covered in Chapter 2, "Management, Planning, and Organization of Information Systems" and are critically important to success in any development process. Your evaluation will primarily focus on interactions with the project managers and those support personnel who they provide for you to interact with related to their development projects. Evaluation of the controls over the development process, their management and motivational styles, and the diligence and importance that they place on good structure and documentation will reflect throughout the development review engagement and ultimately reflect on their ability to successfully develop applications. Your approach will need to be based on an objective approach with scope that everyone agrees with in order to deflect any criticism and to maintain an even-handed result that identifies risks based on principle and in comparison to agreed-upon methodologies. The best way to approach any of these kinds of reviews where personal agendas and careers can be involved is to get everyone to agree on the right way to perform the work before any fieldwork reviews start.

Functional Requirements

All business application systems designs, whether they are for completely new processes and sets of functionalities that have not been addressed programmatically before or for minor enhancements to an existing operational system, need functional requirements definitions as a starting point. These requirements must come from the business users and management and will define what outcome needs to be the result of the application programming solution under development. Often, this wish list must be carefully examined and questioned in order to ensure that the needs are fully understood and to avoid misinterpretation. Your evaluation of a development effort should find that this process of understanding the requirements is in place and ensure that business processes and goals drive it. Coordination between the development team and the business representatives will need to occur in order to define these requirements in a way that is achievable and that will not result in an overly complex solution that does not really meet true business requirements. Gleaning the true business needs from a wishlist is a business analyst's talent, and you should use it as part of the process.

Some amount of effort must be evident in intelligently gathering the requirements, and your review of the documentation should show that these user requirements are documented clearly and completely. The user executives who have authority for making decisions need to be identified, and they should be consciously approving the requirements before any feasibility or preliminary design investigation takes place. These executive sponsors will ensure that the business objective can be satisfied by the planned effort, that the relative priority of this request for design has been assessed among the other tasks and priorities in the cue, and demonstrate that a there is a place for this effort in their long and short-term planning in order to fully satisfy any evaluation concerns related to oversight and control. Support through funding and resource commitment can also help evidence the management oversight and effectiveness potential of a development project.

Part of getting this commitment and approval will of course involve convincing management that the project is worthy of support and funding. This material should be documented and reviewed by the IS auditor as well. Claims of benefit and return on investment should be supported with detailed analysis and documentation that would lead you to draw similar conclusions of support and benefit. Business problems should be defined in the justification, and realistic outcomes should be described that will result from the development effort in a reasonable time with an acceptable payback period. The solutions should fit the business model and culture as well as align with the overall goals and strategic directions of the business. Future needs and expansion accommodation should be part of the justification or be evidenced as part of the requirements to gain assurance that the design is not short-sighted and can accommodate the future directions of the business.

Any opportunities for meeting common needs or solving multiple problems would be examples of well-designed and integrated solution planning. Knowing what other systems might be at the end of their life cycle or planning for major revisions and showing the accommodation of synergistic opportunities would also raise comfort levels that planning and foresight were adequately employed as part of the functionality and inception design phases of the development.

Requirements Definitions

The functional requirements definition should include documentation for all of the interface points, inputs, and outputs needed to meet the defined business functionality needs. All existing systems interface points, including those for systems being replaced or phased out by the new process, should be identified along with the associated process flow changes that are being proposed. Replaced or interfaced systems documentation should be reviewed for completeness and accuracy. Because this process involves other departments, their systems, and feeds to or outputs from their systems, they will need to be addressed within the systems development process. The other businesses' input should be sought and documented, and the impact to their business processes should be assessed as part of the overall cost-benefit analysis that must be included as part of the project request and funding process. Any requirements or opportunities for process improvement for these business departments will need to be defined and included.

Finally, you will want to ensure that proper control and compliance requirements have been included in the requirements definition phase. Data security, regulatory requirements, and privacy measures should be defined in their entirety to ensure that these controls get up-front consideration as hard and fast functional requirements in the definitions identification process.

Part of your assessment of the development project will be to review the documentation and definition processes to determine whether the claims of benefit and need appear to be reasonable and accurate. Are the costs and time frames realistic based on your experience and other projects of a similar size and scope? Do the requirements appear to reflect the overall business strategies and actual needs? Weaknesses might include insufficient justification or support of claims, projects that do not appear to be supported or funded to the extent necessary to result in success, or requirements that are too broad and ambiguous to result in meaningful development without revisiting the functionality and scope many times throughout the course of the development process.

Feasibility Analysis

Once the requirements and need for the project have been initially agreed upon by executive management in support of the project and are defined, including a scope to a sufficient level inclusive of all tangential interface points and process steps, determining the feasibility of the planned development will be the next step. Feasibility is an analytical process that should be documented clearly and sufficiently to show probable success of the planned development effort. This statement does not mean backing into a success formula, however, and you should be on the lookout for mock analyses of this type. Those departments and interfaced processes that have a stake in the success of the development should all have well-documented input to the decision-making process, allowing room for concerns to be voiced, debated, and compromises determined where necessary to ensure that the development will result in an end product that everyone has at least had a say in and at best agrees completely on the approach. The feasibility analysis will dive deeper into the interface requirements and the effects on existing processes and workflows. The objective of the feasibility analysis is either a "go" or "no-go" decision and a firm design and development plan from which the system specifications will be built.

As the feasibility of the proposed application is studied and eventually agreed upon, any significant boundary movement or scope and objective changes in the project definition should initiate a reaffirming of executive approval and business agreement before moving forward. This process might be iterative initially, because new interfaces and impacts might need to be considered first before a second approval of the revised scope and objectives of the development project is sought from upper management. Your assessment should determine that where significant changes to the originally agreed-to functional requirements have occurred, they are documented, substantiated, and approved by the executive sponsorship during this phase of the project development.

One output from the feasibility assessment will be a preliminary design that will be used to determine the extent of the work efforts that will be required, any material costs, and anticipated delivery time frames associated with the development effort. There will be a need for sufficient detail to again assess a cost-benefit analysis of the proposed final design, showing that it will meet the needs of the business and that the impact to all processes and business units affected by the developed product are understood and included in the analysis. This preliminary design should meet the criteria described through the agreed-upon user requirements. You should evaluate the design documentation that is available at this phase of the development to determine whether the detail contained in it is sufficient to support the estimates and analysis and that the level of detail in the design can support any conclusions drawn from the analysis. Evaluate the preliminary design documentation to ensure that it meets the users' requirements as you understand them. Ensure that the regulatory requirements and security and privacy issues will be addressed in the development based on the preliminary design. Review this preliminary design to ensure that it reflects corporate policy and standards that are applicable to the production system for which the solution is being designed and that it meets any IS-specific policies and standards that might be applicable.

You should also expect to see a project plan that is available now at this stage describing the next steps, resource and material needs, and preliminary timelines that will be used to defend the viability of the development effort and will be used in support of a final decision on the proposed design. This project plan should articulate estimated total cost and potential completion dates, which you will evaluate for feasibility. This information should be reconciled to the cost-benefit analysis and any executive decision-making reports—along with a feasibility check on your part of the overall analysis and planning steps as part of your fieldwork.

Impact studies will be part of the process, and you should see a study prepared that identifies the impact of the process changes and the work-flow alterations that will be required to accommodate this new development. Evidence indicating that all major changes resulting from the implementation of this project are understood in terms of impact, that the impact can be addressed, and that the final costs and benefits include these changes as parts of the justification, should be part of the study.

Summing all of this data gathering and analysis into a management steering committee report should be the final part of this process and will need to be evident to the IS auditor performing an evaluation of the project. This feasibility analysis report should contain conclusions that are reasonably drawn for the feasibility study information and include recommendations based on these conclusions and the related analysis. These recommendations should conform to the overall business strategies and directions of the organization. They should be consistent with the existing corporate governance, policy, and practices of the organization. The report should be submitted to the management steering committee for a final decision concerning full funding and support to move forward for development. It should include all relevant information necessary to make the decision, including signoff from all involved departments and especially those who are responsible for the business processes directly affected by the development in concurrence with the recommendations contained in the report.

Finally, if internal audit is involved at all in the project, their opinion at this point should be included as part of the reporting on the process used in determining the feasibility phase of the project. It might be inappropriate for the audit team to give an opinion on the feasibility because it could jeopardize their independence, but certainly an opinion of the process used to arrive at the conclusion is within their review scope. For those projects significant enough in terms of risk and commitment to an organization's future direction, this situation would show due diligence and attempts to ensure that proper processes were being adhered to and that a controlled process was being followed. Also, a relevant milestones report with opinions and recommendations related to the analysis phase should be reviewed when evaluating a development project when available.

System Specifications

When given the green light to move ahead with the project, the project manager must now get down to the task of specifying the system elements in detail, preparing the detailed work plans that will address all of the builds necessary to meet the functional requirements and users' needs. These system specifications detail the expected behavior of the system and include things such as the following:

- Individual scenario proofs
- Documentation templates
- Individual reports criteria
- Individual review criteria checkpoints
- Final use cases against which pilot versions are tested
- Data flows for transactions
- The interface points of the users (navigation device definitions)
- Screen definitions
- Table definitions
- Data interface point definitions
- Standard algorithms
- Process step-through flows
- Single-step flowcharts
- Describing points in the processing where the decision will be made
- Describing points where data will be stored as part of the process
- All of the use cases necessary to satisfy the business functionality requirements

System specifications will need to be documented clearly and thoroughly, and the project scope definitions must now be used as a baseline from which variations will be called into question as changes to agreed-upon direction and scope crop up. This task will require that strict controls be put in place to ensure the success of the project as approved. Significant changes to system design and functionality will need to be formally approved by a predetermined authority that represents the management steering committee and that can act as liaison between them and the project teams—having a full understanding of the management direction and the project direction at the same time. Change control documentation should include impact assessments of those changes in terms of cost and time frames as well as interface and user impact (if significant).

Part of developing the system specifications involves detailing the use cases and ensuring that the planned user experiences will align with the business process needs and expectations. This task can be accomplished through a series of interview sessions with user representatives who will describe their needs and visions of how things need to work in order for them to perform their job requirements. It will be very important to ensure that this task is done and well documented to verify that the users' needs and ideas are captured and included in the system design. User needs should be tabulated and checked off as part of the review process, ensuring that the build processes being planned will satisfy business processes. Efforts should be documented to ensure that all relevant input from every type of expected user is gathered, that screens and workflows are documented for their particular use cases, and that the design specifications accommodate their needs for performing work functions.

As the systems specifications are developed and documented, the associated detailed work plan should be evaluated for adequate detail and for any control or efficiency and effectiveness concerns that the IS auditor might have. The development methodology should be determined by this point, and evidence that it is being adhered to and used effectively as development guidance should be evaluated. Project management and controls systems should be evident and used to adequately manage the systems specification efforts along achievable timelines (with realistic deadlines) and should provide for the deployment of resources as necessary to meet the goals of the specification phase. You will want to review the achievements made during the systems specification phase and determine that they have been reasonably close to previous estimates and assess any significant variances from expectations for trouble spots or unchecked risks. The resources assigned to the task of defining the system specifications should be reviewed for qualifications and adequacy in number to accomplish the objectives. As more detail is fleshed out in the project, appropriate updates to cost and time estimates should be modified to reflect the expectations now used to drive the development teams.

Upon completion of the systems specifications, the associated documentation should be reviewed to ensure that those specifications accurately reflect the approved functional design features and user requirements. Any deviations should be followed up on and assessed for materiality and possible notification of variance to the management oversight authority for reconcilement. Your opinion should be formed as to whether it appears reasonable to expect that the systems specifications as documented can be implemented satisfactorily within the user and data processing environments based on the project plan and performance up to this point. A review of the system specifications for their capability to provide adequate internal controls, information security, privacy, and regulatory compliance should be performed by the IS auditor who is evaluating the development project. Audit features, providing logs and evidence of errors, problems, and follow up, as well as inappropriate use identification and reporting should be included as evaluation points as required.

The hardware, systems architecture, and proposed software solution approach will need to be assessed for appropriateness based on development lead time and resource constraints as well as the approved design and objectives. These solutions should not expose the data or processes to inadequacies of integrity, dependability, confidentiality, or data availability. The specifications will need to undergo a similar analysis as other phases have for appropriate use of policy direction and standards as well as the resultant updates to any relevant impact assessments or scope change that might require additional approval cycles.

Specifications for systems become the road map for the actual development work. To that end, acceptance criteria for the final product should now be formulated along with the testing plans that will prove these acceptance criteria when applied in the testing phases of the development. Data ownership and classification of data sensitivity will be part of the specification documentation—and along with it, plans to protect data and allow access according to its values will need to be documented. Those managing processes that are established within the organization to administer data, access roles, and security administration will need to review and advise on these portions of the planning. You should identify places in the planning process where this situation has occurred and note any concerns made by their review that might impact the project or need a follow up. Other aspects of the security design related to the transfer of sensitive data fit into the security architecture; the approach to managing permissions and access and the need for encryption and segregation should follow similar review and approval processes.

Some kind of project-specific quality control process should be tracking all of these decision and control points to ensure that they are checked, appropriately addressed, and adequately documented. In addition, an objective outside concern such as internal audit or quality control of development at the organizational level should be looking over their shoulder to ensure that all of these processes are monitored. This situation increases the chances for a successful development and implementation at early stages of the project as well as toward the more crucial, final testing stages.

The IS data processing operations should also have a review and approval role in these early phases of the development. As a best practice, the IS auditor would like to see this process in place—which will ensure a more seamless integration with the existing process and provide opportunities for the operations staff to cite potential conflicts with current practices and routines. User department representation should be involved as a review control point in a similar fashion to ensure that their needs will be met and that the screens and interfaces developed are in line with their expectations.

As with the previous development phases, the conclusion of this phase should include updates to risk analysis assumptions, costs estimates, benefit expectations, and functional deliverables as appropriate. Any significant variance to existing expectations should be reported to management and communicated to the involved business departments and stakeholders for signoff and acceptance of change and current position and direction. Management should once again be asked to formally concur with the progress, development, and decisions made up to this point and approve continued development and funding if they agree with the recommendations made in the progress reporting from this phase of the project. Any internal audit review done of the project up to this point, along with associated opinions and recommendations, should also be provided as part of the documentation set for this phase of the development project.

System Design

At this point in the development cycle, final design specifications has been obtained and the complete design will commence in earnest and is probably already in progress to some extent. All of these phases: specification, design, development, and testing will overlap somewhat because it will be more efficient to take some aspects of the work on into the subsequent phases until a natural stopping point is reached for several situations. This design phase will make final decisions in areas where unclear specifications have existed up to this point in the development process. By now the scope should be fairly well set but scope control processes and change order management will still be an important part of the process that you should find in place as part of the development management tool set. Design documentation will be the primary deliverable you would expect to be reviewing as output from this phase and you should find it to be clear and easy to follow for a reasonably qualified developer.

Detailed work plans will need to be prepared for the design phase that should show resource and skill matching to design efforts required. Control over this work plan will be managed through the existing project management processes and follow the systems development methodology consistently as in prior phases of this development effort. Project planning should be reviewed for reasonable expectations, adequate resource allocations, and progress to date against similar measurement criteria. Deadlines should be investigated and timelines that depict the expected progress against those timelines should be evaluated for reasonableness. You will also want to ensure that the output and deliverable expectations are being met, and where they are not, action is taken to both communicate changes and to follow up with corrective measures.

If you are reviewing a development effort that is in progress, it will be relatively difficult to get measurements of progress and reports on design status in real time and gain assurance that things are progressing satisfactorily unless you have a development or programming background and have intimate understanding of the business process and the solution being developed for it. If fact, for smaller and medium sized development efforts, if might be difficult or impossible to draw a clean line between systems specifications and actual design. Especially for development processes that use modeling, RAD development, or object oriented techniques, you will need to adjust your expectations and evaluation criteria to ensure your objectives are met while not trying to force a view of the process into a mold that just will not fit. These approaches will be putting prototypes in front of users for feedback at this point in the process and your concerns will be more those of ensuring the documentation is performed to capture the decisions and final designs as well as looking to the approved scope and requirements for expansion or significant functionality scope creep that often occurs when users start to realize opportunities for adding wish list items into the process.

Most of the same audit and evaluation criteria for ensuring proper oversight and control will apply to each phase and the difference between planning to design and actual designing might be small unless dealing with very complex systems requiring a lot of coding and interrelated pieces of code. The important things to keep in mind when reviewing these design efforts are that the final design meets the original goals and criteria. Along the way you want to ensure that work is properly and clearly documented for change control, and problem management purposes. You want to ensure that, as changes are determined and uncovered, those changes are assessed for impact to users, business processes, deadlines, resource and time constraints, risks, control requirements, cost/benefit justifications and end deliverables and functionality. It will be important to see well defined and consistently used processes for trapping this information into a sufficiently documented form, notifying those who need to know, and seeking approval and decisions from the management authority functions and the business stakeholders. Theses processes repeat themselves again and again throughout out the entire systems development life cycle. In general, the more conference with business process owners and affirmed actions through approval seen in your review of the design and development processes, the more accepting and satisfied the management and businesses will be of the final outcome the more likely a successful overall effort will result.

Review of the final design should go through similar checkpoints as previous stages regardless of what type of development techniques are employed. Do the detailed designs functional features reflect accurately the approved user requirements detail? Can you conclude that there is a reasonable expectation that the designed system can be implemented satisfactorily within the user and data processing environments? Does the design provide adequately for internal controls, regulatory requirements, appropriate segregation of functional duties, and data security requirements? Have the requested audit and logging features been adequately provided for in the design and are appropriate reports related to those audit features being planned? Are corporate standards and practices being followed by the design and for the resultant product being developed? Have quality assurance standards and processes been observed adequately? Has a review and approval cycle been evidenced by operations, business users, and those process owners either providing data to or receiving data from the designed system by way of the products designed interfaces?

Well-documented designs will be the benchmark of a final design phase as mentioned previously. This is also the point in the process where definitions of testing and acceptance criteria should be developed and documented. Before the development commences, it should be determined in writing what kind of tests will be conducted to show that the developed product actually works acceptably and meets the business need criteria. Based on the planned design, you should expect to see testing acceptance criteria that will give the project management team comfort that the needs and requirements of the design have been met by the development about to start. Preliminary test plans should be sketched out and planned for in some amount of detail. This ensures that the rules will not change during the actual development phase. When the achievement of the design criteria seems more difficult to attain than simply changing the rules to meet what has been designed, compromising the original test plans will be a temptation that the preplanning can flag and help correct by requiring results that have to be substantiated.

The final design will specify in detail the architecture of the systems hardware and its configuration required for the design. A review of this design architecture should show that it aligns with the overall IS organization's systems and security architectures and will not create unique scenarios for the network, operations, and security management of it as a production system. Training, staffing, and maintenance issues for these support and production groups, that will result from the planned implementation, will need to be considered, documented, and approved by the affected IS groups in order to conclude that they have been adequately accounted for in the design. Part of the architecture and production readiness review will include assessing the impact of this design as it will fit into the production environment from two aspects. First, the design will need to utilize common processes currently employed by the IS operations environment wherever possible. Standard practices for data back-up, off-site media movement, contingency planning, change control, problem management systems, and any service level agreement processes required by IS standards and best practices will all need to be considered against this design as part of the review for acceptance into the existing production environment. The other aspect will be the impact of placing this system into the existing environment from a resource consumption and workflow perspective. Floor space, process layout, environmentals, power, and support staff perspectives will need to be assessed for impact and change, as examples. Complementary and interrelated processes will need to be evaluated for capacity and growth considerations to ensure a comfortable fit into the environment without causing cascading expansion requirements.

As a final check of the design, you will want to step through the definitions for all inputs and outputs to the system and observe the relative detail of the definitions. By drawing a logical line around the process you will be able to determine what exactly gets input into the system in terms of not only data feeds but also human intervention, and decisions. The form of each input should be documented, the quality related details, timeliness, and sequence order of these inputs should all be known and available for review. In addition the source should be identified and where this source is outside of the system, arrangement should be identified, and notifications initiated to ensure the needed inputs will be available in the quantity and quality required for the development, testing, and subsequent implementation to be successful. Inputs that are identified without a target source or that will result in additional nonexistent processes will be of concern. Each use case should be reviewed to ensure all necessary inputs will be available for the use to be realistic. Similarly, outputs from the system and their next step uses should be identified and documented. The need for output from the system should have been documented in use cases as well and each need will have to be satisfied. Ensuring that output arrangements have been at least been initiated and planned out in some detail will be required for the development of the final product to conclude smoothly with intended outcomes.

Knowing the functional logic required for utilizing these inputs and resulting in these outputs is a natural part of the definition of the design process you will want to see documented in some detail. Each functional process should be reviewed by the affected business units and agreed to as serving their perceived needs and satisfying their expectations of the system to be developed. The next level of detail might also be worth some amount of review by an IS auditor who is more systems knowledgeable. This is a review of the logical file structure and designs for table structures and layouts. Certainly this detail should be thoroughly documented and evidence of data normalization and methodical planning processes should exist with lots of good documentation to go with it. You might want to assess the adequacy of some of these plans but only if your talents allow you to make value added recommendations and if you have some concerns about the effectiveness of this process based on prior experience with this group or track record issues of some kind. It's easy to get in over your head with this level of detail, especially if you are not doing this full time. If you determine that the developers you are reviewing are professionals who work at this level of detail constantly, it's often better to ensure the documentation exists and expect a high degree of accuracy and completeness than try to dig in deep and loose credibility with IS staff and management in the bargain. The desired output of a detailed work plan should provide you with the assurance that the development work will result in a system that meets the agreed to functional requirements in satisfaction of the business leadership. Testing processes will also bear this out. If you cannot read code, you will not be able to add any value here.

Quality Assurance Planning and Review Processes

Quality assurance and the review of the processes managing it cannot exist without a definition of quality that everyone understands and agrees to up front. To step back one step further, an IS organization that does not espouse commitments to quality nor document what those commitments are through standards and procedures to follow cannot expect that a development effort conducted for their benefit will successfully meet a set of criteria that does not exist in advance of the project commencement. Quality goals must therefore be part of the IS organization's documentation initially or some acceptable criteria should be sought by the development project team to use as a benchmark to which the project will be measured for determining quality assurance before the project development starts.

If quality standards exist in sufficiency and applicability to relate directly to the development project, final checks by the IS auditor at the conclusion of each project phase related to quality assurance goals should be performed. The auditor can compare the standards to the work and create a gap analysis to determine the assurance of quality contained in the effort to that point. Certainly the functional requirements will also be evaluation criteria and the program specifications and user procedures developed can be compared to these, previously agreed to benchmarks for achievement determinations. Quality assurance is the testing for the QA criteria and a rigorous review of the development projects processes and the near final code produced to ensure those criteria are met or the work is turned back for making it compliant. These QA goals and standards should not be a surprise to anyone on the project and in fact need to be defined or determined far in advance of the design phase so the design can be built with these goals and criteria in mind all along. Your objective in the review of the completed design will be to ensure that the QA controls exist and were known at the start of the design phase, are then compared to the design, and that any discrepancies were identified and followed up on to the satisfaction of the project lead acting on behalf of the management sponsors.

Independent review from an oversight, QA, or audit function raises the assurance level significantly in most cases. Medium to large system development efforts should have dedicated QA staff that performs several quality related functions on the project teams throughout the course of development. Among those are teaching the team members the QA standards and procedures and how to use them to effectively meet the QA reviews that will occur. Performing these reviews will also be one of their tasks. Reports of these reviews and the compliance to standards performance of the team should be found as part of the documentation trail that result from the QA efforts. Participating and advising in an ongoing fashion with these efforts will lead to higher-quality information systems being produced. The plans for performing these steps and what the acceptable passing criteria will be for the post deployment review should be determined before the building begins and shared with the sponsorship for general agreement.

System Development

Your evaluation of the actual development of a system will not involve passing judgment on the coding techniques for the most part. You will be more interested in assurance that the outcomes achieved are obtained in an efficient, effective manner such that the results match closely to the expectations and that the documentation created throughout the process fairly represents the work and is sufficient to rely on when needed in the future. Processes and procedures used in the development effort will be of interest to you because they are the foundation of good control and structure that leads to predictable and reliable results that have integrity. Mapping work to the detailed work plan that should be complete and available for inspection at this point and used as a roadmap for the work being performed would be a purists approach to tracing the development, but in reality it matters very little to the resulting outcomes and the business process objective.

Of course, development is only one option for providing the software necessary to meet the functional requirements and design criteria. Purchased systems might be used to solve some or all of the need. You should expect to see evidence of build versus buy decisions and associated decision matrices as part of the analysis and design considerations as well at this point, before any development is undertaken. In situations where commercially available packages are available and capable of performing similar if not the same functions as those being developed, the IS auditor should question decisions to develop instead of buy and review the economic and business process factors used to reach conclusions supporting in-house development. Likewise should commercial solutions be favored where massive customization will result in significant maintenance and overhead costs going forward those decisions and the supporting evidence should be analyzed as well. We'll discuss the purchased product and its implementation in the next section.

Whether build or buy decisions are made, the hardware and operating system decisions will now be acted upon and all hardware that is required, not only to support the final product set but any additional requirements for supporting the development and testing environments, will now be negotiated for and purchased along with the initial architecture being configured to manage development and subsequent steps. Risks associated with various hardware and operating systems considerations, their compatibility with the IS organization's infrastructure, and ability to support them going forward are all issues you will want to touch on as part of your review of the decisions and processes followed here. RFP's and the decisions made as the result of the various vendor responses, the impact of those decisions to the development or operations support requirements, if any, will all need to be evaluated as part of your assessment in this area.

Change Control Methodologies

Change control is an extremely important aspect of the development process for several reasons. First, development project changes will need to be closely reviewed and managed in order for the project to conclude successfully, on time, and within budget. The project management aspect of change control that keeps the project on track and manages expectations, matching them with eventual outcomes can be pivotal to the project meeting its objectives. Problems associated with the development might drive change and therefore the problem management procedures should link these two processes together tightly. All problems as identified should be trapped, recorded, and evaluated and any required changes should feed directly into a change control process used by the project management team to control resources, changes over all, and used for general management of the development effort. Significant change that alters the scope and agreed to functional requirements should be raised to the management sponsorship for appraisal and action decisions. In addition, any problems or development changes that result in changes of this magnitude should be thoroughly documented, along with the options evaluated as possible corrective actions and the rationale for making the decisions that became the final course of action.

Change control also has a role to play in the development process itself, as it will ensure that development efforts are not corrupted by multiple developers making simultaneous changes on a module, for example. Managing code movement into the various development sandboxes, logical or physical testing partitions, QA regions, and final production staging areas of the development environment will require a change control procedure that everyone knows and uses consistently in order to allow development to progress as rapidly as possible without losing ground on progress that has already been accepted. Code development should follow change control processes closely, signing out code and reconciling changes to ensure a final product that will work. Version control and schemes for minimizing the number of code set variations floating about will require a disciplined approach. Phasing the development effort into stages that will allow periodic consolidation of efforts to date into one good set of code that works for all of the design criteria at various milestone points in the development process is a common practice for managing complex development efforts. Keeping code progression and changes monitored and recorded can result in a development process where versions and testing can be controlled and managed. Integrated testing of subcomponents will be required when different versions contain different modifications, affecting complimentary business functionality that has to work together on a common set of code in the end.

This concept, referred to as library management, entails keeping strict control of all versions of the code, who has it, what functionality is represents, and what point in time it was last tested with the rest of the code. As developers begin to create code that addresses certain functionality they are typically working with a subset of the whole problem, a module if you will. This module is developed to perform certain functions and supply output to other chunks of code that they will in turn need to perform their routines. Assumptions made at the time this module is created represent the best information available at the time and sometimes placeholders or even dummy information or inputs are used to simulate input processes or yet to be determined supporting processes. As coding and development evolve compromises and corrections in assumptions are made and new sets of current best information are used when creating subsequent and possibly interacting modules of code. Keeping track of who built the code, when, and under what assumptions is difficult for a simple system. But when multiple developers are working on a single module multiplied by several teams developing in differing areas of the same project, the coordination can be a real challenge. Change control and version control management are the only way to ensure some method exists for pulling it all back together into a cohesive system at some point. Testing module A with module B in an integrated test scenario might be invalidated by the introduction of module C that was built with revised assumptions in mind. Changes to module C might not directly affect module B but might affect the interaction of modules A and B indirectly instead. Sorting this all out must be managed through a change control discipline and extensive testing against criteria that is developed prior to developing the modules so that outcome is not tainted by interim assumptions and compromises.

Third-Party Participation

Risks associated with development and your control objective and planned fieldwork testing will vary based on your opinion of the involved parties and their relevant familiarity with good control practices and development methodologies in general. Professional developers carry a lower inherent risk in this area than end users managing the development effort themselves would, for example. Third-party participation decisions also have a risk–reward balance that needs to be considered as part of the overall risk equation of a development effort you might be evaluating.

Third-party programming staff contracts and the integration with other team members will need to be reviewed and evaluated to ensure the code ownership and rights are maintained. Differing styles of working might also impact the productivity and cooperative interaction of the team as a whole. This should not be under estimated. Costs will also be a factor as well, along with the associated impact to delivery dates, driving need for additional resources and increased costs. The good, fast, cheap triangle once again needs to be considered.

Documentation and Standards

Documentation that relates to a systems development effort includes many aspects of both the development work in progress and the use of the final product in production. Program code should be accompanied by documentation that will facilitate future maintenance and support of the code. Authorship should be noted on subsections where multiple development staff are involved to ensure problem resolution can be followed up on, to encourage compliance to standards and methodologies, and for use in managing change control. Training and operational direction will also be derived from the code and design documentation as well as the documentation for support and maintenance manuals.

Procedures for using the functionality provided by the developed software and how it integrates with the overall business process will be important sets of documentation you should review in depth. Process changes can be disruptive to the business workflow and impact customers and users directly. If this information is not well documented and developed in a manner that is user friendly and easy to comprehend poor performance against business objectives might be the result. For example, you will want to consider the following procedural information related to the software development effort:

- Loading server application software and installing clients on user desktops
- Initializing data files
- Performing backups and restores of software and data
- Determining access roles and managing account administration
- Troubleshooting production processes
- Conversion of systems and bulk uploads (and de-conversions) of customer data

- Year-end processing and report generation
- Maintenance, purging, archiving of historic data as a clean up process
- Operations procedures
- Reporting and output creation and control procedures
- Audit and error log use and management
- Tuning and parameter setting
- User preference settings and control
- Customization of user interface, views, and permissions

There are many other examples, depending on the business processes being supported, the intended use cases of the solution being developed, and the operational environment, the unique requirements for integrating systems, and the IS organization's operating practices. You might want to create a list of documentation you see a need for as you review functionality, regulatory, security, audit, and business functional requirements, interface, input, and output requirements and similar specifications that trigger a recognition of the need for procedures or user instructions on process use to following up on during the documentation review portion of the development evaluation. Determining the adequacy of the documentation might be a little difficult in a situation where the development is still in progress and the actual use of it has not yet occurred, but your professional experience with other like systems and the kind of documentation you would need as a reasonably competent user or systems operator will usually give you sufficient guidance to determine material variances. Screen shots and other examples that make the directions and instructions easy to follow and understand will help make them useful.

Standards might also give you some guidance as a benchmark against which you can measure the documentation available from the development effort. Using existing standards as the criteria as well as your knowledge of similar sized efforts in the same or similar organizations and best-practice models, a comparison can be drawn and recommendations for improvement made in a value added manner as appropriate. Any documentation related to standards or the best-practice procedures models agreed to for comparison that are not being addressed adequately will also be cause for follow up communication with the project leadership. A determination will need to be made through this discussion whether these gaps are relevant and therefore need to be addressed or whether to set them aside for this effort.

Data Management, Security, and Audit Functionality

The controls that are built into the application will be part of your evaluation, and, indeed, for those situations in which IS auditors are participating in the actual development process, this is where your expertise and advice will be most valuable. Opportunities to test and validate these controls during construction provide valuable insight to not only the overall comfort level of this applications control scheme but allow you to better understand the issues and opportunities when recommending similar controls to other applications. The overall data management scheme and mapping of all data through the application and transaction processes will be required to ensure access and integrity are controlled in such a way that the data will remain secure and accurate for the processes that need quality data to achieve the desired results. Source and destination will need to be identified for each set of data in each process and then relevant controls applied to ensure quality data every time. A data dictionary is the term used to describe the catalog of data and its qualitative aspects. This dictionary should be created and maintained containing sufficient documentation about each data element to support all of the necessary processing related to that data element.

Boundary Controls

Boundary control refers to the control over gaining access to the system, the data, and processes it represents. Part of the development process (indeed this should be considered in the design phase) is to consider all actions and data that will cross the boundary of the system as it is defined to this development and determine what level of control should be required for these interactions and transfers to occur and how those controls will practically be implemented in the developed system. Understanding the value and sensitivity of the data will be important factors for reviewing how this process resulted in decisions for access and security control and the resultant implementation plan. Assessing the access controls, role based grouping of users, granularity of security permissions assigned, and restrictions placed on application functionality, along with any associated segregation of those access parameters from one user group to another will need to be performed. Knowledge of the business use cases, the business processes, and the roles of the different job functions, as well as their processes and the next steps in each of their functions' support will help the IS auditor determine whether these controls were developed according to the security standards documented by the IS organization and will support the business needs adequately.

All manner of possible user access methods will need to be understood to enable the IS auditor to assess whether the scheme for identifying and authorizing users access and interaction needs have sufficient controls built into them. An evaluation of the chosen control method will validate that the proper choices were made to mitigate risks and provide adequate assurance that the identity of users are valid and that they can perform only those tasks and accesses they have a right to for the business functions they are authorized to perform. Establishing user identity is usually performed by presentation of a user account for validation. This account should be tied to a single user and their business access profile, allowing a fixed set of authorizations to that account whenever it is validated and activated through the presentation of some level of authentication checks. These checks, typically the presentation of a password, will permit the prescribed access to occur and should simultaneously log the fact that access has been approved through the identification and authentication processes.

The compartmentalization of access to files and functions within the application that are available to the users will also need to be reviewed. The perspective of this evaluation will need to consider the business processes and functional segregations required to ensure that integrity and business procedures are maintained while using the application. Access to data and functionality that would violate the business rules in a manual world must be prevented in the logical one as well. Aggregation of otherwise unauthorized information that can be gleaned from insufficient restrictions and controls in multiple disparate processes or locations should be avoided through the development of these boundary controls. Graphical user interface panels should not provide access to unauthorized items and the controls can range from disallowing the functions based on user profile, graying out buttons or otherwise limiting action initiating processes based on authorized roles, to customized panels and user screens that differ completely for each individual role or process being supported. Security levels should be documented and the access decisions should tie back to these security levels. Approvals and concurrence by the organization's security, audit, and the business process owners should be appropriately evidenced based on the IS organization's procedures.

For nonuser related boundary situations, controls over input and output interfaces will need to be considered, to ensure that these transfers of data can be performed with assurances of data integrity and reliability. Encryption of these communications might need to be considered, depending on data quality and the surrounding network environment. If encryption is used, key exchange and processes that ensure sessions and access ports cannot be usurped from the production process, will need to be evaluated, and conclusions related to their sufficiency offered. Standard communication ports in TCP/IP might not be the best way to pass sensitive data and can lead to compromise and hijacking, for example. The understanding of how data will be requested, how those requests will be first recognized then validated, and subsequently honored will need to be developed and documented. Running through several "what if?" scenarios is a good way to check these interface points and assess the control sufficiency. Here again, thinking like a malicious hacker is a helpful skill set for testing the interface development. Investigating the communications and networking environment configurations will give insight into risks and controls that might also need to be considered. Data valuation and the process dependency on the availability and accuracy of the interface will also drive the necessary controls and countermeasures that might be required to ensure availability and accuracy of interface traffic. Output information that can be intercepted or copied without the source application being aware of it could result in downstream failures while the application itself has no operational problems. A series of checkpoints should be developed and validated for each interface point and for the data going into or coming out of the application process.

Input Controls

Computing processes require input that is processed based on logical process steps, considered or combined with other input and then output is produced from the process. Even simple processes like making a table entry require the reception of input, a logical decision or two, processing steps, and the resultant output. The input data must have some controls related to it for the processing to have any hope at all of getting the job done. The alternative is massively complex and expensive analysis processes that would first categorize and characterize the input for the application prior to processing it. Most development seeks to avoid this by making assumptions that the data will be within some range of expectations and can therefore be processed more quickly and effectively. Ensuring that these assumptions are accurate and reasonable require some parameter checking and controls to be put in place. Several aspects of the incoming data that might benefit from such controls can include the following:

- Location of data origination
- Assurance that the data quality arrived uncorrupted or uncompromised
- Timing of data arrival or availability when needed

- Length of the expected character string
- Range of values acceptable for this type of input or reasonableness checks for expected values of data
- Position or layout of the expected string of characters
- Alpha or numeric data quality checks
- Absence of any data at all, null, or zero data values
- Data presented as input that is outside of acceptable parameters
- The presence of a check digit or parity bit to assess the integrity of transmitted input

Keep in mind that input data can also be decisions or instructions and the control checks will be different for each case you evaluate. An examination of what happens when these checks or tests of incoming data fail will also have to be performed to ensure the production process does not come to a halt when rejecting or setting the errant data aside and continuing processing is unacceptable. An IS auditor should determine what level of quality should reasonably be expected, based on risks related to the data types and source of the data. Controls should be identified and subsequently tested to ensure that the control functions perform as intended. Part of your testing will involve presenting out of range input to ensure the controls adequately protect the process and ensure these situations are handled appropriately.

The input method used to introduce the data might be a review point too. If data is input from a keyboard when the process expects a magnetic swipe card to be the input device, for example, there might be a problem. Input validation also has utilization in manual data entry input processes. Screens should be designed that allow for online checking of input and layouts of those screens and should be conducive to accurate and readable input processing. Data entry fields should be user friendly and clearly marked for intuitive use and validation of input prior to committing a transaction for processing. Forcing input into one of several choices rather that accepting free form input can be controlled with graphical interface drop down boxes, for example. This will increase the quality of the input data and can ensure that the input is one of several acceptable choices for which resultant process steps exist. Menu driven inputs and question and answer dialog boxes can help control input solicited from consumers or ad hoc entries that are not repetitive in nature.

Input data must also be controlled so that it cannot overwrite existing data without a validation check to ensure this is a proper action. Direct modification of data in fields where the before and after states of those input fields are not captured is a poorly controlled input situation that should be avoided. Audit trails for input activity will be good practices that you should test for, especially where the change of state can substantially affect the risks associated with the processing functions. Similar to the discussion about database commitment and transaction locking in Chapter 3, "Technical Infrastructure and Operational Practices," knowing the state of the transaction when reads or output is required of the data will require that the input is managed in a controlled manner. You will also want to evaluate the error messaging and error reporting processes to ensure they provide corrective processes that facilitate the business objectives. Obscure error messages or long tedious error reports that are poorly designed will not aid in the problem-solving process and might warrant some improvement related recommendations.

Batch totals are another way of controlling input that is entered manually. By grouping individual transactions into subtotaled batches that are divided up by either physical or logical divisions of the work, the calculated subtotals can then be used to check the quality of that batch and to trace errors back to a particular batch subset of the daily transaction processing input facilitating troubleshooting processes.

Database Controls

A database subsystem is the place where all of the process information will be stored and managed from. Tables relating to various aspects of the business and process will be populated and maintained within the applications databases. Access controls for database tables and their data elements will need to be developed as part of the application design process and should incorporate appropriate levels of control, commensurate with the value of the data, the need to keep its integrity intact, and availability requirements of the processes and users who need it. User access panels and query programs should also be controlled to only allow access that has a demonstrated need to know. The process for establishing data ownership and subsequent permission related decisions should be examined to ensure they align with the design and purpose of the data and supports the solutions designed for the business problems to be solved by this development. Completeness of information and its accuracy will be instrumental in the overall quality of the process and its output, so controls over input and access will need to be reviewed as part of your evaluation.

The database management processes will need to be examined to ensure that the design and development result in well controlled processes that support data tables which have been normalized and simplified as much as possible so that maintenance and tuning can be manageable. Integrity controls that maintain the accuracy of the data and ensure that it is used by appropriate processes and remain available to those processes as required should be evident. Data change logging and validity checks for input and change should be found for all critical data fields along with locking and rollback mechanisms that are used where multiuser systems must handle look ups and transaction input simultaneously. Concurrency controls, mentioned previously, will need to be evaluated for providing effectiveness and sufficiency without impacting the throughput and performance requirements significantly. Encryption might be required for some or all of the data being stored and maintained with the database. Where this requirement exists, the IS auditor should test to ensure that the controls effectively mitigate the risks of unauthorized access in production as well as in maintenance circumstances. Password files are always a good place to start when looking for candidates for table encryption and associated file protection processes. The presence of removable media can also be a factor in determining the need for encryption controls.

Where multitiered client-server configurations are planned and especially with distributed database architectures, data replication and transaction request orphaning should be controlled through reliable means that can be tested and evaluated to the IS auditors satisfaction. Table sizes and functional tuning of the databases should be designed into the maintenance and management procedures for the database and sizing of hardware and memory allocations should be developed to support expected future needs of the production system. Resource consumption of the various production processes and ad-hoc queries should be benchmarked and plotted against available resources to provide for smooth operational processing.

Back up and restore processes should be designed that ensure versions of the current database can be protected and restored if damaged or corrupted. Both master files and transaction history files might be required to permit recovery to the point of failure and contingency planning and disaster recovery should play a role in defining the requirements for the back up processing and storage as well as the need for sufficient documentation related to both recovering and operating the database system. Opportunities for integration of the processes recovery with the rest of the IS organization's recovery plans and procedures should not be overlooked. Database administrator procedures are among the sets of documentation you should evaluate to ensure that proper database controls and management processes are developed. The ability to recover from hardware failure related errors, as well as failures of operating systems, network communications, application software, environmental factors, and human or procedural errors should all be tested as part of your review of database controls. Mirroring and dual recording of critical transactions or recovery logs might be prudent and should be evaluated as part of your review.

Processing Controls

Processing controls reach into the processor subsystems of the development infrastructure and relate to the ways virtual memory is allocated and machine level data management is performed. Ensuring that memory cannot be corrupted by overflowing input register buffers is a prime example of a processing control. While much of this might be integral to the operating system chosen and out of the control of the development team for the most part, parameter settings and coding of software can and will affect processing behavior to some extent and can therefore cause control concerns. The errors and unexpected behavior that comes from this kind of control weakness can be very difficult to troubleshoot and be very hard to explain or understand. For this reason it is important to encourage the development team not to alter or affect the operating system functions if possible.

You will need to determine what controls are in place that addresses situations like transmission errors and transient unexpected data being introduced into the processing. Timing controls should prevent sequence of operations errors or hold up processes that are dependant on others while they are unavailable for proper processing flow. Looping process and "deadly embraces" of processing requests that cannot move forward or back off because of a similar situation with a conflicting process are examples of processing errors for which controls should be established and tested. You will want to see documentation of all instances where the developed code addresses the processor at the machine level and how the potential risk of violating kernel level integrity or instruction protocol might be affected. Any exits in the code that call on routines at the processor level might be opportunities for processor level control situations to occur.

Access controls and procedures for operations level access to operating systems and related utilities will be a testing point you will want to consider in your evaluation. Access to the operating system should be limited and although developers might have access to it in the test and development instances of the environment, plans should be documented that provide for the restriction of access to this level of processing in the final QA and integration testing regions. Audit trails and logging should be part of the design requirements. These can add real value by being turned on and used during the development process for managing changes and keeping track of modifications that might affect other areas of development scheduled when using the same processing instance. Logging is important for security related events but is also valuable for chasing down errors, determining user actions, understanding resource consumption, identifying malfunctions, and performing general troubleshooting of the development process as well.

Communication Controls

Controlling the communication subsystems refers to applying controls over the transport layer of the network supporting the IS organization's infrastructure that the development application is connected to. This information highway brings input into the application programs and sends the output to the peripheral devices accessed by the users or to other applications for further processing. As data is transported across this system its quality can be affected by disruption, attenuation, noise, or interference. Systems and devices remote to the application being developed can fail or degrade in performance, diminishing the effectiveness and reliability of the communication subsystem the application is dependant on. Application messages can also be misrouted or delayed either inadvertently or intentionally. Data can also be copied, read, observed, or intercepted. Many of the information security related attack scenarios are rooted in network communication systems.

Communication layer controls will ensure that the networking system is reliable and available when needed. These controls relate to the design and maintenance of the communication system, maintenance, and troubleshooting routines, and management of the network systems. Single points of failure should be identified and their relative vulnerability and risk factors assessed for possible materiality. Rerouting that occurs automatically when disruption occurs is a control that will help keep traffic flowing even if slow downs and congestion is the resultant compromise. Network management tools that monitor network health and traffic patterns along with proactively notifying network engineers of trouble will help mitigate these risks. Of course, good installation and wiring code practices in the first place cannot be understated. Flow controls like leased cost routing, for example make sense from a network device utilization standpoint as well as from data flow optimization perspectives.

The type of network path chosen for traffic supporting the business will have an affect of the reliability and vulnerability of the application. Leased lines are inherently more secure and trouble free than depending on a public network like the Internet for production critical traffic, for example. Data transfer speeds of the connection, determined by the handling devices at the gateway (a modem, for example), can make a big difference in the production throughput and the amount of errors and re-sends that need to be tolerated in the design. This holds true for bandwidth requirements as well. When the amount of bandwidth necessary for adequate throughput is known through testing and benchmarking exercises and the development leadership has some control over what is available to the process, bandwidth can be managed effectively and results will be predictable for the system. If you are dependant with sharing a resource with others and cannot control the allocation of that resource, the actual experience of application performance might be less than satisfactory.

The security controls applied to these paths in to and out of the application system need to be commensurate to the processing impact of their loss of availability or corruption. Mission-critical inputs should not be left to chance with unreliable communication channels. The quality of the path and the security of the path should be assessed against the risk of the data not being available to the application. The amount of protection required to properly protect the transmitted data will depend on its assigned value. Protective controls include encryption of the transmission or of the packets or payloads themselves, access controls at the port which serves as the entry from the communication system into the application, and limitations on the authorization that this connection would have once allowed into the application's port, based on the parameters identifying the communication signal.

Encryption obscures the data by scrambling it and making it unusable to casual observers. Establishing an encrypted tunnel from the applications port back to the source of the data will protect any data along this path from being observed. This is a good method for controlling access to data streams, but if keys and access codes for the encryption are passed in clear text if will not effectively protect as designed. Encrypting the packets or files and sending the payload to the application for decryption is another method to achieve this end. Keys must be exchanged to transform the payload back into useable information after it has been received and secured from further unauthorized access.

Controls to protect the port from unauthorized access can be implemented a number of ways. Knowing what should be allowed and what should not will give clues to filtering and discarding unsolicited attempts at access to input ports. Ensuring that the quality of the input is only what is expected and rejecting what is not within strict bounds or expectations will keep command line code from being introduced as input data, for example. This is one way to limit what can be done from this port into the application. Other ways involve strict transmission pathing and control of information being introduced to an application through a communication link and involve the application and input controls previously discussed. Controls that track all activity and permissions at a communication port are always a good idea so that a record of what happened should back tracking become necessary for any reason is available.

Output Controls

The output from the application processing is the result of the functions performed and the deliverables of the design criteria. These systems will determine what constitutes output, the method of output, to where, and under what circumstances including permissions and release criteria. The format of the output will be determined by these processes and matched up to the needs of the output destinations. Knowing whom the output is destined for might affect what quality or amount of information is provided in addition to the format it is presented in. Output to another system process will not necessarily require formatting into report styles with headings and cover pages and depending on the need, only a subset of the information should be provided, to protect misuse of the rest of the data. The best way to review and evaluate output controls and the associated output is to spend some time understanding:

- What precisely needs to be outputted
- What it will be used for subsequent to being provided
- Who the recipients will be
- What their level of authorization of access to and use of the data will be
- What time parameters restrict the output (when)
- Where the output is to be delivered and in what kind of format

These are the basic five Ws, who, what, when, where, and why, and need to be compared to the output design and development for each applicable use case to ensure that sufficient information is provided in the quality described, no more, and no less.

For online output, the control situation is similar. In either case, delivery mechanism security, whether it be controls related to the physical proximity to a printer or the encryption of the transmission to the end user terminal will need to be considered dependant upon the risk and the potential materiality of the loss that might occur if compromised. Any audit trails that can track the receipt and verification of what was delivered might be helpful should an investigation become necessary at some point. Preserving the integrity, accuracy, and completeness of the output from creation to destination will also be a potential investigation objective.

Testing and Code Promotion

Quality assurance should be a theme throughout the testing and wrap up of each and every phase of the development. Each module and project subsystem that is developed should be tested for the functional requirements it needs to meet the design criteria and the QA goals and standards appropriate for the particular project subset that is being tested and evaluated. The developed code will need to be reviewed by someone other than the creator for QA and design criteria and the results of that paper walk through test should be documented and followed up on. When satisfactory conclusion of this code review stage is completed, the testing should be promoted to the next step. Each testing step will involve the migration and transition of the developed code through a chain of process in a one-way fashion resulting in fully tested code coming out of the final test phase. The testing process will need to be designed to be cyclical, for if a module fails at the integrated testing phase, it will need to be demoted back to the development sandbox, go through a code review and unit test before being promoted to the integrated testing phase again.

The existence of the test plan will be the first fieldwork review you will perform on the testing process as an IS auditor. Without a test plan, built in advance to keep the process honest, it will be difficult to determine whether test criteria have been satisfactorily met. This test plan should be detailed and in writing. It should cover both unit testing and integrated testing, and test for the QA standards and any other measurement criteria deemed important by the specification process. Each test will need to be carefully crafted to simulate real world use cases and attempt some non-standard inputs and interruptions to ensure these circumstances can be handled gracefully and without loss of process or integrity of data. The test data will need to represent live data but the confidentiality and integrity of actual live data will need to be protected from exposure to this process. Dummy data or de-identified and desensitized data should be used and real data, especially customer files, should never be exposed for privacy and confidentiality reasons. Live production processes will also need protection from the testing and debugging processes and no test systems should have connectivity to the business environment directly, this must be strictly controlled. User interface testing will need to be performed from separate workstations than those used in daily processing, for example. If confusion about which system is being accessed arises, business processing integrity might be a concern. You will want to evaluate the testing scenario from a quality as well as an audit perspective to ensure that the controls, regulatory issues, and security requirements are all being tested thoroughly in the review. QA process goals for the development effort are certainly some of those quality measurements and achieving them helps the project to succeed, without following quality standards and practice expectations the project might ultimately fail when it cannot be integrated into the IS organization or cannot be maintained without large additional investments. Quality assurance is the testing for the QA criteria and a rigorous assessment of the development project's processes and the near final code produced needs performed to ensure those criteria are met or that the work is turned back for making it so.

As code moves through the testing process, change management procedures should control it and ensure that proper documentation, impact, and problem resolution tracking is part of that movement process. Versions of the code, the associated problems, and requirements achievement success will need to be kept track of when further changes and submission for testing solves one problem and causes two new ones. Promotion to the integration testing phase will have similar requirements and the issues of what module worked well with another but not a third will need to be kept straight for corrections to be effectively applied and a final solution to emerge that meets all of the design criteria, functional specifications, and QA goals. Test coordination by one person or team with possible direct involvement of the QA function is a best practice that will help keep the big picture view in perspective. Each test must be documented and the results returned for evaluation and follow up.

As the process matures and evolves toward a final product, more integrated testing will occur and different testing criteria will need to be applied to test for the user aspects, the reporting functions, and the interoperability with other systems and the associated interfaces, for example. Whole system tests and end to end process flow testing will be some of the final stages before actually getting users to perform their functions and interact with the product. At first, interface data will need to be simulated for the testing of the codes reaction to the predefined and expected inputs to the system. Eventually, the interface communications will need to be tested in a manner that does not affect the production process and such that the feed is not expected by a production process therefore failing to complete its mission because of the testing. Finally, the actual interface input (for this example) will need to be tested in an integrated manner with the code to ensure the results are as expected. This scenario will get replayed repeatedly with many fallback steps and moving forward after problem correction. More modules and subsystems will test successfully and subsequently get tested with other checked out subsystems in increasingly more complete test systems using more extensive testing scenarios. Throughout this process change control, problem management and QA functions play a vital role as does a production control like environment that ensures changes are not made on the fly and that all unexpected and undesirable behavior of the tested systems are identified and documented.

When a complete system can be successfully put through all of the paces in the test environment pilot testing, a pseudo production environment will be the next phase. You should expect to see evidence of a planned approach used to introduce the system to the users and educate them about process changes and the use of the new system. The documentation on how to use the product and what to do in certain production situations might not be complete yet, but it should be far enough along that focus groups or pilot team members can use it to begin actual test use of the product in simulated environments. As a best practice, this is an excellent validation and proof of concept for the training material and other instructional manuals as well as the product.

Piloting the production use of the product with a test group of users is a good way to introduce both the product to the production environment and to a small set of agreeable and well trained users to the new product. Both goals of exercising the system in a real world environment and looking for problems, allowing users to use the system and look for deficiencies, can be accomplished simultaneously, if properly planned. Test scenarios or scripts should be followed so that responses and results can be correlated to the expected results of those test cases. Pilot users must agree to taking lots of notes and producing accurate documentation of problems while interacting with the new system in order for the test to be effective. Problem logs and checklists of things to try, including trying to break the system or perform tasks that should not work, should be on the checklist of testing items and validated through the testing process with these knowledgeable business users. This is important because they will more quickly recognize erratic behavior and unacceptable performance from a process and work flow perspective that the developers and QA personnel might. Like all testing, several iterations of this process might be necessary to result in an acceptable product to the pilot users. During an IS audit evaluation you will want to review the test scripts and ensure that all relevant security and audit controls are tested along with the business critical functions that the product requires to be successful. Scanning the feedback forms and problem logs will give you a sense of how the testing process is going and whether any material items are going unaddressed or seem to keep cropping up.

Another way to successfully test a new information system, especially one that will be replacing an existing process, is to test it in parallel with the existing process. Buy matching inputs data element by data element and having knowledgeable users perform similar functions on both systems, outputs can then be analyzed and compared for discrepancies and variance. While this method can be resource intensive and will require a doubling of facility capacity and user tasks for an interim period, it is an excellent way to also introduce the users and production staff to the new system and provide some initial training while working the final bugs out of the system at the same time. Caution must be exercised to avoid mingling test results with accepted production process results during this testing and isolation of interfaces and output feeds must be strictly controlled. Criteria for the testing and expected results should be mapped out prior to performing the test and additional items identified during the test should be noted and followed up on in subsequent unit or integrated testing sequences. Usability and production flow comparisons are often ideal test points that will result from user involvement and participation in developing a system that meets their needs. Having test plans will keep the scope of the testing under control and ensure that results are comparable by performing tests from scripts in a logical and proceduralized fashion.

Operational tests should be conducted to evaluate the facilities and operational aspects of a complete product. Conditions similar to the actual operational environment will substantiate the hardware parameters and environmental requirements. Stress testing of the systems using load simulation software will establish peak load limits and red line caution zones where problems might occur during production processing. This is especially important where user loading is unpredictable and varies greatly throughout the production cycle. Measurements of performance and resource consumption should be used to establish baseline performance metrics during these exercises. This information can then be used to show that functional specifications and requirements have been met and to support the development of key performance indicators for managing the system when it is turned over to productive use. Back up and recovery testing should be performed to ensure the processes can be recreated from scratch should a disruptive loss occur and force a reload of the information system. Recovery back to the point of failure should be the goal of the back up and recovery process development. However, risks and costs might drive a compromise where manual methods might need to be documented into user procedures to maintain transactions between useable off-site back up creation points. Timing of back up media creation and the point where recovered systems can be used in production will need to be considered. In any case, the recovery process functionality as well as benchmark recovery performance and usability of the recovered systems will be outcomes you should expect to see validated when these tests are performed.

All testing will be for naught, if the results are not documented, gathered, and analyzed. At least one level of detailed review should be performed for all testing results prepared and a record of the tests performed and results turned in should be reviewed to ensure this is the case. Problem and issue tracking that comes out of the records of testing can be reconciled to check for adequate identification and tracking of problems if your testing should take you in that direction. Your review of testing will span this continuum:

- Test plans have been developed
- Developed test plans reflect the appropriate needs and testing points (this decision can be a judgment call but should be well rounded, and of course include your favorites from a control perspective)

- Tests are conducted in an environment that fairly represents the production scenarios. In other words, it is a fair test. Repeated tests must use identical test beds to provide comparable results

- Tests are performed by individuals whose characteristics are part of the test criteria. For example, business knowledgeable users should test business functions, network engineers might get involved with testing the interface connectivity, but you wouldn't want to do it the other way around. Repeat testing must use equivalent levels of personnel skill sets to make the test fair

- Tests require documentation of steps performed, results received, and evaluation or comments from the test taker. Problems are logged and severity from the user's perspective is captured on the test report. Tests are ideally proctored to some extent to facilitate the testing and ensure a fair test

- Training is provided to test takers in consistent manner to ensure all testers have the same knowledge basis for a fair test

- Resultant documentation is gathered and analyzed comparing results to expectations of the development testing team. Issues are summarized and prioritized by categories like severity, difficulty to fix, must have, nice to have, and so on

- Results of analysis include problem log items from the testing sessions as well as documented test results feedback

- Overall strategy for correcting deficiencies and planning for retesting should be the result of the pilot testing process

Finding this scenario or some variation that closely follows this outline in your review of testing processes will provide some assurance that a fair and objective test process has been followed that can effectively be used to move the project forward in a manner and will eventually satisfy the needs of the business users.

Security testing and accreditation should be a defined process with clear requirements based in the standards and policies of the organization. Here, security trained personnel should investigate all of the security aspects and test them to see if they can be broken or if controls can be circumvented. Results of this testing should be presented formally to user management along with accreditation, recommendation for changes, if required before acceptance, and the identification of all residual risk that will continue to exist. It will be important that management understands what risk will remain and there is bound to be some that remains, as we've discussed continuously throughout this book. To give a clean bill of health, so to speak, to a system without counseling the user management about risks to which some exposure remains, would lead to a false sense that not only have all risks been secured, but when they are found not to be, will give them reason for blaming those who approved the security for not doing their job adequately.

Training

Training documentation will be vitally important as a final deliverable to the project because without it, how will the users be able to effectively use the tool? Several aspects of training documentation and its presentation need to be considered in a new application development project. It will be difficult to perform much of that documentation until most of the bugs have been worked out and the application's final form takes a solid shape for the most part. Any work done on training documentation for the pilot test phase, for example, will need to be quality checked against changes made because of that process before they can be published in final form. Training the users can help point out flaws in the design and will stand as important testing criteria as well as accomplishing the users training goals. Whether it is an end user or an IS production staff member, if the training seems difficult or hard to understand or if the processes are cumbersome or simply do not make sense or work well in a production environment, the project will be at risk and acceptance from the users could be jeopardized. Production workers deal with these processes day in and day out. They intuitively understand what has to have happened up to the point where their process kicks in, and what just does not look right from the perspectives that are accustomed to. There in-depth knowledge of the business process might not be strong but they are good at recognizing what is different in their scope of familiarity. The process must be easily explainable to them, user friendly, and easy to grasp. Manuals should provide the detailed reference guide necessary for additional questions and learning once the basics have been covered. Training should begin with these basics and avoid the in-depth technical dump until all base functionality is well established and absorbed. Review of the training program will give a sense of the plans and syllabus for training sessions and the level of detail and the skills and knowledge of those doing the training. Incomplete documentation of insufficient training schedules and practice time might result in poor performance of the process initially while learning curve issues are worked out.

Maintenance and support manuals and related documentation might not seem like training material but they will be used to train the support staff on how the product is supposed to behave and what they should expect as a response when certain user configurable parameter settings are adjusted. These maintenance manuals should be evaluated for completeness and accuracy possibly through some hands on testing. This is an excellent way to evaluate the user friendliness and the understandability of the documentation too. Release dates and version numbers should be implemented as part of this documentation to synchronize it with the software versions and any modification or revisions. Troubleshooting matrices and frequently asked questions are good tools to use in this kind of documentation as well as in the user documentation because it gives a quick reference and a way to dig deeper if need be. Here again, contingency planning opportunities might present themselves and if that is part of your review objective, re-reading this documentation with that perspective in mind might surface other concerns you didn't fully consider at first.

User training documentation will need to accommodate the various user roles and types of users and relate to each specific production role's interaction with the application. User manuals should be fairly comprehensive and provide for guidance through the entire spectrum of user interface options, their use, recommended settings, what to do if things go wrong, and where to get additional support for the totally lost user who still cannot figure it out. Frequently asked questions (FAQ) sections of user documentation are a popular way to present quick answers to get users to be productive quickly.

Concluding on the Development Process

After pilot testing has occurred successfully and the project teams believe they are ready, acceptance testing, the formal walk through and sign off by the sponsor, is next. You should expect to see pilot users involved with this process, answering questions, providing testimony and making recommendations to the sponsorship on behalf of the development project. There must be a formal signoff to bring conclusion to this phase. Review of the entire process, goals and agreed to functionality, compromises and scope changes made and approved along they way, and a recap of the budgets numbers would be appropriate activities at such a milestone meeting of the final acceptance testing. All of the components of the information system should be covered by the testing and the final acceptance test should touch on all test work done and show through demonstration that acceptable results have been obtained. This applies not only to the developed software but also to the planned facilities, the documentation, the ability to use the system in a production environment, and the ability to support and maintain it as well. Evidence of this presentation process and any concerns from it for follow up should be reviewed and tracked to conclusion as part of your evaluation of the development process. You should review the same information and be able to draw similar conclusions to those agreed upon, giving attention to decisions that cannot be justified based on the information presented and any information that does not reconcile with your review of the other portions of the development effort.

The formal signoff should evidence the concurrence of the user community, the business processes that will interact with the new application and its processes, and the business leadership and establish agreement that the process or application that has been developed will satisfy their needs and requirements and meet the objectives for which this project was commissioned. Review for approvals should cover all of these stakeholders and any obvious omissions as well as strenuous detractors of the final approval process should be investigated for the materiality of concerns that result.

The IS auditors review should assess the use of project management and control systems throughout the process so far, and this information can then be used to give management a comfort level on the internal control processes followed to date in the project. Use of quality control processes, and the agreed to system's development methodology are part of the review of this development's processes. Serious concerns that are reported about the adequacy of processes control use might prompt management to request a more detailed audit testing for those lesser controlled areas. This more in depth review can augment the process and act as a detective control to assure that actual results are in line with expectations and those positions that are being reported. Naturally, this situation will all depend on the audit scope and objective. Consulting with the audit management and audit sponsors should always be done before significant scope of work or testing changes are made. All of the routine conclusion-of-process steps should be performed by the IS auditor at the end of this project phase like any other. These include:

- Review of budget actuals against projections and estimates
- Review of deliverable timelines achieved against the promised deadlines and expectations
- Review of project accomplishments against agreed to design scope and requirements
- Review of tasks performed against quality control standards and guidelines
- Review of processes and deliverables against regulatory, security, and audit control needs
- Review of resource usage against estimates and objectives achieved with those resources

- Review of problem and issues logs, their resolution, and any outstanding items

- Review of updated cost / benefits analysis, risk analysis, and impact assessments for accuracy and material changes

- Review of approval processes, related recommendations, and outstanding concerns

- Review of plans for the implementation project phase for completeness

Having performed this conclusive review, the IS auditor will report any material findings, their conclusive opinion on this phase, and any related recommendations to the management team for their awareness and attention. Any significant concerns should have action plans for resolution that are committed to such that the timeliness of resolution can be addressed prior to the next phase's processes. Failure to address the material issues prior to beginning the next phase will result in those risks being incompletely addressed and possibly compounded by subsequent implementation of substandard work.

Acquisition

It is equally likely that the requirements and specifications development processes will result in a commercial product being identified for implementation as all or some portion of the solution to developing a new product to provide the needed services. A blend of bought and developed solutions might also fit the bill more ideally. Caution will need to be applied to customized commercial product solutions because of maintenance costs and ongoing support requirements. The aspects of the acquisition process that need to be understood from an IS audit perspective include the following:

- The assessment of potential vendor solutions

- The investigation of the need to customize the vendor application to meet the needs of the business

- The need to maintain the customized code with the application revisions in the future

- The need to reengineer the process to more closely fit the commercial product without extensive enhancements

- The ability to get the vendor to modify their product to meet the business' needs

- The negotiation process and contract provisions including right to audit, escrow, and intellectual property rights issues
- The support, maintenance contract, and performance issues
- The implementation, support expertise, and availability issues
- The integration of vendor solutions into the existing business process flow

Let's cover some of these points, explain their gravity, and how to assess them.

Evaluate the Application System Acquisition and Implementation Process

You will want to see a build versus buy analysis related to any vendor purchase decision. Knowing the criteria for the evaluation of vendors before the vendor identification process begins will be an important risk point to consider. All too often, vendors push product on systems integrators and project management touting the proverbial silver bullet, but always describing it in terms of their solution and not fully considering the real problem at all. Trying to build a problem around a proposed solution has led many a project implementer down the path to disappointment, frustrating the business management and sponsors along the way. You should expect to see time frame requirements that support the basic problem definition and a needs analysis well in advance of any vendor solution or particular product's consideration. The problem definition should be agreed to by the business organization and sponsorship and both build and buy solutions should then be investigated against these well-documented requirements for a solution.

Vendor Selection

The vendor selection and product assessment should always include an evaluation of the vendor's financial and strategic placement in the market place along with their product pitch. This can be only used as a rough indicator of the organization's likely stability, survivability, and ability to provide continued support as we've seen recently in the energy and telecommunications markets. Companies that seem solid and well financed can evaporate overnight too, but less stable organizations are more likely to disappoint when the going gets rough. If the potential investment for a solution will be materially significant to the organization sponsoring the audit, financial statements and audit reports should be reviewed for any serious vendor contending for the successful bid. Your review material for assessing this selection process should include a set of bid documents that provide all vendors the same information from which to make their bid fairly and in like comparison to the other bidders. Any evidence of favoritism or skewed information content where one vendor gets preferential treatment over the rest should be cause for concern. The selected vendor candidates should be fully capable of responding and successfully winning and delivering on the bid package and at least three bidders of sufficient wherewithal should be on the list. Exceptions will always occur, but justification should be included where variances to these best practices exist.

Segregation of duties is a good way to ensure a fair and even bidding process. By separating those who are invested in the technical and project management aspects in the project from the bidding processes, the information flow and fairness can be controlled. Of course, this situation should not be carried to extremes, and project management should have direct control over the final decisions for their project's solutions. Often it is wise to first explore all solutions that are available in the commercial space before committing to a vendors solution. Impact to the business processes will need to be considered where exact fits are not readily available. By first entertaining proposals rather than bids, the project team can assess the various vendor strategies and potential development compromises prior to a final agreement with a vendor.

Hybrid Vendor Development Solutions

There are many hybrid solutions within the range from purely developed solutions to purely commercial solutions. Time and money must be balanced to get an effective solution that meets the needs while remaining economically feasible (good, cheap, and fast). A purely commercial solution might not meet the needs of the business exactly. Understanding how much of a variance to the exact fit the solution represents, will be required in order to determine the options available to the project in meeting their solution requirements completely. If the vendor solution is one that better describes the needed business functionalities and processes than the current organizational solutions and processes, then the option of changing the business processes to align with the vendor solution might be considered prudent. This might be the case if a specific packaged solution has been designed to meet a standard accounting, tracking or regulatory need, for example. Expert advice in the form of a well-known and generally recognized vendor solution might change the business process for the better, reduce overall business risk, and increase the efficiency and effectiveness of the organization overall. This is one possible outcome from a review and compromise toward a vendor solution but it will involve business management and strategic organizational decisions in order to be successful.

Moving down the range, another possibility is to modify the vendor application slightly to meet the needs of the business model more directly. There is often a business requirement that provides no opportunity for compromise in the process requirements and the vendor package can be tweaked slightly to provide a good fit. Some of this is inevitable in reporting, access role development, and interfacing to existing systems within an organization's process. The risks here are maintaining the modifications as the vendor product matures and is updated by the vendor. New releases and upgrades will subsequently require revisiting the customizations made to the installed code, regression testing of the new code on the customized portions of the solution that is in place to ensure that things are not broken by the upgrade, and a review of how the customized code might impact the intended changes the modification provides. This will be a continual need, so maintenance and support costs should be projected into the ROI and cost / benefit analysis when decisions are made to choose this course of action. There will also be a need to document these variances to standard vendor code and how these customizations change the base code to add to the support, cost, and contractual considerations.

Vendor code customization can cover a wide spectrum of slightly modified to hardly recognizable. One of the potentially material concerns that will need to be evaluated is how the agreements and contracts are impacted by any customization of commercial products. This must be reviewed from the perspective of support, primarily. Often when support commitments are part of a vendor agreement, there are clauses in the contract that obligate the user to keep the product in tact in order for support commitments to be honored. This makes sense from the vendor's perspective as customizations are unique to each client's business organization and to maintain an understanding of the impact of modifications on the base code for every potential client would be a monumental task for a vendor. Violation of any commitments to not modify the commercial package might void the warranty or support agreement for this reason. Depending on the situation, the vendor might entertain making and maintaining the customization requirements for you. This is often bundled with a support and management agreement that outsources some portion of application support. These can be costly arrangements and the ability to pull back from them in the future should be carefully considered before making such a commitment. When the expertise does not exist in-house to provide for these needs, there might be little choice, but when the contracts are negotiated and vital systems depend solely on a vendor's ability to support customized production systems, bargaining power is diminished and costs can escalate quickly.

Yet another variation on this theme is to obtain a commercial solution for a subset of the requirements defined in the problem analysis and to develop a solution that integrates this solution into the production processes within the organization. This method can be a successful way to meet the requirements of maintaining vendor solution purity while getting the solution that fits the business need with minimal compromise to process or purchased code. By treating the purchased product as a "black box" of sorts, the interfaces, inputs, and outputs are then designed to transition the existing environment to the fixed parameters of the vendor package. This technique is actually the most common method of minimizing cost and investment while maximizing utilization of vendor solution. Once again, though, support of the interfaces and assessment of vendor upgrade will need to be tested to some extent before implementation. But to the extent that the interface point generically isolate what goes on inside the vendor's application from the other portions of the process, this issue will be minimized. Assessment of the requirements and compartmentalization of them into a set that fits naturally within a commercial solution will need to be part of the build-buy analysis and vendor identification process. The bidding process might change slightly because best fit might also be a criterion to consider.

Vendor Management and Escrow

Once a solution is decided on, negotiations for pricing and contract language are the next steps of the purchasing process. In all likelihood, a long-term relationship will be agreed to, when deciding to use vendor solutions as key production processes for a business. For this reason, service levels and commitments for future interaction should be considered in the negotiations process. Concessions for the long-term commitment and the building of trust between the contracting organizations can reduce risk overall and enhance both parties' positions from both a financial and business perspective. For the IS auditor, there will be a few additional items to consider with the signed agreements before moving on to implementation. Reduced costs for extended service agreements are just one example where you should look to see that effective negotiations were part of the deal making. Consolidation of agreements and anticipation of future business expansions might be opportunities to leverage an agreement. The long-term strategy of the business should be seen as a driving force in contract negotiations as evidenced in the final agreement.

Regardless of the agreements futures and cost structure, you will want to see that the organization is protected by the agreement and that undue risks are not accepted or uncovered by your review of the contracts. If the source code for the software that is being sold as a turnkey application solution is held closely by the vendor as proprietary and unavailable in source form to the organization, a concern will arise should the vendor company become insolvent or otherwise stop supporting code that is vital to the organization's business capabilities. For this reason, insisting that the source code be held in escrow by a neutral and independent third party with contractual obligations to provide it to the organization if the vendor either voluntarily or involuntarily stops supporting the code is good practice. Ongoing review of the vendor's strategic direction and willingness to support the application and its future enhancements and development might also be language you will want to see in the contract. This is especially true if the current version of the application does not fit the business needs as well as promised future versions might and the businesses strategic direction depends on obtaining these future enhancements to pursue its business model to its full effectiveness.

Methods used by the vendor to gather and act on issues and concerns relating to their product should be evaluated as part of the review of the vendor. The objective is to ensure that proper attention and response will be forthcoming to meet the needs of the business. There are several best practices used in the industry worth mentioning here as control techniques. When errors and problems occur with purchased software, a service call is typically placed to the vendor. Like any IS operation, the logging and tracking of these problems should be part of the problem management process. Where mission-critical processes are at risk, arrangements should be contractually agreed to in advance for additional services related to problem management. For example, it might be important to know where outstanding problems are in the vendor's resolution process and what levels of escalation have occurred since the problem was reported or since the last update. Access to reports of outstanding problems, their priority to the vendors overall problem management system, and any interim progress status can sometimes allow for better planning and assessment of service quality. Knowing how many outstanding problems are being tracked in total would be interesting information too, and would give the organization a sense of how problem ridden an application really is, but this information is generally not given out freely.

Some alteration requests and enhancements will require extensive modification to the application in order for them to be accommodated. The percent of the customer population that is experiencing a given problem or wants a particular enhancement will affect its relative priority. A process to request enhancements and participate in setting future direction of the application development efforts might be agreed to with the vendor, depending on the clout and business impact the agreement has to the vendors overall business. The amount of influence that the organization you are evaluating has over the vendor should be assessed and compared to the significance of the investment to the vendor and the business. If there is a mismatch between the amount of attention and influence the business has with the vendor and the investment relative to the parties involved, an opportunity to reduce the risk of not being completely satisfied by the contractual arrangements could be recommended.

You might also want to evaluate any commitments for servicing reported problems for adequacy. Contractually agreed to turn around and escalation processes should be sufficient to support the business processes without jeopardizing the end customer's experience. Problems that affect the ability of the application to function properly and leave the business in a nonfunctioning state should be treated differently from nuisance problems that can be worked around while more permanent solutions are sought. This higher concern category of problem should get immediate attention, appropriate escalation within the vendor's management ranks, and maybe even an on-site response. Response and recourse language should be evaluated to determine the residual risk to the organization. Alternatives for insufficient vendor response might be prudent or even required depending on the contract, penalties, and the risk to the business. Your assessment of the sufficiency of contractual countermeasures should point out residual risks and recommend opportunities to reduce them to acceptable levels. Knowing the total cost as well as realistically describing the benefits and risk mitigation of any recommendations will be necessary to convince the report readers that your suggestions are actionable.

Partnerships and joint ventures are the extreme end of this spectrum of cooperative growth and problem solving. These kinds of agreements not only spread out the risk, but also provide the vendor a test and development environment that provides real business processes to use as a basis for their product enhancements. Some vendors use conferences and user group meetings to review potential enhancements and gather input on the direction of the next revision and future functionality. Lobbying for modifications and voting on priorities at these meetings is also a good way to network with like-minded users who share tips and techniques that can improve the business processes back at home.

A right to audit clause in a contract is typically reserved for service providers and partnerships where company information is actually handled by the vendor or service provider. You might ask that a SAS 70 report be made available or look for other evidences that proper structure and control exists in the potential vendor agreement. Evidence of *International Standards Organization* (ISO) certification or other development rigor such as application of the Software Engineering Institute's *Computer Maturity Model* (CMM) will show that controls and structured processes are important to the vendor's management through quality commitments. Vendor site visits and a walk through of their operations can be staged events with highly controlled access to actual processes but might provide some high level insight into management philosophies and control structures.

Implementation

Once formally accepted, the process of implementing the application into the live production environment will commence. Implementation should be the result of careful planning and scripting of tasks. This process should be documented and proceduralized to minimize impact and error. Fallback strategies should be available for each high-risk process and resource availability should be adjusted to accommodate potential problems without impacting normal operations. At a point in the implementation or conversion where there will be no turning back, a go-no go decision should be made that distills the risks and prospects for success or failure into a business decision made by the key business stakeholders.

By this point in a development project the testing is complete and the approval to place the application into production has been obtained. Users will have been trained and documentation for operators and users alike will be distributed and generally available. An implementation plan with resource requirements, timelines, and problem scenario solution options will have been documented and reviewed by all who are involved with the process. The business sponsors will have signed off on the project, showing their approval and acceptance to move forward based on a set of documentation that you should be able to review and from which you can draw similar conclusions. Hardware should be installed and configured, sized, and set up for production environment work.

The planning for this integration should have been done well before this point in the process, and many things need to be considered for the implementation to happen effectively:

- How will the production data be converted from the old systems to the new systems?

- How will new data elements be integrated into existing and historic data stores and reporting processes?

- What validation will need to occur to ensure that vital production records remain intact throughout the conversion / implementation process and beyond?

- How will the users get trained and cut over to the new system?

- How will interfaces get swung to the new system with minimal re-work and impact to existing processes?

- How will outputs be transitioned from old processes to new ones? For completely new outputs, how will users and clients be notified—and how will the output get integrated into the production processes?

- What situations would be considered candidates for backing out of the conversion process?

- What special problem management and user support resources and processes need to be put in place temporarily to handle the go-live time frames?

In preparation for a go-live sequence of events, preparation for normal and routine maintenance and processing operations will need to be completed. The integration of the new application into the operational environment including all necessary support training, forms, desktop preparation, and scheduling will need to be in place. The actual swinging of production from an old system to a new one can be accomplished in a couple of ways. A new process can simply be turned on and ramped up through first-time use and execution of new processes or functions. Converting historical data and legacy workflows to new ways and uses are more difficult and inherently more risky.

Conversion

Data conversions must be completed as part of any cutover from an old system to a new one performing the similar functions and processing data that was previously managed by systems that will be decommissioned. Adding new clients in bulk or merging two systems into one have similar needs and associated risks. Data integrity is the primary objective with a secondary objective being to ensure the new process can seamlessly transition leaving the data upward and downward compatible. If it has been determined that this situation will not be the case, keeping the old system online in a read-only mode can be an acceptable alternative to extensive data conversion processes. It will be necessary to evaluate the ability to get at the historical data from the post conversion system and compare the capabilities that existed for access to preconversion data before and after applying the conversion process through direct observation, as one way to accomplish this. Using CAAT tools and report generators might also be a successful way to understand any differences in the quality of the data, but care must be taken to prevent data corruption, and to ensure that consistent apples to apples comparisons are performed. Depending on the future need for the data, archiving the data and managing the relevant summaries or period end reports might be sufficient. It will depend on the business process, their needs for the detailed historic data, and what alternatives are reasonable and economically feasible to them.

Testing with the converted data might be prudent to ensure that the future use and access to that information will yield acceptable results. Routines for performing the conversion of data might require design and coding as a mini-project associated with the lagers implementation process. Remember that development of data conversion tools is a process that can be capitalized under SOP 98-1 accounting guidelines. Control over access to the data during a conversion process will be important since normal programmatic and process imbedded controls will most likely not protect this data. Conversion processes normally run outside of a production process and direct access to the tables and data stores often occur without security controls in place to ensure access is limited causing potential exposure of sensitive or confidential data. Ensure that copies are physically and logically protected where possible. Also of concern will be the availability and integrity of the data to be converted. It might seem unlikely that conversions will be tried on live production data impacting its availability for ongoing use and possibly causing damage or corruption to the repository, but you should check the plans just to be sure. What seems like obvious controls to an experienced IS auditor might appear to be needless overhead to the project team already behind schedule and under pressure.

Problem Management and Escalation

During the implementation phase, additional resources and processes should be used to handle problem management and escalation needs beyond those normally expected to handle routine workloads. Even with well-tested processes and extensive training and planning, things can and do go wrong. Rapid assessment of problems during go-live might be critical to heading off catastrophic situations and help keep frustration levels from getting out of hand. Management should be fully informed of progress and significant issues but the implementation team should be given some space to try to address problems without undue pressure from management whose expectations are for a perfect situation. Change is never without risk, and all people involved must be reminded that some amount of disruption from normal flow is bound to occur as a natural part of assimilating changes. If you are involved with oversight or monitoring of implementation processes the best way to add value is often to observe without interference. Controls should be observed to ensure they are working properly but tolerance to interim risk exposure might be acceptable in the short term. Often some amount of duties segregation is bypassed during start up and seen as acceptable short-term risk. Account management and security controls might be temporarily relaxed to facilitate the changes with minimal disruption. You would expect to see good back up documentation for temporarily assuming these risks and procedures to bring them back to normal levels as soon as practical. Audit processes directed at the processing that occurs during the transition periods that more closely examines the data integrity and process controls related errors is one way to mitigate the risks of a conversion process without frustrating the transition team with stringent controls initially. Naturally, procedures will need to be in place to identify run away situations and appropriate escalation procedures should be documented and distributed to the affecting parties should the need to activate them occur. Problems that are not significant in nature should still be recorded and logged for future evaluation, assessment, and prioritization. As time permits and things start to settle into a routine, these should be investigated more thoroughly and corrective actions determined and initiated. Some problems work themselves out and are due to inadequate training or users unfamiliar with procedures, for example and once the routines are performed properly the error conditions no longer exist as issues. Opportunities to observe and address error messages and nonstandard process handling errors might present themselves as one-time situations in these startup situations.

Emergency Change Management

Even during normal production, but especially during a start up, emergency change procedures might need to be used to keep the process going without a complete backout and shut down. Emergency change management processes are typically designed to bypass some of the production control segregation controls allowing programmers more direct access to the production environment than would normally be permitted for routine maintenance and upkeep related changes. Changes must still be logged and recorded in detail but not all of the testing and quality checks might be able to get proper attention due to the time pressures of the implementation schedule and production impact of the waiting system. Post implementation follow up should be planned for these situations and the IS auditor should take note of what level of control degradation was allowed to better understand the risk and potential follow up review that might be required to regain confidence in the code integrity. Production data changes might be required during this phase as well and business management should be directly involved with any decisions and approvals that allow this to occur. Detailed reporting of what was changed and plans to review the access for inappropriate changes, other than those approved, might be prudent. Management review and oversight are certainly minimum controls, albeit manual ones for emergency changes that might be needed. Plans for supporting emergency changes should be made in advance with appropriate procedures and approvals planned out in advance of implementation go-live. The data owners and business management should provide input into what would be acceptable and what would involve additional approval or escalation as part of this planning and procedure documentation.

Post-Implementation

Once the business application has been implemented and it is in production in a stabilized routine, the project will move to its final phase. The post implementation still involves planning and assessment and is where the IS auditor will make a conclusion about the overall effectiveness of the application in meeting the business's needs. Moreover, the businesses will assess the process in terms of their success criteria and prioritize any changes, where their needs are not exactly met. The systems development life cycle is cyclical in nature, by definition, and the ongoing maintenance and maturation of the process and application will continue until it is replaced by better processes that meet the needs better or decommissioned because the needs no longer exist in the way they did at the time the development was taken on as a project.

Acceptance and Post-Implementation Review

In the final analysis of the project, the business management must participate in a review that passes judgment on the application and processes that were developed and the implementation that brought them to the production environment. After the tempers have calmed and the adrenaline of the go-live panic has subsided, an objective review of the application and its ability to meet the business needs should be undertaken as part of the final acceptance and post implementation review. All of the functional requirements should be lined up in a review matrix, and an assessment of how well those needs have been met by the new process along with examples and samples should be performed. Lessons learned analysis can be instructive for IS operational staff and for development teams. It might also be helpful for the business management, where scope changes and incomplete understandings of the requirements drove the process down blind alleys initially. Total costs and expenditures will need to be gathered and processed so that they can be used to determine return on investment and projected payback periods for the time and money invested in the project. Business metrics should be compiled that will compare the new processing to the previous way of doing business so that improvements can be baselined and benchmarked. Improvements should be used to set new production standards and expectations. Situations where the performance standards have degraded should be investigated and corrective measures planned and discussed. Problems that remain outstanding should be prioritized and fixed where this goal can be easily accomplished or scheduled for future enhancements and development cycles as appropriate.

Service levels should be reviewed and assessed to ensure they are realistic and will meet the needs of the customers while not overtaxing the system or its support resources. Ability to meet these commitments should go through an approval process by those who will be accountable for supporting these levels, and they should subsequently be communicated to the users and recipients of the services being offered. The security, regulatory and control related requirements should be given a final evaluation and assessment at this time as well with any concerns about the residual risks that remain, clearly stated in language from which the business leadership can understand the potential impact to the bottom line. Any recommendations or insight into further mitigating risks in a cost-effective manner would be appropriate in this final review as well.

Evaluating the Maintenance and Enhancement Processes

If the development processes were well controlled throughout the life cycle to this point, there should be relatively few surprises in performance and expectation characteristics. No implementation is without at least a few issues and problems. The more complex the process and organizational process in general, the higher chance that some part of the final application will need to be fixed or adjusted to get it just right. Soon after the go-live period ends, and this should be defined by criteria agreed to with business management's involvement in advance of the turn over to production, normal maintenance and operational management processes should take over. This task is necessary for several reasons. It allows for the formal conclusion of the implementation phase, where staff members are stressed and controls are limited for the sake of production impact. This problem needs to be rectified as soon as possible. Also, the normal processes are presumably better able to deal with the processes they were designed to manage and eliminate the possibility of mistakes and oversight from ad-hoc procedures used in an interim fashion. Better control through well-tested processes leads to lower risks and better measurement of what is actually happening as well. You should determine that this demarcation between start up and normal processing does not extend far into the future when reviewing the planning and that definite criteria for transitioning the normal controls into effect happen in a way that minimizes risks to the organization.

Normal problem analysis and error tracking processes should then be used to summarize problems along with the rest of the operations and be prioritized in a similar fashion. By taking the magnifying glass away from the process, so to speak, the overall sense of problem severity can now be weighed along with other operations and production issues. An item's relevant magnitude and the resources necessary to correct it can then be assigned based on total IS organizational requirements, needs, and proper focus. Once this job is done, a fair assessment of the outstanding problems and their impact can be assessed and opportunities to aggregate them with root problem analysis techniques to maximize the efficiency and effectiveness of any applied resources can be identified. By normalizing the change control process, data integrity controls are restored and data validity concerns can be reduced. Keep in mind that extraordinary follow-up auditing of the processed data might have been a requirement for risk mitigation, and the longer this exposure exists the more extra work there will be to do. Normal change control also ensures that changes will be tested and evaluated, providing audit trails and backout processes for their application as fixes. This situation will help stabilize the processes and provide for a more predictable and methodical resolution to any remaining issues related to the application's implementation. Planning of the impact of changes can now be made to limit disruption and ensure that users' experiences are not degraded in unpredictable ways.

Versioning and Release Packaging

As the project implementation fades and more normal processing occurs on a routine basis, lists of enhancements will be formulated from users whose functions continue to mature along with their expectations of the automated solutions they are interacting with on a daily basis. As described earlier in the section about vendor management, several of the enhancement best-practice techniques should be looked to for addressing these needs in a risk mitigating and effective manner. It might be prudent to aggregate changes and enhancements into a newer version of the product, especially if production functions are changing significantly along with the application modifications and new processes or functions are being introduced. This situation enables the reduction of risk because integrated testing and regression testing can evaluate not only more changes at once but also the interaction of these changes with the application and each other. All of the related documentation, procedures, training manuals, users, operations, and maintenance manuals—along with the necessary and important recovery and contingency planning documentation—will need to be kept updated as changes occur. This task is often difficult to do when changes dribble in and overall processes and configurations drift over time until the documentation would not be adequate to serve the purpose it was initially created to address for the organization. Packaging enhancements into version upgrades and new releases is a way to reduce the overhead of change and limit the impact of change to the users at the same time. You should assess changes and the process for planning and implementing them for this opportunity and examine the business needs and change volume to see whether this makes sense. It is usually a more controlled way to introduce change and enables a better-quality product (and ultimately, more customer satisfaction as well).

The system development life cycle then turns on itself because the product releases are no longer sufficient for meeting the challenges of future needs and because product maturity and technological advancements continue over time. Sooner or later, a new product or production idea is presented to management that will replace this process or modify it beyond recognition. A project team will be commissioned to perform some rudimentary functional requirements gathering, and a feasibility analysis will follow. Predictions of change, benefits, and improved cost structures will get the nod—and the process starts all over again.

Resources

- *Information Systems Control and Audit*, Ron Weber, Prentice-Hall, 1999.
- International Organization for Standards (www.iso.ch).
- Carnegie Mellon University, Software Engineering Institute, Capability Maturity Model® for Software (SW-CMM®) at www.sei.cmu.edu/cmm/cmm.html.

Sample Questions

Here is a sampling of questions in the format of the CISA exam. The questions are related to business application systems development, acquisition, implementation, and maintenance and will help test your understanding of this subject. Answers with explanations are provided in Appendix A.

1. When reviewing a systems development project, what would the *most* important objective be for an IS auditor?

   A. Ensuring that the data security controls are adequate to protect the data.

   B. Ensuring that the standards and regulatory commitments are met.

   C. Ensuring that the business requirements are satisfied by the project.

   D. Ensuring that the quality controls and development methodologies are adhered to.

2. When participating in an application development project, which of the following would *not* be appropriate activities for an IS auditor?

   A. Testing the performance and behavior of the system controls to ensure that they are working properly

   B. Attending design and development meetings to monitor progress and provide input on control design options

   C. Reviewing reports of progress to management and contributing to their content based on fieldwork and opinions forms from reviewing documentation provided

   D. Assisting in the development of controls for application modules and user interfaces

3. When reviewing an application development project that uses a prototyping development methodology, with which of the following would the IS auditor be *most* concerned?

   A. The users are testing the systems before the designs are completely documented.

   B. The functional requirements were not documented and agreed to before the prototyping processes began.

   C. The documentation of the coding processes and testing criteria were not complete and well referenced.

   D. The systems specifications were not signed off on before the development processes were started.

4. In a systems development life cycle, the following process steps occur:

   I. Systems Design

   II. Feasibility Analysis

   III. Systems Testing and Acceptance

   IV. Systems Specification Documentation

   V. Functional Requirements Definition

   VI. Systems Development

   What is the natural order of the processes in an SDLC methodology?

   A. V, IV, II, I, VI, III

   B. V, II, IV, I, VI, III

   C. II, IV, V, VI, I, III

   D. II, V, I, VI, III, IV

5. Where would be the ideal place for an IS auditor to find the first consideration of security controls?

   A. During the design phase of the system development process

   B. When determining what the systems specification will need to be

   C. When reviewing the functional requirements for the system

   D. When testing the system for overall compliance to regulatory, privacy, and security requirements

6. The main difference between a functional requirement and a systems specification is:

   A. A functional requirement is a business process need, and a systems specification defines what the system must do to meet that need.

   B. Functional requirements address the details of the need form a data perspective, and systems specifications define them from an operational systems perspective.

   C. Functional requirements define more of what needs to happen, and systems specifications define how something will happen.

   D. Functional requirements define all aspects of the process flow from a business process perspective while systems specifications are more hardware and operating system-specific.

7. Which of the following is *not* a criterion for an effective feasibility analysis report?

   A. An assessment of the proposed solution approach and its viability in the existing business process

   B. An assessment of the impact of the new application on the business processes and workflows

   C. An analysis of the costs and projected benefits of the application, determining overall benefit or detraction from the business prospects of the overall business strategy

   D. An assessment of the systems development methodology proposed for the design of the application

8. If there was a *most* important place for the quality assurance teams to be involved in the development project, where would that place be?

   A. During the testing and code migration from test environments to production-ready code

   B. At the beginning of the project to ensure that quality standards are established and understood by all of the development team members

   C. During the code development to ensure that processes are followed according to standards and are well documented

   D. In the final phases to ensure that all of the quality processes and requirements were met prior to signing off on final acceptance

9. What aspect of the systems development testing process needs to be addressed during the systems design process?

   A. The use cases are documented to show how the product is supposed to work when completed.

   B. The detailed work plans and process steps are defined so that they can be checked for completeness during testing of the development process.

   C. The expectations and outcomes of the development process are defined formally for testing criteria.

   D. The project design is checked against the functional requirements.

10. When reviewing a systems design, an IS auditor would be *least* concerned to find that which of the following was not considered?

    A. The provisions for adequate internal controls and the addressing of regulatory requirements

    B. Increased costs and delays in the project deadlines

    C. The observance of quality assurance standards and processes

    D. The failure to consider environmental and facility needs as part of the design

11. When reviewing a systems development project, an IS auditor observes that the decision has been made to use a purchased vendor package to address the business requirements. The IS auditors should:

    A. Discuss the contract and costs with the vendor to ensure that the best deal has been obtained for the organization

    B. Review the ROI assumptions and decide whether they are still valid

    C. Review the contract for a right to audit clause in the agreement

    D. Review the build versus buy recommendation and determine that the costs and benefits are fairly stated in the recommendations made

12. The *most* important issue with change control during the development of large scale systems is:

    A. Managing the versions of code in development to ensure that testing will result in a workable system

    B. Ensuring that testing and backout procedures have been provided for each change

    C. Ensuring that maintenance and disaster recovery procedures have been documented for each change promoted through the process

    D. Tracking which module has been tested with other modules to understand the development progress

13. When reviewing a development effort where third-party programming staff are used, the IS auditor would be *most* concerned with?

    A. Ensuring that they are qualified and knowledgeable about the tools and techniques being used

    B. Ensuring that the code is reviewed independently from the third-party staff and ensuring that the ownership rights are maintained within the organization

    C. Ensuring that background checks are made for individual third-party staff members to protect the organization from undesirable persons participating in the effort

    D. The impact to the cost and timeline estimates originally presented and approved by management

14. An independent quality assurance function should perform all of the following roles *except*:

    A. Ensuring that the development methods and standards are adhered to throughout the process

    B. Ensuring that the testing assumptions and approved modules of developed code are aligned to give a final product that meets the design criteria

    C. Reviewing the code to ensure that proper documentation and practices were followed

    D. Correcting development deficiencies and resubmitting corrected code through the testing process

15. Which of the following are *not* considered communication controls?

    A. Network traffic monitoring and alert systems

    B. Encryption techniques to limit accessibility to traffic in transit

    C. Access control devices that limit network access

    D. Bandwidth management tools to shift data based on traffic volumes

16. Review of documentation in a systems development review is very important for all of the following reasons *except*:

    A. Training and maintenance efforts require that good documentation be made available for their processes to work effectively

    B. Allowing the IS auditor to review the process without actually having to perform code-level reviews of programming efforts

    C. Disaster recovery and support processes depend on the quality of the systems and user documentation

    D. User effectiveness and production processing depends on the user's ability to read and understand the manuals and procedures associated with the application development process

17. In reviewing a vendor solution bidding process during a systems development review, an IS auditor would be *most* concerned to find that:

    A. A vendor solution had been chosen prior to documenting the vendor criteria.

    B. The chosen vendor's cost was not the lowest of the providers of an acceptable solution.

    C. Some of the vendors received more information about the bid request than the others did.

    D. Some of the bidders on the vendor list were not capable of responding effectively to the bid based on their business model and the product being requested.

18. Which of the following is *not* a risk associated with the decision to use a vendor software solution?

    A. The risk that the vendor might discontinue support of a product that is mission critical to the business

    B. The risk that the costs and contract provisions might adversely impact the business model in the long term

    C. The risk that in-house support expertise might be insufficient to adequately address ongoing support and maintenances need of the product

    D. The risk that business needs for enhancements and corrections might not be addressed in a timely manner

19. During go-live, security and change management controls are often relaxed to facilitate the implementation. What actions are *most* appropriate for the IS auditor during this process?

    A. Raising concerns about the control deficiencies to business management and suggesting additional controls

    B. Waiting until the implementation process is completed and running audit and analysis tools on all transactions during the implementation period

    C. Recommending that the risks of reduced controls be accepted and encouraging the process to move into a more controlled phase as quickly as possible

    D. Observing the implementation process to understand the extent of control risk that is residual to the process and recommending prudent, additional steps to regain assurance of data integrity

20. During the user testing of the application under development, the IS auditor would be *most* concerned if he or she found that:

    A. Users were accessing the test system from their normal workstations to test the system

    B. Production data was being used for testing the system

    C. Users were not all trained to the same level of competency for the testing process

    D. Interfaces were simulated to provide input to testing and were not actually being represented by live input feeds

CHAPTER 7

Business Process Evaluation and Risk Management

This chapter will examine the business process aspects of the information systems auditor's skill requirements and knowledge tool set. The knowledge of this subject matter comprises 15 percent of the CISA exam's content. To be proficient at this set of processes, you must develop intuitive reasoning skills and be able to understand the business compromises and basis for those decisions that are not black and white but many shades of gray. Unlike Chapter 2 where we examined the management processes from an IS perspective, this chapter focuses on the business risks and controls and their management from a business perspective. You will need to master this perspective in order to communicate effectively with the business management—that is the ultimate consumers of your product—if for no other reason. Many of your conclusions and opinions in this area will be based on the documented direction set forth by the business objectives and goals, so you will need these items as a basis for beginning your work in this area.

Understanding every business process and the best practices for the business management of them is beyond the scope of this book and unique to each individual business in many aspects. The Key Performance Indicators (KPIs) that are the drivers for a business process will vary according to

KPI   Key Performance Indicator

the business and the management style. Knowing these two things well about a business before beginning an evaluation of the business processes and the risk management aspects of governing that business is a prerequisite. It will be assumed throughout this chapter that you have a good working knowledge of the business you are reviewing and its market trends, and the best practices currently guiding the business segment in the market. You will need to have spent some time understanding the business and management cultures that are unique to the situational environment in which you are performing this particular evaluation.

Unless you have an extensive real-world work experience in this particular business to back you up, it is unwise to present yourself as an expert in the best practices of the leadership in these areas. Through questioning and probing, you will be able to lead the management of the business into the right direction rather than confronting them with evidence and recommending a change in direction. By stating up front that they are the business experts and you are the risk and control subject matter expert, you can better forge a win-win relationship with the business management team members. Showing your willingness to learn from them and deferring to their experience and yes, egos, in these matters will result in much more cooperation that an arrogant or direct approach will, for the most part. People skills cannot be understated in these situations and choosing your battles to effectively win the war will require that you understand the bigger picture and can be satisfied with incremental wins along the way to get to the end goal.

The goals and objectives of this chapter are to enable you to perform evaluations of how a business uses risk and controls to manage its business goals and objectives, what the best practices are in each of these areas, and how to spot areas for improvement when applying risk and control methods to the business processes. By the end of this chapter, you should have a working understanding of the following:

- How the corporate governance ties the business processes and the information systems into a cohesive, end-to-end process and shows due diligence and proper control
- How to determine whether the information systems are being used effectively within a business to meet its needs
- How to benchmark business processes against the best practices to identify opportunities for improving efficiencies and effectiveness
- How Business Process Reengineering (BPR) can be used to optimize a business and where this process fits into the overall risk management and control process

- How to assess the business processes from performance and customer satisfaction perspectives and to provide value-added recommendations related to improvements in these areas

- What role e-business has in supporting the business processes, where it is appropriate, and how to evaluate its effectiveness

- Various business process control techniques, how they are used to manage the business processes, where they are effective, and what kind of results can be expected from the application of these techniques

- How to review projects intended to change business processes and to ensure that they are properly managed and controlled for the maximum chance of success

- What risk management is, how it is performed, how to evaluate it

- How to use risk assessments and the resulting information as an applicable IS auditing tool

- What other corporate governance controls ought to be in place, such as the audit function, and how to evaluate whether the audit function is managed properly and is sufficient for the needs of the business

Corporate Governance

Corporate governance is the system by which businesses are directed and controlled. The rights and responsibilities of running the company start at the top of the organization. They are subsequently distributed and managed effectively by formal development and deployment as a structure that spells out the policies and procedures for making decisions and declaring the corporation's directives in-line with the business culture and its mission and objectives. By doing this, a governance structure is established that results in the motivation of management and other persons who are deemed accountable to meet companies stated objectives, assuring that these objectives are attained through monitoring and incentive programs.

When evaluating these systems and the overall corporate governance infrastructure, you first must understand what objectives have been established for the business and by whom, and by what root authority that these goals have been established. What is the mission of the company? Is it documented, perhaps, along with a vision statement somewhere in the corporate literature? In order to assess how effective the governance systems are in ensuring an outcome, you will need to be able to articulate what that outcome is. Making money, some say, is the best, others will tell you. You will need to get an agreement from the organization's senior most management through some means in order to review the rest of the structure and ensure that their wishes and directives are being properly addressed. If it is a publicly held company, the shareholders may have some say in the governance of the business and direction may be found in the commitments made by management to these shareholders, which can be helpful in determining the root mission and guiding principles of the organization. If you determine that the authority for the direction sufficiently mandates what is being used as corporate governance directives, you can set about reviewing the rest of the process to see how well it is being done. This authority must be traced back to the top of the organization because the mandate to achieve the goals must come from the root authority of the organization and be articulated in clear unambiguous language.

Assessing the governance process that is used to monitor and encourage the management's and organization's infrastructure ownership to meet the corporate goals then is a matter of working backwards from these documented directives to determine how these accomplishments are managed. How does management ensure that these goals are the objectives of the business units for which they are responsible? Is there a management review process that ensures these goals are adequately incorporated into the next level's business plans and goal setting processes? Are there incentives established that are built around encouraging that these goals are met by tying bonuses or rewards to their achievement? Perhaps minutes from a management meeting can evidence this process of establishing these goals through a meeting's agendas or established evaluation criteria. You will want to encourage the management team to formally guarantee that the appropriate goal setting processes are accounted for at the next level of the organization to show their due diligence in meeting the corporate objectives set from the highest levels of the governance authority. Part of the rationale for performing this process is one of risk mitigation. You will need to convince the organization's management this is not just an audit exercise that has little value. By showing them how the due diligence of formally ensuring these directives are managed well, shows management of the business objectives that their directions are being heard and heeded. Can the business unit's goals you are evaluating be tied back to the corporate goals and overall mission and vision of the organization? A mechanism for proving that this is the case is the justification for the establishment of formal processes, which ensures that the directives are related up through the management ranks and embraced down the line.

What happens if these goals are not met? Are there any examples of disciplinary processes or review procedures that force accountability for achieving these goals? When you establish that processes exist to ensure that the goals trickle down and are the basis for the next level of direction with which to run the business, you will want to see established penalties and enforcement processes and evidence of their use to ensure that the responsibilities are well understood, that the extent of authority is communicated and well-known, and that accountabilities for performance against the goals and objectives are established and taken seriously. The best way to evidence the seriousness of the acceptance of these responsibilities is to show that penalties exist and are applied as a matter of course for nonperformance against those goals and objectives.

Are there adequate measurement techniques and performance indicators that will notify management when achievement of these goals is in question? In order to manage anything effectively you first must be able to measure it. Breaking these objectives into measurable qualities may be a difficult task at first, but without metrics to show verifiable movement toward goals it's all smoke and mirrors. You will need to analyze these metrics and conclude on their effectiveness in showing that the achievement of goals, which they are supposed to represent, can actually be measured by them. Even goals that are not directly measurable in quantifiable production output numbers must have a way of recording movement in the right direction. Goals that cannot be directly measurable will need to be interpreted by management and this may require some back and forth negotiating along with the documentation of those decisions. The resulting agreements must provide direction to the next level of management such that "if these things are accomplished, then we all agree they will represent successful achievement or movement toward that particular corporate goal." Because this will be an interpretive directive, documentation of the agreement and the corresponding accountabilities and authorities for making these agreements will be important for enabling you to conclude that these measurements appropriately represent goal achievement.

Part of your evaluation will be to determine that lower levels of management are held accountable for producing against the goals agreed to with their superiors. What kind of reaction is given to motivate the business unit management to realign with the goals if slippage occurs? You also will want to see evidence that this is not just a paper exercise, but that these metrics are derived from the actual businesses processes in the business units and that they realistically relate to the purported goals of achievement. Reviewing the accuracy and ability of these measurements to represent the actual work being done in support of the business goals also is a function of this assessment process. When the metrics show that the goals are not being met, are the metrics changed or are corrective actions taken to bring the processes in-line with the expected goals? A good way to tell if you have the right metrics or not is through management's commitment to use the metrics to actually drive the business and to make real changes when the metrics show flagging results.

You will possibly need to create a matrix for yourself depicting each overarching goal or governance statement, however vague and lofty these may be, and then set about determining how the management, who is responsible for making these goals happen, ensures they are being met and used for direction. This matrix may be hierarchical in structure but should show that all rights and responsibilities of the company have been given to someone in the organization. These accountabilities should all be documented and incorporated into the business structure as known responsibilities and authorities. This will require an examination at the business unit or next level of the management structure to determine those responsibilities and to ensure that they provide the necessary accountability and authority to achieve their support of the next highest level goals. The tools, which are used to ensure these responsibilities are carried out without fail, should then be evidenced by populating the accountabilities matrix with the delegated authorities and accountabilities on down to the production floor, the product going out the door, and beyond to the customer service personnel. By reviewing the goals down to this level, you then can ensure that any gaps are identified between the goals and directives of the lower levels and those with which their management has been charged.

In order to conclude on the effectiveness of the IS organization, for example, you will want to know what the strategic business direction is, see that it has been documented, that it is being taken seriously by the IS organization's management, and that it guides their direction. This may be evidenced by performing a review of the IS organization's short- and long-term strategies and goals in comparison with the business goals and organization's directives during a similar time frame. In addition, you also will want to ensure that the overall or global business plan is supported by the IS organization's local plan through a mapping of the authorities given to the IS organization's management, the accountability that is documented to support the business goals, and the acceptance of that accountability though the placement of responsibility on the IS organization's management structure for supporting and achieving those business directives. The mandate given to the IS organization to achieve goals that support the overall company governance structure should be reflected in the goals and mission of the IS organization.

Once these chains of authority and governance have been established, stepping back down the organizational tree to the next levels will enable you to ensure that not only is all of the next higher levels of corporate governances, goals, and responsibilities being addressed, but that those delegated to uphold these objectives are being held responsible and accountable for meeting them. Of course, without the authority and mandate to carry out these directives, progress will be uncertain at best. Therefore, part of your review will evaluate whether sufficient authority has been lent to the individuals who are accountable along with the corresponding responsibilities to get the job done. Your analysis and report should be objective and factual, showing clear lines of authority and mandated goals where they exist, and pointing out unclear authority and direction where it does not. Possible suggestions will always involve a formal designation of authority, goals, and agreements on measurable metrics, even when compromises are necessary on both sides of the management line to reach these documented ends.

Management should be asked to ensure that the information they provide, which is being used for material decisions, has a basis and is independently verified as accurate and factual for this reason as well. Your opinion of the governance and management practices of the business will reflect your view of their use of independence to validate the information and decisions with the goal of obtaining some degree of comfort that the management is not performing in a vacuum. Business processes that rely heavily on information, which is not corroborated through some kind of independent assurance mechanisms, at least periodically, can get very far down the wrong path before realizing it is too late.

Evaluating the Effectiveness of the Information Systems in Supporting the Business Process

In addition to being asked about the IS themselves and drawing conclusions about their effectiveness and efficient use, management also will be concerned with how well these systems actually meet the needs of the business, and whether they are providing the right level of support for the business through the deployment of the information systems they have chosen to process their business. There are many shades of gray here and you first will need to establish some criteria from which you can draw comparisons and form opinions on performing an evaluation. Effectiveness can only be determined in relative terms—relative to industry best practices, relative to the amount of investment the company is willing to make to achieve top notch productivity, relative to the competition, and relative to management's expectations. These are all possible ways to examine systems that support the business processes. The first question you will need to ask, possibly to yourself when asked about an evaluation of effectiveness is, " . . . compared to what?"

Effectiveness can be measured against the business needs and service level requirements. This is a relatively simple comparison and evaluation to perform. You must determine what the documented and agreed to processing rates, delivery times, availability rates or other metrics that have been established and required by the business are, and compare those metrics to the actual outputs or services provided by the system. More often though there is a poor understanding of how to measure the effectiveness in the first place, which is really the question being asked of you. "How can I tell if this system is really effective in meeting my needs?" Your services may be provided in an investigative capacity to determine what is important to the business and how those things can be measured and controlled. This is actually a very valuable exercise to the business and can be used in the establishment of a risk management process for the business.

Understanding the business will be vital to this exercise and establishing the pain points will help ensure you understand what the critical time, quantity, and quality-related aspects of the IS outputs really need to be to satisfy the business requirements. Interviewing the business leaders to become familiar with the terminology of the business processes and finding out what the pressure points are then can be translated to the role that the information systems must play in satisfying the business needs. You will want to review any available business reports and evaluate the deliverables and products of the business to get an understanding of what role the information system might have in providing for the success of the business. Talking to the customers of that business is another way to determine what is important. Reviewing the financial statements to determine the revenue or income sources will be input to this understanding as well. Once you have established the critical success factors of the business, you should determine how the information systems contribute to those success factors and identify the ranges of performance and output that are required by the information systems in order to meet the optimum level of business processing. Then, you will be able to evaluate how well the business success factors are being met and conclude on the overall effectiveness of the information system in supporting the business processes. You also will be able to report on what KPIs are best related to the system's effectiveness in supporting the business and possibly help in establishing service level requirements and performance levels where caution and concern then can be applied, should performance vary from these levels.

Best Practice Business Process Design

Often you will seek to compare the business process and its related IS support levels to a benchmark or best practice within the industry that the business is in. Good design methodologies will perform this evaluation first to ensure these methodologies are not proposing outdated solutions and to understand what "state of the art" is before embarking on a system development effort. Just because everyone else is doing it should not be enough reason to change a process that is currently working and meeting business needs successfully, unless other circumstances also are present. You will want to understand the business goals and how and why they are not being met currently to best understand how a best practice analysis can help improve the business process. An assessment of best practices provides an excellent opportunity to understand what issues cropped up with the deployment of these solutions and enables the business to benefit from any lessons learned and mistakes made by others without experiencing them firsthand. Once management is convinced that a best practice solution will better meet their needs than their current process, they then can move forward with a high degree of confidence that the planned approach can successfully be implemented after having seen evidence of success in other examples.

Industry-specific support organizations and research institutions may need to be sought out and engaged at some level to get the information necessary to understanding the business models that are used prevalently and what the trends are for emerging change in the business processes and support models. Once the best practices and trends have been gathered, you must analyze them, along with the organization's business model, looking for a fit with the common goals and directions as appropriate. Decisions on change and new development efforts will need to be weighed fairly, along with the costs and benefits for each possible choice or decision for a new direction. The evaluation of a best practice design should have these steps documented as part of the strategic decision-making process used to determine an approach for the future direction of systems supporting the business. Consideration of the other processes currently used by the business, the companies' strategic direction, and the organizational culture will need to be kept in mind as the information is reviewed and choices for future actions are examined. The risks associated with making a change will need to be weighed with the risk of staying with the current models, the costs related to implementing change, and each of the possible choices associated impact to the business as part of that evaluation, too.

A best practice review also can serve the purpose of validating that the current direction is the right direction strategically. It can be used to assess how to improve the current processes and where improvements and efficiencies can be gained by shortcuts around another company's lessons learned, as mentioned previously. This review also may point out that the business processes currently being used are not conducive to applying the best practice IS solution to them. This is because the processes themselves have inefficiencies or nonstandard practices associated with them, thus precluding any benefit that might have been gained from aligning with a best practice solution model. Close inspection of the business processes may result in a call for change and hard questions on why it is necessary to perform the tasks the way they are currently done, in the current level of detail, or in the manner in which they are currently being performed. Reengineering large portions of the process in this fashion may be the next step in transforming the business and ensuring that the business needs are actually met in the most efficient and effective manner possible.

Management Controls

Management controls are the controls applied to the organization at the management level, which provide overriding guidance and direction for the organization as a whole. These controls include the policy and standards that are applied to everyone in the business. However, they also include management's way of doing business, the culture of the organization, and the governance expectations. The expectations that the organization has of its management's behavior, based on their previous actions, stated direction, and policy, layout a certain control structure that defines the business culture and the behaviors within the infrastructure of the business. A permissive and easy going management style would lead one to use a different disciplinary reaction to a minor policy violation than one used in a strict authoritarian business culture that is characterized by formal dress codes, deviation intolerance from the approved processes, and an inflexibility in the acceptance of personal situations that impact the needs of the business, for an example. There are certain expectations that you can presume with each of these control structures that may carry forward into other aspects of the business as well. This is not a hard and fast rule, but it illustrates how management controls can work in an organization.

When an IS organizational policy exists, requiring that all changes must be controlled, be approved, and thoroughly documented, it doesn't make sense to look for a local policy to that effect in the subsets of the IS organization also because the management overriding control already establishes it as a control. Many aspects of the IS organization and the business processes can benefit from the implementation of controls at the management level of the organization. If background checks are part of the hiring process for all individuals, then it becomes unnecessary to ensure that the security staff has been cleared when reviewing the security department's hiring practices in particular; there are overriding controls applied to all new hires. Many opportunities exist for controls at the management level that will give a more reliable and consistent business performance result to the business outcomes. If all of the business processes use metrics and reporting in a prescribed common manner, then the reports will have meaning and applicability to those representing other aspects of the business processes as well as those intimately familiar with that particular aspect of the business. This can be a great driver for economies of scale adjustments in business processes as well as for further optimizing the process and profits. Centralized management of common issues makes sense where fragmented solutions, all performing the common function, are consuming wasted recourses. Regulatory issues that impact the entire organization and the controls put in place to ensure that compliance is another place where common approaches make a lot of sense.

Your evaluation of the management controls will identify situations where pervasive controls would provide for better processes, more optimal resource usage, and increased effectiveness that might result from controls being applied at higher levels in the management structure, thus breaking down fiefdoms, individual preferences, and political factions. You also will want to note situations where management controls resulted in ineffective processes, increased overhead, and work-around solutions due to many unique business circumstances resulting in multiple exceptions and making the control a cumbersome performance barrier to large portions of the business or information systems. It also will be important to see enforcement and compliance measurements related to these controls just as you would for any other control you were trying to measure for effectiveness. Exceptions are more often found when controls are applied at the management level and all situations do not fit the mold for which the control was intended. Exception processes and the management of exceptions as a natural part of this compromise show that the management is being realistic in their expectations of the controls and their applicability for all cases. In general, bright line principles and mission critical directives are good opportunities for management controls. Management controls also can be applied for all security-related aspects of a business or process and development efforts or change management activities. Many useful places exist to find management controls at work, providing direction for all processes or parts to the business that fall under the category for which they apply.

Key Performance Indicators (KPIs)

Key Performance Indicators were described in Chapter 2, "Management, Planning, and Organization of Information Systems." Like other management controls, their design and use will give the IS auditor some indications of the effectiveness of the business process that the information systems support while at the same time giving the IS organization a view of the system's performance, too. In order to be used effectively, these management tools must be providing the right information to the businesses, enabling the management the ability to use them in making business decisions accurately and effectively. The progress that the business is making toward its production goals and objectives should be monitored and reported on regularly as a natural part of the management controls for the business process. Many of these outcomes also will be information system driven and can be systematically produced and maintained. You will want to review these mechanisms to ensure they are providing good feedback about the business and the systems supporting it to conclude on the overall effectiveness and efficiency of the process in meeting the business objectives.

The ability to draw these conclusions requires that the right information is provided, which best describes to the business leaders how these systems are meeting their needs and requirements. It will not be acceptable to have a system that can show good performance, throughput, uptime, or another system-related metric, while the business requirements are not being met. Key to understanding the effectiveness of the performance indicators to the businesses management therefore will be an understanding of the necessary outcomes and service levels required of the information systems from the perspective of the business. These business requirements then will have to be meaningfully mapped back to the available system measurements and metrics so that the system's information can be used to effectively provide information about the business outcomes.

How well this mapping of system metrics to business outcomes is done will be part of your evaluation when determining the effectiveness of the indictors in providing guidance to the business. This can be an awkward and inexact fit at times, so you will need to pay close attention to assumptions and translations of the business needs to systems metrics in order to conclude that these indicators are useful business decision-making tools. Some historical perspective of the past indicators, related business extrapolations, business decisions resulting from the use of these indicators, and the resultant business adjustments and their relative success in guiding the business outcomes in the right direction will be helpful when concluding that these KPIs actually do represent the business management and control mechanisms. Once you have validated that the KPIs represent the business processing needs adequately, you will want to get some assurance that they are accurate, are maintained and reported on in a timely manner, and are being acted upon in the appropriate way, interpreted correctly, and used to make decisions that can be supported by the information. All of these items will be involved in the evaluation of the KPIs and their use as business drivers and control mechanisms.

Evaluating Business Process Reengineering Projects

Change projects associated with the reengineering of business processes is a complex and high risk endeavor to a company because it will impact the way business is done, putting the existing client base at risk as well as the related business processes. If you are participating in one of these business process change projects, you will find it an insightful and challenging project. Whether you are involved as a participant or charged with evaluating such a project after the fact, there are several pitfalls and traps to be aware of and to test for to ensure a successful deployment. Business Process Reengineering (BPR) implies radical and fundamental changes to the way the business process is done. Unlike Total Quality Management (TQM) techniques, which stress continual improvement over an extended period of time, BPR results in the questioning of even the most basic principles that are held as unshakeable standards. It forces the challenging of every aspect of the business in a search for significant changes that might radically improve the process at its very core. The intentions of BPR are to compress all of this change into a fixed, usually short, time frame regardless of the amount of change that may have to be accommodated to meet that time frame commitment.

BPR is often performed as a redesign or "clean sheet" approach to the business process. Workflows are reestablished often by using independent third parties that are less familiar with the old ways and stigmas of the past trials and errors. Your assessment of this process must ensure that the basic needs and requirements of the business processes are well documented before beginning. To add value to this process, ensure that these needs are truly external requirements and not internally generated as the result of legacy culture from the way things have been done in the past. Unfamiliarity with the internal business climate and culture is actually a benefit in this particular case. The makeup of the team performing this task will be a key element to its success. First of all, change of this magnitude must be driven and fully supported from the topmost management layers of the organization. Their tolerance and patience for this amount of risk and disruption will be required for any hope of success. But at the same time, there must be a grass roots buy-in and a willingness to participate and embrace these changes, or the resistance will make this process very painful at best and a failed experiment in a worst case scenario.

Some of the other attributes of this kind of change process, in contrast with other methods used to improve the design of the business process, are that this is more likely to be a technologically driven approach. The section on application development covered how large-scale vendor solutions, which were specifically designed to solve a business problem, could initiate process changes in order to minimize software modification and customization. This can often be the impetus for a BPR initiative. If the technology is to be leveraged as much as possible, the old ways of doing business must be closely examined to determine what the impact of changing them dramatically in order to align with the out-of-the-box solution may be. How the work is performed in this system must be methodically and systematically analyzed to ensure that each of the steps and tasks are performed so that they add value to the end product, and that each of these steps has no alternative that will suffice at a lower cost or effort, while adding little if any additional risk. Schedules of every set of tasks and each subprocess will need to be mapped out with a workflow diagram. These process flows will be based on the processes that define interaction between organizational entities, result in objects being manipulated, or are required for the management of the operational activities being performed. Each flow must show thorough detailed interconnectivity tracking how it interfaces with other processes, and how various inputs and decisions impact it along the way. Each step, input, and decision point then must be questioned for opportunities to eliminate, automate, or simplify the steps, one at a time, or as an entire process.

The resultant process then is reordered and evaluated as a new design and as a streamlined business process that hopefully has captured the problems and inefficiencies of past business methods and addressed them along the way. Checks should be performed to ensure that the initial issues and requirements list have been satisfactorily addressed by the end design. If the intent was for the resultant processes to align with a turnkey software package of some sort, this alignment should be one of the drivers and the BPR process should seek a good fit of the resultant process to that software package developer's vision of the business process, where possible, while still meeting the business requirements. When change is surely to be a result of this process, it will be important to benchmark the existing processes, business-related metrics, and the historical experience in delivery on the critical requirements before the reengineering process begins. This ideally occurs right after an agreement is reached on what has to survive the process, so that these processes can eventually be compared to the results of the new process, when determining the effectiveness of the resultant process overall. Apples-to-apples comparisons will provide the only real measure of whether the process has actually improved. The costs and work effort may not be measurable accurately for some time due to learning curve issues and working out the bugs of a massive change to the business culture as well as processes.

The approach for reengineering a business process should follow some basic guidelines to be successful. It should strive to

- Focus on the business deliverables or outcomes, not the process steps
- Ensure that the users of the process output understand the process that is needed to get that output for them
- Fully integrate the information systems processes into the business process that produces the final product or information
- Treat all process-related resources as if these processes were a centralized object, even when geographically dispersed
- Link parallel activities rather than integrating them to maximize options for analysis purposes
- Place the decision points as far down into the process as possible, ideally where the work is being performed
- Build controls into the processes rather than adding these controls on later
- Exploit opportunities to gather information only once and at the source

Some of the pitfalls you will want to be ready for have to do with managing expectations and balancing the popular management literature hype with the realities for the business management. For example, the assumption that a radically new and improved process will result from a clean sheet approach may be a bit over ambitious. If it was easy to do, it would have been done by now. Unless the real barriers are removed—some of them being cultural and political in nature—great strides of progress may be limited. For this reason, senior management's commitment to change their behavior and the directives that may be directly or indirectly causing some of these problems will need to be part of the success formula. Another reality is the actual cost and time required to dig into all of this and to redesign an ingrained and imbedded process to the business. A blank check may need to accompany that clean sheet. The phasing of the project into steps may be less dramatic and yield more incremental results, but it also may lower risks and increase buy-in from the workers on the floor. The IS leadership may be important in these processes, certainly if the solution is to be technologically driven and supported, but the reality is that the business owns the process and has to champion changes to their processes and people's work. The "we versus them" mentality will otherwise drive a wedge into the process because IS will be perceived as threatening the jobs and status quo of the business.

The biggest factor for the success of a reengineering project is the human factor. People do not like change—its part of human nature. A grass roots buy-in and enthusiasm will be difficult to get and sustain throughout a difficult and personally risky effort like this. Jobs will be threatened, and the status quo disrupted. Pecking orders will be torn down, new jobs will be created, and reporting relationships will be changed. Upheaval must be confronted as scary and risky to the workers and lots of soothing of egos and calming of fears will be required to ease the pain of change. Processes that keep people informed and keep the big picture goals in front of everyone will help forge the path to the new world. In concluding on this type of effort, follow-up will be an activity that should be recommended in order to give management a more accurate picture of the effectiveness and wins and losses related to a reengineering project. Over time, the metrics can be reevaluated, and by keeping an eye on the true outcomes and how they ultimately improve the bottom line, management will eventually get the answers they are seeking about this kind of project. Not mentioned here specifically is the entire system's development project related list of risks and controls mentioned in some detail in the previous chapter, which also is assumed to be a part of the process and IS auditor would use to assess a reengineering project. These are just the nuances and additional issues related to this specific type of development effort.

Assessing Performance and Customer Satisfaction

Assessing the business' performance and its ability to satisfy the customer base also will require some targets to measure against, which will need to be determined before starting to gather the results against which they will be measured. This recurrent theme should be familiar to you by now. It is always important to determine the expectations of a test before performing it to ensure the fairness and objectivity of the test. The code of ethics standard related to the objectivity of your work supports this kind of approach in all cases. The ability to assess performance adequately within a business is one of the primary control mechanisms a business management team can bring to bear on the management of the processes for which they are accountable. Your assessment should determine that the right aspects of the processes are being monitored to best support the needs and outcomes of the performance and customer satisfaction. You should evaluate whether these aspects fairly and accurately reflect the actual processing and performance situation in the real world through testing and observations that are compared to the reporting to management and by observing the way actual performance is being represented to them.

You should expect to see that metrics relevant to monitoring performance and satisfaction are among those that are routinely reviewed by management and used to guide the processes toward further improvements. Any deficiencies in what you find compared to this expectation, which may be material, should be brought to management's attention. It will be necessary to see that consistent goals are established, against which the business performance is being measured regularly, in order to draw any conclusions on how well the business is performing. Measuring one aspect during one quarter and a different aspect of performance measurement the next will not show performance conclusively over time. Your approach should ask the question, "If I were accountable for this, how would I do it?" This is often a good start in determining where gaps in the logic may lie and will help in seeing how a process, which has been handed off and convoluted over time, may be tuned up to improve the monitoring performance of the related process.

You will need to incorporate any of the changes that have been made to the business process, which could be expected to significantly impact the performance that is being measured over a given span of time. In a similar fashion, dips in the charts showing productivity or other performance measures should be explainable through problem-reporting processes and include records of corrective actions taken from investigations performed by management, who were mobilized as a result of the monitoring of KPIs, for example. Whether the performance is meeting the objectives or not, will be the bottom line conclusion that management will want to see of your evaluation and subsequent report. Valid suggestions for improvement might include improved monitoring or a refocusing on different metrics that better represent the actual performance from a client's or customer's perspective or that more closely relates to the impact on the bottom line in some way.

Customer satisfaction is the goal of the business in most cases because it directly ties to keeping the customer agreeable to coming back and providing more revenue to the organization as the relationship continues. Unless the business is one where repeat customer interaction is not important, or where a poor performance communicated by past customers to new ones by word of mouth will not impact the business (I cannot think of any), it will be important to satisfy the customer and have some assurance, as a business manager, that this is actually occurring according to the business you manage. How do you go about assessing customer satisfaction? This will be the first question asked by the IS auditor during interviews with business management when evaluating this subject mater. You should investigate to determine what mechanism is used to gauge customer satisfaction and evaluate whether it accurately represents that satisfaction, based on your testing and evaluation.

It is very difficult to accurately measure customer satisfaction in an objective and unbiased way. Independent survey organizations are sometimes retained to interview and gather information about customer experiences through questionnaires, surveys, and comment cards that are made available to the customer. Participation is voluntary, however, so a representation of the entire customer group cannot be fully assured. Access to the total population of customers and the percentage that is represented by the satisfaction measurement instrument will be important information in your assessment of the satisfaction rating. Statistical sampling may be employed to extrapolate satisfaction assessments to the entire customer base. You will need to review the assumptions used carefully to ensure that they are reasonable and extendable. Tracking the number of repeat customers is another method that can be used to measure satisfaction—assuming that if customers were not satisfied, they would not come back. You must evaluate the product or service to ensure there are no exit fees or penalty clauses that might taint this assumption as unrealistic in your opinion. Demand for the product or service is often an excellent indicator of customer satisfaction when it can effectively be compared to other alternatives being offered in the marketplace. The organization's overall market share for a given product type also can be indicative of how well received a product is to the consumers. Whatever the measurement tool used, your assessment should review the assumptions, measuring methods, data gathered, benchmark metrics used for comparison, and the reported results for reasonableness, accuracy, and effectiveness in predicting true satisfaction and its use for guiding the business decision-making processes. By driving as much ambiguity and assumption out of the process as possible and focusing on factual and objective information that stands up to scrutiny, the results should give some useful measure that can be used to guide the business effectively.

E-Business Applications in Support of Business

When evaluating the use of e-business applications as a business support mechanism, there are several levels of interest to the IS auditor, so once more it will be important to have clearly defined the scope and objectives before you begin. E-business applications have many technical concerns related to their security, design, and deployment that need to be appropriately recognized and addressed by the business in order to minimize the inherent risks with this communication model. E-business can add significant risks to the businesses technical infrastructure and can provide numerous opportunities for exposure, compromise, and embarrassment to the organization if not properly managed. Just one instance of a Web site defaced with information and characterizations that puts the business at risk and provokes customer outrage will convince you that proper controls need to be put in place and maintained properly. You will want to review the business case that was made for putting this business online and see a justification that defines the benefits a little more clearly that "it's the cool thing to do." The rationale for going online as a business model should be cost justifiable in some way, possibly through savings or an increased customer presence. A "Field of Dreams" rationale (build it and they will come) should be looked at closely for facts that support this expectation and provide evidence supporting the direction to present business processes through an online means. Let's look at some of the ways e-business support can manifest itself, the risks associated with them, the possible benefits of these uses of the Internet, and how they might be examined to assess their usefulness in support of the business model.

Advertising is the most common way to use the World Wide Web. A large percentage of the Web today is really just an online catalog. Costs for advertising this way compared to other ways can easily be gathered and analyzed by tracking the number of hits to an organization's Web page and the amount of time spent on a given page by the viewer. This information then can be compared to other ways of getting similar exposure to potential customers and a cost/benefit analysis also can be performed. Unless a business is derived from the pages directly through a special ordering phone number that enables to business to know that the Web page was the source of the interest or through an online ordering process, it will be difficult to assess how well the Web has actually supported the business process. Advertising on static Web pages can be done economically and the security for these pages is a relatively minor issue to manage as well. However, huge risks exist for the companies that do not take Internet threats seriously, do not keep their systems patched, and do not protect their company environments from these portals to a hostile network environment. Public side access to the servers hosting these pages should be tight or the risk of defacement, the hijacking of server space for illegal use, and the use of the compromised server as a launch point for subsequent attacks internally or to other businesses can be the consequences.

When product ordering, order fulfillment, and business to consumer (B2C) relationships are established and maintained through the Web, the order of the complexity, cost, and security needs increase by an order of magnitude. User and customer accounts will need to be securely managed and programming for shopping carts will need to be bought or built and maintained. The registration of consumers, their credentials, demographic information, and credit card numbers will need to be managed in a secure environment. Liability and risk will need to be examined along with the increased costs of "doing it right" in order to get a fair and accurate measurement of the return on investment for this kind of business model. Proper security measures can tend to be overlooked, adding to the risks and, of course, making the ROI numbers look better than they would with the proper structures and controls in place. The security controls necessary to ensure that the business is not taken advantage of will take on new twists. Pricing and inventory controls will need to be reexamined to ensure the exposure to the Internet does not provide opportunities for the manipulation of data where it has not been authorized. Benchmark sales activity and the amount of customer use on the Web will need to be tracked and monitored accurately to provide data for a cost benefit analysis and to know when something is wrong. Beware of tools that track "hits" on a Web page but do not differentiate new and unique external hits from those that are representative of the internal staff surfing the page and running up the counters.

Use of the Web for Business to Business (B2B) commerce has been the most effective and beneficial way to utilize the Internet environment for businesses in the recent past. The reasons for this relative success are that the business relationships have been previously established, and known quantities and transaction volumes are involved initially so that the efforts can be aimed at economically facilitating existing relationships at a lower cost. Additional revenue and increased business made available by offering this model just adds to the profitability. The movement of files, orders, and transactions, which do not require guaranteed and instantaneous interaction, can be serviced more effectively this way than through faxes, phone calls, couriers, or the mail system for the most part. There are some security issues to consider but because the business on the other end is established as a known entity with a known IP address, the exchange of the cryptographic keys and use of firewall exceptions to closely limit exposure can be accomplished with only moderate efforts and costs. The savings in both labor costs and time can be substantial. If the processing is all occurring in the information system anyway, what better way to serve it up than electronically, already prepared to be inserted right into the system? Controls will need to be in place because this can obviously introduce some risks as well. Without human intervention and the manual handling of paper orders or orders by phone receptionists, mistakes can get further into the system before they are recognized, if proper controls are not built in the process early on.

Applications also are being provided to businesses across the Internet as a way of renting an application or getting an outsourced service; where hosting internally had been the option previously. The Application Service Provider (ASP) model gives the business a portal into an application that is housed and managed centrally out on the Internet and provides the business the look and feel of an in-house operation at reduced costs. The risk associated with this model include the loss of control over customer or company proprietary data. When the provider is managing the business, they are holding the account, data, and transaction information, thus making it more difficult for the business to leverage this information for other needs that might serve to further the business prospects or promote customer relationships. This information instead is available to the ASP for their needs, which may not be in-line with the needs of the business or their customer's wishes, such as selling demographics or mailing lists, for example.

The loss of services without recourse, should the service provider become insolvent and closes down, is another concern. This has often happened recently, without notice, leaving many businesses without their customer lists or their customers without any way to reconnect to the business easily. These vendor providers may not be able to support the business requirements that apply to the individual organization specifically, from a regulatory or security perspective either. This inadequacy often results from state or local laws that the ASP is unfamiliar with or security policies and practices unique to the individual organization that cannot be accommodated by the solutions being offered, due to a narrow focus or technical limitations. You will want to closely review the contracts and agreements made with an ASP to ensure that the rights of ownership are maintained and right to audit clauses are included. Also watch for penalty clauses and exist fees, because an exit strategy should be a natural part of the service-based agreements, in case things should not work out quite the way they are planned.

Evaluating the Design and Implementation of Risk Controls

As you review business processes and information systems used by business processes to perform the work of the organization, you should methodically identify the risks and categorize those risks for each situation and process step you encounter. This defining of "what can go wrong" is part of a risk assessment that can then used to build a risk management program for the process or entity that is being reviewed. Once the risks are identified in raw form, they provide the basis for identifying controls that would reduce the exposure to those risks, making the process less likely to experience the losses associated with the identified risk. Some controls work better than others do, and some cost more than others do to implement and maintain. Finding the correct balance of cost, risk, and controls is the primary area of expertise that IS auditors can develop and offer as a service to their clients over time. You will need to determine what level of risk control and mitigation are required to reduce the exposure to acceptable levels before going any further. The acceptable level is defined by the business process owners because they are the people accountable for the risk of loss and gain by performing the business process in the first place. If they do not agree to a level of acceptable risk, this analysis will become a subjective exercise and its effectiveness will be severely limited. Identifying acceptable risk and unacceptable risk is the first step to any control evaluation you will perform.

Controls cannot be evaluated in a vacuum and must always be weighed in comparison to the risks and their severity, the possible downside costs of doing nothing, and the costs of implementing the controls and managing them in an ongoing fashion. Knowing which controls work best in a given situation will depend on experience, the business culture, and risk tolerance. It also will be helpful to keep in mind the kinds of outcomes that can be typically expected from the various control techniques available. Your evaluation of the implemented controls and their effectiveness also will depend on those expectations. As you assess the effectiveness of a control, you will need to understand the range of utility it can have, what it looks like when it only partially works, how to tell if it is not working at all, and most importantly, how to tell when it is working perfectly but the risk is not being mitigated. One of the most challenging and potentially rewarding aspects of IS auditing is being able to identify an ineffective control and to recommend a better way of controlling the risk at a lower cost to the organization. Many questions on the CISA exam will be geared toward running the cost and risk numbers on a given risk/control pairing to determine whether the control is worth the cost and effort of applying. If fact, these questions may be more geared toward the costs because they are easier to measure, but the effort and disruption to the business also are factors that need to be considered when evaluating the impact of control implementation.

All controls need to have a few basic characteristics to be considered valid and effective. First, they need to be documented. Without a written record of the control and its intent, there is little proof that it really exists and no way to communicate its use to others in a consistent manner. The control needs to be applied in a consistent manner and with as few exceptions as practical, in order to effectively manage the risks that it was put in place to address. Controls need to be timely in their actions and operation. Controls that let you know something went wrong last week may not be effective in reducing losses. These controls need to be specific enough to manage the risk without stopping the other desired things from occurring. The amount of specificity required to describe the boundaries of the controls' actions will be unique to the threats and risks, but some definition of the details will be required in order to be able to determine the controls' effectiveness. A control needs to fit the situation and need of the business. Some controls are better suited to managing certain risks and outcomes than others. A control should not be overkill nor insufficient for the need of the business. Finally, each control applied should be efficient and cost effective. Controls need to be reasonable in terns of cost/benefit in order to be effective. Controls that cost more than the loss expectancy are not worth implementing.

Preventive Controls

Preventive controls are implemented to stop the loss related to a risk from occurring. When the risk situation presents itself, the preventative control kicks in and prevents the loss. Preventative techniques are the most complete form of stop loss control, because the loss is prevented by their nature. You will come to prefer seeing methods that can be used to prevent a bad thing from happening, rather than controlling them after the fact. As the old saying goes, "An ounce of prevention is worth a pound of cure." There are costs associated with preventive controls that also must be considered to get the full picture of the impact to the business, however. Prevention can mean the continuous close examination of each case, performing an analysis for the risk condition, and stopping the risk whenever it is identified. This can be a more expensive way to control than simply enabling the process to perform, identifying errant exceptions after they have occurred, and taking them out of the process stream for corrective actions in due course. While attempting to prevent errors wherever it is cost effective to do so, many production lines in the manufacturing sector also use detective techniques to weed out errors, which is a more cost effective way of dealing with all of the possible permutations of error conditions that may exist in the process. The alternative of building preventative controls for each scenario would be cost prohibitive.

The monitoring and management of the preventive controls also will need to be considered when determining what is best for the business. The prevention of events that would otherwise have occurred must be examined to assess the impact to any downstream processes that may have been expecting an action to occur or even dependant on it happening. How are these processes made whole again? What additional work is needed to keep things on track? If input or output to a process is prevented, it must either get discarded as scrap or captured and set aside to be used proactively for analysis to better the process, and these rejects will need to be managed. To know that preventive controls are working as they were intended to do, some amount of checking and testing needs to be in place showing that the prevention is actually occurring as it was designed to do. Often this is what the IS auditor is tasked to do. You will want to provide errant input of differing severities into the process ahead of the control and ensure the control stops them when it should. Obviously, great care must be used when testing controls in this manner on a live production system, where control failure may impact downstream processes and customers. As an IS auditor, you should shy away from opportunities to directly interact with the production systems. You should instead monitor and observe this kind of testing, leaving the production teams to perform the actual tests.

Part of this control evaluation process is to ensure that good data or otherwise clean scenarios are not prevented by these controls by mistake. Knowing what happens to the rejected input or process flows in the prevented situations will help determine the cost of the control in total. You should review the process used to monitor the control and ensure its accuracy and effectiveness as part of your review. Controls that are put in place but never monitored or tested may not be operating properly and doing more harm than good. A preventive control cannot be assessed as completely effective unless it prevents the loss in all cases. Remember that like security, controls to the 100 percent level will be difficult, if not impossible to implement and afford. For this reason, some amount of error or loss should generally be expected in the control implementations. Often, layered controls will help offset the high cost of a 100-percent effective control need, with relatively little additional process overhead, if designed carefully.

You will want to walk through the control scheme designed to mitigate the risks to ensure that the other control methods would not work better or at a sufficient level with lower costs given the risk and costs, as you determine if the preventive controls are the right technique to apply in a given situation. In situations where the risks are high and losses are great, you would expect to see preventive controls that are monitored closely for effectiveness. Use of the IS auditor's best level-setting question, "So what?" is always useful in this type of evaluation. If the risk does not warrant the prevention of an event, then better control types for the risk at hand should be explored. In addition, you also must consider that if a risk exposure can be prevented for the same or similar costs and impact the process as other control methods, prevention is usually the better option.

Detective Controls

Detective controls are used in situations where it is more important to understand that something has happened that it was to prevent from happening. In some cases, a detective control will ensure that a desirable event did indeed occur, providing feedback that the process is working as intended. Evaluation of the detective controls requires proving that the detection occurs with a high degree of accuracy and reliability. When it is important to detect that an action has occurred, it will be equally important to rely on the control to not miss any valid occurrences where that detection should be taking place and to flag only those valid occurrences of predefined interest. To assess these controls, you will need to understand the trigger event and the mechanism used to identify it. Testing will lead you to conclude that falsely identifying occurrences, which were not valid (False Positives), and falsely ignoring occurrences, which should have been caught (False Negatives), are within some predetermined acceptable range of error rate. Detective controls do not prevent, deter, or correct data or actions associated with an event that is occurring. The risks associated with detective controls are the risks of not knowing a situation or event has occurred. If this failure to detect happens regularly, the control cannot be assessed as effective. When evaluating the cost/benefit for this control type, you must review what happens to the process if the event or situation is not detected and then assess the costs of this scenario against the cost of implementing and maintaining the control.

Corrective Controls

A corrective control fixes errant situations or events as they are identified. It assumes some amount of detection is inherent in its mission of fixing out-of-bounds conditions. These controls are useful when simple corrections are easily found and fixed in a process without a lot of risk and complexity. The risk of not finding and fixing these items must be considered when assessing the total cost and benefit of such a control. It will need to be determined that corrective actions are possible and performed accurately to the satisfaction of the process in order to draw conclusions that these kinds of controls are effective. Determining what is acceptable in terms of corrective actions will be part of this evaluation process. Those situations that are not caught and those fixed that did not require attention will need to be identified and examined for false positive and false negative implications. Comparing this control to one that prevented the need for correction in the first place may be a valid assessment when evaluating whether the right kinds of controls are employed to mitigate risks in a process. The cost to fix along with cost to identify or cost to prevent all will now need to be part of the cost/benefit analysis.

Automated or Programmed Controls

Part of your assessment of the controls will necessitate an evaluation of the use of automated or programmed controls to mitigate risk as opposed to manual controls that also may be implemented to perform similar functions. The common wisdom is that programmatic controls will work without fail because the machine-driven control does not have an opportunity to ignore its programming as a human or manual process might. However, automated controls come at a price. They must be tested, coded, monitored, and maintained to be effective. When circumstances or risks change, these controls must be reconfigured and go through another rigorous development and testing cycle. They will not work just as automatically when systems are not set up correctly as they would work effectively when the implementation of the control is done correctly. Automated systems do not think or recognize bad instructions in most cases. However, they are much more reliable than manual controls and can be assumed to be working in an unattended fashion, with only minor monitoring to ensure continued effectiveness once they are up and running. When drawing conclusions on the overall effectiveness and cost of automated controls, the building, maintaining, and monitoring costs must be offset by the potential losses to best understand the cost effectiveness of the controls. Additionally, the reliability or net effectiveness of the controls, which are assumed higher in automated and programmatic implementations, also must be factored in. Where loss due to risks cannot be left to chance, automated controls should be recommended. Because you will, no doubt, be focusing on the high risk situations as you triage your work and provide risk-based solutions to your clients, these will be your recommendations more often than not. Proper implementation and routine monitoring are a prerequisite.

Manual Controls

It is important to note that there are many things that can be considered as controls for mitigating risks in a business process. Practices and procedures can be very effective in ensuring that the losses associated with a risk are not realized. Sometimes programmatic solutions are not feasible or practical. The process may not lend itself to the automation of the control methods. The costs of programming and maintaining all that automation may be too high to justify automated controls. The risks of missing a few instances of the loss condition may not be high enough to warrant the need for the pervasive automated mitigation of the risks. Manual controls may be perfectly acceptable in these and many other situations used to control risk exposures. Where the process moves from the logical world to the physical world, manual controls often make a lot more sense.

When assessing manual controls, the risk that control-related procedures are not performed will need to be considered. One aspect of management for manual controls to assess is the penalties and enforcement mechanisms in place for assuring compliance with the manual control directives. How well these controls are documented and the processes used to ensure the users are aware of them and trained in their proper use will need to be evaluated though assessments of training and awareness programs related to the controls in question. Evidence of the measurement and monitoring of the effectiveness of any manual controls should be expected in order to give a high confidence level that the controls are in place and being used to effectively mitigate the risks. Many of the scenarios investigated using "what if" situations will need to be reviewed for the appropriate application of the controls like any other control assessment. Are these controls intended to be preventive, detective, corrective, or deterrent in nature? What are the enforcement mechanisms in place and how effective are they? How are potential loss situations identified and what mechanisms validate that situations have not been overlooked or errantly identified? The costs for these controls also need to be reviewed in a similar cost/benefit evaluation treatment, fully considering the opportunity for a missed control application and training, which may not have been applicable to other control scenarios.

Because these controls are manual, the documentation describing them will be part of your assessment material, and in fact may determine how well the control could possibly be implemented. Manual controls must be understood and carried out manually, that is to say by human actions. Therefore, these controls must be documented in a way that enables humans to interpret the intentions and instructions with a high probability of the results being an effective control that has been implemented. How well the control is documented, how recent and accurate the documentation-like procedures are, and how effective the process is in practice, based on the monitoring and reporting processes, will all be input into your evaluation of the manual controls. Procedures that are not written down are difficult to enforce and cannot really be considered as effective controls.

Cost-Benefit Analysis of Control Efforts

Controls must be cost effective to be worth considering as a risk mitigant. The extent to which these controls will not mitigate the risk (the residual risk) will determine the new expectation of losses and the difference between the original ALE and the revised ALE. This difference can be used in comparison to the cost of implementing the control, when determining whether it is cost effective to deploy the control or not. As mentioned previously, controls have other costs associated with them besides the cost to implement that also must be considered. Delays in processing because of the controls and changes to business process flows resulting from control implementations also are costs related to that control. Time also plays a role in this evaluation, too. Loss expectations are typically calculated annually over a time period, for example. The cost of implementing the control has both fixed and recurring costs that will need to be converted into a time-based value to make a fair comparison to the losses expected over that same time period. A $10,000 control that saves losses of $2,000 per year has a defined payback period of five years. If the remaining process life or effective life of the control is only four years, however, the control will actually costs $2,500 per year and may be unjustified compared to the expected loss in the same time frame. It also may be the case that a $500 annual loss in this example is acceptable to the management of the business. If the maximum loss potential remains at $2,000 for this example, then controls with a total implementation and maintenance cost less than $6,000 should not even be considered, given the four-year expected life span remaining for the process. You will be asked to perform several of these calculations over your career as an IS auditor to assess the cost/benefit of the controls you are recommending. Given the extra work involved with implementing a control, do not be surprised when a breakeven offer at control versus loss is turned down and the losses are accepted rather then implementing the control.

Evaluating Risk Management and Governance Implementation

Evaluation of the risk management process used by an organization to manage its risk is an important aspect of the control environment. Risk management should be a visible part of the management strategy for an organization in order for it to be considered a well-controlled company. Because it is impossible to adequately control what you cannot measure, measuring the risks will be a necessary first step to this process. But before the process can be evaluated, there has to be a mandate and requirement in the form of management controls, corporate governance expectations, and organizational policy, which is directing that this process be performed and actively managed by the leadership and on down through the organization.

Why is risk management such a big deal? Why can we not just direct our practices along the lines of best practice processes and controls and call that good enough? Are not our risks similar if not exactly like our competitors, therefore requiring standard control applications, making our control needs and solutions off-the-shelf items? To answer these questions, you will need to come full circle back to the beginning of this book and revisit the discussion about risks. Risks are an inherent part of doing business as you should recall. They are a natural part of the business process and cannot be completely eliminated or there would be no business to be done. The relationship between risk and reward seeks a natural balance in the business world. Higher risks mean higher rewards but also imply higher chances at losses. The best way to maximize the returns of a business is to effectively manage the risks to the benefit of that business and its management team. What may be risky to others could be low risk to your target organization because of inside knowledge, trade secrets, unique expertise, unique contracts or agreements, and many other things that move the balance of risk in the favor of that organization.

There are three basic ways to manage these risks, remain successful, and have above average returns on an ongoing basis. First, you may have a long-running streak of luck that shines on you to the extent that you can do no wrong no matter what happens to your business, which is statistically possible but a highly unlikely scenario. Second, you may have a monopoly situation that enables you an unfair advantage over the competition for an extended time period. This could be a patent, an exclusive contract to provide service, or a corner on the market for a hot commodity of some kind. In these cases, there are no competitors of any substance and you will be the target of the competition and define the benchmark for performance for which everyone else strives. There is little need to be concerned with good controls, prices, or quality of service unless some laws are enacted to force you to pay attention to these things. Governments tend to fall into this category, however, compliance oversight organizations have been put in place to ensure some level of standards are being met. Because no one is lucky enough to be in possession of the proverbial goose that lays golden eggs, the majority of the businesses you perform IS auditing for will fall into the third risk management category.

Businesses that have customers to satisfy and that compete with other companies for a market share and a share of the profits available from the consumer must manage the risks associated with their business well. They must do this to keep from being blindsided by losses that are associated with the risk exposures their company faces on a routine basis. The business that does this best will be the most profitable—they will experience the fewest losses because their exposure is lower and their risks are better managed than the competition. Managing risk means reducing the loss potential to acceptable levels, survivable levels, and ones where the losses can be absorbed without major adjustments to the business' strategy or mission. Many a dot-com business did not survive because of the losses associated with risks they were not prepared to absorb in the e-business world of the early twenty-first century. With unpleasant surprises under control and proactively managed, a business can comfortably take on more growth-related risk, increasing the chance of an improved company position in the marketplace and the opportunities for profits along the way.

Risk Analysis

When you are evaluating a business, you will want to see documentation that the risks inherent to that business have been identified and analyzed, along with the appropriate actions taken to address those risks. This shows that the management has applied a due diligence to their governance responsibilities and is actively trying to understand how to manage the business to improve on its position in the marketplace. Hopefully this process is applied as a management control and performed for all aspects of the business. However, your scope of audit should perform risks assessments even if other areas of the business do not for the reasons previously outlined and as good leading control practices that you would like to see in place.

Every business segment should understand the risks that they are managing too, for their piece of the business. An ideal scenario would push the risk identification and controls management for those risks down into that business segment, ensuring a full understanding of why the controls are needed and the pitfalls of inadequate control implementation or maintenance. The better the business risks are understood at the line management level, the quicker changes to the risk profile can be identified, and the better chance that improved control techniques will be identified to manage those risks, while improving the business process at the same time. In fact, those who are actually performing the work at the unit and line level are more likely to be in the best position to identify the risks related to the business processes because they interact with them everyday. To find a risk analysis that is performed at the senior management level means only that some of the production level risks have been missed or overlooked.

At the same time, these risks need to be communicated to the management and used to augment management's view of the risks that may not be fully understood by the line management. Contractual agreements, business strategies, and regulatory pressures may be shielded from line management in some cases and have to be considered in an aggregate risk model to provide a complete picture of the businesses risks for control analysis purposes. While all of the risks of a business process do not need to be identified, because there is a threshold below which risk identification may not be productive, the frequency of a low risk with loss potential that is likely and occurs frequently can quickly add up to a major loss. The significance of each risk will need to be modeled into an assessment procedure that can be used to manage the risk identification and qualification process. This may be unique to the business segment under review and managed at an organizational level to provide for consistency and control optimization.

Once the significant risks are identified, listed, and sorted by their loss potential and likelihood of occurrence, the assessment of what is acceptable risk (or loss) can begin. Risk appetite is a management decision and must be communicated to the senior management if not made directly by them. Corporate governance may allow for the delegation of risk assessment and controls implementation at lower levels in the organization. However, the risks, which are material to the organization as a whole, and the accountability for those decisions that represent material risk to the organization must be accounted for by those at the top of the organization, along with the acceptance of any residual risk or the decision to implement controls for these significant organizational risks. What constitutes material risks will be part of the decision making that needs to occur as a risk management process is put in place. You should be able to review documentation that describes the different tiers of risk and loss materiality to the organization, which will help you get an insight into the governance structure and the risk tolerance culture of the organization as well.

The delegation of management and responsibility for risks and loss down through the organization hierarchy also should be evidenced through this documentation, enabling you to more directly understand the ownership of the controls and to whom recommendations and suggestions for improvement might be best addressed. Impact from the combination of risks may need to be considered when scenarios exist that could result in several of the losses related to a set of risk exposures simultaneously affecting the organizational entity. The result of this risk analysis should be a rank order listing of the business risks from most significant to least significant, with possibly a line drawn through the list depicting the point below which losses are immaterial and need not be considered for extraordinary control measures. Certainly, the frequency or potential for the occurrence of these risk scenarios must be factored into ranking these raw exposures for analysis. A completely mature and well-implemented process will replay this process at different levels throughout the organization. It will summate the risks further up the organizational structure and push the management of risks with lower significance to the business units where they may be of more interest or hold more impact potential to that unit, will therefore address them there. In this way, the materiality line may be redrawn as the analysis is performed at various organizational levels, each one defining "material" and "significant" as it relates to their profit and loss picture and the individual unit's definition of acceptable risks.

One of the more difficult aspects of defining the inherent risk list is the fact that some control and risk mitigation is occurring in the organization during the identification process. There is a tendency to overlook risks that are well controlled and not seen as an exposure because of the controls currently in place. For this reason, it is often necessary to facilitate the risk identification process with an outsider who can ask questions and drive these risks out into the open. It will be important to identify all significant risks, even those that are currently mitigated to acceptable levels, because they may not always stay that way and will need to be quickly identified as potentially significant, should the controls begin to degrade that protect the business from these risks. There also is an opportunity to aggregate risks. The materiality of a seemingly small risk that everyone has and sees as nothing more than a nuisance could add up to a material risk in aggregate for the entire company, thus warranting a more serious and pervasive approach in controlling it in some way, which may benefit from a more central mitigation approach. At a given level in the organization, a comprehensive list of significant and material risks should exist and be maintained. This list should be reviewed as part of your evaluation of the business risk management to ensure that the list is complete and accurate to the best of your knowledge and research on the subject.

Control Identification

The existing controls, which are currently providing the control over the risks, also will need to be identified. Partial risk mitigation is the more likely scenario, because we know that complete risk elimination is not going to be cost effective or even desirable in many cases. The opportunity to identify controls not currently employed to mitigate the risks now presents itself and may yield additional value to management through this exercise. This is a primary reason for an internal auditor to insist on a risk management scheme and provide the facilitation and participation in the process, to the extent that their objectiveness is not compromised by the involvement and decision making that comes out of the control identification and analysis processes.

Many controls are so ingrained into the daily business process that they may not be seen by the line management as control techniques at all, but they perform this role daily. Management reports and the routine monitoring of processes are prime examples of manual control techniques that may not be understood as mitigating business risks, when, in fact, they do act in this capacity. Like the overlooked or previously mitigated risks, these unrecognized controls also need to be identified in case they change and the risk resurfaces because the relationship of this instrument as a control mechanism was not fully realized previously. The controls need to be paired against the risks so that credit for the risk control can be matched and identified. The objective of this process is to identify uncontrolled risks and position the process to identifying under-controlled risks and over-controlled risks. More than one risk may be addressed by a single control technique. What may act as a preventive control for one risk type may be seen as a detective control for another, and so on. It is not important to track and record what kind of risk control (preventive, detective, corrective, and deterrent) it is, but it may be instrumental information to identifying the best and minimum necessary controls to be used for a given risk, should control consolidation or reduction be called for. Knowing all of the controls that are applicable to a given risk provides options for eliminating redundant controls and reducing inefficiencies and overhead in some cases.

Gap Analysis and Reporting

The degree to which a risk is mitigated can be described as the total reduction of risk from all of the controls being applied to it, which will need to be determined and documented. The list of controls should be mapped to the list of inherent risks showing the level of risk reduction each control affords to the risk in question. A methodology for determining the amount of risk mitigation that is achieved for each of the inherent risks will need to be devised that can provide for a consistent way to "value" the inherent risk and the amount by which that risk level has been reduced. This may end up being a subjective measure, but if it is well documented, logically designed, and consistently applied, it will give relevant results when compared to other risks being assessed by the measurement model being used. By performing this exercise, the residual risk can now be computed.

Residual risk is the remaining risk exposure after the controls have been applied. A resorting of the items now will show the highest residual risk exposure the organization or business unit faces, assuming that the listed controls are operating and in good working condition. Part of your evaluation will be to determine that this is the case. You should be able to do this from your prior audit work or you can check these controls as part of your risk management evaluation, determining the accuracy of the assumptions used in determining the residual risk. If the controls are not working as designed or the "value" of the risks' reduction is different in your assessment from what is stated in the analysis, you will want to question the rationale used for reaching the conclusions that have been made or challenge the assumptions and rating methodology, seeking to gain agreement on the process and its results.

The next step in a risk assessment that you should see documented is the reconciliation of acceptable risk levels to residual risk through a gap analysis process. Each risk needs to be analyzed and a comparison made between the amount of tolerable risk and the amount of risk exposure that remains after the existing and functioning controls are applied. How much unacceptable risk exposure is still unaddressed will be the result of this gap analysis. This new list then can be resorted to prioritize the unacceptable risk that remains and to begin assessing what needs to be done to bring these risks into a proper level of control. There is an opportunity here to determine what controls are redundant, as previously stated, and through a series of "what if" scenarios a determination can now be made of whether some of those controls can be removed without negatively impacting the risk and control balance.

In addition, it also may be determined that the acceptable risk level is above the current level, based on the current compliment of controls enforced to mitigate the risk being analyzed. This is where a big win can potentially be claimed by the effort of going through this process. Remember that some amount of risk is desirable to optimize profitability. Too much control is costly and creates unnecessary overhead. If controls that serve multiple purposes are sufficient to mitigate this particular risk, then additional stand-alone control measures could be discontinued and the resources redirected to better use, for example. Of course, the tendency will be to leave things as they are in over-control cases. This is because of familiarity and fear of exposure. The freeing up of these resources may take some extra investigation and reporting to convince management to take the chance. This is another opportunity to add value to the business through the proper application of risk and control management processes.

Once you have reviewed a process that has been completed and documented similar to this, you will not only have a thorough understanding of the business risks but also the controls, making an audit of the processes relatively simple and reducing those costs to the organization as well. Naturally, this risk matrix will need to be revisited and updated periodically as new threats emerge and processes and controls change over time. Validating the controls and substantiating the risk exposure will be an ongoing business need and the IS auditor is uniquely suited to review them. By ensuring that the majority of the process reflects the work performed by the business unit, ownership of risk assessment is effectively transferred to the business unit as a responsibility where it belongs. Hopefully the business will see the value and savings of performing this process and embrace it as a due diligence and corporate governance requirement.

Independent Assurance

You will have to examine a risk assessment process much more closely if it was created completely with internal resources or without help or input from an objective and independent party. This is partially because of the difficulty insiders have in seeing the risks and controls that they work with everyday for what they really are, but it is also because of the need for the independent assurance of risk and control evaluations. Not only are risks overlooked or sometimes trivialized, but processes, procedures, and reports used everyday can actually be control mechanisms that perform vital functions in guiding the businesses away from risks but are not seen from this perspective. The result of an internally managed risk assessment is often that opportunities are missed to take credit for what is already happening. Overestimating the impact of the risk to the business overall or missing risks completely because of over familiarity with them through daily exposure are other common occurrences. The rational for independent assurance here also is the same as was previously discussed for corporate governance. Residual risk levels used to make important business decisions that have not been validated through some independent means cannot be given the same reliance and audit assurance as those that have. This independent look over the shoulder may cost some money but will be well worth the investment should an oversight of a material nature surface.

One of the most important aspects of corporate governance will be the independent oversight of that governance and the controls' management being used to run the business. While most business management people, left to their own devices, would naturally do the right things, they are not risk and control experts and do not look at the business needs from that perspective on a routine basis. Independent assurance that the controls are in place and working as designed, and that management is using prudent due diligence in its risk management practices, is what the outside investors want to see in order to get some assurance that what management tells them is the truth and that it can be relied upon when making investment decisions. This has recently been challenged and shaken severely by the collapse of Enron and the press implications that their auditors were not performing their jobs in an ethical and legally compliant or independent fashion. Independent assurance is still the best way to ensure the accuracy and integrity of the financial data. Controls to ensure that this independent assurance is in place and that all necessary information is made available to the auditors so they can give the assurance needed by outside directors and investors will need to be strengthened and monitored more closely through improved corporate governance processes in the future.

More often than not, the very fact that you have been asked to evaluate an organization as an external auditor implies the existence of some kind of independent assurance process in place. It could be that the board of directors contracted with your firm to provide this review and evaluation function for them. Major investors or potential business partners may have asked that a review be completed to validate the controls and risk exposure of a business venture they are considering in some capacity. A SAS 70 engagement is often used for this purpose. Independent assurance also is a model you would expect to see in most control assessments in order to rely on it as an adequate control. Certainly without the independence and objectivity of an independent review and the accompanying assurance, a prudent businessperson would be relying on the word of those responsible for the controls that they are functioning properly. By definition, they could not provide an objective opinion. For this reason, your review as an IS auditor will seek to ensure that independent assurance has been used to validate all controls that manage the risk exposures of a material nature. Sometimes that independent review will come from your own efforts. It also may come from other audit and review functions within the organization such as the compliance or internal audit departments. It may, however, be sufficient in many cases to have the controls validated internally but not by those persons who own and maintain the controls, where they are independent. User departments are in a position to validate that processing controls are in place and can be used to check out how well they are working in many cases. As long as the assurance can be determined to be independent, consideration can be given to using that assessment as valid proof that the controls are working. You will want to ensure that your work reflects an independence and objectivity in all aspects to avoid these issues when you are reporting and drawing conclusions.

Security and Internal Control

Information security and internal control functions are perfect examples of where you should expect to find some periodic independent evaluation and oversight. Hearing that others would not understand the process or would not be able to grasp the complexity as excuses for the lack of prior independent assurance should be a big red flag with the IS auditor and result in a much closer look at what is and is not being done. Controls only work if everyone agrees that they work. The risks should be validated in terms of threat and vulnerability so that the controls can be placed where they will do the most good. Funding and resources are never in overabundance. Good, solid risk analysis must drive the application of security and controls so that they can be most efficiently applied for the maximum benefit to the businesses they serve. They need to stand up to the scrutiny of subject matter experts because, if they are to be relied upon for mitigating material risks and changing the risk profile of an organization, there is a need for an independent verification. Either an internal auditor or third-party security experts should be engaged periodically to check the security program and its controls to ensure the plan is sound and the results are accurate and effectively meeting the goals of supporting the business. Business processes depend on these controls to cover their exposures. Without some kind on independent assurance, the business is taking the word of those who would be least likely to speak first if something was wrong. It will be important to note the results of this assurance evaluation and what actions are recommended. Follow-up on the level of action taken from these recommendations to true up the direction based on the feedback also will be of interest. It will be important to ensure that the source of any assurance gained is not only independent but also qualified to make the evaluation and resulting opinions, in order to find them as a reliable source of validation. Qualifications to perform reviews from a technical and business perspective also are qualities businesses will want to see in you as well.

Third-Party Service Providers

Third-party service providers take on business functions and processes for a fee. Some amount of the risk is shared with them because they must provide against a contract and meet certain obligations in order to get paid. It will be important to analyze what risk is transferred and what of the inherent risk within the business process remains with the host organization. This risk assessment will involve a review of the contracts, an assessment of the business models, and how they are linked together. The obligations and penalties associated with the agreements along with an assessment of the legally binding aspects of this agreement to the recourse for nonperformance, will determine how much of the businesses risks have been transferred and how many risks may have been added. Business process risk matrices that show gaps in risk because of provided services need to be investigated further so that new risks and existing risks can be evaluated in light of these third-party arrangements.

Third parties also can add risks to the business as well as give relief. If the service provider is not reputable or has a lot of residual risk within its business, the overall risk may increase at the price of convenience and less-expensive processing. Depending on the contract agreements and recourse stipulated in them, this may be seen as somebody else's problem. But in fact there may be little thought given to the real-time impact of nonperformance to the business processes and the customer impact in the near term, while lawyers sort out contractual obligations. These risks need to be identified and added into the assessment and control evaluation process. The loss of accessibility to the product and information while the service provider is in possession of it, as well as exposures to mishandling and substandard performance, are some of the other risks, that will need to be examined for materiality and mitigation actions, which are related to service provider participation in the business processes.

Multiple vendors and providers, possibly interacting with each other outside of the businesses direct control, can make this an interesting exercise. The independent assessment and assurance of risks, which are additive to the business processes from the service providers, will be necessary to validate the need for additional controls or concern. SAS 70 reviews also can serve this purpose. Evaluation of actual services, reviews of third-party financials, as well as frank discussions with their management, are all control techniques used to define and manage third-party risks. Often, an IS auditor cannot go beyond the scope of the audit into the service provider realm to fully evaluate these risks and fully understand the risks associated with the arrangements that are in place.

Right to audit clauses in the agreements with these service providers may provide some ability to examine third-party service providers more closely and get a sense of their control environment and risks. The scope and objectives of your audit engagement should define these issues early on. Client management should not be lead to believe that an external auditor will gain the same level of access to the internal workings of a remote business process that an internal auditor of that organization would or they will be disappointed. If you do get involved with evaluating third-party service providers who are supporting the primary business you are engaged with, make sure an understanding is documented about how findings at the third-party location will be reported and resolved before performing any fieldwork at that location.

Proactive Audit Involvement

As mentioned previously, the ideal situation for risk assessment is to have the audit teams—primarily internal but also external as well—participate in the risk analysis process and proactively assist in identifying, testing, and seeking value-added solutions to risk and control problems as the evaluation occurs and throughout the business cycle. Audit involvement lowers the risks and acts as a control because of the independent assurance factor that is added to the equation. An auditor is uniquely positioned to proactively enhance the process by looking out for the pitfalls without taking advantage of them, instead they help the business to understand these pitfalls and address those issues to better their business. It is assumed that auditors perform in an independent fashion because their ethical guidelines mandate this to be so. This, of course, assumes that the audit function involved subscribes to the direction of the standards bodies and embraces the process of certification and international auditing organizational practices as their core values. Proactive audit involvement will be difficult to measure in terms of overall risk reduction, but the testing of controls and independent assurance that the risks and controls have been properly identified and evaluated will ensure a solid reliable risk management system with results that will serve the business well.

Laws, Regulatory Requirements, and Contractual Commitments

Risks that relate to the mandates and requirements of laws and regulations also will need to be incorporated into the risk assessment and profile management process. In many highly regulated businesses, staying in business is contingent on satisfying these requirements officially to the oversight authorities. The risks of failing to meet the requirements carry financial and punitive penalties beyond the loss of business and service provider status from the authority bodies. Strategies for staying current on the laws and the risks associated with them will need to be examined and should be provided for as part of the organizational governance and professional due diligence of the management infrastructure. These processes require that someone is held accountable for monitoring the regulations, looking for new laws to assess and to provide an accurate and timely interpretation of these new regulations for compliance strategies, risk assessment, and possible control recommendations. Failure to recognize new and existing legal requirements is one of the risks that will need to be assessed. Failure to adequately comply will be another. Choosing not to comply but instead adding the penalties to the list of acceptable losses, should they occur, also may be within the realm of possibilities to consider. However, the risks associated with reputation and future business impact also should be considered. Your research into the business, during your due diligence phase, will alert you to the regulatory environment that is part of the business landscape of the particular business with which you are engaging. The risks and their magnitude will depend on many factors unique to the business processes and the management governance processes you find in place controlling them.

In a similar fashion, commitments that the business has with other parties will have risks associated with them that also are part of the assessment and risk matrix building process. Understanding these commitments, the risks associated with the failure to meet them, and what controls are in place to ensure this does not happen will be almost a reverse view of the third-party process that we reviewed previously. In this case, the risks might include entertaining third-party audits and the associated disruption and managing the recommendations and sanctions that may come from third-party control assessments.

Provisions for Independent Audits

Coming full circle now, the corporate governance of a business process should require that independent monitoring and reporting on risks and controls to be in place. Unless senior management is able to observe the effectiveness of the control structure firsthand, there is no other way to get the assurance that things are working as designed and that all flaws are surfaced and addressed in a timely and accurate manner. The audit function is designed for such a purpose and reports directly to the body, which is ultimately accountable for corporate governance, so that a direct and clear communication channel exists. Many of the requirements for an audit function were outlined in the first chapter from the perspective of one who would be performing that function. This section will revisit those functions briefly with a perspective of auditing or evaluating the performance of the audit function. Evaluating an audit function that exists within an organization must obviously be performed by an independent audit team that can be objective and impartial in the findings and recommendations to the management to which the subject audit group reports. External auditors and regulatory bodies perform this type of evaluation as part of their assessment of the corporate governance structure routinely and use it to determine how well the overall control and risk management structure has been implemented in the organization under review.

Some audit organizations utilize peer reviews that leverage similar functions at other locations within a larger organization to test the performance and procedures of each other, looking for improvement opportunities. These reviews can help merging organizations find common approaches and add to the quality of future reviews, if handled properly. Finding fault in the details and criticizing in an unconstructive manner can be detrimental to the relationships that were supposed to be strengthened by this process, however. Comparisons of similar practices and reaching an agreement on the best practices among several audit groups performing similar functions also is an objective of local Information Systems Audit and Control Association (ISACA) chapters that are formed in many metropolitan areas throughout the world. These organizations have a formal officer structure and meet regularly to leverage training, networking, and development into a community of experts who can help each other grow professionally. Participation gains visibility for the IS auditor and provides opportunities to practice public speaking, give back to the audit profession, learn from others, meet people, and make friends. These contacts can help you advance your career in the IS audit profession.

Audit Charter

When you are asked to review an audit function, you will perform an assessment using the same steps you would use to evaluate any organization. Start by gaining an understanding of the business (you should already understand this as an IS auditor), the charter, and the scope of the responsibilities of the business. It will be important to see in writing documentation that formally establishes authority, accountability, and independence within the audit function charter. The governance document that grants these authorities should come from the senior-most owners and the management of the business that they serve. This ensures that the mandate to evaluate and report all control weaknesses is clear and unbiased and goes straight to the top of the organization, ensuring success of the audit function. This charter should declare that the audit function subscribes and adheres to all applicable codes of professional ethics and professional standards. This will ensure that the work is objective and performed in a reliable manner. Similar professional performance codes and standards also will apply to the financial auditing as well as to the IS aspects of the audit work performed. You may need some assistance from financial audit resources you are aware of in order to ensure that the charter and direction statements set forth for the financial audit functions meet the best practice requirements for that profession.

Independence

You will want to see that the audit function performs in an independent manner. Direction and influence imposed on the audit function relating to what to audit, and how to test the controls coming from the business units should be looked upon with suspicion. It should be the auditor's function, through their risks assessment process or using that process of the business units after its validation, to determine where the significant risks are and where the audit work needs to be performed. Of course, input also should be sought from the business units. The coordination of schedules and time commitments is always a win-win proposition, however, the final decisions of where the resources need to be applied should be determined by the audit function and presented to the ownership or directors for their concurrence.

It also should be evident that the manner in which the audit function is performed is an independent one in both its perception and appearance as well as in the way it is performed. Auditors should not be affiliated with the business units so there is no question of motive and objectiveness of the performance of their audit work. Reporting structures and organizational charts should be examined. These structures and charts should clearly show that the audit function is outside of the influence of the rest of the organization and has direct reporting lines to senior management who are not part of the business reporting and accountability structure.

The Effect of Non-Audit Roles on the IT Auditor

Because there are independence concerns with auditors performing in nonaudit roles within the organization, care should be taken to ensure this is done without compromising the integrity and independence of the audit function. As we discussed in Chapter 1, audit participation can be of great benefit to development efforts and the auditor's risk and control expertise should be seen as a resource for the betterment of the business processes. An auditor's past involvement in control development and consulting input should be recorded and tracked within the audit department so that conflicts can be readily avoided. For similar reasons, past nonaudit work efforts in the business units also may be seen as sources for audit independence compromise. Auditors, who were at one time responsible for the design and development of systems and controls or production business processes for that matter, may not be suitable for performing audits of those functions due to prior responsibilities related to these items they are now being asked to audit. The audit charter should provide the IS auditor opportunities to declare a conflict and possible independence concern in these situations so that other options can be satisfactorily explored.

Competence

It will be important to your evaluation to determine that those performing the audit function for the business that you are reviewing are competent and qualified to fill these roles. You should request a listing of credentials and educational backgrounds of those individuals who hold management and supervisory audit positions. You will want to ensure that they have a background and education that fits the type of work they are responsible for and are involved in continuing education programs to stay current with the technology, audit techniques, and practices. Certifications and four-year college degrees or better are always a good sign that the people in these positions are professional and career oriented. You also may want to review some of the past work of such people; in fact, you may be using some of it to get a background on the business and management culture. These are excellent opportunities to observe the work ethic and professionalism as evidenced by their work product, reports, and so forth. After reviewing the reports, you should be able to determine that the findings are well researched, based on factual, material concerns, and that the recommendations are value added and presented in a positive and progressive manner.

Membership in organizations that support the continuing education of the audit functions will show that this organization actively pursues competency and professionalism. A review of the technological strengths and weaknesses of the IS audit staff should show a good match to those technologies in use and planned for in the business they are reviewing. Gaps between these competencies and the required technical expertise should be questioned so that strategies for covering the risks and controls related to that technology also are reviewed and understood. Certainly, CISA certification will provide you great assurance that the IS auditors performing any IS audit work are bound by the code of ethics and are knowledgeable of the audit techniques and technology required of them to perform their function.

Planning

The plan that is provided by the audit function to the management for auditing the business should regularly and systematically cover all of the high-risk information service function areas. A risk-based weighting of the audit efforts and priorities is a best practice for determining where the scheduled audit efforts should be directed. Input to this schedule should include new business, prior audit areas that require follow-up and improvement, and areas of high risk that call for more frequent reviews than those of a lesser residual risk level. These schedules should be approved by senior management and completed as approved. Any changes to priorities or scheduled audits should be noted and explained to the management.

Within the IS auditing space, you should be able to match up the planning for IS auditing to the risk assessment analysis and generally agree with the schedule based on the rationale and approach provided along with the plan. Areas of significant risk that are not receiving a proportionate amount of audit attention should be discussed to ensure that reasonable explanations support the lack of attention in high-risk areas. At the next level of detail, the audit programs should show that planning at that level includes risk-based scopes and objectives that will effectively provide the assurance necessary to conclude on the overall residual risk exposure and identify any material control weaknesses. Because the operation and effectiveness of controls change over time, revisiting well controlled but high-risk areas of the business and information systems should be part of the audit planning and scheduling cycle.

Performance

Due professional care will be the benchmark against which the audit work you examine should be measured. You should be able to use the work papers relating to a report and reasonably draw the same or similar conclusions and opinions from that work. Conclusions about the residual risk exposure and the effectiveness of the controls that are in place will be the test of the work performance of the audit staff and supervision. Work papers, which may be called on to support legal claims or investigations, should be professionally documented and compiled, allowing for easy reference and follow through to the testing, results, and key risk area conclusions. You should examine the way that findings move from discovery to validation through the documentation and transference eventually onto the final report. Observe that the gravity of the finding and its recommendation are balanced and hold up to the due professional care standard. Look at the testing procedures and the techniques used to gather evidence to ensure that the testing techniques are suitable for the scope and objectives of the audit that the results hold up and are supported by the testing procedures. Go out into the field and compare what is found there in practice to the work that is documented in the work papers, if you really want to test the performance of the IS audit staff supporting the particular business you are tasked with assessing. You should find that the processes and controls are as described in their work and will be able to note any progress in addressing the identified control weaknesses as you perform this comparison. This also will give you some insight as to how proactive management is in dealing with weaknesses that have been formally identified to them.

Reporting

The reporting, which is coming from the audit organization you are reviewing, will be the most important aspect of your review of the organization's work and performance. This set of documentation represents the organization's final product, and this documentation is most often the only deliverable seen by the primary clients—the owners and directors of the business organization. You should be able to read through a report and get a sense of the overall control effectiveness in the subject area under review. The scope and objective of the audit effort should be clearly defined and plainly state what was reviewed and what was not. All assumptions and caveats related to the audit work performed should be available so that management can make well-informed decisions based on this reporting without getting the wrong impressions from the content or style of the report. These reports should provide a fair and even-handed assessment of the audited environment in a nonconfrontational and positive manner wherever possible. The report should not have an overriding negative tone if management is expected to read and accept its contents.

Audit reports do little good unless they are read and used to provoke change for the betterment of the organization. This should be done through recommendations and suggestions for improvement, which challenge the management to better efficiencies and effectiveness in the process and control environments. You should seek out evidence that the reports are distributed to those persons who are accountable for the governance of the organization, and that the reports are read and responded to in a formal and meaningful manner. Your evaluation should ensure that management takes action based on the reporting that is being provided, and that there are periodic meetings between management and the auditor, where frank and open discussions occur without fear of reprisal by the auditor from the management. Management is responsible for taking the input provided to them from the audit function and acting on it. They may accept the residual risk presented to them and choose not to accept the recommendations of the auditors; this is a perfectly acceptable outcome of the auditor's evaluation process. They should formally accept these risks to show that the audit reports were responded to and considered as input to their decisions when this is the case.

Part of the independence of the auditor's function hinges upon being able to speak directly and frankly with the senior management about concerns they have with other management in the business processes and the way in which they are managing the risks and controls. Sessions to do this are often part of the regularly scheduled audit subcommittee meetings of the board of directors meetings. During these sessions, other members of the management team are usually excused, while the board interfaces directly with the audit management, holding an unobstructed dialog and receiving reports directly from them.

Follow-Up Activities

Follow-up activities for audit work and the action items committed to by management for the corresponding recommendations made in the reports should be a routine part of the ongoing work performed by the audit function. Management is responsible for resolving any outstanding audit comments by either implementing controls, correcting deficiencies in the existing control mechanisms, providing additional information to the audit team that changes the opinion of the materiality of the finding, or by formally accepting the outstanding risk and communicating that to the owners or board for their concurrence. Audits with numerous outstanding control weaknesses or processing effectiveness concerns should be queued for a shorter audit cycle than those with relatively few problem areas and therefore lower residual risk. The follow-up activities should be based on the responses provided to the audit function and reported to the management at the time of the final report issuance. At the time the report is finalized, action items should have been identified along with the names of persons who are accountable for championing the corrective action and a target date by which the item is expected to be completed. The progress related to management's ability to produce against the agreed to target dates and to provide the enhancements to the processes that correct any deficiencies noted in the audit report should be tracked and reported on to the management during the periodic meetings between the management and the audit function of the organization. As these items are addressed, comments and documentation should find its way into the work papers related to the audit in question so that a full accounting of the audit cycle is contained in one central location for future reference.

Resources

- Control Objectives for Information and related Technology—CobiT (www.isaca.org/pubs2.htm#cobit).

Sample Questions

Here is a sampling of questions in the format of the CISA exam. These questions are related to business process evaluation and risk management, and will help test your understanding of this subject. Answers with explanations are provided in Appendix A.

1. Corporate governance can *best* be described as

    A. A formal process of implementing controls across the system

    B. A process that ensures that all risks have controls associated with them

    C. The guiding principles and policies of the organization

    D. The process for ensuring that all risks and accountabilities are managed within a business

2. When reviewing a corporate governance system, an IS auditor would be *most* concerned to find which of the following deficiencies in the process?

    A. Gaps in the handing down of the authority necessary to carry out the responsibilities given to unit management

    B. Lack of an enforcement and disciplinary process for ensuring that governance and direction is in effect

    C. Unit level goals that do not tie directly to the overall mission of the business

    D. Incomplete measurement processes for ensuring that the governance direction is carried out

3. What is the *most* important thing to keep in mind when reviewing a business process for best practice design?

    A. The state of the art solutions that are available in the market to perform these business functions

    B. The current business model and its overall performance metrics

    C. The requirements, business goals, and core competencies defined by the business model

    D. What the competition is doing

4. What is the *primary* role that Key Performance Indicators (KPIs) have in supporting the business process effectiveness?

   A. KPIs show when controls may not be working properly.

   • B. KPIs are used to show that the service levels and business requirements are being met.

   C. KPIs show the percentage of a system's uptime and measure the output volumes and speeds.

   D. KPIs can be used to draw conclusions about the overall performance of the processes and target variances for follow-up analysis.

5. Management controls are intended to do all of the following *except*

   A. Enable for individual units to establish policies to meet their particular needs.

   B. Provide baseline guidance and direction for the entire business culture and style.

   C. Set rules for the business processes that are followed by all units and departments.

   D. Establish a framework for corporate governance and compliance.

6. When evaluating a business process reengineering project, an IS auditor would be *least* concerned to find that

   A. The staff that actually performs the current processes is not involved with the design of the redesign of the process

   B. Management commitment and support is not clearly stated in writing

   C. External facilitators are not involved in the analysis and stream-lining of the existing processes

   D. The scope of the project has not been documented to include all of the existing facets of the business process being examined

7. All of the following are valid ways of measuring customer satisfaction *except*

   A. Sending out questionnaires with the product and asking for feed-back on service and performance

   B. Using internally generated KPIs to see whether the performance levels are being met or exceeded

    C. Measuring repeat business and customer base growth from internal sales and shipping information

    D. Measuring the percentage of overall market share this particular business has in the market and its relative growth over time

8. Which of the following are valid reasons for considering an e-business solution in support of the business process?

    I. The customer base is widely scattered and remote to the physical business location.

    II. The costs of doing business over the Web have been shown to be more efficient for the business than other mechanisms.

    III. Everybody is doing it.

    IV. The sales department believes that adding functionality to the Web presence will move customers from a browse to a buy online model by making this business option available to them.

    V. Real time and immediate support of the business transactions can be best supported by an online transaction model.

    A. I, II, and III only

    B. I, II, III, and IV only

    C. I and II only

    D. I, II, and V only

9. When reviewing the design and implementation of risk controls, it will be *most* important for the IS auditor to determine that

    A. All risks are being completely mitigated through the proper application of control mechanisms.

    B. Controls prevent risks' situations from occurring wherever possible.

    C. As many risks as possible are addressed by the control that is being considered for implementation.

    D. There is a proper balance between the gravity of the risk and the control measure implemented.

10. Preventive controls are primarily used to

    A. Stop a process and notify the operations that an error has occurred

    B. Keep an error situation from occurring by recognizing the condition and denying its occurrence

    C. Monitor and check error conditions that cannot be easily managed in other ways

    D. Address complex ranges of error conditions that can all be addressed by unique prevention condition statements

11. When evaluating the effectiveness of detective controls that are applied to business systems, an IS auditor should consider the following:

    I. Whether preventive controls would be more appropriate for the risk type and possible loss scenario

    II. The error rate and accuracy of the control in identifying out of bounds conditions

    III. The reporting mechanism used to notify management of an error condition

    IV. The cost of the control compared to the potential loss to the system

    V. Whether the risk is significant enough to warrant any controls at all

    A. I, II, and IV only

    B. II, III, and IV only

    C. IV, V, and II only

    D. I, II, III, IV, and V

12. What is the *primary* difference between a corrective control and a detective control where business processes are concerned?

    A. Business processes cannot be corrected in midtransaction, thus making corrective controls less applicable.

    B. Best practices typically indicate preventive controls over either of these other two control choices.

    C. Corrective controls include detection as part of the way these controls operate and then fix the problem as well.

    D. Corrective controls can only fix a small range of errors, while detective controls can detect a far greater scope of possible error conditions.

13. What is the *primary* difference to keep in mind when evaluating automated and manual controls?

   A. Automated controls can operate in an unattended fashion, which requires less testing and monitoring.

   B. Manual controls require human interaction to be successfully deployed and must consider human fallibility as part of the accuracy assessment.

   C. Potential losses are more difficult to measure with manual controls because the error rates are more difficult to measure.

   D. Training and documentation are required for manual controls while automated control do not require such documentation.

14. A risk assessment has determined that the losses that could be potentially incurred with the delivery system of a business may cost up to $10,000 per month. Preventive controls have been recommended that will save the company $7,000 per month, but this control will take three months to implement at a cost of $100,000 and at an ongoing cost of $1,000 per month. The business process has a life span of five years and has been in production for one year. Is the control justified?

   A. Yes, the savings over the remaining life of the process would be $315,000, thus justifying the expense.

   B. No, the $3,000 per month that will be missed over the life of the process ($144,000) exceeds the cost of the control.

   C. Yes, the total cost of the control over the remaining process life is $145,000, while the potential loss without the control would be $480,000.

   D. Maybe, if the potential savings over the remaining life of the process ($315,000) minus the total cost of the control ($145,000) represents a material risk to the company's management ($170,000), management may consider implementing the control and avoiding the risk.

15. The Annual Loss Expectancy (ALE) of a risk without controls is expected to be $35,000 to a business process you are evaluating. You are recommending a control that will save 80 percent of that loss at an annual cost of $20,000 over the life of the process. Is the control justifiable?

    A. No, the savings is insignificant and relative to the cost.

    B. Yes, 80 percent of the loss amounts to $28,000 per year, which exceeds the annual cost by $8,000 per year.

    C. No, ALE is a subjective number and cannot be depended on to make this decision.

    D. Maybe, it depends on the management's appetite for risk and loss.

16. What is the *most* important aspect of risk analysis to keep in mind when reviewing a business process?

    A. Senior management must be held accountable for all risks to the business.

    B. All risks do not need to be eliminated for a business to be profitable.

    C. Risks must be identified and documented in order to perform proper analysis on them.

    D. Line management should be involved in the risk analysis because management sees risks daily that others would not recognize.

17. Before making a recommendation to management for the further mitigation of residual risk during a gap analysis in a risk assessment, the following considerations should be decided upon:

    I.   Management's risk tolerance

    II. The best type of control for the risk scenario and the process

    III. The gap between the acceptable risk and the residual risk

    IV. The state of the art, best practice for the process being reviewed

    V.   Additional risk mitigation that the proposed control would address for the process under review

    A. I, II, III, and V only

    B. II, III, and V only

    C. II, III, IV, and V only

    D. I, II, III, IV, and V

18. What is the *primary* reason for independent assurance as a requirement for relying on control assessment and evaluation?

    A. The review of controls by independent reviewers transfers some amount of the risk to the reviewing body or organization.

    B. IS auditors are more knowledgeable about risks and controls and are better suited to review them and determine their effectiveness.

    C. Unless the controls are reviewed by an independent and objective review process, the quality of the controls cannot be assured.

    D. Management needs to have independent assurance that the risks are managed effectively as part of their corporate governance requirement.

19. What are examples of additional risk to a business that a third party may add to the overall risks of the business?

    A. None, a business will actually take on some of the risk and reduce the overall risks to the business.

    B. A business will take on the risk that they do not have proper processes in place to perform inefficiently.

    C. A business will take on the risks that the contractual commitments do not adequately compensate for poor performance of the third-party vendor.

    D. A business will take on the risk that the customers are impacted by missed service level commitments or the misuse of customer information.

20. When reviewing an audit function for independence, an IS auditor would be most concerned to find that

    A. The internal audit function was made up of people who used to work for the external auditing firm that managed the accounting and auditing of this business

    B. The audit function had an administrative reporting relationship to the controller of finance in the business

    C. Some of the audit staff had previous involvement with the operation of business processes that their group was evaluating

    D. The audit staff had reviewed similar risk and control processes for competing businesses

Answers to Sample Exam Questions

Chapter 1—The IS Audit Process

Here are the answers to the questions in Chapter 1:

1. When planning an IS audit, which of the following factors is *least* likely to be relevant to the scope of the engagement?

   A. The concerns of management for ensuring that controls are sufficient and working properly

   B. The amount of controls currently in place

   C. The type of business, management, culture, and risk tolerance

   D. The complexity of the technology used by the business in performing the business functions

   Answer: B

   The correct answer is B. How many controls are in place has little bearing on what the scope of the audit should be. Scope is a definition of what should be covered in the audit. What management is concerned about (A), what the management risk environment is (C), and how complex the technical environment is (D) could all have an impact of what the scope of a particular audit might be but not the shear number of controls.

2. Which of the following *best* describes how a CISA should treat guidance from the IS audit standards?

    A. IS audit standards are to be treated as guidelines for building binding audit work when applicable.

    B. A CISA should provide input to the audit process when defendable audit work is required.

    C. IS audit standards are mandatory requirements, unless justification exists for deviating from the standards.

    D. IS audit standards are necessary only when regulatory or legal requirements dictate that they must be applied.

    Answer: C

    The correct answer is C. IS audit standards are mandatory to flow at all times unless justification exists for deviating from them. Complying with standards is one of the tenants of the IS Audit Code of Ethics and is not a guideline (A), does not apply only when the work needs to be defendable (B), or when regulatory or legal issues are involved (D).

3. Which of the following is *not* a guideline published for giving direction to IS auditors?

    A. The IT auditor's role in dealing with illegal acts and irregularities

    B. Third-party service provider's effect on IT controls

    C. Auditing IT governance

    D. Completion of the audits when your independence is compromised

    Answer: D

    The correct answer is D. When the perception of auditor independence is questioned, the audit management must investigate and determine whether the situation warrants actions such as removing the auditor or investigating further. There is no standard like the one mentioned, but the subject is covered in the organizational relationship and independence standard. The other answers are guidelines provided by ISACA.

4. Which of the following is *not* part of the IS auditor's code of ethics?

   A. Serve the interest of the employers in a diligent loyal and honest manner.

   B. Maintain the standards of conduct and the appearance of independence through the use of audit information for personal gain.

   C. Maintain competency in the interrelated fields of audit and information systems.

   D. Use due care to document factual client information on which to base conclusions and recommendations.

   Answer: C

   The correct answer is C. Use of client information is unethical and a cause for revocation of your certification. The other three are tenants of the code of ethics.

5. Due care can *best* be described as

   A. A level of diligence that a prudent and competent person would exercise under a given set of circumstances

   B. A level of best effort provided by applying professional judgment

   C. A guarantee that no wrong conclusions are made during the course of the audit work

   D. Someone with lesser skill level that provides a similar level of detail or quality of work

   Answer: A

   The correct answer is A. Due care is a level of diligence applied to work performed. It is a reasonably competent third-party test. It does not ensure that no wrong conclusions are made (C) and is not related on a skill level (D) but a competence and prudence level. It is not a level of best effort (B). It is a benchmark to compare efforts against—that which would have been done in similar circumstances by a prudent and competent person.

6. In a risk-based audit approach, an IS auditor must consider the inherent risk and

   A. How to eliminate the risk through an application of controls

   B. Whether the risk is material, regardless of management's tolerance for risk

    C. The balance of the loss potential and the cost to implement controls

    D. Residual risk being higher than the insurance coverage purchased

Answer: C

The correct answer is C. You do not want to eliminate risk (A), you want to only manage and control it. Management's tolerance of the risk is part of the definition of what is material so whether the risk is material (B) is not a correct answer. Insurance coverage is not necessarily the only control to consider for mitigating residual risk (D). The correct balance of cost to control any potential losses is a very important part of the risk mitigation considerations.

7. Which of the following is *not* a definition of a risk type?

    A. The susceptibility of a business to make an error that is material where no controls are in place

    B. The risk that the controls will not prevent, detect, or correct a risk on a timely basis

    C. The risk that the auditors who are testing procedures will not detect an error that could be material

    D. The risk that the materiality of the finding will not affect the outcome of the audit report

Answer: D

The correct answer is D. Answer A is the definition of an inherent risk, which is a risk in its natural state or without controls. A controls risk (B) is the chance that controls put in place will not solve the problem soon enough to prevent loss. A detection risk (C) occurs when auditing does not discover material errors due to sampling or testing procedures.

8. What part of the audited businesses background is *least* likely to be relevant when assessing risk and planning an IS audit?

    A. A mature technology set in place to perform the business processing functions

    B. The management structure and culture and their relative depth and knowledge of the business processes

C. The type of business and the appropriate model of transaction processing typically used in this type of business

D. The company's reputation for customer satisfaction and the amount of booked business in the processing queue

Answer: A

The correct answer is A. All of the items listed are relevant, however, by itself the maturity of the technology has the least amount of bearing on the risk assessment of an organization. Just because it is a mature technology does not mean it is inherently risky or does not meet the needs of the business.

9. Which statement *best* describes the difference between a detective control and a corrective control?

A. Neither control stops errors from occurring. One control type is applied sooner than the other.

B. One control is used to keep errors from resulting in loss, and the other is used to warn of danger.

C. One is used as a reasonableness check, and the other is used to make management aware that an error has occurred.

D. One control is used to identify that an error has occurred and the other fixes the problems before a loss occurs.

Answer: D

The correct answer is D. While both are after the fact (A), the order of application is not really relevant. While corrective controls keep errors from resulting in loss (B), detective controls do not warn, deterrent controls do. While reasonableness checks can be a detective control, it also is used to make errors known (C).

10. Which of the following controls is *not* an example of a pervasive general control?

A. IS security policy

B. Humidity controls in the data center

C. System-wide change control procedures

D. IS strategic direction, mission, and vision statements

Answer: B

The correct answer is B. The other three are pervasive because they focus on the management and monitoring of the overall IS infrastructure. Humidity controls are specific to a single data center only.

11. One of the *most* important reasons for having the audit organization report to the audit committee of the board is because

    A. Their budgets are more easily managed separate from the other budgets of the organization

    B. The departments resources cannot easily be redirected and used for other projects

    C. The internal audit function is to assist all parts of the organization and no one reporting manager should get priority on this help and support

    D. The audit organization must be independent from influence from reporting structures that do not enable them to communicate directly with the audit committee

Answer: D

The correct answer is D. Independence from influence and for reporting purposes is the primary reason to have reporting lines outside of the corporate reporting structure.

12. Which of the following is *not* a method to identify risks?

    A. Identify the risks, then determine the likelihood of occurrence and cost of a loss.

    B. Identify the threats, their associated vulnerabilities, and the cost of losses.

    C. Identify the vulnerabilities and effort to correct based on the industry's best practices.

    D. Seek managements risk tolerance and determine what threats exist that exceed that tolerance.

Answer: C

The correct answer is C. The industry's best practices must be tempered by management tolerance for risk and their direction. The elimination of risks is not your goal. Risk is only relevant to management's needs.

13. What is the correct formula for annual loss expectancy?

    A. Total actual direct losses divided by the number of years it has been experienced

    B. Indirect and direct potential loss cost times the number of times it might possibly occur

    C. Direct and indirect loss cost estimates times the number of times the loss may occur in a year

    D. The overall value of the risk exposure times the probability for all assets divided by the number of years the asset is held

    Answer: C

    The correct answer is C. Annual loss expectancy is the total losses both direct and indirect times the frequency of occurrence for that loss in a given year.

14. When an audit finding is considered material, it means that

    A. In terms of all possible risk and management risk tolerance, this finding is significant.

    B. It has actual substance in terms of hard assets.

    C. It is important to the audit in terms of the audit objectives and findings related to them.

    D. Management cares about this kind of finding so it needs to be reported regardless of the risk.

    Answer: A

    The correct answer is A. Materiality is a relative, professional judgment call that must take into context management's aggregate tolerance of risk, how this finding stacks up to all of the findings, and the potential cumulative effect of this error.

15. Which of the following is *not* considered an irregularity or illegal act?

    A. Recording transactions that did not happen

    B. Misuse of assets

    C. Omitting the effects of fraudulent transactions

    D. None of the above

    Answer: D

    The correct answer is D. None of the above is *not* an auditing irregularity or a possible illegal act based on the definition in the standard.

16. When identifying the potential for irregularities, the auditor should consider

    A. If a vacation policy exists that requires fixed periods of vacation to be mandatory

    B. How much money is devoted to the payroll

    C. Whether the best practices are deployed in the IS environment

    D. What kind of firewall is installed at the Internet

    Answer: A

    The correct answer is A. While the others have varying relevance to audit testing, they do not indicate possible irregularities by themselves. A vacation policy that does not require staff to be away from work for a fixed period of time—usually one to two full weeks—enables employees to maintain fraudulent schemes without requiring a trained back up employee to step in and perform the process for at least some period of time during the year.

17. Some audit managements choose to use the element of surprise to

    A. Scare the auditees and to see if there are procedures that can be used as a back up

    B. Ensure that staffing is sufficient to manage an audit and daily processing simultaneously

    C. Ensure that supervision is appropriate during surprise inspections

    D. Ensure that policies and procedures coincide with the actual practices in place

    Answer: A

    The correct answer is A. Some of the other answers are nonsensical, but the real reason for using the element of surprise is to ensure that the policies and procedures documents line up with actual practices.

18. Which of the following is *not* a reason to be concerned about auditor independence?

    A. The auditor starts dating the change control librarian.

    B. The auditor invests in the business spin-off of the company.

    C. The auditor used to manage the same business process at a different company.

    D. The auditor is working as consultant for the implementation portion of the project being audited.

Answer: C

The correct answer is C. The fact that this was their job at another company may actually be an advantage for the audit team. The other items listed could lead to a compromise of the auditor's independence and should be investigated.

19. Control objectives are defined in an audit program to

   A. Give the auditor a view of the big picture of what the key control issue are based on the risk and management input

   B. Enable the auditor to scope the audit to only those issues identified in the control objective

   C. Keep the management from changing the scope of the audit

   D. Define what testing steps need to be performed in the program

   Answer: A

   The correct answer is A. The scope is not defined exclusively by the auditor (C) and does not necessarily define testing the related tasks (D). Answer B is somewhat correct; however, Answer A is the best answer.

20. An audit charter serves the following primary purpose:

   A. To describe the audit process used by the auditors

   B. To document the mission and business plan of the audit department

   C. To explain the code of ethics used by the auditor

   D. To provide a clear mandate to perform the audit function in terms of authority and responsibilities

   Answer: D

   The correct answer is D. The charter's main purpose is to define the auditor's roles and responsibilities. It should evidence a clear mandate and authority for the auditors to perform their work. Unlike a mission statement (B) or a process document (A), it describes the bounds of authority. The code of ethics (C) is a nonrelevant answer to this exercise.

21. In order to meet the requirements of audit, evidence sampling must be

    A. Of a 95 percent or higher confidence level, based on repeated pulls of similar sample sizes

    B. Sufficient, reliable, relevant, and useful, and supported by the appropriate analysis

    C. Within two standard deviations of the mean for the entire population of the data

    D. A random selection of the population in which every item has an equal chance of being selected

    Answer: B

    The correct answer is B. Sampling satisfies the evidence requirements that the data is sufficient, reliable, relevant, useful, and supported by the appropriate analysis. A random population section (D) is the definition of a random sample. Answers A and C do not make sense.

22. Audit evidence can take many forms. When determining the types required for an audit, the auditor must consider

    A. CAATs, flowcharts, and narratives

    B. Interviews, observations, and reperformance testing

    C. The best evidence available that is consistent with the importance of the audit objectives

    D. Inspection, confirmation, and substantive testing

    Answer: C

    The correct answer is C. The rest of the answers list types of audit evidence that could be considered, but the auditor must consider the best evidence available and determine what method for gathering and reviewing it as a second step in the audit planning process.

23. The primary thing to consider when planning for the use of CAATs in an audit program is

    A. Whether the sampling error will be at an unacceptable level

    B. Whether you can trust the programmer who developed the tools of the CAATs

C. Whether the source and object codes of the programs of the CAATs match

D. The extent of the invasive access necessary to the production environment

Answer: D

The correct answer is D. There is no sampling error with CAATs, which is one of their strengths (A), you will need to be aware of other participants in the process but that should be under your control (B), and understanding whether the source and object code match is an issue with what you are testing not to itself (C). The best answer is that you should be concerned with the potential impact of your testing on live data.

24. The *most* important aspect of drawing conclusions in an audit report is to

A. Prove your initial assumptions were correct.

B. Identify control weakness based on test work performed.

C. Obtain the goals of the audit objectives and to form an opinion on the sufficiency of the control environment.

D. Determine why the client is at risk at the end of each step.

Answer: C

The correct answer is C. Answer A is not value-added to the client; neither is D unless there is a weakness identified first. Answer B is an okay answer, however, Answer C is the best possible choice.

25. Some things to consider when determining what reportable findings should be are

A. How many findings there are and how long the report would be if all findings were included

B. The materiality of the findings in relevance to the audit objectives and management's tolerance for risk

C. How the recommendations will affect the process and future audit work

D. Whether the test samples were sufficient to support the conclusions

Answer: B

The correct answer is B. Materiality, audit objectives, and management's direction are the key items to consider. Answer D needs resolving long before the findings are reviewed for reportability; Answer A, how many, or Answer C, the effect of the recommendations, is not an issue with whether they should be reported or not.

26. The primary objective of performing a root cause analysis is to

    A. Ask why three times.

    B. Perform an analysis that justifies the recommendations.

    C. Determine the costs and benefits of the proposed recommendations.

    D. Ensure that you are not trying to address symptoms rather than the real problem that needs to be solved.

Answer: D

The correct answer is D. Answers B and C are not correct because they are related to recommendations and not to the root cause. Answer A is a technique used in root cause analysis. The best answer is D.

27. The primary reason for reviewing audit work is to

    A. Ensure that the conclusions, testing, and results were performed with due professional care.

    B. Ensure that the findings are sufficient to warrant the final report rating.

    C. Ensure that all of the work is completed and checked by a supervisor.

    D. Ensure that all of the audits are consistent in style and technique.

Answer: A

The correct answer is A. The other answers are all important but the primary reason is one of ensuring due professional care by checking the work with a reasonably competent third-party review.

Chapter 2—Management, Planning, and Organization of Information Systems

Here are the answers to the questions in Chapter 2:

1. Which criteria would an IS auditor consider to be the *most* important aspect of an organization's IS strategy?

   A. It includes a mission statement.

   B. It identifies a mechanism for charging for its services.

   C. It includes a Web-based e-commerce strategy.

   D. It supports the business objectives.

   Answer: D

   The correct answer is D. While a mission statement (A) is certainly a common component of a strategy documentation, and charging mechanisms (B) can be included as a reference, the most important item to consider is the alignment of the strategy with the business needs and objectives. Web strategies (C) may or may not be relevant to the business at hand.

2. From a segregation of duties standpoint, which of the following job functions should be performed by change control personnel?

   I. Verifying that the source and object code match before moving code into production

   II. Scheduling jobs to run in the production environment

   III. Making changes to production code and data when programs fail

   IV. Applying operating system patches

   A. I only

   B. I, II, and III

   C. II and IV only

   D. I and IV only

Answer: A

The correct answer is A. Scheduling jobs (II) would provide a change control person the opportunity to run jobs in combination with the changes they are applying, thus permitting potential fraud or the abuse of production processing. No direct changes to code or data (III) should ever be permitted by a nonprogrammer who is not acting on behalf of the application or user management. Job function IV could be seen as a change control function, but these systems level upgrades are typically applied by system programmers who are qualified to perform these functions and to ensure they are appropriately installed.

3. In a database management environment, which of the following functions should *not* be performed by the database administrator?

   A. Sizing table space and memory allocations

   B. Testing queries and consulting on table join limitations

   C. Reviewing logs for fraudulent activity or access errors

   D. Performing back ups and recovery procedures

   Answer: C

   The correct answer is C. Sizing database relevant components (A), testing queries and consulting on database access and views (B), and performing back up and recovery functions are all part of the DBA's job. They should not have the responsibility for reviewing audit logs (C) because they have access to modify the logs and are not independent from a capability standpoint. Although they can always change logs to cover up fraudulent activity, the role of review and the assurance that the logs are not tampered with by DBAs should fall to a supervisory position overseeing the DBA function.

4. Many organizations require employees to take a mandatory one to two full weeks of contiguous vacation each year because

   A. The organization wants to ensure that their employee's quality of life provides for happy employees in the workplace.

   B. The organization wants to ensure that potential errors in process or irregularities in processing are identified by forcing a person into the job function as a replacement periodically.

C. The organization wants to ensure that the benefits provided by the company are fully used to enable full employment of replacement staff as much as possible.

D. The organization wants to ensure that their employees are fully cross-trained and able to take over other functions in case of a major disruption or disaster.

Answer: B

The correct answer is B. Employees in sensitive functions should be required to take at least a full weeks vacation annually to ensure that the opportunity for fraudulent or illegal activities are not perpetuated by their uninterrupted daily attendance to systems or processes. The other answers are all valid reasons for providing a job rotation or vacation requirement, but Answer C is the best answer from an audit perspective.

5. Which of the following would be *most* important in evaluating an IS organization's structure?

I. Human Resource policies that adequately describe job functions and duties sufficiently

II. Organization charts that identify clear reporting and authority lines

III. System configurations that are well documented in the system architecture

IV. Training requirements and provisions for cross training that are documented along with roles and responsibilities

A. I and II only

B. I, II, III, and IV

C. I, II, and IV only

D. II and III only

Answer: C

The correct answer is C. Important aspects of an IS strategy, of the items listed, include Human Resource policies, organization charts and clear authority lines, and training requirements. System configurations and architecture are not really related to the strategy of the organization but more to its system design than strategic direction. While training (IV) requirements are not as important in a strategy document as I and II, it is still relevant and the best answer from an audit perspective of those available.

6. In a review of Human Resource policies in an IS organization, an IS auditor would be *most* concerned with the absence of

   A. Requirements for job rotation on a periodic basis

   B. A process for exit interviews to understand the employees' perception of management

   C. The requirement for employees to sign a form signifying that they have read policies

   D. The existence of a termination checklist requiring that keys and company property are obtained and all access permissions are to be revoked upon termination

   Answer: D

   The correct answer is D. The first three answers are good practices to be sure. But the revocation of access privileges and the ability to retain company assets and physical access to property is the most important item listed from an audit perspective.

7. A System Development Life Cycle can be *best* described as

   A. A process used by programmers to document SOP 98-1 compliance

   B. A methodology used to guide the process of software creation project management

   C. A system design methodology that includes all the steps in problem definition, solution identification, testing, implementation, and maintenance of the solution

   D. A process used to manage change control and approval cycles in a development environment

   Answer: C

   The correct answer is C. SDLC methodologies are described by all of the answers provided for this question to some extent. They can guide in change control and approval cycles (D) and the project management of software development. It also can be helpful when analyzing capital- versus expense-related tasks related to development projects, but Answer C best describes the SDLC components and use as a design methodology.

8. What is the *primary* difference between policies and standards?

    A. Policies provide a high-level framework and standards are more dynamic and specific.

    B. Policies take longer to write and are harder to implement than standards.

    C. Standards require interpretation and must have associated procedures.

    D. Policies describe how to do things and standards provide best practices guidance.

    Answer: A

    The correct answer is A. Policies are intended to be high-level guidance by senior management and should not change much over time, while standards are more technology specific and therefore may be more dynamic in nature. Policies are not necessarily harder to write or implement (B) and do not describe how to do things (D), those are called procedures. Policies may require interpretation and standards should be specific and clear for a given situation, which makes Answer C a wrong answer.

9. Which of the following is *not* a standard?

    A. Approved access control methodologies

    B. How to request a new account

    C. Minimum security baseline for hardening a UNIX server

    D. Description of acceptable back up and recovery methods for production data

    Answer: B

    The correct answer is B. How to request clearly spells out a step-by-step process to follow, which is better described as a procedure. Minimums (C), acceptable practices (D), and approved methods (A) all imply standards documentation.

10. Which of the following are *not* key considerations when reviewing third-party services agreements?

    A. Provisions exist to retain ownership of intellectual property and assets.

    B. The lowest price possible is obtained for the service rendered.

C. Business continuity planning and processes are part of the signed agreement.

D. Security and regulatory concerns are identified as risks during negotiations.

Answer: B

The correct answer is B. Lowest cost does not always mean the best arrangement especially from a control standpoint. Ensuring that ownership is retained (A) for the intellectual aspects of the business that would be needed, should the business eventually go to another vendor, are very important to the survivability of the business. (C) BCP processes are an important part of any third-part relationship so alternatives are thought through and well documented before disruptions occur. Additionally, even though it is more important that security and regulatory concerns be addressed directly in the wording of the final agreement signed by both parties, identifying the issues in negotiations it is still more important than the lowest price from an audit and risk perspective.

11. When evaluating project management, which of the following would you be *least* concerned in seeing evidenced?

A. Well-defined project scope and objectives

B. Costs identified with the resources allocated to the project

C. Timelines with achievable milestones

D. Sponsorship and approval by business process management

Answer: B

The correct answer is B. All elements mentioned are important to a successful project and need to be set in place to manage the project successfully. In order of importance to the project, (D) sponsorship and backing is the most critical element, without which you cannot even get started. (A) Knowing where you are going through the scope and objectives also is clearly a key piece in managing anything. (C) Having a time frame documented to measure progress against is necessary to understand the comparative success against management's expectations along the way. (B) Knowing what the costs will be is important but may change through the course of the project, depending on needs to expedite certain sections and on the availability of resources. This can only be estimated throughout the project and only becomes good information after the costs are realized.

12. When evaluating a change control process, the IS auditor would be *most* concerned if he or she observed the following:

    A. Change control personnel permitting systems programmers to patch operating systems

    B. Computer operators running jobs that edit production data

    C. Application programmers correcting data errors in production

    D. Change control personnel copying code from the production for testing purposes

    Answer: C

    The correct answer is C. Programmers should never be permitted to directly access data in the production environment. Computer operators will initiate, by nature of their function, programs that may modify data (B). Systems programmers are permitted to patch systems and in fact, should be the ones performing this function (A). The proper way to test production code is to first copy it from the live production environment to minimize the impact on the user community. No humans should ever directly manipulate the application code or data in the production environment.

13. During the review of a problem management system, it is determined that several problems have been outstanding and unresolved for an excessively long period. Which of the following reasons is *most* questionable to the IS auditor reviewing the management controls of this process?

    A. The problem has been sent to the vendor who will send a fix with the next software release.

    B. The problem has been determined to be a user error and has been referred to the business unit for correction and additional training.

    C. The problem is intermittent and after researching, remains outstanding until reoccurrence.

    D. The problem is seen as a low risk issue and is therefore low on the priority list to be addressed.

    Answer: D

    The correct answer is D. The first three answers are all legitimate reasons to have an outstanding problem on the tracking logs. However, problems can be misleading at first read, and it should never be assumed that because of the way a problem is reported, it is inconsequential. Many security breaches occur in this manner. Management should ensure that all problems are quickly investigated and their root causes are determined. The need to prioritize problems for addressing them implies larger volumes than the organization is equipped to handle, indicating other more severe control and management issues.

14. During the problem analysis and solution design phases of an SDLC methodology, which of the following steps would you be *most* concerned with finding?

    A. Current state analysis and documentation processes

    B. Entity relationship diagramming and process flow definitions

    C. Pilot testing of planned solutions

    D. Gathering of functional requirements from business sponsors

    Answer: C

    The correct answer is C. The other three answers are all part of a well-executed SDLC methodology used to design a system or software. However, the initial problem analysis and design phases of a development cycle are not the appropriate place for the testing of solutions, especially by piloting them with end users.

15. What is the *primary* concern that an IS auditor should consider when reviewing Executive Information Systems (EIS)?

    A. Ensure that senior management actually uses the system to monitor the IS organization.

    B. Ensure that the information being provided is accurate and timely.

    C. Ensure that the information provided fairly summarizes the actual performance of the IS organization so that indicators will be representative of the detailed tracking and monitoring systems.

    D. Ensure that MTBFs are kept to a minimum and within acceptable boundaries.

    Answer: C

    The correct answer is C. EISs must represent real-world information in order for them to be most useful to management. They must summarize the issues in production and enable management to get indicators of the underlying problems that need further investigation. Mean time between failures (D) is only one aspect of information monitoring. Having accurate and timely information (B) does not help if the information that is being reported is not the key indicator needed from which to best run the operation. It is up to management to use the system for it to be useful (A). Certainly, this is reflective of how well management is performing their function, but the quality of the information is the primary concern in a review of the system.

16. SOP 98-1 is an accounting position that needs to be considered by the IS auditor *primarily* because

    A. The AICPA requires all auditors to be aware and comment on this statement of position.

    B. Management may be capitalizing software development tasks that should be expensed.

    C. Keeping track of development efforts from a capital and expense perspective is indicative of good management of IS organizations.

    D. SOP 98-1 tracking systems are required to be interfaced directly to accounting systems and may introduce opportunities for fraudulent accounting.

    Answer: C

    The correct answer is C. The AICPA (A) provides this statement of position as guidance and does not, in general, require auditors to do anything unless it is required based on a risk analysis and professional due care. Although it would be a concern if management was not properly capitalizing development tasks (B), and this should be examined during the review, the use of this statement of position as an indicator of the management processes is the primary aspect of reviewing adherence to this advice. Direct interface with accounting systems (D) is not a hard requirement of this type of accounting method.

17. When reviewing the management processes for overseeing budgeting and spending, the IS auditor should be *least* concerned with which of the following items?

    A. Ensuring that all spending is reconciled to a budgeted line item and the variances to budget are explained

    B. Ensuring that all of the budgeted money is spent in a budget year

C. Ensuring that expenditures are recorded and reported on budgets to IS organizational management

D. Ensuring that SOP 98-1 provisions are adequately documented and appropriately allocated

Answer: B

The correct answer is B. Spending all budgeted monies is of little concern and in fact may be indicative of a well-run organization. The other three items are all relatively important to meeting the functional requirements of oversight and management of an IS organization.

18. When evaluating information security management, which of the following are *not* items the IS auditor would consider commenting on as a potential control weakness?

A. A security program had not been developed using a risk-based approach.

B. The information security officer does not accept responsibility for security decisions in the organization.

C. The use of intrusion detection technologies has not been considered for use in the security program.

D. Account administration processes do not require agreement to acceptable behavior guidelines from all persons requesting accounts.

Answer: B

The correct answer is B. This question uses double negatives to confuse the CISA candidate. The answer is looking for the single item that is acceptable and would not result in an audit concern. Valid concerns include creating a security program without considering risk (A), not at least considering intrusion detection technologies (C) whether they are used or not depends on that analysis, and not making account users aware of their security accountabilities and responsibilities (D). It is not the position of the security management to own the security decisions in an IS organization and (B) it would therefore be considered an appropriate position for information security management to take. That accountability lies with senior management who make their decisions based on expert input from the security management as well as many other sources, including business, finance, human resources, legal, and so forth.

19. In evaluating business continuity management, what three factors are considered important aspects of the overall management of the program by the IS auditor?

    I.   Impact to the businesses has been studied and agreed to from the business management as a basis from which to understand the continuity needs.

    II. Interactions of all affected processes have been identified so that priorities for recovery can be determined.

    III. Recovery tests have been successful and determined to fully meet the needs of the business.

    IV. Contracts have been negotiated with hot site vendors, enabling for the immediate declarations of disaster to result in quicker recovery times.

    V.   The procedures required to manage the business processes without the information systems have been well documented and moved off-site to provide for interim recovery processing.

    A. I, II, and III

    B. I, III, and IV

    C. II, IV, and V

    D. I, II, and V

    Answer: D

    The correct answer is D. Two of the items listed are not considered important aspects of all business continuity process management. Ensuring that recovery testing is successful (III) is not necessary and seldom the case in the real world. In fact, it takes constant testing and adjustments to get even close to a flawless recovery process execution, especially when actual scenarios are seldom what the testing scenarios were. Hot-site contracts (IV) may be applicable in some scenarios but certainly not all and are dependant upon risk tolerance and processing criticality and costs. The other items are required steps and a review of management would ensure that they are all part of the program.

20. Which of the following sets of documentation would an IS auditor expect to find at the off-site facility for business continuity and recovery processes?

I. User manuals and training documentation

II. Current systems configurations

III. Current systems and application code

IV. Operational procedures and required forms and supplies for processing

A. II, III, and IV only

B. I, II, and III only

C. I, III, and IV only

D. All of the above

Answer: D

The correct answer is D. In fact, there is more hard copy documentation that will be required to successfully recover from a complete loss of systems and personnel. Job descriptions, process flows, IS procedure manuals, interim security and control documentation, call lists and rosters, and production data up to the point of failure (to name a few) would all be required in hard copy should you have a need to recover the business from scratch.

Chapter 3—Technical Infrastructure and Operational Practices

Here are the answers to the questions in Chapter 3:

1. The *best* way to understand the security configuration of an operating system is to

A. Consult the vendor's installation manuals

B. Review the security plan for the system

C. Interview the systems programmer who installed the software

D. Review the system-generated configuration parameters

Answer: D

The correct answer is D, review the actual parameters generated from a direct query of the system. The system programmers (C) and the security plan (B) may give you information about the point in time when the system was installed, but patches and modification since that time may have significantly changed the current security since then. The vendor's manual (A) will explain what your options are and may even recommend settings, but they have no bearing on the actual set up.

2. What three things are the most important security controls that should be present when reviewing an operating systems security?

   I. The code comes from a trusted source.

   II. Audit logging is turned on.

   III. Unnecessary services are turned off.

   IV. The default passwords are changed.

   V. Systems administrators do not have any more access than they need to in order to perform their job.

   A. I, II, and III

   B. III, IV, and V

   C. I, III, and IV

   D. I, II, and IV

   Answer: C

   The correct answer is C. Audit logging does need to be turned on (II), but this is only effective when a process is in place to monitor and react to the logs. Systems administrators (V) should use their own account to perform their work, but these accounts will usually be patterned after the root account and the privileges will be very high. Attempting to limit their access is an exercise that adds little value to the risk mitigation process. Default passwords are the most common way for hackers to breach a server (IV) and are very important to change. Any services that are not being used also should be turned off, because they are another common attack avenue (III). Any of the primary security checks would ensure that the code is trusted and has integrity to begin with (I).

3. Databases are complex to evaluate from a risk perspective because

   A. Access controls for application views, query permissions, field level table access, as well as access to reports and query results must be reviewed to assess the security of data.

   B. They can have complex data structures that may be joined through several keys.

C. Data definitions must be maintained in order to understand the data classifications.

D. Data flows and data normalization processes make both table sizing and transaction mapping difficult.

Answer: A

The correct answer is A. Risk is introduced when users have access to data that they have no rights to access. This is very difficult to prevent when so many ways exist to get access to the data that should be protected. Definitions, structures, and flows are important to understanding how the database is meant to operate and whether it will function efficiently, and unless they are seriously flawed, they will not add material risk to the IS organization.

4. In a two-phase commit database transaction, the roll back process is initiated

A. When the client and server cannot agree on a communication protocol

B. In multi-tier architectures that need to reject a proxy request

C. When a committed transaction cannot be completed by all participating servers and clients involved

D. When ownership of the session cannot be assured and committed to

Answer: C

The correct answer is C. In a two-phase commit process on multi-tier client server architectures, transaction processes negotiate a transaction through a commit process that locks data and notifies all of the parties of the intention to process the transaction. If for some reason, this cannot be accomplished to the satisfaction of all involved parties, the roll back process puts everything back to where it was before the transaction started. The other answers are nonsense.

5. Which of the following is *not* a design consideration to investigate when reviewing security packages?

A. What kind of changes and compromises must occur to existing processes

B. How well the security updates and patches are maintained on the security package

C. What weaknesses and deficiencies cause a security package to be considered

D. What kind of support effort will be required to maintain the product adequately

Answer: B

The correct answer is B. The changes and effects of implementing a security package (A) must be part of the design consideration so they can be accommodated in the new processes. Similarly, the additional support effort, which is necessary for the product, must be considered in the design as well (D). The weaknesses that caused a security package to be considered in the first place (C) will be your primary design consideration. How well patches are maintained (B) is not a design criterion, but rather it pertains to how well the maintenance of the system is being performed.

6. Which of the following is *not* normally a concern when reviewing the implementation of an operation console system?

A. Whether the expertise to implement the system is being provided by the vendor to backfill existing functions, enabling the existing staff to learn the new systems

B. Whether the scope and goals of the implementation plan are being met in a cost effective and timely manner

C. Whether the KPIs used to manage the business will be improved by the implementation process

D. Understanding how well the console will interface with other operations components and what compatibility issues exist

Answer: C

The correct answer is C. KPIs are not an important implementation concern but rather are related to the use of the tool after it is installed and working. Knowledge transfer (A), scope creep, cost and deadline overruns (B), and interface issues (D) will be the major issues with this kind of implementation.

7. Which of the following will *not* be information that you would expect to find documented when evaluating a computer hardware installation project?

   A. Procedures for defining the requirements and submitting the requests for proposals and bids

   B. How the hardware installation has improved the process throughputs

   C. Functional requirements for the hardware based on the business plans and needs

   D. Placement and location decisions for equipment installations

   Answer: B

   The correct answer is B. How the process has improved the through-put is something that can be predicted and planned for, but actual results will not be available during the planning and installation of new hardware. The other items need to be evidenced with good documentation.

8. Which of the following is the *most* effective method of assessing the controls over the hardware maintenance process?

   A. Look at the hardware and assess whether the maintenance is current and that the equipment is well kept.

   B. Following the recommended maintenance tasks and maintenance schedules, determine that the procedures are carried out and evidenced as completed by logging and dating the actual main-tenance efforts.

   C. Identify the required maintenance procedures from the vendors information and ensure that these processes are addressed by the IS organizations procedures.

   D. Look at the problem logs and validate whether maintenance processes are determining the mean time between failures when compared to the industry averages.

   Answer: B

   The correct answer is B. The best way to ensure that maintenance processes are in place is to look to a control that evidences the actual completion of the recommended maintenance procedures. Observ-ing hardware conditions (A) will only tell you about most recent activity, not historic behavior. Just because the right procedures are in place (C), you cannot be assured that they are carried out in practice. Just because there are not problems (D), you cannot assume that maintenance is being performed properly.

9. When reviewing voice systems maintenance processes, which of the following is the *least* critical to the audit objective of ensuring customer satisfaction?

   A. Ensuring that as-built drawing modifications are made to the copy of the drawings kept in the office

   B. Ensuring that the support staff is knowledgeable and available to perform the necessary maintenance tasks

   C. Ensuring that the physical security of the PBX devices is managed properly

   D. Ensuring that planning and configurations provide for flexibility with minimal impact to the user base

   Answer: A

   The correct answer is A. Having knowledgeable and available staff (B) is very important to customer satisfaction. Ensuring that designs can change (D) without impacting the users also is important, too. Physical security can prevent malicious behavior that will affect the throughput of the system (C), but a built drawing in the office will have direct and little impact on customers. This is especially the case if built changes are noted in the field copies of the drawings, which is usually where you will find these changes noted. Field drawings should always be consulted as the working copy of what is actually in place.

10. Which of the following should an IS auditor review when performing an assessment of a PBX?

    I. Ensure that the dial-in numbers enabling toll-free outbound access are turned off.

    II. Ensure that voicemail systems do not enable access to phone lines through hijacking.

    III. Ensure that the access codes for the maintenance ports have been changed from the default.

    IV. Ensure that outbound toll numbers, such as 900 numbers, are restricted.

    V. Ensure that excessive phone usage is flagged and investigated for fraud.

A. I, II, III, and IV only

B. II, III, and IV only

C. II, III, IV, and V only

D. I, II, III, IV, and V

Answer: C

The correct answer is C. All of these answers except (I) are necessary activities for a PBX review. Voicemail systems (II) need to be contained to mail traffic only and the ability to use these access points to the system to get a dial tone should be controlled and not enable any hijacking to occur. Access codes for maintenance ports (III) should be strictly controlled and not only changed from their vendor given defaults but changed periodically. 900 numbers and other outbound toll scenarios (IV) should be controlled, and the business decisions should support any allowance for these costs to be incurred. Any excessive call tolls (V) outside of a predetermined boundary should be immediately flagged as potentially fraudulent and investigated if not shut down until an investigation can occur. The ability of obtaining an outbound toll-free line from a dial in number (I) is a business decision and may be turned off, but that is a risk and business decision that should be made by management not the IS auditor. The audit should verify that this is a conscious decision of the business, however.

11. Which of the following would you not expect to find in an Internet DMZ?

    A. DNS servers that advertise addresses to the Internet

    B. Mail relay servers that receive incoming mail and push outgoing mail

    C. Web servers containing content and business logic

    D. Proxy servers that authenticate access requests to internal content

    Answer: C

    The correct answer is C. You would never want to place your business logic in a DMZ where it could become vulnerable to the Internet. This exposes your logic to hijacking and alterations that may provide an avenue for a hacker to get inside the secure domain. The other items you would expect to see in this neutral area and acting as intermediaries. It is assumed that the DNS servers would advertise to internal addresses but only those in the DMZ to the Internet.

12. When reviewing data network architecture, which of the following is not a *primary* review criteria for the IS auditor?

    A. All router access is controlled by secure authentication methods.

    B. Network routing enables for the efficient flow of the businesses critical traffic.

    C. Protocols that are not needed for the business and administration of the network are disabled.

    D. VLANs using layer 2 switching techniques are employed to secure the traffic of critical data.

    Answer: D

    The correct answer is D. The other three issues should always be reviewed when assessing a data network, but layer 2 VLANs are a special case that will be deployed only in certain situations and will not be assessed unless the business case calls for their use.

13. In a well-segregated operational environment, which of the following scenarios would you expect to see?

    A. Computer operators responding to systems messages and initiating problem tickets for failed jobs

    B. Change control librarians making modifications to code only when notified of errors by the application programmers

    C. Tape librarians managing print queues and reloading paper for printers as well as loading off-site storage containers with back up tapes

    D. Operators assisting system programmers with troubleshooting the operating system by adjusting parameters while the programmers observed the results

    Answer: A

    The correct answer is A. This is a properly set of functions that restrict the operator to the role of response and notify. In Answer B, the librarian is making changes to code, which should not be allowed, even if he or she is asked to do so. In Answer C, the librarians have access to both the beginning and end of a process, thereby enabling them to control a process that is not intended. In Answer D, the operator is making changes and should instead support this effort by doing the observation instead of making the change.

14. What are the *most* important criteria to assess when reviewing job descriptions?

    A. The job functions are all defined for the work that needs done, and training is required

    B. Clear authority is established and everyone knows who holds what roles in the organization

    C. Vacations are mandated and job rotation is provided for

    D. Performance is monitored and raises are based on goals that are defined jointly

Answer: B

The correct answer is B. Clear authority and all jobs with an owner are the most important aspects of the job description review. The other items also are important to have, but without clear lines of authority there is no way to enforce the other issues in the first place.

15. The primary purpose of key performance indicators is to

    A. Give management the ability to make sure that the staff is doing their work

    B. Monitor the capacity of the systems equipment and process performance metrics

    C. Provide management with a tool to gauge the overall health of the process and to point to potential trouble spots

    D. Enable operators to know when things are going wrong and whether the SLA is being met

Answer: C

The correct answer is C. KPIs are meant to be a tool for management to get a pulse on the operations quickly and at a glance. They should enable the subsequent drill down to more data, which will better explain the indications provided at a high level by the KPIs. The other answers are not correct.

16. In a media management system review, the IS auditor does *not* need to concern themselves with

    A. Whether the systems catalog accurately reflects the physical library's location of the media

    B. Whether the media is accessed by only those individuals with a "need to know"

C. Whether the media is accurately identified for movement off-site for back up purposes

D. Whether the system adequately retires media and provides for its recycling in a secure manner

Answer: B

The correct answer is B. While this is an important concept in general, it is not the design of the media management system to ensure that access is properly controlled to the data. This is typically the functionality of the security management system. The media system does ensure that the correct jobs request the data, but it makes no decisions on "need to know." The other answers are part of the expected functionality of a media management system.

17. What is the *most* important aspect of a change control system?

A. All changes are documented and approved.

B. Changes are managed through automated tools, preventing access from people.

C. Copies of production are maintained in case the change fails.

D. Quality is ensured through testing and approval.

Answer: A

The correct answer is A. All changes must be recorded and approved in order for a change control system to be any good. Automated tools are nice (B) but not a requirement. Copies can be maintained (C), but any valid back out procedure will do and QC and testing processes (D) are only tangentially tied to a change control process and are not necessarily part of that process.

18. When emergency changes are identified during a change control review, what should the IS auditor also expect to find?

A. A control weakness, because these actions should not be allowed to occur and it should be reported

B. That the changes were applied as necessary and the related problems tickets were logged

C. Disciplinary actions related to enabling the changes to occur without approval by the system owner

D. A process for notifying the system owner of the changes and all associated actions taken with explanation

Answer: D

The correct answer is D. Emergencies happen. Access needs to be permitted for fixes when required. This reduces your possible responses down to Answers B or D. Answers A and C are out of line. Answer B is incorrect because there is no provision for notifying the owner (or approver) that a change was allowed without their approval.

19. Which characteristics of a problem management system are important to the IS auditors review?

    I. All problems are tracked through to conclusion.

    II. All problems are initiated automatically, thus ensuring that the correct data is captured.

    III. Escalation processes ensure that problems do not sit unresolved.

    IV. All relative IS operation areas have access to the system to review and address the problems.

    V. Statistics can be gathered from the system to facilitate the analysis of the IS problems.

    A. I, II, III, IV, and V

    B. I, III, IV, and V only

    C. II, III, IV, and V only

    D. I, III, and V only

Answer: B

The correct answer is B. All of these items except for item II are most important. Item II cannot be implemented practically for all problems. There will always be problems that will be identified and will not originate from automatic sources. These problems also will need to be entered into the management system, and tracked and resolved.

20. Critical aspects of an SLA review include all of these items except

    A. An annual review and re-validation of the business needs

    B. Ensuring that the expected services are clearly defined

    C. Ensuring that monitoring and escalation procedures are in place

    D. Ensuring that the service provider is supplying service to all customers equitably

Answer: D

The correct answer is D. This issue should not be of concern to an individual agreement between one provider and one client. How the provider treats other customers is not part of the agreement being reviewed. The other answers are and should be evaluated.

Chapter 4—Protection of Information Assets

Here are the answers to the questions in Chapter 4:

1. What is the *most* important aspect of performing an evaluation of information security controls on a process or system?

    A. Ensuring that the best practice control techniques are being utilized properly

    B. Understanding the businesses functional requirements of the process to ensure that they can be accomplished

    C. Ensuring that the deployed controls work as part of the overall security architecture program

    D. Making sure that access is strictly controlled based on a need to know

   Answer: B

   The correct answer is B. Best practice control techniques properly utilized (A) will need to be applied relative to the business needs, and they cannot be deployed without considering the goals of the business and the security control parameters that the business process places on the system. It also is important to ensure that the security controls used work well together and compliment other controls used in the architecture providing defense in depth (C), but not without first considering the business goals to ensure the business needs are met. Restricting access based on a need to know (D) also is an important concept and will be a secondary step to ensuring access control that will follow from first understanding the business needs. Those needs define the need to know for the system's users.

2. The concept of data integrity implies that

    A. Access has not been given to those who do not have a need to know

    B. Data can be accessed by processes when necessary to support the business function

    C. Data has not been altered or modified outside of the expected and approved processing steps

    D. Data has not been made available to processes for which the data classification has not been accredited

Answer: C

The correct answer is C. Integrity implies that the data has not been altered from its intended state. Confidentiality is the concept that relates to access control (A), based on data classification (D), and availability is the concept that is used when referring to the data being accessible when needed (B).

3. When reviewing security and business risks, it is *most* important to keep in mind that

   A. Business risks are not as important as the security exposures to potential hackers.

   B. The customer's expectation of privacy should take precedent over the businesses risk tolerance when considering security controls.

   C. Data classification should determine the security controls requirements.

   D. Some compromise of the security controls to accommodate the businesses risk tolerance is a necessary part of doing business.

Answer: D

The correct answer is D. The compromise of security to meet the business needs is a necessary part of doing business in the first place. Without taking risks, there would be no profit margin. The tolerance for the risks taken by the business is the primary security constraint, secondary only to the legal requirements, which may even be arguable. Certainly risks related to hackers (A) should be one of the business risks considered for security controls, but it does not solely define the business risk. Customer expectations (B) should be important to businesses that want to keep their customers, but this does not take precedent over the business risk tolerance. Data classification is important (C), but it is the outcome of a business risk decision process, not a driver.

4. When evaluating the role of the information security officer, you should be *most* concerned to find that

   A. The security officer's role was not well documented as part of the job description.

   B. The security officer's role is defined as a key decision maker on a new product review committee.

C. Part of the defined role was the accountability for ensuring that the security controls kept any security breaches from occurring.

D. The authority for carrying out the role of a security officer was not explicitly tied to the organization's policy.

Answer: C

The item that should cause the most concern to the IS auditor will be Answer C, the expectation that all security breaches can be prevented. This is not possible to accomplish and the security officer will not be successful with this mandate. Poorly defined roles (A) and unclear lines of authority (D) can be corrected and adjusted to bring them in line, but an expectation to solve the security concerns completely is unrealistic. Participating on a product review committee is an appropriate role for an information security officer.

5. When reviewing an information system to assess its privacy risks, an IS auditor would consider all of the following *except*

A. Ensuring that the appropriate consent has been obtained from the customer before the release of sensitive data

B. The business needs for the client data within the processes

C. Proper disclosures to the customer of what the data is used for and how it will be protected

D. The laws and regulations relevant to the industry for privacy controls on customer data

Answer: B

The correct answer is B. The business needs are not related to the privacy risk because they are the original purpose for gathering the data and presumably the one purpose for which the client approves the data be used. Consent (A), disclosure (C), and most importantly the regulations related to the business sector are definitely part of the risk equation. Note: Resale value was originally going to be put in as the wrong answer, but upon reflection the author realized that the value of the data to others is potentially part of the risk assessment and should be considered when determining control needs.

6. While reviewing an information security program the IS auditor determines that the best practices have not been followed as guidelines for developing the program. Which of the following would be the *least* important factor to consider when determining the recommendation related to changes for the program?

   A. Whether a risk assessment was part of the determination of what the program elements should be

   B. Whether the security officer had documented polices and procedures to direct the program

   C. Whether the architectural design of the security deployed an in-depth state-of-the-art defense

   D. Whether any inventory of the existing controls for managing security threats has been done

   Answer: C

   The correct answer is C because state-of-the-art defense in-depth cannot be determined without first looking at the other three answers and additional issues as well. Risk assessments (A), which used the inventories of the existing controls (D), threats, and vulnerabilities, are necessary steps to developing a security program and may preclude many best practice elements, depending on the assessment's outcome. Of course, policy and mandate from the top of the organization (B) is a necessary first step to the program existing at all.

7. Policy for information security is a primary requirement for establishing control in an IS organization. Which of the following is *not* a reason why this is the case?

   A. A policy establishes the steps required to put security in place.

   B. A policy establishes the authority and accountability to get the security job done.

   C. A policy sets the expectations for the employee's behavior as it relates to security.

   D. The policy provides the mandate for putting the security program elements in place.

   Answer: A

   The correct answer is A. Policies are not meant to describe step-by-step processes, which are called procedures. Security policy establishes the authority (B), the management expectations (C), and the mandate for the program (D), but the actual implementation is to be interpreted from the high-level policy.

8. During an IS audit, the IS auditor determines that there is a control weakness due to the lack of available standards. When developing the findings and recommendation for the audit report, which of the following items should *not* be considered for inclusion as reasons for improving standards in the organization?

   A. Standards provide common ground that will increase the efficiency of the operations

   B. Standards creation is an industry best practice

   C. Standards ensure that individual policy interpretation will not result in the establishment of weaker security overall by lowering the minimum security level

   D. Standards provide simplified solutions to problems, enabling leverage of fewer solutions and economies of scale

   Answer: B

   The correct answer is B. Just because they are the industry's best practice is not a good reason to recommend that they be implemented. Management wants to see a value-added recommendation and is not as interested in keeping up the industry's latest fashions. Efficiency (A) and economies of scale (D) are important drivers to management and should be offered as benefits of improving controls whenever possible. Establishing a floor for security (C) also is very important but may need a little more explanation to management to sell the concept.

9. During your review of an information security risk assessment, which of the following elements would you be *least* concerned with if no evidence was available to substantiate it?

   A. The exercise of risk assessment is re-performed periodically.

   B. The threats and vulnerabilities have been determined.

   C. The existing controls have been inventoried and assessed for effectiveness.

   D. The risk assessment included a tactical as well as a strategic initiatives assessment.

Answer: D

The correct answer is D. Tactical and strategic relate more to the resolution of the issues than it does to risks. Assessing risks identifies exposure to bad things happening. It identifies the loss potential and is determined by understanding the threats and vulnerabilities (B), the existing controls in place (C) to manage these threats and vulnerabilities, and should be periodically re-performed (A) to identify changes in the other elements and to reassess the overall risk.

10. When making a recommendation to establish a product review process that includes the security officer as part of the approval team, what should your *strongest* argument in the recommendation be?

    A. Security that is built into a process as part of the initial design can be seven times cheaper than the cost of implementing it after the product is in production.

    B. Plans should be documented and defended to upper management before they are used to implement a new program.

    C. The return on investment for products should be assessed prior to starting development so that these returns can be compared to actual gains after the product has been implemented.

    D. Plans should be evaluated to ensure that they follow the SDLC methodology standard in the organization and that the methodology has input from information security.

    Answer: C

    The correct answer is C. Return on investment is the strongest case that you can make to management and is the primary reason for performing this preliminary assessment if it is not in place. Security controls (A) is secondary to the business needs as is the planning methodology (D) or the plan documentation (B).

11. When reviewing the identification process used to establish user accounts, what is the *most* important aspect of the process?

    A. All of the relevant information is gathered about the person establishing the identity.

    B. Proof is provided to strongly tie the individual presenting themselves as the person for whom the ID is being established.

C. Authorization is obtained for all accounts provided for the individual who is requesting access.

D. The individual is given the opportunity to change their password immediately upon first log in.

Answer: B

The correct answer is B. Tying an actual person to the ID or account is the key factor in the identification process and is what establishing identity is all about. Gathering relevant information is an important administrative function (A) and the authorization processes should always include approvals (C). Good authentication processes will always enable users to create their own password (D) to ensure their identity is maintained, however, establishing identity requires proving you are who you say you are.

12. The security concept of *need to know* implies all of the following except

A. All access allowed within a permission set or role that is approved on a need to know basis can be viewed, copied, or modified because of the permissions granted.

B. Access is required to perform the assigned functions supporting the business process.

C. Data owners and their stewards have explicitly determined that the access by this role or person is acceptable.

D. The least amount of privilege necessary to perform the function has been granted to the role or person receiving this permission.

Answer: A

The correct answer is A. Just because permission has been granted does not mean access within the permitted range is acceptable at all times. Privacy considerations and ethical behavior should take precedence over permissions in situations where broader access, which is necessary for a particular function, is granted to the individual overall. Certainly being granted access implies that this access may be needed in order to perform the function for which it was permitted (B) at some point in time. And the implication is that that permission was a decision made by the data owner or their designated steward (C). It also implies that a least privilege methodology (D) was used to determine what access should be permitted and what should be denied.

13. An IS auditor would expect to see a defense in-depth approach to security or would recommend that one be adopted for all of the following reasons *except*

A. It provides several different security mechanisms that increase the difficulty for hackers and intruders due to the increased knowledge required for compromise.

B. More complex security solutions can lead to higher requirements for training and related support costs including audit requirements.

C. Security solutions never completely solve a problem and a defense in-depth approach provides opportunities to address residual risk from one solution with another solution.

D. Costs can be reduced by multiple iterations of solving most of a problem at a minimal cost and then applying another economic solution to address most of the remaining exposure rather than the extensive and expensive application of one solution set.

Answer: B

The correct answer is B. The one downfall of a defense in-depth solution approach is that it can increase training and maintenance costs. It does, however, provide many benefits that can outweigh this issue, if it is planned and deployed properly. The increased complexity is a barrier to attackers (A) and can provide for a more complete security solution (C). It also can be more economical than trying to solve a problem completely with one solution (D) and the savings could easily overcome the increased costs in training and maintenance.

14. When reviewing role-based access, which of the following parameters should the IS auditor be *least* concerned with?

A. Business functions and job descriptions provide the input to determine that the accesses defined are sufficient to performing the required tasks.

B. The defined role is applicable to a job function or set of job functions that provides a categorization of need that defines a role.

C. The access permissions of a particular role are reconciled to the actual functions performed on a periodic basis.

D. The establishment of new roles is reviewed and approved by the data owner or steward.

Answer: B

The correct answer is B. This is the least important of these aspects of the role-based access definition. From the user's perspective, the role must be relevant and inclusive of the functions to be performed (A). These permissions must be periodically reviewed and validated (C) and changes have to be approved by the data owner to preserve the classification of data that they established (D). Whether these roles are unique to a particular user or applicable to a large number of users is the least important issue.

15. During an evaluation of an account administration process, what should an IS auditor be most concerned about finding?

    A. Employee terminations that did not result in the closing of computer accounts in a timely fashion

    B. Time-of-day restrictions that were not used to limit access to systems

    C. Password aging that was not forced on accounts providing access to the network

    D. Accounts, which were supposed to have been suspended from disuse, were not followed up on and deleted

    Answer: A

    The correct answer is A. Closing computer accounts for those who no longer have a need to know puts data at risk more than the other situation mentioned here. Time-of-day restrictions (B) is an additional constraint, which can be applied to an account that would otherwise have access to the data, and is therefore not a strong control. Password aging (C) is a best practice, but strong passwords may mitigate the risk of not aging the passwords. Closing suspended accounts (D) is a good practice and there is some risk that they could be reopened either inadvertently or through social engineering, but this risk is primarily a housekeeping concern.

16. When evaluating a single sign on implementation, what single factor adds the *most* risk and provides concern for the IS auditor in their review?

    A. The fact that password resets must be effectively propagated across all systems in some way for single sign on to work properly

    B. The issue of systems administrators making changes to a system managed by the single sign on solution, thus putting the accounts out of synchronization

C. The concern that single sign on cannot be effectively achieved unless roles and access needs are defined for all systems on which the user may need to perform their functions

D. The concern that, if compromised, the single sign on access provides a wide range of access where access had been more limited previously

Answer: D

The correct answer is D. Aggregating access through a single key or access point gives only one defense point to many security requirements that were provided separately prior to the single sign on solution. The inconvenience experienced by the users was the trade-off to more security and now being more convenient, there is less control in place. The other issues are important considerations for the implementation review but do not add the highest risk to the implementation.

17. When reviewing application design processes for information security controls, which of the following is *least* likely to be of concern to an IS auditor?

A. The SDLC methodology does not require that security is considered as part of the design criteria.

B. The testing of the application coding does not consider the security requirements identified in the design phase of the system's development process.

C. The sample data used for testing and design is not adequately segregated from the production version of the data.

D. Access permissions of testing and design personnel permits data modification in the test environment.

Answer: D

The correct answer is D. Access permissions during design and testing are the least concern of the items listed here. A process should be in place that ensures that the permissions are not carried through to the production environment, however. The highest concern would be (A) no requirement for security in the design phase. Without this consideration, testing for that design input (B) would not be possible. There also are concerns with production data mixing with test data, because live production data integrity could be negatively impacted.

18. Which of the following are data classification controls?

    I. Labeling the removable media containing classified data with the highest level of data sensitivity contained on the media

    II. Publishing a policy that defines what data classifications are and how these classifications are to be applied

    III. Encrypting data when it is being transmitted across the Internet

    IV. Treating all forms of a given data classification as equal in terms of protection requirements

    V. Regulatory requirements to protect customer data from disclosure without prior consent

    A. I, II, and IV only

    B. I, II, III, and IV only

    C. I, II, III, IV, and V

    D. I, II, IV, and V only

    Answer: B

    The correct answer is B. The only item listed here that is not a control at all (V) is a requirement that does not constitute a control all by itself. The other items are controls that may be put in place to help ensure this requirement is met, but requirements are not controls.

19. Which of the following is not a password control?

    A. Requiring that a password have a minimum length and complexity

    B. Encrypting passwords when in transit and at rest

    C. Limiting the reuse of passwords through the use of a history file

    D. Limiting the number of unique sessions an account can initiate

    Answer: D

    The correct answer is D. The number of times an account can create a unique session is an account control and is not related to password controls. The other items are controls that may be applied to passwords.

20. When evaluating strong authentication usage, what should an IS auditor be *most* concerned with?

    A. Ensuring that the two factors are maintained in separate databases to ensure segregation

    B. Determining the identification process for each factor and ensuring they are synchronized

C. Reviewing the biometric aspects of strong authentication or acceptable type I and type II error rates

D. Reviewing the physical controls related to the storage of the physical tokens or card stock supplies

Answer: B

The correct answer is B. The IS auditor should be most concerned with the matching the identity of the actual user to the various authentication factors. Keeping the various factors separated (A) should not be a consideration at all; in fact, it may be better to secure them simultaneously. Type I (false rejection rate) and type II (false acceptance rate) would be important factors to consider if biometrics were involved, but that is not a criteria in the question. Many strong authentication solutions do not use biometrics as part of the solution. The physical security of a token or card stock not yet issued should be of lesser concern than ensuring that the user's identity has been matched up to the various authentication factors. Again, hardware devices may not be part of the strong authentication solution being evaluated.

21. During a review of a PKI, the IS auditor determines that non-repudiation cannot be assured for a set of transactions. This most likely means that

A. The certificate authority will not stand behind the validation of the certificate used at the time when the transaction occurred.

B. The users certificate was compromised or was expired when the time the transaction occurred.

C. In reviewing the transaction flow and the security related to the use of the certification, it cannot be conclusively proven that no other person could have possibly been responsible for the transaction that had occurred.

D. The transaction did not go through as anticipated, causing a roll back of the request and negating the signed transaction.

Answer: C

The correct answer is C. Non-repudiation implies proof that your request came from you and no one else. There are several reasons why this may be the case, which may include a CA defaulting on their responsibility (A), or a compromise or expiration of the certificate (B). Transaction roll back (D) is not associated with non-repudiation at all, and if it were to occur, there would be no need to prove a transaction.

22. Which of the following would an IS auditor expect to see as part of an information security architecture?

   I. Evidence of the application of a defense in-depth strategy

   II. A risk-based approach to the application and location of the security controls

   III. A plan that takes into consideration the business needs and processes

   IV. The inclusion of the management and operational controls as well as technical controls

   A. I, II, and IV only

   B. I, II, III, and IV

   C. II and IV only

   D. I, II, and III only

   Answer: B

   The correct answer is B. All of the items listed should be found in comprehensive security architecture.

23. When performing a review of the host-based security controls, the risk factors that need to be considered are

   I. The value of the data contained on the server being secured

   II. The functions and tasks required of the server

   III. The services that are not needed in the configuration of the server

   IV. The operating system type and its vulnerabilities

   V. Requirements for encryption related to the services provided by the server

   A. I, II, III, IV, and V

   B. I, II, and IV only

   C. II, III, and V only

   D. III, IV, and V only

   Answer: B

   The correct answer is B. These three items are factors that may introduce risk, operating system type, business needs, and the value of the data. Services that are turned off do not constitute any risk at all (III). Requirements for encryption do not introduce risk unless, of course, this requirement is addressed in a less than optimal fashion.

24. Minimum security baselines (MSBs) and host-based intrusion detection relate to each other in what important aspect?

    A. They both are security controls that apply to a device (server) as opposed to network-based controls.

    B. Host-based intrusion detection cannot be successfully implemented unless MSBs are adequately maintained on the same device.

    C. Host-based intrusion detection controls can be used in place of applying MSBs on the same device.

    D. They should both be implemented on all servers as part of a robust security architecture.

    Answer: A

    The correct answer is A. Both of these items are security controls that apply to devices on the network. While HIDS will be exposed without a good MSB in place (B), it is not a prerequisite. HIDS can in no way replace MSBs on a device (C), one looks for attacks by reviewing the logs, the other is a set of configuration controls, which may enable attacks that a HIDS signature would see as normal and acceptable in most cases. The implementation of both (D) would be recommended only in situations where the risks were significant enough to warrant such an action and certainly not on all servers on the network.

25. During a network security review, the IS auditor determines that the firewall rule set is incorrectly built to protect the organization from the risks that are unacceptable to the business. The IS auditor should

    A. Immediately notify the IS organization management so corrections can be made to prevent further vulnerability.

    B. Discuss the issue with audit management and prepare the findings and recommendations for their report.

    C. Point out the deficiency to the firewall support staff, but note the state the controls were found in at the time of the review.

    D. Look at the rest of the controls to ensure that the risk has not been mitigated by some other method before doing anything.

    Answer: D

    The correct answer is D. Unless the firewall support staff is completely incompetent, there is probably a reason that the controls are set up the way they are, given the risks and environment that this staff manages day to day. Before alerting any management and possibly embarrassing yourself, you would be well advised to first check around for mitigating controls or the acceptance of risk. If that does not satisfy the control need, ask the support staff (C) to ensure they are aware of the situation. Conferring with audit management (B) would be the next step before approaching the IS management (A) and bringing up a potential situation (or possible embarrassment or confrontation) to their attention.

26. What is the *primary* purpose of a DMZ in a network architecture?

    A. To provide a place where authentication can occur before enabling access to sensitive data

    B. To separate business logic from classified data

    C. To provide a neutral zone where transaction requests can be made and honored without affecting the security of either adjacent zone

    D. To provide a location for proxy servers and drop off servers to reside without reducing the security of the more secure adjacent network zone

    Answer: C

    The correct answer is C. DMZs are intended to be a no man's land where neither side is trusted and exchanges or transactions can occur, similar to military DMZs. Business logic should not be housed in a DMZ, and classified data certainly should not be either (B). Authentication may occur in this region but that is not the primary purpose. DMZs do provide a location for proxies and other devices (D) but not to address security on only the more secure adjacent network. DMZs also provide a safe area for the lesser secure networks as well.

27. When evaluating the encryption used to protect a data transmission over the Internet, which of the following is *not* a relevant security control?

    A. Virtual private network

    B. Message digest

    C. Digital certificate technologies

    D. Secure sockets layer technologies

Answer: B

The correct answer is B. A message digest is a computation performed on a message that results in a one-way hash number. This one-way hash number is used to indicate the authenticity of the message received by comparing a reperformed digest computation on the same message to see if the same hash is the result. It is not an encryption-related control, but it is used to validate an encrypted message. The other three items are all encryption-related control techniques used for Internet-based transmission control.

28. Network intrusion detection and incident response are important parts of any security program. What aspects of an audit review *must* be included when evaluating these programs?

    I. Proper staff levels and training of the staff to react and respond to issues as they present themselves

    II. Establishment of a need for using either of these techniques based on the possibility of them actually being required

    III. The response time requirements and the ability of the program in place to meet those needs

    IV. Management's commitment to the programs and their support for enabling them to function when necessary

    A. I, II, III, and IV

    B. I, II, and IV only

    C. II, III, and IV only

    D. I, III, and IV only

Answer: D

The correct answer is D. All of the items listed are important aspects of both network-based intrusion detection systems and an incident response program, except for considering whether there is a possibility of their need or not. Even if the network is completely off-line from other connectivity points, which is unlikely, there will always be a need for an incident response process because security is not foolproof and incidents will always occur at some level. NIDS may be required to a lesser extent, but network-connected systems are attacked continuously from Internet sites and to not use NIDS by choosing to accept the risk would be a rare situation.

29. While evaluating third-party connections in an organization an IS auditor discovers PCAnywhere software resident on a financial workers desktop workstation. Which of the following controls would be seen as the *strongest* risk mitigate to unauthorized network access in this situation?

    A. The software is used only for the remote control of the workstation and access must be authenticated by dial up server controls first.

    B. The software may be correctly configured to use network authentication prior to enabling connection through a modem to it.

    C. The modem is unplugged and only connected when needed.

    D. The software is configured to use dial back and only enables outgoing connections made to known numbers.

    Answer: A

    The correct answer is A. The strongest control is to only allow the software to enable access to the device from a previously authenticated session from a trusted authentication device on the network. The other controls are configurable by the users and no assurance can be made that these settings will not change over time and in changing circumstances. Without a modem connected to the workstation, no outside connection to the network can be gained.

30. In an evaluation of virus protection processes, which three controls cover the *most* risk of those listed here?

    A. Virus protection deployed on every workstation, the blocking of dangerous attachments in all email at the mail servers, and a strong user education program about email viruses

    B. Virus protection active on all mail servers, the blocking of dangerous attachments in all email at the mail servers, and a strong user education program about email viruses

    C. A strong user education program about email viruses and virus protection that is actively enforced on all workstations and the blocking of dangerous attachments in all emails at the mail servers

    D. Virus protection on all mail servers, the blocking of dangerous attachments in all emails at the mail servers, and virus protection that is actively enforced on all workstations

Answer: D

The correct answer is D. The combination of active protection on both the mail servers and workstations, in addition to blocking suspect attachments provides the strongest defense. User awareness (B) and (C) is a good control to have in place but will not be as reliable as up-to-date software controls that are managed centrally. Response (A) only indicates virus protection deployed at the workstation, but it is not necessarily forced to remain on at all times. These controls are often defeated by users when they are given the chance or when the controls are not kept up-to-date, making (D) a better answer.

31. Which of the following is *not* a control to address the risks associated with social engineering attempts?

    A. Asking for a name of a person to call back, documenting all of the requests, and validating the person by some means before granting access

    B. Adding the physical security responsibilities to the systems support people because they know who needs access to the operations center best

    C. Following the rules for access and permissions at all times to avoid opportunities for allowing your guard to be down

    D. Developing a healthy suspicion and learn to "think like an attacker"

Answer: B

The correct answer is B. Adding the physical security responsibilities to the system's support personnel may seen logical, but it will result in segregation of duties problems and lead to unclear primary responsibilities when conflicts arise. These responsibilities also may require the support person to be in two places at one time, leading to the abandonment of one or the other, usually the add-on responsibility. The other controls are all good social engineering controls.

32. What is the *most* important control concern associated with the logging and monitoring of system or network activity?

    A. Ensuring that the information is time synchronized so forensic analysis can be accurately performed

    B. The placement of the sensors and protection of the logs from the systems administrator's access

    C. Developing exception-based reporting and log correlation processes to reduce the amount of log review required

    D. Having the staff support available to read through the logs and take action on the results found

    Answer: D

    The correct answer is D. All of these factors are very important to the implementation of a successful logging and monitoring process, but the most important is being able to read the results and react to the information found. If issues are not identified and actions are not taken, the rest will not help control security.

33. When evaluating personnel safety controls in an IS operation, what is the *best* method to use for evaluating its sufficiency?

    A. Obtaining copies of the safety and emergency evacuation manual to evidence compliance with the requirement for procedures and documentation

    B. Reviewing the records of testing of personal safety devices and their maintenance histories

    C. Spot interviewing a few passing IS staff personnel and asking them about their knowledge of the safety measures and procedures

    D. Looking for posted evacuation signs and personal safety equipment stored in easily accessible locations to the users

    Answer: C

    The correct answer is C. The best way to determine if the staff on-site at an IS organization's facility has been adequately trained and personal safety has been planned for in the area is to ask someone who should know what the response should be when emergencies arise.

These circumstances are immediate and cannot wait while the manual is located and the procedure is looked up. Staff should know at least the basics of what is required to be taught to them on a routine basis.

34. What is the *most* challenging aspect of evaluating physical security controls in an IS organization?

    A. Assessing all of the numerous controls and ensuring that each one is managed properly

    B. Determining how to assess flexible situations such as security movement and the belongings of VIPs and visitors

    C. Being able to obtain proof of the physical security controls effectiveness in preventing or deterring unauthorized acts

    D. Touring the physical site and inspecting the controls to ensure that they are functioning properly

Answer: C

The correct answer is C. The most difficult part of drawing a conclusion when it comes to physical security is determining whether the controls are effective or not. It is easy to tell when a physical control fails because a breach occurs. But unless partial damage occurs when access is attempted, there will be little evidence that the controls are sufficient or not robust enough. This opinion will be a judgment call drawn from the IS auditor's professional opinion.

35. In a review of environmental controls, all of the following are factors that need to be considered *except*

    A. The need for power continuity and the deployment of UPS, batteries, and generators as applicable

    B. The maintenance and testing schedule recorded for the fire suppression systems that protect the information systems

    C. Personnel evacuation plans and emergency exit routes posted in the operations center

    D. Moisture and temperature monitoring and tracking over time

Answer: C

The correct answer is C. Personnel evacuation is not an environmental control concern. If the controls function properly, personnel evacuation will not be necessary. You should ensure that the audit scope adequately defines the boundaries of the audit review in areas like this before proceeding with the engagement.

Chapter 5—Disaster Recovery and Business Continuity

Here are the answers to the questions in Chapter 5:

1. An IS auditor is reviewing an organization's contingency planning and recoverability. What is the *most* important factor to consider for the success of the recovery plan?

   A. The plan has identified all of the critical applications required to be covered for the business to survive.

   B. The plan is stored off-site.

   C. The process is supported by senior management and funded adequately.

   D. Back ups are made and moved off-site regularly.

   Answer: C

   The correct answer is C. The most important factor to consider for the success of a recovery process is the commitment and funding of the solution by management. Without proper support, successful recovery will not be a priority of the organization and funding and resource commitment will not be sufficient to achieve the goals. The other items listed here are necessary attributes of a recovery process, but the support of the leadership is paramount to all other factors.

2. When reviewing business impacts of possible disruption scenarios, which of the following criteria should be considered?

   I. The likelihood customers will take their business somewhere else and not return

   II. The potential losses in terms of buildings and equipment

   III. The costs associated with redeploying a process to replace the one that is lost

   IV. The time it would take to fully recover and return to processing

   V. The losses of current business from not meeting existing commitments

   A. I, II, and III only

   B. I, II, III, IV, and V

   C. I, II, III, and V only

   D. II, III, IV, and V only

Answer: B

The correct answer is B. All of these factors should be considered in a Business Impact Analysis (BIA). Each factor contributes to the decision-making process of how severe a loss might be experienced and what the tolerance may be for loss, if in fact, there are many other factors to consider as well. Even the time it would take to recover (IV) is a factor, because when processing and service cannot be provided, the associated revenue potential cannot be realized. The longer this situation continues, the more loss can be inferred. This also will compound the likelihood that customers will have to turn to other sources for satisfying their needs.

3. An IS auditor determines that external consulting was used to create a recovery plan. Which of the following actions would be *most* appropriate for the IS auditor to take?

   A. Review the costs and contract deliverables for the consulting engagement and assess the adequacy of the contract.

   B. Review the methodology used by the firm and assess its appropriateness for the engaged organization.

   C. Ensure that the decisions made by the consultant seemed reasonable for the given business and organizational structure.

   D. Review the resultant plan and ensure that the business and IS staff were involved in inputting to the final product.

Answer: D

The correct answer is D. The most appropriate action to take is to ensure the organization's business and systems people were involved in building the plan. Recovery plans are unique to the organizations that they represent and cannot be dictated beyond format and approach. The contract and deliverables may be interesting (A) and the methodology should be at least relevant (B). If the consultant is making decisions for the business (C), this would constitute a material weakness because they could not possible know as much about the business and their needs as those who run the business daily.

4. When reviewing a business and systems recovery plan, which of the following will be *most* important to find within the contents of the plan?

   A. Simple checklists depicting the steps that need to be taken to affect a recovery

   B. Change control information related to what has changed since the last plan update

   C. Call trees depicting the recovery teams and their contact information

   D. Inventories of hardware and equipment used on-site

   Answer: A

   The correct answer is A. The single most important element of a recovery plan is the steps needed to affect the recovery. Without these steps, there is no plan to carry out. The other items have relevance in support of the recovery procedure but are not as important as the procedure itself.

5. When reviewing the rationale for recovery options and decisions, which of the following *best* describes the correct approach for determining the appropriate direction for recovery planning?

   A. Planning for a recovery scenario that will not be costly to implement a solution for while still meeting the requirement for a recovery plan

   B. Looking at all options for the worst case disaster scenario and picking the solution that is cheapest while still meeting the needs of the business

   C. Determining the downtime associated with each recovery option and deciding on the one that will recover the business most quickly

   D. Determining the most likely disaster situation and picking the solution that most closely represents the existing processing configuration

Answer: B

The correct answer is B. Obviously, planning for the easy way out and only performing a recovery planning cycle to meet the requirement (A) will not result in a satisfactory recovery process for most businesses. Downtime (C) is not the only consideration when determining recovery strategies, and overall loss reduction should be the paramount determining factor. Even though picking the most likely disaster scenario is the right way to proceed, the existing processing configuration should not matter compared with the ability to recreate the user experience (D). The overall cheapest solution, considering all costs both related to out of pocket and related to downtime and customer impact while still meeting the business need, will be the best answer.

6. A business continuity plan should address the recovery of

   A. All mission critical computer applications

   B. Only those applications related to generating revenue for the business

   C. All applications needing recovery within the first 24 hours after a disruption

   D. Applications and processes determined by management to be high priority to management

   Answer: D

   The correct answer is D. Similar to the security discussions, management has to make the decisions for what needs to be recovered so that the business they are accountable for survives. Business and operations management must educate them and provide them with the expertise to make risk-based decisions that will in the end be their responsibility. They alone must determine whether mission critical should be included on the list (A) or how relevant revenue generation is to the survivability of the business (B). Certainly the first 24 hours will be critical (C), but it is not the only criteria either.

7. Which of the following application attributes are *not* relevant when determining the priority order for recovery?

   A. The dependency of the critical applications on the output of this particular application

   B. The need for critical applications to be recovered in order to supply input to this application

C. The importance of this application to the business processing needs

D. How much downtime is acceptable to the users of this the application

Answer: B

The correct answer is B. Whether critical applications feed this application or not has little bearing on the recovery priority of the application. The dependency of critical applications on the one being examined will affect its relative priority, however (A). The particular applications downtime tolerance (D) and its importance to the business users (C) also will be relevant factors for determining priority.

8. To be effective for disaster recovery, back up copies of computer information should be

   A. Stored on-site in the production environment in a fireproof and watertight container

   B. A series of incremental back ups labeled and stored properly in the media library

   C. Moved off-site as quickly as possible

   D. Labeled and cataloged, corresponding to the recovery plans and sent to the location specified in the plan

   Answer: D

   The correct answer is D. While it is important to move back ups off site quickly (C), without the related documentation, media location identification, and recovery steps mentioned in the correct answer, the recovery would not be effective. Answers A and B are incorrect because the media should not be kept on-site, even if it is labeled properly and stored in fireproof containers.

9. When evaluating recovery plan documentation, an IS auditor determines that the plan's execution will result in the exposure of sensitive data to team members that do not have a need to know for this data. The auditor should

   A. Notify management of a material weakness in their final audit report.

   B. Recommend that stronger controls be applied to the data management during the recovery process.

C. Focus their efforts on the recoverability of the business processes and note the control weakness for follow-up after the recovery is complete.

D. Review the procedures for compensating controls or manual processes to control access during recovery.

Answer: C

The correct answer is C. Recovery plan documentation should be reviewed for its capability to provide for an effective recovery of the business process, not for its ability to protect the data with production level controls during the recovery efforts. This will not be a reportable finding (A) and stronger controls would not be an appropriate recommendation in this case (B) for the most part. Compensating controls may be relevant (D) and give the IS auditor some assurance, but this is not the purpose for evaluating recovery documentation.

10. Incorporating systems and process changes into a recovery plan is an important part of keeping it relevant and viable for the recovery of the business process. Which of the following approaches would *best* meet the needs of the business for ensuring that the changes are appropriately incorporated into the recovery plan documentation?

A. Testing the plan and making changes only as necessary to support the recovery plan process requirements

B. Sending all IS operational changes to the recovery site for inclusion into the recovery documentation

C. Updating the documentation during the periodic review of the plan and incorporating only the relevant changes

D. Making the business unit recovery teams accountable for their respective portions of the recovery plans and related updates

Answer: A

The correct answer is A. Testing the plan is always the best way to ensure that it works and any corrections or changes needed are appropriately addressed. All changes may not be relevant to the plan or its procedures (B) because a full IS system replacement may not be the scope of the recovery process. Updating only during a periodic review (C) may not meet the business needs, especially if major process changes are not updated to the recovery plan documentation in a timely manner. Many teams inputting into a plan (D) will eventually result in unsynchronized changes and processes that will not match up when necessary for recovery purposes.

11. When reviewing a systems disaster recovery plan, an IS auditor should look for operations procedures that

    A. Have been approved by senior management

    B. Follow the procedures used by the IS organization in normal production

    C. Describe how to perform the successful operation of the recovered subset of operations

    D. Describe all aspects of the current process in detail

    Answer: C

    The correct answer is C. Disaster recovery is a stressful situation and the procedures to recover a system should be kept as simple as possible. Describing all current processes in detail (D) may not be relevant to the recovery process and will interfere with getting the job done, in some cases. The procedures used in normal production (B) also may not be relevant as recovery is often the bare minimum necessary to survive. You should not expect to see operational procedures approved by management; they would not understand what they were approving. Only the procedures needed to recover the subset intended to be recovered should be found as procedures in the recovery manual.

12. The declaration of a disaster that invokes a recovery plan process should be

    A. Made by the IS organizational manager as soon as the need is identified

    B. Documented as a process requiring formal approval and an audit trail to provide evidence of the decision

    C. Only done after a repair and restore has been tried and has failed

    D. A decision of the business senior management after considering all alternatives, risks, and costs

    Answer: D

    The correct answer is D. The IS organization should not take it upon themselves to declare a disaster (A) because of the impact to the overall business and disruption a recovery process will make to the business as well as the IS operations. Some repair and restoration may be initiated first (C), but this will depend on the nature of the disruption and damage experienced and is not necessarily the best first step in all cases. Times of emergency are not when audit evidence and formal procedures are called for in a business setting (B), they are a time for decisive action and insistence on approval and evidence is often inappropriate. Senior management should make the decision for the entire affected organization only after considering all of the available alternatives and weighing the cost and benefit of each of them to the long-term survivability of the organization.

13. When reviewing the information recovery procedures, an IS auditor would be *least* concerned with finding procedures that

    A. Lay down the last complete back up and then all of the subsequent incremental back ups that are available

    B. Recover all available information from the available back up tapes and move forward with the available information

    C. Use hard copy transaction records to return the transactions processing history to the time of disaster from the last available back up

    D. Use the best information available and reconcile the inventories to understand the transactions that may have been lost during the disaster or disruption

    Answer: B

    The correct answer is B. A procedure that recognizes that some electronic records are bound to be lost and that requires hard copy transaction information be created and used to recover to the point of failure of the systems is the next best recovery model for a transaction processing system. The best would be mirrored, journaling at an off-site location. The other answers described here do not recognize the transactions in progress since the last back up was taken and will be less effective in providing for a complete recovery.

14. The most important aspect of a recovery plan in the initial hours of a recovery process will be that

    A. Call lists and rosters are included for contacting the recovery teams

    B. People have been trained what to do and where to meet to gather and begin recovery without the documented plan

    C. A disaster is declared by management and the EOC is activated as a control center

    D. Testing results have been included to show current recoverability

Answer: B

The correct answer is B. Knowing what to do without any of the plan documentation is critically important in the first hours of the recovery process when manuals and procedures may not be available from staging and storage areas. Call lists and rosters are critically important to this effort but will not be useable from within the recovery plan stored with the recovery materials or destroyed by the disaster (A). These lists and rosters must be available immediately; the copies with the recovery plan will only be used if all else fails (or as a check to ensure that everything was covered by the interim processes, which were used immediately after the disruption occurred). The other two items (C) and (D) are nice to have but are not as important as the training of key individuals who will lead the initial recovery of gathering and assessment processes.

15. When reviewing a recovery plan, an IS auditor will be *least* concerned with plans for managing the press and media by

    A. Providing a location away from the immediate action where the media and press can be briefed periodically by the designated spokesperson, and allowed the opportunity to ask questions

    B. Providing space for the press and media inside the Emergency Operations Center (EOC) with immediate access to recovery teams

    C. Using a policy to tell the media and press as little as possible and denying all rumors with a "no comment" reply

    D. Using a policy that encourages the media to talk to the workers and ask questions as they come in and out of the recovery area as a way to communicate without interfering with management and the recovery process

Answer: A

The correct answer is A. The best way to deal with the media is to acknowledge their need for information and provide it in a forthright and controlled manner by a person who can provide an authoritative and consistent message that management can control. Direct access to the EOC (B) of the recovery workers (D) may result in reputation damage by unanswered questions as work in progress could provide opportunities for wrong conclusions and unchecked tempers to put the organization in a bad light. Denying access to any information (C) leaves the media to draw their own conclusions, which may not be complimentary to the organization.

16. What is the primary advantage of a hot site over a cold site for recovery planning?

    A. There is less work to do at the time of disaster because the site management will prepare it for you.

    B. Communications have already been tested, thus providing for a higher probability of success.

    C. Testing has occurred at this location in the past, so recovery teams are more familiar with the facilities and how to go about affecting a recovery.

    D. Downtime is minimized because equipment does not have to be configured and installed.

    Answer: D

    The correct answer is D. The primary benefit is the reduced downtime. Costs are generally higher and this trade off here is time for money. If recovery time is critical enough (and this needs to be justified and documented), then the costs will be acceptable compared with the losses that may occur. The other items listed are all benefits of the hot-site recovery plan, but downtime reduction is paramount.

17. When reviewing the plans for business operation recovery, an IS auditor would be *most* concerned to find which of the following unaddressed by the plan?

    A. That there is adequate space for accommodating the business staff in an alternate site

    B. That computer workstations are available with the latest technology on them with which to perform the business processes

    C. That a desktop appropriate for the processing of the recovered business can be made available

    D. That connectivity to the EOC is provided for the business desktops for communication

    Answer: C

    The correct answer is C. Not having the right desktop configuration to perform the necessary business functions will be the most egregious error when planning for business recovery. Adequate space for the business staff may not be necessary (A), depending on the recovery plan and an analysis of what functions are critical and need to be manned for recovery processing. The latest technology (B) is certainly not a requirement for success. Connectivity may be very important to the operational processes (D) but not necessarily to the EOC this is commanding the recovery effort and not the IS operations.

18. When observing the testing of recovery in a dual-site, operational recovery plan configurations, what should an IS auditor expect to see?

    A. Business continues as it normally would with no downtime or disruption

    B. Additional equipment being quickly turned on and added to the configuration at the surviving site to accommodate full processing with minimal disruption

    C. Two identical sets of processing equipment set up for hot fail over from one site to the other with no impact on the users

    D. A procedure that sheds some testing, reporting, and lesser essential functions allowing for the concentration of the surviving site on the critical business processing to be performed

    Answer: D

    The correct answer is D. A dual-site, contingency arrangement is one where a single (sufficiently large) operation splits its processing between two sites, spreading its critical processing across both sites so a single failure will not completely disrupt any one of them. The balance of the sites processing, the lesser critical systems, and spread across the sites provides for the shedding of noncritical operations in support of the critical one if necessary.

19. When reviewing the recovery testing reports to management, an IS auditor will be *most* concerned if the following is not part of the report:

    A. An assessment of the time it takes to recover compared to the management expectations for recovery and a gap analysis of the potential impact that any shortfall may have on management's risk or loss expectations

    B. A comprehensive list of all of the problems and the resultant assigned action items

    C. A description of the process used to test the recovery, depicting the assumptions made about the recovery situation that was being tested

    D. A list of planned goals or milestones with an analysis of the ones that were achieved and those that were not successfully tested

Answer: A

The correct answer is A. The single most important part of communicating with management about disaster recovery testing is to report against the capability to recovery and the adjustment of expectations that management has, by which they make risk-based decisions on a daily basis. Without feedback on the risks and ability to control them through recovery for disaster, management will be unable to provide the correct guidance and direction to lead the company forward in a risk-managed manner. Expectations must be managed and funding and risk tolerance adjustments made through this reporting feedback mechanism. The other items listed may or may not be of interest to management, deepening their appetites for detail related to the progress being made.

Chapter 6—Business Application Systems Development, Acquisition, Implementation, and Maintenance

Here are the answers to the questions in Chapter 6:

1. When reviewing a systems development project, what would the *most* important objective be for an IS auditor?

    A. Ensuring that the data security controls are adequate to protect the data.

    B. Ensuring that the standards and regulatory commitments are met.

    C. Ensuring that the business requirements are satisfied by the project.

    D. Ensuring that the quality controls and development methodologies are adhered to.

Answer: C

The correct answer is C. The most important review objective for any assessment of systems development will be to ensure that the needs of the business are met as the result of the development. This actually incorporates the other objectives at a high level. You will not be able to satisfy the business needs without also addressing the security (A), standards and regulatory requirements (B), and quality objectives (D) as well.

2. When participating in an application development project, which of the following would *not* be appropriate activities for an IS auditor?

    A. Testing the performance and behavior of the system controls to ensure that they are working properly

    B. Attending design and development meetings to monitor progress and provide input on control design options

    C. Reviewing reports of progress to management and contributing to their content based on fieldwork and opinions forms from reviewing documentation provided

    D. Assisting in the development of controls for application modules and user interfaces

    Answer: D

    The correct answer is D. It is a violation of duty segregation for an IS auditor to design and develop systems or controls that they will have to subsequently audit and provide opinions on. Independence and objectiveness are no longer preserved in this case. Testing of controls (A) is an objective and independent function and would be an appropriate contribution to the process. Providing input on control design decisions (B) also would be acceptable as long as the decisions were made by the project team and not by the auditor. Providing input to the reports related to the project's progress and performance (C) also is acceptable as long as the auditor does this in an objective and independent manner.

3. When reviewing an application development project that uses a prototyping development methodology, with which of the following would the IS auditor be *most* concerned?

    A. The users are testing the systems before the designs are completely documented.

    B. The functional requirements were not documented and agreed to before the prototyping processes began.

    C. The documentation of the coding processes and testing criteria were not complete and well referenced.

    D. The systems specifications were not signed off on before the development processes were started.

Answer: B

The correct answer is B. It would be most important in the prototyping development scenario for the business users and management to agree on what the requirements and outcomes are before starting to evaluate the prototypes of new systems. Otherwise, the business problems are not fully known and the solutions presented have little chance of meeting the undocumented need. User testing of designs (A) is a natural part of this process type. Overlap of the functional specification process, the system design process, and the development cycle (C) also is an expected behavior of prototyping methodologies. Strict sign off of the project movement from one phase to another (D) would not be expected in this process as a result.

4. In a systems development life cycle, the following process steps occur:

I. Systems Design

II. Feasibility Analysis

III.Systems Testing and Acceptance

IV. Systems Specification Documentation

V. Functional Requirements Definition

VI.Systems Development

What is the natural order of the processes in an SDLC methodology?

A. V, IV, II, I, VI, III

B. V, II, IV, I, VI, III

C. II, IV, V, VI, I, III

D. II, V, I, VI, III, IV

Answer: A

The correct answer is A. Classic Systems Development Life Cycle (SDLC) methodologies begin by understanding the business or functional requirements and then a feasibility analysis is performed on the solution options. Systems specifications then are further defined based on the accepted solution and approach from which a design is created. That design is developed into an application and that application is tested and finally accepted by the business.

5. Where would be the ideal place for an IS auditor to find the first consideration of security controls?

    A. During the design phase of the system development process

    B. When determining what the systems specification will need to be

    C. When reviewing the functional requirements for the system

    D. When testing the system for overall compliance to regulatory, privacy, and security requirements

    Answer: C

    The correct answer is C. Security should be considered as one of the functional requirements as early in the process as possible. Studies have shown that the security controls are seven times more costly when applied to a system that is already developed as compared to one with security designed into a system as one of its functional requirements. The later in the process that the first consideration of security is identified, the higher the risk is that the security requirements will not easily fit into the process that has been envisioned up to that point.

6. The main difference between a functional requirement and a systems specification is

    A. A functional requirement is a business process need, and a systems specification defines what the system must do to meet that need.

    B. Functional requirements address the details of the need from a data perspective, and systems specifications define them from an operational systems perspective.

    C. Functional requirements define more of what needs to happen, and systems specifications define how something will happen.

    D. Functional requirements define all aspects of the process flow from a business process perspective while systems specifications are more hardware and operating system-specific.

    Answer: A

    The correct answer is A. The most important difference between functional requirements and the systems specification are the business perspective and the solution requirements or system needs perspective. Both sets of information and related documentation require a data and operational view (B), and both are a combination of what and how needs and their solutions might be addressed (C). While functional specifications are a more business driven perspective, systems specifications are not necessarily limited to hardware and operating system perspectives (D). They also need to address application logic-related processes and requirements.

7. Which of the following is *not* a criterion for an effective feasibility analysis report?

   A. An assessment of the proposed solution approach and its viability in the existing business process

   B. An assessment of the impact of the new application on the business processes and workflows

   C. An analysis of the costs and projected benefits of the application, determining overall benefit or detraction from the business prospects of the overall business strategy

   D. An assessment of the systems development methodology proposed for the design of the application

   Answer: D

   The correct answer is D. How the development process may be approached is not part of the feasibility analysis and may not be determined until after all of the requirements and constraints are gathered and analyzed. Assessments of proposed solutions and determining their viability (A) is the objective of the feasibility review. Impact assessments for proposed solutions (B) are part of the determination that must be made to go forward with the project. ROI and a cost/benefit analysis (C) also are important aspects of this assessment.

8. If there was a *most* important place for the quality assurance teams to be involved in the development project, where would that place be?

   A. During the testing and code migration from test environments to production-ready code

   B. At the beginning of the project to ensure that quality standards are established and understood by all of the development team members

C. During the code development to ensure that processes are followed according to standards and are well documented

D. In the final phases to ensure that all of the quality processes and requirements were met prior to signing off on final acceptance

Answer: B

The correct answer is B. Quality Assurance (QA) should be used as a compliance and checking function throughout the systems development process. However, the most important part of the QA process is the establishment of standards and team's education of these requirements. Many other roles are supported and enhanced by the QA function, and they are instrumental in objectively ensuring the processes will be supportable and built according to the organization's methods and conventions (C). They place a key role in checking and testing code migration (A) and ensure the usability of the final product (D). But without established parameters from which to measure efforts, quality cannot be assured.

9. What aspect of the systems development testing process needs to be addressed during the systems design process?

A. The use cases are documented to show how the product is supposed to work when completed.

B. The detailed work plans and process steps are defined so that they can be checked for completeness during testing of the development process.

C. The expectations and outcomes of the development process are defined formally to be used for testing criteria.

D. The project design is checked against the functional requirements.

Answer: C

The correct answer is C. Testing criteria are formulated from the expectations and intentions of the design and its documentation. In fact, test scenarios should be sketched out for the design parameters as part of the design process. This ensures that the design and its incorporation of the requirements and specifications will be honored as testing criteria after the development process is concluded. Work plan steps are not relevant to testing of the systems performance (B) and use cases are only examples (A) and may not be detailed enough to drive out specific testing and evaluation of application development points. The project design should ensure that the functional requirements are all addressed (D), but this does not drive testing criteria directly either.

10. When reviewing a systems design, an IS auditor would be *least* concerned to find that which of the following was not considered?

    A. The provisions for adequate internal controls and the addressing of regulatory requirements

    B. Increased costs and delays in the project deadlines

    C. The observance of quality assurance standards and processes

    D. The failure to consider environmental and facility needs as part of the design

    Answer: B

    The correct answer is B. Time delays and cost overruns may be indicative of project management control issues for the overall project. But when reviewing the design itself, these issues are of the least importance to an IS auditor. The design must have considered the internal control needs (A), the QA requirements (C), and the environmentals (D) to adequately address the needs and result in a acceptable application.

11. When reviewing a systems development project, an IS auditor observes that the decision has been made to use a purchased vendor package to address the business requirements. The IS auditors should

    A. Discuss the contract and costs with the vendor to ensure that the best deal has been obtained for the organization

    B. Review the ROI assumptions and decide whether they are still valid

    C. Review the contract for a right to audit clause in the agreement

    D. Review the build versus buy recommendation and determine that the costs and benefits are fairly stated in the recommendations made

    Answer: D

    The correct answer is D. The correct approach for an IS auditor is to review the decision documentation and to ensure the conclusions made are supported by the problem's risk and benefit analysis. This documentation should be completed for all major decision points in the project to show that the best interests of the business were addressed in the decision. Auditors have no place dealing with vendors directly in any authoritative capacity (A) and contract clauses giving the right to audit will probably not be relevant to a purchased software product vendor (C). ROI assumptions will need to be adjusted after the impact and total cost reassessed, but it is not the auditor's place to make business determinations on validity, for example. It would be more appropriate for the auditor to question documentation found to be deficient, but he or she would not declare something as invalid.

12. The *most* important issue with change control during the development of large scale systems is

   A. Managing the versions of code in development to ensure that testing will result in a workable system

   B. Ensuring that testing and back out procedures have been provided for each change

   C. Ensuring that maintenance and disaster recovery procedures have been documented for each change promoted through the process

   D. Tracking which module has been tested with other modules to understand the development progress

   Answer: A

   The correct answer is A. Ensuring that version control for several concurrent module development efforts can be managed effectively is the most important role that change control plays in the development process from the ones listed in this question. Back out and testing procedures (B) as well as disaster recovery and maintenance documentation (C) are very important aspects of change control in a production system, but they are not as relevant during the development process. The module tracking aspects of change control (D) are more related to the testing than the development phase.

13. When reviewing a development effort where third-party programming staff are used, the IS auditor would be *most* concerned with?

   A. Ensuring that they are qualified and knowledgeable about the tools and techniques being used

   B. Ensuring that the code is reviewed independently from the third-party staff and ensuring that the ownership rights are maintained within the organization

C. Ensuring that background checks are made for individual third-party staff members to protect the organization from undesirable persons participating in the effort

D. The impact to the cost and timeline estimates originally presented and approved by management

Answer: B

The correct answer is B. The most important risks of third-party participation can be addressed with a solid code review integrated as part of the development process and contractually maintaining ownership of the products produced. Qualified personnel also are criteria (A), but this risk that can be mitigated also can be the code review. Background checks are more important than ever (C), especially if these programmers will be in close proximity to the business processes and are relatively unsupervised, which is not always the case. Finally, cost and time aspects are important (D), but this is not as critical to the result and the quality of the code being turned out.

14. An independent quality assurance function should perform all of the following roles *except*

A. Ensuring that the development methods and standards are adhered to throughout the process

B. Ensuring that the testing assumptions and approved modules of developed code are aligned to give a final product that meets the design criteria

C. Reviewing the code to ensure that proper documentation and practices were followed

D. Correcting development deficiencies and resubmitting corrected code through the testing process

Answer: D

The correct answer is D. Independent quality assurance functions cannot modify any code without violating their independence and segregation of duties. The other functions listed are appropriate actions for an independent QA function to perform.

15. Which of the following are *not* considered communication controls?

A. Network traffic monitoring and alert systems

B. Encryption techniques to limit accessibility to traffic in transit

C. Access control devices that limit network access

D. Bandwidth management tools to shift data based on traffic volumes

Answer: C

The correct answer is C. Access controls are boundary controls even when they are applied to the network and communication layers boundary. The other controls work at the communication layer and are communication controls.

16. Review of documentation in a systems development review is very important for all of the following reasons *except*

A. Training and maintenance efforts require that good documentation be made available for their processes to work effectively

B. Allowing the IS auditor to review the process without actually having to perform code-level reviews of programming efforts

C. Disaster recovery and support processes depend on the quality of the systems and user documentation

D. User effectiveness and production processing depends on the user's ability to read and understand the manuals and procedures associated with the application development process

Answer: B

The correct answer is B. Using the documentation as a crutch to avoid detailed review as an IS auditor is not an important use of the development training manuals and systems documentation. The other uses described in the choices given are all necessary and relevant reasons to expect good, accurate, and easily understandable user manuals, training documentation, maintenance manuals, and operational procedures.

17. In reviewing a vendor solution bidding process during a systems development review, an IS auditor would be *most* concerned to find that

A. A vendor solution had been chosen prior to documenting the vendor criteria.

B. The chosen vendor's cost was not the lowest of the providers of an acceptable solution.

C. Some of the vendors received more information about the bid request than the others did.

D. Some of the bidders on the vendor list were not capable of responding effectively to the bid based on their business model and the product being requested.

Answer: A

The correct answer is A. All of these situations are cause for concerns over the bidding process from an IS auditor's perspective, but the most egregious violation of best practice is to have chosen a vendor solution before the problems were formally defined and documented. The other items listed also should be investigated for mitigating controls or valid explanations, but without a problem definition the solution is driving the problem and not the other way around.

18. Which of the following is *not* a risk associated with the decision to use a vendor software solution?

A. The risk that the vendor might discontinue support of a product that is mission critical to the business

B. The risk that the costs and contract provisions might adversely impact the business model in the long term

C. The risk that in-house support expertise might be insufficient to adequately address ongoing support and maintenances need of the product

D. The risk that business needs for enhancements and corrections might not be addressed in a timely manner

Answer: C

The correct answer is C. In-house expertise needs for support and maintenance are greatly reduced by the use of a vendor package solution compared to developed applications, making this answer a risk that is not associated with vendor solutions. The other answers are all considerations of risk that need to be assessed if vendor solutions are being considered.

19. During go-live, security and change management controls are often relaxed to facilitate the implementation. What actions are *most* appropriate for the IS auditor during this process?

    A. Raising concerns about the control deficiencies to business management and suggesting additional controls

    B. Waiting until the implementation process is completed and running audit and analysis tools on all transactions during the implementation period

    C. Recommending that the risks of reduced controls be accepted and encouraging the process to move into a more controlled phase as quickly as possible

    D. Observing the implementation process to understand the extent of control risk that is residual to the process and recommending prudent, additional steps to regain assurance of data integrity

    Answer: D

    The correct answer is D. The best course of action is to observe from a distance and determine the best course of action to mitigate any residual risk exposure from the implementation process. Raising concerns to management (A) will not be seen as value added and may impede progress on the project because some amount of risk must be assumed. Coming in after the fact to analyze for errors (B) will assume a higher risk level than may have actually been the case, resulting in more work than necessary. Accepting the risk and moving forward without assessing the exposure (C) would not be in the best interests of the business owners where the auditor's objectives are to minimize risks and ensure effective application of the controls.

20. During the user testing of the application under development, the IS auditor would be *most* concerned if he or she found that

    A. Users were accessing the test system from their normal workstations to test the system

    B. Production data was being used for testing the system

    C. Users were not all trained to the same level of competency for the testing process

    D. Interfaces were simulated to provide input to testing and were not actually being represented by live input feeds

Answer: B

The correct answer is B. Use of production data for testing purposes may provide real-world examples of data to test with, but it will violate the security and confidentiality of the production data. Even if the data stewards give permission for the use of the data in a testing scenario, client data cannot be exposed to testing without additional controls to ensure that it has not been violated. This can be done effectively in a closed development and testing environment, but that level of controls is not normal for development efforts. The other issues stated here also are of concern to the IS auditor, but the risks and materiality of each case will need to be assessed in order to determine the appropriate level of concern.

Chapter 7—Business Process Evaluation and Risk Management

Here are the answers to the questions in Chapter 7:

1. Corporate governance can *best* be described as

   A. A formal process of implementing controls across the system

   B. A process that ensures that all risks have controls associated with them

   C. The guiding principles and policies of the organization

   D. The process for ensuring that all risks and accountabilities are managed within a business

   Answer: D

   The correct answer is D. Corporate governance can best be described in terms of responsibility and accountability for governing the actions and behavior of the corporation. Implementing controls (A) is only part of the business management process implied by corporate governance. Corporate governance may provide risk and control management (B), but that also is only part of the answer. Guiding principles and overall policy also is part of the overall management of risk and accountability process implied by corporate governance, but ensuring that all of these things are managed well best describes what corporate governance is all about.

2. When reviewing a corporate governance system, an IS auditor would be *most* concerned to find which of the following deficiencies in the process?

   A. Gaps in the handing down of the authority necessary to carry out the responsibilities given to unit management

   B. Lack of an enforcement and disciplinary process for ensuring that governance and direction is in effect

   C. Unit level goals that do not tie directly to the overall mission of the business

   D. Incomplete measurement processes for ensuring that the governance direction is carried out

   Answer: B

   The correct answer is B. All of these items are weaknesses in the corporate governance system. Gaps in the authority to perform against the responsibilities are an all too common problem in business (A). Unit level goals should tie back to the overall goals in some way (C) and measurement processes should completely and accurately show senior management how well the governance direction is being carried out in the business units (D). However, the most significant item of those discussed here is the lack of an enforcement process and means to ensure that the direction is performed against along with sanctions and disciplinary controls to make ensure these things get done. Without this process, there is no penalty for nonperformance and the intent of the governance process must be suspect.

3. What is the *most* important thing to keep in mind when reviewing a business process for best practice design?

   A. The state of the art solutions that are available in the market to perform these business functions

   B. The current business model and its overall performance metrics

   C. The requirements, business goals, and core competencies defined by the business model

   D. What the competition is doing

   Answer: C

   The correct answer is C. The most important aspect to keep in mind when reviewing a business against the state of the art practices is the goals and mission of the business. This should be the prime driver against which change and improvement are to be measured. Knowing what best practices are out in the marketplace (A) will be input to the process, as well the current performance measures (B) and the intelligence about the competition (D). However, the goals of the business should be the driver against which success is measured.

4. What is the *primary* role that Key Performance Indicators (KPIs) have in supporting the business process effectiveness?

   A. KPIs show when controls may not be working properly.

   B. KPIs are used to show that the service levels and business requirements are being met.

   C. KPIs show the percentage of a system's uptime and measure the output volumes and speeds.

   D. KPIs can be used to draw conclusions about the overall performance of the processes and target variances for follow-up analysis.

   Answer: D

   The correct answer is D. KPIs can be used to show many detailed and summary reportable facts and figures, and are also excellent controls in and of themselves for giving management a warning system when the systems and processes are not performing up to their expectations. The primary role of KPIs as it relates to business effectiveness is the big picture view or overall performance conclusions that can be drawn from their review. The other items listed here are all subset information indicators to that overall, primary function.

5. Management controls are intended to do all of the following *except*

   A. Enable for individual units to establish policies to meet their particular needs.

   B. Provide baseline guidance and direction for the entire business culture and style.

   C. Set rules for the business processes that are followed by all units and departments.

   D. Establish a framework for corporate governance and compliance.

Answer: A

The correct answer is A. Management controls are intended to establish overriding rules and principles that act as a baseline for guidance (B) and a corporate governance framework (D) for the entire business. These controls set down the rules for all units to follow (C) but do not usually provide for individual units to deviate or build their own set of policies.

6. When evaluating a business process reengineering project, an IS auditor would be *least* concerned to find that

   A. The staff that actually performs the current processes is not involved with the design of the redesign of the process

   B. Management commitment and support is not clearly stated in writing

   C. External facilitators are not involved in the analysis and streamlining of the existing processes

   D. The scope of the project has not been documented to include all of the existing facets of the business process being examined

Answer: C

The correct answer is C. All of the issues depicted here should be a concern to the review of a reengineering project. Management's commitment and support (B) would be the biggest concern if it were not apparent. Projects of this magnitude and impact cannot be successful without the full support and funding by management. Clearly a red flag should be seen if you find that the processing personnel, who know the current process and deliverables best (A), are not involved in the redesign. The other aspect of this concern would be the need to gain buy-in from those being impacted by the change in order for it to be accepted and succeed. If all of the interfacing aspects of the current process are not considered as part of the project's scope (D), there is definitely going to be some problems, or at a minimum some missed opportunities to capitalize on optimization and efficiencies. The least concern would be the involvement of external facilitators to tease out issues and opportunities that may be overlooked by those who work with the process daily. While the involvement of people unfamiliar with the current process provides opportunities to ask seemingly dumb questions, a rigorous discipline to examine all processes closely can provide this level of analysis as well, making this a less important issue.

7. All of the following are valid ways of measuring customer satisfaction *except*

   A. Sending out questionnaires with the product and asking for feedback on service and performance

   B. Using internally generated KPIs to see whether the performance levels are being met or exceeded

   C. Measuring repeat business and customer base growth from internal sales and shipping information

   D. Measuring the percentage of overall market share this particular business has in the market and its relative growth over time

   Answer: B

   The correct answer is B. Internally generated information, especially that which is not independently verified, is least acceptable as a measurement of external customer satisfaction. Questionnaires seeking direct feedback from the customers (A) and external information about overall market share (D) are independent measurements that show validated evidence of performance against customer expectations. Sales growth and shipping information also can be used to get a sense of this issue (B), but it should be gauged in comparison to the competition and the total market available in order to get the most accurate picture of the actual performance against the potential.

8. Which of the following are valid reasons for considering an e-business solution in support of the business process?

   I. The customer base is widely scattered and remote to the physical business location.

   II. The costs of doing business over the Web have been shown to be more efficient for the business than other mechanisms.

   III. Everybody is doing it.

   IV. The sales department believes that adding functionality to the Web presence will move customers from a browse to a buy online model by making this business option available to them.

   V. Real time and immediate support of the business transactions can be best supported by an online transaction model.

   A. I, II, and III only

   B. I, II, III, and IV only

   C. I and II only

   D. I, II, and V only

Answer: A

The correct answer is A. Items I, II, and III are all valid reasons for considering an online solution for business processing. When customer locations are remote and disperse (I), online solutions add value to these existing customers and provide them options, making this a valid consideration. Anytime there is proof of lowered costs (II) supported by evidence, the consideration is a valid one. You may think that just because everybody is doing it (III) may be the wrong reason, but business trends go that way at times and consideration needs to be made or the business may get left behind. However, just because the sales department believes that if you build it, they will come (IV), the validity of the reasoning must be questioned by the auditor unless some substantiating evidence can by shown. Real-time, immediate needs are the worst rationale (V), because the use of the Internet cannot be assured and certain.

9. When reviewing the design and implementation of risk controls, it will be *most* important for the IS auditor to determine that

    A. All risks are being completely mitigated through the proper application of control mechanisms.

    B. Controls prevent risks' situations from occurring wherever possible.

    C. As many risks as possible are addressed by the control that is being considered for implementation.

    D. There is a proper balance between the gravity of the risk and the control measure implemented.

Answer: D

The correct answer is D. Balance of the controls and the risks they are intended to manage is the most important aspect of a review of control implementation. All risks should not be mitigated completely (A) due to cost and overhead considerations. Preventive controls may be preferable in some instances (B) but certainly not right for all situations. While multiple uses from a single control may certainly simplify control management, it is not the most important aspect of the design and implementation process. Controls should always be applied commensurate with the risk of loss being faced by the residual risk that is being addressed by the implementation.

10. Preventive controls are primarily used to

    A. Stop a process and notify the operations that an error has occurred

    B. Keep an error situation from occurring by recognizing the condition and denying its occurrence

    C. Monitor and check error conditions that cannot be easily managed in other ways

    D. Address complex ranges of error conditions that can all be addressed by unique prevention condition statements

    Answer: B

    The correct answer is B. Preventive controls prevent a predefined error condition from being enabled to occur. Stopping the process (A) is not necessarily part of the way a preventive control may operate and the notification is more of a detective control behavior. Preventive controls must be monitored and checked periodically like any other control (C) making this a wrong answer. Preventive controls need to be defined for every unique situation they are intended to prevent, and they may be expensive and unjustified for complex ranges of error situations (D), which is why this is not the primary use of a preventive control.

11. When evaluating the effectiveness of detective controls that are applied to business systems, an IS auditor should consider the following:

    I.   Whether preventive controls would be more appropriate for the risk type and possible loss scenario.

    II. The error rate and accuracy of the control in identifying out of bounds conditions.

    III. The reporting mechanism used to notify management of an error condition.

    IV. The cost of the control compared to the potential loss to the system.

    V. Whether the risk is significant enough to warrant any controls at all

    A. I, II, and IV only

    B. II, III, and IV only

    C. IV, V, and II only

    D. I, II, III, IV, and V

Answer: D

The correct answer is D. All of the items lists should be considered when evaluating detective controls. Risk and loss potential should be the primary drivers for determining how much control is needed. The way in which the control operates, its success and failure rates, and how it communicates results to management are all important considerations as well.

12. What is the *primary* difference between a corrective control and a detective control where business processes are concerned?

    A. Business processes cannot be corrected in midtransaction, thus making corrective controls less applicable.

    B. Best practices typically indicate preventive controls over either of these other two control choices.

    C. Corrective controls include detection as part of the way these controls operate and then fix the problem as well.

    D. Corrective controls can only fix a small range of errors, while detective controls can detect a far greater scope of possible error conditions.

    Answer: C

    The correct answer is C. Corrective controls correct the problem or error condition after detecting that is has occurred. Business processes are no different than information systems or other processes when it comes to control types used to mitigate risk.

13. What is the *primary* difference to keep in mind when evaluating automated and manual controls?

    A. Automated controls can operate in an unattended fashion, which requires less testing and monitoring.

    B. Manual controls require human interaction to be successfully deployed and must consider human fallibility as part of the accuracy assessment.

    C. Potential losses are more difficult to measure with manual controls because the error rates are more difficult to measure.

    D. Training and documentation are required for manual controls while automated controls do not require such documentation.

Answer: B

The correct answer is B. The human factor is the most important consideration when evaluating manual controls against automated controls. Training and documentation (D) is one aspect of this human interaction as a control mechanism, but there are other aspects, such as human nature, which also play a part in this analysis. Potential loss when using manual controls (C) may be a factor to consider in this evaluation, but it is not the primary concern. Although the automated controls are automatic by design, they still must be monitored and tested (A) commensurate with the risk they are put in place to control.

14. A risk assessment has determined that the losses that could be potentially incurred with the delivery system of a business may cost up to $10,000 per month. Preventive controls have been recommended that will save the company $7,000 per month but this control will take three months to implement at a cost of $100,000 and at an ongoing cost of $1,000 per month. The business process has a life span of five years and has been in production for one year. Is the control justified?

    A. Yes, the savings over the remaining life of the process would be $315,000, thus justifying the expense.

    B. No, the $3,000 per month that will be missed over the life of the process ($144,000) exceeds the cost of the control.

    C. Yes, the total cost of the control over the remaining process life is $145,000, while the potential loss without the control would be $480,000.

    D. Maybe, if the potential savings over the remaining life of the process ($315,000) minus the total cost of the control ($145,000) represents a material risk to the company's management ($170,000), management may consider implementing the control and avoiding the risk.

Answer: D

The correct answer is D. This question is about potential loss not actual loss. The risk of loss is a management decision that must be weighed against the probability of occurrence (not referenced in the problem), and the appetite for risk by management. The cost of funds and other priorities may influence this decision as well. While control looks justifiable on paper (savings exceed cost over the life of the process by a significant amount), the probability of that loss occurring to the business needs to be factored into the decision process.

15. The Annual Loss Expectancy (ALE) of a risk without controls is expected to be $35,000 to a business process you are evaluating. You are recommending a control that will save 80 percent of that loss at an annual cost of $20,000 over the life of the process. Is the control justifiable?

    A. No, the savings is insignificant and relative to the cost.

    B. Yes, 80 percent of the loss amounts to $28,000 per year, which exceeds the annual cost by $8,000 per year.

    C. No, ALE is a subjective number and cannot be depended on to make this decision.

    D. Maybe, it depends on the management's appetite for risk and loss.

    Answer: B

    The correct answer is B. This is a justifiable control mechanism for management to consider for implementation. The significance of the savings compared to the cost (A) is a management decision and not one the IS auditor should be making. While ALE may be somewhat subjective (C), if its source and the method used to derive it is objective and reliable, it is a valid way to determine potential saving or loss over time. While management does have the responsibility for making decisions related to implementing all controls (D), this is still a justifiable control, should management choose to implement it.

16. What is the *most* important aspect of risk analysis to keep in mind when reviewing a business process?

    A. Senior management must be held accountable for all risks to the business.

    B. All risks do not need to be eliminated for a business to be profitable.

    C. Risks must be identified and documented in order to perform proper analysis on them.

    D. Line management should be involved in the risk analysis because management sees risks daily that others would not recognize.

Answer: C

The correct answer is C. In order to manage and control a risk, it first must be recognized as a risk. This implies identifying and documenting all risks no matter how small to perform a rigorous analysis for the business risks. Only after the loss potential and frequency of occurrence have been determined can risk be prioritized for control and mitigation. The other answers are all valid, but this is the most important aspect of risk analysis of those mentioned here.

17. Before making a recommendation to management for the further mitigation of residual risk during a gap analysis in a risk assessment, the following considerations should be decided upon:

   I. Management's risk tolerance

   II. The best type of control for the risk scenario and the process

   III. The gap between the acceptable risk and the residual risk

   IV. The state of the art, best practice for the process being reviewed

   V. Additional risk mitigation that the proposed control would address for the process under review

   A. I, II, III, and V only

   B. II, III, and V only

   C. II, III, IV, and V only

   D. I, II, III, IV, and V

Answer: A

The correct answer is A. All of the items mentioned except for the processing best practice are part of a risk analysis gap assessment. It really does not matter if there is a better way to perform the processing unless a reengineering evaluation is part of the assessment. Risk and control assessment are intended to address existing processes and changing the process should not be a consideration when recommending additional controls to close the gaps between acceptable risk, defined by examining existing controls and management's definition of acceptable risk, and the current state of risk control in effect.

18. What is the *primary* reason for independent assurance as a requirement for relying on control assessment and evaluation?

    A. The review of controls by independent reviewers transfers some amount of the risk to the reviewing body or organization.

    B. IS auditors are more knowledgeable about risks and controls and are better suited to review them and determine their effectiveness.

    C. Unless the controls are reviewed by an independent and objective review process, the quality of the controls cannot be assured.

    D. Management needs to have independent assurance that the risks are managed effectively as part of their corporate governance requirement.

    Answer: C

    The correct answer is C. The primary reason to use independent assurance is to get a second opinion on the effectiveness and efficiency of the controls in mitigating the risks of the business. IS auditors (B) are only one way to get this second opinion and they may not be best suited to evaluate some of the controls. While reviewing and drawing conclusions has some risk in and of itself (A), the risks of the business cannot be transferred by the independent review process. Finally, corporate governance should require that management is accountable for managing the risks of the business as well, but this is not the primary reason for seeking independent assurance.

19. What are examples of additional risk to a business that third party may add to the overall risks of the business?

    A. None, a business will actually take on some of the risk and reduce the overall risks to the business.

    B. A business will take on the risk that they do not have proper processes in place to perform inefficiently.

    C. A business will take on the risks that the contractual commitments do not adequately compensate for poor performance of the third-party vendor.

    D. A business will take on the risk that the customers are impacted by missed service level commitments or the misuse of customer information.

Answer: D

The correct answer is D. Customer impact is an example of additional risk that cannot be contractually compensated for and will be added to the business by engaging third-party vendors as part of the business process. Engaging in business with third parties does not transfer management's accountability or responsibilities for risk (A). Inefficiency in the third parties' business process (B) is not a risk for the host business. Contractually added risk (C) should be addressed when the contracts are negotiated and poor performance of the third party is one of the considerations that should be inputted to the negotiation and contract development process.

20. When reviewing an audit function for independence, an IS auditor would be most concerned to find that

    A. The internal audit function was made up of people who used to work for the external auditing firm that managed the accounting and auditing of the business

    B. The audit function had an administrative reporting relationship to the controller of finance in the business

    C. Some of the audit staff had previous involvement with the operation of business processes that their group was evaluating

    D. The audit staff had reviewed similar risk and control processes for competing businesses

Answer: A

The correct answer is A. The fact that auditors now perform work that their former coworkers are reviewing can be a compromise of independence and has been shown to result in misstated financials and inventories in actual criminal investigations. Administrative reporting within the business organization (B) is a normal way to manage the audit function in an organizational structure. Previous involvement with the business process being evaluated by the audit team (C) may actually be a benefit, as long as the auditors are careful not to compromise their independence by holding direct responsibility for auditing areas that were previously responsible for in the business. In the same way, previous experience with similar risk and control situations (D) may enable the audit function to recommend more value-added options to the business process being assessed. Most competing businesses shy away from sharing audit staff, however. Ethical obligations of the auditors should preclude exposure of other business processes and control secrets to other businesses with which they may be engaged.

What's on the CD-ROM

This appendix provides you with information on the contents of the CD-ROM that accompanies this book. For the latest and greatest information, please refer to the ReadMe file located at the root of the CD.

Here is what you will find:

- System Requirements
- Using the CD with Windows
- What's on the CD-ROM
- Troubleshooting the CD-ROM

System Requirements

Make sure that your computer meets the minimum system requirements listed in this section. If your computer doesn't match up to most of these requirements, you may have a problem using the contents of the CD.

Windows 9x, Windows 2000, Windows NT4 (with SP 4 or later), Windows Me, or Windows XP

- PC with a Pentium processor running at 120 MHz or faster
- At least 32 MB of total RAM installed on your computer; for best performance, we recommend at least 64 MB.
- Ethernet network interface card (NIC) or modem with a speed of at least 28,800 bps
- A CD-ROM drive

Using the CD-ROM with Windows

To install items from the CD to your hard drive, follow these steps:

1. Insert the CD into your computer's CD-ROM drive.
2. A window will appear with the following options: Install, Explore, Links, and Exit.
   - **Install:** Gives you the option to install the supplied software and/or the author-created samples on the CD-ROM.
   - **Explore:** Allows you to view the contents of the CD-ROM in its directory structure.
   - **Links:** Opens a hyperlinked page of Web sites.
   - **Exit:** Closes the auto run window.

If you do not have auto run enabled or if the auto run window does not appear, follow these steps to access the CD:

1. Click Start ➪ Run.
2. In the dialog box that appears, type *d*:**setup.exe**, where *d* is the letter of your CD-ROM drive. This will bring up the auto run window described previously.
3. Choose the Install, Explore, eBook, Links, or Exit option from the menu. (See Step 2 in the preceding list for a description of these options.)

CD-ROM Contents

Included on the CD-ROM is a testing engine that is powered by Boson Software. This program enables you to practice test taking while continuing to learn from the questions and answers provided from the book's examples. The format of the questions is designed to simulate those of the actual test so that you can become familiar with the approach before taking the actual exam. The goal of the testing engine is to make you comfortable with the queston-asking style and the way the answers have to be selected in order to be successful when sitting for the CISA certification exam. The questions that will be used in the testing engine are those presented in the book and cover all seven content area domains of the CISA exam.

When installed and run, the test engine presents you with a multiple-choice, question-and-answer format. Each question deals directly with exam-related material. The categories or content areas can be selected and focused on if certain job content domains need to be emphasized. Right and wrong answers are recorded and tracked for analysis of strengths and weaknesses after each quiz.

After you select what you believe to be the correct answer for each question, the test engine not only notes whether you are correct or not, but also provides information as to why the right answer is right and the wrong answers are wrong, providing you with valuable information for further review. Thus, the test engine gives not only valuable simulated exam experience but useful tutorial direction as well.

Troubleshooting the CD-ROM

If you have difficulty installing or using any of the materials on the companion CD, try the following solutions:

- **Turn off any anti-virus software that you may have running.** Installers sometimes mimic virus activity and can make your computer incorrectly believe that it is being infected by a virus. (Be sure to turn the anti-virus software back on later.)

- **Close all running programs.** The more programs you're running, the less memory is available to other programs. Installers also typically update files and programs; if you keep other programs running, installation may not work properly.

- **Reference the ReadMe file.** Please refer to the ReadMe file located at the root of the CD-ROM for the latest product information at the time of publication.

If you have additional trouble with the CD, please call the Wiley Customer Care phone number: (800) 762-2974. Outside the United States, call 1 (317) 572-3994. You can also contact Wiley Customer Service by email at techsupdum@wiley.com. Wiley will provide technical support only for installation and other general quality control items; for technical support on the applications themselves, consult the program's vendor or author.

Index